SUPER FREAKONOMICS

ALSO BY
STEVEN D. LEVITT & STEPHEN J. DUBNER

FREAKONOMICS
A ROGUE ECONOMIST EXPLORES
THE HIDDEN SIDE OF EVERYTHING

ALSO BY
STEPHEN J. DUBNER

TURBULENT SOULS
A CATHOLIC SON'S RETURN TO HIS JEWISH FAMILY
ALSO PUBLISHED AS
CHOOSING MY RELIGION: A MEMOIR OF A FAMILY BEYOND BELIEF

**CONFESSIONS OF
A HERO-WORSHIPER**

**THE BOY WITH TWO
BELLY BUTTONS**

SUPER FREAKONOMICS

GLOBAL COOLING, PATRIOTIC PROSTITUTES, AND WHY SUICIDE BOMBERS SHOULD BUY LIFE INSURANCE

STEVEN D. LEVITT &
STEPHEN J. DUBNER

wm

WILLIAM MORROW

An Imprint of HarperCollins*Publishers*

Instructor's guides for *SuperFreakonomics* are available at www.HarperAcademic.com.

Designed by Number Seventeen, NYC

ISBN 978-1-61664-309-6

CONTENTS

CHAPTER 4

CHAPTER 5

AN EXPLANATORY NOTE

The time has come to admit that in our first book, we lied. Twice.

The first lie appeared in the introduction, where we wrote that the book had no "unifying theme." Here's what happened. Our publishing house—nice people, smart people—read the first draft of our book and cried out in alarm: "This book has no unifying theme!" Instead, the manuscript was a random heap of stories about cheating teachers, self-dealing Realtors, and crack-selling mama's boys. There was no nifty theoretical foundation upon which these stories could be piled to miraculously add up to more than the sum of their parts.

Our publisher's alarm only grew when we proposed a title for this mishmash of a book: *Freakonomics*. Even over the phone, you could hear the sound of palms smacking foreheads: *This pair of bozos just delivered a manuscript with no unifying theme and a nonsensical, made-up title!*

It was duly suggested that in the published book we concede right up front, in the introduction, that we had no unifying theme. And so, in the interest of keeping the peace (and our book advance), that's what we did.

But in truth, the book *did* have a unifying theme, even if it wasn't obvious at the time, even to us. If pressed, you could boil it down to four words: *People respond to incentives.* If you wanted to get more expansive, you might say this: *People respond to incentives, although not necessarily in ways that are predictable or manifest. Therefore, one of the most powerful laws in the universe is the law of unintended consequences. This applies to schoolteachers and Realtors and crack dealers as well as expectant mothers, sumo wrestlers, bagel salesmen, and the Ku Klux Klan.*

The issue of the book's title, meanwhile, still lay unresolved. After several months and dozens of suggestions, including *Unconventional Wisdom* (eh), *Ain't Necessarily So* (bleh), and *E-Ray Vision* (don't ask), our publisher finally decided that perhaps *Freakonomics* wasn't so bad after all—or, more precisely, it was so bad it might actually be good.

Or maybe they were simply exhausted.

The subtitle promised that the book would explore "the hidden side of everything." This was our second lie. We were sure reasonable people would view such a phrase as intentional hyperbole. But some readers took it literally, complaining that our stories, as motley a collection as they were, did not in fact address "everything." And so, while the subtitle was not intended as a lie, it turned out to be one. We apologize.

Our failure to include "everything" in the first book, however, had an unintended consequence of its own: it created the need for a second book. But let it be noted straightaway that this second book and the first book combined still do not literally comprise "everything."

The two of us have now been collaborators for several years. It began when one of us (Dubner, an author and journalist) wrote a magazine article about the other (Levitt, an academic economist). Adversaries in the beginning, albeit civil ones, we joined forces only when several publishers began to offer significant sums of money for a book. (Remember: *people respond to incentives*—and, despite the common perception, economists and journalists are people too.)

We discussed how the money should be divided. Almost immediately we came to an impasse, for each of us insisted on a 60–40 split. Upon realizing that we each thought the *other* guy should get 60 percent, we knew we'd have a good partnership. So we settled on 50–50 and got to work.

We didn't feel much pressure writing that first book because we genuinely thought few people would read it. (Levitt's father agreed and said it was "immoral" to accept even a penny up front.) These low expectations liberated us to write about any- and everything we found worthwhile. So we had a pretty good time.

We were surprised and thrilled when the book became a hit. As profitable as it might have been to pump out a quick follow-up—think *Freakonomics for Dummies* or *Chicken Soup for the Freakonomics Soul*—we wanted to wait until we had done enough research that we couldn't help but write it all down. So here we finally are, more than four years later, with a second book that we believe is easily better than the first. Of course it is up to you, not us, to say if that is true—or perhaps if it's as bad as some people feared our first book might be.

If nothing else, our publishers have resigned themselves to our unyielding bad taste: when we proposed that this new book be called *SuperFreakonomics,* they didn't even blink.

If this book *is* any good, you have yourselves to thank as well. One of the benefits of writing books in an age of such cheap and easy communication is that authors hear directly from their readers, loudly and clearly and in great number. Good feedback is hard to come by, and extremely valuable. Not only did we receive feedback on what we'd already written but also many suggestions for future topics. Some of you who sent e-mails will see your thoughts reflected in this book. Thank you.

The success of *Freakonomics* had one particularly strange by-product: we were regularly invited, together and separately, to give lectures to all sorts of groups. Often we were presented as the very sort of "experts" that in *Freakonomics* we warned you to watch out for—people who enjoy an informational advantage and have an incentive to exploit it. (We tried our best to disabuse audiences of the notion that we are actually expert in anything.)

These encounters also produced material for future writings. During a lecture at UCLA, one of us (Dubner) talked about how people wash their hands after using the bathroom far less often than they admit. Afterward, a gentleman approached the podium, offered his hand, and said he was a urologist. Despite this unappetizing introduction, the urologist had a fascinating story to tell about hand-washing failures in a high-stakes setting—the hospital where he worked—and the creative incentives the hospital used to overcome these failures. You'll find that story in this book, as well as the heroic story of another, long-ago doctor who also fought poor hand hygiene.

At another lecture, to a group of venture capitalists, Levitt discussed some new research he was doing with Sudhir Venkatesh, the sociologist whose adventures with a crack-selling gang were featured in *Freakonomics*. The new research concerned the hour-by-hour activities of street prostitutes in Chicago. As it happened, one of the venture capitalists (we'll call him John) had a date later that evening with a $300-an-hour prostitute (who goes by the name of Allie). When John arrived at Allie's apartment, he saw a copy of *Freakonomics* on her coffee table.

"Where'd you get *that*?" John asked.

Allie said a girlfriend of hers who was also "in the business" had sent it to her.

Hoping to impress Allie—the male instinct to impress the female is apparently strong even when the sex is already bought and paid for—John said he'd attended a lecture that very day by one of the book's authors. As if that weren't coincidence enough, Levitt mentioned he was doing some research on prostitution.

A few days later, this e-mail landed in Levitt's in-box:

> *I heard through a mutual acquaintance that you are working on a paper about the economics of prostitution, correct? Since I am not really sure if this is a serious project or if my source was putting me on, I just thought I would put myself out there and let you know I would love to be of assistance.*
>
> *Thanks, Allie*

One complication remained: Levitt had to explain to his wife and four kids that he wouldn't be home the following Saturday morning, that instead he'd be having brunch with a prostitute. It was vital, he argued, to meet with her in person to accurately measure the shape of her demand curve. Somehow, they bought it.

And so you will read about Allie in this book as well.

The chain of events that led to her inclusion might be attributed to what economists call *cumulative advantage*. That is, the prominence of our first book produced a series of advantages in writing a second book that a different author may not have enjoyed. Our greatest hope is that we have taken proper advantage of this advantage.

Finally, while writing this book we have tried to rely on a bare minimum of economics jargon, which can be abstruse and unmemorable. So instead of thinking about the Allie affair as an example of *cumulative advantage*, let's just call it . . . well, freaky.

INTRODUCTION

PUTTING THE FREAK IN ECONOMICS

Many of life's decisions are hard. What kind of career should you pursue? Does your ailing mother need to be put in a nursing home? You and your spouse already have two kids; should you have a third?

Such decisions are hard for a number of reasons. For one, the stakes are high. There's also a great deal of uncertainty involved. Above all, decisions like these are rare, which means you don't get much practice making them. You've probably gotten pretty good at buying groceries, since you do it so often, but buying your first house is another thing entirely.

Some decisions, meanwhile, are really, really easy.

Imagine you've gone to a party at a friend's house. He lives only a mile away. You have a great time, perhaps because you drank four glasses of wine. Now the party is breaking up. While draining your last glass, you dig out your car keys. Abruptly you conclude this is a bad idea: you are in no condition to drive home.

For the past few decades, we've been rigorously educated about the risks of driving under the influence of alcohol. A drunk driver is thirteen times more likely to cause an accident than a sober one. And yet a lot of people still drive drunk. In the United States, more than 30 percent of all fatal crashes involve at least one driver who has been drinking. During the late-night hours, when alcohol use is greatest, that proportion rises to nearly 60 percent. Overall, 1 of every 140 miles is driven drunk, or 21 billion miles each year.

Why do so many people get behind the wheel after drinking? Maybe because—and this could be the most sobering statistic yet—drunk drivers are rarely caught. There is just one arrest for every 27,000 miles driven while drunk. That means you could expect to drive all the way across the country, and then back, and then back and forth three more times, chugging beers all the while, before you got pulled over. As with most bad behaviors, drunk driving could probably be wiped out entirely if a strong-enough incentive were instituted—random roadblocks, for instance, where drunk drivers are executed on the spot—but our society probably doesn't have the appetite for that.

Meanwhile, back at your friend's party, you have made what seems to be the easiest decision in history: instead of driving home, you're going to walk. After all, it's only a mile. You find your friend, thank him for the party, and tell him the plan. He heartily applauds your good judgment.

But should he? We all know that drunk driving is terribly risky, but what about drunk walking? *Is* this decision so easy?

Let's look at some numbers. Each year, more than 1,000 drunk pedestrians die in traffic accidents. They step off sidewalks into city streets; they lie down to rest on country roads; they make mad dashes across busy highways. Compared with the total number of people killed in alcohol-related traffic accidents each year—about 13,000—the number of drunk pedestrians is relatively small. But when you're choosing whether to walk or drive, the overall number isn't what counts. Here's the relevant question: on a per-mile basis, is it more dangerous to drive drunk or walk drunk?

The average American walks about a half-mile per day outside the home or workplace. There are some 237 million Americans sixteen and older; all told, that's 43 billion miles walked each year by people of driving age. If we assume that 1 of every 140 of those miles are walked drunk—the same proportion of miles that are driven drunk—then 307 million miles are walked drunk each year.

Doing the math, you find that on a per-mile basis, a drunk walker is *eight times more likely* to get killed than a drunk driver.

There's one important caveat: a drunk walker isn't likely to hurt or kill anyone other than her- or himself. That can't be said of a drunk driver. In fatal accidents involving alcohol, 36 percent of the victims are either passengers, pedestrians, or other drivers. Still, even after factoring in the deaths of those innocents, walking drunk leads to five times as many deaths per mile as driving drunk.

So as you leave your friend's party, the decision should be clear: driving is safer than walking. (It would be even safer, obviously, to drink less, or to call a cab.) The next time you put away four glasses of wine at a party, maybe you'll think through your decision a bit differently. Or, if you're too far gone, maybe your friend will help sort things out. Because friends don't let friends walk drunk.

If you had the option of being born anywhere in the world today, India might not be the wisest choice. Despite its vaunted progress as a major player in the global economy, the country as a whole remains excruciatingly poor. Life expectancy and literacy rates are low; pollution and corruption are high. In the rural areas where more than two-thirds of Indians live, barely half of the households have electricity and only one in four homes has a toilet.

It is especially unlucky to be born female, because many Indian parents express a strong "son preference." Only 10 percent of Indian families with two sons want another child, whereas nearly 40 percent of families with two daughters want to try again. Giving birth to a baby boy is like giving birth to a 401(k) retirement fund. He will grow up to be a wage-earning man who can provide for his parents in their sunset years and, when the time comes, light the funeral pyre. Having a baby girl, meanwhile, means relabeling the retirement fund a dowry fund. Although the dowry system has long been under assault, it is still common for a bride's parents to give the groom or his family cash, cars, or real estate. The bride's family is also expected to pay for the wedding.

The U.S. charity Smile Train, which performs cleft-repair surgery on poor children around the world, recently spent some time in Chennai, India. When one local man was asked how many children he had, he answered "one." The organization later learned that the man did have a son—but he also had five daughters, who apparently didn't warrant a mention. Smile Train also learned that midwives in Chennai were sometimes paid $2.50 to smother a baby girl born with a cleft deformity—and so, putting the lure of incentives to good use, the charity began offering midwives as much as $10 for each baby girl they took to a hospital for cleft surgery.

Girls are so undervalued in India that there are roughly 35 million fewer females than males in the population. Most of these "missing women," as the economist Amartya Sen calls them, are presumed dead, either by indirect means (the girl's parents withheld nutrition or medical care, perhaps to the benefit of a brother), direct harm (the baby girl was killed after birth, whether by a midwife or a parent), or, increasingly, a pre-birth decision. Even in India's smallest villages, where electricity might be sporadic and clean water hard to find, a pregnant woman can pay a technician to scan her belly with an ultrasound and, if the fetus is female, have an abortion. In recent years, as these sex-selective abortions have become more common, the male-female ratio in India—as well as in other son-worshipping countries like China—has grown even more lopsided.

A baby Indian girl who does grow into adulthood faces inequality at nearly every turn. She will earn less money than a man, receive worse health care and less education, and perhaps be subjected to daily atrocities. In a national health survey, 51 percent of Indian men said that wife-beating is justified under certain circumstances; more surprisingly, 54 percent of *women* agreed—if, for instance, a wife burns dinner or leaves the house without permission. More than 100,000 young Indian women die in fires every year, many of them "bride burnings" or other instances of domestic abuse.

Indian women also run an outsize risk of unwanted pregnancy and sexually transmitted disease, including a high rate of HIV/AIDS. One cause is that Indian men's condoms malfunction more than 15 percent of the time. Why such a high fail rate? According to the Indian Council of Medical Research, some 60 percent of Indian men have penises too small for the condoms manufactured to fit World Health Organization specs. That was the conclusion of a two-year study in which more than 1,000 Indian men had their penises measured and photographed by scientists. "The condom," declared one of the researchers, "is not optimized for India."

With such a multitude of problems, what should be done to improve the lives of Indian women, especially the majority who live in the countryside?

The government has tried to help by banning dowries and sex-selective abortions, but these laws have largely been ignored. A number of monetary interventions have also been designed for Indian women. These include Apni Beti, Apna Dhan ("My Daughter, My Pride"), a project that pays rural women not to abort female babies; a vast microcredit industry that makes small-business loans to women; and an array of charitable programs launched by a veritable alphabet soup of international aid agencies.

The Indian government has also vowed to make smaller condoms more readily available.

Unfortunately, most of these projects have proven complicated, costly, and, at best, nominally successful.

A different sort of intervention, meanwhile, *does* seem to have helped. This one, like the ultrasound machine, relies on technology, but it had little to do with women per se and even less to do with baby-making. Nor was it administered by the Indian government or some multinational charity. In fact, it wasn't even designed to help anyone at all, at least not the way we normally think of "help." It was just a plain old entrepreneurial development, called television.

State-run broadcast TV had been around for decades, but poor reception and a dearth of programming meant there simply wasn't much reason to watch. But lately, thanks to a steep fall in the price of equipment and distribution, great swaths of India have been wired for cable and satellite TV. Between 2001 and 2006, some 150 million Indians received cable for the first time, their villages suddenly crackling with the latest game shows and soap operas, newscasts and police procedurals, beamed from the big cities of India and abroad. TV gave many Indian villagers their first good look at the outside world.

But not every village got cable TV, and those that did received it at different times. This staggered introduction produced just the kind of data—a lovely natural experiment—that economists love to exploit. The economists in this case were a pair of young Americans, Emily Oster and Robert Jensen. By measuring the changes in different villages based on whether (and when) each village got cable TV, they were able to tease out the effect of TV on Indian women.

They examined data from a government survey of 2,700 households, most of them rural. Women fifteen and older were asked about their lifestyles, preferences, and familial relationships. As it turned out, the women who recently got cable TV were significantly less willing to tolerate wife-beating, less likely to admit to having a son preference, and more likely to exercise personal autonomy. TV somehow seemed to be empowering women in a way that government interventions had not.

What caused these changes? Did rural Indian women become more autonomous after seeing cosmopolitan images on their TV sets—women who dressed as they pleased, handled their own money, and were treated as neither property nor baby-making machines? Or did such programming simply make the rural women feel embarrassed to admit to a government surveyor that they were treated so badly?

There is good reason to be skeptical of data from personal surveys. There is often a vast gulf between how people say they behave and how they actually behave. (In economist-speak, these two behaviors are known as *declared preferences* and *revealed preferences*.) Furthermore, when it costs almost nothing to fib—as in the case of a government survey like this one—a reasonable amount of fibbing is to be expected. The fibs might even be subconscious, with the subject simply saying what she expects the surveyor wants to hear.

But when you can measure the revealed preference, or the actual behavior, then you're getting somewhere. That's where Oster and Jensen found persuasive evidence of real change. Rural Indian families who got cable TV began to have a lower birthrate than families without TV. (In a country like India, a lower birthrate generally means more autonomy for women and fewer health risks.) Families with TV were also more likely to keep their daughters in school, which suggests that girls were seen as more valuable, or at least deserving of equal treatment. (The enrollment rate for boys, notably, didn't change.) These hard numbers made the self-reported survey data more believable. It appears that cable TV really did empower the women of rural India, even to the point of no longer tolerating domestic abuse.

Or maybe their husbands were just too busy watching cricket.

When the world was lurching into the modern era, it grew magnificently more populous, and in a hurry. Most of this expansion took place in urban centers like London, Paris, New York, and Chicago. In the United States alone, cities grew by 30 million residents during the nineteenth century, with half of that gain in just the final twenty years.

But as this swarm of humanity moved itself, and its goods, from place to place, a problem emerged. The main mode of transportation produced a slew of the by-products that economists call *negative externalities,* including gridlock, high insurance costs, and far too many traffic fatalities. Crops that would have landed on a family's dinner table were sometimes converted into fuel, driving up food prices and causing shortages. Then there were the air pollutants and toxic emissions, endangering the environment as well as individuals' health.

We are talking about the automobile—aren't we?

No, we're not. We are talking about the horse.

The horse, a versatile and powerful helpmate since the days of antiquity, was put to work in many ways as modern cities expanded: pulling streetcars and private coaches, hauling construction materials, unloading freight from ships and trains, even powering the machines that churned out furniture, rope, beer, and clothing. If your young daughter took gravely ill, the doctor rushed to your home on horseback. When a fire broke out, a team of horses charged through the streets with a pumping truck. At the turn of the twentieth century, some 200,000 horses lived and worked in New York City, or 1 for every 17 people.

But oh, the troubles they caused!

Horse-drawn wagons clogged the streets terribly, and when a horse broke down, it was often put to death on the spot. This caused further delays. Many stable owners held life-insurance policies that, to guard against fraud, stipulated the animal be euthanized by a third party. This meant waiting for the police, a veterinarian, or the ASPCA to arrive. Even death didn't end the gridlock. "Dead horses were extremely unwieldy," writes the transportation scholar Eric Morris. "As a result, street cleaners often waited for the corpses to putrefy so they could more easily be sawed into pieces and carted off."

The noise from iron wagon wheels and horseshoes was so disturbing—it purportedly caused widespread nervous disorders—that some cities banned horse traffic on the streets around hospitals and other sensitive areas.

And it was frighteningly easy to be struck down by a horse or wagon, neither of which is as easy to control as they appear in the movies, especially on slick, crowded city streets. In 1900, horse accidents claimed the lives of 200 New Yorkers, or 1 of every 17,000 residents. In 2007, meanwhile, 274 New Yorkers died in auto accidents, or 1 of every 30,000 residents. This means that a New Yorker was nearly twice as likely to die from a horse accident in 1900 than from a car accident today. (There are unfortunately no statistics available on drunk horse-drivers, but we can assume the number would be menacingly high.)

Worst of all was the dung. The average horse produced about 24 pounds of manure a day. With 200,000 horses, that's nearly 5 million pounds of horse manure. A day. Where did it go?

Decades earlier, when horses were less plentiful in cities, there was a smooth-functioning market for manure, with farmers buying it to truck off (via horse, of course) to their fields. But as the urban equine population exploded, there was a massive glut. In vacant lots, horse manure was piled as high as sixty feet. It lined city streets like banks of snow. In the summertime, it stank to the heavens; when the rains came, a soupy stream of horse manure flooded the crosswalks and seeped into people's basements. Today, when you admire old New York brownstones and their elegant stoops, rising from street level to the second-story parlor, keep in mind that this was a design necessity, allowing a homeowner to rise above the sea of horse manure.

All of this dung was terrifically unhealthy. It was a breeding ground for billions of flies that spread a host of deadly diseases. Rats and other vermin swarmed the mountains of manure to pick out undigested oats and other horse feed—crops that were becoming more costly for human consumption thanks to higher horse demand. No one at the time was worried about global warming, but if they had been, the horse would have been Public Enemy No. 1, for its manure emits methane, a powerful greenhouse gas.

In 1898, New York hosted the first international urban planning conference. The agenda was dominated by horse manure, because cities around the world were experiencing the same crisis. But no solution could be found. "Stumped by the crisis," writes Eric Morris, "the urban planning conference declared its work fruitless and broke up in three days instead of the scheduled ten."

The world had seemingly reached the point where its largest cities could not survive without the horse but couldn't survive with it, either.

And then the problem vanished. It was neither government fiat nor divine intervention that did the trick. City dwellers did not rise up in some mass movement of altruism or self-restraint, surrendering all the benefits of horse power. The problem was solved by technological innovation. No, not the invention of a dung-less animal. The horse was kicked to the curb by the electric streetcar and the automobile, both of which were extravagantly cleaner and far more efficient. The automobile, cheaper to own and operate than a horse-drawn vehicle, was proclaimed "an environmental savior." Cities around the world were able to take a deep breath—without holding their noses at last—and resume their march of progress.

The story, unfortunately, does not end there. The solutions that saved the twentieth century seem to have imperiled the twenty-first, because the automobile and electric streetcar carried their own negative externalities. The carbon emissions spat out over the past century by more than 1 billion cars and thousands of coal-burning power plants seem to have warmed the earth's atmosphere. Just as equine activity once threatened to stomp out civilization, there is now a fear that human activity will do the same. Martin Weitzman, an environmental economist at Harvard, argues there is a roughly 5 percent chance that global temperatures will rise enough to "effectively destroy planet Earth as we know it." In some quarters—the media, for instance, which never met a potential apocalypse it didn't like—the fatalism runs even stronger.

This is perhaps not very surprising. When the solution to a given problem doesn't lay right before our eyes, it is easy to assume that no solution exists. But history has shown again and again that such assumptions are wrong.

This is not to say the world is perfect. Nor that all progress is always good. Even widespread societal gains inevitably produce losses for some people. That's why the economist Joseph Schumpeter referred to capitalism as "creative destruction."

But humankind has a great capacity for finding technological solutions to seemingly intractable problems, and this will likely be the case for global warming. It isn't that the problem isn't potentially large. It's just that human ingenuity—when given proper incentives—is bound to be larger. Even more encouraging, technological fixes are often far simpler, and therefore cheaper, than the doomsayers could have imagined. Indeed, in the final chapter of this book we'll meet a band of renegade engineers who have developed not one but three global-warming fixes, any of which could be bought for less than the annual sales tally of all the Thoroughbred horses at Keeneland auction house in Kentucky.

The value of horse manure, incidentally, has rebounded, so much so that the owners of one Massachusetts farm recently called the police to stop a neighbor from hauling it away. The neighbor claimed there was a misunderstanding, that he'd been given permission by the farm's previous owner. But the current owner wouldn't back down, demanding $600 for the manure.

Who was this manure-loving neighbor? None other than Martin Weitzman, the economist with the grave global-warming prediction.

"Congratulations," one colleague wrote to Weitzman when the story hit the papers. "Most economists I know are net exporters of horseshit. And you are, it seems, a net importer."

The vanquishing of horse manure . . . the unintended consequences of cable TV . . . the perils of walking while drunk: what does any of this have to do with economics?

Instead of thinking of such stories as "economics," it is better to see them as illustrating "the economic approach." That's a phrase made popular by Gary Becker, the longtime University of Chicago economist who was awarded a Nobel Prize in 1992. In his acceptance lecture, he explained that the economic approach "does not assume that individuals are motivated solely by selfishness or gain. It is a *method* of analysis, not an assumption about particular motivations. . . . Behavior is driven by a much richer set of values and preferences."

Becker started his career studying topics that weren't typically germane to economics: crime and punishment, drug addiction, the allocation of time, and the costs and benefits of marriage, child rearing, and divorce. Most of his colleagues wouldn't go anywhere near such stuff.

"For a long time," he recalled, "my type of work was either ignored or strongly disliked by most of the leading economists. I was considered way out and perhaps not really an economist."

Well, if what Gary Becker was doing was "not really economics," then we want to do it too. Truth be told, what Becker was doing was actually freakonomics—marrying the economic approach to a rogue, freakish curiosity—but the word hadn't yet been invented.

In his Nobel address, Becker suggested that the economic approach is not a subject matter, nor is it a mathematical means of explaining "the economy." Rather, it is a decision to examine the world a bit differently. It is a systematic means of describing how people make decisions and how they change their minds; how they choose someone to love and marry, someone perhaps to hate and even kill; whether, coming upon a pile of money, they will steal from it, leave it alone, or even add to it; why they may fear one thing and yearn for something only slightly different; why they'll punish one sort of behavior while rewarding a similar one.

How do economists describe such decisions? It usually begins by accumulating data, great gobs of it, which may have been generated on purpose or perhaps left behind by accident. A good set of data can go a long way toward describing human behavior as long as the proper questions are asked of it. Our job in this book is to come up with such questions. This will allow us to describe, for instance, how the typical oncologist or terrorist or college student behaves in a given situation, and why.

Some people may feel uneasy about reducing the vagaries of human behavior to cold numerical probabilities. Who among us wants to describe ourselves as "typical"? If, for instance, you added up all the women and men on the planet, you would find that, on average, the typical adult human being has one breast and one testicle—and yet how many people fit that description? If *your* loved one was killed in a drunk-driving accident, what comfort is there in knowing that walking drunk is more dangerous? If *you* are the young Indian bride who is brutalized by her husband, what cheer can be had from learning that cable TV has empowered the *typical* Indian bride?

These objections are good and true. But while there are exceptions to every rule, it's also good to know the rule. In a complex world where people can be *a*typical in an infinite number of ways, there is great value in discovering the baseline. And knowing what happens on average is a good place to start. By so doing, we insulate ourselves from the tendency to build our thinking—our daily decisions, our laws, our governance—on exceptions and anomalies rather than on reality.

Cast an eye back for a moment to the summer months of 2001, which in the United States came to be known as the Summer of the Shark. The media brought us chilling tales of rampant shark carnage. The prime example was the story of Jessie Arbogast, an eight-year-old boy who was playing in the warm, shallow Gulf waves of Pensacola, Florida, when a bull shark ripped off his right arm and gorged a big piece of his thigh as well. *Time* magazine ran a cover package about shark attacks. Here is the lead of the main article:

> *Sharks come silently, without warning. There are three ways they strike: the hit-and-run, the bump-and-bite and the sneak attack. The hit-and-run is the most common. The shark may see the sole of a swimmer's foot, think it's a fish and take a bite before realizing this isn't its usual prey.*

Scared yet?

A reasonable person might never go near the ocean again. But how many shark attacks do you think actually happened that year?

Take a guess—and then cut your guess in half, and now cut it in half a few more times. During the entire year of 2001, around the world there were just 68 shark attacks, of which 4 were fatal.

Not only are these numbers far lower than the media hysteria implied; they were also no higher than in earlier years or in the years to follow. Between 1995 and 2005, there were on average 60.3 worldwide shark attacks each year, with a high of 79 and a low of 46. There were on average 5.9 fatalities per year, with a high of 11 and a low of 3. In other words, the headlines during the summer of 2001 might just as easily have read "Shark Attacks About Average This Year." But that probably wouldn't have sold many magazines.

So for a moment, instead of thinking about poor Jessie Arbogast and the tragedy he and his family faced, think of this: in a world with more than 6 billion people, only 4 of them died in 2001 from shark attacks. More people are probably run over each year by TV news vans.

Elephants, meanwhile, kill at least 200 people every year. So why aren't we petrified of them? Probably because most of their victims live in places far from the world's media centers. It may also have something to do with the perceptions we glean from the movies. Friendly, entertaining elephants are a staple of children's films (think *Babar* and *Dumbo*); sharks, meanwhile, are inevitably typecast as villains. If sharks had any legal connections whatsoever, they surely would have sued for an injunction against *Jaws*.

And yet the shark scare played out so relentlessly that summer of 2001, with such full-throated horror, that it didn't quiet down until the terrorist attacks on September 11 at the World Trade Center and the Pentagon. Nearly 3,000 people were killed that day—some 2,500 more than have died from shark attacks since the first records were kept, in the late sixteenth century.

So despite its shortcomings, thinking in terms of the typical does have its advantages. We have therefore done our best to tell stories in this book that rely on accumulated data rather than on individual anecdotes, glaring anomalies, personal opinions, emotional outbursts, or moral leanings. Some people may argue that statistics can be made to say anything, to defend indefensible causes or tell pet lies. But the economic approach aims for the opposite: to address a given topic with neither fear nor favor, letting numbers speak the truth. We don't take sides. The introduction of TV, for instance, has substantially helped the women of rural India. This doesn't mean we accept the power of TV as unerringly positive. As you will read in chapter 3, the introduction of TV in the United States produced a devastating societal change.

The economic approach isn't meant to describe the world as any one of us might *want* it to be, or fear that it is, or pray that it becomes—but rather to explain what it actually is. Most of us want to fix or change the world in some fashion. But to change the world, you first have to understand it.

As of this writing, we are roughly one year into a financial crisis that began with a subprime-mortgage binge in the United States and spread, like an extremely communicable disease, around the world. There will be hundreds, if not thousands, of books published on the topic.

This is not one of them.

Why? Mainly because the macroeconomy and its multitude of complex, moving parts is simply not our domain. After recent events, one might wonder if the macroeconomy is the domain of *any* economist. Most economists the public encounters are presented as oracles who can tell you, with alluring certainty, where the stock market or inflation or interest rates are heading. But as we've seen lately, such predictions are generally worthless. Economists have a hard enough time explaining the past, much less predicting the future. (They are still arguing over whether Franklin Delano Roosevelt's policy moves quelled the Great Depression or exacerbated it!) They are not alone, of course.

It seems to be part of the human condition to believe in our own predictive abilities—and, just as well, to quickly forget how bad our predictions turned out to be.

So we have practically nothing to say in this book about what people call "the economy." Our best defense (slim as it may be) is that the topics we *do* write about, while not directly connected to "the economy," may give some insights into actual human behavior. Believe it or not, if you can understand the incentives that lead a schoolteacher or a sumo wrestler to cheat, you can understand how the subprime-mortgage bubble came to pass.

The stories you will read are set in many realms, from the rarefied corridors of academia to the grimiest street corners. Many are based on Levitt's recent academic research; others have been inspired by fellow economists as well as engineers and astrophysicists, psychotic killers and emergency-room doctors, amateur historians and transgender neuroscientists.* Most of the stories fall into one of two categories: things you always thought you knew but didn't; and things you never knew you wanted to know but do.

Many of our findings may not be all that useful, or even conclusive. But that's all right. We are trying to start a conversation, not have the last word. Which means you may find a few things in the following pages to quarrel with.

In fact, we'd be disappointed if you didn't.

---

*To learn about the underlying research on any given section of the book, please read the endnotes (page 221).

CHAPTER 1

HOW IS A STREET PROSTITUTE LIKE A DEPARTMENT-STORE SANTA?

One afternoon not long ago, on a welcoming cool day toward the end of summer, a twenty-nine-year-old woman named LaSheena sat on the hood of an SUV outside the Dearborn Homes, a housing project on the South Side of Chicago. She had a beaten-down look in her eyes but otherwise seemed youthful, her pretty face framed by straightened hair. She was dressed in a baggy black-and-red tracksuit, the kind she'd worn since she was a kid. Her parents rarely had money for new clothes, so she used to get her male cousins' hand-me-downs, and the habit stuck.

LaSheena was talking about how she earns her living. She described four main streams of income: "boosting," "roosting," cutting hair, and turning tricks.

"Boosting," she explained, is shoplifting and selling the swag. "Roosting" means serving as a lookout for the local street gang that sells drugs. She gets $8 for a boy's haircut and $12 for a man's.

Which job is the worst of the four?

"Turning tricks," she says, with no hesitation.

Why?

"'Cause I don't really like men. I guess it bothers me mentally."

And what if prostitution paid twice as much?

"Would I do it more?" she asks. "Yeah!"

Throughout history, it has invariably been easier to be male than female. Yes, this is an overgeneralization and yes, there are exceptions, but by any important measure, women have had it rougher than men. Even though men handled most of the warfare, hunting, and brute-force labor, women had a shorter life expectancy. Some deaths were more senseless than others. Between the thirteenth and nineteenth centuries, as many as 1 million European women, most of them poor and many of them widowed, were executed for witchcraft, taking the blame for bad weather that killed crops.

Women have finally overtaken men in life expectancy, thanks mainly to medical improvements surrounding childbirth. In many countries, however, being female remains a serious handicap even in the twenty-first century. Young women in Cameroon have their breasts "ironed"—beaten or massaged by a wooden pestle or a heated coconut shell—to make them less sexually tempting. In China, foot binding has finally been done away with (after roughly one thousand years), but females are still far more likely than males to be abandoned after birth, to be illiterate, and to commit suicide. And women in rural India, as we wrote earlier, continue to face discrimination in just about every direction.

But especially in the world's developed nations, women's lives have improved dramatically. There is no comparing the prospects of a girl in twenty-first-century America or Britain or Japan with her counterpart from a century or two earlier. In any arena you look—education, legal and voting rights, career opportunities, and so on—it is far better to be a woman today than at any other point in history. In 1872, the earliest year for which such statistics are available, 21 percent of college students in the United States were female. Today, that number is 58 percent and rising. It has truly been a stunning ascendancy.

And yet there is still a considerable economic price to pay for being a woman. For American women twenty-five and older who hold at least a bachelor's degree and work full-time, the national median income is about $47,000. Similar men, meanwhile, make more than $66,000, a premium of 40 percent. The same is true even for women who attend the nation's elite universities. The economists Claudia Goldin and Lawrence Katz found that women who went to Harvard earned *less than half as much* as the average Harvard man. Even when the analysis included only full-time, full-year employees and controlled for college major, profession, and other variables, Goldin and Katz found that the Harvard women still earned about 30 percent less than their male counterparts.

What can possibly account for such a huge wage gap?

There are a variety of factors. Women are more likely to leave the workforce or downshift their careers to raise a family. Even within high-paying occupations like medicine and law, women tend to choose specialties that pay less (general practitioner, for instance, or in-house counsel). And there is likely still a good amount of discrimination. This may range from the overt—denying a woman a promotion purely because she is not a man—to the insidious. A considerable body of research has shown that overweight women suffer a greater wage penalty than overweight men. The same is true for women with bad teeth.

There are some biological wild cards as well. The economists Andrea Ichino and Enrico Moretti, analyzing personnel data from a large Italian bank, found that female employees under forty-five years old tended to miss work consistently on twenty-eight-day cycles. Plotting these absences against employee productivity ratings, the economists determined that this menstrual absenteeism accounted for 14 percent of the difference between female and male earnings at the bank.

Or consider the 1972 U.S. law known as Title IX. While broadly designed to prohibit sex discrimination in educational settings, Title IX also required high schools and colleges to bring their women's sports programs up to the level of their men's programs. Millions of young women subsequently joined these new programs, and as the economist Betsey Stevenson discovered, girls who play high-school sports are more likely to attend college and land a solid job, especially in some of the high-skill fields traditionally dominated by men. That's the good news.

But Title IX also brought some bad news for women. When the law was passed, more than 90 percent of college women's sports teams had female head coaches. Title IX boosted the appeal of such jobs: salaries rose and there was more exposure and excitement. Like the lowly peasant food that is "discovered" by the culinary elite and promptly migrates from roadside shacks into high-end restaurants, these jobs were soon snapped up by a new set of customers: men. These days, barely 40 percent of college women's sports teams are coached by women. Among the most visible coaching jobs in women's sports are those in the Women's National Basketball Association (WNBA), founded thirteen years ago as a corollary to the men's NBA. As of this writing, the WNBA has 13 teams and just 6 of them—again, fewer than 50 percent—are coached by women. This is actually an improvement from the league's tenth anniversary season, when only 3 of the 14 coaches were women.

For all the progress women have made in the twenty-first-century labor market, the typical female would come out well ahead if she had simply had the foresight to be born male.

There *is* one labor market women have always dominated: prostitution.

Its business model is built upon a simple premise. Since time immemorial and all over the world, men have wanted more sex than they could get for free. So what inevitably emerges is a supply of women who, for the right price, are willing to satisfy this demand.

Today prostitution is generally illegal in the United States, albeit with a few exceptions and many inconsistencies in enforcement. In the early years of the nation, prostitution was frowned upon but not criminalized. It was during the Progressive Era, roughly from the 1890s to the 1920s, that this leniency ended. There was a public outcry against "white slavery," in which thousands of women were imprisoned against their will to work as prostitutes.

The white slavery problem turned out to be a wild exaggeration. The reality was perhaps scarier: rather than being forced into prostitution, women were choosing it for themselves. In the early 1910s, the Department of Justice conducted a census of 310 cities in 26 states to tally the number of prostitutes in the United States: "We arrive at the conservative figure of approximately 200,000 women in the regular army of vice."

At the time, the American population included 22 million women between the ages of fifteen and forty-four. If the DOJ numbers are to be believed, 1 of every 110 women in that age range was a prostitute. But most prostitutes, about 85 percent, were in their twenties. In that age range, 1 of every *50* American women was a prostitute.

The market was particularly strong in Chicago, which had more than a thousand known brothels. The mayor assembled a blue-ribbon Vice Commission, comprising religious leaders as well as civic, educational, legal, and medical authorities. Once they got their hands dirty, these good people realized they were up against an enemy even more venal than sex: economics.

"Is it any wonder," the commission declared, "that a tempted girl who receives only $6 per week working with her hands sells her body for $25 per week when she learns that there is demand for it and men are willing to pay the price?"

Converted into today's dollars, the $6-per-week shopgirl had an annual salary of only $6,500. The same woman who took up prostitution at $25 a week earned the modern equivalent of more than $25,000 a year. But the Vice Commission acknowledged that $25 per week was at the very low end of what Chicago prostitutes earned. A woman working in a "dollar house" (some brothels charged as little as 50 cents; others charged $5 or $10) took home an average weekly salary of $70, or the modern equivalent of about $76,000 annually.

At the heart of the Levee, the South Side neighborhood that housed block after block of brothels, stood the Everleigh Club, which the Vice Commission described as "the most famous and luxurious house of prostitution in the country." Its customers included business titans, politicians, athletes, entertainers, and even a few anti-prostitution crusaders. The Everleigh's prostitutes, known as "butterfly girls," were not only attractive, hygienic, and trustworthy, but also good conversationalists who could cite classical poetry if that's what floated a particular gentleman's boat. In the book *Sin in the Second City,* Karen Abbott reports that the Everleigh also offered sexual delicacies that weren't available elsewhere—"French" style, for instance, commonly known today as oral sex.

In an age when a nice dinner cost about $12 in today's currency, the Everleigh's customers were willing to pay the equivalent of $250 just to get into the club and $370 for a bottle of champagne. Relatively speaking, the sex was pretty cheap: about $1,250.

Ada and Minna Everleigh, the sisters who ran the brothel, guarded their assets carefully. Butterflies were provided with a healthful diet, excellent medical care, a well-rounded education, and the best wage going: as much as $400 a week, or the modern equivalent of about $430,000 a year.

To be sure, an Everleigh butterfly's wages were off the charts. But why did even a typical Chicago prostitute one hundred years ago earn so much money?

The best answer is that wages are determined in large part by the laws of supply and demand, which are often more powerful than laws made by legislators.

In the United States especially, politics and economics don't mix well. Politicians have all sorts of reasons to pass all sorts of laws that, as well-meaning as they may be, fail to account for the way real people respond to real-world incentives.

When prostitution was criminalized in the United States, most of the policing energy was directed at the prostitutes rather than their customers. This is pretty typical. As with other illicit markets—think about drug dealing or black-market guns—most governments prefer to punish the people who are supplying the goods and services rather than the people who are consuming them.

But when you lock up a supplier, a scarcity is created that inevitably drives the price higher, and that entices more suppliers to enter the market. The U.S. "war on drugs" has been relatively ineffective precisely because it focuses on sellers and not buyers. While drug buyers obviously outnumber drug sellers, more than 90 percent of all prison time for drug convictions is served by dealers.

Why doesn't the public support punishing users? It may seem unfair to punish the little guy, the user, when he can't help himself from partaking in vice. The suppliers, meanwhile, are much easier to demonize.

But if a government really wanted to crack down on illicit goods and services, it would go after the people who demand them. If, for instance, men convicted of hiring a prostitute were sentenced to castration, the market would contract in a hurry.

In Chicago some one hundred years ago, the risk of punishment fell almost entirely on the prostitute. Besides the constant threat of arrest, there was also the deep social stigma of prostitution. Perhaps the greatest penalty was that a woman who worked as a prostitute would never be able to find a suitable husband. Combine these factors and you can see that a prostitute's wages *had* to be high to entice enough women to satisfy the strong demand.

The biggest money, of course, was taken home by the women at the top of the prostitution pyramid. By the time the Everleigh Club was shut down—the Chicago Vice Commission finally got its way—Ada and Minna Everleigh had accumulated, in today's currency, about $22 million.

The mansion that housed the Everleigh Club is long gone. So is the entire Levee district. The very street grid where the Everleigh stood was wiped away in the 1960s, replaced by a high-rise housing project.

But this is still the South Side of Chicago and prostitutes still work there—like LaSheena, in the black-and-red tracksuit—although you can be pretty sure they won't be quoting you any Greek poetry.

LaSheena is one of the many street prostitutes Sudhir Venkatesh has gotten to know lately. Venkatesh, a sociologist at Columbia University in New York, spent his grad-school years in Chicago and still returns there regularly for research.

When he first arrived, he was a naïve, sheltered, Grateful Dead-loving kid who'd grown up in laid-back California, eager to take the temperature of an intense town where race—particularly black and white—played out with great zeal. Being neither black nor white (he was born in India) worked in Venkatesh's favor, letting him slip behind the battle lines of both academia (which was overwhelmingly white) and the South Side ghettos (which were overwhelmingly black). Before long, he had embedded himself with a street gang that practically ran the neighborhood and made most of its money by selling crack cocaine. (Yes, it was Venkatesh's research that figured prominently in the *Freakonomics* chapter about drug dealers, and yes, we are back now for a second helping.) Along the way, he became an authority on the neighborhood's underground economy, and when he was done with the drug dealers he moved on to the prostitutes.

But an interview or two with a woman like LaSheena can reveal only so much. Anyone who wants to really understand the prostitution market needs to accumulate some real data.

That's easier said than done. Because of the illicit nature of the activity, standard data sources (think of census forms or tax rolls) are no help. Even when prostitutes have been surveyed directly in previous studies, the interviews are often conducted long after the fact and by the kind of agency (a drug-rehab center, for instance, or a church shelter) that doesn't necessarily elicit impartial results.

Moreover, earlier research has shown that when people are surveyed about stigmatizing behavior, they either downplay or exaggerate their participation, depending on what's at stake or who is asking.

Consider the Mexican welfare program Oportunidades. To get aid, applicants have to itemize their personal possessions and household goods. Once an applicant is accepted, a caseworker visits his home and learns whether the applicant was telling the truth.

César Martinelli and Susan W. Parker, two economists who analyzed the data from more than 100,000 Oportunidades clients, found that applicants routinely underreported certain items, including cars, trucks, video recorders, satellite TVs, and washing machines. This shouldn't surprise anyone. People hoping to get welfare benefits have an incentive to make it sound like they are poorer than they truly are. But as Martinelli and Parker discovered, applicants *over*reported other items: indoor plumbing, running water, a gas stove, and a concrete floor. Why on earth would welfare applicants say they had these essentials when they didn't?

Martinelli and Parker attribute it to embarrassment. Even people who are poor enough to need welfare apparently don't want to admit to a welfare clerk that they have a dirt floor or live without a toilet.

Venkatesh, knowing that traditional survey methods don't necessarily produce reliable results for a sensitive topic like prostitution, tried something different: real-time, on-the-spot data collection. He hired trackers to stand on street corners or sit in brothels with the prostitutes, directly observing some facets of their transactions and gathering more intimate details from the prostitutes as soon as the customers were gone.

Most of the trackers were former prostitutes—an important credential because such women were more likely to get honest responses. Venkatesh also paid the prostitutes for participating in the study. If they were willing to have sex for money, he reasoned, surely they'd be willing to talk about having sex for money. And they were. Over the course of nearly two years, Venkatesh accumulated data on roughly 160 prostitutes in three separate South Side neighborhoods, logging more than 2,200 sexual transactions.

The tracking sheets recorded a considerable variety of data, including:

- The specific sexual act performed, and the duration of the trick
- Where the act took place (in a car, outdoors, or indoors)
- Amount received in cash
- Amount received in drugs
- The customer's race

- The customer's approximate age
- The customer's attractiveness (10 = sexy, 1 = disgusting)
- Whether a condom was used
- Whether the customer was new or returning
- If it could be determined, whether the customer was married; employed; affiliated with a gang; from the neighborhood
- Whether the prostitute stole from the customer
- Whether the customer gave the prostitute any trouble, violent or otherwise
- Whether the sex act was paid for, or was a "freebie"

So what can these data tell us?

Let's start with wages. It turns out that the typical street prostitute in Chicago works 13 hours a week, performing 10 sex acts during that period, and earns an hourly wage of approximately $27. So her weekly take-home pay is roughly $350. This includes an average of $20 that a prostitute steals from her customers and acknowledges that some prostitutes accept drugs in lieu of cash—usually crack cocaine or heroin, and usually at a discount. Of all the women in Venkatesh's study, 83 percent were drug addicts.

Like LaSheena, many of these women took on other, non-prostitution work, which Venkatesh also tracked. Prostitution paid about four times more than those jobs. But as high as that wage premium may be, it looks pretty meager when you consider the job's downsides. In a given year, a typical prostitute in Venkatesh's study experienced a dozen incidents of violence. At least 3 of the 160 prostitutes who participated died during the course of the study. "Most of the violence by johns is when, for some reason, they can't consummate or can't get erect," says Venkatesh. "Then he's shamed—'I'm too manly for you' or 'You're too ugly for me!' Then the john wants his money back, and you definitely don't want to negotiate with a man who just lost his masculinity."

Moreover, the women's wage premium pales in comparison to the one enjoyed by even the low-rent prostitutes from a hundred years ago. Compared with them, women like LaSheena are working for next to nothing.

Why has the prostitute's wage fallen so far?

Because demand has fallen dramatically. Not the demand for *sex*. That is still robust. But prostitution, like any industry, is vulnerable to competition.

Who poses the greatest competition to a prostitute? Simple: any woman who is willing to have sex with a man for free.

It is no secret that sexual mores have evolved substantially in recent decades. The phrase "casual sex" didn't exist a century ago (to say nothing of "friends with benefits"). Sex outside of marriage was much harder to come by and carried significantly higher penalties than it does today.

Imagine a young man, just out of college but not ready to settle down, who wants to have some sex. In decades past, prostitution was a likely option. Although illegal, it was never hard to find, and the risk of arrest was minuscule. While relatively expensive in the short term, it provided good long-term value because it didn't carry the potential costs of an unwanted pregnancy or a marriage commitment. At least 20 percent of American men born between 1933 and 1942 had their first sexual intercourse with a prostitute.

Now imagine that same young man twenty years later. The shift in sexual mores has given him a much greater supply of unpaid sex. In his generation, only *5* percent of men lose their virginity to a prostitute.

And it's not that he and his friends are saving themselves for marriage. More than 70 percent of the men in his generation have sex before they marry, compared with just 33 percent in the earlier generation.

So premarital sex emerged as a viable substitute for prostitution. And as the demand for paid sex decreased, so too did the wage of the people who provide it.

If prostitution were a typical industry, it might have hired lobbyists to fight against the encroachment of premarital sex. They would have pushed to have premarital sex criminalized or, at the very least, heavily taxed. When the steelmakers and sugar producers of America began to feel the heat of competition—in the form of cheaper goods from Mexico, China, or Brazil—they got the federal government to impose tariffs that protected their homegrown products.

Such protectionist tendencies are nothing new. More than 150 years ago, the French economist Frédéric Bastiat wrote "The Candlemakers' Petition," said to represent the interests of "the Manufacturers of Candles, Tapers, Lanterns, Candlesticks, Street Lamps, Snuffers, and Extinguishers" as well as "the Producers of Tallow, Oil, Resin, Alcohol, and Generally Everything Connected with Lighting."

These industries, Bastiat complained, "are suffering from the ruinous competition of a foreign rival who apparently works under conditions so far superior to our own for the production of light that he is flooding the domestic market with it at an incredibly low price."

Who was this dastardly foreign rival?

"None other than the sun," wrote Bastiat. He begged the French government to pass a law forbidding all citizens to allow sunlight to enter their homes. (Yes, his petition was a satire; in economists' circles, this is what passes for radical high jinks.)

Alas, the prostitution industry lacks a champion as passionate, even in jest, as Bastiat. And unlike the sugar and steel industries, it holds little sway in Washington's corridors of power—despite, it should be said, its many, many connections with men of high government office. This explains why the industry's fortunes have been so badly buffeted by the naked winds of the free market.

Prostitution is more geographically concentrated than other criminal activity: nearly half of all Chicago prostitution arrests occur in less than one-third of 1 percent of the city's blocks. What do these blocks have in common? They are near train stations and major roads (prostitutes need to be where customers can find them) and have a lot of poor residents—although not, as is common in most poor neighborhoods, an overabundance of female-headed households.

This concentration makes it possible to take Venkatesh's data and merge it with the Chicago Police Department's citywide arrest data to estimate the scope of street prostitution citywide. The conclusion: in any given week, about 4,400 women are working as street prostitutes in Chicago, turning a combined 1.6 million tricks a year for 175,000 different men. That's about the same number of prostitutes who worked in Chicago a hundred years ago. Considering that the city's population has grown by 30 percent since then, the per-capita count of street prostitutes has fallen significantly. One thing that hasn't changed: for the customer at least, prostitution is only barely illegal. The data show that a man who solicits a street prostitute is likely to be arrested about once for every 1,200 visits.

The prostitutes in Venkatesh's study worked in three separate areas of the city: West Pullman, Roseland, and Washington Park. Most of these neighborhoods' residents are African American, as are the prostitutes. West Pullman and Roseland, which adjoin each other, are working-class neighborhoods on the far South Side that used to be almost exclusively white (West Pullman was organized around the Pullman train factory).

Washington Park has been a poor black neighborhood for decades. In all three areas, the race of the prostitutes' clientele is mixed.

Monday is easily the slowest night of the week for these prostitutes. Fridays are the busiest, but on Saturday night a prostitute will typically earn about 20 percent more than on Friday.

Why isn't the busiest night also the most profitable? Because the single greatest determinant of a prostitute's price is the specific trick she is hired to perform. And for whatever reason, Saturday customers purchase more expensive services. Consider the four different sexual acts these prostitutes routinely performed, each with its own price tag:

SEXUAL ACT	AVERAGE PRICE
MANUAL STIMULATION	$26.70
ORAL SEX	$37.26
VAGINAL SEX	$80.05
ANAL SEX	$94.13

It's interesting to note that the price of oral sex has plummeted over time relative to "regular" sexual intercourse. In the days of the Everleigh Club, men paid double or triple for oral sex; now it costs less than half the price of intercourse. Why?

True, oral sex imposes a lower cost on the prostitute because it eliminates the possibility of pregnancy and lessens the risk of sexually transmitted disease. (It also offers what one public-health scholar calls "ease of exit," whereby a prostitute can hurriedly escape the police or a threatening customer.) But oral sex *always* had those benefits. What accounted for the price difference in the old days?

The best answer is that oral sex carried a sort of taboo tax. At the time, it was considered a form of perversion, especially by religious-minded folks, since it satisfied the lust requirements of sex without fulfilling the reproductive requirements. The Everleigh Club was of course happy to profit from this taboo. Indeed, the club's physician avidly endorsed oral sex because it meant higher profits for the establishment and less wear and tear on the butterflies.

But as social attitudes changed, the price fell to reflect the new reality. This shift in preferences has not been confined to prostitution. Among U.S. teenagers, oral sex is on the rise while sexual intercourse and pregnancy have fallen. Some might call it coincidence (or worse), but we call it economics at work.

The lower price for oral sex among prostitutes has been met by strong demand. Here is a breakdown of the market share of each sex act performed by the Chicago prostitutes:

SEXUAL ACT	SHARE OF ALL TRICKS
ORAL SEX	55%
VAGINAL SEX	17%
MANUAL STIMULATION	15%
ANAL SEX	9%
OTHER	4%

Included in the "other" category are nude dancing, "just talk" (an extremely rare event, observed only a handful of times over more than two thousand transactions), and a variety of acts that are the complete opposite of "just talk," so far out of bounds that they would tax the imagination of even the most creative reader. If nothing else, such acts suggest a prime reason that a prostitution market still thrives despite the availability of free sex: men hire prostitutes to do things a girlfriend or wife would never be willing to do. (It should also be said, however, that some of the most deviant acts in our sample actually *include* family members, with every conceivable combination of gender and generation.)

Prostitutes do not charge all customers the same price. Black customers, for instance, pay on average about $9 less per trick than white customers, while Hispanic customers are in the middle. Economists have a name for the practice of charging different prices for the same product: *price discrimination*.

In the business world, it isn't always possible to price-discriminate. At least two conditions must be met:

- Some customers must have clearly identifiable traits that place them in the willing-to-pay-more category. (As identifiable traits go, black or white skin is a pretty good one.)
- The seller must be able to prevent resale of the product, thereby destroying any arbitrage opportunities. (In the case of prostitution, resale is pretty much impossible.)

If these circumstances can be met, most firms will profit from price discriminating whenever they can. Business travelers know this all too well, because they routinely pay three times more for a last-minute airline ticket than the vacationer in the next seat. Women who pay for a salon haircut know it too, since they pay twice as much as men for what is pretty much the same haircut. Or consider the online health-care catalog Dr. Leonard's, which sells a Barber Magic hair trimmer for $12.99 and, elsewhere on its site, the Barber Magic Trim-a-Pet hair trimmer for $7.99. The two products appear to be identical—but Dr. Leonard seems to think that people will spend more to trim their own hair than their pet's.

How do the Chicago street prostitutes price-discriminate? As Venkatesh learned, they use different pricing strategies for white and black customers. When dealing with blacks, the prostitutes usually name the price outright to discourage any negotiation. (Venkatesh observed that black customers are more likely than whites to haggle—perhaps, he reasoned, because they're more familiar with the neighborhood and therefore know the market better.) When doing business with white customers, meanwhile, the prostitute makes the *man* name a price, hoping for a generous offer. As evidenced by the black-white price differential in the data, this strategy seems to work pretty well.

Other factors can knock down the price customers pay a Chicago prostitute. For instance:

	AVERAGE DISCOUNT
PROSTITUTE PAID IN DRUGS RATHER THAN CASH	$7.00
SEX ACT PERFORMED OUTDOORS	$6.50
CUSTOMER USES A CONDOM	$2.00

The drug discount isn't much of a shock considering that most of the prostitutes are drug addicts. The outdoors discount is partially a time discount because tricks performed outdoors tend to be faster. But also, prostitutes charge more for an indoor trick because they usually have to pay for the indoor space. Some women rent a bedroom in someone's home or keep a mattress in the basement; others use a cheap motel or a dollar store that has closed for the night.

The small discount for condom use *is* surprising. Even more surprising is how seldom condoms are used: less than 25 percent of the time even when counting only vaginal and anal sex. (New customers were more likely to use condoms than repeat customers; black customers were less likely than others.) A typical Chicago street prostitute could expect to have about 300 instances of unprotected sex a year. The good news, according to earlier research, is that men who use street prostitutes have a surprisingly low rate of HIV infection, less than 3 percent. (The same is not true for male customers who hire male prostitutes; their rate is above 35 percent.)

So a lot of factors influence a prostitute's pricing: the act itself, certain customer characteristics, even the location.

But amazingly, prices at a given location are virtually the same from one prostitute to the next. You might think one woman would charge more than another who is less desirable. But that rarely happens. Why?

The only sensible explanation is that most customers view the women as what economists call *perfect substitutes,* or commodities that are easily interchanged. Just as a shopper in a grocery store may see one bunch of bananas as pretty much identical to the rest, the same principle seems to hold true for the men who frequent this market.

One surefire way for a customer to get a big discount is to hire the prostitute directly rather than dealing with a pimp. If he does, he'll get the same sex act for about $16 less.

This estimate is based on data from the prostitutes in Roseland and West Pullman. The two neighborhoods are located next to each other and are similar in most regards. But in West Pullman, the prostitutes used pimps, whereas those in Roseland did not. West Pullman is slightly more residential, which creates community pressure to keep prostitutes off the streets. Roseland, meanwhile, has more street-gang activity. Even though Chicago's gangs don't typically get involved in pimping, they don't want anyone else horning in on their black-market economy.

This key difference allows us to measure the impact of the pimp (henceforth known as the *pimpact*). But first, here's an important question: how can we be sure the two populations of prostitutes are in fact comparable? Perhaps the prostitutes who work with pimps have different characteristics than the others. Maybe they're savvier or less drug addicted. If that were the case, we'd merely be measuring two different populations of women rather than the pimpact.

But as it happened, many of the women in Venkatesh's study went back and forth between the two neighborhoods, sometimes working with a pimp and sometimes solo. This enabled us to analyze the data in such a way that isolates the pimpact.

As just noted, customers pay about $16 more if they go through a pimp. But the customers who use pimps also tend to buy more expensive services—no manual stimulation for these gents—which further bumps up the women's wages. So even after the pimps take their typical 25 percent commission, the prostitutes earn more money while turning fewer tricks:

PROSTITUTE	WEEKLY SALARY	AVERAGE TRICKS PER WEEK
WORKING SOLO	$ 325	7.8
WITH PIMP	$ 410	6.2

The secret to the pimps' success is that they go after a different clientele than the street prostitutes can get on their own. As Venkatesh learned, the pimps in West Pullman spent a lot of their time recruiting customers, mostly white ones, in downtown strip clubs and the riverboat casinos in nearby Indiana.

But as the data show, the pimpact goes well beyond producing higher wages. A prostitute who works with a pimp is less likely to be beaten up by a customer or forced into giving freebies to gang members.

So if you are a street prostitute in Chicago, using a pimp looks to be all upside. Even after paying the commission, you come out ahead on just about every front. If only every agent in every industry provided this kind of value.

Consider a different sales environment: residential real estate. Just as you can sell your body with or without the aid of a pimp, you can sell your house with or without a Realtor. While Realtors charge a much lower commission than the pimps—about 5 percent versus 25 percent—

the Realtor's cut is usually in the tens of thousands of dollars for a single sale.

So do Realtors earn their pay?

Three economists recently analyzed home-sales data in Madison, Wisconsin, which has a thriving for-sale-by-owner market (or FSBO, pronounced "FIZZ-bo"). This revolves around the website FSBOMadison.com, which charges homeowners $150 to list a house, with no commission when the home is sold. By comparing FSBO sales in Madison with Realtor-sold homes in Madison along several dimensions—price, house and neighborhood characteristics, time on market, and so on—the economists were able to gauge the Realtor's impact (or, in the interest of symmetry, the *Rimpact*).

What did they find?

The homes sold on FSBOMadison.com typically fetched about the same price as the homes sold by Realtors. That doesn't make the Realtors look very good. Using a Realtor to sell a $400,000 house means paying a commission of about $20,000—versus just $150 to FSBOMadison.com. (Another recent study, meanwhile, found that flat-fee real-estate agents, who typically charge about $500 to list a house, also get about the same price as full-fee Realtors.)

But there are some important caveats. In exchange for the 5 percent commission, someone else does all the work for you. For some home sellers, that's well worth the price. It's also hard to say if the Madison results would hold true in other cities. Furthermore, the study took place during a strong housing market, which probably makes it easier to sell a home yourself. Also, the kind of people who choose to sell their houses without a Realtor may have a better business head to start with. Finally, even though the FSBO homes sold for the same average price as those sold by Realtors, they took twenty days longer to sell. But most people would probably consider it worth $20,000 to live in their old home for an extra twenty days.

A Realtor and a pimp perform the same primary service: marketing your product to potential customers. As this study shows, the Internet is proving to be a pretty powerful substitute for the Realtor. But if you're trying to sell street prostitution, the Internet isn't very good—not yet, at least—at matching sellers to buyers.

So once you consider the value you get for each of these two agents, it seems clear that a pimp's services are considerably more valuable than a Realtor's. Or, for those who prefer their conclusions rendered mathematically:

PIMPACT > RIMPACT

During Venkatesh's study, six pimps managed the prostitution in West Pullman, and he got to know each of them. They were all men. In the old days, prostitution rings in even the poorest Chicago neighborhoods were usually run by women. But men, attracted by the high wages, eventually took over—yet another example in the long history of men stepping in to outearn women.

These six pimps ranged in age from their early thirties to their late forties and "were doing pretty well," Venkatesh says, making roughly $50,000 a year. Some also held legit jobs—car mechanic or store manager—and most owned their homes. None were drug addicts.

One of their most important roles was handling the police. Venkatesh learned that the pimps had a good working relationship with the police, particularly with one officer, named Charles. When he was new on the beat, Charles harassed and arrested the pimps. But this backfired. "When you arrest the pimps, there'll just be fighting to replace them," Venkatesh says, "and the violence is worse than the prostitution."

So instead, Charles extracted some compromises. The pimps agreed to stay away from the park when kids were playing there, and to keep the prostitution hidden. In return, the police would leave the pimps alone—and, importantly, they wouldn't arrest the prostitutes either. Over the course of Venkatesh's study, there was only one official arrest of a prostitute in an area controlled by pimps. Of all the advantages a prostitute gained by using a pimp, not getting arrested was one of the biggest.

But you don't necessarily need a pimp to stay out of jail. The average prostitute in Chicago will turn 450 tricks before she is arrested, and only 1 in 10 arrests leads to a prison sentence.

It's not that the police don't know where the prostitutes are. Nor have the police brass or mayor made a conscious decision to let prostitution thrive. Rather, this is a graphic example of what economists call *the principal-agent problem*. That's what happens when two parties in a given undertaking seem to have the same incentives but in fact may not.

In this case, you could think of the police chief as the principal. He would like to curtail street prostitution. The cop on the street, meanwhile, is the agent. He may also want to curtail prostitution, at least in theory, but he doesn't have a very strong incentive to actually make arrests. As some officers see it, the prostitutes offer something far more appealing than just another arrest tally: sex.

This shows up loud and clear in Venkatesh's study. Of all the tricks turned by the prostitutes he tracked, roughly 3 percent were freebies given to police officers.

The data don't lie: a Chicago street prostitute is more likely to have sex with a cop than to be arrested by one.

It would be hard to overemphasize how undesirable it is to be a street prostitute—the degradation, the risk of disease, the nearly constant threat of violence.

Nowhere were the conditions as bad as in Washington Park, the third neighborhood in Venkatesh's study, which lies about six miles north of Roseland and West Pullman. It is more economically depressed and less accessible to outsiders, especially whites. The prostitution is centered around four locations: two large apartment buildings, a five-block stretch of busy commercial street, and in the park itself, a 372-acre landmark designed in the 1870s by Frederick Law Olmsted and Calvert Vaux. The prostitutes in Washington Park work without pimps, and they earn the lowest wages of any prostitutes in Venkatesh's study.

This might lead you to think that such women would rather be doing anything else but turning tricks. But one feature of a market economy is that prices tend to find a level whereby even the worst conceivable job is worth doing. As bad off as these women are, they would seem to be worse off without prostitution.

Sound absurd?

The strongest evidence for this argument comes from an unlikely source: the long-loved American tradition known as the family reunion. Every summer around the Fourth of July holiday, Washington Park is thronged with families and other large groups who get together for cookouts and parties. For some of these visitors, catching up with Aunt Ida over lemonade isn't quite stimulating enough. It turns out that the demand for prostitutes in Washington Park skyrockets every year during this period.

And the prostitutes do what any good entrepreneur would do: they raise prices by about 30 percent and work as much overtime as they can handle.

Most interestingly, this surge in demand attracts a special kind of worker—a woman who steers clear of prostitution all year long but, during this busy season, drops her other work and starts turning tricks. Most of these part-time prostitutes have children and take care of their households; they aren't drug addicts. But like prospectors at a gold rush or Realtors during a housing boom, they see the chance to cash in and jump at it.

As for the question posed in this chapter's title—*How is a street prostitute like a department-store Santa?*—the answer should be obvious: they both take advantage of short-term job opportunities brought about by holiday spikes in demand.

We've already established that demand for prostitutes is far lower today than it was sixty years ago (if offset a bit by holiday surges), in large part because of the feminist revolution.

If you found that surprising, consider an even more unlikely victim of the feminist revolution: schoolchildren.

Teaching has traditionally been dominated by women. A hundred years ago, it was one of the few jobs available to women that didn't involve cooking, cleaning, or other menial labor. (Nursing was another such profession, but teaching was far more prominent, with six teachers for every nurse.) At the time, nearly 6 percent of the female workforce were teachers, trailing only laborers (19 percent), servants (16 percent), and laundresses (6.5 percent). And by a large margin it was the job of choice among college graduates. As of 1940, an astonishing 55 percent of all college-educated female workers in their early thirties were employed as teachers.

Soon after, however, opportunities for smart women began to multiply. The Equal Pay Act of 1963 and the Civil Rights Act of 1964 were contributing factors, as was the societal shift in the perception of women's roles. As more girls went off to college, more women emerged ready to join the workforce, especially in the desirable professions that had been largely off-limits: law, medicine, business, finance, and so on. (One of the unsung heroes of this revolution was the widespread use of baby formula, which allowed new mothers to get right back to work.)

These demanding, competitive professions offered high wages and attracted the best and brightest women available. No doubt many of these women would have become schoolteachers had they been born a generation earlier.

But they didn't. As a consequence, the schoolteacher corps began to experience a brain drain. In 1960, about 40 percent of female teachers scored in the top quintile of IQ and other aptitude tests, with only 8 percent in the bottom. Twenty years later, fewer than half as many were in the top quintile, with more than twice as many in the bottom. It hardly helped that teachers' wages were falling significantly in relation to those of other jobs. "The quality of teachers has been declining for decades," the chancellor of New York City's public schools declared in 2000, "and no one wants to talk about it."

This isn't to say that there aren't still a lot of great teachers. Of course there are. But overall teacher skill declined during these years, and with it the quality of classroom instruction. Between 1967 and 1980, U.S. test scores fell by about 1.25 grade-level equivalents. The education researcher John Bishop called this decline "historically unprecedented," arguing that it put a serious drag on national productivity that would continue well into the twenty-first century.

But at least things worked out well for the women who went into other professions, right?

Well, sort of. As we wrote earlier, even the best-educated women earn less than their male counterparts. This is especially true in the high-flying financial and corporate sectors—where, moreover, women are vastly underrepresented. The number of female CEOs has increased roughly eightfold in recent years, but women still hold less than 1.5 percent of all CEO positions. Among the top fifteen hundred companies in the United States, only about 2.5 percent of the highest-paying executive positions are held by women. This is especially surprising given that women have earned more than 30 percent of all the master's in business administration (MBA) degrees at the nation's top colleges over the past twenty-five years. Their share today is at its highest yet, 43 percent.

The economists Marianne Bertrand, Claudia Goldin, and Lawrence Katz tried to solve this wage-gap puzzle by analyzing the career outcomes of more than 2,000 male and female MBAs from the University of Chicago.

Their conclusion: while gender discrimination may be a minor contributor to the male-female wage differential, it is desire—or the lack thereof—that accounts for most of the wage gap. The economists identified three main factors:

- Women have slightly lower GPAs than men and, perhaps more important, they take fewer finance courses. All else being equal, there is a strong correlation between a finance background and career earnings.
- Over the first fifteen years of their careers, women work fewer hours than men, 52 per week versus 58. Over fifteen years, that six-hour difference adds up to six months' less experience.
- Women take more career interruptions than men. After ten years in the workforce, only 10 percent of male MBAs went for six months or more without working, compared with 40 percent of female MBAs.

The big issue seems to be that many women, even those with MBAs, love kids. The average female MBA with no children works only 3 percent fewer hours than the average male MBA. But female MBAs *with* children work 24 percent less. "The pecuniary penalties from shorter hours and any job discontinuity among MBAs are enormous," the three economists write. "It appears that many MBA mothers, especially those with well-off spouses, decided to slow down within a few years following their first birth."

This is a strange twist. Many of the best and brightest women in the United States get an MBA so they can earn high wages, but they end up marrying the best and brightest men, who *also* earn high wages—which affords these women the luxury of not having to work so much.

Does this mean the women's investment of time and money in pursuing an MBA was poorly spent? Maybe not. Perhaps they never would have *met* such husbands if they hadn't gone to business school.

There's one more angle to consider when examining the male-female wage gap. Rather than interpreting women's lower wages as a failure, perhaps it should be seen as a sign that a higher wage simply isn't as meaningful an incentive for women as it is for men. Could it be that men have a weakness for money just as women have a weakness for children?

Consider a recent pair of experiments in which young men and women were recruited to take an SAT-style math test with twenty questions. In one version, every participant was paid a flat rate, $5 for showing up and another $15 for completing the test. In the second version, participants were paid the $5 show-up fee and another $2 for each correct answer.

How'd they do?

In the flat-rate version, the men performed only slightly better, getting 1 more correct answer out of 20 than the women. But in the cash-incentive version, the men blew away the women. The women's performance barely budged when compared with the flat-rate version, whereas the average man scored an extra 2 correct questions out of the 20.

Economists do the best they can by assembling data and using complex statistical techniques to tease out the reasons why women earn less than men. The fundamental difficulty, however, is that men and women differ in so many ways. What an economist would *really* like to do is perform an experiment, something like this: take a bunch of women and clone male versions of them; do the reverse for a bunch of men; now sit back and watch. By measuring the labor outcomes of each gender group against their own clones, you could likely gain some real insights.

Or, if cloning weren't an option, you could take a bunch of women, randomly select half of them, and magically switch their gender to male, leaving everything else about them the same, and do the opposite with a bunch of men.

Unfortunately, economists aren't allowed to conduct such experiments. (Yet.) But individuals can if they want to. It's called a sex-change operation.

So what happens when a man decides to employ surgery and hormone therapy to live as a woman (a so-called MTF, or male-to-female transgender) or when a woman decides to live as a man (an FTM, or female-to-male)?

Ben Barres, a Stanford neurobiologist, was born Barbara Barres and became a man in 1997, at the age of forty-two. Neurobiology, like most math and science disciplines, is heavily populated by men. His decision "came as a surprise to my colleagues and students," he notes, but they "have all been terrific about it." Indeed, his intellectual stature seems to have increased. Once, after Barres gave a seminar, a fellow scientist turned to a friend of Barres's in the audience and issued this left-handed compliment: "Ben Barres's work is much better than his sister's." But Barres doesn't have a sister; the commenter was slighting Barres's former, female self.

"It is much harder for men to transition to women than for women to transition to men," Barres admits. The problem, he says, is that males are presumed to be competent in certain fields—especially areas like science and finance—while females are not.

On the other hand, consider Deirdre McCloskey, a prominent economist at the University of Illinois at Chicago. She was born a male, Donald, and decided to become a woman in 1995, at the age of fifty-three. Economics, like neuroscience, is a heavily male field. "I was prepared to move to Spokane and become a secretary in a grain elevator," she says. That proved unnecessary, but McCloskey did "detect a queerness penalty toward me in some of the economics profession. I reckon I'd make a little more money now if I were still Donald."

McCloskey and Barres are just two data points. A pair of researchers named Kristen Schilt and Matthew Wiswall wanted to systematically examine what happens to the salaries of people who switched gender as adults. It is not quite the experiment we proposed above—after all, the set of folks who switch gender aren't exactly a random sample, nor are they the typical woman or man before or after—but still, the results are intriguing. Schilt and Wiswall found that women who become men earn slightly more money after their gender transitions, while men who become women make, on average, nearly one-third less than their previous wage.

Their conclusion comes with a number of caveats. For starters, the sample set was very small: just fourteen MTFs and twenty-four FTMs. Furthermore, the people they studied were mainly recruited at transgender conferences. That puts them in the category of what Deirdre McCloskey calls "professional gender crossers," who aren't necessarily representative.

"One could easily believe," she says, "that people who do not just become women and then get on with their lives, but keep looking back, are not going to be the most successful people in the workplace." (She may have changed gender, but once an economist, always an economist.)

Back in Chicago, in a chic neighborhood just a few miles from where the street prostitutes work, lives someone who was born female, stayed that way, and makes more money than she ever thought possible.

She grew up in a large and largely dysfunctional family in Texas and left home to join the military. She trained in electronics and worked in research and development on navigation systems. When she rejoined the civilian world seven years later, she took a job in computer programming with one of the world's largest corporations. She made a solid five-figure salary and married a man who earned well into six figures as a mortgage broker. Her life was a success, but it was also—well, it was boring.

She got divorced (the couple had no children) and moved back to Texas, in part to help care for a sick relative. Working once again as a computer programmer, she remarried but this marriage also failed.

Her career wasn't going much better. She was smart, capable, technically sophisticated, and she also happened to be physically attractive, a curvaceous and friendly blonde whose attributes were always well appreciated in her corporate setting. But she just didn't like working all that hard. So she became an entrepreneur, launching a one-woman business that enabled her to work just ten or fifteen hours a week and earn five times her old salary. Her name is Allie, and she is a prostitute.

She fell into the profession by accident, or at least on a lark. Her family was devout Southern Baptist, and Allie had grown up "very straitlaced," she says. As an adult, she was the same. "You know, yard-of-the-month in the suburbs, no more than two beers a night and *never* before seven." But as a young divorcée, she started visiting online dating sites—she liked men, and she liked sex—and just for fun listed "escort" on her profile. "I mean, it was so instantaneous," she recalls. "I just thought I'd put it up and see what happens."

Her computer was instantly flooded with replies. "I started hitting *minimize, minimize, minimize,* just so I could keep up!"

She arranged to meet a man at two o'clock on a weekday afternoon at a hotel, in the southwest corner of its parking lot. He'd be driving a black Mercedes. Allie had no idea what to charge. She was thinking about $50.

He was a dentist—physically unintimidating, married, and perfectly kind. Once inside the room, Allie undressed nervously. She can no longer recall the particulars of the sex ("it's all a big blur by this point," she says) but does remember that "it was nothing really kinky or anything."

When they were done, the man put some money on the dresser. "You've never done this before, have you?" he asked.

Allie tried to fib, but it was useless.

"Okay," he said, "this is what you need to do." He began to lecture her. She had to be more careful; she shouldn't be willing to meet a stranger in a parking lot; she needed to know something in advance about her clients.

"He was the perfect first date," Allie says. "To this day, I remain grateful."

Once he left the room, Allie counted the cash on the dresser: $200. "I'd been giving it away for years, and so the fact that someone was going to give me even a penny—well, that was shocking."

She was immediately tempted to take up prostitution full-time, but she was worried her family and friends would find out. So she eased into it, booking mainly out-of-town liaisons. She curtailed her programming hours but even so found the job stultifying. That's when she decided to move to Chicago.

Yes, it was a big city, which Allie found intimidating, but unlike New York or Los Angeles, it was civil enough to make a southern girl feel at home. She built a website (those computer skills came in handy) and, through intensive trial and error, determined which erotic-services sites would help her attract the right kind of client and which ones would waste her ad dollars. (The winners were Eros.com and BigDoggie.net.)

Running a one-woman operation held several advantages, the main one being that she didn't have to share her revenues with anyone. In the old days, Allie probably would have worked for someone like the Everleigh sisters, who paid their girls handsomely but took enough off the top to make themselves truly rich. The Internet let Allie be her own madam and accumulate the riches for herself. Much has been said of the Internet's awesome ability to "disintermediate"—to cut out the agent or middleman—in industries like travel, real estate, insurance, and the sale of stocks and bonds. But it is hard to think of a market more naturally suited to disintermediation than high-end prostitution.

The downside was that Allie had no one but herself to screen potential clients and ensure they wouldn't beat her up or rip her off. She hit upon a solution that was as simple as it was smart. When a new client contacted her online, she wouldn't book an appointment until she had secured his real name and his work telephone number. Then she'd call him the morning of their date, ostensibly just to say how excited she was to meet him.

But the call also acknowledged that she could reach him at will and, if something were to go wrong, she could storm his office. "Nobody wants to see the 'crazy ho' routine," she says with a smile. To date, Allie has resorted to this tactic only once, after a client paid her in counterfeit cash. When Allie visited his office, he promptly located some real money.

She saw clients in her apartment, mainly during the day. Most of them were middle-aged white men, 80 percent of whom were married, and they found it easier to slip off during work hours than explain an evening absence. Allie loved having her evenings free to read, go to the movies, or just relax. She set her fee at $300 an hour—that's what most other women of her caliber seemed to be charging—with a few discount options: $500 for two hours or $2,400 for a twelve-hour sleepover. About 60 percent of her appointments were for a single hour.

Her bedroom—"my office," she calls it with a laugh—is dominated by a massive Victorian four-poster, its carved mahogany pillars draped with an off-white silk crepe. It is not the easiest bed to mount. When asked if any of her clients have difficulty doing so, she confesses that one portly gentleman actually broke the bed not long ago.

What did Allie do?

"I told him that the damn thing was already broken, and I was sorry I hadn't gotten it fixed."

She is the kind of person who sees something good in everyone—and this, she believes, has contributed to her entrepreneurial success. She genuinely likes the men who come to her, and the men therefore like Allie even beyond the fact that she will have sex with them. Often, they bring gifts: a $100 gift certificate from Amazon.com; a nice bottle of wine (she Googles the label afterward to determine the value); and, once, a new MacBook. The men sweet-talk her, and compliment her looks or the decor. They treat her, in many ways, as men are expected to treat their wives but often don't.

Most women of Allie's pay grade call themselves "escorts." When Allie discusses her friends in the business, she simply calls them "girls." But she isn't fussy. "I like *hooker,* I like *whore,* I like them all," she says. "Come on, I know what I do, so I'm not trying to butter it up." Allie mentions one friend whose fee is $500 an hour. "She thinks she's nothing like the girls on the street giving blow jobs for $100, and I'm like, 'Yes, honey, you're the same damn thing.'"

About this, Allie is likely wrong. Although she views herself as similar to a street prostitute, she has less in common with that kind of woman than she does with a trophy wife. Allie is essentially a trophy wife who is rented by the hour. She isn't really selling sex, or at least not sex alone. She sells men the opportunity to trade in their existing wives for a younger, more sexually adventurous version—without the trouble and long-term expense of actually having to go through with it. For an hour or two, she represents the ideal wife: beautiful, attentive, smart, laughing at your jokes and satisfying your lust. She is happy to see you every time you show up at her door. Your favorite music is already playing and your favorite beverage is on ice. She will never ask you to take out the trash.

Allie says she is "a little more liberal" than some prostitutes when it comes to satisfying a client's unusual request. There was, for instance, the fellow back in Texas who still flew her in regularly and asked her to incorporate some devices he kept in a briefcase in a session most people wouldn't even recognize as sex per se. But she categorically insists that her clients wear a condom.

What if a client offered her $1 million to have sex without a condom?

Allie pauses to consider this question. Then, exhibiting a keen understanding of what economists call *adverse selection,* she declares that she still wouldn't do it—because any client crazy enough to offer $1 million for a single round of unprotected sex must be so crazy that he should be avoided at all costs.

When she started out in Chicago, at $300 an hour, the demand was nearly overwhelming. She took on as many clients as she could physically accommodate, working roughly thirty hours a week. She kept that up for a while, but once she paid off her car and built up some cash reserves, she scaled back to fifteen hours a week.

Even so, she began to wonder if one hour of her time was more valuable to her than another $300. As it was, a fifteen-hour workload generated more than $200,000 a year in cash.

Eventually she raised her fee to $350 an hour. She expected demand to fall, but it didn't. So a few months later, she raised it to $400. Again, there was no discernible drop-off in demand. Allie was a bit peeved with herself. Plainly she had been charging too little the whole time. But at least she was able to strategically exploit her fee change by engaging in a little price discrimination. She grandfathered in her favorite clients at the old rate but told her less-favorite clients that an hour now cost $400—and if they balked, she had a handy excuse to cut them loose. There were always more where they came from.

It wasn't long before she raised her fee again, to $450 an hour, and a few months later to $500. In the space of a couple of years, Allie had increased her price by 67 percent, and yet she saw practically no decrease in demand.

Her price hikes revealed another surprise: the more she charged, the less actual sex she was having. At $300 an hour, she had a string of one-hour appointments with each man wanting to get in as much action as he could. But charging $500 an hour, she was often wined and dined—"a four-hour dinner date that ends with a twenty-minute sexual encounter," she says, "even though I was the same girl, dressed the same, and had the same conversations as when I charged $300."

She figured she may have just been profiting from a strong economy. This was during 2006 and 2007, which were go-go years for many of the bankers, lawyers, and real-estate developers she saw. But Allie had found that most people who bought her services were, in the language of economics, *price insensitive.* Demand for sex seemed relatively uncoupled from the broader economy.

Our best estimate is that there are fewer than one thousand prostitutes like Allie in Chicago, either working solo or for an escort service. Street prostitutes like LaSheena might have the worst job in America. But for elite prostitutes like Allie, the circumstances are completely different: high wages, flexible hours, and relatively little risk of violence or arrest. So the real puzzle isn't why someone like Allie becomes a prostitute, but rather why *more* women don't choose this career.

Certainly, prostitution isn't for every woman. You have to like sex enough, and be willing to make some sacrifices, like not having a husband (unless he is very understanding, or very greedy). Still, these negatives just might not seem that important when the wage is $500 an hour. Indeed, when Allie confided to one longtime friend that she had become a prostitute and described her new life, it was only a few weeks before the friend joined Allie in the business.

Allie has never had any trouble with the police, and doesn't expect to. The truth is that she would be distraught if prostitution were legalized, because her stratospherically high wage stems from the fact that the service she provides *cannot* be gotten legally.

Allie had mastered her domain. She was a shrewd entrepreneur who kept her overhead low, maintained quality control, learned to price-discriminate, and understood well the market forces of supply and demand. She also enjoyed her work.

But all that said, Allie began looking for an exit strategy. She was in her early thirties by now and, while still attractive, she understood that her commodity was perishable. She felt sorry for older prostitutes who, like aging athletes, didn't know when to quit. (One such athlete, a future Hall of Fame baseball player, had propositioned Allie while she was vacationing in South America, not knowing that she was a professional. Allie declined, uninterested in a busman's holiday.)

She had also grown tired of living a secret life. Her family and friends didn't know she was a prostitute, and the constant deception wore her out. The only people with whom she could be unguarded were other girls in the business, and they weren't her closest friends.

She had saved money but not enough to retire. So she began casting about for her next career. She got her real-estate license. The housing boom was in full swing, and it seemed pretty simple to transition out of her old job and into the new, since both allowed a flexible schedule. But too many other people had the same idea. The barrier to entry for real-estate agents is so low that every boom inevitably attracts a swarm of new agents—in the previous ten years, membership in the National Association of Realtors had risen 75 percent—which has the effect of depressing their median income. And Allie was aghast when she realized she'd have to give half of her commission to the agency that employed her. That was a steeper cut than any pimp would dare take!

Finally Allie realized what she really wanted to do: go back to college. She would build on everything she'd learned by running her own business and, if all went well, apply this newfound knowledge to some profession that would pay an insanely high wage without relying on her own physical labor.

Her chosen field of study? Economics, of course.

CHAPTER 2

WHY SHOULD SUICIDE BOMBERS BUY LIFE INSURANCE?

If you know someone in southeastern Uganda who is having a baby next year, you should hope with all your heart that the baby isn't born in May. If so, it will be roughly 20 percent more likely to have visual, hearing, or learning disabilities as an adult.

Three years from now, however, May would be a fine month to have a baby. But the danger will have only shifted, not disappeared; April would now be the cruelest month.

What can possibly account for this bizarre pattern? Before you answer, consider this: the same pattern has been identified halfway across the world, in Michigan. In fact, a May birth in Michigan might carry an even greater risk than in Uganda.

The economists Douglas Almond and Bhashkar Mazumder have a simple answer for this strange and troubling phenomenon: Ramadan.

Some parts of Michigan have a substantial Muslim population, as does southeastern Uganda. Islam calls for a daytime fast from food and drink for the entire month of Ramadan. Most Muslim women participate even while pregnant; it's not a round-the-clock fast, after all. Still, as Almond and Mazumder found by analyzing years' worth of natality data, babies that were in utero during Ramadan are more likely to exhibit developmental aftereffects. The magnitude of these effects depends on which month of gestation the baby is in when Ramadan falls. The effects are strongest when fasting coincides with the first month of pregnancy, but they can occur if the mother fasts at any time up to the eighth month.

Islam follows a lunar calendar, so the month of Ramadan begins eleven days earlier each year. In 2009, it ran from August 21 to September 19, which made May 2010 the unluckiest month in which to be born. Three years later, with Ramadan beginning on July 20, April would be the riskiest birth month. The risk is magnified when Ramadan falls during summertime because there are more daylight hours—and, therefore, longer periods without food and drink. That's why the birth effects can be stronger in Michigan, which has fifteen hours of daylight during summer, than in Uganda, which sits at the equator and therefore has roughly equal daylight hours year-round.

It is no exaggeration to say that a person's entire life can be greatly influenced by the fluke of his or her birth, whether the fluke is one of time, place, or circumstance. Even animals are susceptible to this natal roulette. Kentucky, the capital of Thoroughbred horse breeding, was hit by a mysterious disease in 2001 that left 500 foals stillborn and resulted in about 3,000 early fetal losses. In 2004, as this diminished cohort of three-year-olds came of age, two of the three Triple Crown races were won by Smarty Jones, a colt whose dam was impregnated in Kentucky but returned home to Pennsylvania before she could be afflicted.

Such birth effects aren't as rare as you might think. Douglas Almond, examining U.S. Census data from 1960 to 1980, found one group of people whose terrible luck persisted over their whole lives. They had more physical ailments and lower lifetime income than people who'd been born just a few months earlier or a few months later. They stood out in the census record like a layer of volcanic ash stands out in the archaeological record, a thin stripe of ominous sediment nestled between two thick bands of normalcy.

What happened?

These people were in utero during the "Spanish flu" pandemic of 1918. It was a grisly plague, killing more than half a million Americans in just a few months—a casualty toll, as Almond notes, greater than all U.S. combat deaths during all the wars fought in the twentieth century.

More than *25 million* Americans, meanwhile, contracted the flu but survived. This included one of every three women of childbearing age. The infected women who were pregnant during the pandemic had babies who, like the Ramadan babies, ran the risk of carrying lifelong scars from being in their mothers' bellies at the wrong time.

Other birth effects, while not nearly as dire, can exert a significant pull on one's future. It is common practice, especially among economists, to co-write academic papers and list the authors alphabetically by last name. What does this mean for an economist who happened to be born Albert Zyzmor instead of, say, Albert Aab? Two (real) economists addressed this question and found that, all else being equal, Dr. Aab would be more likely to gain tenure at a top university, become a fellow in the Econometric Society (hooray!), and even win the Nobel Prize.

"Indeed," the two economists concluded, "one of us is currently contemplating dropping the first letter of her surname." The offending name: Yariv.

Or consider this: if you visit the locker room of a world-class soccer team early in the calendar year, you are more likely to interrupt a birthday celebration than if you arrive later in the year. A recent tally of the British national youth leagues, for instance, shows that fully half of the players were born between January and March, with the other half spread out over the nine remaining months. On a similar German team, 52 elite players were born between January and March, with just 4 players born between October and December.

Why such a severe birthdate bulge?

Most elite athletes begin playing their sports when they are quite young. Since youth sports are organized by age, the leagues naturally impose a cutoff birthdate. The youth soccer leagues in Europe, like many such leagues, use December 31 as the cutoff date.

Imagine now that you coach in a league for seven-year-old boys and are assessing two players. The first one (his name is Jan) was born on January 1, while the second one (his name is Tomas) was born 364 days later, on December 31. So even though they are both technically seven-year-olds, Jan is a year older than Tomas—which, at this tender age, confers substantial advantages. Jan is likely to be bigger, faster, and more mature than Tomas.

So while you may be seeing maturity rather than raw ability, it doesn't much matter if your goal is to pick the best players for your team. It probably isn't in a coach's interest to play the scrawny younger kid who, if he only had another year of development, might be a star.

And thus the cycle begins. Year after year, the bigger boys like Jan are selected, encouraged, and given feedback and playing time, while boys like Tomas eventually fall away. This "relative-age effect," as it has come to be known, is so strong in many sports that its advantages last all the way through to the professional ranks.

K. Anders Ericsson, an enthusiastic, bearded, and burly Swede, is the ringleader of a merry band of relative-age scholars scattered across the globe. He is now a professor of psychology at Florida State University, where he uses empirical research to learn what share of talent is "natural" and how the rest of it is acquired. His conclusion: the trait we commonly call "raw talent" is vastly overrated. "A lot of people believe there are some inherent limits they were born with," he says. "But there is surprisingly little hard evidence that anyone could attain any kind of exceptional performance without spending a lot of time perfecting it." Or, put another way, expert performers—whether in soccer or piano playing, surgery or computer programming—are nearly always made, not born.*

And yes, just as your grandmother always told you, practice does make perfect. But not just willy-nilly practice. Mastery arrives through what Ericsson calls "deliberate practice." This entails more than simply playing a C-minor scale a hundred times or hitting tennis serves until your shoulder pops out of its socket. Deliberate practice has three key components: setting specific goals; obtaining immediate feedback; and concentrating as much on technique as on outcome.

The people who become excellent at a given thing aren't necessarily the same ones who seemed to be "gifted" at a young age. This suggests that when it comes to choosing a life path, people should do what they love—yes, your nana told you this too—because if you don't love what you're doing, you are unlikely to work hard enough to get very good at it.

Once you start to look, birthdate bulges are everywhere. Consider the case of Major League Baseball players. Most youth leagues in the United States have a July 31 cutoff date. As it turns out, a U.S.-born boy is roughly 50 percent more likely to make the majors if he is born in August instead of July. Unless you are a big, big believer in astrology, it is hard to argue that someone is 50 percent better at hitting a big-league curveball simply because he is a Leo rather than a Cancer.

---

*A few years ago, we wrote a *New York Times Magazine* column, "A Star Is Made," about the birthdate bulge and Ericsson's research on talent. We planned to expand upon it for a chapter in *SuperFreakonomics*. Alas, we ended up discarding the chapter, half-written, for in the time between the column and finishing this book, the field became suddenly crowded with other books that highlighted Ericsson's research, including *Outliers* (by Malcolm Gladwell), *Talent Is Overrated* (by Geoff Colvin), and *The Talent Code* (by Dan Coyle).

But as prevalent as birth effects are, it would be wrong to overemphasize their pull. Birth timing may push a marginal child over the edge, but other forces are far, far more powerful. If you want your child to play Major League Baseball, the most important thing you can do—infinitely more important than timing an August delivery date—is make sure the baby isn't born with two X chromosomes. Now that you've got a son instead of a daughter, you should know about a single factor that makes him *eight hundred times* more likely to play in the majors than a random boy.

What could possibly have such a mighty influence?

Having a father who also played Major League Baseball. So if your son doesn't make the majors, you have no one to blame but yourself: you should have practiced harder when you were a kid.

Some families produce baseball players. Others produce terrorists.

Conventional wisdom holds that the typical terrorist comes from a poor family and is himself poorly educated. This seems sensible. Children who are born into low-income, low-education families are far more likely than average to become criminals, so wouldn't the same be true for terrorists?

To find out, the economist Alan Krueger combed through a Hezbollah newsletter called *Al-Ahd* (*The Oath*) and compiled biographical details on 129 dead *shahids* (martyrs). He then compared them with men from the same age bracket in the general populace of Lebanon. The terrorists, he found, were *less* likely to come from a poor family (28 percent versus 33 percent) and *more* likely to have at least a high-school education (47 percent versus 38 percent).

A similar analysis of Palestinian suicide bombers by Claude Berrebi found that only 16 percent came from impoverished families, versus more than 30 percent of male Palestinians overall. More than 60 percent of the bombers, meanwhile, had gone beyond high school, versus 15 percent of the populace.

In general, Krueger found, "terrorists tend to be drawn from well-educated, middle-class or high-income families." Despite a few exceptions—the Irish Republican Army and perhaps the Tamil Tigers of Sri Lanka (there isn't enough evidence to say)—the trend holds true around the world, from Latin American terrorist groups to the al Qaeda members who carried out the September 11 attacks in the United States.

How can this be explained?

It may be that when you're hungry, you've got better things to worry about than blowing yourself up. It may be that terrorist leaders place a high value on competence, since a terrorist attack requires more orchestration than a typical crime.

Furthermore, as Krueger points out, crime is primarily driven by personal gain, whereas terrorism is fundamentally a political act. In his analysis, the kind of person most likely to become a terrorist is similar to the kind of person most likely to . . . vote. Think of terrorism as civic passion on steroids.

Anyone who has read some history will recognize that Krueger's terrorist profile sounds quite a bit like the typical revolutionary. Fidel Castro and Che Guevara, Ho Chi Minh, Mohandas Gandhi, Leon Trotsky and Vladimir Lenin, Simón Bolívar, and Maximilien Robespierre—you won't find a single lower-class, uneducated lad among them.

But a revolutionary and a terrorist have different goals. Revolutionaries want to overthrow and replace a government. Terrorists want to—well, it isn't always clear. As one sociologist puts it, they might wish to remake the world in their own dystopian image; religious terrorists may want to cripple the secular institutions they despise. Krueger cites more than one hundred different scholarly definitions of terrorism. "At a conference in 2002," he writes, "foreign ministers from over 50 Islamic states agreed to condemn terrorism but could not agree on a definition of what it was that they had condemned."

What makes terrorism particularly maddening is that killing isn't even the main point. Rather, it is a means by which to scare the pants off the living and fracture their normal lives. Terrorism is therefore devilishly efficient, exerting far more leverage than an equal amount of non-terrorist violence.

In October 2002, the Washington, D.C., metropolitan area experienced fifty murders, a fairly typical number. But ten of these murders were different. Rather than the typical domestic disputes or gang killings, these were random and inexplicable shootings. Ordinary people minding their own business were shot while pumping gas or leaving the store or mowing the lawn. After the first few killings, panic set in. As they continued, the region was virtually paralyzed. Schools were closed, outdoor events canceled, and many people wouldn't leave their homes at all.

What kind of sophisticated and well-funded organization had wrought such terror?

Just two people, it turned out: a forty-one-year-old man and his teenage accomplice, firing a Bushmaster .223-caliber rifle from an old Chevy sedan, its roomy trunk converted into a sniper's nest. So simple, so cheap, and so effective: that is the leverage of terror. Imagine that the nineteen hijackers from September 11, rather than going to the trouble of hijacking airplanes and flying them into buildings, had instead spread themselves around the country, nineteen men with nineteen rifles in nineteen cars, each of them driving to a new spot every day and shooting random people at gas stations and schools and restaurants. Had the nineteen of them synchronized their actions, they would have effectively set off a nationwide time bomb every day. They would have been hard to catch, and even if one of them was caught, the other eighteen would carry on. The entire country would have been brought to its knees.

Terrorism is effective because it imposes costs on everyone, not just its direct victims. The most substantial of these indirect costs is fear of a future attack, even though such fear is grossly misplaced. The probability that an average American will die in a given year from a terrorist attack is roughly 1 in 5 million; he is 575 times more likely to commit suicide.

Consider the less obvious costs, too, like the loss of time and liberty. Think about the last time you went through an airport security line and were forced to remove your shoes, shuffle through the metal detector in stocking feet, and then hobble about while gathering up your belongings.

The beauty of terrorism—if you're a terrorist—is that you can succeed even by failing. We perform this shoe routine thanks to a bumbling British national named Richard Reid, who, even though he couldn't ignite his shoe bomb, exacted a huge price. Let's say it takes an average of one minute to remove and replace your shoes in the airport security line. In the United States alone, this procedure happens roughly 560 million times per year. Five hundred and sixty million minutes equals more than 1,065 years—which, divided by 77.8 years (the average U.S. life expectancy at birth), yields a total of nearly 14 person-lives. So even though Richard Reid failed to kill a single person, he levied a tax that is the time equivalent of 14 lives per year.

The direct costs of the September 11 attacks were massive—nearly three thousand lives and economic losses as high as $300 billion—as were the costs of the wars in Afghanistan and Iraq that the United States launched in response. But consider the collateral costs as well. In just the three months following the attacks, there were one thousand extra traffic deaths in the United States. Why?

One contributing factor is that people stopped flying and drove instead. Per mile, driving is much more dangerous than flying. Interestingly, however, the data show that most of these extra traffic deaths occurred not on interstates but on local roads, and they were concentrated in the Northeast, close to the terrorist attacks. Furthermore, these fatalities were more likely than usual to involve drunken and reckless driving. These facts, along with myriad psychological studies of terrorism's aftereffects, suggest that the September 11 attacks led to a spike in alcohol abuse and post-traumatic stress that translated into, among other things, extra driving deaths.

Such trickle-down effects are nearly endless. Thousands of foreign-born university students and professors were kept out of the United States because of new visa restrictions after the September 11 attacks. At least 140 U.S. corporations exploited the ensuing stock-market decline by illegally backdating stock options. In New York City, so many police resources were shifted to terrorism that other areas—the Cold Case Squad, for one, as well as anti-Mafia units—were neglected. A similar pattern was repeated on the national level. Money and manpower that otherwise would have been spent chasing financial scoundrels were instead diverted to chasing terrorists—perhaps contributing to, or at least exacerbating, the recent financial meltdown.

Not all of the September 11 aftereffects were harmful. Thanks to decreased airline traffic, influenza—which travels well on planes—was slower to spread and less dangerous. In Washington, D.C., crime fell whenever the federal terror-alert level went up (thanks to extra police flooding the city). And an increase in border security was a boon to some California farmers—who, as Mexican and Canadian imports declined, grew and sold so much marijuana that it became one of the state's most valuable crops.

When one of the four airplanes hijacked on September 11 crashed into the Pentagon, all of the seriously injured victims, most of whom suffered burns, were taken to Washington Hospital Center, the largest hospital in the city. There were only a handful of patients—corpses were more plentiful—but even so, the burn unit was nearly overwhelmed. Like most hospitals, WHC routinely operated at about 95 percent of capacity, so even a small surge of patients stressed the system. Worse yet, the hospital's phone lines went down, as did local cell service, so anyone needing to make a call had to jump in a car and drive a few miles away.

All things considered, WHC performed well. But for Craig Feied (pronounced *FEE-ed*), an emergency-medicine specialist there, the incident confirmed his greatest fears. If the hospital nearly went haywire with just a few extra burn patients, what would happen during a major disaster, when the ER was most needed?

Even before September 11, Feied had spent thousands of hours thinking such grim thoughts. He was the chief architect of a federally funded pilot program called ER One, which was meant to drag the emergency room into the modern era.

Until the 1960s, hospitals simply weren't designed to treat emergencies. "If you brought someone to a hospital at night," Feied says, "the doors would be locked. You'd ring the bell, a nurse would come down to see what you wanted. She might let you in, then she'd call the doctor at home, and he might or might not come in." Ambulances were often run by the local mortuary. It is hard to think of a better example of misaligned incentives: a funeral director who is put in charge of helping a patient not die!

Today, emergency medicine ranks as the seventh-largest physician specialty (out of thirty-eight), with a fivefold increase in practitioners since 1980. It is a master-of-all-trades endeavor, performed at lightning speed, and the emergency room has become the linchpin of public health. In a given year, there are roughly 115 million ER visits in the United States. Excluding pregnancies, 56 percent of all people admitted to U.S. hospitals come through the ER, up from 46 percent in 1993.

And yet, Feied says, "you could drive a truck through the gaps in our protocols."

September 11 brought home the point that emergency rooms are painfully limited in their surge capacity. If there had been a thousand victims at WHC, would they even have gotten inside?

Such a prospect makes Feied grimace. Most ERs have an ambulance bay that can fit only a few vehicles at a time. The docks are also built too high—"because the people who designed them were used to building loading docks," Feied says. Rooftop helipads are similarly problematic because of the time and space constraints of a single elevator. Feied's idea for getting rid of such bottlenecks is to design an ER more like an airport, with a large convex intake area that could accommodate a multitude of ambulances, buses, or even helicopters.

But these intake issues aren't what worry Feied the most. A hospital that gets hit with something serious and communicable—SARS or anthrax or Ebola or a new strain of lethal influenza—would soon cripple itself. Like most buildings, hospitals recirculate their air, which means that one sick patient could infect hundreds. "You don't want to go to the hospital for a broken ankle and get SARS," Feied says.

The answer is to build hospitals, and especially ERs, with rooms designed for isolation and zero air recirculation. But most hospitals, Feied notes, don't want to spend money on such unsexy, non-revenue-generating features. "There were some nice emergency departments built in 2001, state-of-the-art, and they're completely obsolete today. They were built with open bays, divided by curtains, but if you have a SARS patient in Bed 4, there's not a patient or doctor in the world who will want to go into Bed 5."

And don't even get Feied started on all the hospital patients who die from a cause *other* than what brought them to the hospital: wrong diagnoses (the result of carelessness, hubris, or cognitive bias); medication errors (based, far too often, on sloppy handwriting); technical complications (reading an X-ray backward, for instance); and bacterial infections (the deadliest and most pervasive problem).

"The state of current medical practice is *so* bad right now that there's not very much worth protecting about the old ways of doing things," Feied says. "Nobody in medicine wants to admit this but it's the truth."

Feied grew up in Berkeley, California, during the very raucous 1960s, and he fit right in. He skateboarded everywhere; he occasionally jammed on drums with a local band called the Grateful Dead. He had an aptitude for mechanics, taking apart and reassembling whatever looked interesting, and he was enterprising: by eighteen, he had founded a small technology company. He studied biophysics and mathematics before going into medicine. He became a doctor, he says, because of "the lure of secret knowledge," a desire to understand the human body as well as he understood machines.

Still, you sense that machines remain his first love. He is a fervent early adopter—he put a fax machine in the ER and started riding a Segway when both were novelties—and he excitedly recalls hearing a lecture by the computer scientist Alan Kay more than thirty-five years ago on object-oriented programming. Kay's idea—to encapsulate each chunk of code with logic that enabled it to interact with any other piece—was a miracle of streamlining, making programmers' lives easier and helping turn computers into more robust and flexible tools.

Feied arrived at Washington Hospital Center in 1995, recruited by his longtime colleague Mark Smith to help fix its emergency department. (Smith was also a true believer in technology. He had a master's degree in computer science from Stanford, where his thesis adviser was none other than Alan Kay.) Although some of WHC's specialty departments were well regarded, the ER consistently ranked last in the D.C. area. It was crowded, slow, and disorganized; it ran through a new director every year or so, and the hospital's own medical director called the ER "a pretty undesirable place."

By this time, Feied and Smith had between them treated more than a hundred thousand patients in various emergency rooms. They found one commodity was always in short supply: information. A patient would come in—conscious or unconscious, cooperative or not, sober or high, with a limitless array of potential problems—and the doctor had to decide quickly how to treat him. But there were usually more questions than answers: Was the patient on medication? What was his medical history? Did a low blood count mean acute internal bleeding or just chronic anemia? And where was the CT scan that was supposedly done two hours ago?

"For years, I treated patients with no more information than the patients could tell me," Feied says. "Any other information took too long, so you couldn't factor it in. We often knew what information we needed, and even knew where it was, but it just wasn't available in time. The critical piece of data might have been two hours away or two weeks away. In a busy emergency department, even two *minutes* away is too much. You can't do that when you have forty patients and half of them are trying to die."

The problem agitated Feied so badly that he turned himself into the world's first emergency-medicine informaticist. (He made up the phrase, based on the European term for computer science.) He believed that the best way to improve clinical care in the ER was to improve the flow of information.

Even before taking over at WHC, Feied and Smith hired a bunch of medical students to follow doctors and nurses around the ER and pepper them with questions. Much like Sudhir Venkatesh hired trackers to interview Chicago street prostitutes, they wanted to gather reliable, real-time data that were otherwise hard to get. Here are some of the questions the students asked:

> Since I last talked to you, what information did you need?
>
> How long did it take to get it?
>
> What was the source: Did you make a phone call? Use a reference book? Talk to a medical librarian?*
>
> Did you get a satisfactory answer to your query?
>
> Did you make a medical decision based on that answer?
>
> How did that decision impact patient care?
>
> What was the financial impact of that decision on the hospital?

The diagnosis was clear: the WHC emergency department had a severe case of "datapenia," or low data counts. (Feied invented this word as well, stealing the suffix from "leucopenia," or low white-blood-cell counts.) Doctors were spending about 60 percent of their time on "information management," and only 15 percent on direct patient care. This was a sickening ratio. "Emergency medicine is a specialty defined not by an organ of the body or by an age group but by time," says Mark Smith. "It's about what you do in the first sixty minutes."

Smith and Feied discovered more than three hundred data sources in the hospital that didn't talk to one another, including a mainframe system, handwritten notes, scanned images, lab results, streaming video from cardiac angiograms, and an infection-control tracking

---

*This was in the early days of the Internet, before the advent of the Web.

system that lived on one person's computer on an Excel spreadsheet. "And if *she* went on vacation, God help you if you're trying to track a TB outbreak," says Feied.

To give the ER doctors and nurses what they really needed, a computer system had to be built from the ground up. It had to be encyclopedic (one missing piece of key data would defeat the purpose); it had to be muscular (a single MRI, for instance, ate up a massive amount of data capacity); and it had to be flexible (a system that couldn't incorporate any data from any department in any hospital in the past, present, or future was useless).

It also had to be really, really fast. Not only because slowness kills in an ER but because, as Feied had learned from the scientific literature, a person using a computer experiences "cognitive drift" if more than one second elapses between clicking the mouse and seeing new data on the screen. If ten seconds pass, the person's mind is somewhere else entirely. That's how medical errors are made.

To build this fast, flexible, muscular, encyclopedic system, Feied and Smith turned to their old crush: object-oriented programming. They set to work using a new architecture that they called "data-centric" and "data-atomic." Their system would deconstruct each piece of data from every department and store it in a way that allowed it to interact with any other single piece of data, or any other 1 billion pieces.

Alas, not everyone at WHC was enthusiastic. Institutions are by nature large and inflexible beasts with fiefdoms that must be protected and rules that must not be broken. Some departments considered their data proprietary and wouldn't surrender it. The hospital's strict purchasing codes wouldn't let Feied and Smith buy the computer equipment they needed. One top administrator "hated us," Feied recalls, "and missed no opportunity to try to stonewall and prevent people from working with us. He used to go into the service-request system at night and delete our service requests."

It probably didn't help that Feied was such an odd duck—the contrarianism, the Segway, the original Miró prints on his office wall—or that, when challenged, he wouldn't rest until he found a way to charm or, if need be, threaten his way to victory. Even the name he gave his new computer system seemed grandiose: Azyxxi (*uh-ZICK-see*), which he told people came from the Phoenician for "one who is capable of seeing far"—but which really, he admits with a laugh, "we just made up."

In the end, Feied won—or, really, the data won. Azyxxi went live on a single desktop computer in the WHC emergency room. Feied put a sign on it: "Beta Test: Do Not Use." (No one ever said he wasn't clever.) Like so many Adams and Eves, doctors and nurses began to peck at the forbidden fruit and found it nothing short of miraculous. In a few seconds they could locate practically any information they needed. Within a week, the Azyxxi computer had a waiting line. And it wasn't just ER docs: they came from all over the hospital to drink up the data. At first glance, it seemed like the product of genius. But no, says Feied. It was "a triumph of doggedness."

Within a few years, the WHC emergency department went from worst to first in the Washington region. Even though Azyxxi quadrupled the amount of information that was actually being seen, doctors were spending 25 percent less time on "information management," and more than twice as much time directly treating patients. The old ER wait time averaged eight hours; now, 60 percent of patients were in and out in less than two hours. Patient outcomes were better and doctors were happier (and less error-prone). Annual patient volume doubled, from 40,000 to 80,000, with only a 30 percent increase in staffing. Efficiencies abounded, and this was good for the hospital's bottom line.

As Azyxxi's benefits became clear, many other hospitals came calling. So did, eventually, Microsoft, which bought it, Craig Feied and all. Microsoft renamed it Amalga and, within the first year, installed the system in fourteen major hospitals, including Johns Hopkins, New

York–Presbyterian, and the Mayo Clinic. Although it was developed in an ER, more than 90 percent of its use is currently in other hospital departments. As of this writing, Amalga covers roughly 10 million patients at 350 care sites; for those of you keeping score at home, that's more than 150 terabytes of data.

It would have been enough if Amalga merely improved patient outcomes and made doctors more efficient. But such a massive accumulation of data creates other opportunities. It lets doctors seek out markers for diseases in patients who haven't been diagnosed. It makes billing more efficient. It makes the dream of electronic medical records a straightforward reality. And, because it collects data in real time from all over the country, the system can serve as a Distant Early Warning Line for disease outbreaks or even bioterrorism.

It also allows other, non-medical people—people like us, for instance—to repurpose its data to answer other kinds of questions, such as: who are the best and worst doctors in the ER?

For a variety of reasons, measuring doctor skill is a tricky affair.

The first is selection bias: patients aren't randomly assigned to doctors. Two cardiologists will have two sets of clientele who may differ on many dimensions. The better doctor's patients may even have a *higher* death rate. Why? Perhaps the sicker patients seek out the best cardiologist, so even if he does a good job, his patients are more likely to die than the other doctor's.

It can therefore be misleading to measure doctor skill solely by looking at patient outcomes. That is generally what doctor "report cards" do and, though the idea has obvious appeal, it can produce some undesirable consequences. A doctor who knows he is being graded on patient outcomes may "cream-skim," turning down the high-risk patients who most need treatment so as to not tarnish his score. Indeed, studies have shown that hospital report cards have actually hurt patients precisely because of this kind of perverse physician incentive.

Measuring doctor skill is also tricky because the impact of a doctor's decisions may not be detectable until long after the patient is treated. When a doctor reads a mammogram, for instance, she can't be sure if there is breast cancer or not. She may find out weeks later, if a biopsy is ordered—or, if she missed a tumor that later kills the patient, she may *never* find out. Even when a doctor gets a diagnosis just right and forestalls a potentially serious problem, it's hard to make sure the patient follows directions. Did he take the prescribed medication? Did he change his diet and exercise program as directed? Did he stop scarfing down entire bags of pork rinds?

The data culled by Craig Feied's team from the WHC emergency room turn out to be just the thing to answer some questions about doctor skill. For starters, the data set is huge, recording some 620,000 visits by roughly 240,000 different patients over nearly eight years, and the more than 300 doctors who treated them.

It contains everything you might want to know about a given patient—anonymized, of course, for our analysis—from the moment she walks, rolls, or is carried through the ER door until the time she leaves the hospital, alive or otherwise. The data include demographic information; the patient's complaint upon entering the ER; how long it took to see a doctor; how the patient was diagnosed and treated; whether the patient was admitted to the hospital, and the length of stay; whether the patient was later readmitted; the total cost of the treatment; and if or when the patient died. (Even if the patient died two years later outside the hospital, the death would still be included in our analysis as a result of cross-linking the hospital data with the Social Security Death Index.)

The data also show which doctor treated which patients, and we know a good bit about each doctor as well, including age, gender, medical school attended, hospital where residency was served, and years of experience.

When most people think of ERs, they envision a steady stream of gunshot wounds and accident victims. In reality, dramatic incidents like these represent a tiny fraction of ER traffic and, because WHC has a separate Level I trauma center, such cases are especially rare in our ER data. That said, the main emergency room has an extraordinary array of patient complaints, from the life-threatening to the entirely imaginary.

On average, about 160 patients showed up each day. The busiest day is Monday, and weekend days are the slowest. (This is a good clue that many ailments aren't so serious that they can't wait until the weekend's activities are over.) The peak hour is 11:00 A.M., which is five times busier than the slowest hour, which is 5:00 A.M. Six of every ten patients are female; the average age is forty-seven.

The first thing a patient does upon arrival is tell the triage nurse what's wrong. Some complaints are common: "shortness of breath," "chest pains," "dehydration," "flulike symptoms." Others are far less so: "fish bone stuck in throat," "hit over the head with book," and a variety of bites, including a good number of dog bites (about 300) and insect or spider bites (200). Interestingly, there are more human bites (65) than rat bites and cat bites combined (30), including 1 instance of being "bitten by client at work." (Alas, the intake form didn't reveal the nature of this patient's job.)

The vast majority of patients who come to the ER leave alive. Only 1 of every 250 patients dies within a week; 1 percent die within a month, and about 5 percent die within a year. But knowing whether a condition is life-threatening or not isn't always obvious (especially to the patients themselves). Imagine you're an ER doc with eight patients in the waiting room, one each with one of the following eight common complaints. Four of these conditions have a relatively high death rate while the other four are low. Can you tell which ones are which?

COMPLAINTS	
NUMBNESS	PSYCHIATRIC
CHEST PAINS	SHORTNESS OF BREATH
FEVER	INFECTION
DIZZINESS	CLOT

Here's the answer, based on the likelihood of a patient dying within twelve months:*

HIGH-RISK CONDITIONS	LOW-RISK CONDITIONS
CLOT	CHEST PAINS
FEVER	DIZZINESS
INFECTION	NUMBNESS
SHORTNESS OF BREATH	PSYCHIATRIC

Shortness of breath is by far the most common high-risk condition. (It is usually notated as "SOB," so if someday you see that abbreviation on your chart, don't think the doctor hates you.) To many patients, SOB might seem less scary than something like chest pains. But here's what the data say:

	SOB	CHEST PAINS
AVERAGE AGE OF PATIENT	54.5	51.4
SHARE OF ER PATIENTS WITH COMPLAINT	7.4%	12.1%
ADMITTED TO HOSPITAL	51.3%	41.9%
1-MONTH MORTALITY RATE	2.9%	1.2%
1-YEAR MORTALITY RATE	12.9%	5.3%

*These and other death rates are *risk-adjusted* death rates, controlling for age, other symptoms, etc.

So a patient with chest pains is no more likely than the average ER patient to die within a year, whereas shortness of breath more than doubles the death risk. Similarly, roughly 1 in 10 patients who show up with a clot, a fever, or an infection will be dead within a year; but if a patient is dizzy, is numb, or has a psychiatric condition, the risk of dying is only one-third as high.

With all this in mind, let's get back to the question at hand: given all these data, how do we measure the efficacy of each doctor?

The most obvious course would be to simply look at the raw data for differences in patient outcomes across doctors. Indeed, this method would show radical differences among doctors. If these results were trustworthy, there would be few factors in your life as important as the identity of the doctor who happens to draw your case when you show up at the ER.

But for the same reasons you shouldn't put much faith in doctor report cards, a comparison like this is highly deceptive. Two doctors in the same ER are likely to treat very different pools of patients. The average patient at noon, for instance, is about ten years older than one who comes in the middle of the night. Even two doctors working the same shift might see very different patients, based on their skills and interests. It is the triage nurse's job to match patients and doctors as best as possible. One doc may therefore get all the psychiatric cases on a shift, or all the elderly patients. Because an old person with shortness of breath is much more likely to die than a thirty-year-old with the same condition, we have to be careful not to penalize the doctor who happens to be good with old people.

What you'd *really* like to do is run a randomized, controlled trial so that when patients arrive they are randomly assigned to a doctor, even if that doctor is overwhelmed with other patients or not well equipped to handle a particular ailment.

But we are dealing with one set of real, live human beings who are trying to keep another set of real, live human beings from dying, so this kind of experiment isn't going to happen, and for good reason.

Since we can't do a true randomization, and if simply looking at patient outcomes in the raw data will be misleading, what's the best way to measure doctor skill?

Thanks to the nature of the emergency room, there is another sort of de facto, accidental randomization that can lead us to the truth. The key is that patients generally have no idea which doctors will be working when they arrive at the ER. Therefore, the patients who show up between 2:00 and 3:00 P.M. on one Thursday in October are, on average, likely to be similar to the patients who show up the following Thursday, or the Thursday after that. But the *doctors* working on those three Thursdays will probably be different. So if the patients who came on the first Thursday have worse outcomes than the patients who came on the second or third Thursday, one likely explanation is that the doctors on that shift weren't as good. (In this ER, there were usually two or three doctors per shift.)

There could be other explanations, of course, like bad luck or bad weather or an *E. coli* outbreak. But if you look at a particular doctor's record across hundreds of shifts and see that the patients on those shifts have worse outcomes than is typical, you have a pretty strong indication that the doctor is at the root of the problem.

One last note on methodology: while we exploit information about which doctors are working on a shift, we *don't* factor in which doctor actually treats a particular patient. Why? Because we know that the triage nurse's job is to match patients with doctors, which makes the selection far from random. It might seem counterintuitive—wasteful, even—to ignore the specific doctor-patient match in our analysis. But in scenarios where selection is a problem, the only way to get a true answer is, paradoxically, to *throw away* what at first seems to be valuable information.

So, applying this approach to Craig Feied's massively informative data set, what can we learn about doctor skill?

Or, put another way: if you land in an emergency room with a serious condition, how much does your survival depend on the particular doctor you draw?

The short answer is . . . not all that much. Most of what looks like doctor skill in the raw data is in fact the luck of the draw, the result of some doctors getting more patients with less-threatening ailments.

This isn't to say there's *no* difference between the best and worst doctors in the ER. (And no, we're not going to name them.) In a given year, an excellent ER doctor's patients will have a twelve-month death rate that is nearly 10 percent lower than the average. This may not sound like much, but in a busy ER with tens of thousands of patients, an excellent doctor might save six or seven lives a year relative to the worst doctor.

Interestingly, health outcomes are largely uncorrelated to spending. This means the best doctors don't spend any more money—for tests, hospital admittance, and so on—than the lesser doctors. This is worth pondering in an era when higher health-care spending is widely thought to produce better health-care outcomes. In the United States, the health-care sector accounts for more than 16 percent of GDP, up from 5 percent in 1960, and is projected to reach 20 percent by 2015.

So what are the characteristics of the best doctors?

For the most part, our findings aren't very surprising. An excellent doctor is disproportionately likely to have attended a top-ranked medical school and served a residency at a prestigious hospital. More experience is also valuable: an extra ten years on the job yields the same benefit as having served a residency at a top hospital.

And oh yes: you also want your ER doctor to be a woman. It may have been bad for America's schoolchildren when so many smart women passed up teaching jobs to go to medical school, but it's good to know that, in our analysis at least, such women are slightly better than their male counterparts at keeping people alive.

One factor that *doesn't* seem to matter is whether a doctor is highly rated by his or her colleagues. We asked Feied and the other head physicians at WHC to name the best docs in the ER. The ones they chose turned out to be no better than average at lowering death rates. They were, however, good at spending less money per patient.

So the particular doctor you draw in the ER does matter—but, in the broader scheme of things, not nearly as much as other factors: your ailment, your gender (women are much less likely than men to die within a year of visiting the ER), or your income level (poor patients are much more likely to die than rich ones).

The best news is that most people who are rushed to the ER and think they are going to die are in little danger of dying at all, at least not any time soon.

In fact, they might have been better off if they simply stayed at home. Consider the evidence from a series of widespread doctor strikes in Los Angeles, Israel, and Colombia. It turns out that the death rate dropped significantly in those places, anywhere from 18 percent to 50 percent, when the doctors stopped working!

This effect might be partially explained by patients' putting off elective surgery during the strike. That's what Craig Feied first thought when he read the literature. But he had a chance to observe a similar phenomenon firsthand when a lot of Washington doctors left town at the same time for a medical convention. The result: an across-the-board drop in mortality.

"When there are too many physician-patient interactions, the amplitude gets turned up on everything," he says. "More people with nonfatal problems are taking more medications and having more procedures, many of which are not really helpful and a few of which are harmful, while the people with really fatal illnesses are rarely cured and ultimately die anyway."

So it may be that going to the hospital slightly increases your odds of surviving if you've got a serious problem but increases your odds of dying if you don't. Such are the vagaries of life.

Meanwhile, there *are* some ways to extend your life span that have nothing to do with going to the hospital. You could, for instance, win a Nobel Prize. An analysis covering fifty years of the Nobels in chemistry and physics found that the winners lived longer than those who were merely nominated. (So much for the Hollywood wisdom of "It's an honor just to be nominated.") Nor was the winners' longevity a function of the Nobel Prize money. "Status seems to work a kind of health-giving magic," says Andrew Oswald, one of the study's authors. "Walking across that platform in Stockholm apparently adds about two years to a scientist's life span."

You could also get elected to the Baseball Hall of Fame. A similar analysis shows that men who are voted into the Hall outlive those who are narrowly omitted.

But what about those of us who aren't exceptional at science or sport? Well, you could purchase an annuity, a contract that pays off a set amount of income each year but only as long as you stay alive. People who buy annuities, it turns out, live longer than people who don't, and not because the people who buy annuities are healthier to start with. The evidence suggests that an annuity's steady payout provides a little extra incentive to keep chugging along.

Religion also seems to help. A study of more than 2,800 elderly Christians and Jews found that they were more likely to die in the thirty days after their respective major holidays than in the thirty days before. (One piece of evidence proving a causal link: Jews had no aversion to dying in the thirty days before a *Christian* holiday, nor did Christians disproportionately outlast the Jewish holidays.) In a similar vein, longtime friends and rivals Thomas Jefferson and John Adams each valiantly struggled to forestall death until they'd reached an important landmark. They expired within fifteen hours of each other on July 4, 1826, the fiftieth anniversary of the ratification of the Declaration of Independence.

Holding off death by even a single day can sometimes be worth millions of dollars. Consider the estate tax, which is imposed on the taxable estate of a person upon his or her death. In the United States, the rate in recent years was 45 percent, with an exemption for the first $2 million. In 2009, however, the exemption jumped to $3.5 million—which meant that the heirs of a rich, dying parent had about 1.5 million reasons to console themselves if said parent died on the first day of 2009 rather than the last day of 2008. With this incentive, it's not hard to imagine such heirs giving their parent the best medical care money could buy, at least through the end of the year. Indeed, two Australian scholars found that when their nation abolished its inheritance tax in 1979, a disproportionately high number of people died in the week after the abolition as compared with the week before.

For a time, it looked as if the U.S. estate tax would be temporarily abolished for one year, in 2010. (This was the product of a bipartisan hissy fit in Washington, which, as of this writing, appears to have been resolved.) If the tax *had* been suspended, a parent worth $100 million who died in 2010 could have passed along all $100 million to his or her heirs. But, with a scheduled resumption of the tax in 2011, such heirs would have surrendered more than $40 million if their parent had the temerity to die even one day too late. Perhaps the bickering politicians decided to smooth out the tax law when they realized how many assisted suicides they might have been responsible for during the waning weeks of 2010.

Most people want to fend off death no matter the cost. More than $40 billion is spent worldwide each year on cancer drugs. In the United States, they constitute the second-largest category of pharmaceutical sales, after heart drugs, and are growing twice as fast as the rest of the market. The bulk of this spending goes to chemotherapy, which is used in a variety of ways and has proven effective on some cancers, including leukemia, lymphoma, Hodgkin's disease, and testicular cancer, especially if these cancers are detected early.

But in most other cases, chemotherapy is remarkably *in*effective. An exhaustive analysis of cancer treatment in the United States and Australia showed that the five-year survival rate for all patients was about 63 percent but that chemotherapy contributed barely 2 percent to this result. There is a long list of cancers for which chemotherapy had *zero* discernible effect, including multiple myeloma, soft-tissue sarcoma, melanoma of the skin, and cancers of the pancreas, uterus, prostate, bladder, and kidney.

Consider lung cancer, by far the most prevalent fatal cancer, killing more than 150,000 people a year in the United States. A typical chemotherapy regime for non-small-cell lung cancer costs more than $40,000 but helps extend a patient's life by an average of just two months. Thomas J. Smith, a highly regarded oncology researcher and clinician at Virginia Commonwealth University, examined a promising new chemotherapy treatment for metastasized breast cancer and found that each additional year of healthy life gained from it costs $360,000—if such a gain could actually be had. Unfortunately, it couldn't: the new treatment typically extended a patient's life by less than two months.

Costs like these put a tremendous strain on the entire health-care system. Smith points out that cancer patients make up 20 percent of Medicare cases but consume 40 percent of the Medicare drug budget.

Some oncologists argue that the benefits of chemotherapy aren't necessarily captured in the mortality data, and that while chemotherapy may not help nine out of ten patients, it may do wonders for the tenth. Still, considering its expense, its frequent lack of efficacy, and its toxicity—nearly 30 percent of the lung-cancer patients on one protocol stopped treatment rather than live with its brutal side effects—why is chemotherapy so widely administered?

The profit motive is certainly a factor. Doctors are, after all, human beings who respond to incentives. Oncologists are among the highest-paid doctors, their salaries increasing faster than any other specialists', and they typically derive more than half of their income from selling and administering chemotherapy drugs. Chemotherapy can also help oncologists inflate their survival-rate data. It may not seem all that valuable to give a late-stage victim of lung cancer an extra two months to live, but perhaps the patient was only expected to live four months anyway. On paper, this will look like an impressive feat: the doctor extended the patient's remaining life by 50 percent.

Tom Smith doesn't discount either of these reasons, but he provides two more.

It is tempting, he says, for oncologists to overstate—or perhaps over-*believe* in—the efficacy of chemotherapy. "If your slogan is 'We're winning the war on cancer,' that gets you press and charitable donations and money from Congress," he says. "If your slogan is 'We're still getting our butts kicked by cancer but not as bad as we used to,' that's a different sell. The reality is that for most people with solid tumors—brain, breast, prostate, lung—we aren't getting our butts kicked as badly, but we haven't made much progress."

There's also the fact that oncologists are, once again, human beings who have to tell other human beings they are dying and that, sadly, there isn't much to be done about it. "Doctors like me find it incredibly hard to tell people the very bad news," Smith says, "and how ineffective our medicines sometimes are."

If this task is so hard for doctors, surely it must also be hard for the politicians and insurance executives who subsidize the widespread use of chemotherapy. Despite the mountain of negative evidence, chemotherapy seems to afford cancer patients their last, best hope to nurse what Smith calls "the deep and abiding desire not to be dead." Still, it is easy to envision a point in the future, perhaps fifty years from now, when we collectively look back at the early twenty-first century's cutting-edge cancer treatments and say: We were giving our patients *what*?

The age-adjusted mortality rate for cancer is essentially unchanged over the past half-century, at about 200 deaths per 100,000 people. This is despite President Nixon's declaration of a "war on cancer" more than thirty years ago, which led to a dramatic increase in funding and public awareness.

Believe it or not, this flat mortality rate actually hides some good news. Over the same period, age-adjusted mortality from cardiovascular disease has plummeted, from nearly 600 people per 100,000 to well beneath 300. What does this mean?

Many people who in previous generations would have died from heart disease are now *living long enough to die from cancer* instead. Indeed, nearly 90 percent of newly diagnosed lung-cancer victims are fifty-five or older; the median age is seventy-one.

The flat cancer death rate obscures another hopeful trend. For people twenty and younger, mortality has fallen by more than 50 percent, while people aged twenty to forty have seen a decline of 20 percent. These gains are real and heartening—all the more so because the *incidence* of cancer among those age groups has been increasing. (The reasons for this increase aren't yet clear, but among the suspects are diet, behaviors, and environmental factors.)

With cancer killing fewer people under forty, fighting two wars must surely be driving the death toll higher for young people, no?

From 2002 to 2008, the United States was fighting bloody wars in Afghanistan and Iraq; among active military personnel, there were an average 1,643 fatalities per year. But over the same stretch of time in the early 1980s, with the United States fighting no major wars, there were more than 2,100 military deaths per year. How can this possibly be?

For one, the military used to be much larger: 2.1 million on active duty in 1988 versus 1.4 million in 2008. But even the *rate* of death in 2008 was lower than in certain peacetime years. Some of this improvement is likely due to better medical care. But a surprising fact is that the accidental death rate for soldiers in the early 1980s was higher than the death rate by hostile fire for every year the United States has been fighting in Afghanistan and Iraq. It seems that practicing to fight a war can be just about as dangerous as really fighting one.

And, to further put things in perspective, think about this: since 1982, some 42,000 active U.S. military personnel have been killed—roughly the same number of Americans who die in traffic accidents in a single year.

If someone smokes two packs of cigarettes a day for thirty years and dies of emphysema, at least you can say he brought it on himself and got to enjoy a lifetime of smoking.

There is no such consolation for the victim of a terrorist attack. Not only is your demise sudden and violent but you did nothing to earn it. You are collateral damage; the people who killed you neither knew nor cared a whit about your life, your accomplishments, your loved ones. Your death was a prop.

Terrorism is all the more frustrating because it is so hard to prevent, since terrorists have a virtually unlimited menu of methods and targets. Bombs on a train. An airplane crashed into a skyscraper. Anthrax sent through the mail. After an attack like 9/11 in the United States or 7/7 in London, a massive amount of resources are inevitably deployed to shield the most precious targets, but there is a Sisyphean element to such a task. Rather than walling off every target a terrorist may attack, what you'd really like to do is figure out who the terrorists are *before* they strike and throw them in jail.

The good news is there aren't many terrorists. This is a natural conclusion if you consider the relative ease of carrying out a terrorist attack and the relative scarcity of such attacks. There has been a near absence of terrorism on U.S. soil since September 11; in the United Kingdom, terrorists are probably more prevalent but still exceedingly rare.

The bad news is the scarcity of terrorists makes them hard to find before they do damage. Anti-terror efforts are traditionally built around three activities: gathering human intelligence, which is difficult and dangerous; monitoring electronic "chatter," which can be like trying to sip from a fire hose; and following the international money trail—which, considering the trillions of dollars sloshing around the world's banks every day, is like trying to sift the entire beach for a few particular grains of sand. The nineteen men behind the September 11 attacks funded their entire operation with $303,671.62, or less than $16,000 per person.

Might there be a fourth tactic that could help find terrorists?

Ian Horsley* believes there may. He doesn't work in law enforcement, or in government or the military, nor does anything in his background or manner suggest he might be the least bit heroic. He grew

*This name is, for reasons that will soon become apparent, a pseudonym. All other facts about him are real.

up in the heart of England, the son of an electrical engineer, and is now well into middle age. He still lives happily far from the maddening thrum of London. While perfectly affable, he isn't outgoing or jolly by any measure; Horsley is, in his own words, "completely average and utterly forgettable."

Growing up, he thought he might like to be an accountant. But he left school when his girlfriend's father helped him get a job as a bank cashier. He took on new positions at the bank as they arose, none of them particularly interesting or profitable. One job, in computer programming, turned out to be a bit more intriguing because it gave him "a fundamental understanding of the underlying database that the bank operates on," he says.

Horsley proved to be diligent, a keen observer of human behavior, and a man who plainly knew right from wrong. Eventually he was asked to sniff out fraud among bank employees, and in time he graduated to consumer fraud, which was a far wider threat to the bank. U.K. banks lose about $1.5 billion annually to such fraud. In recent years, it had been facilitated by two forces: the rise of online banking and the fierce competition among banks to snag new business.

For a time, money was so cheap and credit so easy that anyone with a pulse, regardless of employment or citizenship or creditworthiness, could walk into a British bank and walk out with a debit card. (In truth, even a pulse wasn't necessary: fraudsters were happy to use the identities of dead and fictional people as well.) Horsley learned the customs of various subgroups. West African immigrants were master check washers, while Eastern Europeans were the best identity thieves. Such fraudsters were relentless and creative: they would track down a bank's call center and linger outside until an employee exited, offering a bribe for customers' information.

Horsley built a team of data analysts and profilers who wrote computer programs that could crawl through the bank's database and detect fraudulent activity. The programmers were good. The fraudsters were also good, and nimble too, devising new scams as soon as old ones were compromised. These rapid mutations sharpened Horsley's ability to think like a fraudster. Even in his sleep, his mind cruised through billions upon billions of bank data points, seeking out patterns that might betray wrongdoing. His algorithms got tighter and tighter.

We had the good fortune to meet Ian Horsley at about this time and, jointly, we began to wonder: if his algorithms could sift through an endless stream of retail banking data and successfully detect fraudsters, might the same data be coaxed to identify other bad guys, like would-be terrorists?

This hunch was supported by the data trail from the September 11 attacks. The banking histories of those nineteen terrorists revealed some behaviors that, in the aggregate, distinguished them from the typical bank customer:

- They opened their U.S. accounts with cash or cash equivalents, in the average amount of roughly $4,000, usually at a branch of a large, well-known bank.
- They typically used a P.O. box as an address, and the addresses changed frequently.
- Some of them regularly sent and received wire transfers to and from other countries, but these transactions were always below the limit that triggered the bank's reporting requirements.
- They tended to make one large deposit and then withdraw cash in small amounts over time.

- Their banking didn't reflect normal living expenses like rent, utilities, auto payments, insurance, and so on.
- There was no typical monthly consistency in the timing of their deposits or withdrawals.
- They didn't use savings accounts or safe-deposit boxes.
- The ratio of cash withdrawals to checks written was unusually high.

It is obviously easier to retroactively create a banking profile of a proven terrorist than to build one that would identify a terrorist before he acts. Nor would a profile of these nineteen men—foreign nationals living in the United States who were training to hijack jetliners—necessarily fit the profile of, say, a homegrown suicide bomber in London.

Furthermore, when data have been used in the past to identify wrongdoing—like the cheating schoolteachers and collusive sumo wrestlers we wrote about in *Freakonomics*—there was a relatively high prevalence of fraud among a targeted population. But in this case, the population was gigantic (Horsley's bank alone had many millions of customers) while the number of potential terrorists was very small.

Let's say, however, you *could* develop a banking algorithm that was 99 percent accurate. We'll assume the United Kingdom has 500 terrorists. The algorithm would correctly identify 495 of them, or 99 percent. But there are roughly 50 million adults in the United Kingdom who have nothing to do with terrorism, and the algorithm would also wrongly identify 1 percent of *them*, or 500,000 people. At the end of the day, this wonderful, 99-percent-accurate algorithm spits out too many false positives—half a million people who would be rightly indignant when they were hauled in by the authorities on suspicion of terrorism.

Nor, of course, could the authorities handle the workload.

This is a common problem in health care. A review of a recent cancer-screening trial showed that 50 percent of the 68,000 participants got at least 1 false-positive result after undergoing 14 tests. So although health-care advocates may urge universal screening for all sorts of maladies, the reality is that the system would be overwhelmed by false positives and the sick would be crowded out. The baseball player Mike Lowell, a recent World Series MVP, underscored a related problem while discussing a plan to test every ballplayer in the league for human growth hormone. "If it's 99 percent accurate, that's going to be 7 false positives," Lowell said. "What if one of the false positives is Cal Ripken? Doesn't it put a black mark on his career?"

Similarly, if you want to hunt terrorists, 99 percent accurate is not even close to good enough.

On July 7, 2005, four Islamic suicide bombers struck in London, one on a crowded bus and three in the Underground. The murder toll was fifty-two. "Personally, I was devastated by it," Horsley recalls. "We were just starting to work on identifying terrorists and I thought maybe, just maybe, if we had started a couple years earlier, would we have stopped it?"

The 7/7 bombers left behind some banking data, but not much. In the coming months, however, a flock of suspicious characters accommodated our terrorist-detection project by getting themselves arrested by the British police. Granted, none of these men were *proven* terrorists; most of them would never be convicted of anything. But if they resembled a terrorist closely enough to get arrested, perhaps their banking habits could be mined to create a useful algorithm. As luck would have it, more than a hundred of these suspects were customers at Horsley's bank.

The procedure would require two steps. First, assemble all the available data on these hundred-plus suspects and create an algorithm based on the patterns that set these men apart from the general population. Once the algorithm was successfully fine-tuned, it could be used to dredge through the bank's database to identify other potential bad guys.

Given that the United Kingdom was battling Islamic fundamentalists and no longer, for instance, Irish militants, the arrested suspects invariably had Muslim names. This would turn out to be one of the strongest demographic markers for the algorithm. A person with neither a first nor a last Muslim name stood only a 1 in 500,000 chance of being a suspected terrorist. The likelihood for a person with a first *or* a last Muslim name was 1 in 30,000. For a person with first *and* last Muslim names, however, the likelihood jumped to 1 in 2,000.

The likely terrorists were predominately men, most commonly between the ages of twenty-six and thirty-five. Furthermore, they were disproportionately likely to:

- Own a mobile phone
- Be a student
- Rent, rather than own, a home

These traits, on their own, would hardly be grounds for arrest. (They describe just about every research assistant the two of us have ever had, and we are pretty sure none of them are terrorists.) But, when stacked atop the Muslim-name markers, even these common traits began to add power to the algorithm.

Once the preceding factors were taken into account, several other characteristics proved fundamentally neutral, not identifying terrorists one way or another. They included:

- Employment status
- Marital status
- Living in close proximity to a mosque

So contrary to common perception, a single, unemployed, twenty-six-year-old man who lived next door to a mosque was no more likely to be a terrorist than another twenty-six-year-old who had a wife, a job, and lived five miles from the mosque.

There were also some prominent negative indicators. The data showed that a would-be terrorist was disproportionately *un*likely to:

- Have a savings account
- Withdraw money from an ATM on a Friday afternoon
- Buy life insurance

The no-ATM-on-Friday metric would seem to be a proxy for a Muslim who attends that day's mandatory prayer service. The life-insurance marker is a bit more interesting. Let's say you're a twenty-six-year-old man, married with two young children. It probably makes sense to buy some life insurance so your family can survive if you happen to die young. But insurance companies don't pay out if the policyholder commits suicide. So a twenty-six-year-old family man who suspects he may one day blow himself up probably isn't going to waste money on life insurance.

This all suggests that if a budding terrorist wants to cover his tracks, he should go down to the bank and change the name on his account to something very un-Muslim (Ian, perhaps). It also wouldn't hurt to buy some life insurance. Horsley's own bank offers starter policies for just a few quid per month.

All these metrics, once combined, did a pretty good job of creating an algorithm that could distill the bank's entire customer base into a relatively small group of potential terrorists.

It was a tight net but not yet tight enough. What finally made it work was one last metric that dramatically sharpened the algorithm. In the interest of national security, we have been asked to not disclose the particulars; we'll call it Variable X.

What makes Variable X so special? For one, it is a behavioral metric, not a demographic one. The dream of anti-terrorist authorities everywhere is to somehow become a fly on the wall in a roomful of terrorists. In one small, important way, Variable X accomplishes that. Unlike most other metrics in the algorithm, which produce a yes or no answer, Variable X measures the *intensity* of a particular banking activity. While not unusual in low intensities among the general population, this behavior occurs in high intensities much more frequently among those who have other terrorist markers.

This ultimately gave the algorithm great predictive power. Starting with a database of millions of bank customers, Horsley was able to generate a list of about 30 highly suspicious individuals. According to his rather conservative estimate, at least 5 of those 30 are almost certainly involved in terrorist activities. Five out of 30 isn't perfect—the algorithm misses many terrorists and still falsely identifies some innocents—but it sure beats 495 out of 500,495.

As of this writing, Horsley has handed off the list of 30 to his superiors, who in turn have handed it off to the proper authorities. Horsley has done his work; now it is time for them to do theirs. Given the nature of the problem, Horsley may never know for certain if he was successful. And you, the reader, are even less likely to see direct evidence of his success because it would be invisible, manifesting itself in terrorist attacks that never happen.

But perhaps you'll find yourself in a British pub some distant day, one stool away from an unassuming, slightly standoffish stranger. You have a pint with him, and then another and a third. With his tongue loosened a bit, he mentions, almost sheepishly, that he has recently gained an honorific: he is now known as Sir Ian Horsley. He's not at liberty to discuss the deeds that led to his knighthood, but it has something to do with protecting civil society from those who would do it great harm. You thank him profusely for the great service he has performed, and buy him another pint, and then a few more. When the pub at last closes, the two of you stumble outside. And then, just as he is about to set off on foot down a darkened lane, you think of a very small way to repay his service. You push him back onto the curb, hail a taxi, and stuff him inside. Because, remember, friends don't let friends walk drunk.

CHAPTER 3

UNBELIEVABLE STORIES ABOUT APATHY AND ALTRUISM

In March 1964, late on a cold and damp Thursday night, something terrible happened in New York City, something suggesting that human beings are the most brutally selfish animals to ever roam the planet.

A twenty-eight-year-old woman named Kitty Genovese drove home from work and parked, as usual, in the lot at the Long Island Rail Road station. She lived in Kew Gardens, Queens, roughly twenty minutes by train from Manhattan. It was a nice neighborhood, with tidy homes on shaded lots, a handful of apartment buildings, and a small commercial district.

Genovese lived above a row of shops that fronted Austin Street. The entrance to her apartment was around the rear. She got out of her car and locked it; almost immediately, a man started chasing her and stabbed her in the back. Genovese screamed. The assault took place on the sidewalk in front of the Austin Street shops and across the street from a ten-story apartment building called the Mowbray.

The assailant, whose name was Winston Moseley, retreated to his car, a white Corvair parked at the curb some sixty yards away. He put the car in reverse and backed it down the block, passing out of view.

Genovese, meanwhile, staggered to her feet and made her way around to the back of her building. But in a short time Moseley returned. He sexually assaulted her and stabbed her again, leaving Genovese to die. Then he got back in his car and drove home. Like Genovese, he was young, twenty-nine years old, and he too lived in Queens. His wife was a registered nurse; they had two children. On the drive home, Moseley noticed another car stopped at a red light, its driver asleep at the wheel. Moseley got out and woke the man. He didn't hurt or rob him. The next morning, Moseley went to work as usual.

The crime soon became infamous. But not because Moseley was a psychopath—a seemingly normal family man who, although he had no criminal record, turned out to have a history of grotesque sexual violence. And it wasn't because Genovese was a colorful character herself, a tavern manager who happened to be a lesbian and had a prior gambling arrest. Nor was it because Genovese was white and Moseley was black.

The Kitty Genovese murder became infamous because of an article published on the front page of *The New York Times*. It began like this:

> *For more than half an hour 38 respectable, law-abiding citizens in Queens watched a killer stalk and stab a woman in three separate attacks in Kew Gardens. . . . Not one person telephoned the police during the assault; one witness called after the woman was dead.*

The murder took about thirty-five minutes from start to finish. "If we had been called when he first attacked," said a police inspector, "the woman might not be dead now."

The police had interviewed Genovese's neighbors the morning after the murder, and the *Times*'s reporter reinterviewed some of them. When asked why they hadn't intervened or at least called the police, they offered a variety of excuses:

"We thought it was a lovers' quarrel."

"We went to the window to see what was happening but the light from our bedroom made it difficult to see the street."

"I was tired. I went back to bed."

The article wasn't very long—barely fourteen hundred words—but its impact was immediate and explosive. There seemed to be general agreement that the thirty-eight witnesses in Kew Gardens represented a new low in human civilization. Politicians, theologians, and editorial writers lambasted the neighbors for their apathy. Some even called for the neighbors' addresses to be published so justice could be done.

The incident so deeply shook the nation that over the next twenty years, it inspired more academic research on bystander apathy than the Holocaust.

To mark the thirtieth anniversary, President Bill Clinton visited New York City and spoke about the crime: "It sent a chilling message about what had happened at that time in a society, suggesting that we were each of us not simply in danger but fundamentally alone."

More than thirty-five years later, the horror lived on in *The Tipping Point,* Malcolm Gladwell's groundbreaking book about social behavior, as an example of the "bystander effect," whereby the presence of multiple witnesses at a tragedy can actually *inhibit* intervention.

Today, more than forty years later, the Kitty Genovese saga appears in all ten of the top-selling undergraduate textbooks for social psychology. One text describes the witnesses remaining "at their windows in fascination for the 30 minutes it took her assailant to complete his grisly deed, during which he returned for three separate attacks."

How on earth could thirty-eight people stand by and watch as their neighbor was brutalized? Yes, economists always talk about how self-interested we are, but doesn't this demonstration of self-interest practically defy logic? Does our apathy really run so deep?

The Genovese murder, coming just a few months after President John F. Kennedy's assassination, seemed to signal a sort of social apocalypse. Crime was exploding in cities all across the United States, and no one seemed capable of stopping it.

For decades, the rate of violent and property crimes in the United States had been steady and relatively low. But levels began to rise in the mid-1950s. By 1960, the crime rate was 50 percent higher than it had been in 1950; by 1970, the rate had *quadrupled.*

Why?

It was hard to say. So many changes were simultaneously rippling through American society in the 1960s—a population explosion, a growing anti-authoritarian sentiment, the expansion of civil rights, a wholesale shift in popular culture—that it wasn't easy to isolate the factors driving crime.

Imagine, for instance, you want to know whether putting more people in prison really lowers the crime rate. This question isn't as obvious as it may seem. Perhaps the resources devoted to catching and jailing criminals could have been used more productively. Perhaps every time a bad guy is put away, another criminal rises up to take his place.

To answer this question with some kind of scientific certainty, what you'd really like to do is conduct an experiment. Pretend you could randomly select a group of states and command each of them to release 10,000 prisoners. At the same time, you could randomly select a different group of states and have them lock up 10,000 people, misdemeanor offenders perhaps, who otherwise wouldn't have gone to prison. Now sit back, wait a few years, and measure the crime rate in those two sets of states. Voilà! You've just run the kind of randomized, controlled experiment that lets you determine the relationship between variables.

Unfortunately, the governors of those random states probably wouldn't take too kindly to your experiment. Nor would the people you sent to prison in some states or the next-door neighbors of the prisoners you freed in others. So your chances of actually conducting this experiment are zero.

That's why researchers often rely on what is known as a *natural experiment,* a set of conditions that mimic the experiment you want to conduct but, for whatever reason, cannot. In this instance, what you want is a radical change in the prison population of various states for reasons that have nothing to do with the amount of crime in those states.

Happily, the American Civil Liberties Union was good enough to create just such an experiment. In recent decades, the ACLU has filed lawsuits against dozens of states to protest overcrowded prisons. Granted, the choice of states is hardly random. The ACLU sues where prisons are most crowded and where it has the best chance of winning. But the crime trends in states sued by the ACLU look very similar to trends in other states.

The ACLU wins virtually all of these cases, after which the state is ordered to reduce overcrowding by letting some prisoners free. In the three years after such court decisions, the prison population in these states falls by 15 percent relative to the rest of the country.

What do those freed prisoners do? A whole lot of crime. In the three years after the ACLU wins a case, violent crime rises by 10 percent and property crime by 5 percent in the affected states.

So it takes some work, but using indirect approaches like natural experiments can help us look back at the dramatic crime increase of the 1960s and find some explanations.

One major factor was the criminal-justice system itself. The ratio of arrests per crime fell dramatically during the 1960s, for both property and violent crime. But not only were the police catching a smaller share of the criminals; the courts were less likely to lock up those who were caught. In 1970, a criminal could expect to spend an astonishing 60 percent less time behind bars than he would have for the same crime committed a decade earlier. Overall, the decrease in punishment during the 1960s seems to be responsible for roughly 30 percent of the rise in crime.

The postwar baby boom was another factor. Between 1960 and 1980, the fraction of the U.S. population between the ages of fifteen and twenty-four rose by nearly 40 percent, an unprecedented surge in the age group most at risk for criminal involvement. But even such a radical demographic shift can only account for about 10 percent of the increase in crime.

So together, the baby boom and the declining rate of imprisonment explain less than half of the crime spike. Although a host of other hypotheses have been advanced—including the great migration of African Americans from the rural South to northern cities and the return of Vietnam vets scarred by war—all of them combined still cannot explain the crime surge. Decades later, most criminologists remain perplexed.

The answer might be right in front of our faces, literally: television. Maybe Beaver Cleaver and his picture-perfect TV family weren't just a casualty of the changing times (*Leave It to Beaver* was canceled in 1963, the same year Kennedy was assassinated). Maybe they were actually a *cause* of the problem.

People have long posited that violent TV shows lead to violent behavior, but that claim is not supported by data. We are making an entirely different argument here. Our claim is that children who grew up watching a lot of TV, even the most innocuous family-friendly shows, were more likely to engage in crime when they got older.

Testing this hypothesis isn't easy. You can't just compare a random bunch of kids who watched a lot of TV with those who didn't. The ones who were glued to the TV are sure to differ from the other children in countless ways beyond their viewing habits.

A more believable strategy might be to compare cities that got TV early with those that got it much later.

We wrote earlier that cable TV came to different parts of India at different times, a staggered effect that made it possible to measure TV's impact on rural Indian women. The initial rollout of TV in the United States was even bumpier. This was mainly due to a four-year interruption, from 1948 to 1952, when the Federal Communications Commission declared a moratorium on new stations so the broadcast spectrum could be reconfigured.

Some places in the United States started receiving signals in the mid-1940s while others had no TV until a decade later. As it turns out, there is a stark difference in crime trends between cities that got TV early and those that got it late. These two sets of cities had similar rates of violent crime before the introduction of TV. But by 1970, violent crime was twice as high in the cities that got TV early relative to those that got it late. For property crime, the early-TV cities started with much *lower* rates in the 1940s than the late-TV cities, but ended up with much higher rates.

There may of course be other differences between the early-TV cities and the late-TV cities. To get around that, we can compare children born in the *same* city in, say, 1950 and 1955. So in a city that got TV in 1954, we are comparing one age group that had no TV for the first four years of life with another that had TV the entire time. Because of the staggered introduction of TV, the cutoff between the age groups that grew up with and without TV in their early years varies widely across cities. This leads to specific predictions about which cities will see crime rise earlier than others—as well as the age of the criminals doing the crimes.

So did the introduction of TV have any discernible effect on a given city's crime rate?

The answer seems to be yes, indeed. For every extra year a young person was exposed to TV in his first 15 years, we see a 4 percent increase in the number of property-crime arrests later in life and a 2 percent increase in violent-crime arrests. According to our analysis, the total impact of TV on crime in the 1960s was an increase of 50 percent in property crimes and 25 percent in violent crimes.

Why did TV have this dramatic effect?

Our data offer no firm answers. The effect is largest for children who had extra TV exposure from birth to age four. Since most four-year-olds weren't watching violent shows, it's hard to argue that content was the problem.

It may be that kids who watched a lot of TV never got properly socialized, or never learned to entertain themselves. Perhaps TV made the have-nots want the things the haves had, even if it meant stealing them. Or maybe it had nothing to do with the kids at all; maybe Mom and Dad became derelict when they discovered that watching TV was a lot more entertaining than taking care of the kids.

Or maybe early TV programs somehow *encouraged* criminal behavior. *The Andy Griffith Show,* a huge hit that debuted in 1960, featured a friendly sheriff who didn't carry a gun and his extravagantly inept deputy, named Barney Fife. Could it be that all the would-be criminals who watched this pair on TV concluded that the police simply weren't worth being afraid of?

As a society, we've come to accept that some bad apples will commit crimes. But that still doesn't explain why none of Kitty Genovese's neighbors—regular people, good people—stepped in to help. We all witness acts of altruism, large and small, just about every day. (We may even commit some ourselves.) So why didn't a single person exhibit altruism on that night in Queens?

A question like this may seem to fall beyond the realm of economics. Sure, liquidity crunches and oil prices and even collateralized debt obligations—but social behaviors like altruism? Is that really what economists do?

For hundreds of years, the answer was no. But around the time of the Genovese murder, a few renegade economists had begun to care deeply about such things. Chief among them was Gary Becker, whom we met earlier, in this book's introduction. Not satisfied with just measuring the economic choices people make, Becker tried to incorporate the sentiments they attached to such choices.

Some of Becker's most compelling research concerned altruism. He argued, for instance, that the same person who might be purely selfish in business could be exceedingly altruistic among people he knew—although, importantly (Becker *is* an economist, after all), he predicted that altruism even within a family would have a strategic element. Years later, the economists Doug Bernheim, Andrei Shleifer, and Larry Summers empirically demonstrated Becker's point. Using data from a U.S. government longitudinal study, they showed that an elderly parent in a retirement home is more likely to be visited by his grown children if they are expecting a sizable inheritance.

But wait, you say: maybe the offspring of wealthy families are simply more caring toward their elderly parents?

A reasonable conjecture—in which case you'd expect an only child of wealthy parents to be especially dutiful. But the data show no increase in retirement-home visits if a wealthy family has only one grown child; there need to be at least two. This suggests that the visits increase because of competition between siblings for the parent's estate. What might look like good old-fashioned intrafamilial altruism may be a sort of prepaid inheritance tax.

Some governments, wise to the ways of the world, have gone so far as to legally require grown children to visit or support their aging moms and dads. In Singapore, the law is known as the Maintenance of Parents Act.

Still, people appear to be extraordinarily altruistic, and not just within their own families. Americans in particular are famously generous, donating about $300 billion a year to charity, more than 2 percent of the nation's GDP. Just think back to the last hurricane or earthquake that killed a lot of people, and recall how Good Samaritans rushed forward with their money and time.

But why?

Economists have traditionally assumed that the typical person makes rational decisions in line with his own self-interest. So why should this rational fellow—*Homo economicus,* he is usually called—give away some of his hard-earned cash to someone he doesn't know in a place he can't pronounce in return for nothing more than a warm, fuzzy glow?

Building on Gary Becker's work, a new generation of economists decided it was time to understand altruism in the world at large. But how? How can we know whether an act is altruistic or self-serving? If you help rebuild a neighbor's barn, is it because you're a moral person or because you know your own barn might burn down someday? When a donor gives millions to his alma mater, is it because he cares about the pursuit of knowledge or because he gets his name plastered on the football stadium?

Sorting out such things in the real world is extremely hard. While it is easy to observe actions—or, in the Kitty Genovese case, *in*action—it is much harder to understand the intentions behind an action.

Is it possible to use natural experiments, like the ACLU-prison scenario, to measure altruism? You might consider, for instance, looking at a series of calamities to see how much charitable contribution they produce. But with so many variables, it would be hard to tease out the altruism from everything else. A crippling earthquake in China is not the same as a scorching drought in Africa, which is not the same as a devastating hurricane in New Orleans. Each disaster has its own sort of "appeal"—and, just as important, donations are heavily influenced by media coverage. One recent academic study found that a given disaster received an 18 percent spike in charitable aid for each seven-hundred-word newspaper article and a 13 percent spike for every sixty seconds of TV news coverage. (Anyone hoping to raise money for a Third World disaster had better hope it happens on a slow news day.) And such disasters are by their nature anomalies—especially noisy ones, like shark attacks—that probably don't have much to say about our baseline altruism.

In time, those renegade economists took a different approach: since altruism is so hard to measure in the real world, why not peel away all the real world's inherent complexities by bringing the subject into the laboratory?

Laboratory experiments are of course a pillar of the physical sciences and have been since Galileo Galilei rolled a bronze ball down a length of wooden molding to test his theory of acceleration. Galileo believed—correctly, as it turned out—that a small creation like his could lead to a better understanding of the greatest creations known to humankind: the earth's forces, the order of the skies, the workings of human life itself.

More than three centuries later, the physicist Richard Feynman reasserted the primacy of this belief. "The test of all knowledge is experiment," he said. "Experiment is the sole judge of scientific 'truth.'" The electricity you use, the cholesterol drug you swallow, the page or screen or speaker from which you are consuming these very words—they are all the product of a great deal of experimentation.

Economists, however, have never been as reliant on the lab. Most of the problems they traditionally worry about—the effect of tax increases, for instance, or the causes of inflation—are difficult to capture there. But if the lab could unravel the scientific mysteries of the universe, surely it could help figure out something as benign as altruism.

These new experiments typically took the form of a game, run by college professors and played by their students. This path had been paved by the beautiful mind of John Nash and other economists who, in the 1950s, experimented broadly with the Prisoner's Dilemma, a game-theory problem that came to be seen as a classic test of strategic cooperation. (It was invented to glean insights about the nuclear standoff between the United States and the Soviet Union.)

By the early 1980s, the Prisoner's Dilemma had inspired a lab game called Ultimatum, which works as follows. Two players, who remain anonymous to each other, have a onetime chance to split a sum of money. Player 1 (let's call her Annika) is given $20 and is instructed to offer any amount, from $0 to $20, to Player 2 (we'll call her Zelda). Zelda must decide whether to accept or reject Annika's offer. If she accepts, they split the money according to Annika's offer. But if she rejects, they both go home empty-handed. Both players know all these rules coming into the game.

To an economist, the strategy is obvious. Since even a penny is more valuable than nothing, it makes sense for Zelda to accept an offer as low as a penny—and, therefore, it makes sense for Annika to *offer* just a penny, keeping $19.99 for herself.

But, economists be damned, that's not how normal people played the game. The Zeldas usually rejected offers below $3. They were apparently so disgusted by a lowball offer that they were willing to pay to express their disgust. Not that lowball offers happened very often. On average, the Annikas offered the Zeldas more than $6. Given how the game works, an offer this large was clearly meant to ward off rejection.

But still, an average of $6—almost a third of the total amount—seemed pretty generous.

Does that make it altruism?

Maybe, but probably not. The Ultimatum player making the offer has something to gain—the avoidance of rejection—by giving more generously. As often happens in the real world, seemingly kind behaviors in Ultimatum are inextricably tied in with potentially selfish motivations.

Enter, therefore, a new and ingenious variant of Ultimatum, this one called Dictator. Once again, a small pool of money is divided between two people. But in this case, only one person gets to make a decision. (Thus the name: the "dictator" is the only player who matters.)

The original Dictator experiment went like this. Annika was given $20 and told she could split the money with some anonymous Zelda in one of two ways: (1) right down the middle, with each person getting $10; or (2) with Annika keeping $18 and giving Zelda just $2.

Dictator was brilliant in its simplicity. As a one-shot game between two anonymous parties, it seemed to strip out all the complicating factors of real-world altruism. Generosity could not be rewarded, nor could selfishness be punished, because the second player (the one who wasn't the dictator) had no recourse to punish the dictator if the dictator acted selfishly. The anonymity, meanwhile, eliminated whatever personal feeling the donor might have for the recipient. The typical American, for instance, is bound to feel different toward the victims of Hurricane Katrina than the victims of a Chinese earthquake or an African drought. She is also likely to feel different about a hurricane victim and an AIDS victim.

So the Dictator game seemed to go straight to the core of our altruistic impulse. How would *you* play it? Imagine that you're the dictator, faced with the choice of giving away half of your $20 or giving just $2.

The odds are you would . . . divide the money evenly. That's what three of every four participants did in the first Dictator experiments. Amazing!

Dictator and Ultimatum yielded such compelling results that the games soon caught fire in the academic community. They were conducted hundreds of times in myriad versions and settings, by economists as well as psychologists, sociologists, and anthropologists. In a landmark study published in book form as *Foundations of Human Sociality,* a group of preeminent scholars traveled the world to test altruism in fifteen small-scale societies, including Tanzanian hunter-gatherers, the Ache Indians of Paraguay, and Mongols and Kazakhs in western Mongolia.

As it turns out, it didn't matter if the experiment was run in western Mongolia or the South Side of Chicago: people gave. By now the game was usually configured so that the dictator could give any amount (from $0 to $20), rather than being limited to the original two options ($2 or $10). Under this construct, people gave on average about $4, or 20 percent of their money.

The message couldn't have been much clearer: human beings indeed seemed to be hardwired for altruism. Not only was this conclusion uplifting—at the very least, it seemed to indicate that Kitty Genovese's neighbors were nothing but a nasty anomaly—but it rocked the very foundation of traditional economics. "Over the past decade," *Foundations of Human Sociality* claimed, "research in experimental economics has emphatically falsified the textbook representation of *Homo economicus.*"

Non-economists could be forgiven if they felt like crowing with satisfaction. *Homo economicus,* that hyper-rational, self-interested creature that dismal scientists had embraced since the beginning of time, was dead (if he ever really existed). Hallelujah!

If this new paradigm—*Homo altruisticus*?—was bad news for traditional economists, it looked good to nearly everyone else. The philanthropy and disaster-relief sectors in particular had reason to cheer. But there were far broader implications. Anyone from a high government official down to a parent hoping to raise civic-minded children had to gain inspiration from the Dictator findings—for if people are innately altruistic, then society should be able to rely on its altruism to solve even the most vexing problems.

Consider the case of organ transplantation. The first successful kidney transplant was performed in 1954. To the layperson, it looked rather like a miracle: someone who would surely have died of kidney failure could now live on by having a replacement organ plunked inside him.

Where did this new kidney come from? The most convenient source was a fresh cadaver, the victim of an automobile accident perhaps or some other type of death that left behind healthy organs. The fact that one person's death saved the life of another only heightened the sense of the miraculous.

But over time, transplantation became a victim of its own success. The normal supply of cadavers couldn't keep up with the demand for organs. In the United States, the rate of traffic fatalities was declining, which was great news for drivers but bad news for patients awaiting a lifesaving kidney. (At least motorcycle deaths kept up, thanks in part to many state laws allowing motorcyclists—or, as transplant surgeons call them, "donorcyclists"—to ride without helmets.) In Europe, some countries passed laws of "presumed consent"; rather than requesting that a person donate his organs in the event of an accident, the state assumed the right to harvest his organs unless he or his family specifically opted out. But even so, there were never enough kidneys to go around.

Fortunately, cadavers aren't the only source of organs. We are born with two kidneys but need only one to live—the second kidney is a happy evolutionary artifact—which means that a living donor can surrender one kidney to save someone's life and still carry on a normal life himself. Talk about altruism!

Stories abounded of one spouse giving a kidney to the other, a brother coming through for his sister, a grown woman for her aging parent, even kidneys donated between long-ago playground friends. But what if you were dying and didn't have a friend or relative willing to give you a kidney?

One country, Iran, was so worried about the kidney shortage that it enacted a program many other nations would consider barbaric. It sounded like the kind of idea some economist might have dreamed up, drunk on his belief in *Homo economicus:* the Iranian government would *pay* people to give up a kidney, roughly $1,200, with an additional sum paid by the kidney recipient.

In the United States, meanwhile, during a 1983 congressional hearing, an enterprising doctor named Barry Jacobs described his own pay-for-organs plan. His company, International Kidney Exchange, Ltd., would bring Third World citizens to the United States, remove one of their kidneys, give them some money, and send them back home. Jacobs was savaged for even raising the idea. His most vigorous critic was a young Tennessee congressman named Al Gore, who wondered if these kidney harvestees "might be willing to give you a cut-rate price just for the chance to see the Statue of Liberty or the Capitol or something."

Congress promptly passed the National Organ Transplant Act, which made it illegal "for any person to knowingly acquire, receive, or otherwise transfer any human organ for valuable consideration for use in human transplantation."

Sure, a country like Iran might let people buy and sell human organs as if they were live chickens at a market. But surely the United States had neither the stomach nor the need for such a desperate maneuver. After all, some of the nation's most brilliant academic researchers had scientifically established that human beings are altruistic by their very nature. Perhaps this altruism was just an ancient evolutionary leftover, like that second kidney. But who cared *why* it existed? The United States would lead the way, a light unto the nations, relying proudly on our innate altruism to procure enough donated kidneys to save tens of thousands of lives every year.

The Ultimatum and Dictator games inspired a boom in experimental economics, which in turn inspired a new subfield called behavioral economics. A blend of traditional economics and psychology, it sought to capture the elusive and often puzzling human motivations Gary Becker had been thinking about for decades.

With their experiments, behavioral economists continued to sully the reputation of *Homo economicus*. He was starting to look less self-interested every day—and if you had a problem with that conclusion, well, just look at the latest lab results on altruism, cooperation, and fairness.

One of the most prolific experimental economists among the new generation was a native of Sun Prairie, Wisconsin, named John List. He became an economist by accident and had a far less polished academic pedigree than his peers and elders. He came from a family of truckers. "My grandfather moved here from Germany, and he was a farmer," List says. "Then he saw that truckers were making more money than he was just to take his grain to the mill, so he decided to sell everything and buy one truck."

The Lists were a smart, hardworking, athletic family, but academics were not of paramount importance. John's father started driving trucks when he was twelve, and John too was expected to join the family business. But he rebelled by going to college. This happened only because he earned a partial golf and academic scholarship to the

University of Wisconsin–Stevens Point. During school breaks he'd help his father unload calf feed or haul a load of paper goods down to Chicago, three and a half hours away.

During golf practice at Stevens Point, List noticed a group of professors who had time to play golf just about every afternoon. They taught economics. That's when List decided to become an economics professor too. (It helped that he liked the subject.)

For graduate school he chose the University of Wyoming. It was hardly a top-tier program, but even so he felt overmatched. On the first day, when students went around the classroom and gave a bit of personal background, List felt everyone staring at him when he said he'd graduated from Stevens Point. They had all gone to places like Columbia and the University of Virginia. He decided his only chance was to outwork them. Over the next few years, he wrote more papers and took more qualifying exams than anyone else—and, like many young economists, started to dabble with lab experiments.

When it was time to apply for a teaching job, List sent out 150 applications. The response was, shall we say, muted. He did land a job at the University of Central Florida, in Orlando, where he took on a heavy teaching load and also coached the men's and women's waterskiing teams. He was a blue-collar economist if ever there was one. He was still writing paper after paper and running lots of experiments; his water-skiers even qualified for the national championships.

After a few years, List was invited to join Vernon Smith, the godfather of economic lab experiments, at the University of Arizona. The job would pay $63,000, considerably more than his UCF salary. Out of loyalty, List presented the offer to his dean, expecting UCF to at least match the offer.

"For $63,000," he was told, "we think we can replace you."

His stay at Arizona was brief, for he was soon recruited by the University of Maryland. While teaching there, he also served on the President's Council of Economic Advisors; List was the lone economist on a forty-two-person U.S. delegation to India to help negotiate the Kyoto Protocol.

He was by now firmly at the center of experimental economics, a field that had never been hotter. In 2002, the Nobel Prize for economics was shared by Vernon Smith and Daniel Kahneman, a psychologist whose research on decision-making laid the groundwork for behavioral economics. These men and others of their generation had built a canon of research that fundamentally challenged the status quo of classical economics, and List was following firmly in their footsteps, running variants of Dictator and other behavioralist lab games.

But since his days at Stevens Point, he had also been conducting quirky field experiments—studies where the participants didn't know an experiment was going on—and found that the lab findings didn't always hold up in the real world. (Economists are known to admire theoretical proofs; thus the old quip: *Sure, it works in practice, but does it work in theory?*)

Some of his most interesting experiments took place at a baseball-card show in Virginia. List had been attending such shows for years. As an undergrad, he sold sports cards to earn cash, driving as far as Des Moines, Chicago, or Minneapolis, wherever there was a good market.

In Virginia, List cruised the trading floor and randomly recruited customers and dealers, asking them to step into a back room for an economics experiment. It went like this. A customer would state how much he was willing to pay for a single baseball card, choosing from one of five prices that List established. These offers ranged from low-ball ($4) to premium ($50). Then the dealer would give the customer a card that was supposed to correspond to the offered price. Every customer and dealer did five such transactions, though with a different partner for each round.

When the customer has to name his price first—like the white men who visit Chicago street prostitutes—the dealer is plainly in a position to cheat, by giving a card that's worth less than the offer. The dealer is also in a better position to know each card's true worth. But the buyers had some leverage, too: if they thought the sellers *would* cheat, they could simply make a lowball offer each round.

So what happened? On average, the customers made fairly high offers and the dealers offered cards of commensurate value. This suggests that the buyers trusted the sellers and the buyers' trust was rewarded fairly.

This didn't surprise List. He had simply demonstrated that the results you get in a lab with college students could be replicated outside the lab with sport-card traders, at least when the participants know a researcher is carefully recording their actions.

Then he ran a different experiment, out on the real trading floor. Once again, he recruited random customers. But this time he had them approach dealers at their booths, and the dealers didn't know they were being watched.

The protocol was simple. A customer would make a dealer one of two offers: "Give me the best Frank Thomas card you can for $20" or "Give me the best Frank Thomas card you can for $65."

What happened?

Unlike their scrupulous behavior in the back room, the dealers consistently ripped off the customers, giving them lower-quality cards than the offer warranted. This was true for both the $20 offer and the $65 offer. In the data, List found an interesting split: the out-of-town dealers cheated more often than the locals. This made sense. A local dealer was probably more concerned with protecting his reputation. He might even have been worried about retribution—a baseball bat upside the head, perhaps, after a customer went home, got online, and found out he'd been hustled.

The trade-floor cheating made List wonder if perhaps all the "trust" and "fairness" he'd witnessed in the back room weren't trust and fairness at all. What if they were just a product of the experimenter's scrutiny? And what if the same was true for altruism?

Despite all the lab evidence of altruism collected by his peers and elders, List was skeptical. His own field experiments pointed in a different direction, as did his personal experience. Back when he was nineteen years old, he delivered a load of paper goods to Chicago. His girlfriend, Jennifer, came along for the ride. (They'd later marry and have five kids.) When they got to the warehouse, four men were in the loading bay, sitting on a couch. It was the dead of summer and punishingly hot. One man said they were on break.

List asked how long the break would last.

"Well, we don't know," the man said, "so why don't you just start unloading yourself."

It was customary for warehouse workers to unload a trucker's truck, or at least help. Plainly that wasn't going to happen.

"Well, if you guys don't want to help, that's fine," List said. "Just give me the keys to the forklift."

They laughed and told him the keys were lost.

So List, along with Jennifer, began unloading the truck, box by box. Drenched in sweat and thoroughly miserable, they labored under the mocking eyes of the four workmen. Finally only a few boxes were left. One of the workmen suddenly found the keys to the forklift and drove it over to List's truck.

Encounters like this had made John List seriously question whether altruism truly runs wild through the veins of humankind, as Dictator and other lab experiments argued.

Yes, that research had won much acclaim, including a Nobel Prize. But the more List thought about it, the more he wondered if perhaps those findings were simply—well, wrong.

In 2005, thanks largely to his field experiments, List was offered a tenured professor position at the University of Chicago, perhaps the most storied economics program in the world. This wasn't supposed to happen. It is a nearly inexorable law of academia that when a professor lands a tenured job, he does so at an institution less prestigious than the one where he began teaching, and also less prestigious than where he received his Ph.D. John List, meanwhile, was like a salmon who swam downstream to spawn, into the open water. Back in Wisconsin, his family was unimpressed. "They wonder why I've failed so miserably," he says, "why I'm not still in Orlando, where the weather is really great, instead of Chicago, where the crime is really high."

By now he knew the literature on altruism experiments as well as anyone. And he knew the real world a bit better. "What is puzzling," he wrote, "is that neither I nor any of my family or friends (or their families or friends) have ever received an anonymous envelope stuffed with cash. How can this be, given that scores of students around the world have outwardly exhibited their preferences for giving in laboratory experiments by sending anonymous cash gifts to anonymous souls?"

So List set out to definitively determine if people are altruistic by nature. His weapon of choice was Dictator, the same tool that created the conventional wisdom. But List had a few modifications up his sleeve. This meant recruiting a whole bunch of student volunteers and running a few different versions of the experiment.

He began with classic Dictator. The first player (whom we'll call Annika once again) was given some cash and had to decide whether to give none, some, or even all of it to some anonymous Zelda. List found that 70 percent of the Annikas gave some money to Zelda, and the average "donation" was about 25 percent of the total. This result was perfectly in line with the typical Dictator findings, and perfectly consistent with altruism.

In the second version, List gave Annika another option: she could still give Zelda any amount of her money but, if she preferred, she could instead *take* $1 from Zelda. If the dictators were altruistic, this tweak to the game shouldn't matter at all; it should only affect the people who otherwise would have given nothing. All List did was expand the dictator's "choice set" in a way that was irrelevant for all but the stingiest of players.

But only 35 percent of the Annikas in this modified, steal-a-dollar-if-you-want version gave any money to Zelda. That was just half the number who gave in the original Dictator. Nearly 45 percent, meanwhile, didn't give a penny, while the remaining 20 percent *took* a dollar from Zelda.

Hey, what happened to all the altruism?

But List didn't stop there. In the third version, Annika was told that Zelda had been given the same amount of money that she, Annika, was given. And Annika could steal Zelda's entire payment—or, if she preferred, she could give Zelda any portion of her own money.

What happened? Now only 10 percent of the Annikas gave Zelda any money, while more than 60 percent of the Annikas took from Zelda. More than 40 percent of the Annikas took *all* of Zelda's money. Under List's guidance, a band of altruists had suddenly—and quite easily—been turned into a gang of thieves.

The fourth and final version of List's experiment was identical to the third—the dictator could steal the other player's entire pile of money—but with one simple twist. Instead of being handed some money to play the game, as is standard in such lab experiments, Annika and Zelda first had to work for it. (List needed some envelopes stuffed for another experiment, and with limited research funds he was killing two birds with one stone.)

After they worked, it was time to play. Annika still had the option of taking all of Zelda's money, as more than 60 percent of the Annikas did in the previous version. But now, with both players having earned their money, only 28 percent of the Annikas took from Zelda. Fully two-thirds of the Annikas neither gave nor took a penny.

So what had John List done, and what does it mean?

He upended the conventional wisdom on altruism by introducing new elements to a clever lab experiment to make it look a bit more like the real world. If your only option in the lab is to give away some money, you probably will. But in the real world, that is rarely your only option. The final version of his experiment, with the envelope-stuffing, was perhaps most compelling. It suggests that when a person comes into some money honestly and believes that another person has done the same, she neither gives away what she earned nor takes what doesn't belong to her.

But what about all the prizewinning behavioral economists who had identified altruism in the wild?

"I think it's pretty clear that most people are misinterpreting their data," List says. "To me, these experiments put the knife in it. It's certainly not altruism we've been seeing."

List had painstakingly worked his way up from truck driver's son to the center of an elite group of scholars who were rewriting the rules of economic behavior. Now, in order to stay true to his scientific principles, he had to betray them. As word of his findings began to trickle out, he suddenly became, as he puts it, "clearly the most hated guy in the field."

List can at least be consoled by knowing that he is almost certainly correct. Let's consider some of the forces that make such lab stories unbelievable.

The first is selection bias. Think back to the tricky nature of doctor report cards. The best cardiologist in town probably attracts the sickest and most desperate patients. So if you're keeping score solely by death rate, that doctor may get a failing grade even though he is excellent.

Similarly, are the people who volunteer to play Dictator more cooperative than average? Quite likely yes. Scholars long before John List pointed out that behavioral experiments in a college lab are "the science of just those sophomores who volunteer to participate in research and who also keep their appointment with the investigator." Moreover, such volunteers tend to be "scientific do-gooders" who "typically have . . . [a] higher need for approval and lower authoritarianism than non-volunteers."

Or maybe, if you're *not* a do-gooder, you simply don't participate in this kind of experiment. That's what List observed during his baseball-card study. When he was recruiting volunteers for the first round, which he clearly identified as an economics experiment, he made note of which dealers declined to participate. In the second round, when List dispatched customers to see if unwitting dealers would rip them off, he found that the dealers who declined to participate in the first round were, on average, the biggest cheaters.

Another factor that pollutes laboratory experiments is scrutiny. When a scientist brings a lump of uranium into a lab, or a mealworm or a colony of bacteria, that object isn't likely to change its behavior just because it's being watched by someone in a white lab coat.

For human beings, however, scrutiny has a powerful effect. Do you run a red light when there's a police car—or, increasingly these days, a mounted camera—at the intersection? Thought not. Are you more likely to wash your hands in the office restroom if your boss is already washing hers? Thought so.

Our behavior can be changed by even subtler levels of scrutiny. At the University of Newcastle upon Tyne in England, a psychology professor named Melissa Bateson surreptitiously ran an experiment in her own department's break room. Customarily, faculty members paid for coffee and other drinks by dropping money into an "honesty box." Each week, Bateson posted a new price list. The prices never changed, but the small photograph atop the list did. On odd weeks, there was a picture of flowers; on even weeks, a pair of human eyes. When the eyes were watching, Bateson's colleagues left *nearly three times as much* money in the honesty box. So the next time you laugh when a bird is frightened off by a silly scarecrow, remember that scarecrows work on human beings too.

How does scrutiny affect the Dictator game? Imagine you're a student—a sophomore, probably—who volunteered to play. The professor running the experiment may stay in the background, but he's plainly there to record which choices the participants are making. Keep in mind that the stakes are relatively low, just $20. Keep in mind also that you got the $20 just for showing up, so you didn't work for the money.

Now you are asked if you'd like to give some of your money to an anonymous student who *didn't* get $20 for free. You didn't really want to keep all that money, did you? You may not like this particular professor; you might even actively dislike him—but no one wants to look cheap in front of somebody else. *What the heck,* you decide, *I'll give away a few of my dollars.* But even a cockeyed optimist wouldn't call that altruism.

In addition to scrutiny and selection bias, there's one more factor to consider. Human behavior is influenced by a dazzlingly complex set of incentives, social norms, framing references, and the lessons gleaned from past experience—in a word, context. We act as we do because, given the choices and incentives at play in a particular circumstance, it seems most productive to act that way. This is also known as rational behavior, which is what economics is all about.

It isn't that the Dictator participants didn't behave in context. They did. But the lab context is unavoidably artificial. As one academic researcher wrote more than a century ago, lab experiments have the power to turn a person into "a stupid automaton" who may exhibit a "cheerful willingness to assist the investigator in every possible way by reporting to him those very things which he is most eager to find." The psychiatrist Martin Orne warned that the lab encouraged what might best be called forced cooperation. "Just about any request which could conceivably be asked of the subject by a reputable investigator," he wrote, "is legitimized by the quasi-magical phrase 'This is an experiment.'"

Orne's point was borne out rather spectacularly by at least two infamous lab experiments. In a 1961–62 study designed to understand why Nazi officers obeyed their superiors' brutal orders, the Yale psychologist Stanley Milgram got volunteers to follow his instructions and administer a series of increasingly painful electric shocks—at least they *thought* the shocks were painful; the whole thing was a setup—to unseen lab partners. In 1971, the Stanford psychologist Philip Zimbardo conducted a prison experiment, with some volunteers playing guards and others playing inmates. The guards started behaving so sadistically that Zimbardo had to shut down the experiment.

When you consider what Zimbardo and Milgram got their lab volunteers to do, it is no wonder that the esteemed researchers who ran the Dictator game, with its innocuous goal of transferring a few dollars from one undergrad to another, could, as List puts it, "induce almost any level of giving they desire."

When you look at the world through the eyes of an economist like John List, you realize that many seemingly altruistic acts no longer seem so altruistic.

It may appear altruistic when you donate $100 to your local public-radio station, but in exchange you get a year of guilt-free listening (and, if you're lucky, a canvas tote bag). U.S. citizens are easily the world's leaders in per-capita charitable contributions, but the U.S. tax code is among the most generous in allowing deductions for those contributions.

Most giving is, as economists call it, *impure altruism* or *warm-glow altruism*. You give not only because you want to help but because it makes you look good, or feel good, or perhaps feel less bad.

Consider the panhandler. Gary Becker once wrote that most people who give money to panhandlers do so only because "the unpleasant appearance or persuasive appeal of beggars makes them feel uncomfortable or guilty." That's why people often cross the street to avoid a panhandler but rarely cross over to visit one.

And what about U.S. organ-donation policy, based on its unyielding belief that altruism will satisfy the demand for organs—how has that worked out?

Not so well. There are currently 80,000 people in the United States on a waiting list for a new kidney, but only some 16,000 transplants will be performed this year. This gap grows larger every year. More than 50,000 people on the list have died over the past twenty years, with at least 13,000 more falling off the list as they became too ill to have the operation.

If altruism were the answer, this demand for kidneys would have been met by a ready supply of donors. But it hasn't been. This has led some people—including, not surprisingly, Gary Becker—to call for a well-regulated market in human organs, whereby a person who surrenders an organ would be compensated in cash, a college scholarship, a tax break, or some other form. This proposal has so far been greeted with widespread repugnance and seems for now politically untenable.

Recall, meanwhile, that Iran established a similar market nearly thirty years ago. Although this market has its flaws, anyone in Iran needing a kidney transplant does not have to go on a waiting list. The demand for transplantable kidneys is being fully met. The average American may not consider Iran the most forward-thinking nation in the world, but surely some credit should go to the only country that has recognized altruism for what it is—and, importantly, what it's not.

If John List's research proves anything, it's that a question like "Are people innately altruistic?" is the wrong kind of question to ask. People aren't "good" or "bad." People are people, and they respond to incentives. They can nearly always be manipulated—for good *or* ill—if only you find the right levers.

So are human beings capable of generous, selfless, even heroic behavior? Absolutely. Are they also capable of heartless acts of apathy? Absolutely.

The thirty-eight witnesses who watched Kitty Genovese's brutal murder come to mind. What's so puzzling about this case is how little altruism was required for someone to have called the police from the safety of his or her home. That's why the same question—how could those people have acted so horribly?—has lingered all these years.

But perhaps there's a better question: *did* they act so horribly?

The foundation for nearly everything ever written or said about Genovese's murder was that provocative *New York Times* article, which wasn't published until two weeks after the crime. It had been conceived at a lunch between two men: A.M. Rosenthal, the paper's metro editor, and Michael Joseph Murphy, the city's police commissioner.

Genovese's killer, Winston Moseley, was already under arrest and had confessed to the crime. The story wasn't big news, especially in the *Times*. It was just another murder, way out in Queens, not the kind of thing the paper of record gave much space.

Strangely, though, Moseley also confessed to a second murder even though the police had already arrested a different man for that crime.

"What about that double confession out in Queens?" Rosenthal asked Murphy at lunch. "What's that story all about anyway?"

Instead of answering, Murphy changed the subject.

"That Queens story is something else," he said, and then told Rosenthal that thirty-eight people had watched Kitty Genovese be murdered without calling the police.

"Thirty-eight?" Rosenthal asked.

"Yes, thirty-eight," Murphy said. "I've been in this business a long time, but this beats everything."

Rosenthal, as he later wrote, "was sure that the Commissioner was exaggerating." If so, Murphy may have had sufficient incentive. A story about two men arrested for the same murder clearly had the potential to embarrass the police. Furthermore, given the prolonged and brutal nature of the Genovese murder, the police may have been touchy about who caught the blame. Why *hadn't* they been able to stop it?

Despite Rosenthal's skepticism, he sent Martin Gansberg, a longtime copy editor who'd recently become a reporter, to Kew Gardens. Four days later, one of the most indelible first sentences in newspaper history appeared on the *Times*'s front page:

> *For more than half an hour 38 respectable, law-abiding citizens in Queens watched a killer stalk and stab a woman in three separate attacks in Kew Gardens.*

For a brand-new reporter like Gansberg and an ambitious editor like Rosenthal—he later wrote a book, *Thirty-Eight Witnesses,* about the case and became the *Times*'s top editor—it was an unqualified blockbuster. It isn't often that a pair of lowly newspapermen can tell a tale that will set the public agenda, for decades hence, on a topic as heady as civic apathy. So *they* certainly had strong incentives to tell the story.

But was it true?

The best person to answer that question may be Joseph De May Jr., a sixty-year-old maritime lawyer who lives in Kew Gardens. He has an open face, thinning black hair, hazel eyes, and a hearty disposition. On a brisk Sunday morning not long ago, he gave us a tour of the neighborhood.

"Now the first attack occurred roughly in here," he said, pausing on the sidewalk in front of a small shop on Austin Street. "And Kitty parked her car over there, in the train station parking lot," he said, gesturing to an area perhaps thirty-five yards away.

The neighborhood has changed little since the crime. The buildings, streets, sidewalks, and parking areas remain as they were. The Mowbray, a well-kept brick apartment house, still stands across the street from the scene of the first attack.

De May moved to the neighborhood in 1974, a decade after Genovese was killed. The murder wasn't something he thought about much. Several years ago, De May, a member of the local historical society, built a website devoted to Kew Gardens history. After a time, he felt he should add a section about the Genovese murder, since it was the only reason Kew Gardens was known to the outside world, if it was known at all.

As he gathered old photographs and news clippings, he began to find discrepancies with the official Genovese history. The more intently he reconstructed the crime, chasing down legal documents and interviewing old-timers, the more convinced he became that the legendary story of the thirty-eight apathetic witnesses was—well, a bit too heavy on legend. Like the lawyer he is, De May dissected the *Times* article and identified six factual errors in the first paragraph alone.

The legend held that thirty-eight people "remained at their windows in fascination" and "watched a killer stalk and stab a woman in three separate attacks" but "not one person telephoned the police during the assault."

The real story, according to De May, went more like this:

The first attack occurred at about 3:20 A.M., when most people were asleep. Genovese cried out for help when Moseley stabbed her in the back. This awoke some Mowbray tenants, who rushed to their windows.

The sidewalk was not well lit, so it may have been hard to make sense of what was happening. As Moseley later testified, "[I]t was late at night and I was pretty sure that nobody could see that well out of the window." What someone likely *would* have seen at that point was a man standing over a woman on the ground.

At least one Mowbray tenant, a man, shouted out the window: "Leave that girl alone!" This prompted Moseley to run back to his car, which was parked less than a block away. "I could see that she had gotten up and wasn't dead," Moseley testified. He backed his car down the street, he said, to obscure his license plate.

Genovese struggled to her feet and slowly made her way around to the back of the building, toward her apartment's entrance. But she didn't make it all the way, collapsing inside the vestibule of a neighboring apartment.

Roughly ten minutes after the first attack, Moseley returned. It is unclear how he tracked her in the dark; he may have followed a trail of blood. He attacked her again inside the vestibule, then fled for good.

The *Times* article, as with most crime articles, especially of that era, relied heavily on information given by the police. At first the police said Moseley attacked Genovese three separate times, so that is what the newspaper published. But only two attacks occurred. (The police eventually corrected this but, as in a game of Telephone, the error took on a life of its own.)

So the first attack, which was brief, occurred in the middle of the night on a darkened sidewalk. And the second attack occurred some time later, in an enclosed vestibule, out of view of anyone who might have seen the first attack.

Who, then, were "the thirty-eight witnesses"?

That number, also supplied by the police, was apparently a whopping overstatement. "We only found half a dozen that saw what was going on, that we could use," one of the prosecutors later recalled. This included one neighbor who, according to De May, may have witnessed part of the second attack, but was apparently so drunk that he was reluctant to phone the police.

But still: even if the murder was not a bloody and prolonged spectacle that took place in full view of dozens of neighbors, why didn't anyone call the police for help?

Even that part of the legend may be false. When De May's website went live, one reader who found it was named Mike Hoffman. He was just shy of fifteen years old when Genovese was murdered, and he lived on the Mowbray's second floor.

As Hoffman recalls, he was awakened by a commotion on the street. He opened his bedroom window but still couldn't make out what was being said. He thought perhaps it was a lovers' quarrel and, more angry than concerned, he "yelled for them to 'Shut the fuck up!'"

Hoffman says he heard other people shouting, and when he looked out the window, he saw a man run away. To keep the man in view, Hoffman went to the other window in his room, but the figure faded into the darkness. Hoffman returned to the first window and saw a woman on the sidewalk stagger to her feet. "That's when my dad came in my room and yelled at me for yelling and waking *him* up."

Hoffman told his father what happened. "This guy just beat up a lady and ran away!" Hoffman and his father watched as the woman, walking with great difficulty, rounded the corner. Then everything was quiet. "Dad called the police in case she was hurt badly and needed medical attention," Hoffman says. "In those days, there was no 9-1-1. We had to dial the operator and wait for the eventual connection to the police operator. It took several minutes to get connected to the police and my father told them what we had seen and heard, and that she did walk away but appeared dazed. At that point we couldn't see or hear anything else and we all went back to sleep."

It wasn't until morning that the Hoffmans found out what happened. "We were interviewed by detectives and learned that she had went around the back of the building across the street, and the guy came back to finish her off," Hoffman says. "I remember my dad saying to them that if they had come when we called them, she'd probably still be alive."

Hoffman believes the police response was slow because the situation his father described was not a murder in progress but rather a domestic disturbance—which, by the looks of it, had concluded. The attacker had fled and the victim had walked off, if shakily, under her own power. With a low-priority call like that, Hoffman says, "the cops don't put down the donuts as fast as if it were to come across as a homicide call."

The police acknowledged that someone did call after the second attack, in the vestibule, and they arrived shortly thereafter. But Hoffman believes their response may have been based on his father's original call. Or, perhaps, there was more than one call: Joseph De May has heard from other Mowbray tenants who claim to have phoned the police after the first attack.

It is hard to say how reliable Hoffman's memory of the events may be. (He did write and sign an affidavit of his recollections.) It is also hard to say if De May's revisionist history is fully accurate. (To his credit, he points out that "an undetermined number of ear witnesses reacted badly" that night, and perhaps could have done more to help;

he is also reluctant to cast himself as the infallible source on all things Genovese.)

De May and Hoffman both have an incentive to exonerate their neighborhood from the black eye the Genovese murder gave it. That said, De May strives hard to not be an apologist, and Hoffman seems to be a pretty good witness—a man who, now in his late fifties and living in Florida, spent twenty years as a New York City policeman and retired as a lieutenant.

Now, considering the various incentives at play, which is more unbelievable: the De May–Hoffman version of events or the conventional wisdom that a whole neighborhood of people stood around and watched, refusing to help, as a man murdered a woman?

Before you answer, consider also the circumstances under which Winston Moseley was ultimately arrested. It happened a few days after the Genovese murder. At about three o'clock in the afternoon in Corona, another Queens neighborhood, Moseley was seen carrying a television out of a home belonging to a family named Bannister and loading it into his car.

A neighbor approached and asked what he was doing. Moseley said he was helping the Bannisters move. The neighbor went back in his house and phoned another neighbor to ask if the Bannisters were really moving.

"Absolutely not," said the second neighbor. He called the police while the first neighbor went back outside and loosened the distributor cap on Moseley's car.

When Moseley returned to his car and found it wouldn't start, he fled on foot but was soon chased down by a policeman. Under interrogation, he freely admitted to killing Kitty Genovese a few nights earlier.

Which means that a man who became infamous because he murdered a woman whose neighbors failed to intervene was ultimately captured because of . . . a neighbor's intervention.

CHAPTER 4

THE FIX IS IN—AND IT'S CHEAP AND SIMPLE

It is a fact of life that people love to complain, particularly about how terrible the modern world is compared with the past.

They are nearly always wrong. On just about any dimension you can think of—warfare, crime, income, education, transportation, worker safety, health—the twenty-first century is far more hospitable to the average human than any earlier time.

Consider childbirth. In industrialized nations, the current rate of maternal death during childbirth is 9 women per 100,000 births. Just one hundred years ago, the rate was *more than fifty times* higher.

One of the gravest threats of childbearing was a condition known as puerperal fever, which was often fatal to both mother and child. During the 1840s, some of the best hospitals in Europe—the London General Lying-in Hospital, the Paris Maternité, the Dresden Maternity Hospital—were plagued by it. Women would arrive healthy at the hospital to deliver a baby and then, shortly thereafter, contract a raging fever and die.

Perhaps the finest hospital at the time was the Allgemeine Krankenhaus, or General Hospital, in Vienna. Between 1841 and 1846, doctors there delivered more than 20,000 babies; nearly 2,000 of the mothers, or 1 of every 10, died. In 1847, the situation worsened: *1 of every 6* mothers died from puerperal fever.

That was the year Ignatz Semmelweis, a young Hungarian-born doctor, became assistant to the director of Vienna General's maternity clinic. Semmelweis was a sensitive man, very much attuned to the suffering of others, and he was so distraught by the rampant loss of life that he became obsessed with stopping it.

Unlike many sensitive people, Semmelweis was able to put aside emotion and focus on the facts, known and unknown.

The first smart thing he did was acknowledge that doctors really had no idea what caused puerperal fever. They might *say* they knew, but the exorbitant death rate argued otherwise. A look back at the suspected causes of the fever reveals an array of wild guesses:

- "[M]isconduct in the early part of pregnancy, such as tight stays and petticoat bindings, which, together with the weight of the uterus, detain the faeces in the intestines, the thin putrid parts of which are taken up into the blood."
- "[A]n atmosphere, a miasma, or . . . by milk metastasis, lochial suppression, cosmo-telluric influences, personal predisposition . . ."
- Foul air in the delivery wards.
- The presence of male doctors, which perhaps "wounded the modesty of parturient mothers, leading to the pathological change."
- "Catching a chill, errors in diet, rising in the labor room too soon after delivery in order to walk back to bed."

It is interesting to note that the women were generally held to blame. This may have had something to do with the fact that all doctors at the time were male. Although nineteenth-century medicine may seem primitive today, doctors were considered nearly godlike in their wisdom and authority. And yet puerperal fever presented a troubling contradiction: when women delivered babies at home with a midwife, as was still common, they were at least sixty times *less* likely to die of puerperal fever than if they delivered in a hospital.

How could it be more dangerous to have a baby in a modern hospital with the best-trained doctors than on a lumpy mattress at home with a village midwife?

To solve this puzzle, Semmelweis became a data detective. Gathering statistics on the death rate at his own hospital, he discovered a bizarre pattern. The hospital had two separate wards, one staffed by male doctors and trainees, the other by female midwives and trainees. There was a huge gap between the two wards' death rates:

	DOCTORS' WARD			MIDWIVES' WARD		
YEAR	BIRTHS	DEATHS	RATE	BIRTHS	DEATHS	RATE
1841	3,036	237	7.8%	2,442	86	3.5%
1842	3,287	518	15.8%	2,659	202	7.6%
1843	3,060	274	9.0%	2,739	164	6.0%
1844	3,157	260	8.2%	2,956	68	2.3%
1845	3,492	241	6.9%	3,241	66	2.0%
1846	4,010	459	11.4%	3,754	105	2.8%
TOTAL	**20,042**	**1,989**		**17,791**	**691**	
AVERAGE RATE			**9.9%**			**3.9%**

Why on earth was the death rate in the doctors' ward more than twice as high?

Semmelweis wondered if the women patients admitted to the doctors' ward were sicker, weaker, or in some other way compromised.

No, that couldn't be it. Patients were assigned to the wards in alternating twenty-four-hour cycles, depending on the day of the week they arrived. Given the nature of pregnancy, an expectant mother came to the hospital when it was time to have the baby, not on a day that was convenient. This assignment methodology wasn't quite as rigorous as a randomized, controlled trial, but for Semmelweis's purpose it did suggest that the divergent death rates weren't the result of a difference in patient populations.

So perhaps one of the wild guesses listed above *was* correct: did the very presence of men in such a delicate feminine enterprise somehow kill the mothers?

Semmelweis concluded that this too was improbable. After examining the death rate for *newborns* in the two wards, he again found that the doctors' ward was far more lethal than the midwives': 7.6 percent versus 3.7 percent. Nor was there any difference in the death rate of male babies versus females. As Semmelweis noted, it was unlikely that newborns would "be offended by having been delivered in the presence of men." So it was unreasonable to suspect that male presence was responsible for the mothers' deaths.

There was also a theory that patients admitted to the doctors' ward, having heard of its high death rate, were "so frightened that they contract the disease." Semmelweis didn't buy this explanation either: "We can assume that many soldiers engaged in murderous battle must also fear death. However, these soldiers do not contract childbed fever."

No, some other factor unique to the doctors' ward had to figure in the fever.

Semmelweis had by now established a few facts:

- Even the poorest women who delivered their babies on the street and *then* came to the hospital did not get the fever.
- Women who were dilated for more than twenty-four hours "almost invariably became ill."
- Doctors did not contract the disease from the women or newborns, so it was almost certainly not contagious.

Still, he remained puzzled. "Everything was in question; everything seemed inexplicable; everything was doubtful," he wrote. "Only the large number of deaths was an unquestionable reality."

The answer finally came to him in the wake of a tragedy. An older professor whom Semmelweis admired died quite suddenly after a mishap. He had been leading a student through an autopsy when the student's knife slipped and cut the professor's finger. The maladies he suffered before dying—bilateral pleurisy, pericarditis, peritonitis, and meningitis—were, Semmelweis observed, "identical to that from which so many hundred maternity patients had also died."

The professor's case held little mystery. He died from "cadaverous particles that were introduced into his vascular system," Semmelweis noted. Were the dying women also getting such particles in their bloodstream?

Of course!

In recent years, Vienna General and other first-rate teaching hospitals had become increasingly devoted to understanding anatomy. The ultimate teaching tool was the autopsy. What better way for a medical student to limn the contours of illness than to hold in his hands the failed organs, to sift for clues in the blood and urine and bile? At

Vienna General, every single deceased patient—including the women who died of puerperal fever—was taken directly to the autopsy room.

But doctors and students often went to the maternity ward straight from the autopsy table with, at best, a cursory cleansing of their hands. Although it would be another decade or two before the medical community accepted germ theory—which established that many diseases are caused by living microorganisms and not animal spirits or stale air or too-tight corsets—Semmelweis understood what was going on. It was the *doctors* who were responsible for puerperal fever, transferring "cadaverous particles" from the dead bodies to the women giving birth.

This explained why the death rate in the doctors' ward was so much higher than in the midwives' ward. It also explained why women in the doctors' ward died more often than women who gave birth at home or even in the streets, and why women in a longer state of dilation were more susceptible to the fever: the longer a woman lay in that state, the more often her uterus was poked and prodded by a gaggle of doctors and medical students, their hands still dripping with the remnants of their latest autopsy.

"None of us knew," as Semmelweis later lamented, "that *we* were causing the numerous deaths."

Thanks to him, the plague could finally be halted. He ordered all doctors and students to disinfect their hands in a chlorinated wash after performing autopsies. The death rate in the doctors' maternity ward fell to barely 1 percent. Over the next twelve months, Semmelweis's intervention saved the lives of 300 mothers and 250 babies—and that was just in a single maternity ward in a single hospital.

As we wrote earlier, the law of unintended consequences is among the most potent laws in existence. Governments, for instance, often enact legislation meant to protect their most vulnerable charges but that instead ends up hurting them.

Consider the Americans with Disabilities Act (ADA), which was intended to safeguard disabled workers from discrimination. A noble intention, yes? Absolutely—but the data convincingly show that the net result was *fewer* jobs for Americans with disabilities. Why? After the ADA became law, employers were so worried they wouldn't be able to discipline or fire bad workers who had a disability that they avoided hiring such workers in the first place.

The Endangered Species Act created a similarly perverse incentive. When landowners fear their property is an attractive habitat for an endangered animal, or even an animal that is being considered for such status, they rush to cut down trees to make it less attractive. Among the recent victims of such shenanigans are the cactus ferruginous pygmy owl and the red-cockaded woodpecker. Some environmental economists have argued that "the Endangered Species Act is actually endangering, rather than protecting, species."

Politicians sometimes try to think like economists and use price to encourage good behavior. In recent years, many governments have started to base their trash-pickup fees on volume. If people have to pay for each extra bag of garbage, the thinking goes, they'll have a strong incentive to produce less of it.

But this new way of pricing also gives people an incentive to stuff their bags ever fuller (a tactic now known by trash officers the world around as the "Seattle Stomp") or just dump their trash in the woods (which is what happened in Charlottesville, Virginia). In Germany, trash-tax avoiders flushed so much uneaten food down the toilet that the sewers became infested with rats. A new garbage tax in Ireland generated a spike in backyard trash burning—which was bad not only for the environment but for public health too: St. James's Hospital in Dublin recorded a near tripling of patients who'd set themselves on fire while burning trash.

Well-intentioned laws have been backfiring for millennia. A Jewish statute recorded in the Bible required creditors to forgive all debts every sabbatical, or seventh year. For borrowers, the appeal of unilateral debt relief cannot be overstated, as the penalties for defaulting on a loan were severe: a creditor could even take a debtor's children into bondage.

If you were a creditor, however, you saw this debt-forgiveness program differently. Why loan money to some sandal maker if he could just tear up the note in Year Seven?

So creditors gamed the system by making loans in the years right after a sabbatical and pulling tight the purse strings in Years Five and Six. The result was a cyclical credit crunch that punished the very people the law was intended to help.

But in the history of unintended consequences, few match the one uncovered by Ignatz Semmelweis: medical doctors, while in pursuit of lifesaving knowledge, conducted thousands upon thousands of autopsies, which, in turn, led to the loss of thousands upon thousands of lives.

It is heartening, of course, that Semmelweis's brilliant data deduction showed how to end this scourge. But our larger point, and the point of this chapter, is that Semmelweis's solution—sprinkling a bit of chloride of lime in the doctors' hand-wash—was remarkably simple and remarkably cheap. In a prosperous world, simple and cheap fixes sometimes get a bad rap; we are here to defend them.

There is another powerful, if bittersweet, example from the realm of childbirth: the forceps. It used to be that when a baby presented itself feet- or derriere-first, there was a good chance it would get stuck in the uterus, endangering both mother and child. The forceps, a simple set of metal tongs, allowed a doctor or midwife to turn a baby inside the uterus and adroitly pluck it out, headfirst, like a roast suckling pig from the oven.

As effective as it was, the forceps did not save as many lives as it should have. It is thought to have been invented in the early seventeenth century by a London obstetrician named Peter Chamberlen. The forceps worked so well that Chamberlen kept it a secret, sharing it only with sons and grandsons who continued in the family business. It wasn't until the mid-eighteenth century that the forceps passed into general use.

What was the cost of this technological hoarding? According to the surgeon and author Atul Gawande, "it had to have been millions of lives lost."

The most amazing thing about cheap and simple fixes is they often address problems that seem impervious to *any* solution. And yet almost invariably, a Semmelweis or a team of Semmelweises ride into view and save the day. History is studded with examples.

At the start of the Common Era, just over two thousand years ago, there were roughly 200 million people on earth. By the year 1000, that number had risen only to 300 million. Even by 1750, there were just 800 million people. Famine was a constant worry, and the smart money said the planet couldn't possibly support much more growth. The population in England had been *decreasing*—"essentially because," as one historian wrote, "agriculture could not respond to the pressure of feeding extra people."

Enter the Agricultural Revolution. A variety of innovations, none particularly complex—they included higher-yielding crops, better tools, and a more efficient use of capital—changed farming and, subsequently, the face of the earth. In late eighteenth-century America, "it took 19 out of 20 workers to feed the country's inhabitants and provide a surplus for export," wrote the economist Milton Friedman. Two hundred years later, only 1 of 20 American workers was needed to feed a far larger population while also making the United States "the largest single exporter of food in the world."

The Agricultural Revolution freed up millions of hands that went on to power the Industrial Revolution. By 1850, worldwide population had grown to 1.3 billion; by 1900, 1.7 billion; by 1950, 2.6 billion. And then things *really* took off. Over the next fifty years, the population more than doubled, reaching well beyond 6 billion. If you had to pick a single silver bullet that allowed this surge, it would be ammonium nitrate, an astonishingly cheap and effective crop fertilizer. It wouldn't be much of an overstatement to say that ammonium nitrate feeds the world. If it disappeared overnight, says the agricultural economist Will Masters, "most people's diets would revert to heaps of cereal grains and root crops, with animal products and fruits only for special occasions and for the rich."

Or consider the whale. Hunted since antiquity, by the nineteenth century it had become an economic engine that helped turn the United States into a powerhouse. Every square inch of it could be turned into *something*, so the whale afforded one-stop shopping for a fast-growing nation: material for the manufacture of paint and varnish; textiles and leather; candles and soap; clothing and of course food (the tongue was a particular delicacy). The whale was especially beloved by the finer sex, surrendering its body parts for corsets, collars, parasols, perfume, hairbrushes, and red fabric dye. (This last product was derived from, of all things, the whale's excrement.) Most valuable was whale oil, a lubricant for all sorts of machinery but most crucially used for lamp fuel. As the author Eric Jay Dolin declares in *Leviathan*, "American whale oil lit the world."

Out of a worldwide fleet of 900 whaling ships, 735 of them were American, hunting in all four oceans. Between 1835 and 1872, these ships reaped nearly 300,000 whales, an average of more than 7,700 a year. In a good year, the total take from oil and baleen (the whale's bonelike "teeth") exceeded $10 million, today's equivalent of roughly $200 million. Whaling was dangerous and difficult work, but it was the fifth-largest industry in the United States, employing 70,000 people.

And then what appeared to be an inexhaustible resource was—quite suddenly and, in retrospect, quite obviously—heading toward exhaustion. Too many ships were hunting for too few whales. A ship that once took a year at sea to fill its hold with whale oil now needed four years. Oil prices spiked accordingly, rocking the economy back home. Today, such an industry might be considered "too big to fail," but the whaling industry was failing indeed, with grim repercussions for all America.

That's when a retired railway man named Edwin L. Drake, using a steam engine to power a drill through seventy feet of shale and bedrock, struck oil in Titusville, Pennsylvania. The future bubbled to the surface. Why risk life and limb chasing underwater leviathans around the world, having to catch and carve them up, when so much energy was just waiting, in the nation's basement, to be pumped upstairs?

Oil was not only a cheap and simple fix but, like the whale, extraordinarily versatile. It could be used as lamp oil, a lubricant, and as a fuel for automobiles and home heating; it could be made into plastic and even nylon stockings. The new oil industry also provided lots of jobs for unemployed whalers and, as a bonus, functioned as the original Endangered Species Act, saving the whale from near-certain extinction.

By the early twentieth century, most infectious diseases—smallpox, tuberculosis, diphtheria, and the like—were on their way out. But polio refused to surrender.

It would be hard to invent a more frightening illness. "It was a children's disease; there was no prevention; there was no cure; every child everywhere was at risk," says David M. Oshinsky, author of the Pulitzer Prize–winning *Polio: An American Story*. "And what this really meant was that parents were absolutely frantic."

Polio was also a great mystery, spiking in summertime, its cause unknown. (In a classic case of mistaking correlation and causality, some researchers suspected that ice cream—consumed in far greater quantities in the summer—caused polio.) It was first thought to target immigrant slum children, especially boys, but it struck girls too, as well as kids in the leafiest suburbs. Even Franklin Delano Roosevelt, who was far removed from immigrant slums and, at thirty-nine, from childhood as well, contracted the disease.

Every outbreak prompted a new round of quarantines and panic. Parents kept their kids away from friends, from pools and parks and libraries. In 1916, the worst polio epidemic to date struck New York City. Out of 8,900 reported cases, 2,400 people died, most of them children under five. The disease roared on. Nineteen fifty-two was the worst year yet, with 57,000 reported cases nationwide, 3,000 of them fatal and 21,000 resulting in permanent paralysis.

Surviving a bad case of polio was only marginally better than dying. Some victims lost the use of their legs and lived in constant pain. Those with respiratory paralysis practically lived inside an "iron lung," a huge tank that did the work of their failed chest muscles. As the population of living polio victims grew, the cost of their medical care was staggering. "At a time when less than ten percent of the nation's families had any form of health insurance," Oshinsky writes, "the expense of boarding a polio patient (about $900 a year) actually exceeded the average annual wage ($875)."

America was by now the most powerful country on earth, the victor in two world wars, possessor of a blindingly bright future. But there was legitimate concern that this single disease would consume such a large share of future health-care dollars that it would cripple the nation.

And then a vaccine was developed—a series of vaccines, really—and polio was effectively stamped out.

To call the vaccine a "simple" fix might seem to discount the tireless efforts of everyone who helped stop polio: the medical researchers (Jonas Salk and Albert Sabin chief among them); the fund-raising volunteers (the March of Dimes, Oshinsky writes, was "the largest charitable army the country had ever known"); even the non-human martyrs (thousands of monkeys were imported to be given experimental vaccines).

On the other hand, there is no simpler medical fix than a vaccine. Consider two of the major ways we try to thwart disease. The first is to invent a procedure or technology that helps fix a problem once it's arisen (open-heart surgery, for instance); these tend to be very costly. The second is to invent a medicine to prevent the problem before it happens; in the long run, these tend to be extraordinarily cheap. Health-care researchers have estimated that if a polio vaccine hadn't been invented, the United States would currently be caring for at least 250,000 long-term patients at an annual cost of at least $30 billion. And that doesn't even include "the intangible costs of suffering and death and of averted fear."

Polio is a stark example, but there are countless cheap and simple medical fixes. New ulcer drugs reduced the rate of surgery by roughly 60 percent; a later round of even cheaper drugs saved ulcer patients some $800 million a year. In the first twenty-five years after lithium was introduced to treat manic depression, it saved nearly $150 billion in hospitalization costs. Even the simple addition of fluoride to water systems has saved about $10 billion per year in dental bills.

As we noted earlier, deaths from heart disease have fallen substantially over the past few decades. Surely this can be attributed to expensive treatments like grafts, angioplasties, and stents, yes?

Actually, no: such procedures are responsible for a remarkably small share of the improvement. Roughly half of the decline has come from reductions in risk factors like high cholesterol and high blood pressure, both of which are treated by relatively cheap medicines. And much of the remaining decline is thanks to ridiculously inexpensive treatments like aspirin, heparin, ACE inhibitors, and beta-blockers.

By the early 1950s, automobile travel had become fantastically popular in the United States, with about 40 million cars on the road. But at the thirty-fifth annual convention of the National Automobile Dealers Association, held in January 1952, a vice president of the BFGoodrich tire company warned that the smooth ride might be over: "If the death rate continues upward it will seriously hurt the automobile business, as many people will quit driving."

Nearly 40,000 people died in U.S. traffic accidents in 1950. That's roughly the same number of deaths as today, but a straight-up comparison is very misleading, because far fewer miles were driven back then. The rate of death per mile driven was five times higher in 1950 than it is today.

Why so many fatalities then? Suspects were legion—faulty cars, poorly designed roads, careless drivers—but not much was known about the mechanics of car crashes. Nor was the auto industry exactly burning to find out.

Enter Robert Strange McNamara. Today he is best remembered as the much-maligned secretary of defense during the Vietnam War. One reason McNamara was so maligned was that he tended to make decisions based on statistical analysis rather than emotion or political considerations. In other words, he behaved like an economist.

This was no coincidence. He studied economics at Berkeley and went on to the Harvard Business School, where he stayed on as a young professor of accounting. McNamara volunteered when World War II broke out, and his analytical skills landed him in the Statistical Control Office of the Army Air Forces.

His team used data as a weapon to fight the war. For example, the abort rate among American bombers leaving England for daytime sorties over Germany was found to be unnaturally high, about 20 percent. The pilots gave a variety of explanations for failing to reach the target: a malfunctioning electrical system, a spotty radio, or illness. But a closer analysis of the data led McNamara to conclude that these reasons were "baloney." The real explanation, he said, was fear. "A helluva lot of them were going to be killed, they knew that, and they found reasons to not go over the target."

McNamara reported this to the commanding officer, the notoriously headstrong Curtis LeMay, who responded by flying the lead plane on bombing missions and vowing to court-martial any pilot who turned back. The abort rate, McNamara says, "dropped overnight."

After the war, the Ford Motor Company asked McNamara and others from his unit to bring their statistical wizardry to the auto industry. McNamara wanted to return to Harvard, but he and his wife had both racked up huge medical bills—from polio, of all things. So he took the job at Ford. He quickly rose through the ranks even though he wasn't a "car guy" in any traditional sense. "Instead," as one historian later wrote, "he was absorbed by such novel concepts as safety, fuel economy, and basic utility."

McNamara was particularly concerned with the deaths and injuries from automobile accidents. He asked the car guys what caused the problem. There were few statistics available, he was told.

Some aeronautical researchers at Cornell were trying to prevent airplane deaths, so McNamara commissioned them to look into auto crashes. They experimented by wrapping human skulls in different materials and dropping them down the stairwells in Cornell's dormitories. It turned out that human beings were no match for the hard materials used in car interiors. "In a crash, the driver was often impaled on the steering wheel," McNamara says. "The passenger was often injured because he'd hit the windshield or the header bar or the instrument panel." McNamara ordered new Ford models to have a safer steering wheel and a padded instrument panel.

But the best fix, he realized, was also the simplest one. Rather than worrying about what a passenger's head would hit when he was flung about during an accident, wouldn't it be better to keep him from being flung at all? McNamara knew that airplanes had seat belts; why not cars?

"I calculated the number of deaths we'd prevent each year, which was very high," he says. "And this came at essentially no cost, with no great penalty for wearing them."

McNamara had all of Ford's company cars outfitted with seat belts. "I flew down to visit an assembly plant in Texas," he recalls. "The manager met me at the plane. I buckled my seat belt, and he said, 'What's the matter, you afraid of my driving?' "

That manager, it turned out, reflected a widespread sentiment about seat belts. McNamara's bosses saw them as "inconvenient, costly, and just a bunch of damn nonsense," he says. Even so, they followed his lead and put seat belts in the new Ford models.

McNamara was of course right: the seat belt would eventually save many lives. But the key word here is "eventually."

The brilliant rationalist had encountered a central, frustrating tenet of human nature: *behavior change is hard.* The cleverest engineer or economist or politician or parent may come up with a cheap, simple solution to a problem, but if it requires people to change their behavior, it may not work. Every day, billions of people around the world engage in behaviors they know are bad for them—smoking cigarettes, gambling excessively, riding a motorcycle without a helmet.

Why? Because they want to! They derive pleasure from it, or a thrill, or just a break from the daily humdrum. And getting them to change their behavior, even with a fiercely rational argument, isn't easy.

And so it was with the seat belt. Congress began setting federal safety standards in the mid-1960s, but even fifteen years later, seat belt use was laughably low: just 11 percent. Over time, the numbers crept upward, thanks to a variety of nudges: the threat of a traffic ticket; expansive public-awareness campaigns; annoying beeps and flashing dashboard lights if the belt wasn't buckled; and, eventually, a societal acceptance that wearing a seat belt wasn't an insult to anyone's driving ability. Seat-belt use rose to 21 percent by the mid-1980s, 49 percent by 1990, 61 percent by the mid-1990s, and today it is over 80 percent.

That's a big reason the per-mile auto fatality rate has fallen so much in the United States. Seat belts reduce the risk of death by as much as 70 percent; since 1975 they have saved roughly 250,000 lives. Traffic fatalities still claim more than 40,000 lives a year, but relatively speaking, driving isn't all that dangerous anymore. What makes the death toll so high is that so many Americans spend an enormous amount of time in their cars, racking up some 3 trillion miles per year. That translates into one death for every 75 million miles driven—or, put another way, if you drove 24 hours a day at 30 miles per hour, you could expect to die in a car accident only after driving for 285 straight years. Compared with the death rates in many countries in Africa, Asia, and the Middle East, where seat-belt use is far less prevalent, driving in the United States isn't much more dangerous than sitting on your couch.

And seat belts, at about $25 a pop, are one of the most cost-effective lifesaving devices ever invented. In a given year, it costs roughly $500 million to put them in every U.S. vehicle, which yields a rough estimate of $30,000 for every life saved. How does this compare with a far more complex safety feature like air bags? At an annual U.S. price of more than $4 billion, air bags cost about $1.8 *million* per life saved.

Robert McNamara, who recently passed away at the age of ninety-three, told us shortly before his death that he still wanted to get to 100 percent compliance on seat belts. "A lot of women often don't use the shoulder belt because they're uncomfortable, they're not designed to take account of the breasts," he said. "I think with very little thought, belts could be designed that are more comfortable and therefore increase the percentage of use."

He may or may not be right about women and seat belts. But without doubt there *is* one group of people for whom seat belts are poorly designed: children.

Sometimes it pays to be low status. When a family of four goes for a drive, the kids usually get shunted to the backseat while the mom or dad rides shotgun. The kids are luckier than they know: in the event of a crash, the backseat is far safer than the front. This is even truer for adults, who are larger and therefore more likely to smack into something hard when they sit up front. Unfortunately, while it's okay to consign the low-status kids to the rear seat, if the parents go out for a drive alone, it's a bit awkward for one of them to ride in the back while leaving the other up front in the martyr's seat.

Seat belts are now standard issue in the rear seat of all cars. But they were designed to fit grown-ups, not kids. If you try to strap in your three-year-old darling, the lap belt will be too loose and the shoulder belt will come across his neck or nose or eyebrows instead of his shoulder.

Fortunately, we live in a world that cherishes and protects children, and a solution was found: the child safety seat, commonly known as a car seat. Introduced in the 1960s, it was first embraced by only the most vigilant parents. Thanks to the advocacy of doctors, traffic-safety experts, and—surprise!—car-seat manufacturers, it came into wider use, and the government eventually joined the party. Between 1978 and 1985, every state in the United States made it illegal for children to ride in a car unless they were buckled into a safety seat that met federal crash-test standards.

Motor-vehicle accidents were the leading cause of death for U.S. children back then, and they still are today, but the rate of death has been falling dramatically. Most of the credit has gone to the car seat.

Safety isn't free, of course. Americans spend more than $300 million a year buying 4 million car seats. A single kid will typically inhabit three different seats over time: a rear-facing seat for infants; a larger, front-facing seat for toddlers; and a booster seat for older children. Moreover, if that kid has a sibling or two, his parents may have to buy an SUV or minivan to accommodate the width of the car seats.

Nor is the car-seat solution as simple as most people might like. Any given seat is a tangle of straps, tethers, and harnesses, built by one of dozens of manufacturers, and it must be anchored in place by a car's existing seat belt—whose configuration varies depending on *its* manufacturer, as does the shape and contour of the rear seat itself. Furthermore, those seat belts were designed to batten down a large human being, not a small, inanimate hunk of plastic. According to the National Highway Traffic Safety Administration (NHTSA), more than 80 percent of car seats are improperly installed. That's why so many parents trek to the local police station or firehouse for help with the seats. And that's why NHTSA runs a four-day National Standardized Child Passenger Safety Training Program for public-safety personnel, using a 345-page manual to teach proper installation.

But who cares if car seats aren't so simple or cheap? Not every solution can be as elegant as we might like. Isn't it worth a police officer sacrificing four days of work to master such a valuable safety device?

What matters is that car seats are *effective*, that they save children's lives. And according to NHTSA, they do, reducing the risk of fatality by a whopping 54 percent for children ages one to four.

Curious parents may have a question: a 54 percent reduction compared with *what*?

That answer can easily be found on NHTSA's own website. The agency maintains a trove of government data called the Fatality Analysis Reporting System (FARS), a compilation of police reports from all fatal crashes in the United States since 1975. It records every imaginable variable—the type and number of vehicles involved, their speed, time of day, where the passengers were sitting in the car—including what kind of safety restraints, if any, were being worn.

It turns out that a child in a car seat is 54 percent less likely to die than a child riding completely unrestrained—that is, with no car seat, no seat belt, no nothing. That makes sense. A car crash is a violent affair, and a lot of terrible things can happen to a mass of flesh and bone when it is traveling fast inside a heavy metal object that suddenly stops moving.

But how much better is the complicated and costly new solution (the car seat) than the cheap and simple old solution (the seat belt), even though the simple solution wasn't meant for kids?

Seat belts plainly won't do for children under two years old. They are simply too small, and a car seat is the best practical way to secure them. But what about older children? Laws vary by state, but in many cases car seats are mandatory until a child is six or seven years old. How much do those kids benefit from car seats?

A quick look at the raw FARS data from nearly thirty years of crashes reveals a surprising result. For children two and older, the rate of death in crashes involving at least one fatality is almost identical for those riding in car seats and those wearing seat belts:

MODE OF RESTRAINT	INCIDENTS	DEATHS	CHILD'S DEATH RATE
CHILD SAFETY SEAT	6,835	1,241	18.2%
ADULT SEAT BELT	9,664	1,750	18.1%

It may be that these raw data are misleading. Perhaps kids who ride in car seats are in more violent crashes. Or maybe their parents drive more at night, or on more dangerous roads, or in less-safe vehicles?

But even the most rigorous econometric analysis of the FARS data yields the same results. In recent crashes and old ones, in vehicles large and small, in single-car crashes and pileups, there is no evidence that car seats are better than seat belts in saving the lives of children two and older. In certain kinds of crashes—rear-enders, for instance—car seats actually perform slightly worse.

So maybe the problem is, as NHTSA admits, that too many car seats are installed improperly. (You might argue that a forty-year-old safety device that only 20 percent of its users can install correctly may not be a great safety device to begin with; compared with car seats, the condoms worn by Indian men seem practically infallible.) Could it be that the car seat *is* a miracle device but that we just haven't learned to use it properly?

To answer this, we sought out crash-test data for a side-by-side comparison of seat belts and car seats. You wouldn't think this would be hard to find. After all, every car seat brought to the market must undergo crash testing to gain federal approval. But it appears that researchers have rarely, if ever, run parallel tests on child-sized crash-test dummies. So we decided to do it ourselves.

The idea was simple: we would commission two crash tests, one with a three-year-old-sized dummy in a car seat versus a three-year-old dummy in a lap-and-shoulder belt, the other with a six-year-old-sized dummy in a booster seat versus a six-year-old dummy in a lap-and-shoulder belt. In each case, the test would simulate a thirty-mile-per-hour frontal collision.

We had a hard time finding a crash-test lab that would do our tests, even though we were willing to pay the $3,000 fee. (Hey, science doesn't come cheap.) After being turned down by what felt like every facility in America, we finally found one willing to take our money. Its director told us we couldn't name the lab, however, out of concern he might lose work from the car-seat manufacturers that were the core of his business. But, he said, he was "a fan of science," and he too wanted to know how things would turn out.

After flying in to this undisclosable location, we bought some new car seats at a Toys "R" Us and drove to the lab. But once the engineer on duty heard the particulars of our test, he refused to participate. It was an idiotic experiment, he said: *of course* the car seats would perform better—and besides, if we put one of his expensive dummies in a lap-and-shoulder belt, the impact would probably rip it to pieces.

It seemed odd to worry over the health of a crash-test dummy—aren't they made to be crashed?—but once we agreed to reimburse the lab if the seat-belted dummy was damaged, the engineer got to work, grumbling under his breath.

The lab conditions guaranteed that the car seats would perform optimally. They were strapped to old-fashioned bench-style rear seats, which give a flush fit, by an experienced crash-test engineer who was presumably far better at securing a car seat than the average parent.

The chore was gruesome, from start to finish. Each child dummy, dressed in shorts, T-shirt, and sneakers, had a skein of wires snaking out of its body to measure head and chest damage.

First came the pair of three-year-olds, one in a car seat and the other in a lap-and-shoulder belt. The pneumatic sled was fired with a frightening bang. In real time, you couldn't see much (except that, to our relief, the seat-belted dummy remained in one piece). But watching the super-slow-motion video replay, you saw each dummy's head, legs, and arms jerk forward, fingers flailing in the air, before the head snapped back. The six-year-old dummies were next.

Within minutes, we had our results: the adult seat belts passed the crash test with flying colors. Based on the head- and chest-impact data, neither the children in the safety seats nor those in the seat belts would likely have been injured in this crash.

So how well did the old-fashioned seat belts work?

They exceeded every requirement for how a child safety seat should perform. Think of it this way: if we submitted our data from the seat-belted dummies to the federal government and said it came from the latest and greatest car seat, our "new" product—which is pretty much the same nylon strap Robert McNamara pushed for back in the 1950s—would easily win approval. Since a plain old seat belt can meet the government's safety standard for car seats, perhaps it's not very surprising that car-seat manufacturers turn out a product that can't beat the seat belt. Sad, perhaps, but not surprising.

As one can imagine, our lack of appreciation for car seats places us in a slim minority. (If we didn't have six young children between us, we might well be labeled child haters.) One compelling argument against our thesis is called "seat-belt syndrome." A group of prominent child-safety researchers, warning that crash-test dummies typically don't have sensors to measure neck and abdomen injuries, tell grisly emergency-room tales of the damage seat belts inflict upon children. These researchers gathered data by interviewing parents whose children were in car accidents, and concluded that booster seats reduce significant injury by roughly 60 percent relative to seat belts.

These researchers, many of whom actively care for injured children, are surely well-meaning. But are they right?

There are a variety of reasons why interviewing parents is not the ideal way to get reliable data. Parents may have been traumatized by the crash and will perhaps misremember details. There's also the question of whether the parents—whose names the researchers harvested from an insurance company's database—are being truthful. If your child was riding unrestrained in a car crash, you might feel strong social pressure (or, if you think the insurance company will raise your rates, financial pressure) to say your child was restrained. The police report will show whether or not the vehicle had a car seat, so you can't readily lie about that. But every backseat has a seat belt, so even if your child wasn't wearing one, you could say he was, and it would be difficult for anyone to prove otherwise.

Are there data sources other than parent interviews that could help us answer this important question about child injuries?

The FARS data set won't work because it covers only fatal accidents. We did, however, locate three other data sets that contain information on all crashes. One was a nationally representative database and two were from individual states, New Jersey and Wisconsin. Together, they cover more than 9 million crashes. The Wisconsin data set was particularly useful because it linked each crash to hospital-discharge data, allowing us to better measure the extent of the injuries.

What does an analysis of these data reveal?

For preventing *serious* injury, lap-and-shoulder belts once again performed as well as child safety seats for children aged two through six. But for more minor injuries, car seats did a better job, reducing the likelihood of injury by roughly 25 percent compared with seat belts.

So don't go throwing out your car seats just yet. (That would be illegal in all fifty states.) Children are such valuable cargo that even the relatively small benefit car seats seem to provide in preventing minor injuries may make them a worthwhile investment. There's another benefit that's hard to put a price tag on: a parent's peace of mind.

Or, looking at it another way, maybe that's the greatest *cost* of car seats. They give parents a misplaced sense of security, a belief they've done everything possible to protect their children. This complacency keeps us from striving for a better solution, one that may well be simpler and cheaper, and would save even more lives.

Imagine you were charged with starting from scratch to ensure the safety of all children who travel in cars. Do you really think the best solution is to begin with a device optimized for adults and use it to strap down some second, child-sized contraption? Would you really stipulate that this contraption be made by dozens of different manufacturers, and yet had to work in all vehicles even though each vehicle's seat has its own design?

So here's a radical thought: considering that half of all passengers who ride in the backseat of cars are children, what if seat belts were designed *to fit them in the first place*? Wouldn't it make more sense to take a proven solution—one that happens to be cheap and simple—and adapt it, whether through adjustable belts or fold-down seat inserts (which do exist, though not widely)—rather than relying on a costly, cumbersome solution that doesn't work very well?

But things seem to be moving in the opposite direction. Instead of pushing for a better solution to child auto safety, state governments across the United States have been raising the age when kids can graduate from car seats. The European Union has gone even further, requiring most children to stay in booster seats until they are twelve.

Alas, governments aren't exactly famous for cheap or simple solutions; they tend to prefer the costly-and-cumbersome route. Note that none of the earlier examples in this chapter were the brainchild of a government official. Even the polio vaccine was primarily developed by a private group, the National Foundation for Infant Paralysis. President Roosevelt personally provided the seed money—it's interesting that even a sitting president chose the private sector for such a task—and the foundation then raised money and conducted the drug trials.

Nor was it the government that put seat belts in cars. Robert McNamara thought they would give Ford a competitive advantage. He was dead wrong. Ford had a hard time marketing the seat belt, since it seemed to remind customers that driving was inherently unsafe. This led Henry Ford II to complain to a reporter: "McNamara is selling safety but Chevrolet is selling cars."

Some problems, meanwhile, seem beyond the reach of any solution, simple or otherwise. Think of the devastation Mother Nature regularly dishes out. By comparison, traffic fatalities seem eminently manageable.

Since 1900 more than 1.3 million people worldwide have been killed by hurricanes (or, as they are called in some places, typhoons or tropical cyclones). In the United States, the carnage has been lighter—roughly 20,000 deaths—but the financial losses have been steep, averaging more than $10 billion per year. In the space of just two recent years, 2004 and 2005, six hurricanes, including the killer Katrina, did a combined $153 billion in damages to the southeastern United States.

Why so much damage of late? More people have been moving to hurricane-prone areas (it's nice to live near the ocean, after all), and a lot of them built expensive vacation properties (which drive up the property-damage totals). The irony is that many of these homeowners were lured to the ocean because of the *scarcity* of hurricanes in recent decades—and, perhaps, by the correspondingly low insurance rates.

From the mid-1960s until the mid-1990s, hurricane activity was depressed by the Atlantic Multidecadal Oscillation, a long-recurring climate cycle of sixty to eighty years during which the Atlantic Ocean gradually cools and then warms up again. The temperature change isn't drastic, just a couple of degrees. But it's enough to discourage hurricanes during the cool years and, as we've seen recently, empower them during the warm.

In some regards, hurricanes wouldn't seem to be such a hard problem to solve. Unlike other problems—cancer, for instance—their cause is well established, their location is predictable, and even their timing is known. Atlantic hurricanes generally strike between August 15 and November 15. They travel westward through "Hurricane Alley," a horizontal stretch of ocean running from the west coast of Africa through the Caribbean and into the southeastern United States. And they are essentially heat engines, massive storms created when the topmost layer of ocean water edges above a certain temperature (80 degrees Fahrenheit, or 26.7 degrees Celsius). That's why they start forming only toward summer's end, after the sun has had a few months to warm up the ocean.

And yet for all their predictability, hurricanes represent a battle that humans seem to have lost. By the time a hurricane forms, there's really no way to fight it. All you can do is run away.

But outside of Seattle lives an intellectually venturesome fellow named Nathan who believes, along with some friends, that they've got a good hurricane solution. Nathan has a physics background, which is key, because that means he understands the thermal properties that define a hurricane. A hurricane isn't just a dynamo; it's a dynamo that comes without an "off" switch. Once it's begun amassing energy it cannot be shut down, and it's far too powerful to be blown back out to sea with a big fan.

That's why Nathan and his friends—most of whom are, like him, science geeks of some sort—want to dissipate the thermal energy *before* it has a chance to accumulate. In other words: prevent the water in Hurricane Alley from getting warm enough to form a destructive hurricane in the first place. Armies sometimes engage in a "scorched earth" policy, destroying anything that might be of value to the enemy. Nathan and his friends want to practice a "chilled ocean" policy to keep the enemy from destroying anything of value.

But, one might be tempted to ask, doesn't this constitute playing with Mother Nature?

"Of *course* it's playing with Mother Nature!" Nathan cackles. "You say that like it's a bad thing!"

Indeed, if we hadn't played with Mother Nature by using ammonium nitrate to raise our crop yields, many readers of this book probably wouldn't exist today. (Or they would at least be too busy to read, spending all day scrounging for roots and berries.) Stopping polio was also a form of playing with Mother Nature. As are the levees we use to control hurricane flooding—even if, as in Hurricane Katrina, they sometimes fail.

The anti-hurricane solution Nathan proposes is so simple that a Boy Scout might have dreamt it up (a very clever one, at least). It can be built with materials bought at a Home Depot, or maybe even filched from the dump.

"The trick is to modify the surface temperature of the water," Nathan says. "Now the interesting thing is that the surface layer of warm water is very thin, often less than 100 feet. And right beneath it is a bulk of very cold water. If you're skin-diving in many of these areas, you can feel the huge difference."

The warm surface layer is lighter than the cold water beneath, and therefore stays on the surface. "So what we need to do is fix that," he says.

It is a tantalizing puzzle—all that cold water, trillions upon trillions of gallons, lying just beneath the warm surface and yet impotent to defuse the potential disaster.

But Nathan has a solution. It is basically "an inner tube with a skirt," he says with a laugh. That is, a large floating ring, anywhere from thirty to three hundred feet across, with a long flexible cylinder affixed to the inside. The ring might be made from old truck tires, filled with foamed concrete and lashed together with steel cable. The cylinder, extending perhaps six hundred feet deep into the ocean, could be fashioned from polyethylene, aka the plastic used in shopping bags.

"That's it!" Nathan crows.

How does it work? Imagine one of these skirted inner tubes—a giant, funky, man-made jellyfish—floating in the ocean. As a warm wave splashes over the top, the water level inside the ring rises until it is higher than the surrounding ocean. "When you have water elevated above the surface in a tube like that," Nathan explains, "it's called 'hydraulic head.'"

Hydraulic head is a force, created by the energy put into the waves by wind. This force would push the warm surface water down into the long plastic cylinder, ultimately flushing it out at the bottom, far beneath the surface. As long as the waves keep coming—and they always do—the hydraulic head's force would keep pushing surface water into the cooler depths, which inevitably lowers the ocean's surface temperature. The process is low-impact, non-polluting, and slow: a molecule of warm surface water would take about three hours to be flushed out the bottom of the plastic cylinder.

Now imagine deploying these floats en masse in the patches of ocean where hurricanes grow. Nathan envisions "a picket fence" of them between Cuba and the Yucatán and another skein off the southeastern seaboard of the United States. They'd also be valuable in the South China Sea and in the Coral Sea off the coast of Australia. How many would be needed? Depending on their size, a few thousand floats might be able to stop hurricanes in the Caribbean and the Gulf of Mexico.

A simple throwaway version of this contraption could be built for roughly $100 apiece, although the larger costs would come in towing and anchoring the floats. There's also the possibility of more durable and sophisticated versions, remote-controlled units that could be relocated to where they are most needed. A "smart" version could even adjust the rate at which it cools the surface water by varying the volume of warm water it takes in.

The most expensive float Nathan envisions would cost $100,000. Even at that price, allocating 10,000 of them around the world would cost just $1 billion—or one-tenth the amount of hurricane property damage incurred in a single year in the United States alone. As Ignatz Semmelweis learned about hand-washing and as millions of heart patients learned about cheap pills like aspirin and statins, an ounce of prevention can be worth a few tons of cure.

Nathan isn't yet sure the float will work. For months it has been undergoing intense computer modeling; soon it will be tried out in real water. But all indications are that he and his friends have invented a hurricane killer.

Even if it were capable of eliminating tropical storms entirely, that wouldn't be wise, since storms are part of the natural climate cycle and deliver much-needed rainfall to land. The real value comes from cooling down a Category 5 storm into a less destructive one. "You might be able to manipulate the monsoon rain cycle in tropical areas," Nathan enthuses, "and smooth out the boom-or-bust nature of rainfall in the Sahel in Africa, aiming to prevent starvation."

The float might also improve the ocean's ecology. As surface water heats up each summer, it becomes depleted of oxygen and nutrients, creating a dead zone. Flushing the warm water downward would bring rich, oxygenated cold water to the surface, which ought to substantially enhance sea life. (The same effect can be seen today around offshore oil platforms.) The float might also help sink some of the excess carbon dioxide that has been absorbed by the ocean's surface in recent decades.

There remains, of course, the question of how, and by whom, these floats would be deployed. The Department of Homeland Security recently solicited hurricane-mitigation ideas from various scientists, including Nathan and his friends. Although such agencies rarely opt for cheap and simple solutions—it simply isn't in their DNA—perhaps an exception will be made in this case, for the potential upside is large and the harm in trying seems minimal.

As dangerous as hurricanes are, there looms within the realm of nature a far larger problem, one that threatens to end civilization as we know it: global warming. If only Nathan and his friends, such smart and creative thinkers who aren't afraid of simple solutions, could do something about *that* . . .

CHAPTER 5

WHAT DO AL GORE AND MOUNT PINATUBO HAVE IN COMMON?

The headlines have been harrowing, to say the least.

"Some experts believe that mankind is on the threshold of a new pattern of adverse global climate for which it is ill-prepared," one *New York Times* article declared. It quoted climate researchers who argued that "this climatic change poses a threat to the people of the world."

A *Newsweek* article, citing a National Academy of Sciences report, warned that climate change "would force economic and social adjustments on a worldwide scale." Worse yet, "climatologists are pessimistic that political leaders will take any positive action to compensate for the climatic change or even to allay its effects."

Who in his or her right mind wouldn't be scared of global warming?

But that's not what these scientists were talking about. These articles, published in the mid-1970s, were predicting the effects of global *cooling*.

Alarm bells had rung because the average ground temperature in the Northern Hemisphere had fallen by .5 degrees Fahrenheit (.28 degrees Celsius) from 1945 to 1968. Furthermore, there had been a large increase in snow cover and, between 1964 and 1972, a decrease of 1.3 percent in the amount of sunshine hitting the United States. *Newsweek* reported that the temperature decline, while relatively small in absolute terms, "has taken the planet about a sixth of the way toward the Ice Age average."

The big fear was a collapse of the agricultural system. In Britain, cooling had already shortened the growing season by two weeks. "[T]he resulting famines could be catastrophic," warned the *Newsweek* article. Some scientists proposed radical warming solutions such as "melting the arctic ice cap by covering it with black soot."

These days, of course, the threat is the opposite. The earth is no longer thought to be too cool but rather too warm. And black soot, rather than saving us, is seen as a chief villain. We have cast endless streams of carbon emissions skyward, the residue of all the fossil fuels we burn to heat and cool and feed and transport and entertain ourselves.

By so doing, we have apparently turned our tender planet into a greenhouse, fashioning in the sky a chemical scrim that traps too much of the sun's warmth and prevents it from escaping back into space. The "global cooling" phase notwithstanding, the average global ground temperature over the past hundred years has risen 1.3 degrees Fahrenheit (.7 degrees Celsius), and this warming has accelerated of late.

"[W]e are now so abusing the Earth," writes James Lovelock, the renowned environmental scientist, "that it may rise and move back to the hot state it was in fifty-five million years ago, and if it does most of us, and our descendants, will die."

There is essentially a consensus among climate scientists that the earth's temperature has been rising and, increasingly, agreement that human activity has played an important role. But the ways humans affect the climate aren't always as obvious as they seem.

It is generally believed that cars and trucks and airplanes contribute an ungodly share of greenhouse gases. This has recently led many right-minded people to buy a Prius or other hybrid car. But every time a Prius owner drives to the grocery store, she may be canceling out its emission-reducing benefit, at least if she shops in the meat section.

How so? Because cows—as well as sheep and other cud-chewing animals called ruminants—are wicked polluters. Their exhalation and flatulence and belching and manure emit methane, which by one common measure is about *twenty-five times more potent* as a greenhouse gas than the carbon dioxide released by cars (and, by the way, humans). The world's ruminants are responsible for about 50 percent more greenhouse gas than the entire transportation sector.

Even the "locavore" movement, which encourages people to eat locally grown food, doesn't help in this regard. A recent study by two Carnegie Mellon researchers, Christopher Weber and H. Scott Matthews, found that buying locally produced food actually *increases* greenhouse-gas emissions. Why?

More than 80 percent of the emissions associated with food are in the production phase, and big farms are far more efficient than small farms. Transportation represents only 11 percent of food emissions, with delivery from producer to retailer representing only 4 percent. The best way to help, Weber and Matthews suggest, is to subtly change your diet. "Shifting less than one day per week's worth of calories from red meat and dairy products to chicken, fish, eggs, or a vegetable-based diet achieves more greenhouse-gas reduction than buying all locally sourced food," they write.

You could also switch from eating beef to eating kangaroo—because kangaroo farts, as fate would have it, don't contain methane. But just imagine the marketing campaign that would be needed to get Americans to take up 'roo-burgers. And think how hard the cattle ranchers would lobby Washington to ban kangaroo meat. Fortunately, a team of

Australian scientists is attacking this problem from the opposite direction, trying to replicate the digestive bacteria in kangaroos' stomachs so it can be transplanted to cows.

For a variety of reasons, global warming is a uniquely thorny problem.

First, climate scientists can't run experiments. In this regard, they are more like economists than physicists or biologists, their goal being to tease out relationships from existing data without the ability to, say, invoke a ten-year ban on cars (or cows).

Second, the science is extraordinarily complex. The impact of any single human activity—let's pretend we tripled the number of airplane flights, for instance—depends on many different factors: the gases emitted, yes, but also how the planes affect things like convection and cloud formation.

To predict global surface temperatures, one must take into account these and many other factors, including evaporation, rainfall, and, yes, animal emissions. But even the most sophisticated climate models don't do a very good job of representing such variables, and that obviously makes predicting the climatic future very difficult. By comparison, the risk models used by modern financial institutions seem quite reliable—but, as recent banking meltdowns have shown, that isn't always the case.

The imprecision inherent in climate science means we don't know with any certainty whether our current path will lead temperatures to rise two degrees or ten degrees. Nor do we really know if even a steep rise means an inconvenience or the end of civilization as we know it.

It is this specter of catastrophe, no matter how remote, that has propelled global warming to the forefront of public policy. If we were certain that warming would impose large and defined costs, the economics of the problem would come down to a simple cost-benefit analysis. Do the future benefits from cutting emissions outweigh the costs of doing so? Or are we better off waiting to cut emissions later—or even, perhaps, polluting at will and just learning to live in a hotter world?

The economist Martin Weitzman analyzed the best available climate models and concluded the future holds a 5 percent chance of a terrible-case scenario—a rise of more than 10 degrees Celsius.

There is of course great uncertainty even in this estimate of uncertainty. So how should we place a value on this relatively small chance of worldwide catastrophe?

The economist Nicholas Stern, who prepared an encyclopedic report on global warming for the British government, suggested we spend 1.5 percent of global gross domestic product each year—that would be a $1.2 trillion bill as of today—to attack the problem.

But as most economists know, people are generally unwilling to spend a lot of money to avert a future problem, especially when its likelihood is so uncertain. One good reason for waiting is that we might have options in the future to avert the problem that cost far less than today's options.

Although economists are trained to be cold-blooded enough to sit around and calmly discuss the trade-offs involved in global catastrophe, the rest of us are a bit more excitable. And most people respond to uncertainty with more emotion—fear, blame, paralysis—than might be advisable. Uncertainty also has a nasty way of making us conjure up the very worst possibilities. (Think about the last time you heard a bump in the night outside your bedroom door.) With global warming, the worst possibilities are downright biblical: rising seas, hellish temperatures, plague upon plague, a planet in chaos.

It is understandable, therefore, that the movement to stop global warming has taken on the feel of a religion. The core belief is that humankind inherited a pristine Eden, has sinned greatly by polluting it, and must now suffer lest we all perish in a fiery apocalypse. James Lovelock, who might be considered a high priest of this religion, writes in a confessional language that would feel at home in any liturgy: "[W]e misused energy and overpopulated the Earth . . . [I]t is much too late for sustainable development; what we need is a sustainable retreat."

A "sustainable retreat" sounds a bit like wearing a sackcloth. To citizens of the developed world in particular, this would mean consuming less, using less, driving less—and, though it's uncouth to say it aloud, learning to live with a gradual depopulation of the earth.

If the modern conservation movement has a patron saint, it is surely Al Gore, the former vice president and recent Nobel laureate. His documentary film *An Inconvenient Truth* hammered home for millions the dangers of overconsumption. He has since founded the Alliance for Climate Protection, which describes itself as "an unprecedented mass persuasion exercise." Its centerpiece is a $300 million public-service campaign called "We," which urges Americans to change their profligate ways.

Any religion, meanwhile, has its heretics, and global warming is no exception. Boris Johnson, a classically educated journalist who managed to become mayor of London, has read Lovelock—he calls him a "sacerdotal figure"—and concluded the following: "Like all the best religions, fear of climate change satisfies our need for guilt, and self-disgust, and that eternal human sense that technological progress must be punished by the gods. And the fear of climate change is like a religion in this vital sense, that it is veiled in mystery, and you can never tell whether your acts of propitiation or atonement have been in any way successful."

So while the true believers bemoan the desecration of our earthly Eden, the heretics point out that this Eden, long before humans arrived, once became so naturally thick with methane smog that it was rendered nearly lifeless. When Al Gore urges the citizenry to sacrifice their plastic shopping bags, their air-conditioning, their extraneous travel, the agnostics grumble that human activity accounts for just 2 percent of global carbon-dioxide emissions, with the remainder generated by natural processes like plant decay.

Once you strip away the religious fervor and scientific complexity, an incredibly simple dilemma lies at the heart of global warming. Economists fondly call it an *externality.*

What's an externality? It's what happens when someone takes an action but someone else, without agreeing, pays some or all the costs of that action. An externality is an economic version of taxation without representation.

If you happen to live downwind from a fertilizer factory, the ammonium stench is an externality. When your neighbors throw a big party (and don't have the courtesy to invite you), their ruckus is an externality. Secondhand cigarette smoke is an externality, as is the stray gunshot one drug dealer meant for another that instead hit a child on the playground.

The greenhouse gases thought to be responsible for global warming are primarily externalities. When you have a bonfire in your backyard, you're not just toasting marshmallows. You're also emitting gases that, in a tiny way, help to heat the whole planet. Every time you get behind the wheel of a car, or eat a hamburger, or fly in an airplane, you are generating some by-products you're not paying for.

Imagine a fellow named Jack who lives in a lovely house—he built it himself—and comes home from work on the first warm day of summer. All he wants is to relax and cool off. So he cranks the air conditioner all the way up. Maybe he thinks for a moment about the extra dollar or two he'll pay on his next electricity bill, but the cost isn't enough to deter him.

What he *doesn't* think about is the black smoke from the power plant that burns the coal that heats the water that turns to steam that fills the turbine that spins the generator that makes the power that cools the house that Jack built.

Nor will he think about the environmental costs associated with mining and trucking away that coal, or the associated dangers. In the United States alone, more than 100,000 coal miners died on the job over the past century, with another estimated 200,000 dying later from black lung disease. Now *those* are externalities. Thankfully, coal-mining deaths have plummeted in the United States, to a current average of about 36 per year. But if Jack happened to live in China, the local death externality would be much steeper: at least 3,000 Chinese coal miners die on the job each year.

It's hard to blame Jack for not thinking about externalities. Modern technology is so proficient that it often masks the costs associated with our consumption. There's nothing visibly dirty about the electricity that feeds Jack's air conditioner. It just magically appears, as if out of a fairy tale.

If there were only a few Jacks in the world, or even a few million, no one would care. But as the global population hurtles toward 7 billion, all those externalities add up. So who should be paying for them?

In principle, this shouldn't be such a hard problem. If we knew how much it cost humankind every time someone used a tank of gas, we could simply levy a tax of that magnitude on the driver. The tax wouldn't necessarily convince him to cancel his trip, nor should it. The point of the tax is to make sure the driver faces the full costs of his actions (or, in economist-speak, to *internalize the externality*).

The revenues raised from these taxes could then be spread out across the folks who suffer the effects of a changing climate—people living in Bangladeshi lowlands, for instance, who will be flooded if the oceans rise precipitously. If we chose exactly the right tax, the revenues could properly compensate the victims of climate change.

But when it comes to *actually* solving climate-change externalities through taxes, all we can say is good luck. Besides the obvious obstacles—like determining the right size of the tax and getting someone to collect it—there's the fact that greenhouse gases do not adhere to national boundaries. The earth's atmosphere is in constant, complex motion, which means that your emissions become mine and mine yours. Thus, *global* warming.

If, say, Australia decided overnight to eliminate its carbon emissions, that fine nation wouldn't enjoy the benefits of its costly and painful behavior unless everyone else joined in. Nor does one nation have the right to tell another what to do. The United States has in recent years sporadically attempted to lower its emissions. But when it leans on China or India to do the same, those countries can hardly be blamed for saying, *Hey, you got to free-ride your way to industrial superpowerdom, so why shouldn't we?*

When people aren't compelled to pay the full cost of their actions, they have little incentive to change their behavior. Back when the world's big cities were choked with horse manure, people didn't switch to the car because it was good for society; they switched because it was in their economic interest to do so. Today, people are being asked to change their behavior not out of self-interest but rather out of selflessness. This might make global warming seem like a hopeless problem unless—and this is what Al Gore is banking on—people are willing to put aside their self-interest and do the right thing even if it's personally costly. Gore is appealing to our altruistic selves, our externality-hating better angels.

Keep in mind that externalities aren't always as obvious as they seem.

To keep their cars from being stolen off the street, a lot of people lock the steering wheel with an anti-theft device like the Club. The

Club is big and highly visible (it even comes in neon pink). By using a Club, you are explicitly telling a potential thief that your car will be hard to steal. The *implicit* signal, meanwhile, is that your neighbor's car—the one without a Club—is a much better target. So your Club produces a negative externality for your non-Club-using neighbor in the form of a higher risk that *his* car will be stolen. The Club is a perfect exercise in self-interest.

A device called LoJack, meanwhile, is in many ways the opposite of the Club. It is a small radio transmitter, not much larger than a deck of cards, hidden somewhere in or beneath the car where a thief can't see it. But if the car is stolen, the police can remotely activate the transmitter and follow its signal straight to the car.

Unlike the Club, LoJack doesn't stop a thief from stealing your car. So why bother installing it?

For one, it helps you recover the car, and fast. When it comes to auto theft, fast is important. Once your car has been missing more than a few days, you generally don't *want* it back, because it likely will have been stripped. Even if you don't want your car to be found, your insurance company does. So a second reason to install LoJack is that insurers will discount your premium. But perhaps the best reason is that LoJack actually makes it fun to have your car stolen.

There's a certain thrill to tracking a LoJack-equipped car, as if the hounds have just been released. The police spring into action, follow the radio signal, and nab the car thief before he knows what's happening. If you're lucky, he may even have filled up the gas tank for you.

Most stolen cars end up in chop shops, clandestine mini-factories that remove the car's most valuable parts and scrap the remains. The police have a hard time rooting out these operations—until, that is, LoJack comes around. Now the police simply follow the radio signal and, often, find the chop shop.

The people who run chop shops aren't stupid, of course. Once they realize what's happening, they change their procedure. The thief, rather than driving the car straight to the shop, will leave it in a parking lot for a few days. If the car is gone when he returns, he knows it had LoJack. If not, he assumes it's safe to deliver it to the chop shop.

But the police aren't stupid either. When they find a stolen car in a parking lot, they may choose not to reclaim it right away. Instead, they watch the vehicle until the thief returns and let him lead them to the chop shop.

Just how difficult has LoJack made life for auto thieves?

For every additional percentage point of cars that have LoJack in a given city, overall thefts fall by as much as 20 percent. Since a thief can't tell which cars have LoJack, he's less willing to take a chance on any car. LoJack is relatively expensive, about $700, which means it isn't all that popular, installed in fewer than 2 percent of new cars. Even so, those cars create a rare and wonderful thing—a *positive* externality—for all the drivers who are too cheap to buy LoJack, because it protects their cars too.

That's right: not all externalities are negative. Good public schools create positive externalities because we all benefit from a society of well-educated people. (They also drive up property values.) Fruit farmers and beekeepers create positive externalities for each other: the trees provide free pollen for the bees and the bees pollinate the fruit trees, also at no charge. That's why beekeepers and fruit farmers often set up shop next to each other.

One of the unlikeliest positive externalities on record came cloaked in a natural disaster.

In 1991, an eroded, wooded mountain on the Philippine island of Luzon began to rumble and spew sulfuric ash. It turned out that beloved old Mount Pinatubo was a dormant volcano. The nearby farmers and townspeople were reluctant to evacuate, but the geologists, seismologists, and volcanologists who rushed in ultimately persuaded most of them to leave.

Good thing, too: on June 15, Pinatubo erupted for nine furious hours. The explosions were so massive that the top of the mountain caved in on itself, forming what is known as a caldera, a huge bowl-shaped crater, its new peak 850 feet lower than the original mountaintop. Worse yet, the region was simultaneously being lashed by a typhoon. According to one account, the sky poured down "heavy rain and ash with pumice lumps the size of golf balls." Around 250 people died, mainly from collapsed roofs, and more died in the following days from mudslides. Still, thanks to the scientists' warnings, the death toll was relatively small.

Mount Pinatubo was the most powerful volcanic eruption in nearly one hundred years. Within two hours of the main blast, sulfuric ash had reached twenty-two miles into the sky. By the time it was done, Pinatubo had discharged more than 20 million tons of sulfur dioxide into the stratosphere. What effect did that have on the environment?

As it turned out, the stratospheric haze of sulfur dioxide acted like a layer of sunscreen, reducing the amount of solar radiation reaching the earth. For the next two years, as the haze was settling out, the earth cooled off by an average of nearly 1 degree Fahrenheit, or .5 degrees Celsius. A single volcanic eruption practically reversed, albeit temporarily, the cumulative global warming of the previous hundred years.

Pinatubo created some other positive externalities too. Forests around the world grew more vigorously because trees prefer their sunlight a bit diffused. And all that sulfur dioxide in the stratosphere created some of the prettiest sunsets that people had ever seen.

Of course it was the global cooling that got scientists' attention. A paper in *Science* concluded that a Pinatubo-size eruption every few years would "offset much of the anthropogenic warming expected over the next century."

Even James Lovelock conceded the point: "[W]e might be saved," he wrote, "by an unexpected event such as a series of volcanic eruptions severe enough to block out sunlight and so cool the Earth. But only losers would bet their lives on such poor odds."

True, it probably would take a loser, or at least a fool, to believe a volcano could be persuaded to spew its protective effluvia into the sky at the proper intervals. But what if some foolish people thought Pinatubo could perhaps serve as a blueprint to stop global warming? The same sort of fools who, for instance, once believed that women *didn't* have to die in childbirth, that worldwide famine was *not* foreordained? While they're at it, could they also make their solution cheap and simple?

And if so, where might such fools be found?

In a nondescript section of Bellevue, Washington, a suburb of Seattle, lies a particularly nondescript series of buildings. There's a heating-and-air-conditioning company, a boat maker, a shop that fabricates marble tiles, and another building that used to be a Harley-Davidson repair shop. This last one is a windowless, charmless structure of about twenty thousand square feet whose occupant is identified only by a sheet of paper taped to the glass door. It reads "Intellectual Ventures."

Inside is one of the most unusual laboratories in the world. There are lathes and mold makers and 3D printers and many powerful computers, of course, but there is also an insectary where mosquitoes are bred so they can be placed in an empty fish tank and, from more than a hundred feet away, assassinated by a laser. This experiment is designed to thwart malaria. The disease is spread only by certain species of female mosquito, so the laser's tracking system identifies the females by wing-beat frequency—they flap more slowly than males because they are heavier—and zaps them.

Intellectual Ventures is an invention company. The lab, in addition to all the gear, is stocked with an elite assemblage of brainpower, scientists and puzzle-solvers of every variety. They dream up processes and products and then file patent applications, more than five hundred a year. The company also acquires patents from outside inventors, ranging from Fortune 500 companies to solo geniuses toiling in basements. IV operates much like a private-equity firm, raising investment capital and paying returns when its patents are licensed. The company currently controls more than twenty thousand patents, more than all but a few dozen companies in the world. This has led to some grumbling that IV is a "patent troll," accumulating patents so it can extort money from other companies, via lawsuit if necessary. But there is little hard evidence for such claims. A more realistic assessment is that IV has created the first mass market for intellectual property.

Its ringleader is a gregarious man named Nathan, the same Nathan we met earlier, the one who hopes to enfeeble hurricanes by seeding the ocean with skirted truck tires. Yes, that apparatus is an IV invention. Internally it is known as the Salter Sink because it sinks warm surface water and was originally developed by Stephen Salter, a renowned British engineer who has been working for decades to harness the power of ocean waves.

By now it should be apparent that Nathan isn't just some weekend inventor. He is Nathan Myhrvold, the former chief technology officer at Microsoft. He co-founded IV in 2000 with Edward Jung, a biophysicist who was Microsoft's chief software architect. Myhrvold played a variety of roles at Microsoft: futurist, strategist, founder of its research lab, and whisperer-in-chief to Bill Gates. "I don't know anyone I would say is smarter than Nathan," Gates once observed.

Myhrvold, who is fifty years old, has been smart for a long time. Growing up in Seattle, he graduated from high school at fourteen and by the time he was twenty-three had earned, primarily at UCLA and

Princeton, a bachelor's degree (mathematics), two master's degrees (geophysics/space physics and mathematical economics), and a Ph.D. (mathematical physics). He then went to Cambridge University to do quantum cosmology research with Stephen Hawking.

Myhrvold recalls watching the British science-fiction TV show *Dr. Who* when he was young: "The Doctor introduces himself to someone, who says, 'Doctor? Are you some kind of scientist?' And he says, 'Sir, I am *every* kind of scientist.' And I was, like, Yes! *Yes!* That is what I want to be: *every* kind of scientist!"

He is so polymathic as to make an everyday polymath tremble with shame. In addition to his scientific interests, he is an accomplished nature photographer, chef, mountain climber, and a collector of rare books, rocket engines, antique scientific instruments, and, especially, dinosaur bones: he is co-leader of a project that has dug up more *T. rex* skeletons than anyone else in the world. He is also—and this is hardly unrelated to his hobbies—very wealthy. In 1999, when he left Microsoft, he appeared on the Forbes list of the four hundred richest Americans.

At the same time—and this is how Myhrvold has managed to *stay* wealthy—he is famously cheap. As he walks through the IV lab pointing out his favorite tools and gadgets, his greatest pride is reserved for the items he bought on eBay or at bankruptcy sales. Though Myhrvold understands complexity as well as anyone, he is a firm believer that solutions should be cheap and simple whenever possible.

He and his compatriots are currently working on, among other projects: a better internal combustion engine; a way to reduce an airplane's "skin drag" and thus increase its fuel efficiency; and a new kind of nuclear power plant that would radically improve the future of worldwide electricity production. Although many of their ideas are just that—ideas—some have already started saving lives. The company has invented a process whereby a neurosurgeon who is attempting to repair an aneurysm can send IV the patient's brain-scan data, which are fed into a 3D printer that produces a life-size plastic model of the aneurysm. The model is shipped overnight to the surgeon, who can make a detailed plan to attack the aneurysm *before* cutting through the patient's skull.

It takes a healthy dose of collective arrogance for a small group of scientists and engineers to think they could simultaneously tackle many of the world's toughest problems. Fortunately, these folks have the requisite amount. They have already sent satellites to the moon, helped defend the United States against missile attack and, via computing advances, changed the way the world works. (Bill Gates is not only an investor in IV but an occasional inventor as well. The mosquito-zapping laser was a response to his philanthropic quest to eradicate malaria.) They have also conducted definitive scientific research in many fields, including climate science.

So it was only a matter of time before they began thinking about global warming. On the day we visited IV, Myhrvold convened roughly a dozen of his colleagues to talk about the problem and possible solutions. They sat around a long oval conference table, Myhrvold near one end.

They are a roomful of wizards, and yet without doubt Myhrvold is their Harry Potter. For the next ten or so hours, fueled by an astonishing amount of diet soda, he prodded and amplified, interjected and challenged.

Everyone in the room agrees that the earth has been getting warmer and they generally suspect that human activity has something to do with it. But they also agree that the standard global-warming rhetoric in the media and political circles is oversimplified and exaggerated. Too many accounts, Myhrvold says, suffer from "people who get on their high horse and say that that our species will be exterminated."

Does he believe this?

"Probably not."

When *An Inconvenient Truth* is mentioned, the table erupts in a sea of groans. The film's purpose, Myhrvold believes, was "to scare the crap out of people." Although Al Gore "isn't technically lying," he says, some of the nightmare scenarios Gore describes—the state of Florida disappearing under rising seas, for instance—"don't have any basis in physical reality in any reasonable time frame. No climate model shows them happening."

But the scientific community is also at fault. The current generation of climate-prediction models are, as Lowell Wood puts it, "enormously crude." Wood is a heavyset and spectacularly talkative astrophysicist in his sixties who calls to mind a sane Ignatius P. Reilly. Long ago, Wood was Myhrvold's academic mentor. (Wood himself was a protégé of the physicist Edward Teller.) Myhrvold thinks Wood is one the smartest men in the universe. Off the top of his head, Wood seems to know quite a bit about practically anything: the melt rate of the Greenland ice core (80 cubic kilometers per year); the percentage of unsanctioned Chinese power plants that went online in the previous year (about 20 percent); the number of times that metastatic cancer cells travel through the bloodstream before they land ("as many as a million").

Wood has achieved a great deal in science, on behalf of universities, private firms, and the U.S. government. It was Wood who dreamed up IV's mosquito laser assassination system—which, if it seems vaguely familiar, is because Wood also worked on the "Star Wars" missile-defense system at the Lawrence Livermore National Laboratory, from which he recently retired. (From fighting Soviet nukes to malarial mosquitoes: talk about a peace dividend!)

Today, at the IV think session, Wood is wearing a rainbow tie-dyed short-sleeve dress shirt with a matching necktie.

"The climate models are crude in space and they're crude in time," he continues. "So there's an enormous amount of natural phenomena they can't model. They can't do even giant storms like hurricanes."

There are several reasons for this, Myhrvold explains. Today's models use a grid of cells to map the earth, and those grids are too large to allow for the modeling of actual weather. Smaller and more accurate grids would require better modeling software, which would require more computing power. "We're trying to predict climate change twenty to thirty years from now," he says, "but it will take us almost the same amount of time for the computer industry to give us fast enough computers to do the job."

That said, most current climate models tend to produce similar predictions. This might lead one to reasonably conclude that climate scientists have a pretty good handle on the future.

Not so, says Wood.

"Everybody turns their knobs"—that is, adjusts the control parameters and coefficients of their models—"so they aren't the outlier, because the outlying model is going to have difficulty getting funded." In other words, the economic reality of research funding, rather than a disinterested and uncoordinated scientific consensus, leads the models to approximately match one another. It isn't that current climate models should be ignored, Wood says—but, when considering the fate of the planet, one should properly appreciate their limited nature.

As Wood, Myhrvold, and the other scientists discuss the various conventional wisdoms surrounding global warming, few, if any, survive unscathed.

The emphasis on carbon dioxide? "Misplaced," says Wood.

Why?

"Because carbon dioxide is not the major greenhouse gas. The major greenhouse gas is water vapor." But current climate models "do not know how to handle water vapor and various types of clouds. That is the elephant in the corner of this room. I hope we'll have good numbers on water vapor by 2020 or thereabouts."

Myhrvold cites a recent paper asserting that carbon dioxide may have had little to do with recent warming. Instead, all the heavy-particulate pollution we generated in earlier decades seems to have *cooled* the atmosphere by dimming the sun. That was the global cooling that caught scientists' attention in the 1970s. The trend began to reverse when we started cleaning up our air.

"So most of the warming seen over the past few decades," Myhrvold says, "might actually be due to *good environmental stewardship*!"

Not so many years ago, schoolchildren were taught that carbon dioxide is the naturally occurring lifeblood of plants, just as oxygen is ours. Today, children are more likely to think of carbon dioxide as a poison. That's because the amount of carbon dioxide in the atmosphere has increased substantially over the past one hundred years, from about 280 parts per million to 380.

But what people don't know, the IV scientists say, is that the carbon dioxide level some 80 million years ago—back when our mammalian ancestors were evolving—was at least 1,000 parts per million. In fact, that is the concentration of carbon dioxide you regularly breathe if you work in a new energy-efficient office building, for that is the level established by the engineering group that sets standards for heating and ventilation systems.

So not only is carbon dioxide plainly not poisonous, but changes in carbon-dioxide levels don't necessarily mirror human activity. Nor does atmospheric carbon dioxide necessarily warm the earth: ice-cap evidence shows that over the past several hundred thousand years, carbon dioxide levels have risen *after* a rise in temperature, not the other way around.

Beside Myhrvold sits Ken Caldeira, a soft-spoken man with a boyish face and a halo of curly hair. He runs an ecology lab at Stanford for the Carnegie Institution. Caldeira is among the most respected climate scientists in the world, his research cited approvingly by the most fervent environmentalists. He and a co-author coined the phrase "ocean acidification," the process by which the seas absorb so much carbon dioxide that corals and other shallow-water organisms are threatened. He also contributes research to the Intergovernmental Panel on Climate Change, which shared the 2007 Nobel Peace Prize with Al Gore for sounding the alarm on global warming. (Yes, Caldeira got a Nobel certificate.)

If you met Caldeira at a party, you would likely place him in the fervent-environmentalist camp himself. He was a philosophy major in college, for goodness' sake, and his very name—a variant of *caldera*, the craterlike rim of a volcano—aligns him with the natural world. In his youth (he is fifty-three now), he was a hard-charging environmental activist and all-around peacenik.

Caldeira is thoroughly convinced that human activity is responsible for some global warming and is more pessimistic than Myhrvold about how future climate will affect humankind. He believes "we are being incredibly foolish emitting carbon dioxide" as we currently do.

Yet his research tells him that carbon dioxide is not the right villain in this fight. For starters, as greenhouse gases go, it's not particularly efficient. "A doubling of carbon dioxide traps less than 2 percent of the outgoing radiation emitted by the earth," he says. Furthermore, atmospheric carbon dioxide is governed by the law of diminishing returns: each gigaton added to the air has less radiative impact than the previous one.

Caldeira mentions a study he undertook that considered the impact of higher carbon-dioxide levels on plant life. While plants get their water from the soil, they get their food—carbon dioxide, that is—from the air.

"Plants pay exceedingly dearly for carbon dioxide," Lowell Wood jumps in. "A plant has to raise about a hundred times as much water from the soil as it gets carbon dioxide from the air, on a molecule-lost-per-molecule-gained basis. Most plants, especially during the active part of the growing season, are water-stressed. They bleed very seriously to get their food."

So an increase in carbon dioxide means that plants require less water to grow. And what happens to productivity?

Caldeira's study showed that doubling the amount of carbon dioxide while holding steady all other inputs—water, nutrients, and so forth—yields a 70 percent increase in plant growth, an obvious boon to agricultural productivity.

"That's why most commercial hydroponic greenhouses have supplemental carbon dioxide," Myhrvold says. "And they typically run at 1,400 parts per million."

"Twenty thousand years ago," Caldeira says, "carbon-dioxide levels were lower, sea level was lower—and trees were in a near state of asphyxiation for lack of carbon dioxide. There's nothing special about today's carbon-dioxide level, or today's sea level, or today's temperature. What damages us are *rapid* rates of change. Overall, more carbon dioxide is probably a *good* thing for the biosphere—it's just that it's increasing too fast."

The gentlemen of IV abound with further examples of global warming memes that are all wrong.

Rising sea levels, for instance, "aren't being driven primarily by glaciers melting," Wood says, no matter how useful that image may be for environmental activists. The truth is far less sexy. "It is driven mostly by water-warming—literally, the thermal expansion of ocean water as it warms up."

Sea levels *are* rising, Wood says—and have been for roughly twelve thousand years, since the end of the last ice age. The oceans are about 425 feet higher today, but the bulk of that rise occurred in the first thousand years. In the past century, the seas have risen less than eight inches.

As to the future: rather than the catastrophic thirty-foot rise some people have predicted over the next century—good-bye, Florida!—Wood notes that the most authoritative literature on the subject suggests a rise of about one and a half feet by 2100. That's much less than the twice-daily tidal variation in most coastal locations. "So it's a little bit difficult," he says, "to understand what the purported crisis is about."

Caldeira, with something of a pained look on his face, mentions a most surprising environmental scourge: trees. Yes, trees. As much as Caldeira personally lives the green life—his Stanford office is cooled by a misting water chamber rather than air-conditioning—his research has found that planting trees in certain locations actually exacerbates warming because comparatively dark leaves absorb more incoming sunlight than, say, grassy plains, sandy deserts, or snow-covered expanses.

Then there's this little-discussed fact about global warming: while the drumbeat of doom has grown louder over the past several years, the average global temperature during that time has in fact *decreased*.

In the darkened conference room, Myhrvold cues up an overhead slide that summarizes IV's views of the current slate of proposed global-warming solutions. The slide says:

- Too little
- Too late
- Too optimistic

Too little means that typical conservation efforts simply won't make much of a difference. "If you believe there's a problem worth solving," Myhrvold says, "then these solutions won't be enough to solve it. Wind power and most other alternative energy things are cute, but they don't scale to a sufficient degree. At this point, wind farms are a government subsidy scheme, fundamentally." What about the beloved Prius and other low-emission vehicles? "They're great," he says, "except that transportation is just not that big of a sector."

Also, coal is so cheap that trying to generate electricity without it would be economic suicide, especially for developing countries. Myhrvold argues that cap-and-trade agreements, whereby coal emissions are limited by quota and cost, can't help much, in part because it is already . . .

Too late. The half-life of atmospheric carbon dioxide is roughly one hundred years, and some of it remains in the atmosphere for thousands of years. So even if humankind immediately stopped burning all fossil fuel, the existing carbon dioxide would remain in the atmosphere for several generations. Pretend the United States (and perhaps Europe) miraculously converted overnight and became zero-carbon societies. Then pretend they persuaded China (and perhaps India) to demolish every coal-burning power plant and diesel truck. As far as atmospheric carbon dioxide is concerned, it might not matter all that much. And by the way, that zero-carbon society you were dreamily thinking about is way . . .

Too optimistic. "A lot of the things that people say would be a good thing probably aren't," Myhrvold says. As an example he points to solar power. "The problem with solar cells is that they're black, because they are designed to absorb light from the sun. But only about 12 percent gets turned into electricity, and the rest is reradiated as heat—which contributes to global warming."

Although a widespread conversion to solar power might seem appealing, the reality is tricky. The energy consumed by building the thousands of new solar plants necessary to replace coal-burning and other power plants would create a huge long-term "warming debt," as Myhrvold calls it. "Eventually, we'd have a great carbon-free energy infrastructure but only after making emissions and global warming worse every year until we're done building out the solar plants, which could take thirty to fifty years."

This hardly means the energy problem should be dismissed. That's why IV—along with inventors all over the world—are working toward the holy grail: cheaper and cleaner forms of energy.

But from an atmospheric perspective, energy represents what might be called the input dilemma. How about the *output* dilemma? What if the greenhouse gases we've already emitted *do* produce an ecological disaster?

Myhrvold is not blind to the possibility. He has probably thought about such scenarios in greater scientific detail than any climate doomsayer: a collapse of massive ice sheets in Greenland or Antarctica; a release of huge amounts of methane caused by the melting of arctic permafrost; and, as he describes it, "a breakdown of the thermohaline circulation system in the North Atlantic, which would put an end to the Gulf Stream."

So what happens if the doomsayers turn out to be right? What if the earth *is* becoming dangerously warmer, whether because of our fossil-fuel profligacy or some natural climate cycle? We don't really want to sit back and stew in our own juices, do we?

In 1980, when Myhrvold was a grad student at Princeton, Mount St. Helens erupted back home in Washington State. Even though he was nearly three thousand miles away, Myhrvold saw a thin layer of ash accumulating on his windowsill. "It's hard not to think about volcanic dust when it's raining down on your dorm room," he says, "although to be honest, my room was messy in many other ways."

Even as a kid, Myhrvold was fascinated by geophysical phenomena—volcanoes, sunspots, and the like—and their history of affecting the climate. The Little Ice Age intrigued him so much that he forced his family to visit the northern tip of Newfoundland, where Leif Eriksson and his Vikings reputedly made camp a thousand years earlier.

The connection between volcanoes and climate is hardly a new idea. Another polymath, Benjamin Franklin, wrote what seems to be the first scientific paper on the topic. In "Meteorological Imaginations and Conjectures," published in 1784, Franklin posited that recent volcanic eruptions in Iceland had caused a particularly harsh winter and a cool summer with "constant fog over all Europe, and [a] great part of North America." In 1815, the gargantuan eruption of Mount Tambora in Indonesia produced "The Year Without a Summer," a worldwide disaster that killed crops, prompted widespread starvation and food riots, and brought snow to New England as late as June.

As Myhrvold puts it: "All really big-ass volcanoes have some climate effects."

Volcanoes erupt all the time, all over the world, but truly "big-ass" ones are rare. If they weren't—well, we probably wouldn't be around to worry about global warming. The anthropologist Stanley Ambrose has argued that a supervolcanic explosion at Lake Toba on Sumatra, roughly seventy thousand years ago, blocked the sun so badly that it triggered an ice age that nearly wiped out *Homo sapiens*.

What distinguishes a big-ass volcano isn't just how much stuff it ejaculates, but where the ejaculate goes. The typical volcano sends sulfur dioxide into the troposphere, the atmospheric layer closest to the earth's surface. This is similar to what a coal-burning power plant does with its sulfur emissions. In both cases, the gas stays in the sky only a week or so before falling back to the ground as acid rain, generally within a few hundred miles of its origin.

But a big volcano shoots sulfur dioxide far higher, into the stratosphere. That's the layer that begins at about seven miles above the earth's surface, or six miles at the poles. Above that threshold altitude, there is a drastic change in a variety of atmospheric phenomena. The sulfur dioxide, rather than quickly returning to the earth's surface, absorbs stratospheric water vapor and forms an aerosol cloud that circulates rapidly, blanketing most of the globe. In the stratosphere, sulfur dioxide can linger for a year or more, and will thereby affect the global climate.

That's what happened in 1991 when Mount Pinatubo erupted in the Philippines. Pinatubo made Mount St. Helens look like a hiccup; it put more sulfur dioxide into the stratosphere than any volcano since Krakatoa, more than a century earlier. In the period between those two eruptions, the state of science had progressed considerably. A worldwide cadre of scientists was on watch at Pinatubo, equipped with modern technology to capture every measurable piece of data. The atmospheric aftereffects of Pinatubo were undeniable: a decrease in ozone, more diffuse sunlight, and, yes, a sustained drop in global temperature.

Nathan Myhrvold was working at Microsoft then, but he still followed the scientific literature on geophysical phenomena. He took note of the Pinatubo climate effects and, one year later, a 900-page report from the National Academy of Sciences called *Policy Implications of Greenhouse Warming*. It included a chapter on geoengineering, which the NAS defined as "large-scale engineering of our environment in order to combat or counteract the effects of changes in atmospheric chemistry."

In other words: if human activity is warming up the planet, could human ingenuity cool it down?

People have been trying to manipulate the weather forever. Just about every religion ever invented has a rain-making prayer. But secularists have stepped it up in recent decades. In the late 1940s, three General Electric scientists in Schenectady, New York, successfully seeded clouds with silver iodide. The trio included a chemist named

Bernard Vonnegut; the project's public-relations man was his younger brother Kurt, who went on to become a world-class novelist—and in his writing, he used a good bit of the far-out science he picked up in Schenectady.

The 1992 NAS report gave a credibility boost to geoengineering, which until then had largely been seen as the province of crackpots and rogue governments. Still, some of the NAS proposals would have seemed outlandish even in a Vonnegut novel. A "multiple balloon screen," for instance, was meant to deflect sunlight by launching billions of aluminized balloons into the sky. A "space mirror" scheme called for fifty-five thousand reflective sails to orbit high above the earth.

The NAS report also raised the possibility of intentionally spreading sulfur dioxide in the stratosphere. The idea was attributed to a Belarusian climate scientist named Mikhail Budyko. After Pinatubo, there was no doubt that stratospheric sulfur dioxide cooled the earth. But wouldn't it be nice to not have to rely on volcanoes to do the job?

Unfortunately, the proposals for getting sulfur dioxide into the stratosphere were complex, costly, and impractical. Loading up artillery shells, for instance, and firing them into the sky. Or launching a fleet of fighter jets with high-sulfur fuel and letting their exhaust paint the stratosphere. "It was more science fiction than science," says Myhrvold. "None of the plans made any economic or practical sense."

The other problem was that many scientists, particularly nature-friendly ones like Ken Caldeira, found the very idea abhorrent. Dump chemicals in the atmosphere to reverse the damage caused by . . . dumping chemicals in the atmosphere? It was a crazy, hair-of-the-dog scheme that seemed to violate every tenet of environmentalism. Those who saw global warming as a religious issue could hardly imagine a more grievous sacrilege.

But the best reason to reject the idea, Caldeira thought, was that it simply wouldn't work.

That was his conclusion after hearing Lowell Wood give a lecture on stratospheric sulfur dioxide at a 1998 climate conference in Aspen. But being a scientist who prefers data to dogma—even if the environmental dogma in this case lay close to his heart—Caldeira ran a climate model to test Wood's claims. "The intent," he says, "was to put an end to all the geoengineering talk."

He failed. As much as Caldeira disliked the concept, his model backed up Wood's claims that geoengineering could stabilize the climate even in the face of a large spike in atmospheric carbon dioxide, and he wrote a paper saying so. Caldeira, the most reluctant geoengineer imaginable, became a convert—willing, at least, to explore the idea.

Which is how it comes to pass that, more than ten years later, Caldeira, Wood, and Myhrvold—the onetime peacenik, the onetime weapons architect, and the onetime Viking fanboy—are huddled together in a former Harley-Davidson repair shop showing off their scheme to stop global warming.

It wasn't just the cooling potential of stratospheric sulfur dioxide that surprised Caldeira. It was how little was needed to do the job: about thirty-four gallons per minute, not much more than the amount of water that comes out of a heavy-duty garden hose.

Warming is largely a polar phenomenon, which means that high-latitude areas are four times more sensitive to climate change than the equator. By IV's estimations, 100,000 tons of sulfur dioxide per year would effectively reverse warming in the high Arctic and reduce it in much of the Northern Hemisphere.

That may sound like a lot but, relatively speaking, it is a smidge. At least 200 *million* tons of sulfur dioxide already go into the atmosphere each year, roughly 25 percent from volcanoes, 25 percent from human sources like motor vehicles and coal-fired power plants, and the rest from other natural sources like sea spray.

So all that would be needed to produce a globe-changing effect is one-twentieth of 1 percent of current sulfur emissions, simply relocated to a higher point in the sky. How can this be? Myhrvold's answer: "Leverage!"

Leverage is the secret ingredient that distinguishes physics from, say, chemistry. Think back to the Salter Sink, IV's device for preventing hurricanes. Hurricanes are destructive because they gather up the thermal energy in the ocean's surface and convert it into physical force, a primordial act of leverage creation. The Salter Sink ruptures that process by using wave power to continually sink the warm water all through hurricane season.

"A kilogram of sulfur dioxide, emitted by a truck or a bus or a power plant into the troposphere, does much less good for you than in the stratosphere," Myhrvold says. "So you get a huge leverage, and that's a pretty cool thing. That's why Archimedes said, 'If you give me a fulcrum, I can move the world.'"*

So once you eliminate the moralism and the angst, the task of reversing global warming boils down to a straightforward engineering problem: how to get thirty-four gallons per minute of sulfur dioxide into the stratosphere?

The answer: a very long hose.

That's what IV calls this project—a "garden hose to the sky." Or, when they're feeling slightly more technical, a "stratospheric shield for climate stabilization." Considering its scientific forebear and the way it wraps the planet in a protective layer, perhaps it should be called Budyko's Blanket.

---

*Lowell Wood challenged Myhrvold's quote of Archimedes: "Actually, he asked for a sufficiently long *lever*." To which Myhrvold huffed: "He needed a fulcrum too!"

For anyone who loves cheap and simple solutions, things don't get much better. Here's how it works. At a base station, sulfur would be burned into sulfur dioxide and then liquefied. "The technology for doing this is well known," says Wood, "because early in the twentieth century, sulfur dioxide was the major refrigerant gas."

The hose, stretching from the base station into the stratosphere, would be about eighteen miles long but extremely light. "The diameter is just a couple inches, not some giant-ass pipe," says Myhrvold. "It's literally a specialized fire hose."

The hose would be suspended from a series of high-strength, helium-filled balloons fastened to the hose at 100- to 300-yard intervals (a "string of pearls," IV calls it), ranging in diameter from 25 feet near the ground to 100 feet near the top.

The liquefied sulfur dioxide would be sent skyward by a series of pumps, affixed to the hose at every 100 yards. These too would be relatively light, about forty-five pounds each—"smaller than the pumps in my swimming pool," Myhrvold says. There are several advantages to using many small pumps rather than one monster pump at the base station: a big ground pump would create more pressure, which, in turn, would require a far heavier hose; even if a few of the small pumps failed, the mission itself wouldn't; and using small, standardized units would keep costs down.

At the end of the hose, a cluster of nozzles would spritz the stratosphere with a fine mist of colorless liquid sulfur dioxide.

Thanks to stratospheric winds that typically reach one hundred miles per hour, the spritz would wrap around the earth in roughly ten days' time. That's how long it would take to create Budyko's Blanket. Because stratospheric air naturally spirals toward the poles, and because the arctic regions are more vulnerable to global warming, it makes sense to spray the sulfur aerosol at high latitude—with perhaps one hose in the Southern Hemisphere and another in the Northern.

Myhrvold, in his recent travels, happened upon one potentially perfect site. Along with Bill Gates and Warren Buffett, he was taking a whirlwind educational tour of various energy producers—a nuclear plant, a wind farm, and so on. One of their destinations was the Athabasca Oil Sands in northern Alberta, Canada.

Billions of barrels of petroleum can be found there, but it is heavy, mucky crude. Rather than lying in a liquid pool beneath the earth's crust, it is mixed in, like molasses, with the surface dirt. In Athabasca you don't drill for oil; you mine it, scooping up gigantic shovels of earth and then separating the oil from its waste components.

One of the most plentiful waste components is sulfur, which commands such a low price that oil companies simply stockpile it. "There were big yellow mountains of it, like a hundred meters high by a thousand meters wide!" says Myhrvold. "And they stair-step them, like a Mexican pyramid. So you could put one little pumping facility up there, and with one corner of one of those sulfur mountains, you could solve the whole global warming problem for the Northern Hemisphere."

It is interesting to think what might have happened if Myhrvold was around one hundred years ago, when New York and other cities were choking on horse manure. One wonders if, while everyone else looked at the mountains of dung and saw calamity, he might have seen opportunity.

On balance, Budyko's Blanket is a fiendishly simple plan. Considering the complexity of climate in general and how much we don't know, it probably makes sense to start small. With the fire-hose approach, you could begin with a trickle of sulfur and monitor the results. The amount could be easily dialed up or down—or, if need be, turned off. There is nothing permanent or irreversible about the process.

And it would be startlingly cheap. IV estimates the "Save the Arctic" plan could be set up in just two years at a cost of roughly $20 million, with an annual operating cost of about $10 million. If cooling the poles alone proved insufficient, IV has drawn up a "Save the Planet" version, with five worldwide base stations instead of two, and three hoses at each site. This would put about three to five times the amount of sulfur dioxide into the stratosphere. Even so, that would still represent less than 1 percent of current worldwide sulfur emissions. IV estimates this plan could be up and running in about three years, with a startup cost of $150 million and annual operating costs of $100 million.

So Budyko's Blanket could effectively reverse global warming at a total cost of $250 million. Compared with the $1.2 trillion that Nicholas Stern proposes spending each year to attack the problem, IV's idea is, well, practically free. It would cost $50 million less to stop global warming than what Al Gore's foundation is paying just to increase public awareness about global warming.

And there lies the key to the question we asked at the beginning of this chapter: *What do Al Gore and Mount Pinatubo have in common?* The answer is that Gore and Pinatubo both suggest a way to cool the planet, albeit with methods whose cost-effectiveness are a universe apart.

This is not to dismiss the potential objections to Budyko's Blanket, which are legion. First of all, would it work?

The scientific evidence says yes. It is basically a controlled mimicry of Mount Pinatubo's eruption, whose cooling effects were exhaustively studied and remain unchallenged.

Perhaps the stoutest scientific argument in favor of the plan came from Paul Crutzen, a Dutch atmospheric scientist whose environmentalist bona fides run even deeper than Caldeira's. Crutzen won a Nobel Prize in 1995 for his research on atmospheric ozone depletion. And yet in 2006, he wrote an essay in the journal *Climatic Change* lamenting the "grossly unsuccessful" efforts to emit fewer greenhouse gases and acknowledging that an injection of sulfur in the stratosphere "is the only option available to rapidly reduce temperature rises and counteract other climatic effects."

Crutzen's embrace of geoengineering was considered such a heresy within the climate-science community that some peers tried to stop publication of his essay. How could the man reverently known as "Dr. Ozone" possibly endorse such a scheme? Wouldn't the environmental damage outweigh the benefits?

Actually, no. Crutzen concluded that damage to the ozone would be minimal. The sulfur dioxide would eventually settle out in the polar regions but in such relatively small amounts that there, too, significant harm was unlikely. If a problem did arise, Crutzen wrote, the sulfur injection "could be stopped on short notice . . . which would allow the atmosphere to return to its prior state within a few years."

Another fundamental objection to geoengineering is that it intentionally alters the earth's natural state. To that, Myhrvold has a simple answer: "We've *already* geoengineered the earth."

In just a few centuries, we will have burned up most of the fossil fuel that took 300 million years of biological accumulation to make. Compared with that, injecting a bit of sulfur into the sky seems pretty mild. As Lowell Wood points out, sulfur isn't even the optimal chemical for a stratospheric shield. Other, less noxious-sounding materials—aluminized plastic micro beads, for instance—could make an even more efficient sunscreen. But sulfur is the most palatable choice "simply because we've got the volcano proof of feasibility," Wood says, "and along with that, a proof of harmlessness."

Wood and Myhrvold do worry that Budyko's Blanket might create an "excuse to pollute." That is, rather than buying time for us to create new energy solutions, it would lure people into complacency. But blaming geoengineering for this, Myhrvold says, is like blaming a heart surgeon for saving the life of someone who fails to exercise and eats too many french fries.

Perhaps the single best objection to the garden hose idea is that it is *too* simple and *too* cheap. As of this writing, there is no regulatory framework to prohibit anyone—a government, a private institution, even an individual—from putting sulfur dioxide in the atmosphere. (If there were, many of the world's nearly eight thousand coal-burning electricity units would be in a lot of trouble.) Still, Myhrvold admits that "it would freak people out" if someone unilaterally built the thing. But of course this depends on the individual. If it were Al Gore, he might snag a second Nobel Peace Prize. If it were Hugo Chávez, he'd probably get a prompt visit from some U.S. fighter jets.

One can also imagine the wars that might break out over who controls the dials on Budyko's Blanket. A government that depends on high oil prices might like to crank up the sulfur to keep things extra cool; others, meanwhile, might be happier with longer growing seasons.

Lowell Wood recounts a lecture he once gave, during which he mentioned that a stratospheric shield could also filter out damaging ultraviolet rays. An audience member suggested that fewer ultraviolet rays would lead to more people getting rickets.

"My response," Wood says, "was that your pharmacist can take care of that with vitamin D, and it'll be better for your overall health as well."

All the rocket scientists, climate scientists, physicists, and engineers around the IV conference table chuckle at Wood's riposte. Then someone asks if IV, with Budyko's Blanket up its sleeve, should be working toward a rickets-prevention patent. Now they laugh louder.

But it's not entirely a joke. Unlike most of the patents IV owns, Budyko's Blanket has no clear route to profits. "If you were an investor of mine," Myhrvold says, "you might ask: 'Remind me again why you're working on this?'" Indeed, many of IV's most time-consuming projects, including a variety of AIDS and malaria solutions, are substantially pro bono work.

"This is the world's greatest philanthropist sitting on the other side of the table," Wood says with a chuckle and a nod toward Myhrvold. "Involuntarily so, but there he is."

As dismissive as Myhrvold can be toward the prevailing sentiments on global warming, he is quick to deny that he dismisses global warming itself. (If that were the case, he'd hardly spend so much of his company's resources working on solutions.) Nor is he arguing for an immediate deployment of Budyko's Blanket—but, rather, that technologies like it be researched and tested so they are ready to use if the worst climate predictions were to come true.

"It's a bit like having fire sprinklers in a building," he says. "On the one hand, you should make every effort not to have a fire. But you also need something to fall back on in case the fire occurs anyway." Just as important, he says, "it gives you breathing room to move to carbon-free energy sources."

He is also eager to get geoengineering moving forward because of what he sees as "a real head of steam" that global-warming activists have gathered in recent years.

"They are seriously proposing doing a set of things that could have enormous impact—and we think probably negative impact—on human life," he says. "They want to divert a huge amount of economic value toward immediate and precipitous anti-carbon initiatives, without thinking things through. This will have a huge drag on the world economy. There are billions of poor people who will be greatly delayed, if not entirely precluded, from attaining a First World standard of living. In this country, we can pretty much afford the luxury of doing whatever we want on the energy-and-environment front, but other parts of the world would seriously suffer."

Certain new ideas, no matter how useful, are invariably seen as repugnant. As we mentioned earlier, a market for human organs—even though it might save tens of thousands of lives each year—is one such example.

Over time, some ideas do cross the repugnance barrier to become reality. Charging interest on loans. Selling human sperm and eggs. Profiting from a loved one's premature death. This last example of course describes how life insurance works. Today it is standard practice to wager on your own death in order to provide for your family. Until the mid–nineteenth century, life insurance was considered "a profanation," as the sociologist Viviana Zelizer writes, "which transformed the sacred event of death into a vulgar commodity."

Budyko's Blanket may simply be too repugnant a scheme to ever be given a chance. Intentional pollution? Futzing with the stratosphere? Putting the planet's weather in the hands of a few arrogant souls from Seattle? It is one thing for climate heavyweights like Paul Crutzen and Ken Caldeira to endorse such a solution. But they are mere scientists. The real heavyweights in this fight are people like Al Gore.

And what does he think of geoengineering?

"In a word," Gore says, "I think it's nuts."

If the garden-hose-to-the-sky idea doesn't fly, IV has another proposal that relies on the same science but is perhaps slightly less repugnant. As it turns out, the amount of stratospheric sulfur necessary to cool the planet is equal to the amount that just a handful of coal-burning power plants already belch out. This second plan calls for simply extending the smokestacks at a few strategically located plants. So instead of spewing their sulfur-laden smoke several hundred feet into the air, these smokestacks would release it some eighteen miles high, into the stratosphere, where it would have the same net cooling effect as the garden-hose scheme.

This plan is appealing because it simply repurposes existing pollution without adding any more. Although an eighteen-mile-high smokestack might sound like a hard thing to build, IV has figured out how—essentially by attaching a long, skinny hot-air balloon to an existing power-plant smokestack, creating a channel that lets the hot sulfur gases rise by their own buoyancy into the stratosphere. This project is dubbed, naturally, "chimney to the sky."

And if even *that* plan is too repugnant, IV has something entirely different, a plan that is practically heavenly: a sky full of puffy white clouds.

This is the brainchild of John Latham, a British climate scientist who recently joined the IV stable of inventors. Latham is a gentle, soft-spoken man in his late sixties who is also a rather serious poet. So it caught his ear when, long ago, he stood on a mountaintop in North Wales with his eight-year-old son Mike, gazing down at a sunset, and the boy, pointing out how shiny the clouds were, called them "soggy mirrors."

Precisely!

"On balance, the role of clouds is to produce a cooling," says Latham. "If clouds didn't exist in the atmosphere, the earth would be a lot hotter than it is now."

Even man-made clouds—the contrails from a jet plane, for instance—have a cooling effect. After the September 11 terrorist attacks, all commercial flights in the United States were grounded for three days. Using data from more than four thousand weather stations across the country, scientists found that the sudden absence of contrails accounted for a subsequent rise in ground temperature of nearly 2 degrees Fahrenheit, or 1.1 degrees Celsius.

There are at least three essential ingredients for the formation of clouds: ascending air, water vapor, and solid particles known as cloud condensation nuclei. When planes fly, particles in the exhaust plume serve as the nuclei. Over landmasses, dust particles do the job. But there are far fewer cloud-friendly nuclei over the world's oceans, Latham explains, so the clouds contain fewer droplets and are therefore less reflective. As a result, more sunlight reaches the earth's surface. The ocean, because it is dark, is particularly good at absorbing the sun's heat.

By Latham's calculations, an increase of just 10 or 12 percent of the reflectivity of oceanic clouds would cool the earth enough to counteract even a doubling of current greenhouse gas levels. His solution: use the ocean itself to make more clouds.

As it happens, the salt-rich spray from seawater creates excellent nuclei for cloud formation. All you have to do is get the spray into the air several yards above the ocean's surface. From there, it naturally lofts upward to the altitude where clouds form.

IV has considered a variety of ways to make this happen. At the moment, the favorite idea is a fleet of wind-powered fiberglass boats, designed by Stephen Salter, with underwater turbines that produce enough thrust to kick up a steady stream of spray. Because there is no engine, there is no pollution. The only ingredients—seawater and air—are of course free. The volume of spray (and, therefore, of cloud reflectivity) would be easily adjustable. Nor would the clouds reach land, where sunshine is so important to agriculture. The estimated price tag: less than $50 million for the first prototypes and then a few billion dollars for a fleet of vessels large enough to offset projected warming at least until 2050. In the annals of cheap and simple solutions to vexing problems, it is hard to think of a more elegant example than John Latham's soggy mirrors—geoengineering that the greenest green could love.

That said, Myhrvold fears that even IV's gentlest proposals will find little favor within certain environmentalist circles. To him, this doesn't compute.

"If you believe that the scary stories could be true, or even possible, then you should also admit that relying only on reducing carbon-dioxide emissions is not a very good answer," he says. In other words: it's illogical to believe in a carbon-induced warming apocalypse *and* believe that such an apocalypse can be averted simply by curtailing new carbon emissions. "The scary scenarios could occur even if we make herculean efforts to reduce our emissions, in which case the only real answer is geoengineering."

Al Gore, meanwhile, counters with his own logic. "If we don't know enough to stop putting 70 million tons of global-warming pollution into the atmosphere every day," he says, "how in God's name can we know enough to precisely counteract that?"

But if you think like a cold-blooded economist instead of a warm-hearted humanist, Gore's reasoning doesn't track. It's not that we don't *know how* to stop polluting the atmosphere. We don't *want* to stop, or aren't willing to pay the price.

Most pollution, remember, is a negative externality of our consumption. As hard as engineering or physics may be, getting human beings to change their behavior is probably harder. At present, the rewards for limiting consumption are weak, as are the penalties for overconsuming. Gore and other environmentalists are pleading for humankind to consume less and therefore pollute less, and that is a noble invitation. But as incentives go, it's not a very strong one.

And *collective* behavior change, as beguiling as that may sound, can be maddeningly elusive. Just ask Ignatz Semmelweis.

Back in 1847, when he solved the mystery of puerperal fever, Semmelweis was hailed as a hero—wasn't he?

Quite the opposite. Yes, the death rate in Vienna General's maternity ward plummeted when he ordered doctors to wash their hands after performing autopsies. Elsewhere, however, doctors ignored

Semmelweis's findings. They even ridiculed him. Surely, they reasoned, such a ravaging illness could not be prevented simply by washing one's hands! Moreover, doctors of that era—not the humblest lot—couldn't accept the idea that they were the root of the trouble.

Semmelweis grew frustrated, and in time his frustration curdled into vitriol. He cast himself as a scorned messiah, labeling every critic of his theory a murderer of women and babies. His arguments were often nonsensical; his personal behavior became odd, marked by lewdness and sexual impropriety. In retrospect, it's safe to say that Ignatz Semmelweis was going mad. At the age of forty-seven, he was tricked into entering a sanitarium. He tried to escape, was forcibly restrained, and died within two weeks, his reputation shattered.

But that doesn't mean he wasn't right. Semmelweis was posthumously vindicated by Louis Pasteur's research in germ theory, after which it became standard practice for doctors to scrupulously clean their hands before treating patients.

So do contemporary doctors follow Semmelweis's orders?

A raft of recent studies have shown that hospital personnel wash or disinfect their hands in *fewer than half* the instances they should. And doctors are the worst offenders, more lax than either nurses or aides.

This failure seems puzzling. In the modern world, we tend to believe that dangerous behaviors are best solved by education. That is the thinking behind nearly every public-awareness campaign ever undertaken, from global warming to AIDS prevention to drunk driving. And doctors are the most educated people in the hospital.

In a 1999 report called "To Err Is Human," the Institute of Medicine estimated that between 44,000 and 98,000 Americans die each year because of preventable hospital errors—more than deaths from motor-vehicle crashes or breast cancer—and that one of the leading errors is wound infection. The best medicine for stopping infections? Getting doctors to wash their hands more frequently.

In the wake of this report, hospitals all over the country hustled to fix the problem. Even a world-class hospital like Cedars-Sinai Medical Center in Los Angeles found it needed improvement, with a hand-hygiene rate of just 65 percent. Its senior administrators formed a committee to identify the reasons for this failure.

For one, they acknowledged, doctors are incredibly busy, and time spent washing hands is time not spent treating patients. Craig Feied, our emergency-room revolutionary from Washington, estimates that he often interacted with more than one hundred patients per shift. "If I ran to wash my hands every time I touched a patient, following the protocol, I'd spend nearly half my time just standing over a sink."

Sinks, furthermore, aren't always as accessible as they should be and, in patient rooms especially, they are sometimes barricaded by equipment or furniture. Cedars-Sinai, like a lot of other hospitals, had wall-mounted Purell dispensers for handy disinfection, but these too were often ignored.

Doctors' hand-washing failures also seem to have psychological components. The first might be (generously) called a perception deficit. During a five-month study in the intensive-care unit of an Australian children's hospital, doctors were asked to track their own hand-washing frequency. Their self-reported rate? Seventy-three percent. Not perfect, but not so terrible either.

Unbeknownst to these doctors, however, their nurses were spying on them, and recorded the docs' actual hand-hygiene rate: a paltry 9 percent.

Paul Silka, an emergency-room doctor at Cedars-Sinai who also served as the hospital's chief of staff, points to a second psychological factor: arrogance. "The ego can kick in after you've been in practice a while," he explains. "You say: 'Hey, *I* couldn't be carrying the bad bugs. It's the *other* hospital personnel.'"

Silka and the other administrators at Cedars-Sinai set out to change their colleagues' behavior. They tried all sorts of incentives: gentle cajoling via posters and e-mail messages; greeting doctors every morning with a bottle of Purell; establishing a Hand Hygiene Safety Posse that roamed the wards, giving a $10 Starbucks card to doctors who were seen properly washing their hands. You might think the highest earners in a hospital would be immune to a $10 incentive. "But none of them turned down the card," Silka says.

After several weeks, the hand-hygiene rate at Cedars-Sinai had increased but not nearly enough. This news was delivered by Rekha Murthy, the hospital's epidemiologist, during a lunch meeting of the Chief of Staff Advisory Committee. There were roughly twenty members, most of them top doctors in the hospital. They were openly discouraged by the report. When lunch was over, Murthy handed each of them an agar plate—a sterile petri dish loaded with a spongy layer of agar. "I would love to culture your hand," she told them.

They pressed their palms into the plates, which Murthy sent to the lab. The resulting images, Silka recalls, "were disgusting and striking, with gobs of colonies of bacteria."

Here were the most important people in the hospital, telling everyone else how to change their behavior, and yet even their own hands weren't clean! (And, most disturbingly, this took place at a lunch meeting.)

It may have been tempting to sweep this information under the rug. Instead, the administration decided to harness the disgusting power of the bacteria-laden handprints by installing one of them as the screen saver on computers throughout the hospital. For doctors—lifesavers by training, and by oath—this grisly warning proved more powerful than any other incentive. Hand-hygiene compliance at Cedars-Sinai promptly shot up to nearly 100 percent.

As word got around, other hospitals began copying the screen-saver solution. And why not? It was cheap, simple, and effective.

A happy ending, right?

Yes, but . . . think about it for a moment. Why did it take so much effort to persuade doctors to do what they have known to do since the age of Semmelweis? Why was it so hard to change their behavior when the price of compliance (a simple hand-wash) is so low and the potential cost of failure (the loss of a human life) so high?

Once again, as with pollution, the answer has to do with externalities.

When a doctor fails to wash his hands, his own life isn't the one that is primarily endangered. It is the next patient he treats, the one with the open wound or the compromised immune system. The dangerous bacteria that patient receives are a negative externality of the doctor's actions—just as pollution is a negative externality of anyone who drives a car, jacks up the air conditioner, or sends coal exhaust up a smokestack. The polluter has insufficient incentive to not pollute, and the doctor has insufficient incentive to wash his hands.

This is what makes the science of behavior change so difficult.

So instead of collectively wringing our filthy hands about behavior that is so hard to change, what if we can come up with engineering or design or incentive solutions that supersede the need for such change?

That's what Intellectual Ventures has in mind for global warming, and that is what public-health officials have finally embraced to cut down on hospital-acquired infections. Among the best solutions: using disposable blood-pressure cuffs on incoming patients; infusing hospital equipment with silver ion particles to create an antimicrobial shield; and forbidding doctors to wear neckties because, as the U.K. Department of Health has noted, they "are rarely laundered," "perform no beneficial function in patient care," and "have been shown to be colonized by pathogens."

That's why Craig Feied has worn bow ties for years. He has also helped develop a virtual-reality interface that allows a gowned and gloved-up surgeon to scroll through X-rays on a computer without actually touching it—because computer keyboards and mice tend to collect pathogens at least as effectively as a doctor's necktie. And the next time you find yourself in a hospital room, don't pick up the TV remote control until you've disinfected the daylights out of it.

Perhaps it's not so surprising that it's hard to change people's behavior when someone else stands to reap most of the benefit. But surely we are capable of behavior change when our own welfare is at stake, yes?

Sadly, no. If we were, every diet would always work (and there would be no need for diets in the first place). If we were, most smokers would be ex-smokers. If we were, no one who ever took a sex-ed class would be party to an unwanted pregnancy. But knowing and doing are two different things, especially when pleasure is involved.

Consider the high rate of HIV and AIDS in Africa. For years, public-health officials from around the world have been fighting this problem. They have preached all sorts of behavior change—using condoms, limiting the number of sexual partners, and so on. Recently, however, a French researcher named Bertran Auvert ran a medical trial in South Africa and came upon findings so encouraging that the trial was halted so the new preventive measure could be applied at once.

What was this magical treatment?

Circumcision. For reasons Auvert and other scientists do not fully understand, circumcision was found to reduce the risk of HIV transmission by as much as 60 percent in heterosexual men. Subsequent studies in Kenya and Uganda corroborated Auvert's results.

All over Africa, foreskins began to fall. "People are used to policies that target behaviors," said one South African health official, "but circumcision is a surgical intervention—it's cold, hard steel."

The decision to undergo an adult circumcision is obviously a deeply personal one. We would hardly presume to counsel anyone in either direction. But for those who *do* choose circumcision, a simple word of advice: before the doctor gets anywhere near you, please make sure he washes his hands.

EPILOGUE

MONKEYS ARE PEOPLE TOO

The branch of economics concerned with issues like inflation, recessions, and financial shocks is known as macroeconomics. When the economy is going well, macroeconomists are lauded as heroes; when it turns sour, as it did recently, they catch a lot of the blame. In either case, the headlines go to the macroeconomists.

We hope that after reading this book, you'll realize there is a whole different breed of economist out there—*micro*economists—lurking in the shadows. They seek to understand the choices that individuals make, not just in terms of what they buy but also how often they wash their hands and whether they become terrorists.

Some of these microeconomists do not even limit their research to the human race.

Keith Chen, the son of Chinese immigrants, is a hyper-verbal, sharp-dressing thirty-three-year-old with spiky hair. After an itinerant upbringing in the rural Midwest, Chen attended Stanford, where after a brief infatuation with Marxism, he made an about-face and took up economics. Now he is an associate professor of economics at Yale.

His research agenda was inspired by something written long ago by Adam Smith, the founder of classical economics: "Nobody ever saw a dog make a fair and deliberate exchange of one bone for another with another dog. Nobody ever saw one animal by its gestures and natural cries signify to another, *this is mine, that yours; I am willing to give this for that.*"

In other words, Smith was certain that humankind alone had a knack for monetary exchange.

But was he right?

In economics, as in life, you'll never find the answer to a question unless you're willing to ask it, as silly as it may seem. Chen's question was simply this: *What would happen if I could teach a bunch of monkeys to use money?*

Chen's monkey of choice was the capuchin, a cute, brown New World monkey about the size of a one-year-old child, or at least a scrawny one-year-old who has a very long tail. "The capuchin has a small brain," Chen says, "and it's pretty much focused on food and sex." (This, we would argue, doesn't make the capuchin so different from many people we know, but that's another story.) "You should really think of a capuchin as a bottomless stomach of want. You can feed them marshmallows all day, they'll throw up, and then come back for more."

To an economist, this makes the capuchin an excellent research subject.

Chen, along with Venkat Lakshminarayanan, went to work with seven capuchins at a lab set up by the psychologist Laurie Santos at Yale–New Haven Hospital. In the tradition of monkey labs everywhere, the capuchins were given names—in this case, derived from characters in James Bond films. There were four females and three males. The alpha male was named Felix, after the CIA agent Felix Leiter. He was Chen's favorite.

The monkeys lived together in a large, open cage. Down at one end was a much smaller cage, the testing chamber, where one monkey at a time could enter to take part in experiments. For currency, Chen settled on a one-inch silver disc with a hole in the middle—"kind of like Chinese money," he says.

The first step was to teach the monkeys that the coins had value. This took some effort. If you give a capuchin a coin, he will sniff it and, after determining he can't eat it (or have sex with it), he'll toss it aside. If you repeat this several times, he may start tossing the coins *at you,* and hard.

So Chen and his colleagues gave the monkey a coin and then showed a treat. Whenever the monkey gave the coin back to the researcher, it got the treat. It took many months, but the monkeys eventually learned that the coins could buy the treats.

It turned out that individual monkeys had strong preferences for different treats. A capuchin would be presented with twelve coins on a tray—his budget constraint—and then be offered, say, Jell-O cubes by one researcher and apple slices by another. The monkey would hand his coins to whichever researcher held the food he preferred, and the researcher would fork over the goodies.

Chen now introduced price shocks and income shocks to the monkeys' economy. Let's say Felix's favorite food was Jell-O, and he was accustomed to getting three cubes of it for one coin. How would he respond if one coin suddenly bought just two cubes?

To Chen's surprise, Felix and the others responded rationally. When the price of a given food rose, the monkeys bought less of it, and when the price fell, they bought more. The most basic law of economics—that the demand curve slopes downward—held for monkeys as well as humans.

Now that he had witnessed their rational behavior, Chen wanted to test the capuchins for *ir*rational behavior. He set up two gambling games. In the first, a capuchin was shown one grape and, dependent on a coin flip, either got only that grape or won a bonus grape as well. In the second game, the capuchin started out seeing two grapes, but if the coin flip went against him, the researchers took away one grape and the monkey got only one.

In both cases, the monkey got the same number of grapes on average. But the first gamble was framed as a potential gain while the second was framed as a potential loss.

How did the capuchins react?

Given that the monkeys aren't very smart in the first place, you might assume that any gambling strategy was well beyond their capabilities. In that case, you'd expect them to prefer it when a researcher initially offered them two grapes instead of one. But precisely the opposite happened! Once the monkeys figured out that the two-grape researcher sometimes withheld the second grape and that the one-grape researcher sometimes added a bonus grape, the monkeys strongly preferred the one-grape researcher. A rational monkey wouldn't have cared, but these irrational monkeys suffered from what psychologists call "loss aversion." They behaved as if the pain from losing a grape was greater than the pleasure from gaining one.

Up to now, the monkeys appeared to be as rational as humans in their use of money. But surely this last experiment showed the vast gulf that lay between monkey and man.

Or did it?

The fact is that similar experiments with human beings—day traders, for instance—had found that people make the same kind of irrational decisions at a nearly identical rate. The data generated by the capuchin monkeys, Chen says, "make them statistically indistinguishable from most stock-market investors."

So the parallels between human beings and these tiny-brained, food-and-sex monkeys remained intact. And then, as if Chen needed any further evidence of these parallels, the strangest thing happened in the lab.

Felix scurried into the testing chamber, just as he'd done countless times before, but on this day, for reasons Chen could never understand, Felix did not gather up the twelve coins on the tray and use them to buy food. Instead, he flung the entire tray's worth of coins back into the communal cage and, fleeing the testing chamber, dashed in after them—a bank heist followed by a jailbreak.

There was chaos in the big cage, with twelve coins on the floor and seven monkeys going after them. When Chen and the other researchers went inside to get the coins, the monkeys wouldn't give them up. After all, they had learned that the coins had value. So the humans resorted to bribing the capuchins with treats. This taught the monkeys another valuable lesson: crime pays.

Then, out of the corner of his eye, Chen saw something remarkable. One monkey, rather than handing his coin over to the humans for a grape or a slice of apple, instead approached a second monkey and gave it to her. Chen had done earlier research in which monkeys were found to be altruistic. Had he just witnessed an unprompted act of monkey altruism?

After a few seconds of grooming—*bam!*—the two capuchins were having sex.

What Chen had seen wasn't altruism at all, but rather the first instance of monkey prostitution in the recorded history of science.

And then, just to prove how thoroughly the monkeys had assimilated the concept of money, as soon as the sex was over—it lasted about eight seconds; they're monkeys, after all—the capuchin who'd received the coin promptly brought it over to Chen to purchase some grapes.

This episode sent Chen's mind spinning. Until now, the researchers had run narrowly defined money experiments with one monkey at a time. What if Chen could introduce money directly into the monkeys' lives? The research possibilities were endless.

Alas, Chen's dream of capuchin capitalism never came to pass. The authorities who oversaw the monkey lab feared that introducing money to the capuchins would irreparably damage their social structure.

They were probably right.

If the capuchins were so quick to turn to prostitution as soon as they got hold of some money, just imagine how quickly the world would be overrun with monkey murderers and monkey terrorists, with monkey polluters who contribute to global warming and monkey doctors who fail to wash their hands. Future generations of monkeys, of course, would come along and solve these problems. But there would always be something to fix—like the monkeys' pigheaded insistence that all their children ride in car seats . . .

ACKNOWLEDGMENTS

Jointly, we'd first like to thank all the people who let us tell their stories in this book. For every person named in the text, there were usually five or ten more who contributed in various ways. Thanks to all of you. We are also greatly indebted to the many scholars and researchers whose work is cited in the book.

Suzanne Gluck of William Morris Endeavor is an agent like no other, and we are lucky to have her. She has many extraordinary colleagues, including Tracy Fisher, Raffaella De Angelis, Cathryn Summerhayes, Erin Malone, Sarah Ceglarski, Caroline Donofrio, and Eric Zohn, all of whom have been a big help, as have others at WME, past and present.

At William Morrow/HarperCollins, we've had a great time working with our wonderful editor Henry Ferris, and Dee Dee DeBartlo is unfailingly hardworking and cheerful. There are many others to thank—Brian Murray, Michael Morrison, Liate Stehlik, Lynn Grady, Peter

Hubbard, Danny Goldstein, and Frank Albanese among them—as well as those who've moved on, especially Jane Friedman and Lisa Gallagher. For tea, sympathy, and more, thanks to Will Goodlad and Stefan McGrath at Penguin UK (who also provide excellent British children's books for our offspring).

The New York Times has allowed us, in its pages and on our blog, to run some of this book's ideas up the flagpole. Thanks especially to Gerry Marzorati, Paul Tough, Aaron Retica, Andy Rosenthal, David Shipley, Sasha Koren, Jason Kleinman, Brian Ernst, and Jeremy Zilar.

To the women of Number 17: what fun! And there is more to come.

The Harry Walker Agency has given us more opportunities to meet more incredible people than we ever thought possible, and they are a joy to work with. Thanks to Don Walker, Beth Gargano, Cynthia Rice, Kim Nisbet, Mirjana Novkovic, and everyone else there.

Linda Jines continues to prove that she has no peer when it comes to naming things.

And thanks especially to all the readers who take the time to send along their clever, fascinating, devious, and maddening ideas for us to pursue.

PERSONAL ACKNOWLEDGMENTS

I owe an enormous debt to my many co-authors and colleagues, whose great ideas fill this book, and to all the kind people who have taken the time to teach me what I know about economics and life. My wife, Jeannette, and our children, Amanda, Olivia, Nicholas, and Sophie, make every day a joy, even though we miss Andrew so much. I thank my parents, who showed me it was okay to be different. Most of all, I want to thank my good friend and co-author Stephen Dubner, who is a brilliant writer and a creative genius.

S.D.L.

People like Sudhir Venkatesh, Allie, Craig Feied, Ian Horsley, Joe De May Jr., John List, Nathan Myhrvold, and Lowell Wood make me grateful every day that I became a writer. They are full of insights and surprises that are a joy to learn. Steve Levitt is not only a great collaborator but a wonderful economics teacher as well. For outstanding research assistance, thanks to Rhena Tantisunthorn, Rachel Fershleiser, Nicole Tourtelot, Danielle Holtz, and especially Ryan Hagen, who did great work on this book and will write great books of his own one day. To Ellen, my extraordinary wife, and to the fantastic creatures known as Solomon and Anya: you are all pretty damn swell.

S.J.D.

NOTES

INTRODUCTION: PUTTING THE FREAK IN ECONOMICS

1–3 THE PERILS OF WALKING DRUNK: The brilliant economist Kevin Murphy called our attention to the relative risk of walking drunk. For background on **the dangers of drunk driving,** see Steven D. Levitt and Jack Porter, "How Dangerous Are Drinking Drivers?" *Journal of Political Economy* 109, no. 6 (2001). / 2 One of the benefits of a cumbersome federal bureaucracy is that it hires tens of thousands of employees to staff hundreds of agencies that collect and organize endless reams of statistical data. The National Highway Traffic Safety Administration (NHTSA) is one such agency, and it supplies definitive and valuable data on traffic safety. Regarding the **proportion of miles driven drunk,** see "Impaired Driving in the United States," NHTSA, 2006. / 2 For **drunk pedestrian deaths,** see "Pedestrian Roadway Fatalities," NHTSA, DOT HS 809 456, April 2003. / 2 For **drunk driving deaths,** see "Traffic Safety Facts 2006," NHTSA, DOT HS 810 801, March 2008. / 2 **"They lie down to rest on country roads":** see William E. Schmidt,

"A Rural Phenomenon: Lying-in-the-Road Deaths," *The New York Times*, June 30, 1986. / 3 The **number of Americans of driving age:** here and elsewhere in this book, population statistics and characteristics are generally drawn from U.S. Census Bureau data. / 3 **"Friends Don't Let Friends . . .":** By total happenstance, we recently met one of the creators of the original slogan "Friends Don't Let Friends Drive Drunk." Her name is Susan Wershba Zerin. In the early 1980s, she worked at the Leber Katz Partners ad agency in New York and was the account manager on a pro bono anti-drunk-driving campaign for the U.S. Department of Transportation. "Elizabeth Dole, the secretary of transportation, was our key contact," she recalls. The phrase "Friends Don't Let Friends Drive Drunk" was written as the campaign's internal strategic statement, but it proved so memorable in-house that it was adopted as the campaign's tagline.

3–8 THE UNLIKELY SAVIOR OF INDIAN WOMEN: This section draws substantially from Robert Jensen and Emily Oster, "The Power of TV: Cable Television and Women's Status in India," *Quarterly Journal of Economics*, forthcoming. For more on **living standards in India,** see the United Nations Human Development Report for India; "National Family Health Survey (NFHS-3), 2005-06, India," The International Institute for Population Sciences and Macro Intl.; and "India Corruption Study 2005," Center for Media Studies, Transparency International, India. / 4 On the **unwantedness of girls in India** and the use of ultrasounds to identify them for abortion, see NFHS-3 report; and Peter Wonacott, "India's Skewed Sex Ratio Puts GE Sales in Spotlight," *The Wall Street Journal*, April 19, 2007; and Neil Samson Katz and Marisa Sherry, "India: The Missing Girls," *Frontline*, April 26, 2007. / 4 For more on the persistence of **dowry in India,** see Siwan Anderson, "Why Dowry Payments Declined with Modernization in Europe but Are Rising in India," *Journal of Political Economy* 111, no. 2 (April 2003); Sharda Srinivasan and Arjun S. Bedi, "Domestic Violence and Dowry: Evidence from a South Indian Village," *World Development* 35, no. 5 (2007); and Amelia Gentleman, "Indian Brides Pay a High Price," *The International Herald Tribune*, October 22, 2006. / 4 The **Smile Train** story comes from author interviews with Brian Mullaney of

Smile Train; see also Stephen J. Dubner and Steven D. Levitt, "Bottom-Line Philanthropy," *The New York Times Magazine,* March 9, 2008. / 4 For more on **the "missing women" of India,** see Amartya Sen, "More Than 100 Million Women Are Missing," *The New York Review of Books,* December 20, 1990; Stephan Klasen and Claudia Wink, published in K. Basu and R. Kanbur (eds.), *Social Welfare, Moral Philosophy and Development: Essays in Honour of Amartya Sen's Seventy-Fifth Birthday* (Oxford University Press, 2008); and Swami Agnivesh, Rama Mani, and Angelika Koster-Lossack, "Missing: 50 Million Indian Girls," *The New York Times,* November 25, 2005. See also Stephen J. Dubner and Steven D. Levitt, "The Search for 100 Million Missing Women," *Slate,* May 24, 2005, which reported on Emily Oster's finding of a connection between missing women and hepatitis B; but see also Steven D. Levitt, "An Academic Does the Right Thing," Freakonomics blog, *The New York Times,* May 22, 2008, in which the hepatitis conclusion was found to be faulty. / 5 **Son worship in China:** see Therese Hesketh and Zhu Wei Xing, "Abnormal Sex Ratios in Human Populations: Causes and Consequences," *Proceedings of the National Academy of Sciences,* September 5, 2006; and Sharon LaFraniere, "Chinese Bias for Baby Boys Creates a Gap of 32 Million," *The New York Times,* April 10, 2009. / 5 Information about **bride burning, wife beating, and other domestic atrocities** can be found in Virendra Kumar, Sarita Kanth, "Bride Burning," *The Lancet* 364, supp. 1 (December 18, 2004); B. R. Sharma, "Social Etiology of Violence Against Women in India," *Social Science Journal* 42, no. 3 (2005); "India HIV and AIDS Statistics," AVERT, available at www.avert.org/indiaaids.htm; and Kounteya Sinha, "Many Women Justify Wife Beating," *The Times of India,* October 12, 2007. / 5 **"The condom is not optimized for India":** see Rohit Sharma, "Project Launched in India to Measure Size of Men's Penises," *British Medical Journal,* October 13, 2001; Damian Grammaticus, "Condoms 'Too Big' for Indian Men," *BBC News,* December 8, 2006; and Madhavi Rajadhyaksha, "Indian Men Don't Measure Up," *The Times of India,* December 8, 2006. / 5 **Apni Beti, Apna Dhan** is described in Fahmida Jabeen and Ravi Karkara, "Government Support to Parenting in Bangladesh and India," Save the Children, December 2005.

8–12 DROWNING IN HORSE MANURE: See Joel Tarr and Clay McShane, "The Centrality of the Horse to the Nineteenth-Century American City," in *The Making of Urban America*, ed. Raymond Mohl (Rowman & Littlefield, 1997); Eric Morris, "From Horse Power to Horsepower," *Access*, no. 30, Spring 2007; Ann Norton Greene, *Horses at Work: Harnessing Power in Industrial America* (Harvard University Press, 2008). Also based on author interviews with Morris, McShane, and David Rosner, Ronald H. Lauterstein Professor of Sociomedical Sciences at Columbia University. / 11 **Climate change will "destroy planet Earth as we know it":** see Martin Weitzman, "On Modeling and Interpreting the Economics of Catastrophic Climate Change," *The Review of Economics and Statistics* 91, no. 1 (February 2009). / 12 **The case of the stolen horse manure** is recounted in two *Boston Globe* articles by Kay Lazar: "It's Not a Dung Deal," June 26, 2005; and "Economics Professor Set to Pay for Manure," August 2, 2005.

12–14 WHAT IS "FREAKONOMICS," ANYWAY? **Gary Becker, the original freakonomist,** has written many books, papers, and articles that should be widely read, including *The Economic Approach to Human Behavior*, *A Treatise on the Human Family*, and *Human Capital*. See also his Nobel Prize acceptance speech, "The Economic Way of Looking at Life," Nobel Lecture, University of Chicago, December 9, 1992; and *The Nobel Prizes/Les Prix Nobel 1992: Nobel Prizes, Presentations, Biographies, and Lectures*, ed. Tore Frängsmyr (The Nobel Foundation, 1993). / 13 **"Our job in this book is to come up with such questions":** as the renowned statistician John Tukey once reportedly said, "An approximate answer to the right question is worth a great deal more than a precise answer to the wrong question." / 13 **One breast, one testicle:** for this thought, a hat tip to the futurist Watts Wacker.

14–15 SHARK-ATTACK HYSTERIA: The *Time* magazine cover package appeared on July 30, 2001, and included Timothy Roche, "Saving Jessie Arbogast." / 15 The definitive source for **shark attack statistics** is the International Shark Attack File, compiled by the Florida Museum of Natural History at the University of Florida. / 15 **Elephant deaths:** see *People and Wildlife, Conflict or*

Co-existence, ed. Rosie Woodroffe, Simon Thirgood, and Alan Rabinowitz (Cambridge University Press, 2005). For more on elephants attacking humans, see Charles Siebert, "An Elephant Crackup?" *The New York Times Magazine,* October 8, 2006.

CHAPTER 1: HOW IS A STREET PROSTITUTE LIKE A DEPARTMENT-STORE SANTA?

19–20 MEET LASHEENA: She is one of the many street prostitutes who participated in Sudhir Venkatesh's fieldwork, summarized in much further detail later in the chapter and contained in Steven D. Levitt and Sudhir Alladi Venkatesh, "An Empirical Analysis of Street-Level Prostitution," working paper.

20 HARD TO BE A WOMAN: For historic life expectancy, see Vern Bullough and Cameron Campbell, "Female Longevity and Diet in the Middle Ages," *Speculum* 55, no. 2 (April 1980). / 20 **Executed as witches:** see Emily Oster, "Witchcraft, Weather and Economic Growth in Renaissance Europe," *Journal of Economic Perspectives* 18, no. 1 (Winter 2004). / 20 **Breast ironing:** see Randy Joe Sa'ah, "Cameroon Girls Battle 'Breast Ironing,'" *BBC News,* June 23, 2006; as many as 26 percent of Cameroonian girls undergo the procedure, often by their mothers, upon reaching puberty. / 20 **The plight of Chinese women:** see the U.S. State Department's "2007 Country Reports on Human Rights Practices"; for long-term consequences of foot binding, see Steven Cummings, Xu Ling, and Katie Stone, "Consequences of Foot Binding Among Older Women in Beijing, China," *American Journal of Public Health* 87, no. 10 (1997).

20–22 DRAMATIC IMPROVEMENT IN WOMEN'S LIVES: The **advancement of women in higher education** is derived from two reports by the U.S. Department of Education's National Center for Education Statistics: *120 Years of American Education: A Statistical Portrait* (1993); and *Postsecondary Institutions in the United States: Fall 2007, Degrees and Other Awards Conferred: 2006–07, and 12-Month Enrollment: 2006–07* (2008). / 21 **Even Ivy League women** trail men in salaries: see Claudia Goldin and Lawrence F. Katz, "Transitions: Career and Family Lifecycles of the Educational Elite," *AEA*

Papers and Proceedings, May 2008. / 21 **Wage penalty for overweight women:** see Dalton Conley and Rebecca Glauber, "Gender, Body Mass and Economic Status," National Bureau of Economics Research working paper, May 2005. / 21 **Women with bad teeth:** see Sherry Glied and Matthew Neidell, "The Economic Value of Teeth," NBER working paper, March 2008. / 21 **The price of menstruation:** see Andrea Ichino and Enrico Moretti, "Biological Gender Differences, Absenteeism and the Earnings Gap," *American Economic Journal: Applied Economics* 1, no. 1 (2009). / 22 **Title IX creates jobs for women; men take them:** see Betsey Stevenson, "Beyond the Classroom: Using Title IX to Measure the Return to High School Sports," The Wharton School, University of Pennsylvania, June 2008; Linda Jean Carpenter and R. Vivian Acosta, "Women in Intercollegiate Sport: A Longitudinal, National Study Twenty-Seven-Year Update, 1977–2004"; and Christina A. Cruz, *Gender Games: Why Women Coaches Are Losing the Field* (VDM Verlag, 2009). For the WNBA disparity, see Mike Terry, "Men Dominate WNBA Coaching Ranks," *The Los Angeles Times,* August 2, 2006.

23–26 PREWAR PROSTITUTION: The section was drawn from a variety of archival sources and books, including: *The Social Evil in Chicago* (aka the Chicago Vice Commission report), American Vigilance Association, 1911; George Jackson Kneeland and Katharine Bement Davis, *Commercialized Prostitution in New York City* (The Century Co., 1913); Howard Brown Woolston, *Prostitution in the United States,* vol. 1, *Prior to the Entrance of the United States into the World War* (The Century Co., 1921); and *The Lost Sisterhood: Prostitution in America, 1900–1918* (The Johns Hopkins University Press, 1983). For more information on the Everleigh Club, see Karen Abbott's fascinating book *Sin in the Second City* (Random House, 2007).

25 DRUG DEALERS, NOT BUYERS, DO THE TIME: See Ilyana Kuziemko and Steven D. Levitt, "An Empirical Analysis of Imprisoning Drug Offenders," *Journal of Public Economics* 88 (2004); also, the U.S. Sentencing Commission's *2008 Sourcebook of Federal Sentencing Statistics.*

26–43 THE STREET PROSTITUTES OF CHICAGO: This section is largely drawn from Steven D. Levitt and Sudhir Alladi Venkatesh, "An Empirical Analysis of Street-Level Prostitution," working paper.

27–28 LYING TO THE OPORTUNIDADES CLERK: See César Martinelli and Susan Parker, "Deception and Misreporting in a Social Program," *Journal of European Economics Association* 7, no. 4 (2009). This paper was brought to our attention by the journalist Tina Rosenberg.

30 LOSING VIRGINITY TO A PROSTITUTE, THEN AND NOW: See Charles Winick and Paul M. Kinsie, *The Lively Commerce: Prostitution in the United States* (Quadrangle Books, 1971), citing a paper by P. H. Gebhard presented to the December 1967 meeting of the American Association for the Advancement of Science; and Edward O. Laumann, John H. Gagnon, Robert T. Michael, and Stuart Michaels, *The Social Organization of Sexuality: Sexual Practices in the United States* (The University of Chicago Press, 1994).

33–34 WHY DID ORAL SEX GET SO CHEAP? See Bonnie L. Halpern-Felsher, Jodi L. Cornell, Rhonda Y. Kropp, and Jeanne M. Tschann, "Oral Versus Vaginal Sex Among Adolescents: Perceptions, Attitudes, and Behavior," *Pediatrics* 115 (2005); Stephen J. Dubner and Steven D. Levitt, "The Economy of Desire," *The New York Times Magazine,* December 11, 2005; Tim Harford, "A Cock-and-Bull Story: Explaining the Huge Rise in Teen Oral Sex," *Slate,* September 2, 2006. / 33 **"Ease of exit"** is a phrase used by Dr. Michael Rekart of the University of British Columbia in an author interview; see also Michael Rekart, "Sex-Work Harm Reduction," *Lancet* 366 (2005).

35 PRICE DISCRIMINATION: For more information on Dr. Leonard's hair and pet trimmers, see Daniel Hamermesh, "To Discriminate You Need to Separate," Freakonomics blog, *The New York Times,* May 8, 2008.

36 HIGH AIDS RATE AMONG MALE PROSTITUTES' CUSTOMERS: See K. W. Elifson, J. Boles, W. W. Darrow, and C. E. Sterk, "HIV Seroprevalence and Risk Factors Among Clients of Female and Male

Prostitutes," *Journal of Acquired Immune Deficiency Syndromes and Human Retrovirology* 20, no. 2 (1999).

37–40 PIMPACT > RIMPACT: See Igal Hendel, Aviv Nevo, and Francois Ortalo-Magne, "The Relative Performance of Real Estate Marketing Platforms: MLS Versus FSBOMadison.com," *American Economic Review,* forthcoming; and Steven D. Levitt and Chad Syverson, "Antitrust Implications of Outcomes When Home Sellers Use Flat-Fee Real Estate Agents," *Brookings-Wharton Papers on Urban Affairs,* 2008.

43–44 FEMINISM AND TEACHING: The **occupations of women in 1910** are taken from the 1910 U.S. Census. / 43 **Percentage of women as teachers**: see Claudia Goldin, Lawrence F. Katz, and Ilyana Kuziemko, "The Homecoming of American College Women: The Reversal of the College Gender Gap," *Journal of Economic Perspectives* 20, no. 4 (Fall 2006). Thanks to Kuziemko for additional calculations. / 43 **Work opportunities multiplying:** see Raymond F. Gregory, *Women and Workplace Discrimination: Overcoming Barriers to Gender Equality* (Rutgers University Press, 2003). / 43 **Baby formula as "unsung hero":** see Stefania Albanesi and Claudia Olivetti, "Gender Roles and Technological Progress," National Bureau of Economic Research working paper, June 2007. / 44 The **erosion of teacher quality**: see Marigee P. Bacolod, "Do Alternative Opportunities Matter? The Role of Female Labor Markets in the Decline of Teacher Supply and Teacher Quality, 1940–1990," *Review of Economics and Statistics* 89, no. 4 (November 2007); Harold O. Levy, "Why the Best Don't Teach," *The New York Times,* September 9, 2000; and John H. Bishop, "Is the Test Score Decline Responsible for the Productivity Growth Decline," *American Economic Review* 79, no. 1 (March 1989).

44–46 EVEN TOP WOMEN EARN LESS: See Justin Wolfers, "Diagnosing Discrimination: Stock Returns and CEO Gender," *Journal of the European Economic Association* 4, nos. 2–3 (April–May 2006); and Marianne Bertrand, Claudia Goldin, and Lawrence F. Katz, "Dynamics of the Gender Gap for Young Professionals in the Financial and Corporate Sectors," National Bureau of Economic Research working paper, January 2009.

46 DO MEN LOVE MONEY THE WAY WOMEN LOVE KIDS? The **cash-incentive gender-gap experiment** was reported in Roland G. Fryer, Steven D. Levitt, and John A. List, "Exploring the Impact of Financial Incentives on Stereotype Threat: Evidence from a Pilot Study," *AEA Papers and Proceedings* 98, no. 2 (2008).

47–48 CAN A SEX CHANGE BOOST YOUR SALARY? See Kristen Schilt and Matthew Wiswall, "Before and After: Gender Transitions, Human Capital, and Workplace Experiences," *B.E. Journal of Economic Analysis & Policy* 8, no. 1 (2008). Further information for this section was drawn from author interviews with Ben Barres and Deirdre McCloskey; see also Robin Wilson, "Leading Economist Stuns Field by Deciding to Become a Woman," *Chronicle of Higher Education,* February 16, 1996; and Shankar Vedantam, "He, Once a She, Offers Own View on Science Spat," *The Wall Street Journal,* July 13, 2006.

49–56 WHY AREN'T THERE MORE WOMEN LIKE ALLIE? As detailed in this book's explanatory note, we met Allie thanks to a mutual acquaintance. Allie is not her real name, but all other facts about her are true. Over the past few years, we have both spent a considerable amount of time with her (all fully clothed), as this section was based on extensive interviews, a review of her ledgers, and the occasional guest lectures she delivered at the University of Chicago for Levitt's class "The Economics of Crime." Several students said this was the single-best lecture they had in all their years at the university, which is both a firm testament to Allie's insights and a brutal indictment of Levitt and the other professors. See also Stephen J. Dubner, "A Call Girl's View of the Spitzer Affair," Freakonomics blog, *The New York Times,* March 12, 2008.

56 REALTORS FLOCK TO A REAL-ESTATE BOOM: See Stephen J. Dubner and Steven D. Levitt, "Endangered Species," *The New York Times Magazine,* March 5, 2006.

CHAPTER 2: WHY SHOULD SUICIDE BOMBERS BUY LIFE INSURANCE?

57–59 RAMADAN AND OTHER BIRTH EFFECTS: The section on **prenatal day-time fasting** was drawn from Douglas Almond and Bhashkar Mazumder, "The Effects of Maternal Fasting During Ramadan on Birth and Adult Outcomes," National Bureau of Economic Research working paper, October 2008. / 58 **The natal roulette affects horses too:** see Bill Mooney, "Horse Racing; A Study on the Loss of Foals," *The New York Times,* May 2, 2002; and Frank Fitzpatrick, "Fate Stepped in for Smarty," *The Philadelphia Inquirer,* May 26, 2004. / 59 **The "Spanish Flu" effect:** see Douglas Almond, "Is the 1918 Influenza Pandemic Over? Long-Term Effects of *In Utero* Influenza Exposure in the Post-1940 U.S. Population," *Journal of Political Economy* 114, no. 4 (2006); and Douglas Almond and Bhashkar Mazumder, "The 1918 Influenza Pandemic and Subsequent Health Outcomes: An Analysis of SIPP Data," *Recent Developments in Health Economics* 95, no. 2 (May 2005). / 59 **Albert Aab versus Albert Zyzmor:** see Liran Einav and Leeat Yariv, "What's in a Surname? The Effects of Surname Initials on Academic Success," *Journal of Economic Perspectives* 20, no. 1 (2006); and C. Mirjam van Praag and Bernard M.S. van Praag, "The Benefits of Being Economics Professor A (and not Z)," Institute for the Study of Labor discussion paper, March 2007.

59–62 THE BIRTHDATE BULGE AND THE RELATIVE-AGE EFFECT: See Stephen J. Dubner and Steven D. Levitt, "A Star Is Made," *The New York Times Magazine,* May 7, 2006; K. Anders Ericsson, Neil Charness, Paul J. Feltovich, and Robert R. Hoffman, *The Cambridge Handbook of Expertise and Expert Performance* (Cambridge University Press, 2006); K. Anders Ericsson, Ralf Th. Krampe, and Clemens Tesch-Romer, "The Role of Deliberate Practice in the Acquisition of Expert Performance," *Psychological Review* 100, no. 3 (1993); Werner Helsen, Jan Van Winckel, and A. Mark Williams, "The Relative Age Effect in Youth Soccer Across Europe," *Journal of Sports Sciences* 23, no. 6 (June 2005); and Greg Spira, "The Boys of Late Summer," *Slate,* April 16, 2008. As explained in a footnote to this section, we originally planned to write a chapter in *SuperFreakonomics* on how talent is acquired—that is, when a person is very good at a given thing, what is it that makes him or her so good? But our plans changed when several books were recently published on this theme. A lot of people gave generously of their time and thoughts in our reporting on this abandoned chapter, and we remain indebted to them. Anders Ericsson was extremely helpful, as were Werner Helsen, Paula Barnsley, Gus Thompson, and many others. We are especially grateful to Takeru Kobayashi, the competitive-eating champion from Japan, for his time, insights, and willingness during a New York visit to try out a Papaya King hot dog as well as a Hebrew National, even though he's not particularly fond of hot dogs except when he's eating eight or ten of them per minute. It was the ultimate busman's holiday, and Kobayashi could not have been more gracious.

62–64 WHO BECOMES A TERRORIST? See Alan B. Krueger, *What Makes a Terrorist* (Princeton University Press, 2007); Claude Berrebi, "Evidence About the Link Between Education, Poverty and Terrorism Among Palestinians," Princeton University Industrial Relations Section working paper, 2003; and Krueger and Jita Maleckova, "Education, Poverty and Terrorism: Is There a Causal Connection?" *Journal of Economic Perspectives* 17, no. 4 (Fall 2003). / 63 For more on **terrorists' goals,** see Mark Juergensmeyer, *Terror in the Mind of God* (University of California Press, 2001). / 63–64 **Terrorism hard to define:** see "Muslim Nations Fail to Define Terrorism," Associated Press, April 3, 2002.

64–66 WHY TERRORISM IS SO CHEAP AND EASY: **The murder count in the Washington, D.C., metro area** was provided by the Federal Bureau of Investigation, which collects crime statistics from local police departments. The Washington, D.C., Metropolitan Statistical Area includes the district itself and surrounding counties in Maryland, Virginia, and West Virginia. For more on the **impact of the Washington sniper attacks,** see Jeffrey Schulden et al., "Psychological Responses to the Sniper Attacks: Washington D.C., Area, October 2002," *American Journal of Preventative Medicine* 31, no. 4 (October 2006). / 65 Figures for **airport security screenings** come from the Federal Bureau of Transportation

Statistics. / 65 **Financial impact of 9/11:** see Dick K. Nanto, "9/11 Terrorism: Global Economic Costs," *Congressional Research Service,* 2004. / 65–66 **Extra driving deaths after 9/11:** see Garrick Blalock, Vrinda Kadiyali, and Daniel Simon, "Driving Fatalities after 9/11: A Hidden Cost of Terrorism," Cornell University Department of Applied Economics and Management working paper, 2005; Gerd Gigerenzer, "Dread Risk, September 11, and Fatal Traffic Accidents," *Psychological Science* 15, no. 4 (2004); Michael Sivak and Michael J. Flannagan, "Consequences for Road Traffic Fatalities of the Reduction in Flying Following September 11, 2001," *Transportation Research* 7, nos. 4–5 (July–September 2004); and Jenny C. Su et al., "Driving Under the Influence (of Stress): Evidence of a Regional Increase in Impaired Driving and Traffic Fatalities After the September 11 Terrorist Attacks," *Psychological Science* 20, no. 1 (December 2008). / 66 **Back-dated stock options:** see Mark Maremont, Charles Forelle, and James Bandler, "Companies Say Backdating Used in Days After 9/11," *The Wall Street Journal,* March 7, 2007. / 66 **Police resources shifted to terrorism:** see Selwyn Raab, *Five Families: The Rise, Decline and Resurgence of America's Most Powerful Mafia Empires* (Macmillan, 2005); Janelle Nanos, "Stiffed," *New York,* November 6, 2006; Suzy Jagger, "F.B.I. Diverts Anti-Terror Agents to Bernard Madoff $50 Billion Swindle," *The Times* (London), December 22, 2008; and Eric Lichtblau, "Federal Cases of Stock Fraud Drop Sharply," *The New York Times,* December 24, 2008. / 66 **Influenza and airline travel:** see John Brownstein, Cecily Wolfe, and Kenneth Mandl, "Empirical Evidence for the Effect of Airline Travel on Interregional Influenza Spread in the United States," *PloS Medicine,* October 2006. / 66 **Crime drop in D.C.:** see Jonathan Klick and Alexander Tabarrok, "Using Terror Alert Levels to Estimate the Effect of Police on Crime," *Journal of Law and Economics* 48, no. 1 (April 2005). / 66 **A California pot bonanza:** see "Home-Grown," *The Economist,* October 18, 2007; and Jeffrey Miron, "The Budgetary Implications of Drug Prohibition," Harvard University, December 2008.

66–74 THE MAN WHO FIXES HOSPITALS: This section is based primarily on author interviews with Craig Feied as well as other members of his team, including Mark Smith. We also benefited substantially from Rosabeth Moss Kanter and Michelle Heskett, "Washington Hospital Center," a four-part series in *Harvard Business School,* July 21, 2002, N9-303-010 through N9-303-022. / 67 **Emergency medicine as a specialty:** see Derek R. Smart, *Physician Characteristics and Distribution in the U.S.* (American Medical Association Press, 2007). / 67 **E.R. statistics:** see Eric W. Nawar, Richard W. Niska, and Jiamin Xu, "National Hospital Ambulatory Medical Care Survey: 2005 Emergency Department Summary," *Advance Data from Vital and Health Statistics,* Centers for Disease Control, June 29, 2007; and information gleaned from the Federal Agency for Healthcare Research and Quality (AHRQ), as well as these AHRQ reports: Pamela Horsleys and Anne Elixhauser, "Hospital Admissions That Began in the Emergency Department, 2003," and Healthcare Cost and Utilization Project (H-CUP) Statistical Brief No. 1., February 2006. / 71 **"It's about what you do in the first sixty minutes":** drawn from Fred D. Baldwin, "It's All About Speed," *Healthcare Informatics,* November 2000. / 72 **"Cognitive drift":** see R. Miller, "Response Time in Man-Computer Conversational Transactions," *Proceedings of the AFIPS Fall Joint Computer Conference,* 1968; and B. Shneiderman, "Response Time and Display Rate in Human Performance with Computers," *Computing Surveys,* 1984.

74–82 WHO ARE THE BEST AND WORST DOCTORS IN THE ER?: This section is based primarily on Mark Duggan and Steven D. Levitt, "Assessing Differences in Skill Across Emergency Room Physicians," working paper. / 74–75 The **negative effect of doctor report cards:** see David Dranove, Daniel Kessler, Mark McClellan, and Mark Satterthwaite, "Is More Information Better?" *Journal of Political Economy* 111, no. 3 (2003). / 81–82 **Do doctors' strikes save lives?:** see Robert S. Mendelsohn, *Confessions of a Medical Heretic* (Contemporary Books, 1979); and Solveig Argeseanu Cunningham, Kristina Mitchell, K. M. Venkat Narayan, and Salim Yusuf, "Doctors' Strikes and Mortality: A Review," *Social Science and Medicine* 67, no. 11 (December 2008).

82–84 WAYS TO POSTPONE DEATH: **Win a Nobel Prize:** see Matthew D. Rablen and Andrew J. Oswald, "Mortality and Immortality,"

University of Warwick, January 2007; and Donald MacLeod, "Nobel Winners Live Longer, Say Researchers," *The Guardian*, January 17, 2007. **Make the Hall of Fame:** see David J. Becker, Kenneth Y. Chay, and Shailender Swaminathan, "Mortality and the Baseball Hall of Fame: An Investigation into the Role of Status in Life Expectancy," iHEA 2007 6th World Congress: Explorations in Health Economics paper. **Buy annuities:** see Thomas J. Phillipson and Gary S. Becker, "Old-Age Longevity and Mortality-Contingent Claims," *Journal of Political Economy* 106, no. 3 (1998). **Be religious:** see Ellen L. Idler and Stanislav V. Kasl, "Religion, Disability, Depression, and the Timing of Death," *American Journal of Sociology* 97, no. 4 (January 1992). **Be patriotic:** see David McCullough, *John Adams* (Simon & Schuster, 2001). **Beat the estate tax:** Joshua Gans and Andrew Leigh, "Did the Death of Australian Inheritance Taxes Affect Deaths?" *Topics in Economic Analysis and Policy* (Berkeley Electronic Press, 2006).

84–86 THE TRUTHS ABOUT CHEMOTHERAPY: This section was drawn in part from interviews with practicing oncologists and oncology researchers including Thomas J. Smith, Max Wicha, Peter D. Eisenberg, Jerome Groopman, as well as several participants at "Requirements for the Cure for Cancer," an off-the-record 2007 conference organized by Arny Glazier and the Van Andel Research Institute. (Thanks to Rafe Furst for the invitation.) See also: Thomas G. Roberts Jr., Thomas J. Lynch Jr., Bruce A. Chabner, "Choosing Chemotherapy for Lung Cancer Based on Cost: Not Yet," *Oncologist*, June 1, 2002; Scott Ramsey et al., "Economic Analysis of Vinorelbine Plus Cisplatin Versus Paclitaxel Plus Carboplatin for Advanced Non-Small-Cell Lung Cancer," *Journal of the National Cancer Institute* 94, no. 4 (February 20, 2002); Graeme Morgan, Robyn Wardy, and Michael Bartonz, "The Contribution of Cytotoxic Chemotherapy to 5-year Survival in Adult Malignancies," *Clinical Oncology* 16 (2004); Guy Faguet, *The War on Cancer: An Anatomy of Failure, a Blueprint for the Future* (Springer Netherlands, 2005); Neal J. Meropol and Kevin A. Schulman, "Cost of Cancer Care: Issues and Implications," *Clinical Oncology* 25, no. 2 (January 2007); and Bruce

Hillner and Thomas J. Smith, "Efficacy Does Not Necessarily Translate to Cost Effectiveness: A Case Study in the Challenges Associated with 21st Century Cancer Drug Pricing," *Journal of Clinical Oncology* 27, no. 13 (May 2009). / 86 **"The deep and abiding desire not to be dead":** Thomas Smith offered this quotation from memory, attributing it to his colleague Thomas Finucane, writing in "How Gravely Ill Becomes Dying: A Key to End-of-Life Care," *Journal of the American Medical Association* 282 (1999). But Smith had, in his memory, slightly improved Finucane's original quote, which was "the widespread and deeply held desire not to be dead."

86 LIVING LONG ENOUGH TO DIE FROM CANCER: See Bo E. Honore and Adriana Lleras-Muney, "Bounds in Competing Risks Models and the War on Cancer," *Econometrica* 76, no. 6 (November 2006).

87 WAR: NOT AS DANGEROUS AS YOU THINK?: Derived from "U.S. Active Duty Military Deaths 1980 through 2008 (as of April 22, 2009)," prepared by the Defense Manpower Data Center for Department of Defense; thanks to a reader named Adam Smith (seriously) for alerting us to these data.

87–96 HOW TO CATCH A TERRORIST: This section is drawn from "Identifying Terrorists Using Banking Data," Steven D. Levitt and A. Danger Powers, working paper; and from author interviews with Ian Horsley (a pseudonym), primarily in London. / 89 **Bank fraud in the U.K.:** gleaned from the Association for Payment Clearing Services (APACS). / 92 **False positives in cancer screening:** see Jennifer Miller Croswell et al., "Cumulative Incidence of False-Positive Results in Repeated, Multimodal Cancer Screening," *Annals of Family Medicine* 7 (2009). / 92 **Mike Lowell:** see Jimmy Golen, "Lowell: Baseball Held to Higher Standard," The Associated Press, January 18, 2008. / 92 **Release of terror suspects:** see Alan Travis, "Two-Thirds of U.K. Terror Suspects Released Without Charge," *The Guardian,* May 12, 2009.

CHAPTER 3: UNBELIEVABLE STORIES ABOUT APATHY AND ALTRUISM

97–100 KITTY GENOVESE AND THE "38 WITNESSES": This section, as well as the section at the end of the chapter about Kitty Genovese, benefited greatly from the time and input of Joseph De May Jr., who has created a repository of documentary evidence about the murder at www.kewgardenshistory.com. We are also indebted to many others who contributed their knowledge of the case in interviews or correspondence, including Andrew Blauner, Mike Hoffman, Jim Rasenberger, Charles Skoller, Jim Solomon, and Harold Takooshian. And we drew extensively from some of the many books and articles written about the murder, including: Martin Gansberg, "37 Who Saw Murder Didn't Call the Police: Apathy at Stabbing of Queens Woman Shocks Inspector," *The New York Times,* March 27, 1964; A.M. Rosenthal, *Thirty-Eight Witnesses: The Kitty Genovese Case* (Melville House, 2008; originally published 1964 by McGraw-Hill); Elliot Aronson, *The Social Animal,* 5th ed. (W.H. Freeman and Co., 1988); Joe Sexton, "Reviving Kitty Genovese Case, and Its Passions," *The New York Times,* July 25, 1995; Malcolm Gladwell, *The Tipping Point* (Little, Brown, 2000); Jim Rasenberger, "Nightmare on Austin Street," *American Heritage,* October 2006; Charles Skoller, *Twisted Confessions* (Bridgeway Books, 2008); Rachel Manning, Mark Levine, and Alan Collins, "The Kitty Genovese Murder and the Social Psychology of Helping: The Parable of the 38 Witnesses," *American Psychologist* 62, no. 6 (2007). / 97 **Weather conditions in Queens** were provided by the National Weather Service. / 99 **Genovese and the Holocaust:** see Maureen Dowd, "20 Years After the Murder of Kitty Genovese, the Question Remains: Why?" *The New York Times,* March 12, 1984. Dowd cites R. Lance Shotland, a professor of psychology at Pennsylvania State University, who noted that "probably no single incident has caused social psychologists to pay as much attention to an aspect of social behavior as Kitty Genovese's murder." / 99 **Bill Clinton's statement** about the Genovese murder comes from his remarks at the AmeriCorps Public Safety Forum in New York City, March 10, 1994.

100–104 CRIME AND TELEVISION IN AMERICA: This section is primarily drawn from Steven D. Levitt and Matthew Gentzkow, "Measuring the

Impact of TV's Introduction on Crime," working paper. See also: Matthew Gentzkow, "Television and Voter Turnout," *Quarterly Journal of Economics* 121, no. 3 (August 2006); and Matthew Gentzkow and Jesse M. Shapiro, "Preschool Television Viewing and Adolescent Test Scores: Historical Evidence from the Coleman Study," *Quarterly Journal of Economics* 123, no. 1 (February 2008). / 101 **Prison overcrowding and the ACLU "experiment":** see Steven D. Levitt, "The Effect of Prison Population Size on Crime Rates: Evidence from Prison Overcrowding Litigation," *The Quarterly Journal of Economics* 11, no. 2 (May 1996).

105 FAMILY ALTRUISM?: See Gary Becker, "Altruism in the Family and Selfishness in the Marketplace," *Economica* 48, no. 189, New Series (February 1981); and B. Douglas Bernheim, Andrei Shleifer, and Lawrence H. Summers, "The Strategic Bequest Motive," *Journal of Political Economy* 93, no. 6 (December 1985).

106–107 AMERICANS ARE FAMOUSLY ALTRUISTIC: These figures are drawn from an Indiana University Center on Philanthropy study. From 1996 to 2006, overall American giving increased from $139 billion to $295 billion (inflation-adjusted), which represents an increase from 1.7% of GDP to 2.6% of GDP. See also David Leonhardt, "What Makes People Give," *The New York Times,* March 9, 2008. / 107 For more on **disaster donations and TV coverage,** see Philip H. Brown and Jessica H. Minty, "Media Coverage and Charitable Giving After the 2004 Tsunami," *Southern Economic Journal* 75, no. 1 (2008).

107 THE VALUE OF LAB EXPERIMENTS: **Galileo's acceleration experiment** is related in Galileo Galilei, *Dialogue Concerning Two New Sciences,* trans. Henry Crew and Alfonso de Salvio, 1914. **Richard Feynman's point** about the primacy of experimentation comes from his *Lectures on Physics,* ed. Matthew Linzee Sands (Addison-Wesley, 1963).

108–111 ULTIMATUM AND DICTATOR: The first paper on **Ultimatum** as it is commonly known is Werner Guth, Rolf Schmittberger, and Bernd Schwarze, "An Experimental Analysis of Ultimatum Bargaining," *Journal of Economic Behavior and Organization* 3, no. 4 (1982). For a good background on the evolution of such games, see Steven D. Levitt and John A. List, "What Do Laboratory Experiments Measuring Social Preferences Tell Us About the Real World," *Journal of Economic Perspectives* 21, no. 2 (2007). See also: Daniel Kahneman, Jack L. Knetsch, and Richard Thaler, "Fairness as a Constraint on Profit Seeking: Entitlements in the Market," *American Economic Review* 76, no. 4 (September 1986); Robert Forsythe, Joel L. Horowitz, N. E. Savin, and Martin Sefton, "Fairness in Simple Bargaining Experiments," *Games and Economic Behavior* 6, no. 3 (May 1994); Colin F. Camerer, *Behavioral Game Theory* (Princeton University Press, 2003); and John A. List, "Dictator Game Giving Is an Experimental Artifact," working paper, 2005.

111–113 ORGAN TRANSPLANTS: The **first successful long-term kidney transplant** was performed at the Peter Bent Brigham Hospital in Boston by Joseph Murray in December 1954, as related in Nicholas Tilney, *Transplant: From Myth to Reality* (Yale University Press, 2003). / 111 **"Donorcyclists":** see Stacy Dickert-Conlin, Todd Elder, and Brian Moore, "Donorcycles: Do Motorcycle Helmet Laws Reduce Organ Donations?" Michigan State University working paper, 2009. / 111 **"Presumed consent"** laws in Europe: see Alberto Abadie and Sebastien Gay, "The Impact of Presumed Consent Legislation on Cadaveric Organ Donation: A Cross Country Study," *Journal of Health Economics* 25, no. 4 (July 2006). / 112 **The Iranian kidney program** is described in Ahad J. Ghods and Shekoufeh Savaj, "Iranian Model of Paid and Regulated Living-Unrelated Kidney Donation," *Clinical Journal of the American Society of Nephrology* 1 (October 2006); and Benjamin E. Hippen, "Organ Sales and Moral Travails: Lessons from the Living Kidney Vendor Program in Iran," Cato Institute, *Policy Analysis,* no. 614, March 20, 2008. / 112 The **exchange between Dr. Barry Jacobs and Rep. Al Gore** took place in the Hearings before the Subcommittee on Health and the Environment to consider H.R. 4080, October 17, 1983.

113–123 JOHN LIST, GAME-CHANGER: This section is drawn primarily from author interviews with John A. List as well as a number of his many, many papers, several written in collaboration with Steven D. Levitt. These papers include: List, "Does Market Experience

Eliminate Market Anomalies?" *Quarterly Journal of Economics* 118, no. 1 (2003); Glenn Harrison and List, "Field Experiments," *Journal of Economic Literature* 42 (December 2004); List, "Dictator Game Giving Is an Experimental Artifact," working paper, 2005; List, "The Behavioralist Meets the Market: Measuring Social Preferences and Reputation Effects in Actual Transactions," *Journal of Political Economy* 14, no. 1 (2006); Levitt and List, "Viewpoint: On the Generalizability of Lab Behaviour to the Field," *Canadian Journal of Economics* 40, no. 2 (May 2007); Levitt and List, "What Do Laboratory Experiments Measuring Social Preferences Tell Us About the Real World," *Journal of Economic Perspectives* 21, no. 2 (2007); List, "On the Interpretation of Giving in Dictator Games," *Journal of Political Economy* 115, no. 3 (2007); List and Todd L. Cherry, "Examining the Role of Fairness in High Stakes Allocation Decisions," *Journal of Economic Behavior & Organization* 65, no. 1 (2008); Levitt and List, "Homo Economicus Evolves," *Science,* February 15, 2008; Levitt, List, and David Reiley, "What Happens in the Field Stays in the Field: Professionals Do Not Play Minimax in Laboratory Experiments," *Econometrica* (forthcoming, 2009); Levitt and List, "Field Experiments in Economics: The Past, the Present, and the Future," *European Economic Review* (forthcoming, 2009). Note that other researchers have begun questioning whether altruism seen in the lab is an artifact of the experiment itself; notably, see Nicholas Bardsley, "Experimental Economics and the Artificiality of Alteration," *Journal of Economic Methodology* 12, no. 2 (2005). / 121 **"Just those sophomores"** and "scientific do-gooders": see R. L. Rosenthal, *Artifact in Behavioral Research* (Academic Press, 1969). / 121 **"Higher need for approval":** see Richard L. Doty and Colin Silverthorne, "Influence of Menstrual Cycle on Volunteering Behavior," *Nature,* 1975. / 121 **The boss washing her hands:** see Kristen Munger and Shelby J. Harris, "Effects of an Observer on Hand Washing in a Public Restroom," *Perceptual and Motor Skills* 69 (1989). / 122 **The "honesty box" experiment:** see Melissa Bateson, Daniel Nettle, and Gilbert Roberts, "Cues of Being Watched Enhance Cooperation in a Real-World Setting," *Biology Letters,* 2006. Along these same lines, consider another clever field experiment, this one conducted in thirty Dutch churches by a young economist named Adriaan R. Soetevent. In these churches, the collection was taken up in a closed bag that was passed along from person to person, row to row. Soetevent got the churches to let him switch things up, randomly substituting an open collection basket for the closed bags over a period of several months. He wanted to know if the added scrutiny changed the donation patterns. (An open basket lets you see how much money has already been collected as well as how much your neighbor puts in.) Indeed it did: with open baskets, the churchgoers gave more money, including fewer small-denomination coins, than with closed bags—although, interestingly, the effect petered out once the open baskets had been around for a while. See Soetevent, "Anonymity in Giving in a Natural Context—a Field Experiment in 30 Churches," *Journal of Public Economics* 89 (2005). / 123 A **"stupid automaton":** see A.H. Pierce, "The Subconscious Again," *Journal of Philosophy, Psychology, & Scientific Methods* 5 (1908). / 123 **"Forced cooperation":** see Martin T. Orne, "On the Social Psychological Experiment: With Particular Reference to Demand Characteristics and Their Implications," *American Psychologist* 17, no. 10 (1962). / 123 **"Why Nazi officers obeyed":** see Stanley Milgram, "Behavioral Study of Obedience," *Journal of Abnormal and Social Psychology* 67, no. 4 (1963). / 123 The **Stanford prison experiments:** see Craig Haney, Curtis Banks, and Philip Zimbardo, "Interpersonal Dynamics in a Simulated Prison," *International Journal of Criminology and Penology* 1 (1973).

123–125 "IMPURE ALTRUISM": **Americans as top givers:** see "International Comparisons of Charitable Giving," Charities Aid Foundation briefing paper, November 2006. And for the correspondingly strong tax incentives, see David Roodman and Scott Standley, "Tax Policies to Promote Private Charitable Giving in DAC Countries," *Center for Global Development*, working paper, January 2006. / 124 **"Impure" and "warm-glow" altruism:** see James Andreoni, "Giving with Impure Altruism: Applications to Charity and Ricardian Equivalence," *Journal of Political Economy* 97 (December 1989); and Andreoni, "Impure Altruism and Donations to Public Goods: A Theory of Warm-Glow Giving," *Economic Journal* 100 (June 1990). / 124 **The economics of panhandling:** see Gary S. Becker, "Spouses and Beggars: Love and Sympathy," in *Accounting for Tastes* (Harvard University Press, 1998). / 124 **Organ transplant waiting lists:** this information was gleaned from the U.S. Department of Health and Human Services' Organ Procurement and Transplant Network website, at www.optn.org. Further material was generated by the economist Julio Jorge Elias of State University of New York, Buffalo. See also Becker and Elias, "Introducing Incentives in the Market for Live and Cadaveric Organ Donations," *Journal of Economic Perspectives* 21, no. 3 (Summer 2007); and Stephen J. Dubner and Steven D. Levitt, "Flesh Trade," *The New York Times Magazine*, July 9, 2006. / 124–125 **No waiting list in Iran:** see Benjamin E. Hippen, "Organ Sales and Moral Travails: Lessons from the Living Kidney Vendor Program in Iran," Cato Institute, *Policy Analysis*, no. 614, March 20, 2008; and Stephen J. Dubner, "Human Organs for Sale, Legally, in . . . *Which* Country?" Freakonomics blog, *The New York Times*, April 29, 2008.

125–131 KITTY GENOVESE REVISITED: See the notes at the top of this chapter section for a list of the sources we relied upon for the reappraisal of the case. This second section drew substantially on interviews with Joseph De May Jr. and Mike Hoffman, as well as A.M. Rosenthal's book *Thirty-Eight Witnesses*. . . . One of us (Dubner) had the opportunity to work with Rosenthal as the latter's days at the *Times* expired. Even toward the end of his life (he died in 2006), Rosenthal remained a forceful journalist and an exceedingly sharp-opinioned man who didn't suffer fools or, as some have argued, dissenting opinions. In 2004, Rosenthal participated in a symposium at Fordham University in New York to mark the fortieth anniversary of the Genovese murder. He offered a singular explanation for his obsession with the case: "Why did the Genovese incident move me so deeply? I tell you this. I had five sisters, and I was the youngest. What loving and magnificent sisters I had. But one of my sisters was murdered. Young Bess was returning home two nights before New Year's through a path in Van Cortlandt Park, when a sexual pervert jumped out of the bushes and exposed himself to her. In shock, she escaped, and ran home one mile, sweaty in the chill weather. Within two days, Bess fell ill and died. I still miss our darling Bess, and feel Bess was murdered by this criminal who took her life away, no less than the monster who killed Kitty Genovese." . . . The Genovese murder caused many pundits to dust off a famous remark uttered by Edmund Burke two centuries earlier: "The only thing necessary for the triumph of evil is for good men to do nothing." It seemed to perfectly sum up what happened that night. But Fred Shapiro, editor of *The Yale Book of Quotations,* could never find anything like this line in Burke's writings. Which means that this famous quotation—along with, seemingly, half the quotes attributed to Mark Twain and Oscar Wilde—appears to be as apocryphal as the story of the thirty-eight witnesses.

CHAPTER 4: THE FIX IS IN—AND IT'S CHEAP AND SIMPLE

133 MATERNAL DEATH RATES: For recent figures, see "Maternal Mortality in 2005: Estimates Developed by WHO, UNICEF, UNFPA, and the World Bank," World Health Organization, 2007. For historical rates, see Irvine Loudon, "Maternal Mortality in the Past and Its Relevance to Developing Countries Today," *American Journal of Clinical Nutrition* 72, no. 1 (July 2000).

134–138 IGNATZ SEMMELWEIS COMES TO THE RESCUE: The story of Ignatz Semmelweis has been told variously over the years, but perhaps the most impressive telling is Sherwin B. Nuland, *The Doctor's Plague: Germs, Childbed Fever, and the Strange Story of Ignatz Semmelweis* (Atlas Books, 2003). This may be because Nuland is a physician himself. We have drawn substantially from his book, and we are greatly indebted. See also: Ignatz Semmelweis, "The Etiology, Concept, and Prophylaxis of Childbed Fever," trans. K. Codell Carter (University of Wisconsin Press, 1983; originally published 1861). Note: *Puerpera* is Latin for a woman who has given birth.

138–140 UNINTENDED CONSEQUENCES: For an overview, see Stephen J. Dubner and Steven D. Levitt, "Unintended Consequence," *The New*

York Times Magazine, January 20, 2008. / 139 For the **Americans with Disabilities Act,** see Daron Acemoglu and Joshua D. Angrist, "Consequences of Employment Protection? The Case of the Americans with Disabilities Act," *Journal of Political Economy* 109, no. 5 (2001). / 139 For the **Endangered Species Act,** see Dean Lueck and Jeffrey A. Michael, "Preemptive Habitat Destruction Under the Endangered Species Act," *Journal of Law and Economics* 46 (April 2003); and John A. List, Michael Margolis, and Daniel E. Osgood, "Is the Endangered Species Act Endangering Species?" National Bureau of Economic Research working paper, December 2006. / 139 **Avoiding the trash tax:** for the **"Seattle Stomp,"** the **Charlottesville woods-dumping,** and other tactics, see Don Fullerton and Thomas C. Kinnaman, "Household Responses to Pricing Garbage by the Bag," *American Economic Review* 86, no. 4 (September 1996); for **German food-flushing,** see Roger Boyes, "Children Beware: The Rats Are Back and Hamelin Needs a New Piper," *The Times* (London), December 17, 2008; for **backyard burning in Dublin,** see S.M. Murphy, C. Davidson, A.M. Kennedy, P.A. Eadie, and C. Lawlor, "Backyard Burning," *Journal of Plastic, Reconstructive & Aesthetic Surgery* 61, no. 1 (February 2008). / 140 **The sabbatical backlash**: see Solomon Zeitlin, "Prosbol: A Study in Tannaitic Jurisprudence," *The Jewish Quarterly Review* 37, no. 4 (April 1947). (Thanks to Leon Morris for the tip.)

141 FORCEPS HOARDING: See James Hobson Aveling, *The Chamberlens and the Midwifery Forceps* (J. & A. Churchill, 1882); Atul Gawande, "The Score: How Childbirth Went Industrial," *The New Yorker,* October 2, 2006; and Stephen J. Dubner, "Medical Failures, and Successes Too: A Q&A with Atul Gawande," Freakonomics blog, *The New York Times,* June 25, 2007.

141–142 MORE FOOD, MORE PEOPLE: See "The World at Six Billion," *United Nations,* 1999; Mark Overton, *Agricultural Revolution in England: The Transformation of the Agrarian Economy, 1500–1850* (Cambridge University Press, 1996); and Milton Friedman and Rose Friedman, *Free to Choose* (Harvest, 1990; originally published 1979). Information from Will Masters, a professor of agricultural economics at Purdue, came from an author interview.

For a stunning exhibition of Masters's mastery at setting theories of agricultural economics to verse, see Stephen J. Dubner, "Why Are Kiwis So Cheap?" Freakonomics blog, *The New York Times,* June 4, 2009.

142–143 CONSIDER THE WHALE: The rise and fall of whale hunting is beautifully told in Eric Jay Dolin, *Leviathan: The History of Whaling in America* (W.W. Norton & Company, 2007). See also: Charles Melville Scammon, *The Marine Mammals of the Northwestern Coast of North America: Together with an Account of the American Whale-Fishery,* 1874; Alexander Starbuck, *History of the American Whale Fishery From Its Earliest Inception to the Year 1876,* published by the author, 1878; and Paul Gilmour, "Saving the Whales, Circa 1852," Letter to the Editor, *The Wall Street Journal,* December 6, 2008.

143–146 THE MYSTERIES OF POLIO: See David M. Oshinsky, *Polio: An American Story* (Oxford University Press, 2005), a truly excellent book on the topic; and "The Battle Against Polio," *NewsHour with Jim Lehrer,* PBS, April 24, 2006. / 144 The **fallacious polio/ice-cream link** was raised by David Alan Grier, a statistician at George Washington University, in Steve Lohr, "For Today's Graduate, Just One Word: Statistics," *The New York Times,* August 5, 2009. / 145 For estimated **cost savings of the polio vaccines,** see Kimberly M. Thompson and Radboud J. Duintjer Tebbens, "Retrospective Cost-Effectiveness Analysis for Polio Vaccination in the United States," *Risk Analysis* 26, no. 6 (2006); and Tebbens et al., "A Dynamic Model of Poliomyelitis Outbreaks: Learning from the Past to Help Inform the Future," *American Journal of Epidemiology* 162, no. 4 (July 2005). / 145–146 For **other cheap and simple medical fixes,** see Marc W. Kirschner, Elizabeth Marincola, and Elizabeth Olmsted Teisberg, "The Role of Biomedical Research in Health Care Reform," *Science* 266 (October 7, 1994); and Earl S. Ford et al., "Explaining the Decrease in U.S. Deaths from Coronary Disease, 1980–2000," *New England Journal of Medicine* 356, no. 23 (June 7, 2007).

146 THE KILLER CAR: For **number of cars in the 1950s,** see "Topics and Sidelights of the Day in Wall Street: Fuel Consumption," *The New*

York Times, May 25, 1951. For **industry fears** over safety concerns, see "Fear Seen Cutting Car Traffic, Sales," *The New York Times,* January 29, 1952.

146–150 THE STRANGE STORY OF ROBERT MCNAMARA'S SEAT BELT: This section is based on a number of sources, including author interviews with McNamara shortly before his death. See also: "A Life in Public Service: Conversation with Robert McNamara," April 16, 1996, by Harry Kreisler, part of the Conversations with History series, Institute of International Studies, University of California, Berkeley; *The Fog of War: Eleven Lessons from the Life of Robert S. McNamara,* directed by Errol Morris, 2003, Sony Pictures Classics; Richard Alan Johnson, *Six Men Who Built the Modern Auto Industry* (MotorBooks/MBI Publishing Company, 2005); and Johnson, "The Outsider: How Robert McNamara Changed the Automobile Industry," *American Heritage,* Summer 2007. / 149 **Seat belt usage over time:** see Steven D. Levitt and Jack Porter, "Sample Selection in the Estimation of Air Bag and Seat Belt Effectiveness," *The Review of Economics and Statistics* 83, no. 4 (November 2001). / 149 For **lives saved by seat belts,** see Donna Glassbrenner, "Estimating the Lives Saved by Safety Belts and Air Bags," National Highway Traffic Safety Administration, paper no. 500; and "Lives Saved in 2008 by Restraint Use and Minimum Drinking Age Laws," NHTSA, June 2009. / 149 **3 trillion miles driven per year:** gleaned from U.S. Bureau of Transportation Statistics . . . / 149 **Dangerous roads on other continents:** see "Road Safety: A Public Health Issue," World Health Organization, March 29, 2004. / 149–150 The **cost of a life saved by a seat belt versus an air bag:** see Levitt and Porter, "Sample Selection in the Estimation of Air Bag and Seat Belt Effectiveness," *The Review of Economics and Statistics* 83, no. 4 (November 2001).

150–158 HOW MUCH GOOD DO CAR SEATS DO? This section is primarily based on Steven D. Levitt, "Evidence That Seat Belts Are as Effective as Child Safety Seats in Preventing Death for Children," *The Review of Economics and Statistics* 90, no. 1 (February 2008); Levitt and Joseph J. Doyle, "Evaluating the Effectiveness of Child Safety Seats and Seat Belts in Protecting Children from Injury," *Economic Inquiry,* forthcoming; and Levitt and Stephen J. Dubner,

"The Seat-Belt Solution," *The New York Times Magazine,* July 10, 2005. For a brief **history of child safety seats,** see: Charles J. Kahane, "An Evaluation of Child Passenger Safety: The Effectiveness and Benefits of Safety Seats," National Highway Traffic Safety Administration, February 1986. / 155–156 **"A group of prominent child-safety researchers":** see Flaura K. Winston, Dennis R. Durbin, Michael J. Kallan, and Elisa K. Moll, "The Danger of Premature Graduation to Seat Belts for Young Children," *Pediatrics* 105 (2000); and Dennis R. Durbin, Michael R. Elliott, and Flaura K. Winston, "Belt-Positioning Booster Seats and Reduction in Risk of Injury Among Children in Vehicle Crashes," *Journal of the American Medical Association* 289, no. 21 (June 4, 2003).

158–159 HURRICANE STATISTICS: Data on **worldwide hurricane deaths** were provided by the Emergency Events Database, hosted by the Université catholique de Louvain; the U.S. death count was obtained from the National Hurricane Research Division of the National Oceanic and Atmospheric Association. The **economic cost in the United States alone:** see Roger Pielke Jr. et al., "Normalized Hurricane Damage in the United States: 1900–2005," *Natural Hazards Review,* February 2008. For more on **the Atlantic Multidecadal Oscillation,** see Stephen Gray, Lisa Graumlich, Julio Betancourt, and Gregory Pederson, "A Tree-Ring Based Reconstruction of the Atlantic Multidecadal Oscillation Since 1567 A.D.," *Geophysical Research Letters* 21 (June 17, 2004); Mihai Dima, "A Hemispheric Mechanism for the Atlantic Multidecadal Oscillation," *Journal of Climate* 20 (October 2006); David Enfield, Alberto Mestas-Nuñez, and Paul Trimble, "The Atlantic Multidecadal Oscillation and Its Relation to Rainfall and River Flows in the Continental U.S.," *Geophysical Research Letters* 28 (May 15, 2001); and Clive Thompson, "The Five-Year Forecast," *New York,* November 27, 2006.

159–163 "AN INTELLECTUALLY VENTURESOME FELLOW NAMED NATHAN": This section is drawn from author interviews with Nathan and his colleagues, whom the reader will meet in fuller detail in Chapter 5. Neal Stephenson—yes, the same one who writes phantasmagorical novels—was particularly helpful in walking us through some of the details and showing computer simulations. The hurricane killer described is also known as Jeffrey A. Bowers et al., "Water Alteration Structure Applications and Methods," U.S. Patent Application 20090173366, July 9, 2009. Among the "et al." authors is one William H. Gates III. The abstract from the patent application reads like this: "A method is generally described which includes environmental alteration. The method includes determining a placement of at least one vessel capable of moving water to lower depths in the water via wave induced downwelling. The method also includes placing at least one vessel in the determined placement. Further, the method includes generating movement of the water adjacent the surface of the water in response to the placing."

CHAPTER 5: WHAT DO AL GORE AND MOUNT PINATUBO HAVE IN COMMON?

165–166 LET'S MELT THE ICE CAP!: For the section on **global cooling,** see: Harold M. Schmeck Jr., "Climate Changes Endanger World's Food Output," *The New York Times,* August 8, 1974; Peter Gwynne, "The Cooling World," *Newsweek,* April 28, 1975; Walter Sullivan, "Scientists Ask Why World Climate Is Changing; Major Cooling May Be Ahead," *The New York Times,* May 21, 1975. Ground temperatures over the past 100 years can be found in "Climate Change 2007: Synthesis Report," U.N. Intergovernmental Panel on Climate Change (IPCC).

166 JAMES LOVELOCK: All Lovelock quotes in this chapter can be found in *The Revenge of Gaia: Earth's Climate Crisis and the Fate of Humanity* (Basic Books, 2006). Lovelock is a scientist perhaps best known as the originator of the Gaia hypothesis, which argues that the earth is essentially a living organism much like (but in many ways superior to) a human being. He has written several books on the subject, including the foundational *Gaia: The Practical Science of Planetary Medicine* (Gaia Books, 1991).

167 COWS ARE WICKED POLLUTERS: **The potency of methane** as a greenhouse gas as compared with carbon dioxide was calculated by the climate scientist Ken Caldeira, of the Carnegie Institution for

Science, based on the IPCC's Third Assessment Report. **Ruminants produce more greenhouse gas than transportation sector:** see "Livestock's Long Shadow: Environmental Issues and Options," Food and Agriculture Organization of the United Nations, Rome, 2006; and Shigeki Kobayashi, "Transport and Its Infrastructure," chapter 5 from IPCC Third Assessment Report, September 25, 2007.

167 WELL-MEANING LOCAVORES: See Christopher L. Weber and H. Scott Matthews, "Food-Miles and the Relative Climate Impacts of Food Choices in the United States," *Environmental Science and Technology* 42, no. 10 (April 2008); see also James McWilliams, "On Locavorism," Freakonomics blog, *The New York Times,* August 26, 2008; and McWilliams's forthcoming book, *Just Food* (Little, Brown, 2009).

167–168 EAT MORE KANGAROO: See "Eco-friendly Kangaroo Farts Could Help Global Warming: Scientists," Agence France-Press, December 5, 2007.

168–171 GLOBAL WARMING AS A "UNIQUELY THORNY PROBLEM": For the **"terrible-case scenario,"** see Martin L. Weitzman, "On Modeling and Interpreting the Economics of Catastrophic Climate Change," *The Review of Economics and Statistics* 91, no. 1 (February 2009). / 169 **A Stern warning:** see Nicholas Herbert Stern, *The Economics of Climate Change: The Stern Review* (Cambridge University Press, 2007). / 169 There is much to be read about **the influence of uncertainty,** especially as it compares with its cousin risk. The Israeli psychologists Amos Tversky and Daniel Kahneman, whose work is generally credited with giving ultimate birth to behavioral economics, conducted pioneering research on how people make decisions under pressure and found that uncertainty leads to "severe and systematic errors" in judgment. (See "Judgment Under Uncertainty: Heuristics and Biases," from *Judgment Under Uncertainty: Heuristics and Biases,* ed. Daniel Kahneman, Paul Slovic, and Amos Tversky [Cambridge University Press, 1982].) We wrote about the difference between risk and uncertainty in a *New York Times Magazine* column ("The Jane Fonda Effect," September 16, 2007) about the fear over nuclear power: "[The economist Frank Knight] made a distinction between two key factors in decision making: risk and uncertainty. The cardinal difference, Knight declared, is that risk—however great—can be measured, whereas uncertainty cannot. How do people weigh risk versus uncertainty? Consider a famous experiment that illustrates what is known as the Ellsberg Paradox. There are two urns. The first urn, you are told, contains 50 red balls and 50 black balls. The second one also contains 100 red and black balls, but the number of each color is unknown. If your task is to pick a red ball out of either urn, which urn do you choose? Most people pick the first urn, which suggests that they prefer a measurable risk to an immeasurable uncertainty. (This condition is known to economists as *ambiguity aversion.*) Could it be that nuclear energy, risks and all, is now seen as preferable to the uncertainties of global warming?" / 170 **Al Gore's "We" campaign:** see www.climateprotect.org and Andrew C. Revkin, "Gore Group Plans Ad Blitz on Global Warming," *The New York Times,* April 1, 2008. / 170 **The heretic Boris Johnson:** see Boris Johnson, "We've Lost Our Fear of Hellfire, but Put Climate Change in Its Place," *The Telegraph,* February 2, 2006. / 170 **"Rendered nearly lifeless":** see Peter Ward, *The Medea Hypothesis: Is Life on Earth Ultimately Self-Destructive?* (Princeton University Press, 2009); and Drake Bennett, "Dark Green: A Scientist Argues That the Natural World Isn't Benevolent and Sustaining: It's Bent on Self-Destruction," *The Boston Globe,* January 11, 2009. / 170–171 **Human activity and carbon emissions:** see Kenneth Chang, "Satellite Will Track Carbon Dioxide," *The New York Times,* February 22, 2009; read more about NASA's view of carbon dioxide at http://oco.jpl.nasa.gov/science/.

172 THE NEGATIVE EXTERNALITIES OF COAL MINING: For **American coal worker deaths**, see the U.S. Department of Labor, Mine Safety and Health Administration, "Coal Fatalities for 1900 Through 2008"; and Jeff Goodell, *Big Coal: The Dirty Secret Behind America's Energy Future* (Houghton Mifflin, 2007). Deaths from black lung were gleaned from National Institute for Occupational Safety and Health reports. **Chinese coal worker deaths**

were reported by the Chinese government to be 4,746 in 2006, 3,786 in 2007, and 3,215 in 2008; these numbers are likely underestimates. See "China Sees Coal Mine Deaths Fall, but Outlook Grim," Reuters, January 11, 2007; and "Correction: 3,215 Coal Mining Deaths in 2008," *China.org.cn,* February 9, 2009.

174–175 LOJACK: See Ian Ayres and Steven D. Levitt, "Measuring Positive Externalities from Unobservable Victim Precaution: An Empirical Analysis of LoJack," *Quarterly Journal of Economics* 113, no. 8 (February 1998).

175 APPLE TREES AND HONEY BEES: See J. E. Meade, "External Economies and Diseconomies in a Competitive Situation," *Economic Journal* 62, no. 245 (March 1952); and Steven N. S. Cheung, "The Fable of the Bees: An Economic Investigation," *Journal of Law and Economics* 16, no. 1 (April 1973). Cheung, in his paper, writes a remarkable sentence: "Facts, like jade, are not only costly to obtain but also difficult to authenticate." For a very strange twist on this insight, see Stephen J. Dubner, "Not as Authentic as It Seems," Freakonomics blog, *The New York Times,* March 23, 2009.

175–176 MOUNT PINATUBO: For one dramatic telling of the eruption, see Barbara Decker, *Volcanoes* (Macmillan, 2005). For its effect on global climate, see: Richard Kerr, "Pinatubo Global Cooling on Target," *Science,* January 1993; P. Minnis et al., "Radiative Climate Forcing by the Mount Pinatubo Eruption," *Science,* March 1993; Gregg J. S. Bluth et al., "Stratospheric Loading of Sulfur from Explosive Volcanic Eruptions," *Journal of Geology,* 1997; Brian J. Soden et al., "Global Cooling After the Eruption of Mount Pinatubo: A Test of Climate Feedback by Water Vapor," *Science,* April 2002; and T.M.L. Wigley, "A Combined Mitigation/Geoengineering Approach to Climate Stabilization," *Science,* October 2006.

177–203 INTELLECTUAL VENTURES AND GEOENGINEERING: This section is primarily drawn from a visit we made to the Intellectual Ventures lab in Bellevue, Washington, in early 2008, and from subsequent interviews and correspondence with Nathan Myhrvold, Ken Caldeira, Lowell Wood, John Latham, Bill Gates, Rod Hyde, Neal

Stephenson, Pablos Holman, and others. During our visit to IV, several other people contributed to the conversation, including Shelby Barnes, Wayt Gibbs, John Gilleand, Jordin Kare, Casey Tegreene, and Chuck Witmer. . . . **Conor and Cameron Myhrvold,** Nathan's college-age sons, also participated. They have already stepped into the invention racket themselves with a "wearable/portable protection system for a body," or a human air bag. From the patent application: "In an embodiment, system 100 may be worn by a locomotion-challenged person to cushion against prospective falls or collisions with environmental objects. In another embodiment, system 100 may be worn by athletes in lieu of traditional body-padding, helmets, and/or guards. In another embodiment, system 100 may be worn by people riding bicycles, skate-boarding, skating, skiing, snow-boarding, sledding and/or while engaged in various other sports or activities." . . . **For some interesting further reading on their father,** see: Ken Auletta, "The Microsoft Provocateur," *The New Yorker,* May 12, 1997; "Patent Quality and Improvement," Myhrvold's testimony before the Subcommittee on the Courts, the Internet and Intellectual Property, Committee on the Judiciary, House of Representatives, Congress of the United States, April 28, 2005; Jonathan Reynolds, "Kitchen Voyeur," *The New York Times Magazine,* October 16, 2005; Nicholas Varchaver, "Who's Afraid of Nathan Myhrvold," *Fortune,* July 10, 2006; Malcolm Gladwell, "In the Air; Annals of Innovation," *The New Yorker,* May 12, 2008; Amol Sharma and Don Clark, "Tech Guru Riles the Industry by Seeking Huge Patent Fees," *The Wall Street Journal,* September 18, 2008; Mike Ullman, "The Problem Solver," *Washington CEO,* December 2008. . . . **Myhrvold is himself famous** for writing—in particular, many long, provocative, extravagantly detailed memos that are intended primarily for internal use. See Auletta, above, for a good discussion of some of Myhrvold's Microsoft memos. Perhaps his greatest memo to date is one he wrote for his current company, back in 2003. It is called "What Makes a Great Invention?" We hope it will someday be made available for public consumption. / 177 **Mosquito laser assassination:** for more fascinating detail, see Robert A. Guth, "Rocket Scientists Shoot Down Mosquitoes with Lasers," *The Wall Street Journal,* March 14–15,

2009. / 178 "I don't know anyone [who] is smarter than Nathan": see Auletta, above. / 179 **More *T. rex* skeletons:** see Gladwell, above; based also on correspondence with the paleontologist Jack Horner, with whom Myhrvold collaborates in hunting for dinosaur bones. / 180 **Definitive research . . . including climate science:** see, e.g., Edward Teller, Lowell Wood, and Roderick Hyde, "Global Warming and Ice Ages: I. Prospects for Physics-Based Modulation of Global Change," 22nd International Seminar on Planetary Emergencies, Erice (Sicily), Italy, August 20–23, 1997; Ken Caldeira and Lowell Wood, "Global and Arctic Climate Engineering: Numerical Model Studies," *Philosophical Transactions of the Royal Society,* November 13, 2008. / 180 **For the next ten hours or so:** During a break, if you were to casually ask Myhrvold a question of interest—his take on, say, whether an asteroid strike was indeed responsible for the extinction of dinosaurs—he is apt to regale you with a long narrative history of the various competing theories, the logic (and caveats) behind the ultimate winning theory, and the fallacies (and lesser truths) behind the losers. On this particular question, Myhrvold's short answer is: yes. / 181 **Wood himself was a protégé:** for an excellent exploration of geoengineering that is also a dual profile of Lowell Wood and Ken Caldeira, see Chris Mooney, "Can a Million Tons of Sulfur Dioxide Combat Climate Change?" *Wired,* June 23, 2008. / 181 **"As many as a million":** see Gladwell, above. / 182–183 **Myhrvold cites a recent paper:** see Robert Vautard, Pascal Yiou, and Geert Jan van Oldenborgh, "Decline of Fog, Mist and Haze in Europe Over the Past 30 Years," *Nature Geoscience* 2, no. 115 (2009); and Rolf Philipona, Klaus Behrens, and Christian Ruckstuhl, "How Declining Aerosols and Rising Greenhouse Gases Forced Rapid Warming in Europe Since the 1980s," *Geophysical Research Letters* 36 (2009). / 183 **The carbon dioxide you breathe in a new office building:** derived from guidelines of the American Society of Heating, Refrigerating, and Air-Conditioning Engineers. / 183 **Carbon dioxide is not poison:** for a trenchant overview of the current state of thinking about atmospheric carbon dioxide, see William Happer, "Climate Change," Statement before the U.S. Senate Environment and Public Works Committee, February 25, 2009; data also gleaned from the Department of Energy's

Carbon Dioxide Information Analysis Center. / 183 **Carbon dioxide levels rise *after* a rise in temperature:** see Jeff Severinghaus, "What Does the Lag of CO_2 Behind Temperature in Ice Cores Tell Us About Global Warming," *RealClimate*, December 3, 2004. / 183–184 **"Ocean acidification":** see Ken Caldeira and Michael E. Wickett, "Oceanography: Anthropogenic Carbon and Ocean pH," *Nature* 425 (September 2003); and Elizabeth Kolbert, "The Darkening Sea," *The New Yorker*, November 20, 2006. / 184 **Hard-charging environmental activist:** see Mooney, above, for interesting reading on Caldeira's background / 184 **Caldeira mentions a study:** see Caldeira et al., "Impact of Geoengineering Schemes on the Terrestrial Biosphere," *Geophysical Research Letters* 29, no. 22 (2002). / 186 **Trees as environmental scourge:** see Caldeira et al., "Climate Effects of Global Land Cover Change," *Geophysical Research Letters* 32 (2005); and Caldeira et al., "Combined Climate and Carbon-Cycle Effects of Large-Scale Deforestation," *Proceedings of the National Academy of Sciences* 104, no. 16 (April 17, 2007). / 187 **The half-life of atmospheric carbon:** see Archer et al., "Atmospheric Lifetime of Fossil Fuel Carbon Dioxide," *Annual Review of Earth and Planetary Sciences* 37 (2009). / 188 **"Would put an end to the Gulf Stream":** see Thomas F. Stocker and Andreas Schmittner, "Influence of Carbon Dioxide Emission Rates on the Stability of the Thermohaline Circulation," *Nature* 388 (1997); and Brad Lemley, "The Next Ice Age," *Discover*, September 2002. / 189 **The northern tip of Newfoundland:** this former Norse settlement is known as L'Anse aux Meadows. / 189 **Benjamin Franklin's volcanic suspicion:** see Benjamin Franklin, "Meteorological Imaginations and Conjectures," *Memoirs of the Literary and Philosophical Society of Manchester*, December 22, 1784; and Karen Harpp, "How Do Volcanoes Affect World Climate?" *Scientific American*, October 4, 2005. / 189 **"Year Without a Summer":** see Robert Evans, "Blast from the Past," *Smithsonian*, July 2002. / 189 **Lake Toba super volcano:** see Stanley H. Ambrose, "Late Pleistocene Human Population Bottlenecks, Volcanic Winter, and Differentiation of Modern Humans," *Journal of Human Evolution* 34, no. 6 (1998). / 191 **The Vonnegut brothers make rain:** see William Langewiesche, "Stealing Weather," *Vanity Fair*, May 2008. / 191 **The idea**

was attributed to . . . Mikhail Budyko: see M. I. Budyko, "Climatic Changes," American Geophysical Society, Washington, D.C., 1977. Improbably, Ken Caldeira did postdoctoral work at Budyko's institute in Leningrad and met his future wife there. / 196–197 **Perhaps the stoutest scientific argument:** see Paul J. Crutzen, "Albedo Enhancement by Stratospheric Sulfur Injections: A Contribution to Resolve a Policy Dilemma?" *Climatic Change,* 2006. / 198 **There is no regulatory framework:** for further reading, see "The Sun Blotted Out from the Sky," Elizabeth Svoboda, *Salon.com,* April 2, 2008. / 199 **Certain new ideas . . . are invariably seen as repugnant:** the dean of repugnance studies is the Harvard economist Alvin E. Roth, whose work can be see at the Market Design blog. See also: Stephen J. Dubner and Steven D. Levitt, "Flesh Trade," *The New York Times Magazine,* July 9, 2006; and Viviana A. Zelizer, "Human Values and the Market: The Case of Life Insurance and Death in 19th Century America," *American Journal of Sociology* 84, no. 3 (November 1978). / 200 **Al Gore is quoted** here and elsewhere in Leonard David, "Al Gore: Earth Is in 'Full-Scale Planetary Emergency,'" *Space.com,* October 26, 2006. / 201–202 **The "soggy mirrors" plan:** see John Latham, "Amelioration of Global Warming by Controlled Enhancement of the Albedo and Longevity of Low-Level Maritime Clouds," *Atmospheric Science Letters* 3, no. 2 (2002). / 201 **Contrail clouds:** see David J. Travis, Andrew M. Carleton, and Ryan G. Lauritsen, "Climatology: Contrails Reduce Daily Temperature Range," *Nature,* August 8, 2002; Travis, "Regional Variations in U.S. Diurnal Temperature Range for the 11–14 September 2001 Aircraft Groundings: Evidence of Jet Contrail Influence on Climate," *Journal of Climate* 17 (March 1, 2004); and Andrew M. Carleton et al., "Composite Atmospheric Environments of Jet Contrail Outbreaks for the United States," *Journal of Applied Meteorology and Climatology* 47 (February 2008). / 203 **Fighting global warming with individual behavior change:** the difficulty of this endeavor was illustrated, if indirectly, by Barack Obama as he ran for president in 2008. While preparing for a debate, Obama was caught on tape complaining about how shallow the debates could be: "So when Brian Williams [of NBC News] is asking me about what's a personal thing that you've done [that's green], and I say, you know, 'Well, I planted a bunch of trees.' And he says, 'I'm talking about personal.' What I'm thinking in my head is, 'Well, the truth is, Brian, we can't solve global warming because *I* f—ing changed light bulbs in my house. It's because of something collective.'" As reported in "Hackers and Spending Sprees," *Newsweek* web exclusive, November 5, 2008.

203–208 DIRTY HANDS AND DEADLY DOCTORS: For **Semmelweis's sad ending,** see Sherwin B. Nuland, *The Doctor's Plague: Germs, Childbed Fever, and the Strange Story of Ignatz Semmelweis* (Atlas Books, 2003). / 204 **"A raft of recent studies":** see Didier Pittet, "Improving Adherence to Hand Hygiene Practice: A Multidisciplinary Approach," *Emerging Infectious Diseases*, March–April 2001. / 204–205 **"To Err Is Human":** Linda T. Kohn, Janet Corrigan, and Molla S. Donaldson, *To Err Is Human: Building a Safer Health System* (National Academies Press, 2000). It should be noted that hospitals had already been trying for years to increase doctors' hand-washing rates. In the 1980s, the National Institutes of Health launched a campaign to promote hand-washing in pediatric wards. The promotional giveaway was a stuffed teddy bear called T. Bear. Kids and doctors alike loved T. Bear—but they weren't the only ones. When a few dozen T. Bears were pulled from the wards to be examined after just one week, every one of them was found to have acquired at least one of a host of new friends: *Staphylococcus aureus, E. coli, Pseudomonas, Klebsiella,* and several others. / 205–206 **Cedars-Sinai Medical Center:** see Stephen J. Dubner and Steven D. Levitt, "Selling Soap," *The New York Times Magazine,* September 24, 2006. It was Dr. Leon Bender, a urologist at Cedars-Sinai, who led us to this story. / 205 **The Australian study:** see J. Tibbals, "Teaching Hospital Medical Staff to Handwash," *Medical Journal of Australia* 164 (1996). / 207 **"Among the best solutions":** for disposable blood-pressure cuffs, see Kevin Sack, "Swabs in Hand, Hospital Cuts Deadly Infections," *The New York Times,* July 27, 2007; for the silver-ion antimicrobial shield, see Craig Feied, "Novel Antimicrobial Surface Coatings and the Potential for Reduced Fomite Transmission of SARS and Other Pathogens," unpublished manuscript, 2004; for neckties, see "British Hospitals Ban Long

Sleeves and Neckties to Fight Infection," Associated Press, September 17, 2007.

208–209 FORESKINS ARE FALLING: See Ingrid T. Katz and Alexi A. Wright, "Circumcision—A Surgical Strategy for HIV Prevention in Africa," *New England Journal of Medicine* 359, no. 23 (December 4, 2008); also drawn from author interview with Katz.

EPILOGUE: MONKEYS ARE PEOPLE TOO

211–216 See Stephen J. Dubner and Steven D. Levitt, "Monkey Business," *The New York Times Magazine*, June 5, 2005; Venkat Lakshminarayanan, M. Keith Chen, and Laurie R. Santos, "Endowment Effect in Capuchin Monkeys," *Philosophical Transactions of the Royal Society* 363 (October 2008); and M. Keith Chen and Laurie Santos, "The Evolution of Rational and Irrational Economic Behavior: Evidence and Insight from a Non-Human Primate Species," chapter from *Neuroeconomics: Decision Making and the Brain*, ed. Paul Glimcher, Colin Camerer, Ernst Fehr, and Russell Poldrack (Academic Press, Elsevier, 2009). / 212 **"Nobody ever saw a dog"**: see Adam Smith, *An Inquiry into the Nature and Causes of the Wealth of Nations*, ed. Edwin Cannon (University of Chicago Press, 1976; originally published in 1776). / 214 **Day traders are also loss-averse:** see Terrance Odean, "Are Investors Reluctant to Realize Their Losses?" *Journal of Finance* 53, no. 5 (October 1998).

INDEX

THE GREAT FAILURE

ALSO BY NATALIE GOLDBERG

Chicken and in Love

Writing Down the Bones: Freeing the Writer Within

Wild Mind: Living the Writer's Life

Long Quiet Highway: Waking Up in America

Banana Rose: A Novel

Thunder and Lightning: Cracking Open the Writer's Craft

Top of My Lungs: Poems and Paintings

Living Color: A Writer Paints Her World

The Essential Writer's Notebook

THE GREAT FAILURE

My Unexpected Path to Truth

NATALIE GOLDBERG

HarperSanFrancisco
A Division of HarperCollins*Publishers*

In certain cases, names, descriptions, and places have been changed to protect individuals' privacy.

Dogen poem from *The Sea and the Honeycomb: A Book of Tiny Poems,* ed. by Robert Bly © 1971 by Robert Bly. Reprinted by permission of Robert Bly.

Excerpt from "Case 13: Te-shan: Bowls in Hand" *The Gateless Barrier* translated by Robert Aitken. Copyright © 1991 by Diamond Sangha. Reprinted by permission of North Point Press, a division of Farrar, Straus and Giroux, LLC.

A small portion of this book was published in *Shambhala Sun,* July 2002.

HarperCollins books may be purchased for educational, business, or sales promotional use. For information please write: Special Markets Department, HarperCollins Publishers, 10 East 53rd Street, New York, NY 10022.

HarperCollins Web site: http://www.harpercollins.com

FIRST HARPERCOLLINS PAPERBACK EDITION PUBLISHED IN 2005

Library of Congress Cataloging-in-Publication Data is available.
ISBN-13: 978–0–06–081612–4
ISBN-10: 0–06–081612–0

05 06 07 08 09 RRD(H) 10 9 8 7 6 5 4 3 2 1

For Michèle

Acknowledgments

THANK YOU TO Erik Storlie, Tamara Kaiser, Rob Wilder, Eddie Lewis, Wendy Johnson, Judith Ragir, Jisho Warner, Jean Leyshon, and Liz Visick. Also to Dunn Brothers in Minneapolis, Bread and Chocolate in St. Paul, Minnesota, the Four Arts Society Library in Palm Beach, Florida, the Menlo Park Public Library, and the Prolific Oven Bakery in Palo Alto, California, where I wrote much of this.

The following books were very helpful: *Zen's Chinese Heritage* by Andrew Ferguson (Wisdom Publications, 2000), *Book of Serenity,* translated by Thomas Cleary (Shambhala, 1988), and *The Blue Cliff Record,* translated by Thomas Cleary and J. C. Cleary.

Geri Thoma, my agent, Gideon Weil, my editor—I appreciate you.

THE GREAT FAILURE

Introduction

She knows there's no success like failure,
And that failure's no success at all.
—Bob Dylan

After my Zen teacher died, a fellow practitioner said to me, "Natalie, your writing succeeded. You didn't follow the teachings. Everything Roshi taught us was about how to fail."

We both laughed.

But I think it was true that we were trained in defeat. Downfall brings us to the ground, facing the nitty-gritty, things as they are with no glitter. Success cannot last forever. Everyone's time runs out. This is not a popular notion, but it is true.

Achievement solidifies us. Believing we are invincible, we want more and more. It makes us hungry. But we can be caught in the opposite too. Human beings manage to also drown in the pool of despair, seeped in the mud of depression. We spend our life on a roller coaster with rusty tracks, stuck to highs and lows, riding from one, trying to grab the other.

To heal ourselves from this painful cycle—the severe split we create and then the quasi equilibrium we try to maintain—we have to crash. Only then can we drop through to a more authentic self.

Zen transmits its legacy from this deeper place. It is a different kind of failure: the Great Failure, a boundless surrender. Nothing to hold on to and nothing to lose. Sitting still, feeling our breath, we watch the electric animals of desire and aggression arise and pass away. Our arms spread wide, we welcome it all. In the Great Failure we find the Great Success. They are no longer different from one another. Both dissolve into the moment. Illusions break open and we can be real with ourselves and the people around us. When obstructions are swept away, we can see clearly. Here we are, with our lives in our hands. Who were we? Who are we?

I write about my two fathers, my natural one and my spiritual one. Each was a powerful man. I loved them both. I tell incidents that happened, matters not often talked about. I am looking down the raw throat of their lives. In doing this I am also facing my own. How I was deceived, disregarded, offended, how I was naïve, ignorant, foolish—the things no one wants to behold.

Why am I doing this? Because it is a way to liberation, bringing us into intimate connection with human life. And what is the best approach? Of course, the hardest and most obvious: through the people we are close to. Not through some flashy movie star on the screen, but in contact with our wrinkles, our scars, with the sad way a father missed his chance in love, as though he thought time would last forever.

The Great Failure is a boundless embrace, leaving nothing out. We hear the words "repression," "denial," "rationalization," any method to squirm away. But in the end this kind of coping only leads to more pain. Entire wars have been based on our inability to see.

I wanted to learn the truth, to become whole. If I could touch the dark nature in someone else, I could know it in myself. I wrote this book in the hope of meeting what's real. It is my humble effort to illuminate the path of honesty.

PART 1

Don't worry if you write the truth. It doesn't hurt people, it helps them.

—Dainin Katagiri Roshi

With orange leaves still clinging to branches in that unusually mild stretch of late fall, on a sweet street in quiet St. Paul, I was about to slip my key into the front door of the apartment building. I was returning from Zen Center, where I came to study for two months. It was Monday at nine in the evening; no one was on the street. Suddenly I jerked my head to the right. One step below me in the entryway stood a beautiful man, shining face, almost clear eyes, in his late teens, aiming the barrel of a shotgun right at my neck. Feeling the small opening circle on my skin, I jerked my head.

"How dare you!" I was about to be outraged when he hissed, "Don't make a move. Give me your purse."

On my left shoulder dangled a small black backpack with three hundred dollars in twenty-dollar bills. Just that day I had been to the bank. To my chest I clutched my spiral notebook, the hefty 463-page *Book of Serenity* containing one hundred Zen dialogues, and a thinner black paperback, *Transmission of Light*.

On my right shoulder was a big blue plastic bag advertising a pharmaceutical company in white letters. My friend, a dermatologist, had picked it up for me at a medical convention. This bag held my old brown sneakers, black pants I bought when I returned a gift sweater that was too small, a Bob Dylan T-shirt a student had given me fifteen years ago, and a pair of good socks. I had gone to the gym only three times in the last month. That afternoon was my third time.

"C'mon, give it up."

I looked at him. He was nervous. Was this his first? Or was he on drugs? In a magnanimous moment I handed over my exercise bag.

"This is your purse?" He took a step back and surveyed me.

"Yes," I said emphatically.

"You sure?" I nodded my head up and down in earnest. We were having a fashion disagreement.

He turned and ran. I bolted through the front door. I had fooled him. He could keep those worn gym shoes. I felt a small victory.

Five days later I was standing on the podium during a conference at a Marriott Hotel in Fort Lauderdale, Florida. Seven hundred people were staring up at me. The title of my talk was "Riding Your Wild Horses." I was supposed to be speaking about creative writing, but the night before I had decided to change the whole lecture. In St. Paul I'd been studying Zen koans, short interchanges between teachers and students from eighth- and ninth-century China that cut through conditioned ways of seeing, enabling a person to experience one's true nature. I wanted to talk about that in my keynote speech, then to link it up to my being robbed, another kind of wake-up experience. I was sure it would work. I loved giving talks. Eventually, I'd meander over and tie it up with writing to fulfill the obligation of my original contract. This felt adventuresome and I was pleased. I made three notes on the smallest torn-off corner of a piece of paper and went to bed.

A tall lovely man who had read my books introduced me. I stepped onto the stage and thanked him. I took a sip of water and began by telling an ancient teaching tale.

Te-shan, a learned Buddhist scholar, piled up all his sutras—they weighed a lot—put them in a bag on his back, and headed south. Te-shan thought the Zen practitioners in southern China who espoused direct insight not dependent on book learning had it all wrong, and he was going to set them straight. On the way—of course he walked, maybe for a portion of the journey taking a boat down the Yangtze—he met an old woman selling tea cakes on the side of the road. He stopped for some refreshment. But the old woman, instead of setting out the provisions, inquired, "What's on your back?"

"They are commentaries and teachings of the Buddha."

"They are indeed! Well, if you're so learned, may I ask you a question? If you can answer it, the food is free, but if you fail, you get nothing."

Our Te-shan with all his book learning thought this would be simple, like taking candy from a babe. He agreed.

The woman then asked—and with her question I could feel my audience fading, that vital link between speaker and listener suddenly going limp—"If the mind does not exist in the past, and the present mind does not exist, and there's also no mind in the future, tell me with what mind will you receive these cakes?"

What is she talking about? Before the old woman's question, the audience was willing to come along. After all, everyone loves a story, and certainly Natalie Goldberg was leading up to those wild horses advertised in the catalog. Maybe the old woman will even pull them out of her cakes. Oh, the audience was hopeful. I could feel it. This was a conference full of crystals, psychics, healing dances, drums, auras, afterlives.

The question stunned Te-shan. He could not fathom an answer. Speechless, he wasn't even a match for a roadside cake seller, no less an ordinary woman. He knew he had to abandon his bold decision to challenge the southern teachers of Zen. All his scholarly learning had led to nothing. No lunch for him.

Now, it was here in my talk that I planned to swoop down and point out that these unnamed old women in koans appear to have great wisdom, but they happen to be. . . what was I talking about anyway? Where did I think this was going to lead? Was I attempting to compare the old woman with my robber? The old woman had blown Te-shan's mind. My mind had been blown too, but it was only five days after I was accosted—it was too soon for me to make any sense of it. Besides, this audience did not have to witness my struggle for personal realization. What was I doing standing up in front of everyone anyway? I wanted my stolen brown shoes and my Dylan shirt back. Every face in the audience was suddenly the same—the face of my thief. They had signed up for this lovely New Age weekend down in Florida—what was going on with this Natalie Goldberg? I knew only a handful had read any of my books. How was I going to leap over this mess smoothly and talk about writing practice, where I was on solid ground? I mentioned the horses from the title—ahh, relief on their faces—they had come to the correct lecture hall after all.

Then everything dropped away. I had nothing to say. I glanced at my little white piece of paper. No help there. I looked at my wristwatch. I was supposed to be up there for a full hour. Forty-five more minutes to go. I was being paid big bucks for this talk.

Total silence. Into a long pause I asked, "Would you like to hear a poem?"

Everyone nodded, relieved.

I knew one poem by heart. "It's by Dogen, a thirteenth-century Zen master."

Nobody's face registered any recognition. I plunged ahead anyway:

This slowly drifting cloud is pitiful;
What dreamwalkers men become.

Awakened, I hear the one true thing—
Black rain on the roof of Fukakusa temple.

It went over like a dead—not a wild—horse.

"Would you like to hear it again?" Of course, they wouldn't, but I dove in and recited it even more dramatically a second time. Then I asked the dumbest question. "How many of you liked it?" I already knew the answer. Eight people out of seven hundred raised their hands.

People in the back of the room were getting up and leaving. "Well, does anyone have a question?" I asked brightly.

Immediately ushers rushed into the aisles with mikes. The organizers must have felt relief—she's doing something. Questioners formed small lines, awaiting their chance to speak.

A man's amplified voice: "How do you know if you're writing something good? I mean, you could be working on something for six months, and it could be shit."

Now here was my medium. There was no angle of writing for which I couldn't come up with a helpful answer. But instead of launching into my authoritative voice, I just stood there and quietly said, "I don't know. It's up to each one of us to find our own way."

He nodded seriously.

A frail young woman in sandals and a gray and white checkered shift stepped to the mike. "I want to write this story. It's partly true, about my brother, but I'm afraid he'll kill me if he reads it."

This is an old question about privacy. I'd answered it many times and been, I think, helpful.

Instead, I cocked my head and just kept looking at this woman. I noticed, but without thinking about it, more like the way a clay plate registers the placement on its surface of a carrot, a radish and a slice of cucumber—open and indifferent—that she wore small turquoise earrings, one gold bangle on her right wrist, had a long thin scar from her left ankle up to right below her shinbone. I understood right then that I couldn't help anyone.

It came to mind that she wanted an answer to her question. "You have to make your own decision." I meant it with all my heart—but not particularly to that specific inquiry.

A few more people fumbled up to the mike, while most of the audience dashed for the exits. I glanced at my watch. "Only five minutes left," I said cheerily. "One more person."

"What's it like to be a famous writer?"

Now things were getting loopy. I smiled so my substantial teeth and pink gums showed. I gave a little bow—the Buddhist way, with hands together in front of me—and then I slithered off the stage. Please no one ever see me again. Should I go to the officials and tell them to keep their big check? I'd never goofed like this. Maybe I was just imagining how bad I was. Then I remembered the old tea-cake woman's question and winced. Yeah, I was terrible. No one wanted to hear this stuff, especially from me. I didn't know what I was talking about.

I left the building looking straight ahead, glancing neither right nor left. I made it to my rented Hyundai and barreled out of the parking lot, heading north to the small seaside town of Lake Worth.

The plan was to visit my parents after the conference. They lived ten miles inland in a senior community called Buttonwood, where squat, unattached units lined up behind well-trimmed lawns. Bougainvillea, palms, and wandering jews edged along the front walks. Houseplants that were put out one day while the cleaning person mopped were forgotten and grew into towering trees.

Though I had made good time, my parents were waiting for me eagerly as though I were late.

"Was there traffic? Here, sit." My father scooped chicken onto his plate. "Get your own, Nat." This was business. Take your fill and eat.

My mother rushed back and forth, to the stove for sweet potatoes, then to the refrigerator for applesauce. "You want water? It's cold. I took it from the tap and put it in the freezer just before you came." She reached in for an old brown prune-juice jar now full of water.

"Any Perrier?" I asked.

My father raised his left eyebrow—both are substantial, thick, silver, bushy, above piercing blue eyes. "That stuff is toilet water. They bottle it, and then the fools hand over their good dollar bills. What a racket."

"So, Nat, how did your talk go?" my mother asked with her mouth full of lettuce. This question was unusual. When I visited them, my individual life dropped away. Never was there a mention of my life beyond the arms of the family. I was fifty years old. It made no difference. My father's only comment on the phone when I told him at thirty-five that I was getting a divorce was, "So now will you move back home?"

But why this time would my mother ask, this single time when I'd failed miserably?

I ignored the question. This usually is a good tactic. I commented on the meal. The interest in food would sweep any conversation under.

A moment later she actually asked again. "Tell us about your talk." Not only that, but my father stopped eating, poultry leg dangling halfway to his mouth, grease around his lips. He too wanted to hear how it went.

"Oh, really good." That should have been enough.

But it wasn't. "How many people were there?" my mother wanted to know.

"This kasha is really good. I like the onions."

"How many?" My father put down the leg.

"Seven hundred."

"What did you tell them?" No one but me was eating now.

"Oh, a Zen story—a koan—and then I brought it over to writing." Of course, I never mentioned the mugging. At all costs protect your parents.

"What's a koan?" I was backed into a corner. They were paying attention.

"A teaching story."

"Well, c'mon, Nat. Tell it to us. You know, like we were the audience. Talk."

By now I had become as pale as the turnip on my plate. I took a deep breath. "Well, Te-shan is a learned man who lives in northern China . . ."

They were listening intently. I could feel their raw attention, as palpable as a small animal in my hand. All at once I was transmitting the dharma in my parents' Florida kitchen. My head was whirling. If these teachings were able to reach my father's ears—I glanced over at his big floppy lobes—then Zen could truly take root in this country.

I encouraged myself: keep going, Nat. I got to the old woman. My mother's eyes narrowed. "What kind of cakes?" she asked.

I made it up. "Honey cakes with poppy seeds."

"Mmm, must have been good. That man was hungry," my mother said. "It was a long trip."

"So what's the question the old woman's gonna ask?" My father was impatient. He was a gambler. He wanted to see if Te-shan could win the cake.

"Okay." I spoke in a gruff storytelling whisper. This

time I was going to make the story work. "She holds a morsel in front of his nose. She speaks, 'If present mind does not exist, if past mind does not exist'"—with these few utterances from the ancient woman again I've lost my audience. That warm furry animal I held in the palm of my hand dashed out. I clenched an empty fist.

My father crinkled his nose as if something near him stunk. Once more I smelled the dead horse. My mother stuck out her tongue.

My father's nostrils quivered. "They paid you all that money for that?"

I nodded, my lips pressed together in a tight rib of agreement. I commiserated with him. Life just doesn't make sense.

I've been through all this before. I never learn. The time before was at the beginning of a weeklong visit. My father and I went to the Gourmet Deli for lunch. We hadn't seen each other in eight months. Things felt fresh, and we were both hungry. I ordered a corned beef sandwich. He wanted two big specials, large beefy hot dogs with plenty of sauerkraut and mustard, and fries. He ordered an IBC root beer. Recently he had found this beverage in a store and acted as though he had discovered America. "Nat, these are the greatest. You should have one." Then he scrunched his face. "Naa, forget it. They're expensive. Stay with the free water." My father must have really loved them. Usually he wouldn't have spent extra money.

After the waitress took our order and left, we sat cheered in anticipation of a good meal and a week together. In a madras shirt, material taut, the two buttons over his middle strained, the plaid zigzagging, his thick-fisted hands clenched together in front of him, my father tried to think what next to say to his educated daughter. He had owned a tough bar on Long Island for thirty years and day after day watched those from the seedier side of life drink themselves under. He had risen with his own tough nature to meet their pain and make his living. But now he suddenly had a question, and he asked it enthusiastically—life at that moment seemed full of possibility. "Nat, so tell me—what is Buddhism anyway? They talk about it on TV. I even read about it in *Time* magazine. I don't get it. Explain it to me."

I'd spent hundreds of hours doing zazen, back straight, legs crossed, feeling my breath go in and out, and now here was my chance. My father wanted to know what I surely must understand.

I chose my words carefully and tried to keep it simple and direct. "Well, Dad, it's about being present, moment by moment. So when you're drinking a glass of water, you just drink a glass of water. When you walk, you walk—"

My father's eyes bugged out of his head, and he leaned in over the table. "You've got to be kidding," he interrupted me. "That's ridiculous."

My head jerked back: he's right. What had I been

thinking? Why couldn't I have followed his example? His mind always stayed dead ahead of him. His life was congruent. One thing followed another. Nothing in the way. He went to war, he came home, he married, he worked, he had children, he grew old and retired to Florida. What was the problem? What else was there? Sure, once in a while he wondered about his dead mother, Rose, or what it would have been like to have had a son, but these were only brief musings. My father's life was the horse in front of him. He got on it and rode.

Then for a moment he softened. He put his big paw over mine, "Nat . . ." But he never finished the sentence. The waitress had come and laid those plates of juicy meat in front of us. Words dropped. We dug in.

THE VERY FIRST TIME my parents challenged my zen life happened in New Mexico, that land of coyotes, sage, dirt roads, woodstoves—absurd things, but because their daughter was there, Ben and Syl Goldberg schlepped out.

They are visiting me in my new home in Santa Fe. Already they have let me know I've gotten a bad deal on the house. I paid much too much. Now in the cool late July afternoon we are sitting on the porch. Amazingly, we're not eating. We are sitting in a line. I am in the middle.

"Hey, Nat," my father begins, "what is meditation?"

"It's hard to explain." Then because I am still incredibly foolish, I have a brilliant, daring idea. "Do you want to try?" And before they can answer I run into the house and get a bell.

Accoutrements, I think, will make it official.

"Okay, when I ring the bell you just sit and feel your breath go in and out at your nose. If your mind wanders, just bring it back gently to your breath. We'll sit for ten minutes."

"Okay," they both say, suddenly eager—this will be fun—and they wriggle in their chairs to compose themselves.

The bell sounds three times, and we settle into this most ordinary thing—people breathing next to each other. My father is on my right, my mother on my left. I cannot believe this is happening. Here we are, all paying attention. The ten minutes feel spacious, luscious, and forever. The shade is cool. We're all quiet. This must be what heaven is.

The time is up. I ring the bell once to mark the end of meditation.

"Well, how was it?" I ask. "Did you have a lot of distractions?"

My father shrugs his shoulders. "What's the big deal?"

"Well, did you discover how much you think? Was it hard to concentrate?"

"No, I didn't have a single thought."

"None?" I ask surprised.

"Not a one."

"Well, did you feel peaceful?"

"Not particularly. It was like how it always is when you don't talk. That's why human beings talk. Nothing is happening otherwise."

I turn to my mother. "I was aggravated the whole time about your friend. She must think I'm awful."

The night before, my mother had blurted out at dinner that she thought the chapters of my novel were awful, and my friend Frances, who was there, told me later that my mother was jealous.

I had confronted my mother that morning, and she apologized profusely. "I don't know what came over me. Your chapters are lovely."

"Let's try again," my mother says. "This time I'll do it right."

I start to explain there's no right or wrong, but instead just say, "Okay."

"This time I want to ring the bell," my father says, grabbing the stick. He ceremoniously hits the bell three times.

We are sitting for two and a half minutes when my father suddenly belts out, "Hello, Dolly. Well, hello, Dolly. It's so nice to have you back where you belong," while ringing the bell continuously to accompany himself.

"Buddy, please," my mother tries to stop him, struggling to reach across me to grab the bell, but my father keeps going. He's having a ball.

I'm the only one staring straight ahead at the high adobe wall a hundred feet in front of us, still attempting to notice my breath.

I decide right then that I don't have to save my parents. They don't count as sentient beings. They are in another category entirely.

I imagine the Enlightened One's talk under the bodhi tree. "There are ten kinds of beings"—and now Buddha turns his head and addresses me personally—"and, Natalie, your father is the eleventh kind—out of this universe."

THREE STRIKES AND YOU'RE OUT. The Te-shan story was my final dharma defeat with my parents. They were victorious forever. I had a terrible headache as I sat in their kitchen.

"This has been a long day," I said, excusing myself.

My parents gazed over across the table at me with the grace and assurance of great Thoroughbreds striding way ahead of the loser.

My father nodded his large head. "I'll meet you early tomorrow morning."

I didn't stay with them anymore—for the past ten years I'd stayed at a pink hotel on the beach, "Florida the way it used to be," the last small place in a towering strip of deluxe condominiums.

I said good night and drove alone through the dark to my hotel.

I didn't use the air conditioner, and at six in the morning I could hear my father calling out my name, "Nat, Naat," through the open screened window.

I dashed to the door in my nightgown and beckoned him to number twenty-four. "Dad, you're early. It's still dark out." He slept little at night now, dozing off intermittently in his blue TV chair.

Five months ago he had had surgery for colon cancer. When he came out of the anesthetic he bit the nurse, who was trying to prick his arm. "You've got all the blood you're gonna get out of me."

The staff couldn't wait to get rid of him. They wanted to send him to rehab right away, but he wouldn't go. He declared loudly to me on the phone, while my sister and mother sat opposite him in the hospital room, "I love you, Natalie. I love my wife. I love Romi. But so help me, if your mother doesn't take me home, I'll leave all of you. I know my body better than anyone else. I don't care what they say. I want to go home." This was his last great fight after World War II—all those enemies in the white sanitary building trying to murder him.

I looked at my father in the early morning light. His skin was yellow, and he was too thin. All at once my father had become an old man. His strong swimmer legs were like bowed sticks in his blue Bermuda shorts and sockless loafers. He had already outlived the rest of his family by twenty years. All the other Goldbergs died in their early sixties.

"Wait for me by those deck chairs." I pointed. "Watch the sun rise over the ocean. I have to do my half hour of walking."

"Okay," he easily agreed. This was enjoyable for him. Something to do, a place to be. He'd been retired for over twenty years, and life had become boring.

Before the operation, we drove to consultations with different oncologists. I wanted my father to have the best care. I didn't like the first one we visited. He was too abrupt, too sure of himself.

As we sat in the waiting room for a second opinion, my father asked where Michèle was. She had been my partner for the last five years, and we had recently moved in together. She often came down to Florida with me to visit my parents, and my mother and father had grown fond of her.

"It was hard for her yesterday, seeing all these cancer doctors. It brought up feelings about her dad."

"Didn't he die ten years ago?"

"Yes."

"So what's the problem?"

"It reminded her of how it was when he was sick."

"But it was ten years ago."

"Dad, a person can still have feelings."

"I don't understand. It was years ago. Why didn't she come?"

I rolled my eyes. "Never mind."

This doctor we liked. He complimented my father on the Hawaiian shirt he was wearing.

"My daughter gave it to me."

When he walked out of the room for a moment, my father said, "Well, at least he admires my clothes."

What other criteria did we really have? The first doctor didn't even physically examine him. This one did.

"Thank you," my father said when we were back in the car. He added no qualifier. He was genuinely appreciative. He didn't like the first physician either, but felt too helpless to stick up for himself.

In the distance at the end of the pier fishing boats were gathering bait.

"How was it?" I was sweating in my white shorts and sneakers after my walk.

My father turned up his nose. "No big deal. It was the sunrise. Let's go eat."

Even for the short distance to the restaurant he turned on the car air conditioner full blast. He put his big right hand over mine. I looked at his ruby ring, the one his mother gave him on his twentieth birthday. He'd never taken it off. One of the two small diamonds was missing, and all edges of the red gem had been rubbed smooth by wear. Once swimming in the Indian Ocean while stationed in India during the war, he came up, breaking the water's surface, and saw it was missing. With no hesitation he dove under again and grabbed two handfuls of sand. When he opened his fingers and the saltwater rushed through, the ring was in his left palm.

I fingered this ring while we drove.

I'd never met his parents. They died before I was born. His mother of Parkinson's disease.

"My mama, she was sweet. She made me mashed-potato cones for snacks when I was young. We didn't have a lot of money."

In the summers between the last years of elementary school and junior high, he took the subway alone to Coney Island. In his navy blue shorts he dove off the pier and swam day after day. He'd read about Johnny Weissmuller, another Jew, who was a swimming star. If he could do it, my father could too. Hand over hand, he had a lone determination. By the time he arrived in high school in ninth grade, they let him use the school pool. Now he could swim in the late fall, through the dark months of winter, and on into spring. At seventeen he won the freestyle. None of his family attended the meet to see him slap the edge one moment before the kid from Tilden High. So close and tight was his win that the slap was like two consecutive sounds—slap! slap! my father's and the other boy's—but his was first. The coach reached down and pulled him out of the water to the roar of the Lincoln home crowd. My father was the champion—self-taught—in all of Brooklyn.

But when he talked about it there was no glory. It was just luck, he said.

But for me he was champion of the world. I loved his close effort, his power. When I was young, I watched him dive over and over into the ocean at Jones Beach. He taught me to swim. I'd stand on his shoulders, and when the great waves came, the two of us charged right into them, me on top, he on the bottom.

From age twelve to sixteen I attended summer camp and learned lake swimming. All four years I made tremendous effort in the swim meets, but no matter how hard I tried to be my father, I always came in second after a thin dark-haired girl from Queens.

We got a seat right away at John G.'s near a wooden column. "Dad, should we move? You don't have a view of the sea."

He shrugged. "I know it's there. I don't have to see it." He ordered his favorite: salami and eggs.

I had my camera.

He put his hand over the lens. "Not now."

"Oh, come on. I need photos of my model." I had drawn him often in the last five years. Mostly he had been in his large reclining chair in front of the TV and being still had come naturally now.

Recently I'd sold a portrait. I called to tell him.

"You're kidding. A woman bought it? How old is she?"

"Twenty-six."

"Send her a real picture of me, in the army. She can see how I really look. She paid that much? She must be in love with me."

"Dad, she liked *my painting*."

"Don't be silly. Give me her address. I'll send her a Christmas card. Forget it. I'll marry her." Then he paused. "Hey, what's my cut?"

He reached for the single yellow rose in a thin glass vase in the center of the table, held it next to his cheek, and posed. Just as I was about to click, he stuck out his tongue.

"C'mon, Daddy. Be serious."

"Why?"

"Because I need your good looks."

"Yes, I am handsome," he smiled, and I snapped.

"Now you." He seized the camera and handed me the flower.

I didn't like being photographed here in Florida. My hair in the humidity twirled, curled, and formed wisps where it wasn't supposed to. I tried to smile.

On our way out, we stopped for toothpicks at the cashier's counter. A full cup of pennies was offered for use in a gum ball machine that gave M&Ms. My father and I each put in a coin and filled our hands with colored candy that fell down a shoot. We walked out popping the candy in our mouths and rolling the toothpicks across our lips.

It was not always this sweet between us. Nine years earlier I had written him a long letter. "Did you ever wonder what my childhood looked like to me?" Well, of course, he hadn't, but I thought—after hours of group and individual therapy—to inform him.

"You never knocked before you entered my bedroom. You commented often at the dinner table about my young breasts, and you tried to kiss me on the lips in a way that made me uncomfortable. I carried constant anger around as a defense, to ward you off. You tried to peek at me when I was an adolescent, naked in the shower. I didn't feel safe. You called me gooney, made fun of my nose, the shadow on my upper lip, my eyebrows growing across the bridge of my nose."

I wrote him that he was a terrible father, never came to my school, never asked about my homework. Sure, once he rode bicycles with me for a Girl Scout cookout, and once he brought a hundred boxes of Scout cookies to the bar and handed them out instead of change for beer purchases. His customers were outraged. "You don't like mint? Here's a box of pecan sandies." He grabbed the one box away and gave the other. I won the award for the most cookies sold. I remembered once when I was nine, sitting at the edge of my bed engrossed in reading a book, he walked in, rubbed my head, and said with obvious pride, "You're reading again?"

But that was it, I wrote. I hated my childhood.

When he received my letter, he tried to call, but after I said briskly, "Write me. No more phone calls," I hung up.

Two weeks later I received a thin envelope addressed in my father's crooked hand. I imagined a gorilla gripping a pen. "I don't know what you're talking about, but don't worry. I'll never leave you."

That was exactly him. My father knew two things: determination and animal devotion. My father would be eternally loyal to me. I was his daughter. He was my father. For my whole life we would stand in relationship to each other. That was it. I knew I'd get no more.

But I did not give up. I wrote back, "Your letter's not good enough." My father had not treated his young daughter well, and my mother did not protect me.

As soon as I left home at eighteen, I tried to figure out what went on in my family. I attended college in Washington, D.C. Freshman students were offered free counseling. I quickly took advantage of it and made an appointment.

In this new city, both strange and wonderful, I turned at the entrance of a corner brownstone only blocks from the White House and walked into a dank waiting room. I whispered to the receptionist, "I'm supposed to see someone at two." I wanted to keep the secrets of my life sealed until I entered the inner sanctum of that therapist's office.

A woman wearing a beige skirt, white blouse, single strand of pearls, and short black heels beckoned me into her room and then pointed to a dark wooden seat across from her desk.

I began by telling her that my boyfriend and I had

broken up a little while ago. Sex between us had died out. But I had a new boyfriend, and I occasionally saw the old one. Lovemaking was hot again with the old one, but I was numb with the person I liked now.

I told her that these two men were my first sexual partners. I knew something felt askew and I sensed that somehow it had to do with my father.

"Well, what new technique is your old boyfriend doing that's turning you on?" She removed her eye-glasses, exhaled on one lens, and rubbed it with a tissue.

"He's not doing anything different." I was no Sigmund Freud, but I knew this therapist wasn't catching on. I was trying to tell her something about myself, about my history. My forehead furrowed. I wanted her to lead me into my subconscious—wasn't that what it was all about?

"Your old boyfriend must be doing something different. Otherwise, you wouldn't feel excited." She put her glasses back on.

I tried to tell her again how uncomfortable I felt around my father. I explained that I wanted to feel good with the person I was dating, not with the sideshow.

She insisted my old boyfriend had a new technique.

I gave up. "I'll have to think about it," I said. Then sarcasm slid off my tongue. "That's right," I snapped my fingers, "he was wearing my red underpants."

"There you go," she brightened. The problem was solved.

I slinked out of there, marched down the streets of the capital of our great country, stormed into my dormitory, and never went back to college counseling again.

After I graduated, I moved to Detroit to live with a boyfriend and tried therapy again at a free clinic. The man sitting opposite me was a foreign graduate student. He explained he was getting his Ph.D.

I told him my problem. "I can be turned on as long as I'm not involved. Become my boyfriend, and it's the end of sex." I was older now, more experienced at verbalizing the dilemma, but the basic phenomenon was the same.

"I understand." He had a clipped accent. "If you become close, you think it is your father. You are afraid of having sex with your father."

"Yeah," I said. We were getting somewhere. "So what should I do?"

"It's rather simple. If you let yourself imagine having sex with your father, you will no longer be afraid. We are only afraid of the unknown."

I nodded. I wanted badly to solve this.

"I can help you."

I was elated.

"Lie down." He pointed to a green vinyl couch with no arms or back. I slid onto it. "Close your eyes and envision what I say."

I relaxed and shut my eyes.

He proceeded. "Your father has walked into the room. He comes to you. Can you see that?"

"Uh-huh." My lids closed tighter, and I gripped my

hands into fists, but I went along with him. He was going to cure me.

I heard "the penis entering the vagina" in the staccato rhythm of English spoken as a second language. I was floating above the room. I had just met this psychologist, and we had genitals going in and out of each other—my father's, no less. I thought, well, this therapy is free. He can't take too much time with each client. He has to get down to business. He punctuated the words "penis" and "vagina" as he repeated them over and over. Did they talk about this stuff in Japan? Maybe he came here to learn special American techniques. My mind was working fast. I didn't want to know what my father's genitals looked like, much less felt like. I was trying, but I was nauseous. It wasn't working.

"Okay, open your eyes."

I popped up, and the vinyl tore from my skin.

"Well, how do you feel?"

"Is this what you're doing your dissertation on?" I was overly friendly, tapping my foot up and down. Then I blurted out, "I feel the same." In truth I felt much worse, withdrawn and wooden.

He lifted his eyebrows, glanced at the clock on the back wall. "Sorry. The session is up."

I walked out of there like a stiff puppet.

Twenty years later, I was almost forty; my life was full of Zen practice and writing. In fact, I was about to finish a novel, the most difficult thing I'd ever attempted.

The main character, a loose copy of myself, was sleeping with too many men right before her marriage. It was true in real life, but it wasn't believable. It didn't work in the fiction. I was slashing whole paragraphs.

Outside the cafés and libraries I wrote in, women were whispering "sexual abuse." People all over the country were meeting in incest survivor groups. Everywhere I went I saw a thick white book entitled *The Courage to Heal* on coffee tables, lining shelves of bookstores, on friends' desks. Did I want to drag that old dog out? Who had the time? I had learned to cope. Besides, nothing as radical as intercourse happened between me and my father. I just was uncomfortable with him. He was inappropriate with me. I had language now. I had "inappropriate." I had a novel to finish. I was a woman now of singular focus.

The snow was deep the Monday in January when I returned to my house tired. I did not lock my front door. I was an old hippie and liked to believe in trusting the world. Sometimes I forgot my keys in my car. A year before, my blue Rabbit was stolen, but I didn't learn. I made a grilled cheese sandwich for dinner and read in bed until I fell asleep.

Around one in the morning I heard a vague rattling, turned over in bed, and then suddenly sat bolt upright. A naked man with a hairy chest and a nylon stocking over his head was standing over me. I could see his large body clearly in the moonlight pouring through the window.

I let out a scream so loud I did not hear it, but it filled my entire body. I only felt pure silence, but the sound pierced the old thick-walled adobe. Neighbors slammed on lights and dashed open doors, and the naked man in an instant was gone. I ran to the back door and let Steve, Juan, and Linda in. Someone else had already called the police. We could hear a distant siren. We walked gingerly to the front of the house. No trace of his clothes anywhere, but he couldn't have grabbed everything that fast. The door was ajar. We held open the useless screen. Bare footprints in the snow ran to the left and were lost under the streaks of car tires in the street's slush. Did he come in naked? Walk to my front door bare-assed? It was freezing outside. He must have lived right nearby. He couldn't have walked nude down Galisteo Street in the cold checking for an unlocked door.

The police arrived and told us they'd been after this guy. He never touched the women. The door was always unlocked. He just gazed. He had repeated this weekly for the last three months.

I made a quick, logical conclusion: lock my door. Then I'd be safe. I couldn't afford to engage my imagination. I had to use it for the novel.

The next morning I marched out of the house only a half hour later than usual to the Galisteo Newsstand, where I wrote. I would let nothing deter me. But I couldn't ward off the awful feeling that I was being watched. That that naked man lived across the street, down the block, kitty-corner to my place. At the café I was okay; later in my locked house I felt secure. It was the distance between the two that was terrorizing.

A month and a half later I finished my first draft. Then my close reserve exploded. That man was like my father! He never touched me; he just looked. I marched over to the rape crisis center and joined an abuse group.

These women were not like me. My father didn't do what their fathers, brothers, uncles, aunts, mothers, babysitters did to them. The walls of the room were a sickening green. Usually I loved groups, especially after the loneliness of writing each day, but I was squirming in my chair. I hated this meeting. I remembered how cute, funny my father was.

The frizzy-haired woman with large glasses across from me described how she shaved her pubic hair when it first came out so no one could see she was maturing. My face fell. I did the same thing. My sister had seen the thin downy first strands while we were in the bathroom, and she'd announced it at dinner. Then my father would try to walk in on me after a shower, so he too could see.

I didn't lock the door then either, and if I did, it was easy to pick the lock with an unbent paper clip. I learned early locks were useless. My puberty was filled with yelling at my father to shut the door, holding a pink towel in front of myself. I cut my pubic hair so my sister would shut her mouth. But I could not also cut off my breasts, the forming curve of my hips. My adolescence was an agony. I was the last girl in my seventh grade to get a bra, to wear nylons. I never wore jewelry, lipstick, eye shadow. I did not want to be noticed by the man in our house.

A pale woman in light green pedal pushers and high brown boots spoke next. She told how she tried at all costs to avoid being in a room alone with her father. I could hardly breathe. I'd come down the stairs from the bedroom, go out the front door, and come in the back to go up to the kitchen, all to avoid walking through the living room, where my father sat on the couch.

"This will be our text." The leader of the group held up that big white book I'd seen everywhere. Each chapter ended with a writing assignment. We were to come back the next week with our notebooks.

I began to write in a thin green one. As my pen scratched across the page, the world of my childhood started to coalesce. Too many things I'd forgotten, never uttered I was now describing, and then it was affirmed by the experience of these women. A case was being built. I wasn't crazy. Something did happen.

Each week no matter what the assignment, I'd open that notebook and scream with my pen, "Fuck you, fuck you, fuck you." A whole book filled with little more than those two words. In group I watched women who'd never written before take satisfaction in describing a certain dress, meal, house.

The leader would encourage. "Very vivid. Good. Good."

My turn would come. I was an inarticulate banshee. I couldn't believe this man I had loved with all my young heart had been so disrespectful to me, treated me like a "broad," a "hussy," behaved as though I didn't matter, as though I wasn't his daughter. He didn't love me. He couldn't. Then I'd stop. What about *his* mean father, his childhood? He didn't know any better. It was the fifties—he could only see women as sex objects. I'd make excuses. But I was his flesh and blood. My mind whirled. I couldn't put the two together. "How could you be my father and handle me like this?" I'd howl in my pillow at night, "But I was your daughter. I was your daughter."

Then I'd stop trying to understand; I just burned. I cried in uncontrollable convulsions several times a day as though I were vomiting. I felt my thin ten-year-old-girl legs under the kitchen table as we ate dinner and he made snide comments when an uncle was visiting. "Hey, Nat has baby hairs under her arms. Come over and show it." I had on a sleeveless shirt. I couldn't see any in the mirror. I'd show them they were mistaken. My father held up my arm, and they peered close. "See?" my father pointed with his thick forefinger, just grazing the two frail growths. I pulled away and ran to the medicine-chest mirror to look. Even in the dead heat of July I wore sleeves after that.

Where was my mother? This wasn't clandestine mistreatment; we were at the dinner table, for heaven's sake. She was busy spooning the onion gravy over the pot roast;

she was taking her apron off to sit down; she was reaching into the refrigerator for some milk. I had no protector. Everything was in the open, and no one stopped it. Was the rest of the house occupied by ghosts? Where was everyone?

But I loved him. He taught me to swim.

Whenever I'd soften, I'd think, Hitler had a bad childhood. Was that an excuse? It would reignite me. But I'd also watch the depth of my own doubt, how I wanted to shut off what I didn't want to know.

I experienced all my withheld rage in my legs. I wanted to run as hard as I could as far as I could from that house in Farmingdale, New York. In Santa Fe I started a women's running club and found a coach, who encouraged us to run like animals. My desire was to scorch the track, burn up my past; instead, I was the slowest, most quietly faithful one in the group. Wherever I had to travel to teach writing, Manhattan, Kansas City, Boulder, I'd put on those rubber shoes and pound the streets with my feet.

The big word I learned was "boundary." "Here's where I end. You begin over there. Daddy, get the hell out of my way." I was experiencing the death of my father, of some dream I was brought up to believe about daddies and their daughters.

One night as soon as the meeting at the rape crisis center was over, I dashed over to the Zia Diner and shoved meat loaf and mashed potatoes down my throat. I noticed a familiar woman at another booth. We locked eyes for a moment, almost nodded, then looked away. Just ten minutes earlier we'd been divulging our deepest pains. Outside we acted as if we had nothing in common. Camaraderie or closeness was unbearable. I stayed distant from the other women. I was frightened to get too close.

No one in the group knew I was a writer. The truth was I don't think I ever even heard the writing topics that were assigned. Only anger fueled my hand. And grief. This was the end of the world. The statistics were startling: one out of every four children, then I'd hear one out of six. The numbers stopped mattering. I was learning something true and mean about the world. Rabbis, priests, parents, siblings, cousins, teachers—this was oppression, close up and personal. And insidious—it quietly ruled and ruined lives. Just twenty years ago no one could help me. Therapists were ignorant. It was important for women to help each other, to hear the stories and recognize ourselves. The process was slow and painful, but I was no longer under my father's thumb.

For the next year my mother wrote, "Dear Natalie, we loved you so much. We didn't mean to make a mistake," and then in another letter, "We did the best we could," and "This isn't fair."

Six months later they sent an old photo they'd blown up as a gift: Rhoda, in a diaper, is one year old with dark big eyes and a head of curly hair, sitting on my mother's left knee. My mother, with full lips, bright eyes, and thick hair, is looking down lovingly at her. And I, at four in a plaid dress, barrette in my hair, am leaning on her right leg, trying to get her attention.

All that photo did was ignite my wrath. My mother never saw me, and it was right there in the framed picture. She was getting off easy in the letters I sent. She had basically ignored me for my whole childhood. Simple questions—What yellow school bus do I take to first grade? What do I wear to school? How do I find the classroom?—were never answered, as though she were on drugs and never heard me. And in fact, she often was. Sleeping pills, Valium, diet pills were dispensed liberally by her brother, the doctor. I mustered a confident air, but was shattered inside. Finally at the end of the first day at Main Street Elementary, I broke down sobbing, my face hidden in my arms leaning on the wooden desk. Already there was an acknowledgment that I was on my own, set adrift in a huge world at an early age.

I think even worse than being taunted by my father was being neglected by my mother. It created no affirmation of my existence. It was probably even a deeper wound, but I wasn't ready to take on both parents at once.

I thought, all my work, and this was their response? They enclosed a note, "See how happy we were?"

"No, I don't," I wrote back. How blind could they be?

I did not see them for another six months. The last letter from my mother read, "Please, Nat, let's go back to before this all began, when we were all content."

Content! I crumpled up the paper and tossed it in the wastebasket. More time passed. My parents were never going to understand.

I WAS AT A RECONCILIATION RETREAT in New York with Thich Nhat Hanh, the Vietnamese Buddhist monk. In 1968 Martin Luther King Jr. nominated him for the Nobel Peace Prize. Besides regular practitioners, Vietnam vets were invited to attend. Thirty came. Thay, as we called this spiritual teacher, wanted to meet with these American soldiers who had been at war with his country. It was 1991. He felt they still suffered terribly, and he wanted to tell them to forgive themselves, let go, go on, help someone now, no matter what happened in the past.

Many of these vets had not seen a Vietnamese person since they were in the war in Asia. Scores of them hadn't had a night's sleep since they left the jungle. Some were just getting off alcohol and drugs. A few hadn't touched another human being since they returned.

I was asked to lead twelve vets in a group discussion. We went off to a grassy knoll. I was the only woman. I asked the man to my right with close-cut hair, a mustache, wearing army fatigues to begin. "Share how it feels to be here."

I had no training for this, but I'd been a teacher and a meditator for a long time. I'd run groups, but most important, I'd seen into my own family's darkness.

I listened patiently, evenly, quietly. I did not comment. I just let people talk. Once the ground of acceptance had been laid, I was the silent witness. As soon as the men began to share, they could not stop. Every once in a while they glanced over at me. Was I wincing at their tales?

They became more bold, divulged more horrifying stories, but I wasn't judging, nor was I shocked.

The men told me how grateful they were that I could listen. It was my turn to speak. "I've seen what close relatives, families, people you're supposed to trust can do to each other. If that is possible, why should we be surprised what people do to others they have never met, people we think are foreigners from another land."

A gray-eyed man sitting directly across from me chimed in, "'Nam looked like a party compared to what went on in my family in Boston before I enlisted at eighteen."

I nodded. I was no longer that bookish girl with hair pulled straight back, ending in a ponytail, who still carried a schoolbag in high school, silent, hiding from the bewildering truth of her family. The inner work I had been doing about my father was necessary. I knew that. It wasn't about sex alone, but an essential stance I had in relation to the world.

In September of that year, my friend Carol, the dermatologist from the Twin Cities, called, and we planned a trip to Prague for three weeks. We left in November.

Something about travel in a foreign country loosens your perceptions. As we walked back and forth across the ancient bridge over the Vltava River, many thoughts came to me.

I remembered hearing a story fifteen years earlier about my second cousins Eric, seventeen, and David, eighteen. Neither of them had a father: one father had died too young, and the other had abandoned his family. Even though these two boys were his blood, I doubt that my father was trying to be paternally helpful; more likely he was bored when he made his offer at a family gathering. "Hey," he turned to them, a cup of tea in his hand, two rugalach on his plate. "It's not too late. Let's hit Aqueduct for a couple of races. I'll show you boys the real world."

They jumped in the car and turned the clover onto the Long Island Expressway. Both cousins had driver's licenses, but my father manned the car. He was their great-uncle Buddy, older than history (he must have been sixty), and he had a predilection for driving slow, very, very slow. He was going forty in the left lane, cars whizzing by on the right.

"C'mon, Uncle Buddy, we'll never get there," David whined from the passenger seat.

"Never mind. Look at the scenery. You live in Connecticut. Enjoy Long Island." He flicked his cigar ashes in the open tray.

"We'll never make it," Eric from the backseat chimed in. David turned around, they looked at each other, and they both fell over laughing.

"No rush. No rush. The horses are waiting for us. Eric, you're a smart boy. Aren't you going to Harvard? You should know speed is for the astronauts."

They pulled into the full parking lot and found a spot far from the entrance. They could hear the cheers in the stands. Suddenly, Uncle Buddy's legs were in motion, the slow man driving a car could really move in the parking lot, the glint off the chrome only exciting him more.

"But I'm under age!" Eric yelled after his great-uncle's back.

My father stopped dead, then turned. "Eric, a smart boy like you, how could you do this to me? C'mon, let's see what I've got in the trunk."

He pulled out baggy trousers. "Here, put them on." He plopped a fedora on his head. It fell below his eyes.

My father stood back. "I don't know," he mused. Then he bent down, picked up two handfuls of dirt, and rubbed it on Eric's cheeks.

"Now walk with a limp like you've got arthritis. No one will stop you."

Eric began to protest.

"Let's go." My father charged ahead.

The authorities grabbed Eric immediately. "What kind of joke is this?"

My father was aching for a winning ticket. He had no time. He ignored the police and spoke directly to his great-nephew. "I'll tell you what." He stuck his hand in his pocket. "Here's the keys. You go back and wait in the car. David and I will just watch two races. We'll bet on one for you."

It was dusk, many races later, when they returned. My father had only won one out of eight. They weaved among the field of cars.

"Where did we park?" my father called to David as they fanned out.

"There's the car." David pointed in the distance at a blue Buick.

"But where's Eric?" They rushed toward the vehicle.

He was crumpled in the backseat. My father knocked on the glass with his knuckles. Eric didn't rouse. He knocked harder.

My father went for his keys and then remembered Eric had them. "Oh, my God, he locked the doors."

"Jeez, it was sweltering all day," David whispered. "There's no open windows. Do you think he's alive?"

"Sure. C'mon," my father jumped on the trunk and rocked the car.

"You bang," he ordered David. "Son of a gun, that kid can sleep."

Eric slowly lifted his head as though he was moving it through wet cement. The first thing he saw was my father's face, his nose smashed against the window. "Open the door."

David on the other side of the car raised his fists high

in the air. "Uncle Buddy did it again—he raised the dead from the living."

My father peered across the car hood, "Kid, you got it all backwards. Your Uncle Buddy got the sleeping to wake up."

The car door swung open. My father jumped in and lit the ignition. "Now, you boys, tell both your mothers you had a very educational time. That your uncle could have been a professor, why even a doctor of philosophy."

They both started to jeer.

"I did go the College of Hard Knocks, you know."

I smiled. It was all there: the thoughtlessness, the inconsideration. Oh, but was he fun! My whole childhood I wanted so badly for him to play with me, but I was a girl. I only interested him in narrow ways.

By the time I reached Prague, I had not seen my parents in over three years. During the whole trip one thought plagued me: "Two people on this earth look like me, carry the same genes."

I returned to the States determined to reconnect. My parents would never respond to my accusations the way I wanted them to. My father was a disrespectful bully, and he could be a cruel tease. But something had turned for me. I knew he would never mistreat me again. I had withdrawn, and he could not bear that. He had no savvy about psychological things, but he did not want to lose me. In a way I did not wholly understand, by having drawn an invisible line he could not cross, I also gave him freedom from his own confused boundaries.

I called on a Saturday night, and my father and I were soon arguing: Who will visit first?

"So what you're saying is you'll never visit us again?" he screamed into the phone. "I'm hanging up." He slammed the phone down. My mother was on another phone. I was breathing heavily. I felt the old hate, but I remembered my vow to reconnect. "Mom, tell him to get back on."

He got back on. You could feel the electric rage between us, but deeper there was determination. "Natalie, you know that vacuum cleaner you want?" he managed to say through gulps of air, "Well, I think you should get a Hoover."

"Do you need it for carpet or wood floors?" He proceeded. He spoke for three full minutes about cleaner parts. He was desperate to keep the connection going. My father was a vacuum salesman before he bought the bar and was now using anything he knew.

I agreed I wanted a stand-up, then no, maybe he was right, an Electrolux might be better.

He talked on, so thick with appliance details I was certain I was in training to become a salesman, just like he had been.

Then he paused, "Don't buy one. Wait. We'll come to New Mexico in May, and I'll help you choose one."

I understood: no psychology talk. This is how my

father communicated. This man, however ignorantly, must love me.

Five months later they flew out.

My parents wasted no time. They launched right back into my spiritual education on the second day of their visit after three years of being apart. That was when my father belted out "Hello Dolly" on the porch using my meditation bell. No Zen master was able to smash false notions the way my parents could. I saw I still was gullible at the core.

It was exactly right that I had talked about Te-shan at that conference. I was merely acting out his dilemma in another dimension. He had the tea-cake woman at the side of the road. I had Syl and Bud from Brooklyn, who were so enlightened they had no idea they were even awake. They were much too busy befuddling me, revealing my ignorance to myself.

On the third afternoon we drank some lemonade in the kitchen—my father preferred his root beer or at least Canada Dry ginger ale—but he was attempting good behavior, and he tried to be polite. He drank his glass of lemonade.

When my mother went off into the bedroom to call my sister, my father leaned in like a coconspirator. "So tell me, Nat, what was wrong—all those letters? Really. I didn't get it. Were you on drugs?"

I'd just taken a gulp of lemonade. The glass was at my mouth. Full of disbelief, I burst out laughing, spraying the drink all over my hand.

"No, really, you broke our hearts." He tapped my forearm. "What kind of trouble were you in?"

All the thousands of dollars I had spent in therapy—the intimate hours of study of my family flashed before me. Useless, all useless. "Well, Dad—" I began.

He cut me off. "You went to a psychiatrist?" He was in shock.

I corrected him. "A psychologist."

He waved that off. "What's the difference? Why, our whole family's nutty. You could have asked me."

Then he moved in closer to ensure that no one else could hear. "You didn't talk about me? What did he say?"

"Dad, it was a woman. She said—"

He didn't wait for an answer. He could not imagine a woman doctor. "Nat, I had a lousy childhood. My father was a mean son of a bitch. With Jews at the time we'd call our fathers 'Pop.' In second grade, in the public schools I heard them say 'Dad' and 'Daddy.'" He brushed his forehead with the palm of his hand. "So I tried it out. When my father came home from work, I said, 'Hi, Dad,' and he looked me straight in the face and said, 'What? You're a sissy?'"

My father shook his head. "We were miserable, but we didn't *talk* about it." He gulped down the last of his lemonade.

Just then my mother walked in and sensed something was amiss. "What have you been talking about?"

"Oh, we had a little friendly father-daughter exchange." He was proud of himself.

My mother looked from one to the other of us nervously. She wanted things to go smoothly.

I interjected, "Joan Mitchell, an American painter who lived in France most of her life, is being shown nearby."

My father brightened. For some reason he liked paintings. He never could believe people could make realistic pictures on canvas. He thought it was a wonder. "The artist came all the way from France to visit?"

"No, but the paintings did."

"Sure, let's go," he said.

My mother was only relieved the subject had changed; also she liked to pretend an interest in culture. After all, her brother was a doctor, and besides, it was an excuse to switch into another outfit. "Give me just a minute."

Walking into the new yellow stuccoed building on Read Street, we were immediately hit with canvases, each as big as a small Volkswagen, splashed with color.

Stepping over to the first one, my father peered closely at the oils. Then he stepped back. "Hey, Nat," he said excitedly. "I know how the painter made it. He filled a cannon with paint and then let it rip."

"Very funny," I said and stepped to the next one, too engrossed to bother correcting his gender assumptions again.

He followed after me, and we looked together at two more. My mother had wandered off.

"I've seen enough," he said. "My knees hurt." My father's legs, after thirty years of standing behind the bar serving drinks, felt tired now. "Find me a chair. I'll just sit and wait."

"A chair is in the back down the hall," the woman behind the desk pointed.

"I'll find it." He trailed off.

I couldn't believe I was getting to see so many of these pictures in person. I was in the process of writing a book about painting, and Mitchell was one of the women painters I had discovered and admired the most.

I came to the end of the show. Out of the corner of my eye I saw my mother heading for the bathroom.

I stepped into the gallery library, a soft gray–carpeted room, and my father was so intently bent over a book on his lap, he didn't hear me come in. I peeked over his right shoulder. He was looking at an abstract pastel by Mitchell, touching the page with his forefinger.

He was suddenly aware of me. "Nat, tell me. What's this a picture of? I'm looking and looking, and I can't figure it out. Is it a tree? A house? I can't find anything."

"Dad," I placed my hand on his shoulder, "it's abstract. It's not supposed to represent anything."

He did not pursue this. His moment of curiosity was over. "You done? Let's go. I've had enough." He slammed the book shut.

We met my mother in the hall, and as we headed out, I asked the same woman behind the desk, "How much?"

She glanced up. "Two fifty."

My father caught the number and was working it around in his brain. We stepped outside and blinked. Though it was late afternoon, the New Mexico light was penetrating.

"Well, I guess that's fair," my father said. "There's a lot of paint and those big canvases. The materials could easily cost that much."

"Dad, she meant two hundred and fifty *thousand*."

We were crossing the street. His face fell. For the first time ever, he could not respond. This was too much to grasp, too beyond his reach. As we drove to the restaurant for dinner, he was totally silent, looking straight ahead out the windshield.

I enjoyed this moment. My father was stumped.

After that visit in Santa Fe, I traveled down to Florida three months later. I knew they were aging, and I wanted to see them whenever I could. My mother mysteriously moved from room to room in her nightgown. I supposed she was not feeling well, but I did not worry so much about her. She often seemed distracted.

The last time I'd visited—before the letters began—I'd invited her repeatedly to come to lunch with me in Palm Beach, just the two of us. When she finally agreed and I took her to a swanky restaurant I thought she'd enjoy, also to impress her that her daughter could afford ten-dollar salads, she said over and over, "I have to get home to your father."

"Why?" I entreated. "He's fine on his own."

"I don't like to be away too long."

Two hours was too long? I wouldn't be visiting for another six months. The continual message I received throughout my childhood was I wasn't worth taking time for. Here it was again being stamped on my forehead.

The other thing she did at this luncheon was comment, on every third bite of food, "This is robbery. We could have gone to a place near our house that gives you twice as much for half the price."

We, of course, never approached the simple conversation I longed for: a question or show of interest in what I was doing or how I felt. Nor did she ever share anything about herself.

As soon as we arrived home, she dashed to the back bedroom to call my sister across the country. Together they commiserated about the poor restaurant choice I made. They were as tight as thieves, and I was left out. It was an old family story I experienced in a hundred ways. I stood at the front door diminished to insignificance.

Nothing had ever been physically wrong with my mother before. My mother's people seemed to live forever. Sam Edelstein, her father, died at ninety-two and her mother, Rose, at ninety-four. But I often thought she could use some of that old-fashioned psychology I had swallowed in gulps. Simple things like: What do you *feel?* What were your dreams, Mom, before you were submerged by your overbearing husband? What is it *you* want to eat when you look at a menu, rather than first checking to see what everyone else is going to order? But I left well enough alone this time. I was tired of being the only one to stir the deep waters. Besides, I enjoyed this new connection with my father. My mother seemed oddly relieved when we left the house and went off on our own.

On the second afternoon of my visit, my father and I picked up the newspaper and drove to my hotel. We planned to go to the races, and he was perusing the Daily Racing Form at the small kitchen table.

"I'm betting on the first two races. Only two. Read me the names. I have an intuition about these things," I said to him.

"Humph," my father let out a long breath.

"C'mon, read them."

"Nightline. Cosmos. Baby's Head. Long Whistle. Vermont Air. Last Puzzle. Kiddin' Around. Blue Will. Zumbro."

I twisted up my face, conjuring the winner. Zumbro had snap. Plus I used to have a boyfriend who lived near the Zumbro River in Minnesota.

"You gotta be kidding. That horse has the worst odds."

"Exactly. When he wins, I'll win big."

"You don't know what you're talking about. Where's the trash?" He threw in a banana peel. "We don't have to bother going to the track. You might as well dump your money in the garbage."

I insisted I knew what I was doing.

My father was half disgusted—he took gambling seriously. Then something big came over him. "I'll tell you what! Let's bet on which horse falls down first." Our eyes locked across the table—a hiatus like a sensation of space in a haiku stopped us dead. We burst into hard laughter. My father's head dropped to the table. He leaned on his arms, drool forming at the corner of his mouth. Everything shimmered, shook: the window over the sink, the burners on the stove, the refrigerator, our water glasses on the table. I was almost choking.

For moments we were free of aches and pains, even free of the weight of the roles of father and daughter. We were in Florida, a whole new state from New York, and we'd known each other for fifty years.

In great delight I rose up and grabbed a blank piece of hotel stationery from the counter. With a black pen, I wrote: "I, Benjamin Goldberg, have received five dollars from Natalie Goldberg, and I will bet it on number nine in the first race. If I neglect to bet it and Zumbro wins, I owe Natalie the money at twenty to one."

I pushed the paper across the yellow Formica table and said, "Sign this. I'm going swimming. I'm not going to the racetrack. I'll give you the five."

He read my formal printing.

"Give me the pen." He reached out his arm. "BULL SHIT" he wrote in caps in his shaky hand, and then signed and handed it back. He was gleeful. "I haven't laughed like that in I don't know when. You know, I'm not going to the track either." His eyes were gleaming. He had taken a great leap. He suddenly saw things in a whole new way.

My FATHER HAD WON AND LOST hundreds, probably thousands, of dollars gambling on horses. My mother said we would have been rich, if it weren't for his betting. I never quite believed how wealthy we would have been.

One Passover when I was eleven, we were in Brooklyn with my mother's oldest brother, the doctor. Paintings from Europe were on the walls, and we passed matzo to each other wrapped in a fresh linen napkin. The meal had an elegant dignity. My grandmother, who lived with us, had made the gefilte fish. Just two days earlier the fresh carp had been swimming in our bathtub. Grandma was proud of her son, and he adored her cooking, put extra beet horseradish on his plate. And those plates! Gold trimmed with a royal blue circle. Even as a young girl I knew the plates were imported from across the Atlantic. Was it England? Belgium? I could never remember. We munched on moist sponge cake, small chocolate truffles for dessert.

I was happy in the special blue dress I wore. Here in Flatbush we were surrounded by Jews, our people. Passover was close to Easter, and at home on Long Island we lived in an all-Catholic neighborhood. To feel comfortable back in Farmingdale we wore Easter hats, white ones with red ribbons, and new spring coats with black velvet trim.

But here in Flatbush, when dessert was over, we put on our new garb to stroll to Martense Street, just ten blocks away, to my father's relatives for a little visit, maybe a second Passover dessert. My mother didn't come with us. My sister and I each held one of my father's hands. At different intervals Rhoda skipped, and I wouldn't step on the sidewalk cracks. My father wore a tan overcoat, unbuttoned, flapping open, and a brown fedora. He was moving fast, not paying a lot of attention to us. This was not unusual, but still it was special to have time alone with him.

We rang the bell to the upstairs half of the white clapboard duplex, and the ring came back to us. My father quickly turned the knob. Aunt Lil, with her dyed flaming-red hair, my father's oldest sister, along with Uncle Sam, his oldest brother, and Junie, my skinny red-headed, red-freckled cousin, who was somehow becoming beautiful as she grew older, all leaned out the door above the long brown-carpeted stairway, shouting, "It's Buddy. C'mon up," and we dashed up the flight, jumping into their arms.

Here in Aunt Lil's living room were big print couches you could flop on and dishes of pretzels, potato chips, and hard candies in twists of bright foil paper. I quickly unwrapped a caramel and popped it into my mouth, grabbed for a fistful of greasy chips. I knew no one here would notice or reprimand me.

My father's relations all seemed larger than life. Aunt Lil's hair was long and wild, pulled back in a barrette, and her laugh was full of gusto. Her husband, Uncle Seymour, had wavy short black hair and a full face. Something about him? I never could put my finger on it. He wasn't unfriendly. He just seemed awkward in the yellow nylon shirts he always wore. What was going on with him? He never laughed like the rest of them, only smiled, not showing any teeth. (We found out years later after he died that at that very same time he was with us, he had a whole second, hidden family with two sons, living in a suburb of Newark, New Jersey.) But my thoughts couldn't linger on him. Aunt Rae, the other sister, the one with the nose job, was now bringing out from the back room Easter baskets for me and Rhoda. Yippee! I snapped off the head of the chocolate bunny and shoved it in my mouth. All the polite manners I exercised at Uncle Manny's could be done away with here. I acted as though they hadn't served a thing over there. This freedom was dizzying.

Aunt Rae lived downstairs with Uncle Sam, but he wasn't there very much. Neither of them ever married. Though I heard that once Aunt Rae ran off to Florida when she was seventeen with a no-good, but Aunt Lil, the older sister, went down to get her and had the marriage annulled. The legend was that Rae and Lil had great legs, real sets of gams, and even my father had gorgeous legs. My mother didn't. All legs would have been the same to me—I was an unsuspecting child who even at eleven did not know about menstrual periods—but value was constantly being put on body parts in my family. Often I heard how one cousin had long piano fingers, a distant uncle had a good nose but a blunt chin, and another relative's lips were too thin.

My Aunt Rae sat opposite us on a stuffed chair, her ankles crossed, one hand holding the wrist of the other. She was smiling, half at us, half in her own dream. Once a few years back when we were alone, she told me about all the beaus she had had, and she showed me costume jewelry they had given her. I cocked my head to look more closely at her nose job. I knew my father loved her. She was the one who looked after him, the youngest in the family. Once as a joke as we were saying good-bye, he stuck his tongue in her mouth. She pulled back and said in a motherly tone, "Buddy, stop that."

Aunt Rae used to get paid to dance with men at a bar in Manhattan. They would buy her drinks, but the bartender only gave her water, my family explained to me. Why would someone treat her to water? I wondered. Everyone seemed relieved when she landed a job selling nylons at a new Alexander's downtown. Then something about Uncle Sam making up the difference in her salary.

During that long summer afternoon in Brooklyn she slipped me peeks at photos, kept in a hidden pocket of her purse, in which she sat at a nightclub table, her flower-patterned dress cut low, two or three idiot men leering at her and gripping whiskey glasses.

I peered at the pictures, then back at her. I understood at an early age that my Aunt Rae was a truly innocent woman with a big and simple heart who did not question the hearts of the men she encountered. Contrary to family opinion, my Aunt Rae seemed fond of her late twenties and thirties when she was beautiful and men desired her.

She was unerringly sweet to me. I started in on the white jelly beans. After all, who else remembered to give me an Easter basket?

I glanced over at Uncle Sam, Aunt Lil, and my father, who were huddled at a corner of the dining room table, gesturing wildly and telling jokes. My aunt hit my father on the upper arm with her open palm, "Oh, Buddy," her eyes full of tears, but she wasn't crying. She was laughing.

I began to eat all the greens, then the yellows.

I watched Uncle Sam. He was always the oddest, with his wiry body, broken Yiddish, mismatched clothing, and loud voice. He was the family genius. My father enlisted twice for active duty in World War II, so his older brother didn't have to go once.

I heard the story many times that money ran short and Uncle Sam couldn't finish medical school, so he became a druggist instead. Bored selling Chiclets and iron pills to old people in the area, he mixed chemicals and tried them on his own body. My parents showed him my A's in math and science, and he offered to put me through pharmacy school when I grew up. My mother raised her eyebrows. This was a good deal, but a girl pharmacist? Shouldn't she be a teacher?

I was curious about Uncle Sam. I had often cajoled my mother into telling me about him. After all, I reasoned to her, I needed to know what a pharmacist's life would be like. My mother put her erect index finger in front of her lips, indicating the secrecy of this story she was about to tell. Above the pharmacy was a two-bedroom flat he rented to a night salesman and his wife, whose name was Charlotte. She was lonely when Murray was away and often came down to talk to Sam, who worked behind the counter till eleven at night in a white button-down shirt. They talked uninterrupted for hours, because the old customers stayed home at night. She confessed to Sam that she still loved salads with marshmallows in them, and she swore she heard crickets once in the middle of winter in upstate New York, back in high school, as she walked home from a dance.

Sam told her about the way his mom used to cook only kosher food, and then he told her what kosher food was, how the pink dishes were for dairy only and the white ones were for meat. On Friday nights they ate braided egg bread and wore small skullcaps. He could speak a language called Yiddish and read Hebrew, where the sentences started from the wrong side of the page.

I wanted my mother to keep going. I didn't care if this had anything to do with my future trade. She hesitated and then continued.

Sam was strange to her, but night after night, talking a counter width away from each other, they fell in love. She was twenty-five and he was already thirty, never having had a girlfriend before.

And there was friendship, my mother said. They'd go off fishing together, and they whistled. Charlotte in sneakers, no socks, rolled up dungarees, and Uncle Sam in old white shorts, shirtless, those few small hairs coming out where his heart was.

This was where my mother stopped the story, but I begged more details out of her.

Murray had no whiff of the affair at first or else didn't care. Sam, who was spending more and more time in Manhattan with Charlotte, rather than at his duplex in Brooklyn that he shared with Aunt Rae, finally rented the second bedroom from Charlotte's husband, Murray, in the apartment above the pharmacy that they actually rented from him.

"Do you get it?" My mother paused in the narrative. It was so *meshugas* (which meant "crazy").

So Uncle Sam spent nights with Charlotte while Murray worked, and Murray spent days with her while Sam worked. Everyone grew comfortable together, like old shoes. Sundays they sat around the table, Charlotte frying eggs and bacon, toasting bagels, and Murray and Sam reading the paper, throwing out facts about the mayor, Washington, and the low temperature the day before.

I leaned my head on my hand and tried to act nonplussed, so she'd go on. But I needn't have worried. My mother was lost in the story now. Nothing could have stopped her.

In the summers Sam closed the pharmacy, and he and Charlotte spent two months at Twin Oaks, the old dilapidated mansion on the south shore of Long Island that his family a long time ago had bought for a song. Murray would come out on weekends.

It was at Twin Oaks when I knew Charlotte and Sam the best. I was five or six, and I remembered the smell of turpentine, the wooden ladder, the white hens in the tall grass as Sam and Charlotte painted the trim on the endless summer home. Charlotte and I sat in the white kitchen at Twin Oaks making up songs about Uncle Sam, while Charlotte cut up carrots for coleslaw with the tan dog Fluffy at her feet. I never knew Charlotte's last name.

My mother continued. Charlotte must have known Sam was nuts, or odd or temperamental, but she loved him. Once when Uncle Sam heard raccoons running on top of the roof, he ran for a gun and shot at them through the bedroom ceiling. White plaster filled in cracks in the old wooden floor and covered everything for days.

In Uncle Sam's bedroom there was at least a thousand

dollars' worth of hi-fi equipment next to a thin mattress on the floor. Sam was wild about classical music. He turned the hi-fi so loud Dad would run up the stairs—

I interjected, "Didn't I follow after him? Wasn't I real young?"

Yes, she nodded, and went on. He banged on the door, but Uncle Sam couldn't hear. He wanted Charlotte to listen to a new record he'd bought, and when it was done he turned to her and whispered, "Did you like that?"

My mother moved her head closer to mine, and there was urgency in her telling.

One January they went to Carnegie Hall to hear a live performance. He was loaded, but he was so cheap he would spend the money for tickets only once a year. After the concert was over, Sam stood up in the balcony, put two fingers in his mouth, and let out a shrill whistle like an ump at a Dodgers' game. He stuck thumbs-up with his other hand and shouted, "Atta boy, Isaac!"

"You know who Isaac was, don't you?" My mother didn't wait for me to answer. "Only Isaac Stern, the greatest violinist in the world." Just then I noticed a raised mole on my mother's upper lip.

She moved deeper into the story. Then he helped Charlotte put her coat over her pink satin dress—can you imagine wearing that to a concert?—and, with rubbers on their feet, they walked through the winter slush to the subway. Over and over Uncle Sam heard the concert in his head.

Eventually Murray died and Charlotte and Uncle Sam married in an Israeli restaurant—suddenly my reverie was interrupted. "C'mon, girls. It's time to go." My father stood up from Aunt Lil's table.

Just as we were hugging everyone good-bye, my father said aloud, "Last week at the races I made an extra five hundred dollars, but I didn't tell Sylvia." He said it to show off to his older siblings. I even understood that then, but all I cared about was that he betrayed my mother, whom we left, still visiting her brother, our Uncle Manny, several city blocks away.

"Oh, Buddy, you shouldn't," my Aunt Lil said.

I didn't say a word as we walked back to my uncle's, but as soon as the door was opened, I ran to my mother, cupped my hand over her ear, and whispered, "Daddy won five hundred dollars and didn't tell you."

I dashed into the bathroom and vomited my Easter candy into the toilet.

As we drove the hour out to Farmingdale, huddled into the Buick, all six of us, including my grandmother and grandfather, my mother didn't say a word, but I felt vindicated anyway. I had held a rage beneath the surface, and now I had proof of his violation.

Usually, my mother had no problem screaming in front of the immediate family but, oddly, it was quiet in the house for the next three days. I forgot about the whole incident.

On the fourth day, it was a Wednesday—I remember

clearly because that was the day each week after school I went to my Girl Scout troop meeting—I met my father on the walkway leading up to the front door of our split level. He worked nights; it was a little after five and he was running late. When he saw me, his face turned ugly. "Because of you, your mother and I almost divorced." Then he belted me across the face with his fist. My head jerked back, but I quickly turned and looked straight at him. I did not utter a word. I was no longer young. He hurried past me to his car. I marched stunned into the house and sat down at the kitchen table, in the center of which my grandmother was about to place a platter of lamb chops. I silently ate the mashed potatoes she lovingly put back into the skin.

My father had never hit me before. He was a big man and doubled as the bouncer in his own bar. Years later he told me that that incident in front of our house unraveled him. He expected me to burst out crying.

Even at eleven I was honing myself to meet him head-on and stand up. My father had an inner power that could recognize the integral power in others. I think he recognized the crude beginnings of mine that day.

On the last night of my visit in Florida, I said goodbye to my mother. She still seemed removed, but when I asked her about it, she said she'd just been tired. My mother and I hugged. She told me to have a safe trip. My plane left early the next day.

My father drove me back to the hotel. At the first sign of any yellow light he braked. He timed it perfectly, so he didn't miss one red light. His driving was maddening.

As we sat in the car waiting for green, he gnawed on one end of an unlit Bering Plaza cigar. I could see he did not want to let me go. "Did I ever tell you about this one anti-Semite who came to the bar regularly in the early sixties."

Yes, he had told me, but I said, "Vaguely. Tell it to me again."

My father relished bitterness and revenge. "I turned green every time I handed this man a whiskey. The man talked of hebes and kikes and then ordered another drink on the rocks. I poured it like it was gasoline. I wanted to burn this man. He had a scar above his right eye, I remember. Weeks passed. This was a good-paying customer, but I tasted bile whenever this man stepped up to the barstool.

"You were, I think, in junior high school. One Saturday we visited Uncle Sam at the pharmacy in Manhattan."

I nodded. I remember licking a cone of coffee ice cream at the counter, when my father leaned over to his brother. By then my uncle's teeth were yellow and browned at the roots. He had a prominent skull that jutted out from his thin neck, and he wore a narrow mustache above almost invisible lips. He rolled down his white shirtsleeves as he listened to his only brother.

"Sam, I wanna get this anti-Semite. I don't want to do

him in—I only want to make him real uncomfortable. The son of a bitch."

My uncle's face was the color of putty in the gray light from the big front windows.

"Buddy, you have to be careful." Then my uncle smiled, and I saw those teeth again. I licked down to the sugar cone and took my first bite. "I do have something. It's a horse laxative. But you only can use the tiniest bit—a man is not a horse—otherwise, you'll kill him."

My father lit up.

Uncle Sam slipped him a brown bottle with a rubber dropper, just as my mother came out of the ladies' room in a black velvet hat with a red bird on top. A fresh smear of lipstick was across her face. My father palmed the bottle into his trouser pocket.

"Careful, Buddy," my uncle said again and then, "Sylvia, you look beautiful." My mother flashed her dark eyes.

Another red traffic light. My father pulled out the ashtray and balanced his cigar on the edge. Then he continued, "When that lousy man came in again and ordered his third drink, I turned my back to the bar to pour it. I touched, just touched, the rim of the glass with that golden liquid in the dropper. I slapped that glass on the bar, 'This one's on me,' and I leaned back and watched."

The light changed to green. The car behind us honked its horn. My father took his foot off the brake and ever so slightly applied the gas. Then he continued, "The man bolted down the drink, and faster than his mind could think," he smiled at the rhyme and at the memory, "the laxative ran through his body. He was about to say, 'Where's the bathroom?' but he'd already done his business. And I just nodded congenial-like. He turned red and ran out the door."

"What if you killed him?" I asked.

"I didn't kill that tough bastard, but I never saw him again."

"What was his name?"

My father turned and looked at me suspiciously. "You're not going to write about it?"

"No, of course not."

"Ahh, what the hell. He deserved it."

We parked the car and were standing on the concrete step in front of my room. He grabbed me by the shoulders. "I love you." He paused. "I love you—I *really* love you." These weren't just words family members said to one another. A connection was being made. Here we were together, this one lifetime, me and him. He loved his daughter.

He started to take off the ruby ring. "It's your inheritance. Take it now."

I shook my head and put my hand on his wrist.

"You wear it," I said.

I never wanted him to die.

THE NEXT MORNING I was sitting at gate thirty-four, Delta, waiting to board the plane at five fifteen. Was that my father in the empty distance down at gate twenty-three, coming toward me walking his lopsided walk, heavy to the right, in a blue T-shirt and khaki Bermudas, carrying a bag?

"Gee, I was afraid you'd already left. I grabbed some fruit. You'll get hungry." He reached out the sack and was pleased.

I looked in—a brown banana and two apples. "I got them from the kitchen." I looked up at him. His smile hardly revealed his small teeth, darkened and close together in front.

At least four or five of his back teeth had been pulled. When the dentist told him how much a root canal would cost and then the capping, he said straight out, "Pull."

The dentist stuttered, tried to explain the necessity of—

My father cut him off. "You've got to be kidding—twelve hundred dollars! I don't like my teeth that much." He opened his mouth wide. "Go ahead. Do as I say, pull."

I thanked him for the fruit. "I do get hungry on these long flights."

He nodded, satisfied that he knew to do the right thing. "Well, I won't hang around. I got things to do." At eighty-two he no longer played golf or tennis. He mostly spent his days in front of the TV with the shades pulled against the southern sun.

"Sure," I said.

He raised his big paw, turned, and I watched him walk away. From the back I saw his right hand raised to his face. He was wiping away tears.

Time felt convoluted. I'd tumbled from youth, and my father had shot through to old age.

PART 2

I can write a beautiful piece about the red rock desert, but if I don't talk about the fact that if you just switch your eyes a little bit to the left you'll see the results of oil and gas leases . . . that doesn't quite seem honest. And a hundred years from now, I don't want someone to say, where was she? Why didn't she tell us the truth?

—Terry Tempest Williams

Te-shan asked the old tea-cake woman, "Who is your teacher? Where did you learn this?"

She pointed to a monastery a half mile away.

Te-shan visited Lung-t'an and questioned him far into the night. Finally when it was very late, Lung-t'an said, "Why don't you go and rest now?"

Te-shan thanked him and opened the door. "It's dark outside. I can't see."

Lung-t'an lit a candle for him, but just as Te-shan turned and reached out to take it, Lung-t'an blew it out.

At that moment Te-shan had a great enlightenment. Full of gratitude, he bowed deeply to Lung-t'an.

The next day Lung-t'an praised Te-shan to the assembly of monks. Te-shan brought his books and commentaries in front of the building and lit them on fire, saying, "These notes are nothing, like placing a hair in vast space."

Then bowing again to his teacher, he left.

THE THURSDAY NIGHT I flew into Minneapolis and saw Katagiri Roshi's body laid out in the zendo (meditation hall), dead eighteen hours from a cancer he fought for over a year, was also the night I had slipped the original letter to my father into the blue mailbox. I flipped the stone-cold metal lid and heard the long white envelope hit the bottom. I was standing across the street from Zen Center at the edge of Lake Calhoun, where the solid ice was only beginning to break up. Even though it was past midnight, thick gray clouds hovered low in the sky. I'd carried that letter in my purse for over a month. The immense disappointment at seeing Roshi dead shocked me into finally sending it. Now I would lose both fathers.

But mail is slower than we think. The date was March first. It was probably picked up on March second. My father did not receive it until the morning of March seventh, his birthday. I never planned it that way. I didn't think about it. My father, ordinarily not a thoughtful man, did. "My birthday? Why would you do that?" My father liked his birthday and wanted to enjoy his day.

It was incomprehensible that I would never see my beloved teacher again. My father was the only one I knew who had sneered at death's bleak face as he fought in the righteous war that marked his life. Of everyone I knew, he alone did not seem afraid of the great darkness. "Nat, you're here and then you're not. Don't worry about it. It's not a big deal," he told me as he placed a pile of army photos on my lap. "The Japanese, you have to give it to 'em. They could really fight. Tough, good soldiers." Then he held up a black-and-white. "Here's your handsome daddy overseas."

Roshi also fought as a young man in World War II. He told a story about not wanting to kill and shooting in the air above enemy heads. I told that to my father. "What a lot of malarkey," my father sneered. "You don't believe that, do you? You're in battle, you fight."

My father met my teacher only once, about a year after I had married. We had just bought the lower half of a duplex on a leafy tree–lined one-way street six blocks from Zen Center in Minneapolis. I was in my early thirties, and my parents drove out for a week in July. They were still young, in their early sixties.

In the middle of one afternoon when no one was around, we slipped off our shoes and stepped onto the high-shined wooden floor of the zendo. My parents peered at bare white walls, black cushions, and a simple wooden altar with a statue and some flowers.

I heard the door in the hall open. "I bet that's Roshi."

My father's eyes grew wide. His face swung to the large screened window, and for a moment I thought he was going to crash through in a grand escape. Pearls of sweat formed on his upper lip.

Roshi turned the corner. They stood across the room from each other. The meeting was brief. They never shook hands. My father was subdued, withdrawn, and Roshi too wasn't his usual animated self.

I remember thinking, my father has become shy in front of a Zen master—finally someone tamed him.

I got it all wrong. He didn't give a shit about that. He had just encountered the enemy face-to-face. After Roshi exited, he hissed, "I fought them, and now you're studying with them."

"If this were your last moment on earth," Roshi cut the silence with these words late at night, "how would you sit?" We were waiting for the bell to ring. It was the end of a weeklong retreat. Our knees and backs ached. The candle flame hissed; the smell of incense from Eiheiji monastery (the Japanese training center for Soto Zen), shipped in cartons to Minnesota, soaked our clothes.

"You've got to be kidding. Just ring the damn bell," was the only thought that raced through my head.

On other occasions when he asked similar questions, my mind froze. Me, die? Not possible.

Death was something aesthetic, artistic; it had to do with the grand words "forever," "eternity," "emptiness." I never had known anyone who had died before. It was merely a practice point: everything is impermanent. Sure, sure. But really it was inconceivable that my body would not be my body. I was lean, young, and everything worked. I had a name, an identity: Natalie Goldberg.

What a shock it was for me to see my great teacher's stiff body. This was for real? The man I had studied with for twelve years was gone? Stars, moon, hope stopped.

Ocean waves and ants froze. Even rocks would not grow. This truth I could not bear.

Wait a minute! Wasn't he the one who urged me to create writing as a Zen practice? Didn't I do that—and wrote a book about it? Vice presidents of insurance agencies, factory workers in Nebraska, quarry diggers in Missouri, lawyers, doctors, housewives, all with secret, tender hearts yearning to step forward and speak, were sending me fan letters. After eons of fear from stiff school curriculums, I gave them the tools to write. I was doing my part for Zen in this country, saving sentient Americans all over the place.

And, Roshi, I did it for you. I couldn't have done it alone. You were always at my back. And now you're dead? Impossible. I'm out there alone? My breath caught. This can't be. I won't take death seriously—you must be someplace. I'll come find you. Heaven? Hell? Give me a minute. I'll figure it out. I'm coming for you.

My panic was real. I only had one tool: I immediately dove into creating another book. Writing was all-powerful for me. I would keep him alive this way. I would write about the cuffed jeans he wore when he worked on the land, the wild smile that showed the bottom of his teeth, his thick arms, how he fell off the zafu (meditation cushion) laughing when I'd tell him a marriage problem. I'd tug at his priest robe. "Very funny, yes. Now help me."

For the two years I wrote, he stayed vividly alive. He was with me.

Although I didn't speak to my father for a long time after the trauma of sending the letter, I still considered myself a lucky woman, as I leaned over my notebook writing the book about Roshi. Maybe my childhood wasn't so great, but look who I had found, this man from another country. I could step out of my own skin and be free. I began the first pages explaining in detail my lost suburban childhood and then on page one hundred, bingo! I met Roshi.

I was guided by three great teachings I received from him:

Continue Under All Circumstances
Don't Be Tossed Away—Don't Let Anything Stop You
Make Positive Effort for the Good

The last one Roshi told me when I was divorcing and couldn't get out of bed.

"If nothing else, get up and brush your teeth." He paused. "I can never get up when the alarm goes off. Nevertheless," he nodded, "I get up."

Once in the early days I was perplexed about trees. I asked at the end of a lecture, "Roshi, do the elms suffer?"

He answered.

"What? Could you tell me again? Do they really suffer?" I couldn't take it in.

He shot back his reply.

It pinged off my forehead and did not penetrate. I was

caught in thinking mind, too busy trying to understand everything.

But my confusion had drive. I raised my hand a third time. "Roshi, just once more. I don't get it. I mean do trees *really* suffer."

He looked straight at me. "Shut up."

That went in.

The amazing thing was I did not take it personally. He was directly commanding my monkey mind to stop. I'd already been studying with him for a while. Those two words were a relief. Dead end. Quit. I rested back into my sitting position and felt my breath go in and out at my nose. The thought about trees that evening stopped grabbing me by the throat.

With him extraneous things were cut away. My life force stepped forward. After a sleepy childhood I was seen and understood. Glory! Glory! I had found a great teacher in the deep north of this country. Maybe that had been the purpose of my short marriage: to bring me here. Both Roshi and I did not belong in Minnesota, yet we had found each other.

I positioned Roshi in the deep gash I had in my heart. He took the place of loneliness and desolation, and with him as a bolster I felt whole. But the deal was he had to stay alive, continue existing, for this configuration to work.

I sat by the hot oven as his body was cremated. All that was left was ashes. I took two years to finish the book about him and then I really faced the end: Where was he?

I traveled to Czechoslovakia with my friend Carol to celebrate the book's completion, but there was no rejoicing. That was when it all came home: I was deeply, deeply alone. No Zen teacher, and no blood father either.

We were in Karlovy Vary, a beautiful resort town, a hiatus in all the destructive history of Czechoslovakia.

Carol wrote down the most precise directions for me to meet her at the bus station to ride back to Prague at the end of the day: walk down the main avenue, cross the railroad tracks, make a left, a right . . . She could tell I was preoccupied, and she didn't want me to miss the bus back.

"Uh-huh," I nodded and stuck the paper slip in my pocket.

Large chestnut trees lined the park; the leaves' broad edges had turned yellow, red, and orange. I bent to pocket three large mahogany nuts for a friend in New Mexico.

"Karlovy Vary," I repeated like a chant. Writers have come to you. What is it you have?

Goethe was an old man when he visited with a very young consort. It would have been scandalous, but it was Goethe—he was a great literary figure—and it was Europe. Worse things had happened. Rilke was here for refuge and relaxation. I liked this place. I felt connected.

Shadows were lengthening. I finished the pistachio ice cream I ate out of a silver dish, put some coins on the small round marble table, and pulled the crumpled note from my pocket.

I reread the directions. I'd wandered far from the place that Carol's directions began from. No matter. I pursed my lips and set out. Travel imbued me with a poignancy; I felt a grand weight for each step, brick, storefront. None of this will last forever. Each moment vividly presented itself. I felt a lump in my throat, a thump in my heart, the pulse of my blood. Now and now and now. I was back in the romance of eternity.

I realized I hadn't thought of Roshi in days. What a relief! I congratulated myself. Then at the edge of a line of shops, I turned at a souvenir cart—I don't know how to say this—in the twilight I saw a tree. At least ten feet tall, buoyant, arms extended, leaves bright green. But the tree was nameless. I dropped my suitcase. How was it possible? I lowered myself onto a bench. People rushed by.

"So this is where you've ended up? While they carry your ashes to Tassajara in Carmel Valley and Hokyoji in Minnesota and Taisoin in Japan, you have escaped into a tree."

I sat contentedly in the growing dark. I never wanted to leave.

Suddenly, my happiness cracked. I remembered: the bus! Carol! Czechoslovakia! My God! I ripped myself away from the ten thousand leaves and tore through the cobbled streets toward the narrow highway where the station was. I flew into the ticket man's chest as he tried to signal with his hands: no more buses.

"No, no, no," I screamed, dropping any pretense of being human.

A cry from the back of a receding bus, a screech of brakes, and then my name yelled out in the dark. I grabbed my bag and ran. Carol beckoned through the window with her arms.

I flung myself into the backseat. We tilted as the vehicle swung around a curve and banged us on the hard wooden seats.

"We were late in leaving," she explained.

I looked at her and nodded. I leaned my cheek against the cold glass as we rolled through the mysterious countryside. "Karlovy Vary, Karlovy Vary," I whispered. Goethe found love. Rilke, poetry. And what do you know? I found Roshi.

But that elation did not last.

Soon after our visit to Prague, the book came out, and my publisher arranged a tour. For my first two books, I hadn't gone on one. I'd heard hard stories from other writers about late planes, missed interviews, being stranded in the wrong city, getting a cold and sounding like a foghorn, losing bearings and referring on radio to the wrong town, the one you were in last week. But for Roshi I would do it. Even if I no longer had him, he should be shared with others. Maybe they would benefit as I had. Maybe too I wouldn't feel so alone in my grief. I kept wondering who I would write for now. What great purpose would again spring me into action?

In the back of cabs going to airports from Minneapolis, St. Louis, Washington, D.C., Boston, Milwaukee, my body collapsed with exhaustion. I can't do this anymore—and then, miraculously, I experienced energy fill me from some source outside myself. I was so pleased, I did not question it.

In Seattle, my tenth city, the escort, who took me to radio stations, bookstore readings, the hotel, was particularly lovely. "You seem to be doing okay." She eyed me cautiously in the passenger seat as she drove me to the airport. "The last one I drove around two days ago caught a stomach flu and sat with a bucket between her legs." She turned a corner. "If you know even one person in the audience, it seems to help and make a difference. You don't feel so dislocated."

Yes, it was true. I was lucky. I did know people everywhere I went. But Portland, Oregon, was next. I'd never been there. I didn't know a single soul. I'd held out well, but I was worn out.

The short plane ride from Seattle to Portland left at five in the morning. The publisher wanted to make sure nothing would keep me from a newspaper interview at ten. At six thirty the new escort, Deirdre, was waiting at the gate. She began talking as soon as she saw me. "I've made a decision this year to tell every author I work with about political issues I think are important."

"Please don't," I said silently as I looked out the window. A terrible headache was converging over my eyebrows. We were stuck in traffic. She launched into a tirade about lesbians, then one on abortion, and another on the evils of taxes.

I sunk deeper in the car seat. I had no energy to assert my opinion.

"You have a noon brown bag at Cat Bird Seat Bookstore downtown. The idea is that people can come hear you during their lunch hour. But no one ever comes. You'll be lucky if you sell one book. We can be late." Deirdre pressed both hands against the top of the steering wheel. "Would you like to stop at the hotel first?"

"Yes!" I almost jumped through the roof of the car. A moment to get away. Yes, yes, yes.

When we pulled up in front of the bookstore, it was jammed. I had so thoroughly believed Deirdre that I turned to the manager, who rushed at me, and asked, "Did you have a speaker today?"

"Yes—you're late." She grabbed my elbow and hurried me up front.

I looked out on a crowded room; most people were sitting on the carpeted floor. I read a short piece about how I first met Roshi, then opened it up for discussion.

The audience's questions surprised me. "How many of you are Zen students?" I asked.

No one raised their hand. "In no other group all over the country did anyone ask me anything about Buddhism, even though this," I held up my book, "is about my twelve-year relationship with a Zen teacher. But your comments are detailed and technical about aspects of sitting. No center here either?"

People shook their heads.

"Hmmm." I looked at the clock above their heads. "I better sign books. Lunch hour is almost up."

A long line formed out the door. I settled into a seat at the table. This would take a while. I was lonely, and I was tired. I knew no one in this town, but I tried my best.

I signed a new book on the title page.

I signed the next woman's. She had an old copy of my first.

The third woman held a pile of three book-club copies, two used and one new. "You've got them all," I teased her.

She was in a flutter and wanted certain pages signed in each one.

Ahh, I'll take a little rest while she opens them. I had no other thought in my head. I leaned back in the chair and glanced over to the checkout—there he was! leaning his elbows on the counter. The arms of his koromo (priest robe) were tied back like they were when he swept the walk, raked under the elm out back of the zendo. Every time the cash register rang, the drawer snapped open and he broke into laughter, rubbing his shaved head with his hand. Many people were buying this book about him. Another purchase, another ring. The change tray flew out, and again he laughed, this time with his chin in his chunky muscled hand. I don't think it was the book sales that delighted him. It was the silly mechanism of the spirited register that caused his glee, a bonus he hadn't expected. He was here to pay a visit to his former student, so she wouldn't be lost in an unknown town.

And his old student drank in his presence for as long as she could—one very good long moment.

The woman cleared her throat to get my attention. Her opened books were piled in front of me on the table. She had found her places.

"Oh, yes," I said and dragged my attention away from Roshi.

I picked up my pen and wrote my name in the top one. I dated it: the month, the year, the day, even the time. I wrote "in Portland, Oregon" with great assurance. Then I drew a small heart next to the state name to stamp the secret in place, that he was here.

The last time I saw Roshi alive he was lying in bed in his apartment above the zendo in Minneapolis, Minnesota. His wife was reading him a letter from a former student. He'd received a lot of mail. In his last months he had been dismayed that he hadn't done very much in America, but the messages overwhelmingly thanked him for how he'd changed lives. He was listening attentively to the words his wife read. I didn't want to interrupt, so I stayed briefly. I was returning to New Mexico the next day. Just as I opened the door to leave, he called out, "I'll see you again."

"Sure," I agreed, but I knew he was dying. In all our interactions he was careful to make teaching points. He was never casual with me. Maybe he was worn out from making any point. This one time perhaps he just threw out an American colloquialism, "See ya again." Or could he have been in denial about his sickness?

I leaned over past the next person, who was handing me a book, but Roshi was gone. I knew, though, with certainty that he'd kept his promise. But this was no magic, no white knight who came to save me. Great effort, not my individual will, had harnessed these forces, allowed this moment to coalesce. He manifested in support not of me but of the dharma, of the sharing of teachings.

Deirdre came to get me. I gave her a big grin. It was then that I fell into a trap: thinking the visit was personal and maybe if I kept making effort, he'd keep returning, death be damned. But in a moment I let go, and as we walked to the Chevy, I only felt happy: I got to see him again.

A BOOK IS A PUBLIC THING. I became known as Katagiri Roshi's student. I felt lucky to have known him, but my heart was tied to a dead man. I couldn't let go, and I couldn't go on.

The third year after his death was the worst in my life. Through the book people were loving Roshi, but there was no one to love, only an image made of words. I wrote those words, and while I was writing I was oblivious to the finality of his passing. But in that third year, I felt the strong winds of New Mexico blow through the hole in my chest.

Our process had been cut short. In a healthy teacher-student relationship, the teacher calls out of the student a large vision of what is possible. I finally dared to feel the great true dream I had inside. I projected it onto this person who was my teacher. This projection was part of spiritual development. It allowed me to discover the largeness of my own psyche, but it wasn't based on some illusion. Roshi possessed many of these projected qualities, but each student was individual. When I asked other practitioners what impressed them about Katagiri Roshi, the reported qualities were different for each person. One woman in Santa Cruz admired his unerring self-confidence. When she visited me in New Mexico she stood up and imitated his physical stance. She said that even when no one understood his English and we weren't sure of the Buddhist concepts he discussed, he bowed in front of the altar and walked out after his lecture as though all time and the universe were backing him.

I'd never even taken note of that. What I loved was his enthusiasm, his ability to be in the moment and not judge and categorize me. He had a great sense of humor. I admired his dedication to practice and to all beings and his willingness to tell me the truth, with no effort to sweeten it.

Eventually, as the teacher-student relationship matures, the student manifests these qualities herself and learns to stand on her own two feet. The projections are reclaimed. What we saw in him is also inside us. We close the gap between who we think the teacher is and who we think we are not. We become whole.

Roshi died before this process was finished. I felt like a green fruit. I still needed the sun, the rain, the nutrients of the tree. Instead, the great oak withered; I dangled for a while and then fell to the ground, very undernourished.

How many of us get to live out the full maturation process? Our modern lives are built on speed. We move fast, never settle. Most of us grab what we can, a little from here, then there. For twelve years I had one source. I should have been satisfied. He gave me everything. I knew that when I saw his dead body, but how to live it inside myself?

This projection process also can get more complicated if we haven't individuated from our original parents. Then we present to the teacher those undeveloped parts too. Here the teacher needs to be savvy, alert, and committed in order to avoid taking advantage of vulnerable students. I have read about Zen ancestors who practiced with their teachers for forty years in a single monastery, and I understand why. There would be no half-baked characters in those ancient lineages.

But, oddly enough, Te-shan only had that one meeting with Lung-t'an, and he woke up. Of course, he was a serious scholar of the dharma for a long time. Who is to say scholarly pursuits—studying books intently and writing commentary—don't prepare the mind as well as sweeping bamboo-lined walkways, sitting long hours, or preparing monastery meals?

Zen training is physical. But what isn't physical while we have a body on this earth? Sitting bent over books, our eyes following a line of print, is physical too. So that when Te-shan had that single evening in Lung-t'an's room, he was already very ripe. Lung-t'an merely had to push him off the tree, and Te-shan was prepared to fall into the tremendous empty dark with no clinging.

Te-shan was shown true darkness when Lung-t'an blew out the light; he held at last a dharma candle to guide his way, but he still had a lot of maturation ahead of him. Don't forget the next morning he made that grandiose gesture of burning his books in front of the assembly of monks. He was still acting out, choosing this and leaving that. He was not yet able to honor his whole journey, to respect everything that brought him to this moment. Te-shan still envisioned things in dualistic terms: now only direct insight mattered; books needed to be destroyed. He didn't see that all those years of study had created a foundation that supported his awakening with Lung-t'an. Originally he traveled from the north with his sutras on his back to enlighten the southern barbarians. Here he was doing a complete reversal, torching his past and revering his present experience. Someday he would embrace the north and the south, unify all of China in his heart, and attain a peaceful mind. But he was not there yet. We see him engaged in drama, presenting a flaming pageant in front of the other monks.

His life had not yet settled and become calm.

After he left Lung-t'an, he wandered for a long time, looking to be tested and sharpened. He already had left his place in northern China to wander among what he thought were the southern barbarians. He might be the precursor to our fractured American way of searching for peace.

How can anyone survive if the way is so splintered? What we learn is it's all whole, been whole all along. It is our perception that is broken and that creates a shattered world. But each of us has to discover this in our own lives. That is what is so hard.

"I wish you'd gotten to meet him," I'd tell writing students.

"We are," they'd say, meaning they did through knowing me.

I scoffed. "You don't know what you're talking about."

At a party in San Francisco, Ed Brown, a longtime Zen practitioner and author of many books, pulled me over. "Nat, I have another story about Katagiri for you to steal."

I laughed. I'd asked his permission and acknowledged him with the last one I used. I put my arm around him. "Sure, Ed, give it to me. I'd love to steal from you again."

He began, "I'd been practicing for twenty years when the thought suddenly came to me, 'Ed, maybe you can just hear what your heart is saying. You can be quiet and pay attention to yourself.' It was a big moment of relief for me. Tears filled my eyes."

He showed me with his fingers how they fell down his cheeks. "I'd tried so hard all my life. Made such effort, lived in a monastery since I was young. And now this. Could it be that simple?

"The next day I had an interview with Katagiri. I asked him, 'Do you think it's okay to just listen to yourself?'

"He looked down, then he looked up. 'Ed, I tried very hard to practice Dogen's Zen. After twenty years I realized there was no Dogen's Zen.'"

Dogen was a strict patriarch from thirteenth-century Japan. We chanted his words each morning. He was a yardstick by which we measured ourselves.

I felt my legs buckle. I reached out for the back of a chair. Just us. No heaven Zen in some Asian sky out there.

I put my hand on Ed's shoulder. "Ed, I vow to once again misappropriate your story." He nodded, satisfied.

I was reminded how simple, sincere, earnest Roshi was. I was happy, and then it ignited my anger. I was mad he died. I had found the perfect teacher.

I tried practicing other places. I did two fall practice periods at Green Gulch, part of the San Francisco Zen

Center. While I was there, an old student told me about the early years at the Zen monastery in Carmel Valley.

Tassajara was in a narrow valley. The sun didn't reach it until late morning, rising over an eastern mountain, and it dropped early behind the slope of a western one. The practice was difficult, and the days and nights were frigid and damp. But American students of the late sixties were fervent about this path to liberate their lives. One particular winter retreat that lasted for a hundred days was being led by Katagiri, fresh from Japan.

One young zealous woman, a fierce practitioner, a bit Zen crazed, was having a hard time. She was full of resistance when the four o'clock wake-up bell rang on the fifth day of Rohatsu sesshin, an intense week that honored Buddha's enlightenment and signaled almost the finish of the long retreat. Practice that day would again be from four thirty in the morning until ten at night with few breaks except for short walking meditations (kinhin) and an hour work period after lunch. It was her turn that morning to carry the kyosaku, that long narrow board administered in the zendo to sleepy students' shoulders. Her hands were frozen and her bare feet were ice on the cold wooden floor when she got there. She picked up the wake-up stick and passed quietly by the altar to do the ritual bow to Katagiri, the head teacher, who was facing into the room. The flame on the candle was strong. The incense wafted through the air. The practitioners were settled onto their cushions, facing out toward the wall.

A thought inflamed her just as she was about to bow in front of Katagiri: it's easy for him. He's Asian. He's been doing this all his life. It's second nature. His body just folds into position.

Though it is a rule of retreat that people do not look at each other, in order to limit social interaction and provide psychic space for going deeply within, at this moment she glanced up at Roshi. She was stunned to see pearls of sweat forming on his upper lip. Only one reason he could have been perspiring in this frozen zendo: great effort. It wasn't any easier for him than anyone else. Was she ever wrong in her assumptions. She had gotten close enough to see what no one was supposed to see. All her rage and stereotyping crumbled.

My heart jumped. I imagined the small hard dark hairs above his lip—he did not shave for the whole week during sesshins. I recalled the shadow building on his cheeks and shaved head as the days went on, how he bowed with his hands pressed together in front of him, elbows out, and shoulders erect. His small beautiful foot as he placed a step on the floor during kinhin. Though retreats were austere, singular, solitary, there was also a rare intimacy that was shared in silence and practice together.

Just two weeks before the end of the second Green Gulch retreat, in December 1995, almost six years after Katagiri Roshi had died, in a stunning moment in the zendo that shot through me like a hot steel bolt, I realized this regimented practice no longer fit me. The known world blanked out, and I was lost in the moving weight of a waterfall. For me, the structure *was* Katagiri Roshi. I learned it all from him. If I stepped out of it, I'd lose my great teacher. I knew how to wake at four o'clock in the morning, to sit still for forty-minute periods, to eat with three bowls in concentration—it was over, other parts of me needed care. Structure had saved my life, given me a foundation, and now it was cracking. It was a big opening, but I wasn't up to it.

After the practice period I stayed at a friend's south of San Francisco, recuperating from one of those terrible winter flus that flatten a person for three weeks. Below the surface of sneezing and blowing my nose, in the place I could not touch, I feared I would lose Roshi. I wanted so bad to keep him alive, and I thought the fierce structure of Zen was the way. The conflict of holding on and needing to let go made me sick and gloomy, as I lay in bed.

My friend handed me a cup of hot tea. Right before she went to the movies, she changed the bedsheets, while I took a shower. As I slipped into the fresh linen, the phone rang. I almost didn't answer. Let the machine pick it up. It couldn't be for me. Hardly anyone knew I was there. The phone was on a small table on the left side of the bed. The humidifier was whistling as I lifted the mouthpiece and in a nasal voice whispered, "Hello."

"Natalie, it's Peter." He had been at the Minnesota Zen Center, but we rarely had reason to speak in the last two or three years. How did he find me here? "I have something to tell you."

My eyes were swollen, and my ears hurt. "What?" I innocently asked.

"Roshi's priests were in a teachers' meeting, and it came out that Roshi had slept with a student."

My nose was running. Where were my tissues? "Huh?" I asked. I must have misheard.

"A student had lodged a complaint about a sexual indiscretion with one of Roshi's dharma heirs, and Eleanor got all heated up and suddenly blurted out, 'I don't know what the big deal is. Roshi and I had a reationship for a year and—' Then she abruptly stopped and threw her hand over her mouth. She realized what she'd said. We all turned to her—no one cared about the other problem anymore. We just stared at her."

I pictured the whole thing in my groggy head. I knew all the dharma heirs well, the twelve priests Roshi had given transmission to, added their names to his ancient lineage just before he died. We'd all practiced together. He said no one was ready to take over, but he hoped to avoid his heirs becoming competitive and political, and maybe in time someone would ripen and step forward. I wanted that transmission too, but couldn't get it. I wasn't a priest. I could see them at the meeting, sitting in a circle at the old center, a house on Lake Calhoun. Eleanor's freckled face came on in a high flush, while the other faces went white and numb. Their suddenly weighted heads bent over like ripe sunflowers, too heavy for their necks, as they stared at her in a boundless silence.

I too was silent. I didn't know what to say, so Peter continued.

At the same time almost to the day that we found out about Eleanor, another dharma teacher out in California discovered that a Zen student in Detroit had acted as a confidante for Roshi and had helped him out with at least one other woman Zen student in that city.

I put my hand to my forehead. Was I running a fever? I couldn't possibly be hearing what I was hearing.

The actions were so discreet it took six years after my teacher's death for them to be unveiled. Then the secret, unviewed for so long, suddenly unreeled, exposing itself across the country.

A splitting headache over my left eye was coming on as Peter continued to speak. It must be this flu. I shook my head to push the ache away.

Peter was profoundly disturbed, but I could come up with only one dumb comment. "Well, at least he was getting some all those years." Then I scrunched deeper under the covers. I felt unsafe.

I thanked him for calling. I placed the phone down as if it were a bad-smelling fish. I wanted it out of my hand.

For two hours I blanked out and denied Peter had called. I just lay in bed and stared up at the ceiling. I even forgot I ever studied Zen, that I crossed my legs in a sitting meditation position, that I knew where Japan or Minneapolis was on the globe of the world.

When my friend returned, I asked her about the movie. A man was in love with a woman, but she wasn't sure about him. He drove a Mercedes and she liked that, but something about him scared her. My friend loved to tell every detail. Usually I interrupted her and said I didn't want a blow-by-blow synopsis. Only kids do that: "This happened, then this." I usually told her to give me the texture, analysis, conflict point—we were old Jewish friends and could be blunt with each other—but this evening I nodded my head as one detail after another, one scene and then another unrolled. I was the thirteenth sunflower in Katagiri's lineage, nodding my heavy head. Uh-huh, uh-huh, uh-huh.

At first my friend was delighted—I was listening to her rehash—but then she stopped. "What's wrong?"

"Roshi had relations with one of his female students." My feeble body couldn't hold back the movement of an ancient glacier, an old crystallized story. "I'm exhausted. I'm going to sleep."

This was the same thing that happened with my father, different but the same. My heart loved them both, but now I held raw knowledge—betrayal dripped off my gripped hand.

Five days later, I flew home from California. Taos seemed empty—not the empty I loved there in winter, the sky a deeper blue, the distant mountaintops crested with snow, the bite of a dry, clear cold, and the smell of cedar and piñon fires—but just vacant. I tried hard to keep my balance after this landslide of new knowledge. I rationalized he was a Japanese man. The attitude of Japanese men about relationships with women was different. Maybe it was acceptable to be married and have mistresses or affairs. I asked myself a pragmatic question: What power did you project on Roshi that you can now claim for yourself? That's the one all my friends asked. That's all I had to do, they said: take back the power. I tried to grab hold with that one, but I knew it did not come close to the hurricane I felt inside.

I MET ROSHI WHEN I WAS THIRTY. Because of his support, I wrote books. His great betrayal before this had been that he died, left me too early. I had made him perfect, so I could feel safe to go deep and let my life bloom. Because of my family abuse, I was driven to get what I had longed for in my family—clear recognition with no sexual overtones—and with Roshi nothing was going to interrupt it.

My father was sleeping on a couch at his in-laws' apartment in Brooklyn and my mother was in a daze, unconscious on drugs, when I zoomed out between her legs into the abundant world. No one was there to welcome me. I was raised in the somnambulant suburbs. When I met Roshi, I recognized life in this shining man before me. I needed to be reflected in another. By the time

I encountered him, I was ravenous. Unknowingly, Roshi became my mother, my father, my Zen master.

While sex scandals broke up other Zen and Eastern religious communities, I felt safe with my teacher. Everyone knew he was clean. Robert Aitken, an American Zen teacher in Hawaii, had been known to repeat, "Thank god for Katagiri Roshi—he's the one who gives us hope." My childhood had been preoccupied with protecting myself from my father. In Zen, with its strict structure, I felt free to explore whole parts of myself without keeping my guard up.

I felt gratitude toward Peter for calling, directly, before the information was covered up or reduced to some half rumor, swallowed into a secret silence, people turning their backs if someone poked around. I'd seen it happen before in other communities. Nevertheless, the information was devastating. I could not find an easy conclusion. I no longer had any ground below me. Every time I tried to find my feet, the foothold crumbled.

I sat at my desk on the mesa one afternoon. I needed to get back to the novel I was working on, I told myself. The pen hovered above the page, but I looked blankly ahead out the window, not seeing the newly planted piñons. Instead, I was remembering the first floor of a duplex on Emerson Avenue near Zen Center. I was newly married. We were having a potluck in our living room. Even our simple home had a built-in oak commode with leaded-glass windows. The gray carpet was thin and rubbed raw in spots. All the Zen students were there that early summer evening. My first book of poetry had just been published by a small Minnesota press, and there was some publicity in the local uptown neighborhood newspaper.

Roshi, who had a can of beer in his hand, came up to me. He beamed with his shaved head. We were about the same height. He was in his early fifties, twenty years older than me, full of vitality, wearing jeans and a white T-shirt.

"I saw your photograph in the newspaper," he spoke in a broken English, but by this time I understood him easily.

I nodded and smiled. I was proud and happy he had noticed my accomplishment.

"You are very beautiful."

I did not expect this. "Thank you," I said cheerily, covering up my confusion, acting extra innocent, young, girlish. Roshi had never talked this way before.

He saw that I was not recording the hidden significance of my beauty. He repeated again with more intensity and emphasis, "No, you are very beautiful. Do you know that?" His words were now directly pointed at me, obviously full of innuendo.

I was confused, something was terribly askew—we were in another dimension.

Yet I was not a complete fool—I knew what he was getting at—but this couldn't be Roshi. This man was too creepy. I blithely thanked him for his compliment, walked away, and stayed away the rest of the evening.

It must have been the beer. Roshi's wife had been out of town, his two sons off somewhere. I forgot the incident, and I never mentioned it to anyone, not even my husband. I continued to study with him for the next ten years. Luckily, it never came up again.

The sound of ravens' wings flapping over my house heading east brought me back to the huge stillness on the mesa. But right then nothing could hold me. My thoughts pressed on.

I didn't realize it, but after that encounter I was unconsciously more diligent about our interactions. I kept my relationship with Roshi narrow, assiduously defined the parameters of our interactions—practice periods, work periods, retreats, formal settings. I stayed one-pointed in my encounters with him. No after-dinner meetings, being a board member, driving him places alone. After a lifetime of childhood training fending off my father, I wasn't going to be threatened by that one time. I had it all under lock and key.

Then I remembered hearing that a similar incident happened to another student the same weekend. Could this experience have been repeated: Roshi threw out a hook, and if there was no bite, he'd let go? I grimaced as I sat all alone in my studio next to the zendo I had built in his honor.

Two days after I returned home I received a call from a friend living in Australia. She said back when she was practicing with Roshi, she spoke to him about her marriage troubles. "What he advised stunned me—he told me I should have an affair! At the time I just thought, 'I don't understand this Zen.' I wonder now what he was really getting at."

My teeth ground together. This was hard to hear. But what were we doing going to him about relationship, work, probably even car problems? We were mixed up about Roshi's position. We wanted to learn Zen from him, but wasn't Zen in everything? Because his role was never clarified, we filled the vacuum with our expectations. Wouldn't he also know about plumbing? There was nothing a Zen master didn't understand.

This probably was not a problem in Japan, where a priest's position was clearly defined and built into society's fabric. But here in the United States, where Zen perfume, Zen beds, Zen beads were sold, we could project wildly on Zen's true purpose.

At first Roshi must have been surprised by what we brought to him. Then curiosity might have taken over. He was a man sincerely motivated by wanting to help human beings. But somewhere along the line, I guess, he became confused by the female abundance he found at American centers, so different from Japanese monasteries.

The last of December moved farther into darkness, the evenings coming early, the sun rising late over the mountain. I sat by myself through the shadowy days, but I could not get a handle on this new information. I didn't talk about it with New Mexico friends. They didn't know Roshi, and it was too easy to hear "Roshi slept with a student" and just write him off. I still felt protective.

In the middle of January I conducted a weeklong writing workshop at the Mabel Dodge Luhan House in Taos. Sixty people from all over the country attended. I taught well and was certain I had a handle on all this Roshi stuff. Then on Wednesday morning, standing up in front of the class, I didn't feel well. After class I noticed blisters had formed along my left hip. They burned and itched badly enough that during lunch I called my friend Carol, the dermatologist, in Minnesota. I described the symptoms.

"What's going on?" I had to be with my students in fifteen minutes.

"It sounds like shingles."

"Not again!" I had had an outbreak for the first and only time six years earlier when Roshi died.

"But that time was on the left side of your face?" Carol's a good friend and remembers these details. "Nat, further outbreaks, I'm almost certain, always happen in the same place. I've never heard of it breaking out in another place, but it definitely sounds like shingles."

She told me at this point there was nothing much I could do, but after the workshop I should have a dermatologist look at it anyway.

I moaned. With no dermatologist in Taos, I'd have to drive an hour and a half to Santa Fe.

"Have you been under a lot of stress lately?" Carol asked.

We hung up. My mind began to unravel. The old world, the one I constructed for so many years with Roshi at the helm, was collapsing, and no logic I perfunctorily grabbed was going to stop it.

In a dream I had two years after Katagiri died, I wandered the world homeless in one torn shirt and one pair of pants. At the end of the year I ended up at his vacant Japanese monastery in a cold gray cavernous, cathedral-like room. With hair matted, mouth frothing, eyes bulging, I stomped my feet and screamed "No" from my guts, and the whole building resounded. "I will not allow this. I will not accept the loss of this man." I woke up.

These shingles shocked and alerted me that I was not handling this new information well. As soon as the workshop was over, I cancelled everything and settled into winter on the lonesome mesa.

Each morning I went across to my studio. But instead of working or meditating, I sat in an old rocker, and the cinema just rolled. I played in my head the early mornings, the afternoons, the twilights I spent in the zendo in Minneapolis, Minnesota. The scenes came easily without any prodding.

Eleanor is sewing a black robe in the basement, humming to herself. Her chin has some chapped skin, and her fingers are nimble, quick. Another scene: I see them together in the hall. They flirt. Roshi says something. His smile could shatter an ice age. She laughs like sparkling champagne. I winced. It was obvious, right in front of us, if we'd paid attention.

I recall a talk he gave: a man is diving from a board one hundred feet high into twelve inches of water. Roshi had seen this demonstrated on a TV show. He loved to take popular media into a whole new dimension.

"No way from ordinary perspective can this man survive," he explains.

The diver had to transform into something flexible, holding no fixed idea that this feat was impossible. He had to become not who he was—or thought he was. His skeletal structure had to melt.

This sounds odd, funny, but Roshi was serious and enthusiastic, and I loved him for it. His way of seeing took me beyond my usual perceptions; boundaries liquefied; the world enlarged. I felt happy, whole. Naturally, his explanation might not have made logical sense, but neither did diving a long way into a foot of water. If you thought about it, it was a dumb thing to try to do.

That was the point. "My job is to make you very dumb," he often said.

"Dumb" in Zen was a compliment. It meant you weren't running ahead of yourself, planning, organizing, strategizing. You were open to receive the world as it was.

I could relate to that. A writer needed a certain dumb quality. I often told my students that in a downpour people rush for cover. A writer stands unprotected near a puddle, fascinated by the ripples the drops make, bewitched by the way they bounce on pavement, letting the rain hit her naked head. Both writers—and Zen students—needed to step into life fresh and experience it anew. Being smart was beside the point.

When I began studying with Roshi in 1978, there was not a lot of reading material on Zen. I guess we were more like Te-shan when he burned his books. We were sixties kids bent on direct experience.

Roshi didn't explain the practice; instead, we practiced it. It was hard physical labor to sit hour after hour on a cushion with our legs crossed. I experienced my conceptions and ideas melting into an intimacy with what was simply in front of me.

And Roshi was there, also sitting. Side by side, we practiced.

At the second lecture I ever heard him give, on a Saturday morning in June, he began, "I have been reading your Descartes."

I perked right up. Six years earlier I'd finished a master's degree in Great Books. At St. John's we were only to read the text. This impressed me. I was required to meet Socrates, Kant, Hegel, Spinoza directly, using no secondary sources. For a whole eight weeks in a two-hour seminar twice weekly, we wrestled with Descartes. What could this philosopher possibly mean?

Now so many years later, sitting up straight, what would this Zen teacher have to say on the subject?

"I think; therefore, I am," Roshi quoted Descartes's famous line. "I'm sure he knew, but forgot to mention," and here Roshi took a long pause, "I don't think; therefore, I'm not."

My mouth dropped open. In that moment all of Western civilization fell off a cliff. In that whole two-month class no one ever thought of that angle. We had tried every perspective to unlock Descartes's meaning. We leaned, exasperated, over that broad seminar table—there were eight of us and a St. John's tutor—and all we produced were thoughts on thoughts. That was a long July and a dry August in Santa Fe, New Mexico.

Roshi's simple statement, which seemed so obvious and ordinary to him, the slant to reality he'd lived with all his life, stripped my brain cells, flushed out my vision—at the back of thinking is nonthinking, on the other side of existence is nonexistence.

At the end of the lecture we chanted the *Heart Sutra* printed on cards. "No eyes, no ears, no nose, no tongue, no body . . . no color, no sound, no taste, no touch . . ."—we enumerated all these things and said they weren't. It was an antidote to the firm Western belief in our solid presence on the earth. No old age, no death, no stopping, no path, nothing to attain.

My time at that college, that study of René Descartes, prepared me to receive Katagiri Roshi's words when I heard him speak that late spring day in the green of Minnesota. This would have seemed crazy and very scary, but all that work at St. John's actually created a foundation. I understood the world would now be flipped on its ear, thrown over, belly-up. Nothing would ever be the same.

I stumbled out of that zendo with recognition alive in me, not from Descartes's thinking existence, but from Katagiri Roshi's nonthinking nonexistence.

I dove right into that deep pool of emptiness, moved across town to be within six blocks of Zen Center, and in a private meeting a few weeks later formally asked that man with a shaved head to be my teacher.

But eighteen years later on the mesa in Taos, New Mexico, staring out the window, I wondered what Katagiri Roshi really meant. Did he know what he was talking about? Maybe the diver on TV just had a trick up his sleeve?

In late January Peter called, and we compared notes. We were both dumbfounded. How could we have been that naïve? "I once drove home from a retreat at Hokyoji with Eleanor and asked playfully, 'Hey, how come I never hear about a boyfriend?'

"Right in the car she told me the whole truth. 'Oh, a while ago for over a year I had an affair with a married man, and it didn't work out. I guess I was disappointed and stopped after that.'"

We rehashed an early morning board meeting when one Zen student stomped in in his snow boots before the sun had even risen and demanded to know what was going on between Roshi and Clay. He had heard them at night in the house. This wasn't Eleanor. This was a student who came later, who adored everything Japanese, and she worshiped Roshi.

This went right over all our heads. There was a stunned silence. No one budged. Roshi looked straight ahead and finally whispered without even looking up at Clay, "You don't know what you're talking about."

Clay moved home to Lexington, Kentucky, and never came back.

I remembered how much I liked Clay. During the first retreat I ever sat at the Minnesota Zen Center in 1978, he sat next to me. I wanted to call him right then and say, "Clay, you're not crazy."

I cried a lot in that rocker. The shock finally shattered any veneer I attempted to create. I didn't want to know these things. I didn't want to know how human Roshi was; I didn't want to come up close and personal with him.

Sure, out of the corner of my eye I sometimes saw he wasn't happy. After the last retreat I sat with him, we drove the three hours back along the Mississippi to Minneapolis together. He'd been inspiring during the long hours of practice, and his daily talks had been vibrant, full of a generous vision of the world. He'd given his lectures after the evening meal, after a break, just as the last of twilight visited the farming valley where the monastery was. The rolling green hills, red barns, fields of corn and sunflowers, the Winnebago Creek slowly winding below the bluffs of the Mississippi, the insects lifting their voices—how idyllic could it get for this girl from Long Island?

The last night of that last retreat with him by the Mississippi I raised my hand and asked a question that bore little relation to what he'd been speaking about. The question had come up during the day—it was important to me—and it turned out it was the last one I ever was able to ask him in a formal teacher-student configuration (after a year's sabbatical he found out he had cancer). "Roshi, if we were living in Germany during World War II and we were Buddhists, how should we act?"

I felt the German woman sitting across the zendo from me tense up. She was in her mid-twenties. I hadn't spoken to her, since we were on silence all week. I doubt if I would have mentioned anything about this in an informal setting, but the long days of practice had cut to the heart.

Roshi spoke clearly into the kerosene-lit night: "Buddhism has no prescriptions. If your family is starving, and they hand you a gun and tell you to fight, you don't know what you'll do. That's why I tell you to practice. Maybe something fresh will come up."

The German woman began to cry. You could feel her relief. No standard condemnation. What space and freedom, a chance to let go and not be frozen in history. This was immense, compassionate, and simple.

But next to me in the passenger's seat driving home along the banks of the great river, Roshi seemed small, dejected, lost. He couldn't even respond to small talk, so I stopped trying.

Two Zen students were compiling his lectures for a first book with a publisher I knew. Roshi loved and respected books. When he was in San Francisco, he asked a student to drive him to a Japanese bookstore with floor-to-ceiling shelves. The student watched him walk down the aisles, stopping intermittently to run his hand along book spines, caressing the titles.

I knew he was afraid his talks weren't up to publishing standards, that no one would understand what he said. He thought his English wasn't good enough. This wasn't true. He made wild, wonderful, uncanny connections. I remembered one in which he discussed a tick in a tree patiently waiting for years for a warm body to pass underneath. And then plop! he demonstrated with his hands, it would drop itself onto the skin of a passerby.

My throat tightened. What had he been comparing this to?

Waves of anger rose in me. He encouraged me to open up. I was vulnerable. He held the position of teacher, but breached it.

At the time he gave that talk I made my own odd connections. I loved his lectures most of all. It was language turned on its elbow. Roshi was giving a true speech. I was becoming a true writer—

Was I willing to see true now? I'd rise to the challenge, speak in my studio to the space in front of me,

"Roshi, I'm deconstructing the way I idealized you"—and then I'd stop.

If I let go of my solid vision of him, what would I have? How dull the world seemed.

During our drive back to the Twin Cities, I broke the silence in the car by suggesting to Roshi that I tell the editors of his book that it was not necessary to get formal approval from him on finished chapters, that they should just go ahead and trust their judgment. He sunk deeper into the fake velour car seat. He was so relieved. He couldn't bear to read his own words, though he told me none of this. Instead, he just nodded in agreement.

When I helped him carry his sleeping bag and duffel into Zen Center, he didn't look around or wave. I watched his back as he walked upstairs to his apartment.

I had a glimmer then of the chasm between the Zen master and the lonely, insecure man. That moment was an opportunity to hold contradictory parts of him, to understand life doesn't work in a neat package the way I wanted it to. I could have come closer to his humanity—and mine. But I wasn't ready or willing. I had a need for him only to be great, to hold my projections. In freezing him on a pedestal I had only contributed to his isolation.

I sat in the rocker, feeling sad and missing him.

He was the youngest of six children. His mother barely had time for him. He'd spoken fondly of the single hour that he once had with her when she took him shopping. No other brothers and sisters. Just the heaven of his mother all to himself.

My mother was mostly absent in my life, not because she was busy, but because she was vacant. She woke in the morning, put on her girdle, straight wool skirt, and cashmere sweater, and then sat in a chair in her bedroom, staring out the window.

"Mom, I'm sick and want to stay home from school."

"That's fine."

The next day I wrote the absentee note for the teacher, and she signed without glancing at it. I was hungrier than I knew. I wanted someone to contact me, even if it was to simply say, "Natalie, you are not sick. That wouldn't be honest. As a matter of fact, you look lovely today." As a kid I needed a reflection of my existence, that I was, indeed, here on this earth. The attention I received from my father was invasive and uncomfortable. I hoped at least for my mother's affirmation, but there wasn't any.

Roshi was the one person who directly spoke to this hunger. When I went in for dokusan (an individual face-to-face interview with the teacher), we sat cross-legged on cushions, opposite each other. He wasn't distracted, "aggravated," or impatient. He was right there, which inspired me to meet him in that moment. I had friends, acquaintances I interacted with, and we sat facing each other across luncheon tables, but this was a man whose life's work was to arrive in the present. The effect was stunning. Life seemed to beam out of every cell in his body. His facial expressions were animated.

I could ask him a question, and he would respond from no stuck, formulated place. I think it was the constant awareness of emptiness: that although this cushion, this floor, this person in front of you, and you yourself are here, it isn't of permanent duration. Knowing this in his bones and muscles, not just as a philosophical idea, allowed him a spontaneity and honesty.

"Roshi, now that I am divorced, it is very lonely."

"Tell me. What do you do when you are alone in the house?"

I'd never thought of that. I became interested. "Well, I water the plants," I faltered, then continued, "I wash a few dishes, call a friend." The momentum built. "I sit on the couch for hours and stare at the bare branches out the window. I play over and over Paul Simon's new album about New Mexico—I miss it there."

His attention encouraged me. "Lately, I've been sitting at my dining-room table and painting little pictures." I looked at him. Suddenly my solitary life had a texture.

"Is there anything wrong with loneliness?" he asked in a low voice.

I shook my head. All at once I saw it was a natural condition of life, like sadness, grief, even joy. When I was sitting with him, it didn't feel ominous or unbearable.

"Anyone who wants to go to the source is lonely. There are many people at Zen Center. Those who are practicing deeply are only with themselves."

"Are you lonely?" I entreated.

"Yes," he nodded. "But I don't let it toss me away. It's just loneliness."

"Do you ever get over it?"

"I take an ice-cold shower every morning. I never get used to it. It shocks me each time, but I've learned to stand up in it." He pointed at me. "Can you stand up in loneliness?"

He continued, "Being alone is the terminal abode. You can't go any deeper in your practice if you run from it."

He spoke to me evenly, honestly. My hunger was satiated—the ignored little girl still inside me and the adult seeker—both were nourished.

I understood that Roshi too had been neglected in his childhood.

Even though he had tremendous perseverance, he was human, with needs and desires. All of us want something—even the vastly wise like a good cookie with their tea and delight in good-quality tea. Maybe it was that very perseverance that broke him. He couldn't keep it up, and his human needs leaked out. "Continue under all circumstances," he barked out, so often that that dictum even penetrated my lazy mind and became a strong tool for my life. But as I grew older I understood its drawbacks: if you are crossing a street and a semi is coming, step aside. If you have hemorrhoids, don't push the sitting; take a hot bath. That one tactic—perseverance—can put you on a dead-end road, and then what do you do? Continue to march deep into a blind alley?

The hidden life of Roshi was being exposed. It took a long time. The teacher who stepped forward was very radiant. It was hard to see the darkness at his back, but unless I could see his, I was vulnerable to being shortsighted in my own.

Touching Roshi's frailty finally brought him closer to me, unraveled my solid grief. At the end of January I had a painful backache that lasted all day. At midnight in my flannel pajamas I got up out of bed, went to the window, and looked out at the star-studded clear, cold night sky with Taos Mountain in the distance.

"Where are you? Come back!" I demanded. "We have things to settle."

I let out a scream that cracked the dark, but one raw fact did not change: nothing made him return, and I was left to make sense of his life—and mine.

I WAS BROUGHT UP in a culture that lived through World War II. It was called the "just war," the righteous one, but those who fought in it had seen things no one spoke of. One friend's father was one of the soldiers who liberated Bergen-Belsen. His wife said he didn't return the same man. Besides his career as a lawyer, he was only interested in the roses he tended each summer.

We had a country full of bewildered men who were bolstered by the fact that it was "a good war." But war was war, and they saw horrors, things that nothing prepared them for. How do you come back to red-lipped women in high heels and stylish feathered hats, to ice in tall glasses, tablecloths, bus stops, public libraries, neckties, and sidewalks lined with maples?

My father, an old man when we sat in the last row of a movie theater watching the invasion of Normandy, wept, reaching for tissues and clutching my hand. "I didn't know they suffered so bad over there." He had had it easy, dropping bombs from a distance on the Pacific theater. The truth was, for all my father's bravado I felt a powerful depression saturating him. My sister and I in our white and pink pinafore dresses turned somersaults, danced, and sang trying to get him to notice us, to cheer up, to be glad to be with us. We thought we were the cause of his unhappiness. No young girl could fathom the depth of those blues.

My generation was raised on something askew, not spoken of, and we felt it. Why did so many smart kids go so wholeheartedly and blindly into Eastern religions? We longed for something congruent, something that held up. How odd now to think I went to a man from the very country my father bombed. How naïve to think Roshi might not have had some of the same problems my father did from across the sea.

I've heard Roshi was depressed in the last years before he died. In some Zen circles in Japan there is an understanding that if teachers face a life-threatening illness in their mature years, their late fifties or sixties, and survive it, their depth is even greater than before. Roshi, my beloved teacher, did not pass through. I don't know if the "closed system," his attitude of silence, contributed to his early death. But how I wish in our desperation to keep him alive in the long, slow year that he was fighting for his life, one Zen student had bent close and whispered, "Speak. Unload your heart."

I am not saying repressed feelings are the cause of cancer. We live in human bodies that will die someday of one thing or another. Cancer is a disease. Some people die of it. Yet in the same way I urged my writing students, I could have urged him in hushed tones on his sickbed, "Whatever you need to say. Tell it all."

We tried everything else—chemotherapy, radiation, acupuncture, visualization—why didn't I, at least, grace him with what I shared across the country with so many thousands of writing students?

Perhaps I didn't ask him because I neglected to stop and ask myself the same question. "Natalie, what have you not come clean with?"

Maybe it's only now that I know the answer—or am willing to look at it. I left my husband. While his mother was dying of cancer and he visited her every day as she grew bone-thin, I went on Zen retreats. When his father died six months later, I signed up for a hundred-day practice period. Every morning I was gone at four o'clock to sit three hours before I went to work. Every evening I sat another two. On weekends I was at Zen Center sewing, pulling weeds, raking leaves, studying a passage in a dharma book.

My husband lost both his parents while they were still in their fifties. He had just turned thirty. Neither of us knew anything about death. I rang the bell in the zendo tolling impermanence while my husband wept, growing out of youth on our red couch in the living room.

He was the love of my life. When I met him, my heart fell open. Seven years after we met, three years after we took marriage vows, I divorced him. I walked out.

I continued to sit in the zendo in perfect posture, in the cool illusion of serenity, while a furnace roared at my back. Instead of feeling all the way down through my emotions in zazen, I split them off to escape my suffering. If fear came, I severed it. I fostered fantasy, daydreaming. I slept with unnamed men—one was a violinist, another a housepainter, a third an executive at Honeywell—and plowed under the intimacy I had known with Neil.

Fifteen years later I still missed him. Nothing changed, because there was pain in my core I wouldn't look at. Finally, I think I betrayed myself. Maybe that's what betrayal essentially is. We don't abandon someone else without forgetting part of ourself. I was split off from my heart center. I kept repeating my affairs out of desperation and took myself farther and farther from the source of my own love and well-being.

The worst was that Neil never knew how broken I was. He thought I didn't care.

Zen is about plunging oneself into the hot center of life and death. Nothing hidden, nothing not revealed. When there is a secret, the dharma can't grow direct from the root. It has to twist itself looking for sun.

Roshi's dharma heirs, the twelve priests designated to carry on his teachings, not only inherited his strengths, but also carried his shadow, the unclaimed, unseen part of their former leader.

Of course, we are drawn to teachers who unconsciously mirror our own psychology. None of us are clean. We all make mistakes. It's the repetition of those mistakes and the refusal to look at them that compound the suffering and assure their continuation.

Five years after the news leaked out, a former board member referred to Roshi as having "immaculate morality." I was surprised. I knew he knew better.

Having lunch with a dharma teacher, I was startled by her denial: "Oh, people exaggerate. It's not for sure."

Another Zen teacher at another lunch said, "In my day we didn't ever stand up to male authority. Good luck. What about his wife? You'll hurt her."

"I'm writing Roshi's wife to let her know what I'm doing. I don't want to hurt his family, but I also have to be faithful to the legacy he gave me: to write honestly."

Suddenly I could hear my mother's voice, "Why write anything? It only causes trouble."

A man on a Minnesota call-in public radio show asked me on the air: "I thought writers were supposed to tell the truth. I read your book after your teacher died. Recently I heard about some secrets, but you never mentioned them in your work."

"I didn't know about it then. I would have written it."

So I had to now, but I became increasingly nervous. I didn't want to injure anyone. This was the last thing I ever expected I'd have to face. I wanted him to live, even after his death, but in a real way. With Roshi I found Natalie. He gave me what I needed to stand up and go through this. This wasn't Roshi's story anymore. It was our story, the people who studied with him—and it's my story. It's part of how the dharma came to us. Nothing will ever change how this man opened my life. And not only mine—all the people who practiced with him were forever helped. We forsook him by freezing him in some pure image for our own selfish needs even when we had learned otherwise. To not be real about our teacher is not to be real about ourselves. It is to twist the dharma.

But I was afraid. I realized I would meet resistance. I began to doubt what I was doing. Was it right or wrong? The few lunches I'd had with Zen friends surprised me. Everyone was not going to applaud with "Good girl, Natalie." I had an abiding love for the people I practiced with. I didn't want to lose them.

Then something in me snapped. I had to face all this before when I confronted my father. This was familiar territory. No one was happy. My sister even laughed at me. Why was I making such a big deal? My family wanted to keep the idealized dream of who we were. Natalie, as a hurting individual, did not matter. All they knew was she was disrupting the plan.

I determined that anything I said had to be backed up. I had to know for sure as much as possible. I made a trip up to Minnesota. As I flew on the plane, I began to muse, to question things that had been hearsay: What was the actual story about Roshi's priest who lost his psychology license? What occurred and why? I was living in New Mexico when it happened.

I called the state psychology board when I arrived in town. They had to have the information.

"If he lost his license, it should be on the Web. Tell me his name. I'll look it up," said the receptionist.

Thirty seconds later, she was back. "Yup. He 'surrendered' it in 1990."

That was the very year Roshi died. I felt creepy. I wanted to hang up. This was none of my business.

"Surrendered? That's not the same as revoked?" I asked. Maybe he didn't care about being a psychologist anymore.

"Why don't you just come down and look at the file yourself. You'll have to give us a driver's license. Wanna make sure no one walks off with it."

"I don't need a psychology degree? I mean, I'm not a therapist."

"Nope, it's public knowledge. In fact, if you're coming today I'll just copy it for you so you don't have to wait. It'll cost four dollars."

I jotted down the address. Was I really going to do this?

I drove across the line from Minneapolis into St. Paul. The numbers suddenly switched, and I was lost. Didn't I have something better to do on a June afternoon? I felt like a snoop. I should have gone swimming in one of the city lakes instead.

I found the six-story board building and rose in the elevator to the third floor.

"Here it is," the receptionist reached out a six-page file before I even said my name.

I dug in my wallet and only had three ones and a ten.

She took the three. "Never mind. No one will know but you and me."

As soon as I left the building, I plopped down on the outside stairs and opened the file on my lap. It was half humid out. It was not yet the full flowering of a Minnesota summer. I liked this softer air after years in the dry Southwest. But at this moment I didn't care about the weather. I was not even sure I'd understand the jargon in the report.

I fumbled through the first page. He waived any formal hearing. I turned the page over. A client he had for two years had lodged a complaint. They'd gone out to dinner once and had a luncheon in a public place. A sideways hug, maybe a patted knee. Ordinary gestures, but this was a therapist and a client. Professional lines were blurred.

The licensee denied some of the accusations, said the hug was an encouraging display in a public place.

A breeze lifted the page I was reading.

None of us were very clear. I remember another therapist at Zen Center who gave me and Neil free individual therapy sessions. I knew she lingered after the hour visiting with Neil, so I pushed our conversation past the hour too. We were already separated. I heard she was getting a ride down to the next retreat in Neil's car. Something broke in me—I knew this was wrong, that it made me crazy, but at the time I knew nothing of boundaries. I called her screaming and crying. She did not console me. We never spoke again.

Many years later when visiting Minnesota I decided to confront her. Why carry around a rock in my heart?

She didn't remember the incident. She said, "I probably held the phone in my hand and wondered, 'Why is Natalie so upset?' It seemed back then we knew nothing of proper limits."

I was glad to have finally spoken to her.

A semi rumbled down University Avenue. I saw a meat hook painted in red and the letters "PRIME BEEF" in bright orange. Then the truck passed, and only a tangle of green trees across the street was left.

Were we all confused back then? I was a fledgling poet. Neil was a pianist. We held no professional positions, we could come in front of no board, but even before we took the vow of marriage, we said we could sleep around. What were we thinking? We knew that Neil's father had affairs, and we saw his mother's suffering. But we never translated it to our marriage.

Maybe we were all one big unhinged, bewildered fishy stew back then at Zen Center, but we thought Roshi was clear. He was not part of us, not part of our muddled humanity.

During our first retreat, Neil whispered to me, "This man knows who he is. He knows what he thinks. Who else can you say that about?"

On page six of the file: the licensee could be relicensed, but first he had to meet with an ethical consultant at least one hour per month for a period of two years. Five more pages of conditions followed.

My eyes fell on the word "religious." He had to "separate religious affiliations from the provision of psychological services."

I knew he never retrieved his professional standing. I think he wasn't interested. He went on to establish a Zen monastery.

I drove back to the Uptown area in Minneapolis near Lake Calhoun where I was staying, near where the center is. The whole two weeks of my visit I never went there to practice, but sometimes at night I walked in the alley behind the building. I saw weeds growing in the cracks of the sidewalk leading up to the entrance. It was now twelve years since Roshi lived there. I tried to recall what it was like, the heaven of it. Yes, with all the confusion, it was still the best thing I had ever known. I spent my thirties sitting still. At the age when others were investing their energy in building careers, a vast opportunity was presented to me—to meet my own mind and "to have kind consideration for all sentient beings every moment forever." That was a big job Zen and Roshi proposed, probably an impossible one, but it offered me an enormous vision of human life, so different from the one I was brought up with.

"Don't trust anyone. They're all out to get you," was often quoted by my father. I longed for a different perspective.

I could see the moon through the elm leaves. "Roshi, what I'm doing now is part of what you taught me. I want to see unfettered, all the way down. Who we were—what a human being is."

A mind that rests at zero. No good or bad. No criticism, blame—also no praise. That is how we were trained by Roshi. In a world of bonuses, competition, fear of failure, yearning for applause, receiving evaluations, grades, tests, reproaches, and condemnations, it was actually frightening to enter the zendo, where those things did not apply. Who was I, if I wasn't running after affirmation and dodging negation? A crow just crowed; a flower bloomed. Could I just show up at five each morning to sit for no reason?

"I'll be here whether you are or not. I'm not sitting for Minnesota Zen Center. I'm sitting for all sentient beings."

To wake up that early and to walk the six blocks to the center or to drive there, getting into my old car, parked on the street through the night in subzero temperatures—I could do it maybe once or twice to try to impress the teacher. But that motivation couldn't have sustained my effort. It was a waste of time anyway. Roshi wasn't impressed. And when I didn't show up, no one came to drag me out of bed or called to chastise me.

I'd wrestle with myself when the four-thirty alarm went off. "I'm going. I'm not going." Roshi called it "fighting with tofu." It's ridiculous; it gets you nowhere.

For the first three years that I practiced at Zen Center, I felt certain Roshi would kick me out. Finally, he would have to admit I was hopeless. I imagined my exit—it would be dramatic. I'd be sitting facing the wall, he'd run up behind me, scream, "I can't take it anymore," grab me by my collar and the seat of my pants, and fling me crashing through the window, wooden frame collapsing as I flew through.

Other times I envisioned him exclaiming to the whole group, "There is one enlightened one among you. Here, Natalie, please take my seat." And of course I would be gracious and humble, exclaiming to everyone there my sincere hope that they too someday—in some distant future—could realize the way.

It took those full three years for me to finally drop the need to be loved or maligned and to just appear. To accept that something in me wanted to be there in the same way a tree in spring sprouts leaves or a fish in water swims.

Often I told my writing students: "Look over your shoulder. No one's there. No one cares whether you write or not. You must step forward, pick up the pen, and begin." I'd smile. "If you do, maybe beings seen and unseen will help." Pause. "But don't wait around for that. Get to work."

I remembered Roshi said to me once in the dokusan room, "Look around you. The sangha [the spiritual community] is a microcosm of human society. You can watch it all right here."

Did he know how real that statement was?

I believe he did. Even betrayal was part of life. The whole sangha was going to die someday. Everyone I ever loved would sometime leave me. By not being willing to see things as they were I deluded myself. I was trying to hold out against reality.

THE NEXT DAY I LOCATED the phone number of the woman in Detroit whom Peter had originally told me about so long ago in that first phone call in California, the woman who had been Roshi's confidante. My heart raced as I heard the first ring. Don't be home, I thought. I can forget this. She's going to call me a busybody, a meddler. Let dead dogs lie.

On the third ring, a man's voice said hello. "No, this is her center, not her home. I can give her a message. Hey, aren't you the writer? Oh, she'll love to speak with you."

Oh, no, she won't, I thought as I hung up. So she has her own Zen place now.

The next day she called. She said we met once briefly five years ago.

I took a deep breath. "I want to ask you what happened with Roshi and the woman he was allegedly involved with."

"Oh," she paused. "I am happy to tell you.

"Yes, she was very unstable. They met in the Minneapolis Zen Center. She had slept with Tibetan lamas and other teachers before. She lost her job and moved to Detroit to live with her parents. At some point she was having a breakdown, and she called him a lot. He wouldn't answer the phone. Her frantic parents tried to call him too. This was when he asked me for help. He told me not to commit her. It might expose him. I was a therapist. He put me in an awful situation. Finally, I went along with his wishes, but then the woman called me all the time. She threatened to hurt my children. I was terrified."

She was talking faster than I could keep up. She was relieved to speak about it.

"People know you. They'll believe you when you write.

"After that I stopped practicing with Roshi. I'd had trouble with another Zen teacher. So I was crushed when this happened. I thought I could trust Roshi. I thought he was clean."

My heart sunk. Years ago I had heard she'd left the community. No one knew why, but the unspoken implication was that she wasn't a serious student. She had left silently to protect Roshi.

Hearing all this directly, rather than from intermediaries, gave it a clarity. I respected her forthrightness, and it urged me on. Suddenly, this investigation seemed so simple and direct. But I knew it wasn't. I was very alone. People wanted to minimize these events. We were all dedicated to our dream of him.

I remembered the effort it had taken to stand up to my father. I'd felt as if I'd taken on the whole institution of fatherdom. Everything had been set in concrete, and I wanted to budge it.

In the first letter I sent home, I told my father I only wanted to converse through the mail. I needed a way to protect myself. I was afraid I'd crumble if I spoke to him directly. As soon as he received the letter, he called.

"Dad, only through the mail."

"Natalie, that's ridiculous—"

I cut him off, "Only by mail. I'm hanging up." And I did just that. I'd shattered a universe. I was excited and amazed. You mean you don't have to do what your father wants?

While I was in Minnesota I also needed to find out if Clay's accusations about Roshi and his housemate at that early morning board meeting had any validity. Had anyone else ever seen or heard anything?

I could find no verification, so I decided to not mention the whole situation in my writing.

I was leaving the next day. The phone rang. It was an old Zen friend. We hadn't seen each other in years.

"Couldn't we at least go for a quick walk by the lake? I'll come around nine. You'll have time to finish packing."

I was tired, and the plane took off very early the next day. I hesitated, then gave in.

I was glad to see her, and the lake at night looked beautiful. She'd become a successful painter and showed at the Walker.

"So what are you writing now?"

I told her briefly.

"You included Maria, didn't you?"

"No, it's not for sure."

"Yes, it is."

I turned. City lights glinted off the water. "How?"

"I walked in on them. In the basement, where the washing machine was."

"You did?"

"Yeah, years ago when I first started practicing. The door had been shut and it was dark in there."

"What did you see?"

"I saw Roshi and Maria in an embrace. I had startled them and they looked like deer caught in the headlights."

"What did you think? Did you tell anyone?"

"I was embarrassed. I felt foolish. I didn't know what to think—I ran upstairs. I didn't mention it to anyone."

I slept little that night. The few blocks around the center had been home to me. They held so much.

When my husband and I were breaking up, Roshi told me to only speak to Neil when I could express myself clearly. I managed it on the phone every third day for short periods of time. I guessed it felt okay, but I had hurt, wrath, indignation underneath. I had loved this man, moved up to the strange Midwest to be with him, and it was all dissolving. In my early thirties, all passions warred in me. Now I was trying to be good on the phone. It lasted for three short conversations, and then the next time we spoke what I repressed exploded.

I described it to Roshi: it was as though a rabid red dog ran out of my mouth and bit my old husband's face.

"That's a good one." He laughed and laughed.

I was defeated once again and my emotions became a battleground.

With Zen practice I saw the difference between clinging rage and the red-hot wake-up of a flash of energy. I began to have an honest appreciation of anger's sheer reflexive, self-protective side and its destructive side; the anger that finally moves us, motivates us to change inwardly; the anger that is pure, like a first thought, comes through us, cleanses us, and passes. What was important for me was that it wasn't denied and shuffled off into a passive-aggressive mode.

But what I also understand now is that you can know about anger clearly with half of yourself while the other half is cut off and never gets the benefit of any of your clear knowledge. We've seen examples in great artists who are enlightened in their work and function cruelly and ignorantly in their personal lives. Unfortunately we have also discovered this about spiritual leaders. I think my generation hoped that Eastern teachers would be different, free of these problems, but the splitting off seems to be cross-cultural and across religions. No one is immune. Roshi was sincere about his vows, but in a split the one part doesn't live by the same rules as the other part. So a person could practice deeply, have great understanding and aspiration for compassion, and simultaneously act out in a way that blurs boundaries between teacher and student.

During a retreat I was finished with my dishwashing job, but the bell had already rung. Waiting until the next period in order to enter the zendo, I lingered in the kitchen popping spoonfuls of gomasio, toasted sesame salt we ground by hand, into my mouth.

Tony walked in, saw me, and screamed that I wasn't supposed to do that. Earlier that year after a lecture he had yelled at me for asking Roshi how he met his wife. He also said I wasn't supposed to do that.

I was startled by his aggression that afternoon. I felt vulnerable and tender after four days of silence and practice.

I didn't say anything. I went downstairs to the bathroom. When I came out, he was standing by the shoe rack.

"Tony, I don't know why you attacked me." I was hoping for some closure, for an apology so I could go back and sit in peace.

Instead, he attacked me again. "You do exactly what you want. You don't follow the rules."

Innocent me felt self-righteous. "Go to hell," I said and stormed up the stairs for the next sit. Wait until I tell Roshi. He'll comfort me. He'll protect me from that brute Tony.

Finally, my turn for dokusan arrived. I marched into Roshi's study, did my prerequisite bows, and then plopped myself on the cushion.

I told Roshi exactly what happened.

His response: stop causing trouble. He rang the bell for me to leave.

I couldn't believe it. I went back to the zendo and decided he misunderstood the situation. I waited for the last person to receive an interview, then I marched myself upstairs again.

I explained the whole situation again with more detail, the gomasio spoon, dishwashing, shoe rack. I enunciated clearly—maybe it was my English he hadn't understood. Maybe when I got upset my New York accent became heavier. (Of course, this had never been an impediment between us before.)

"You are a troublemaker. I know you very well. Cut it out."

"Roshi, you got it all wrong. It's Tony who's causing the disturbance."

"You and Tony are alike. Whenever you see commotion, you dive in."

I was never so insulted. Such injustice. I left the room, again marched down the stairs, and sulked.

It took ten years to see it a different way. I was telling my friend Eddie about it over lunch, explaining to him about the gomasio—I stopped. My brain flipped to a past page. Just that morning the cook had announced that all retreatants were to stay out of the kitchen, except for when they had jobs to do, and then he asked that we not eat any kitchen food except at meals. There had been a problem with pilfering late at night. I even had another vague memory: Didn't he say something about the gomasio supply dwindling?

I whispered across the table to Eddie, "I did start the whole thing. Roshi was right."

How could this man have been so clear, seeing into my

own nature, and then in another pocket of time been so unclear in his behavior toward some of his women students?

Several years after my divorce, Roshi assigned me the practice of not approaching those who hurt me with anger, but waiting until my intention was to create peace with them. I was older, calmer. I agreed. I'd already tasted the suffering from my breakup and didn't want to react blindly anymore. I knew those consequences.

Immediately after I made that promise, I encountered an old friend, the kind who manages to drop innuendoes about your weight, your lover, another friend, your writing. When you leave her, you're foaming at the mouth, gnashing your teeth, and you aren't sure why. After all, you were both smiling. You've known each other a long time. She was familiar, you have history together.

This time I went away from her as usual feeling like a maniac, but I had made a firm commitment to harmony. I didn't run back and start an argument. Instead, I held torturously steady inside myself. Peace, I hissed through my teeth, steam blowing off the top of my head. I felt as though I'd swallowed a whole crazed animal that jerked inside the container of my skin. She was trying to cut loose out of my arm—I saw the bulge try to break through my thigh, my chest, my belly. There it was trying to escape out my back.

Six weeks later—it took six hard weeks—I had a date with my old friend at a sushi restaurant for dinner.

Maybe I imagined it, but she seemed nervous. I think she honestly knew she'd blown it last time we'd seen each other. I felt spacious. We ate slabs of raw fish. I don't remember exactly what I said, but it was simple, short. I had no self-centered agenda, but I told her clearly I didn't like it when she said this or that about me and that I wanted to be able to honor our friendship. I do recall the awed look on her face, the respect, curiosity, surprise.

The miso soup was served. It was delicious, with small floating cubes of tofu and fresh chopped green onion. I was happy and at peace. I felt a great victory.

When I think back on my experience with Roshi at that one potluck at my house, it seems that he didn't think at all, that he never calculated any consequences. Another person stepped forward, the unknown, isolated hungry one. He even looked different—his skin was sallow as though he hadn't seen much of daylight. That person had been hiding away, perhaps waiting for a chance to have his needs met, however remote.

He told us when he first came to San Francisco in the sixties he was appalled by all the unkempt hippies who sat with him. He said he would preach acceptance and then go up to his room and cry because he hated all these wild Americans. We seemed so strange.

That kind of real honesty was what I came to expect of him. It made his breach of trust even more shocking.

I've heard some men say, well, they were adult women—what's the problem?

We were not peers with him. It wasn't equal consent; it wasn't two independent individuals with a horizontal relationship.

Even if the women involved were okay with it, it was a betrayal of the community. Something hidden was going on.

Once I went to Roshi disturbed by Trungpa Rinpoche, a Tibetan meditation master I'd studied with in Boulder before I moved to Minneapolis. "Roshi, he was really terrific, but he had affairs with a lot of his students. I can't make sense of it. It felt weird." Trungpa's relationships were public knowledge, but they still crossed a primary boundary, and even in my naïve early thirties I was uncomfortable with it.

I cringe as I think of this interchange now. Roshi's reply: "Buddhism is Buddhism." I could tell by the straight horizontal line his lips made, his eyes looking ahead, that he was incensed by my question. He rang the bell with no further discussion.

I think it was the exact year he was having an affair with Eleanor. I was a sincere, albeit shortsighted, Zen student. What had I said that upset him? For a long time I contemplated the depth of that statement, "Buddhism is Buddhism."

One of the great things I felt around Roshi was that we were all equally seen and cared about. But was that true?

I questioned it now. Were some student connections more advantageous? Was he thinking about Eleanor when he was sitting? What went on during retreats when they had dokusan?

Eleanor was tall—almost six feet, highly freckled, fair, with shocking red hair and a noticeable mole above the left side of her lip—was that the type he liked? Did he find that darker brown spot on her face sexy? Why did he choose her and not continue to pursue me? She got more time with him. With all this in my head, my thoughts ran murky. I was glad I didn't know about it while it was happening. There would have been only confusion for me in the zendo.

But not knowing created misconceptions, a divide between what I thought was happening and what was really occurring. I went over endlessly in my head my connection with Roshi. I felt shattered, but I also began to feel the essential ground of my practice. I was glaring down inside the long narrow neck of what was:

Roshi, I'm calling you. Do you hear me? Get into form again. I want to speak with you, just one more time, and then I'll open my hand and let go.

I'm invoking you back into sight, sound, taste, back into color and smell, the felt world from whatever saw-dust, ash, Huge Mind you have dissolved into, whatever task you are attending to in what other universe. Put down your dust rag, your job of cleaning the altar in another dimension, and be with me. We have to talk.

When you first died, I would have gone anywhere, climbed down into boiling water, crawled through vomit, swarms of biting insects to find you. But I would have been looking in the wrong places. Instead, I discovered you in your passion, need. In your human frailty I see you again. I might even have gone off searching for you in lofty places, heavenly realms, but all along the only spot I would really find you is back here on earth, in the raw meat of your swollen, agitated heart.

You taught me that it was in the continual meeting of yourself that we wake up, that we stay alive through clouds and sidewalks, trees and human eyes. Maybe it was the cancer, the being in America too long with no peers, having a secret so well hidden for so long that cut you off from yourself and separated you from everyone else. Added isolation to the original loneliness you were so good at talking about. My teacher of loneliness was lonely, alone with the Alone.

Oh, Roshi, what turmoil, but it spread farther than your own private heart. You passed suffering down beyond your death. One long black slash on your enormous life.

I feel you again in the thick snow of the Midwest, how it would fall all night and fill the streets, in the dark tangled branches before dawn along Irving where I'd walk to morning zazen, the streaks of early car wheels in the white street, the heavy gray weight of the sky. I walked through a mysterious world with some large assurance. I was in the heart of your teachings.

We came to you eager and open with our early confusion and a huge sincerity for finding the way. We must have been overwhelming. But I'm sorry, Roshi, you should have toed the line, let out an unequivocal scream in your bald head: NO! White-knuckled it if you had to, but left us alone. It's still unclear exactly what or who was involved, so no one knows the truth in its fullness.

I sense you were conflicted. Was this when you went to Japan and visited an important lineage teacher? Perhaps, you spoke to him about the American women—monasteries in Japan were all men. When you returned, you declared yourself celibate. I was living in New Mexico by then and thought it peculiar. I did not know then about your private life.

My generation longed for something pure, untouched, celestial. That was our mistake. Running from one disillusion, we jumped into the arms of another.

Roshi, how do I hold you now? More real, more honest. You gave me everything in those years when I lived six blocks away. My thirties, your fifties. The black terns on the September lake at breaks in autumn sesshin. When I sit or stand, I feel you. When I write, I hear you whisper, "Be yourself."

We've had a long drought in New Mexico. Piñons have turned brown in the hills, their deep roots no longer able to find water. Great ancient cottonwoods that border the pueblo land and the road into town have given up. They stand now like ghosts of winter at the end of August. But this morning in middle September, it rained. I could hear thunder in the mountains and a pounding on the tin roof. The sage, the Russian olive at last showed their true turquoise color, and the chamisa bloomed its yellow pungent fall flowers. Snow was on the top of Wheeler Peak, the tallest mountain in our state. Its height has reached into another season.

Lung-t'an handed Te-shan the light, but then just as Te-shan was about to reach for the candle, Lung-t'an blew it out. And with that, everything was revealed. Night and day, fall and spring, the stars swirling in the open sky. What did Te-shan see in the new dark? His hand empty, he could not hold on to anything?

Did Roshi, knowing or not knowing, blow out our lights? Now we were on our own. Would we take advantage of this timely jolt from the other side, use it to wake up, or would we crawl under the warm covers in the dark and go to sleep?

LONG AFTER THAT SEASON that I ensconced myself on the mesa, I was at a conference in southern Arizona. I knew Eleanor lived nearby. I called her and made a date for dinner. What was it I wanted to ask? I'd always liked her, and I knew she was a serious practitioner.

We sat across a white linen tablecloth on a Thursday evening. We chattered about this and that. All the while in my head I urged, "Go ahead, broach the subject. You are a coward. Say something."

And then another voice sounded. "Shut up. What will you gain? Leave well enough alone."

One, two, three, I breathed and blurted out, "You know, I heard about you and Roshi."

The space between us froze. Her face became wooden—

At that very moment, the waiter appeared at our side. "Oh, goodness, you need rolls," and he shoved in front of us a basket of hot buns wrapped in a checkered cloth.

I reached for one. "Oh, they're good," I declared.

Eleanor quickly scooped butter into hers.

That bread had given me an escape. It was as though I'd never uttered a word.

After dinner I drove past tall saguaro cactus in my rented car to drop her off in front of her driveway. As I pulled away, I looked back through the rearview mirror. She had already gone inside. I knew she had loved him. I heard their laughter again filling the hall of the zendo. I wanted to feel a wild fury, but instead I felt heavyhearted.

A few months later the Minnesota Zen Center sent out a long letter referring to problems at Zen Center and the recently discovered indiscretions of the founding teacher. They were developing guidelines now to avoid these student-teacher problems in the future. But the language was so abstract, no one would have had any idea what it was about unless they already knew the situation.

Soon after it was mailed out, I ran into a longtime

Zen student in San Francisco. "I got a letter from Minnesota—I guess I'm still on their mailing list. I read it through three times, but I couldn't figure out what they were talking about."

I told him bluntly.

"You're kidding! I would never have guessed. From the letter, it never occurred to me that it was even about Katagiri."

Yes, none of us would have guessed. We were all in our own dreamworld of how we wanted things to be. Even when we knew differently, it was hard to face.

I think I finally freed myself in a single afternoon. I was already late, rushing to the plaza, with Taos Mountain at my back, to meet someone I didn't know. Glancing over at a big gallery window—usually it displayed large eccentric landscapes of a painter I loved—I saw that this time the window was empty. I halted in front of the glass. I put my hand to the pane. I don't know how to say this—in one stunning moment I fell through. I was in vast space. I wasn't myself. I was Katagiri Roshi, looking at Natalie. I experienced his love and admiration. I always thought it had been one-way, but he needed me as much as I needed him. I had believed in him. He couldn't have been a teacher without a student.

All of us in that small zendo across from Lake Calhoun had created something beautiful together. The love was equal; we all were part of the commitment and dedication.

Roshi wasn't some piece of heaven that marched through our midst and then left. Roshi, me, the students from Minnesota, the ones who migrated from Iowa and Tennessee, the ones who fell asleep on the cushion, the ones who came late, those who shaved their heads, who married, who showed up only to help at the summer rummage sale, even the floor, the walls, the breaking cold, the trembling early daffodils, the doorway, the altar—all were part of "dependent coorigination." He repeated the phrase often: nothing exists by itself. We were all interconnected and interpenetrated.

I wasn't less than Roshi; we were all good enough, ample, sufficient. Standing on this zero spot, this level, steady view, I could step forth and speak. Unfettered, I could let go.

PART 3

wife daughters friends this is for you
satori is mistake after mistake
—Ikkyu

On March 1, exactly nine years to the day that Roshi died, I drove up to Boulder, setting the cruise control at seventy-five, the Colorado highway speed limit. I was going up there to record *Long Quiet Highway*, the book I'd written seven years earlier about Roshi. This time there would be an addendum: what we heard about his relationships after he died.

I was adjusting the tape deck so the same song would play over and over. If I like a song, fifty repetitions are not too much. It drives passengers mad, so I reserve the pleasure for when I'm driving alone. I am of that lineage that lands one song and is happy to wire her nervous system to its beat, its words, the breath of the singer. I like those agonizing songs, the ones that shatter the mind and then link your life to something larger. In listening to a song like that continuously I'm carried to a bigger place. After that, no matter where I hear it—as background music in a café, in a passing automobile, hummed by a pedestrian on a busy street—my body splays open, and a huge world is available to me. Who else's songs can do this year after year but the Jew from the Iron Range in northern Minnesota, the alien in a cold place, who has seen some tough things?

This new car had a button I could press that slid the tape back over the same two feet of sound again and again. If only I could find it and coordinate the pressing of it with the end of the first play. Was that how it worked? Michèle explained it before I left.

I hunger for sound the way a wrestler wants touch. This is a five-hour trip. I need to fill my ears. I am focused on the buttons. I forget everything else.

I glance up. My car is heading for the side of the road. I jerk the wheel too fast to steer away from the shoulder. The car careens in circles, spins hard off pavement, hits dirt mounds, tangles in sage, eats up lumps of grass, then smacks against a big hill. My large green suitcase is flung out the back window with glass shattered everywhere, landing across the divider line in the south lane. In seconds, I am no longer in a car but inside an accordion. The backseat is caved in and the trunk is pushed up against me. In front an air bag is pressed on my chest. The tape deck is stuck on my one song: Bob Dylan wails, "Death is not the end" over and over.

I don't know if I'm alive or dead. I certainly am vacant of thought or feeling. I push open the door and crawl out. The hills are yellow and bare but for a bit of gray scrub. I sit on the side of the road. A van filled to the brim with a large Hispanic family pulls over, and they ask if I'm okay. I nod, and the mother with soft eyes sends her small son over to give me a can of juice. She knows I am not okay though my body is intact.

Some cars fly by. I just sit there. Finally the police arrive and tell me an ambulance from Pueblo is on its way.

Though I can walk, they strap me on a gurney, and as the ambulance whines down the highway, the technicians ask me questions. I know my date of birth, my address, even my Social Security number.

The driver calls back, "You don't look in your fifties. I thought mid-thirties."

I smile weakly.

I break down in front of two officers after being carried into the hospital. I tell them I am not appearing before a court in two weeks. "I can't drive up again. My car is all broken." They leave me alone with a forty-dollar ticket.

The X rays say I am fine. But I no longer trust my life, that it will stay with me.

Michèle drives up from Taos. We stay in a hotel that night. I only want Häagen-Dazs coffee ice cream and Coca-Cola.

So this is what a human being clings to when she's come a hair's breadth from death, I think as I spoon the dessert into my mouth. No great satori or sudden freedom? Just this. I feel the cold on my tongue.

The truth was I'd gotten two or three speeding tickets in the last six months. Outside of Española the police chased me for a full two minutes before I pulled over. I was blasting a tape so loud I hadn't heard the siren. Another time in Rinconada I tired of trailing behind three cars all dutifully doing the speed limit on a two-lane highway because a police vehicle was in front. I pulled into the left lane, jammed on my gas, passed the Goody Two-shoes vehicles at least twenty miles over the limit, and veered back into the right, ahead of the state patroller, gassing it even more, my taillights receding in his windshield.

Immediately, he put on his siren and flashed his red lights. I didn't care. I didn't want to be a good citizen anymore.

"Do you realize you almost hit a car coming in the other direction? Not to mention your speed." He leaned into my rolled-down window.

I glared at him. So what? I was a moment away from saying, "Fuck you." I imagined myself entering another layer of society—prison, detention, courts. Then shooting smack, sharing needles in back alleys. A grave restlessness reigned in me. It was as though I was between worlds—or pushing to enter some underworld. I'd left one, but hadn't been born in another. If there was no Roshi, what was there? The argument that Katagiri was the finger pointing to the moon didn't help. I didn't want the moon. But what did I want? I could watch my life slip away.

The day after my car accident, we stopped at the junkyard in Canyon City where they had towed my car. A thin man with gray hair and a Maine accent unlocked the gate.

"There it is," I pointed.

He looked at the heap of metal in the corner and then back at me. "You're not supposed to be alive," he whistled through his teeth, shaking his head. "Nobody gets out of a wreck like that."

On the trip home in Michèle's Jeep, every bump hurt. I kept repeating, "Slow down."

After Te-shan burned his books at Lung-t'an's monastery, he ventured on to wander through southern China. He heard that Kuei-shan's teachings were flourishing, so he traveled to meet him. But now Te-shan was an adept, someone who had seen into the heart of things, when that candle was blown out.

Carrying his bundle straight into the teaching hall, Te-shan crossed from east to west, back and forth. He looked around and said, "There's nothing, no one." Then he went out.

But when he got to the monastery gate, he said, "Still, I shouldn't be so rude." He wanted to bring out his innermost guts in dharma combat with Kuei-shan. He hoped to be challenged and deepened—tenderized.

So he reentered to meet Kuei-shan, who was sitting in the hall. Kuei-shan did not move. With full ceremony this time Te-shan greeted him, "Teacher!" Kuei-shan reached for his whisk, but Te-shan shouted, shook out his sleeves, and left.

Turning his back on the teaching hall, he put on his straw sandals and went on his way.

That evening Kuei-shan asked the head monk, "Where is that newcomer?"

The head monk answered, "He turned his back on the teaching hall, put on his straw sandals, and left."

Kuei-shan said, "Hereafter that lad will go to the summit of a solitary peak, build a grass hut, and go on scolding the Buddhas and reviling the patriarchs."

Remember when Te-shan met the old tea-cake woman when he had the pile of commentaries on the *Diamond Sutra* on his back? Now he carried a new bundle—the monk's—into the hall. He's still stuck, this time in the Absolute. He can't come down to the ground after the awakening he had with Lung-t'an.

At first he clung to his books; now he's attached to emptiness. Like a cat caught in flypaper, he roams the countryside looking for help. Kuei-shan could have helped him, but Te-shan couldn't stay still long enough.

Kuei-shan waited all the way till evening to ask after that strange monk. Unlike Te-shan, he was in no hurry. When the head monk said he left, Kuei-shan made a pronouncement, but saying that he was going to go to an isolated summit and rail against the lineage was not a compliment about Te-shan's future. Kuei-shan was saying that Te-shan, no matter what insight he recently had, was still upholding the pattern of his suffering. He continued to be distant, fervent, caustic. It doesn't mean that having understanding causes one to suddenly become someone else, all at once a tender sweetheart. A person has a bundle of qualities that make up his or her character, but these sets of energies, if that person is lucky and is filled with inspiration and effort, evolve. Sometimes for better—or worse.

Te-shan's whole lifetime way of meeting the world was understood by this old teacher. Te-shan here was still living in a cave and not free. In this quick meeting, he was seen through by Kuei-shan.

I COULD NO LONGER quite trust any teacher I studied with, not in the way I had been devoted to Roshi—and I still hadn't lodged that trust deep in myself. I could not settle down.

In April, a month after the car accident, I traveled to Florida. I was to be a speaker at a book fair in Palm Beach. This was near my parents' home, so they came along, but of course I didn't tell them about the car accident, in the same way I didn't tell them about the mugging in St. Paul. It would have upset them.

Behind heavy curtains on the stage of the convention center my father discovered tables of brownies, punch, small sandwiches, Danish. "Nat, it's free." He held up a can of Pepsi. He'd already eaten three rugalach. "Free," he repeated. "Free."

"Yes, for the volunteers and presenters," a woman nearby in diamond-studded glasses and a T-shirt with a glittering palm tree chimed in.

"Yes, and for their parents," my father twirled over to the cheese display, undeterred even for a moment.

He was so happy that he almost bought a book later when we walked around on the main floor peering into stalls.

"Young man," he said to the owner of a small press, his hand clamped on the Midwesterner's shoulder, "I'd like to purchase something, but my daughter here is a published writer, and I still have her books to read."

Then I could hear his loud whisper, "Free food behind that wall," and he pointed with his thick finger.

My mother was about to buy a bookmark farther down the aisle. He scurried up. "Syl, we don't need that. Here," he withdrew a cocktail napkin from his pocket. "Just use this to hold your place." He smiled broadly. "Look, it's got the name of this fair."

My mother, flustered, let go of her purchase.

For almost the whole visit my father was in high spirits. One night in their living room, he put on a show of different characters. Disappearing into the hall, he returned with a black patent leather matador hat on his head, and he waved a dishrag in front of himself, repeating, "Bolero." He was enticing a bull into the dining room. For act two he hobbled over to us like a bum, wearing an old brown felt fedora and a plaid wool jacket. For his final act, he was Sherlock Holmes, pipe in his mouth, checkered hat with flaps tied at the top, visor in the back and front. He held a spyglass to his eye, inspecting the couch for clues to crack the crime. Then he came over to my hair.

"Let's see what this dandruff reveals."

"Daddy," I yelled, trying to grab his hand, and fell into peals of laughter.

The last night of my visit we went to the Gourmet Deli, the scene of my famous second dharma defeat years before. It was a mile from their house. We had had such a good visit I almost forgot the recent car accident and the pain and fear I still felt. We'd already ordered when my father leaned in close.

The weight of our imminent departure (Michèle had come with me) was on all our minds. "I'm going to miss you" is what I expected him to whisper. I bent to hear what he had to say.

"You need to lose weight," he hissed in my ear.

I shot up in my seat, tears sprung in my eyes. Was that what he was noticing all week? My father, always overweight but not caring, carrying it with a flair, had dropped decades of pounds since his operation almost a year ago.

I was speechless, hurt to the core. I couldn't look up. I picked at my hamburger. Our last meal was a tragedy. The bill came, and I ran to the car.

My father wasn't quite sure what he'd done. I told him he should apologize, my weight wasn't his business.

When we came home, he just stared at the TV.

The next morning I phoned them from the airport.

"Are we still pals?" he asked. I knew this was as much as I would get.

"Yes," I hesitated, "but I'm not fat."

In late July every time I phoned, my sister, who was visiting, and my mother were always out shopping. Usually my father never picked up the phone. If no one else was there, he'd let it ring. (They never owned an answering machine.) I think now he felt the weight of his loneliness.

"Oh, Nat, when are you coming?"

"Remember—this Monday, August 2."

"When's that?" My father in the last two months had become confused. "Gee, I hope I last that long."

"You will, Daddy." He'd never said anything like that before.

For the last weeks he'd been sleeping a lot—and in the bed, not dozing in his blue TV chair.

Sunday morning he woke up to go swimming as he always did. Then he decided not to go.

Sunday afternoon he'd told my mother to call 911. He didn't feel well. When the paramedics came, they took his vital signs. They were all fine.

"Take me anyway," he said. "I'm not well." This was not like my father. He hated hospitals.

In the ambulance he had a heart attack. Not a bad one, they said.

As soon as I arrived Monday night, I drove to the hospital. He was sedated, tossing his head back and forth, his hands tied down. They had tubes in his nose. Even unconscious, he was trying to pull them out.

I sat beside him a long time. Then I noticed he wasn't wearing his ruby ring.

The next day my sister kept repeating, "I don't understand. It's the doctors. They did it to him."

A few days before, they'd gone to the beach. She told me that out of the blue he turned to her while driving and said, "You know, Romi, everyone has to die someday."

"Not you, Daddy." She clutched his hand.

"I'm sorry. No one gets away," he shook his head.

All kinds of monitors buzzed and clicked.

"What can you do?" my sister grabbed the nurse's arm. "His kidneys, I saw the monitor screen, they're getting better?"

The doctor came in. We all stood around my father's bed.

"Well," the young physician in white sighed deeply. He'd seen this before. "His kidneys aren't functioning—"

"They will, though, they will." My sister held a fistful of the white sheets.

My mother backed away from the bed. She was afraid of hospitals, of my father like this.

His legs hung out of a thin pale hospital gown decorated with small blue diamond shapes. His feet were beautiful. All the swelling from bursitis was gone. But this was not my father tied down like this. He was full of small motions. Sometimes his eyes fluttered open, but he wasn't seeing.

Have I said his eyes were blue? Yes, they were blue, but now they were vacant.

Michèle and I went back to the hotel in late afternoon. We dropped my mother off at home. My sister stayed, trying to convince the staff to get his liver up and going. "Just two days ago we swam in the waves," I heard her say. "It's this hospital that did it to him. Now, please, fix it."

I sat on the beach in early evening. This was it.

Early the next morning the phone rang. "Daddy is on life support."

"I'll be right there."

Now he was breathing into an aspirator.

"Romi, we have to let go. There's nothing we can do."

"Let's meet with doctors. Hear what they have to say."

She didn't get it, but I didn't roll my eyes. That would mean I still possessed irony, humor, sarcasm. Instead, I was as dull as lead, but in a sudden moment of inspiration, I actually addressed my father directly. The only time anyone thought to do this. I bent low and spoke into his ear, "Daddy, is there anything we can do?"

From the depths of another world, he breathed out one singular last human word, "No-o-o-thing."

I thought I might be imagining it, but the nurse tucking in his sheet repeated it. "See, even he knows."

We meet in another room again with the young doctor.

Without saying he's as good as dead, he tells us all his organs have given out. He suggests hospice. He makes a call on a beige phone.

"So how long will he be there? Three months?" my sister asks.

I'm watching all this now as if it were a play. I know as soon as the plugs are pulled, he will be gone.

"Romi, we have to let him go," I tell her.

The doctor turns to my mother, "Mrs. Goldberg?"

"Well, whatever you say."

"It's over." I look straight at my mother. She doesn't look back.

"How do we proceed?" I ask the social worker, who has joined us. It is clear we are taking him off life support.

My sister pleads, "Well, maybe we don't know he could go the other way."

"Each of you individually can go in and say good-bye, tell him what you want." I watch her thin neck working up and down as she speaks. She's wearing a gold heart on a narrow chain.

My sister goes down the hall first. She comes back sobbing, her small nose bright red and pale around the nostrils.

I go next, tears running down my cheeks. His large head cocked to his left shoulder, he's on his back, facing the ceiling. I observe the stubble over his paunchy cheek, the pale eyelashes, his receding hairline, and steel gray hair. He is still handsome. He can't be a man subject to the laws of life and death. He must be something else, an avalanche. But here it is: my father is dying, his last tumble in all his years. My words blow breath on his long earlobe. "Daddy, I've come to say good-bye. You can let go and go on. I have always loved you. Take my love with you. I love you." I repeated those three words over and over. "Thank you for being my father. I'll miss everything about you. You were a great man. Thank you for my life. Everything is complete. Go on." There was a slow tear rolling down his right cheek. "Forever I'll love you."

I leave and walk down the empty hall. Michèle passes me on her way in. She's known my father for two years and wants to pay her respects.

Then my mother goes in and comes out. The male nurse beckons us back. We stand around the bed. We all touch him—I hold his right foot and leg—as the nurse undoes the wiring and tubes.

"It's so final," my mother whispers. I put my hand on her shoulder.

When the wrist restraints are untied, the full life of my father roars out and fills the room. He is a wild thing, a white lion. He arches his back and faces the window, the death rattle comes from his throat, and he is free, gone. He does not look back; he does not linger. You feel it. Something much brighter than this life calls him, and he charges on.

I know death will never scare me again. It isn't some foreign dark cave at the end of life. It is the most natural, ordinary thing. It is as though a hand turns over from palm up to palm down, or a leaf flutters and we glimpse its silver underside. It is almost as if nothing happens—the big emptiness is just there as it always has been.

Ben Goldberg was merely a squiggle on open space—his love of Bing cherries, horse racing, the odd funny twist of his humor, the year of his birth, 1916, the first woman he loved, the last time he ate rye bread, saw Brooklyn, drove a car—all dissolved. We, human beings, his daughters who stood by his deathbed, wanted to believe he was forever, solid and dependable. Not so. He had passed on. My father, whoever he was, was gone.

It was four in the afternoon. A blue sky and palm trees lined the boulevard outside my father's window. When the service sent him to Miami to teach swimming to the officers, he never got over the place. After the war he returned to New York and told his mother about the flamingoes, the white buildings, the forever summer. He brought my mother down here on their honeymoon. Now he ended up in his paradise. He'd made it.

Michèle drove my mother home. My sister and I sat for a short while in the room. I knew about being with the body to help the soul on its journey, but clearly the man had moved on. No spirit was hovering in this hospital.

Back at the hotel late that night old, past fears ignited. I'd learned to control my father by putting up fierce boundaries. Now he had no body. He was amorphous. He could creep into my bedroom, and I did not know how to block him.

Suddenly it felt as though his death left behind vapors. That creepy part of him descended like smoke, surrounding me with a putrid smell.

The week before, I'd sent a present to my sister at my parents' home. My father blithely told me on the phone he'd opened it.

I clenched the phone's mouthpiece. "You have no right." Nothing had changed.

He laughed. "It's no big deal. I just wrapped it back up."

I was helpless all over again.

The next day we went to the funeral home. His body would be refrigerated and flown up to New York the following Monday. We'd have a graveside ceremony at the old Hebrew cemetery in Elmont, Long Island, where the family owned a plot. Even his parents had been buried there in another area a long time ago.

My sister, mother, Michèle, and I would first go that

Sunday to a cousin's wedding in Westchester, New York, and the following day all the relatives, conveniently gathered, would drive out for the funeral. Much discussion ensued about exactly where in the plot Buddy's body would be placed. Not next to Aunt Priscilla, but it would serve her right. She once put him down when he used a big word, "You don't know the meaning of that," and he never forgot it. Now the snob and the man who never finished high school could duke it out in heaven. But if not there, he'd have to lie next to Grandma, my mother's mother, and he wasn't a blood relative. Besides, wasn't Uncle Manny, her favorite, going to be laid there? And then Cousin Nancy wasn't even sure in thirty years that she wanted to be buried in New York. So another potential space opened up.

We chose a plain pine box, not because my father was Orthodox, but because it was cheap. My father had said, "Don't spend money on my coffin. Just another way they can rip you off." It was exactly like the one that they had cremated Roshi in nine years earlier. These simple boxes are often used by Orthodox Jews for burial. The Zen students removed the Star of David from Roshi's and saved it for me. This Jewish star attached to my father's coffin would be buried with him.

It was a beautiful Monday in August. Not humid, not hot, but the sun shone, and we could hear the shouting at

Belmont Park, a mile to the north. It was the fifth race of the afternoon, and the Thoroughbreds were making their last turn into the homestretch, when the limousine pulled up with my father's body. I'm sure he strained through the black metal of the long car to hear who'd won. But more likely he was hovering over the track right then, angelic arms outspread, mouthing in a whisper like a green breeze, "Four-legged animals, turf, jockeys, silk shirts, bets, hopes, dollars, tickets, bleachers, outdoor stands, men with cigars plugged in the corner of your mouths, and women with brassieres, nylons, and high heels, adieu, adieu."

Meanwhile, his family stood empty-handed around the box they were lifting out of the back hatch. The man in charge needed a witness, someone to look in one last time and make sure they shipped the right corpse to the right place.

My sister and I stepped forward. His face looked like wax. His beard hadn't grown. Looking straight up, his eyes were opened, the blue incandescent.

My sister talked nervously to the attendant. "He looks like a sculpture. I was an art major in college twenty years ago . . ." and she started to tell him about using clay for modeling.

He had on the blue silk Hawaiian shirt that he refused to take off for a full month after I bought it for him. We'd given it to the undertaker. Now he could wear it forever.

"It's him," I nodded, and they closed the lid.

Relatives piled in cars to drive the length of three city blocks to the grave site. I walked there slowly, the way I'd been taught by Roshi. Mindful of each step, I repeated, "This is your father you're burying today. This is it."

But it felt more as if I was in someone else's movie. Whose father? Whose daughter? What town? You know someday your parents will die, but it's always a future occurrence. I passed gravestone after gravestone, old upright aging markers with Hebrew characters carved with filigree and hearts.

Everyone was gathering in front of plot eight. The hole was already dug and the dirt piled high. My mother and cousin Esther sat in white plastic chairs Michèle and I had purchased at a neighborhood grocer before the ceremony. A local Reform rabbi was there to perform the service. I told him that I would take over. Then I asked if anyone had anything to share about my father.

One cousin recalled the way he loved to buy fresh roasted chichi nuts from a vendor in New York.

Esther told how he took her husband, Venty, to a strip joint the night before their wedding. That he dragged him to a front-row seat and gave him two singles to put in the stripper's cleavage. She turned to me. "Your father loved to shock people."

A great-niece recalled how he pulled her out of bed one very early morning when she was visiting to take her to the pier in Lake Worth to watch the seagulls and the fishermen, how when they passed young boys eyeing her, my father put his arm around her shoulder and told them, "She's my wife."

My sister read a poem torn from a notebook. It was about how she would miss her father.

My mother said he was a wonderful son-in-law to her parents.

I read from a book I'd written about painting, what it was like to sit in front of my father and draw him.

Then the coffin was lowered into the ground. The leaves on the old sycamores lining the walk tilted in a slight current of air. I knew it was no longer Benjamin Goldberg, but it was also that man, the last of him in this life.

The rabbi now wanted to say Kaddish. He had mentioned earlier to me that it is traditional to throw dirt in after the coffin, but it was too emotional, so he wasn't going to ask anyone to do it. I held up my hand for him not to begin just yet. I stepped forward, bent down, grabbed loose soil in both my hands, lifted the soil to my mouth, kissed it, then released it over the opening in the earth. My sister was right behind me. Wasn't this how it always was? The younger sibling following the older. The rest of the family took turns with the small shovel. Some held back. The two widows in their eighties continued to sit in their plastic chairs.

I nodded to the rabbi. He recited the ancient Hebrew. People cried. I held another position—the guide at my father's farewell. I did not cry again for months.

It was over. We all lingered. The sweetness of being together. Life was hard—and now there was one less. We handed out Pepperidge Farm cookies I picked up when we bought the plastic chairs.

I heard the gruff sound of someone clearing his throat. I looked up. Three men in plaid shirts, leaning on shovels, dirt on their faces, were waiting at the edge of the plot.

"Oh," the rabbi tried to shoo us away, "they're on union time."

"Go ahead," I nodded, and they stepped onto our grave property and dirt flew. In moments the hole was filled.

Most of us drove on the Long Island Expressway headed for the heart of the city, straight to the Carnegie Delicatessen. A long table in the back was reserved. We ordered thick pastrami and corned beef, tongue and brisket piled high on rye, specials—those big hot dogs my father loved—coleslaw, kosher pickles, potato pancakes, one plate of cheese blintzes. My sister wanted chicken soup with matzo balls. We had a plate of herring in sour cream, many RC root beers. With each bite someone pledged to my father.

"Buddy would have loved this."

These were second cousins, nieces, nephews, a first niece-in-law, his two daughters, his wife. No aunts or uncles, no brothers or sisters. They had long passed away. At the table sat the generation of American Jews who'd gone to college, donned running shoes, and lived in Westport, Manhattan, Boston, or Westchester. Uncle Buddy, even if he wasn't truly their uncle, was the one who introduced them to this food from the old country of Brooklyn. It was their touch with the past. He didn't know what a fax, a cell phone, or a computer was all about—and he didn't care.

We chomped on rugalach and bobka for dessert.

"Wait a minute! Wouldn't he have liked some strawberry cheesecake?" We ordered half a cake.

Across the table Michèle looked green and excused herself. I followed her to the bathroom.

"I've been nauseous all evening, ever since I drove you, your mother, and sister from the cemetery."

Walking back to the table, I knew sometimes it took the outsider, the non–blood relation, to witness and carry the suffering that is in the back of every relative's mind.

My mother, after a lifetime of good health, fell apart. She had spinal stenosis, then bad teeth, then heart palpitations. Cataracts were removed. She had glaucoma. Whenever she was lonely, she called 911 with a new ailment. None were fatal; some couldn't be corroborated upon examination and testing. Still, she was in pain, and she'd never been alone in her life.

A person went to work and came home. He went on vacation and returned. He went to the bank and drove the same streets, again to reappear. He went to his death—maybe the wait was a little longer, but the coming back was programmed into me. I wasn't fully grieving. I was on standby. But two springs had flowered, almost two summers had passed in which he did not swim, two birthdays when he did not age.

Hiking in Bandelier National Park outside of Santa Fe one Saturday when dusk came and the visitors had to leave, I did not want to go with them. The presence of an ancient people among the pueblo ruins was palpable. Finally, a forest-service ranger politely addressed me directly, "The gates will be closing soon down by the entrance."

I thought of hiding behind a boulder where a yucca was growing, then reluctantly obeyed the law. But I could not drive the hour and a half home. Something compelled me to linger. I stayed in a cheap hotel in nearby White Rock and slept long into the next morning.

I hadn't planned to be gone overnight. I had no toothbrush. I splashed water on my face, slipped on the same clothes I wore the day before, and headed back to Bandelier.

During the night I had dreamed that my father slept next to me, and I told him to rest, that I would take care of things now. It was a simple dream, but it was the first I'd had of him in the long months since he died.

Instead of hiking down through the falls, I turned right toward Frijoles Canyon. Thirteen years earlier was the last time I backpacked down there with my friend Frances. We camped near red cliffs and a cold stream. We'd seen deer, and I wrote the pivotal chapter of a book in which I clearly enunciated what wild mind was. All at once I had to find the ponderosa I leaned against when I wrote. I hadn't eaten breakfast. I had little water, no food. Could so much have changed in all these dozen years? Where was the meadow where Frances told me she realized she loved David, the man she eventually married and divorced? Where was the high narrow cliff we circumambulated, the knife we lost in the tall weeds? I pushed on at a furious pace way beyond where visitors were treading that day. Perspiration poured down my face. My feet hurt, and my socks were stiff with sweat.

Breathing heavily at the top of a thin incline, I stopped. What was I really looking for?

Wild mind, I had written, was outside our normal perception, beyond our constant discursive thoughts, as big as the sky. All we need to do is take one step backward, and we live in that mind, one with everything, not limited to the boundaries of our skin. It is the place where birds, clouds, old memories, horses move through us.

My heart fell into my stomach. I was out there looking

for my father. I wouldn't find him in the old way. He'd gone beyond being a human being.

Exhausted, I turned back toward the trailhead.

All the rest of that summer I hiked up to Heart Lake north of Questa, up Elliot Barker Trail toward Angel Fire, Divisidero off Cañon. I spotted a herd of thirty to forty elk through my binoculars off Latir Mesa way up above Cabresto Lake. I sat and watched them for a full hour.

That spring I had dreamed that elk came to me, and the biggest one, the leader, tried to break into my house. I was afraid and hid under a table with my friend Wendy, who also in real life had lost her father. Finally, I let the big elk in, and we sat opposite each other. He tried painfully to communicate, but we didn't speak even close to the same language.

When I saw the herd that afternoon in late summer, I felt peaceful and at ease. I knew I had found my father again.

One day Te-shan descended to the dining hall, bowls in hand. Hsüeh-feng asked him, "Where are you going with your bowls in hand, Old Teacher? The bell has not rung, and the drum has not sounded." Te-shan turned and went back to his room.

Hsüeh-feng brought up this matter with Yen-t'ou. Yen-t'ou said, "Te-shan, great as he is, does not yet know the last word."

Hearing about this, Te-shan sent for Yen-t'ou and asked, "Don't you approve of this old monk?" Yen-t'ou whispered his meaning. Te-shan said nothing further.

Next day, when Te-shan took the high seat before his assembly, his presentation was different from usual. Yen-t'ou came to the front of the hall, rubbing his hands and laughing loudly, saying, "How delightful! Our Old Boss has got hold of the last word. From now on, no one under heaven can outdo him!"

THE LAST TIME we see Te-shan in the ancient texts he is an old man and an able teacher. He has his own monastery with many students and is renowned for his nonverbal teaching. This philosopher of the *Diamond Sutra* became a master who taught almost without words.

When his students came to him, he energetically used the kyosaku, the hitting stick, which Americans are horrified by and associate with the toughness of Zen. Te-shan would say to his students, "If you speak, you get thirty blows. If you do not speak, you get thirty blows."

But Te-shan was not a maniac who arbitrarily cornered his students and beat them. By now Te-shan was a seasoned teacher, not stuck in the wandering heart of the young man who journeyed to see Kuei-shan and then left immediately. His character had matured during the thirty years he lived in obscurity after the visit to Kuei-shan. During this time his taciturn, stern nature allowed him to develop a presence of penetrating silence. Now he had become the teacher of Hsüeh-feng and Yen-t'ou, and out of his lineage would eventually emerge the Yunmen and Fayen schools.

These blows were more an expression of the Middle Way—words, but not words. What is the sense of what he is saying? He'll hit you either way, speaking or not? You're thrown back on yourself.

In our final meeting with Te-shan, he is heading toward the monastery dining room, his eating bowls in hand.

Hsüeh-feng, who is the cook, sees Te-shan from the kitchen. Hsüeh-feng is an ardent student who has not yet attained realization. He calls out, "Where are you going with your bowls in hand, Old Teacher? The bell has not yet rung."

Te-shan simply turns and goes back to his room.

No fight. No reprimand—how dare you talk to me like that? No correction—why is the meal late? Understand: Te-shan did not suddenly become a doddering pushover. He was capable of immense power, but he did not need to exercise it anymore. He was deeply at home in himself, in harmony with the universe.

There is a saying in Zen: a pearl rolling in a silver bowl. A smooth ride, no bumps, no jagged edges. No resistance, no fight, desire, need. The precious metal and the gem meet perfectly.

This rolling pearl was the mind of Te-shan at the end of his life. It contained multitudes—contradictions, paradoxes, life, and death all were embraced. Nothing caught him or tossed him away—or perhaps he was completely tossed away, at one with all things.

The story goes on a bit with an effort by a fellow monk, Yen-t'ou, to help enlighten Hsüeh-feng, the cook, who misunderstood Te-shan's simple turning as an example that the old teacher was failing. But it's not necessary for us to go on. We can end with our friend, turning in the hallway, his bowls in hand, open, surrendered, at ease, living in vast acceptance. We all know the one hard road he traveled to find himself here.

In May, almost three years after my father's death, I visit my mother, living alone in Florida, now eighty-six years old. She is very thin, walks slowly with a cane, and has trouble seeing.

I'm telling her some grievances I had from the past. (I seem to never give up.) I'm sharing in the hope of closing the distance between us. I'm trying to see my father's absence as an opportunity. Death will also claim her, and I want some reconciliation before she goes.

She is hard of hearing. I have to speak loudly even though I am sitting on the couch across from her. The discussion is not going well. She bristles and denies anything but the glorious childhood she perceives that I had.

She affirms her position with an example. "Don't you remember when you were inducted into the Junior Honor Society? I was so proud."

I am not deterred. I push ahead. I know this is my last chance. "Mom, my memory of that day is that you were arguing bitterly with Daddy and your only comment to me was, 'You are the only pleasure I get.' You didn't really acknowledge *me*."

I know I am going over her head. A daughter of immigrants, my mother has three basic concerns: Did you eat? Did you sleep? Were you warm? Psychology is a field that developed in another country, not Brooklyn.

She is quiet. We are at an impasse. I do know that in the last years by herself she has mulled over her past, grieved her mother's death that happened almost twenty years ago.

"Why didn't I fly up when the nursing home called and said Grandma was fading? What was the matter with me?" She has cried herself to sleep many nights in the lonesome bedroom.

Now she turns to me. "Natli, I was a very unhappy woman. I think your father was having an affair."

My eyes widen, my head jerks. I was not expecting this. I sit up straight. Did I hear right? "What?" I ask, incredulous.

She nods. "With Ruth. Remember the barmaid who worked at the Aero for twenty years. She still sends Christmas cards. When your father's hands were too shaky to write her back, he'd ask me to. He was always worried about her arthritis. Oh, he was so happy when he heard she was feeling better." My mother makes a face.

"Wait a minute. What makes you think—"

"I'm sitting here realizing what a dolt I was. Your father always worked Tuesday nights—do you recall? They closed the bar at four, but sometimes he didn't get home till six thirty.

"I'd say, 'Buddy, where were you?' He'd say, 'I had some drinks with the boys.'

"After she was working there a year, we came home from visiting you up in camp, and there was an unsigned letter in the mail for me. 'Where is your husband on Tuesday nights?' was written with a pencil in a terrible handwriting. I showed it to him, and he said, 'It's one of the guys pulling a prank. Give it to me. I'll figure out who it was and get even.' He acted indignant. I handed it over and never thought about it again. But, let me tell you, where there's smoke, there's fire."

"Wait a minute. Why do you think it was Ruth?"

"I got a Christmas card this year from her with a note that said, 'Ben was so good to me. He was a good friend.' Why did she need to say that? When I read it, I remembered that old letter, and suddenly I put two and two together." Her eyes filled with tears. "What a damn fool I was."

I don't want to believe this. "Didn't she have a husband?"

"She did. He worked nights."

"Doing what?"

"Painting prisons."

"Mom, are you sure? I never heard of a job like that."

"It's true. She left her last job because she was having an affair with the owner of the bar. That's how Daddy hired her."

"Then she repeated it?"

My mother nods. "He always said a penis has no morals."

Never ever before in all the years of my life did my mother infer that my father had genitals. And now they are even going in the wrong place? All along it was right in front of her—someone even notified her—but now she is facing up to it?

Wasn't this true with Roshi too, when I pictured him and Eleanor in the zendo together? It was right there. And my father's abuse with me? No one wanted to see it. Anyone who looked could have known.

My mother gazes across the room at me. Her black eyes are glowing. Her mouth is determined, lips pressed together. She opens and then clenches her hands on the two arms of the old TV chair that used to be my father's. A gold band is still on her left third finger.

I feel nauseous. I get up to open a window. I can hardly breathe.

"Don't do that. The rain'll come in."

A burst of thunder cracks in the distance. I jump and slam the window shut.

"You met her once. You were a little girl."

I fumble with the venetian blind. "I don't remember." She is not going to change this subject.

"Do you have a phone number?" I ask. I should get to the bottom of this—who am I kidding? We have already gotten there. We are right at the rudiment, the bone, the core.

Was this what made her so unhappy in my childhood? Why she was always preoccupied and ignored her young daughter?

The roles have been switched. The rug has once again been pulled out from under me. My mother wants to get to the truth that underscored her life.

I sit down on the edge of the couch. I can't stay still. I jump up again. "I'm going to the pool."

Her mouth falls open. "In the rain? At night? Are you crazy? You'll get electrocuted."

"I'll take a shower." I run into the bathroom before she can say another word.

I've had a disdain for Tuesdays all my life and never could figure out why. I had no aversion for any other day of the week. I thought it was some personal idiosyncrasy. In my thirties I wrote a poem that began, "A girl sometimes wonders / if her father slept around." I took a leap into what I thought was my imagination for the next stanza, "My father did / I didn't want to believe it / but my father did sleep around."

I didn't mention Tuesday in that poem. But standing

naked in the brown-tiled shower my father and mother stood up in a thousand times before, I know that that second workday of the week, the one I pictured as a sickening yellow, should have been in my verse. When I'd read that poem publicly, the room of people always moved into a deep apprehensive silence, the way they did when I recited the one about my father and World War II. Was there a connection? How many daughters had fathers who had extramarital affairs while they were growing up?

I reach for the hot knob and turn it off, stand in the blazing cold water that no human ever gets used to, and let it penetrate me.

TE-SHAN'S DISCIPLE Yen-t'ou eventually became Teshan's lineage holder and an extraordinary teacher with many students. This was at the end of the Tang dynasty, when there was much disruption in the land. Bandits roamed freely everywhere. The frightened monks left the monastery and hid in the surrounding forest. Only Yen-t'ou remained at the temple, where he continued to meditate.

One day the head bandit stalked through the temple grounds. Enraged that there were no treasures, he pulled out his sword. In front of him sat Yen-t'ou totally composed. The thief ran the blade through the great Zen adept.

Yen-t'ou let out a scream that was heard in the woods for thirty miles around. And then he died.

Was he scared, angry, horrified? What are we to make of that yell? A shout that resounded that far a distance had to plumb the depths. It was the total expression of his life. Whatever was there he encountered it. He did not turn away. This time what he came upon was his death. He faced it completely.

Much later he was given the name "Clear Severity."

I GRAB THE YELLOW TOWEL from the hook behind the door. How old would Ruth be now? Late sixties?

I bend over to wipe my feet, run the cloth over my calves.

I see the Aero Tavern in my mind's eye, the place my father worked for thirty years in the town where I was brought up. My father is handing a glass of whiskey to Harry, an old regular who sways over to the bathroom. Ruth is drying down the counter. The distributor rolls in a keg through the front door, the Rheingold light flashes, and the phone is ringing. Above it hangs a round plaster print of my hand that I made for my father in kindergarten. My mother is calling to tell her husband to pick up a quart of milk and a loaf of bread for dinner on the way home. But now I see something else too: a trapdoor on the ceiling. I remember my father mentioning it once, another way out, in case there was trouble. The Mafia, the cops, you never know. Could my father and Ruth, half-dressed, have climbed out?

I stand up and shake out my wet head. There never is another way out. Only the straight way. My mother has revealed herself to me.

I take a deep breath. I throw on one of her nightgowns and march right back into the living room.

I fold my arms around her, leaning over the chair.

My mother looks up and says, “I love you,” touches my elbow.

My heart is pounding. I almost hesitate. I say it back. And I mean it. I actually truly mean it.

"These were big in the twenties and thirties. It has the same structure as a ruby, only it's synthetic." The clerk was bald with thick eyebrows.

I had one of those rings at home in a small black velvet box—my inheritance. I'd never seen another before. I left the store and felt my father all over the place. This was his world.

I stood on the corner curb. You live and then you die, I thought. It's good to have some good times. My father certainly did that. When people used to say to him, you have such a talented daughter, he'd reply, "My wife and I are ordinary. She did this all on her own."

I don't wonder much what he would have thought about this writing.

"You got it all wrong," he might have said. "You always were a rotten kid. You thought too much." He'd pause. "Make sure to tell them I loved your mother, how beautiful my eyes were, how good my girls were—yeah, you and the little one." He'd stop again. "And, Nat, I'm proud of you. I don't understand what you do, but you've got a heck of a lot of nerve."

When my father first opened the tavern, two beefy men marched in, and behind them three movers plunked down along the north wall a jukebox and a cigarette machine.

"You pay us. We collect once a week." They turned and left.

My father served fourteen drinks in the next hour, eight of which were tap ale. Four football players from the nearby agricultural college were standing at the bar.

"Fellas, help push these out."

He left the equipment on the street. Word got around, and the Mafia arrived within the hour.

"I didn't order anything from you." My father stared them down.

"I got dumb lucky. They left and never bothered me again."

Any nerve I got I inherited from him.

And then I wonder what Roshi, dead now thirteen years, would have thought. I've even stopped waiting for his return. Could he ever have existed? It feels as though he's taken his place as a distant star. I won't say this too loudly, because I don't want my adored father to hear, but Katagiri Roshi was the most important human being in my life.

After I die and my ashes are sprinkled in the places I love—the Jewish cemetery in Taos, the artists' cemetery in Woodstock, by the Mississippi near New Albin, Iowa, with my blood family on Long Island—I wouldn't want people to say of me only "She was a great teacher" or "I loved her writing." I would like at least one person to come closer, to add, "She was also lonely, she suffered a lot. She was mixed up. She made some big mistakes." Then tell those mistakes and sum up: "But she was important to me." Then I would feel really honored, as though someone had seen and known me.

Roshi was a private man. He came from a private culture. It is American to march out our feelings, the particulars of our life, to meet someone at a party, pat them on the back, tell them all our stories.

Roshi knew my deep history, beyond where I was born, who my parents were, my favorite food, what colors I liked. In every human existence, we are telling the history of a people. Roshi reached beyond the details to show me the patterns of suffering and pointed out the path to freedom. But it wasn't holy or abstract. We sat across from each other, and he knew me—the stinky Natalie, as he would say, and the great one.

I'm not sure he would have thanked me for what I have written. A long time ago he had thanked me for my effort. Once for four years I pursued Gary Snyder to come to Minnesota and do a benefit for Zen Center. When Snyder finally arrived, I was in Israel on a poetry fellowship. But three months later when I returned, Roshi acknowledged me. It was a simple thing. I was sitting across the table from him the first time back at the center.

"Gary Snyder was here." He nodded. "Thank you." There was a long pause—time enough for me to feel his appreciation.

In those days I felt the power of silence. Since then I have also understood something else: that silence protects no one. I have heard it often repeated: keep it in the family. That only continues the suffering.

But Roshi deserves the same treatment he gave to me. I can also look beyond "stinky Katagiri." With his own great effort, he planted the seed of an enormous gift into the soil of this country. And he did it person to person. I could have read a book about Buddhism, Zen, meditation. Instead, he practiced with me moment by moment. He taught me the most simple, democratic thing—how to sit still in the center of this busy world. You need no fancy equipment, no special intelligence or talent. This one thing turned my whole life—affected how I write, eat, walk, think, and don't think. It has rooted inside me, so that after everything else has been said, every story told, I will never forget it. Even after my ashes are spread, something will abound with an endless gratitude.

About the Author

How I Wrote *The Great Failure*

I wrote this book on the sly; part of me never believed—or was frightened and aghast—that I was revealing these secrets about my father, about the Zen teacher I studied with, and ultimately about myself. This was not a book I planned to write. In a sense, I backed into it. Sometimes we don't get to choose our subjects—they choose us.

In March 2000, I attended a weeklong retreat in St. Paul, Minnesota. I'd just moved back there to practice for a year and a half. On the second day, curled into the cross-legged position, I could not stop thinking of the mugging I'd experienced two years earlier while visiting St. Paul. My mind would not settle. After the third forty-minute period of restless sitting, out of sheer exasperation, I made a bargain with myself: Listen, if you let go now and stop thinking about it, I promise when this sesshin is over, I'll write down the whole story.

To my amazement, the plea worked. The story line dropped away, and the rest of that week I sat in relative calm.

Two weeks later, I remembered my promise and thought: I'd better do it; otherwise, my mind won't believe me the next time. I had no

"I had no urgency to write. I'd written book after book over the last twelve years and was hoping for a little break, but knowing how the mind works, I felt I should keep my side of the contract."

"Where did I think all this writing would lead me? I asked myself."

urgency to write. I'd written book after book over the last twelve years and was hoping for a little break, but knowing how the mind works, I felt I should keep my side of the contract. The next day I nonchalantly sauntered over to a café on Grand Avenue and wrote for an hour and a half.

It was rather pleasant; I was engaged. I had an urge to continue the story. For a full month I went to the café almost every day, each time beginning from the last sentence of the day before and adding. I was curious to see what I would write and excited, remembering just how much fun writing could be. Then whammo! On a Wednesday morning I wrote myself right into the darkness. Spread out in my notebook in my hefty handwriting were the details of my childhood with my father. I looked up. The café was jammed. Hats and scarves were shoved up against ledges, and thick winter jackets were piled on the backs of chairs. People's faces were ashen from many months of overcast sky and cold weather. I glanced down at the page again. I felt dizzy; images blurred. Then suddenly I laid my head in my crossed arms on the small table and wept.

Where did I think all this writing would lead me? I asked myself.

I didn't care that people were sipping caffe lattes and biting into moist sponge cake close at hand. I knew I was in the Midwest. They would pretend I wasn't sobbing. I let it rip.

I'd been happily whistling through words, the pen flying in my agile hand. I was back to my old love affair. I was young again, funny and full of energy. Writing seduced me, then brought me to the edge of a pit and dropped me in. Whatever I thought I was writing about backpedaled me into the thing I most wanted to avoid. I collided smack into the mother lode, the jugular vein.

I grabbed at my napkin, dabbed at my swollen eyes.

I saw the whole scenario in front of me. This was a book I'd unwittingly begun. And I knew clearly where it was leading—through my father to Katagiri. I would burn in hell. This book would be difficult, but it was what was presented to me. I knew if I didn't write it, if I tried to dodge it, no other book would come.

Even deeper than my momentary good luck at settling my mind that one day at that one retreat was my large vow to write, to tell the truth as I knew it, to let the life of writing do its work on me. I had to step out of the way and let writing do writing. This does not mean I was in some trance state, that I was a clairvoyant medium. I was an adult. I knew my responsibility.

"This time I was asking them to swallow cod liver oil, and I was saying, It might be bitter, but it's good for you."

Unfortunately, I have a strong urge to be liked, to be accepted. I was fortunate to have written books people wanted. This time I was asking them to swallow cod liver oil, and I was saying, It might be bitter, but it's good for you. Failure, betrayal, disappointment are the guts of our life. We need to look at these things or we will never be free. We will spend out days on the run, avoiding them.

I went on a grueling book tour in the fall when *The Great Failure* came out. Audiences in Chicago, Boston, New York resisted even the

> *"Out of exasperation, I looked out at the audience and asked, 'Okay, how many of you have never failed? Please raise your hand.'"*

word *failure.* "That's why I put it in the title. Up front. Let's look at what we are afraid of."

They didn't blink. They acted as though I'd written a four-letter word across the cover. I recalled the first thing one editor, who wanted to buy the book, had said to me: "You can't sell failure in America. The title has to go."

Out of exasperation, I looked out at the audience and asked, "Okay, how many of you have never failed? Please raise your hand." A stunned silence ensued. Not a single hand went up.

"Do you see?" I said triumphantly. "We are all in the same boat. Failure is a truth of life. What can we learn from it? Not the old adage, failure will build character, but instead, what gold can we mine from our darkness?"

The audience softened. The relief was palpable. They weren't the only ones who had failed.

And then they asked the next question: What about your family? What did they think? Did they read the book?

Rarely had my family opened any of my books, so I didn't worry about them. But of course, suddenly my relatives all became literary giants and devoured this one. They didn't comment on the contents. Instead, they were momentarily awkward before taking their usual possession of me. I was theirs no matter what, but they didn't want to talk about what they had read.

I did receive a surprising e-mail from a second cousin: "I will always love Uncle Buddy. I sometimes wondered about your relationship, why you seemed to disappear for long periods of time. Now things are clear. When I was a young girl I, too, was uncomfortable with your father. He kissed me in ways that made me back off. "Then she said she was proud of me for my honesty. I was elated. She has my undying loyalty.

"We often have a hope that some book we write will bring about reconciliation, give us love."

In the Zen world, I've had to face a lot of silence and cold shoulders. I lost some friends. It has not been easy.

Each writer has to decide what she is willing to write and bear up under. Sometimes support comes from unexpected places. I received a wonderful review in a liberal Catholic journal. They've had to face some hard things in recent years, and it has opened them.

Some people were upset I wasn't angry enough.

I told them this book was written after many years of digesting the circumstances. I went through rage—sometimes it still flares—despair, disbelief. I wanted to write a book that showed another angle, a place of hard-earned equanimity. I couldn't skip the difficult emotions, but some resolution is possible. A writer can't change the world, but she can try to see it clearly and write down what she sees.

When my father was still alive and he protested something I'd written in an earlier book, I said, "If you don't like it, sit down and write your own version."

We often have a hope that some book we write will bring about reconciliation, give us love. We can't count on that. Fifty percent of the people who read it might hate us; we

might have saved the lives of the other fifty percent. Writing can be part of the healing process, taking all our disparate parts into our arms. In here, in us, is a great wealth. We meet ourselves and close a yawning gap; that hole gets knit together. Knowing this wholeness, the world becomes whole. No inside, no outside. No here and no there. No one too foreign or difficult not to be embraced.

Finally, this is my story. I wrote it. I stand behind it.

Beyond Betrayal

(From the Spring 2005 issue of *Tricycle* magazine; www.tricycle.com)

"Disappointment and failure bring us down to the ground so we can see through our ideas to the way things really are."

Caryl Göpfert speaks with bestselling author Natalie Goldberg about her "failed" relationship with her teacher, Katagiri Roshi.

The author of ten books, Natalie Goldberg is perhaps best known for her 1986 classic *Writing Down the Bones: Freeing the Writer Within.* Her 1993 book, *Long Quiet Highway: Waking Up in America,* is a glowing memoir of her relationship with her revered Zen master, Katagiri Roshi, who died on March 1, 1990.

In her most recent work, *The Great Failure: My Unexpected Path to Truth,* Goldberg revisits her memories of Katagiri Roshi in the light of the posthumous discovery that he had been sexually involved with a few of his female students. *The Great Failure* examines her connection with both Roshi, whom she views as her spiritual father, and her own biological father—two men whom she loved deeply, but by whom she felt disappointed and betrayed.

Zen teacher Caryl Göpfert spoke with Goldberg last fall in Stanford, California, about *The Great Failure* and the lessons she continues to learn from her disillusionment.

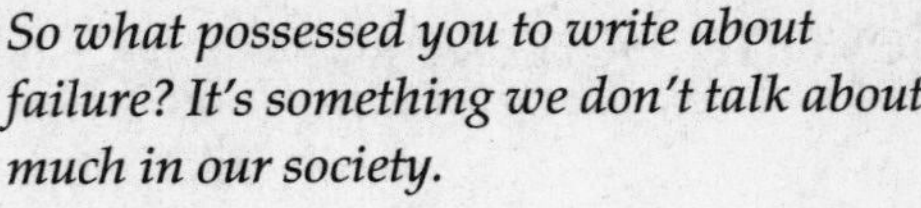

So what possessed you to write about failure? It's something we don't talk about much in our society.

In our society we're always running from failure and running after success. I knew that failure was the underbelly, the thing we keep hidden, the thing that we're most frightened of. Usually the things that we're frightened of have a lot of juice, a lot of power. And my understanding of Zen practice is that it's about really sitting down with the underbelly, facing things like death and betrayal and disappointment that we never want to look at.

I don't necessarily make a judgment when I say failure. *The Great Failure* is beyond good and bad. It's about seeing through illusion to how things really are. I had a lot of deluded ideas about what it is to have a relationship with a father. Some of them were wonderful, but they didn't really match up with my experience. And I had the dream of perfection with Katagiri Roshi. I had him up on a pedestal. Six years after he died, information came out about him that didn't fit my idea of perfection, and so it broke down that illusion. And that helped me to wake up a lot.

Disappointment and failure bring us down to the ground so we can see through our ideas to the way things really are. And when that happens, it is really the Great Success.

Do you see a direct connection between your relationship with your father and your relationship with Katagiri Roshi?

Because there was pain in my relationship with my father, I unconsciously went seeking for someone I could believe was perfect, a relationship where I could feel safe enough to let my true heart out. And I did feel safe enough with Katagiri. I was lucky. I could keep my illusions for a long time. And through those illusions, I was able to connect with my true heart—connect with all the love that, with my father, I was always holding back in terrible fear. If I opened up to my father, I was afraid I'd be grabbed. So I never got to experience who I truly was with him. And with Katagiri, I did.

"If I opened up to my father, I was afraid I'd be grabbed."

After Katagiri died, my heart was broken. But that heartbreak was also the entryway to waking up on a deeper level, by breaking through my misjudgments about who he was.

What was your inner landscape like when you found out that Katagiri Roshi had been sleeping with students?

I was in incredible shock. I went into complete denial for several days after I heard the news. I couldn't digest it. It was so far from my idea of who he was or my experience of him. And then, slowly, I took it in. I actually took off for three months. I canceled everything and went up to the Mesa, where I lived, and just sat with it.

I cried a lot. I found myself remembering all the years I practiced with him in the zendo. It was almost like watching a movie that would run in front of my eyes automatically, without my calling it up. I watched that movie of him in the zendo, and I realized this behavior had been right in front of me all along. He flirted a lot, and he even came on to me. I just wasn't willing to see it.

"He flirted a lot, and he even came on to me. I just wasn't willing to see it."

I went through hating him. I went through missing him terribly, really wishing I could speak to him about it—and yet knowing that, because he came from a very reserved Japanese culture, he probably wouldn't be willing to talk about it, even if he were alive. But I really wanted one more time with him where I could say, "What the fuck did you do?"

It was agony. I had an outbreak of shingles from the stress. I just could not find equilibrium. It completely tossed me away, because he was such a strong foundation for me. I was heartbroken. But going all the way into it brought me to my own awakening, brought me to stand more solidly on the ground.

Why do you think it affected you so strongly? As some of your critics have pointed out, it wasn't your boundaries he had violated.

If you put poison in one side of a lake, it doesn't stay there. It poisons the whole lake. What a teacher does affects the whole community. We thought there was one thing going on, and something entirely different was happening. There was a secret. We didn't really know who this teacher was. There was a part of him that we didn't know about, a part that was suffering and dark and unclear. There was a shadow over our community and our prac-

MOON HANDBOOKS

YELLOWSTONE ~GRAND TETON HANDBOOK

MAP SYMBOLS

Primary Road
Secondary Road
Hiking Trail
U.S. Highway
State Highway
City
Town
Point of Interest
Accommodation
Restaurant/Bar
Other Location
Golf Course
Ski Area
Campground
Unique Natural Feature

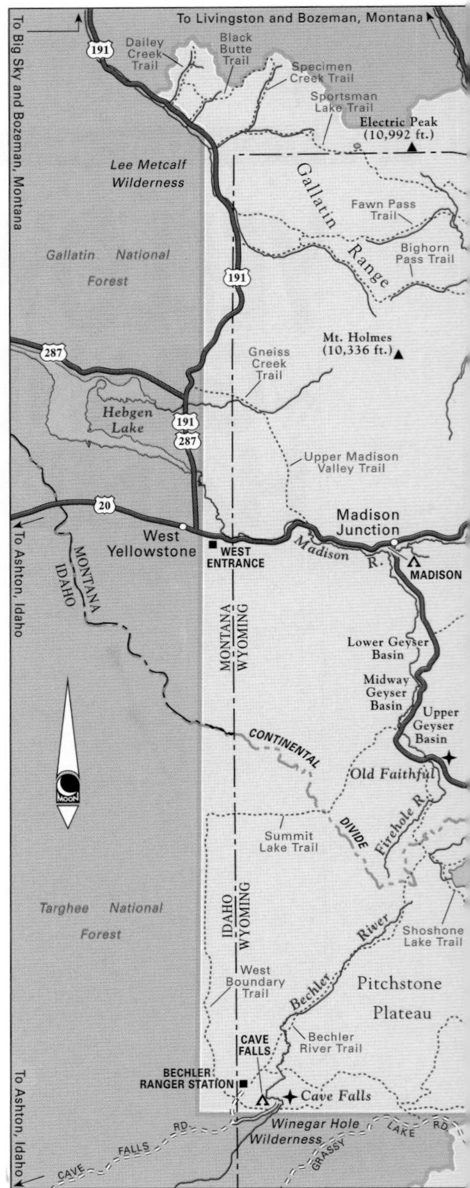

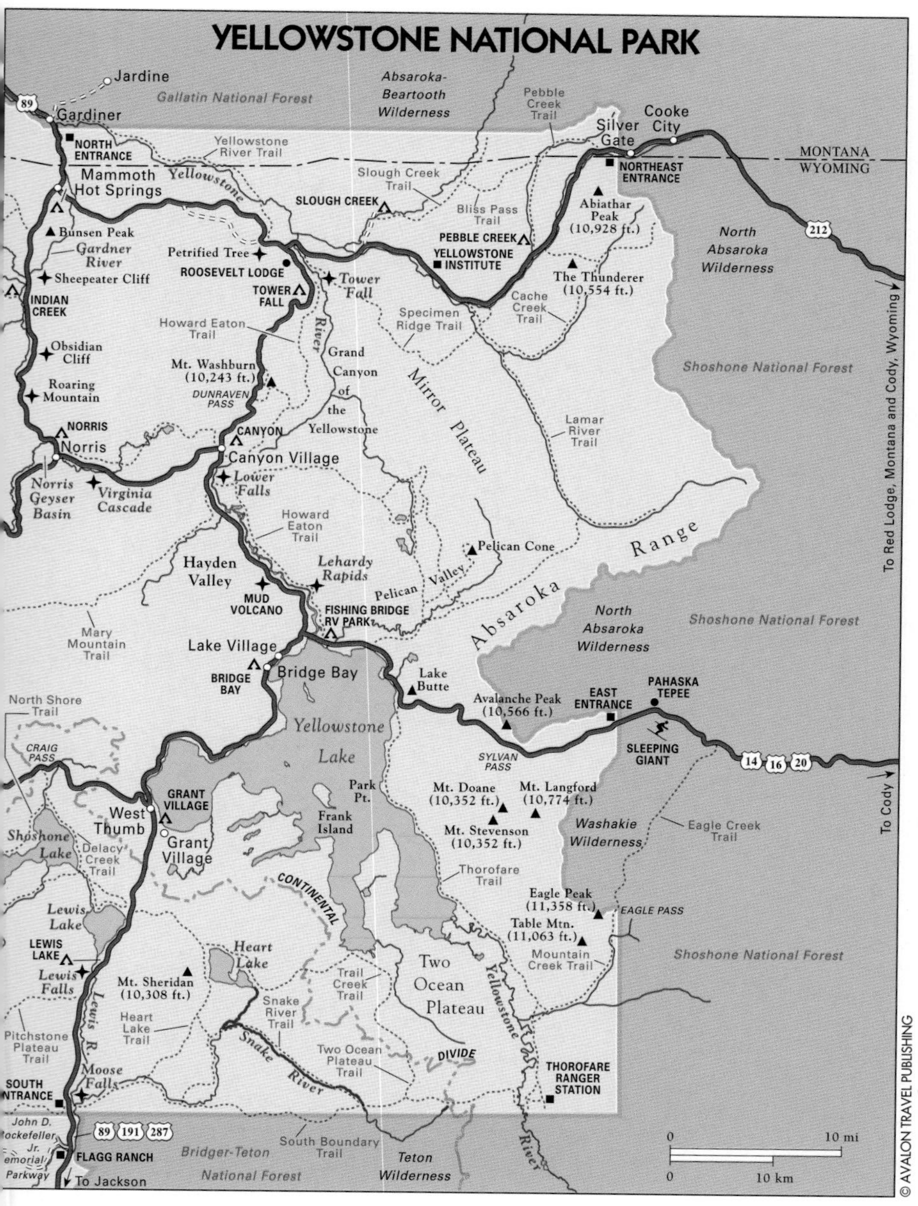
YELLOWSTONE NATIONAL PARK
Jardine
Gallatin National Forest
Absaroka-Beartooth Wilderness
Pebble Creek Trail
Cooke City
Silver Gate
Gardiner
NORTH ENTRANCE
Yellowstone River Trail
MONTANA
WYOMING
NORTHEAST ENTRANCE
Mammoth Hot Springs
Yellowstone
Slough Creek Trail
SLOUGH CREEK
Bliss Pass Trail
Abiathar Peak (10,928 ft.)
Bunsen Peak
Gardner River
Petrified Tree
PEBBLE CREEK
YELLOWSTONE INSTITUTE
North Absaroka Wilderness
Sheepeater Cliff
ROOSEVELT LODGE
TOWER FALL
Tower Fall
The Thunderer (10,554 ft.)
INDIAN CREEK
Cache Creek Trail
Howard Eaton Trail
Specimen Ridge Trail
Obsidian Cliff
River
Grand Canyon of the Yellowstone
Mt. Washburn (10,243 ft.)
DUNRAVEN PASS
Mirror Plateau
Shoshone National Forest
Roaring Mountain
NORRIS
Norris
CANYON
Canyon Village
Lamar River Trail
Norris Geyser Basin
Virginia Cascade
Lower Falls
Howard Eaton Trail
Pelican Cone
Range
Hayden Valley
Lehardy Rapids
Pelican Valley
MUD VOLCANO
FISHING BRIDGE RV PARK
Absaroka
North Absaroka Wilderness
Shoshone National Forest
Mary Mountain Trail
Lake Village
BRIDGE BAY
Bridge Bay
Lake Butte
Avalanche Peak (10,566 ft.)
EAST ENTRANCE
PAHASKA TEPEE
North Shore Trail
CRAIG PASS
Yellowstone Lake
SYLVAN PASS
SLEEPING GIANT
GRANT VILLAGE
West Thumb
Park Pt.
Frank Island
Mt. Doane (10,352 ft.)
Mt. Langford (10,774 ft.)
Mt. Stevenson (10,352 ft.)
Washakie Wilderness
Eagle Creek Trail
Shoshone Lake
Delacy Creek Trail
Grant Village
Thorofare Trail
CONTINENTAL
Eagle Peak (11,358 ft.)
EAGLE PASS
Table Mtn. (11,063 ft.)
Lewis Lake
LEWIS LAKE
Heart Lake
Two Ocean Plateau
Mountain Creek Trail
Shoshone National Forest
Lewis Falls
Mt. Sheridan (10,308 ft.)
Trail Creek Trail
Snake River Trail
Yellowstone
Lewis R.
Heart Lake Trail
Pitchstone Plateau Trail
Snake River
Two Ocean Plateau Trail
DIVIDE
THOROFARE RANGER STATION
SOUTH ENTRANCE
Moose Falls
John D. Rockefeller, Jr. Memorial Parkway
FLAGG RANCH
Bridger-Teton National Forest
South Boundary Trail
Teton Wilderness
River
To Jackson
0
10 mi
0
10 km
89
191
287
212
14
16
20
To Red Lodge, Montana and Cody, Wyoming
To Cody

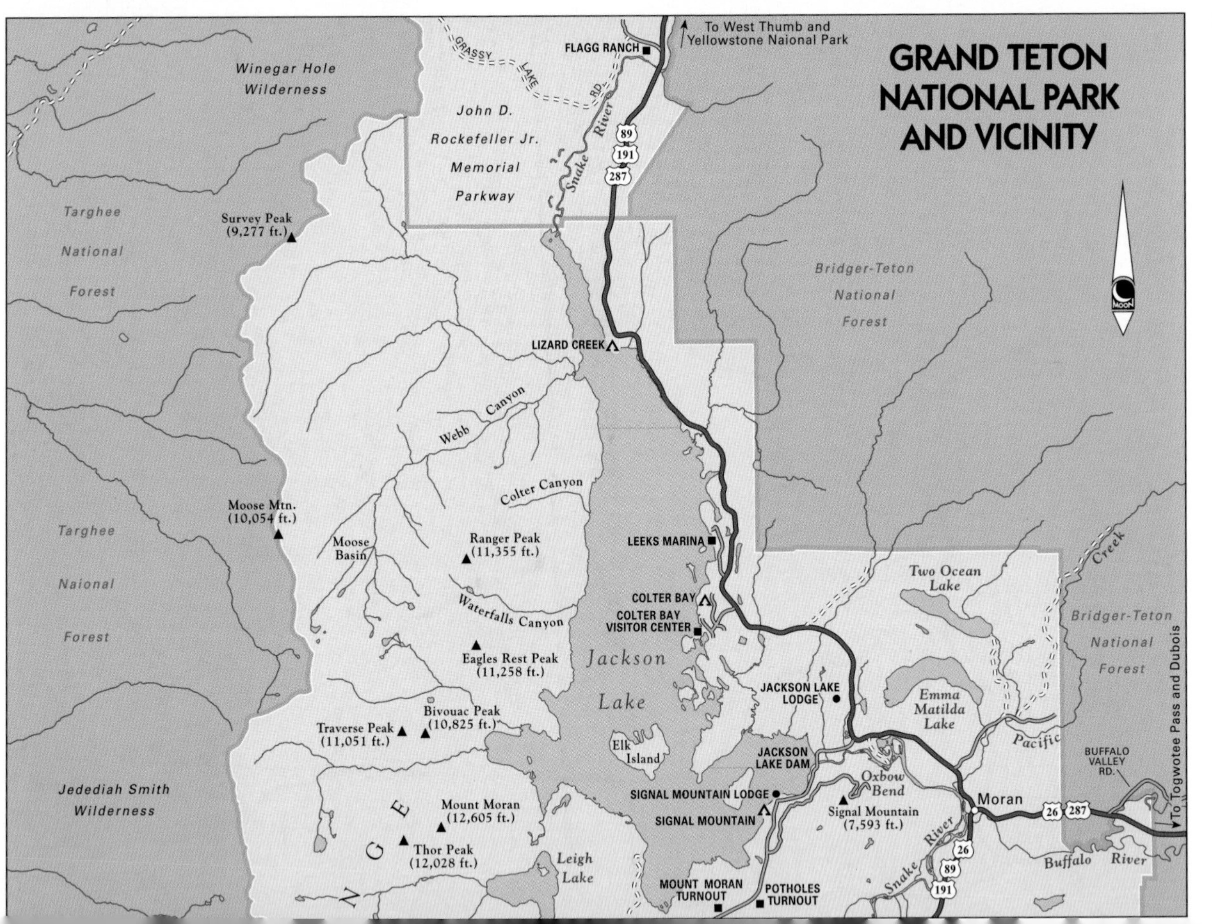
GRAND TETON NATIONAL PARK AND VICINITY
MOON
To West Thumb and Yellowstone Naional Park
FLAGG RANCH
GRASSY LAKE RD.
Snake River
89
191
287
Winegar Hole Wilderness
John D. Rockefeller Jr. Memorial Parkway
Targhee National Forest
Survey Peak (9,277 ft.)
Bridger-Teton National Forest
LIZARD CREEK
Webb Canyon
Colter Canyon
Moose Mtn. (10,054 ft.)
Targhee Naional Forest
Moose Basin
Ranger Peak (11,355 ft.)
LEEKS MARINA
Waterfalls Canyon
COLTER BAY
COLTER BAY VISITOR CENTER
Eagles Rest Peak (11,258 ft.)
Jackson Lake
Two Ocean Lake
Creek
Bridger-Teton National Forest
To Togwotee Pass and Dubois
JACKSON LAKE LODGE
Emma Matilda Lake
Bivouac Peak (10,825 ft.)
Traverse Peak (11,051 ft.)
Elk Island
JACKSON LAKE DAM
Pacific
BUFFALO VALLEY RD.
Jedediah Smith Wilderness
SIGNAL MOUNTAIN LODGE
Oxbow Bend
Signal Mountain (7,593 ft.)
Moran
26
287
SIGNAL MOUNTAIN
Mount Moran (12,605 ft.)
Thor Peak (12,028 ft.)
N
G
E
Leigh Lake
Snake River
26
89
191
Buffalo River
MOUNT MORAN TURNOUT
POTHOLES TURNOUT

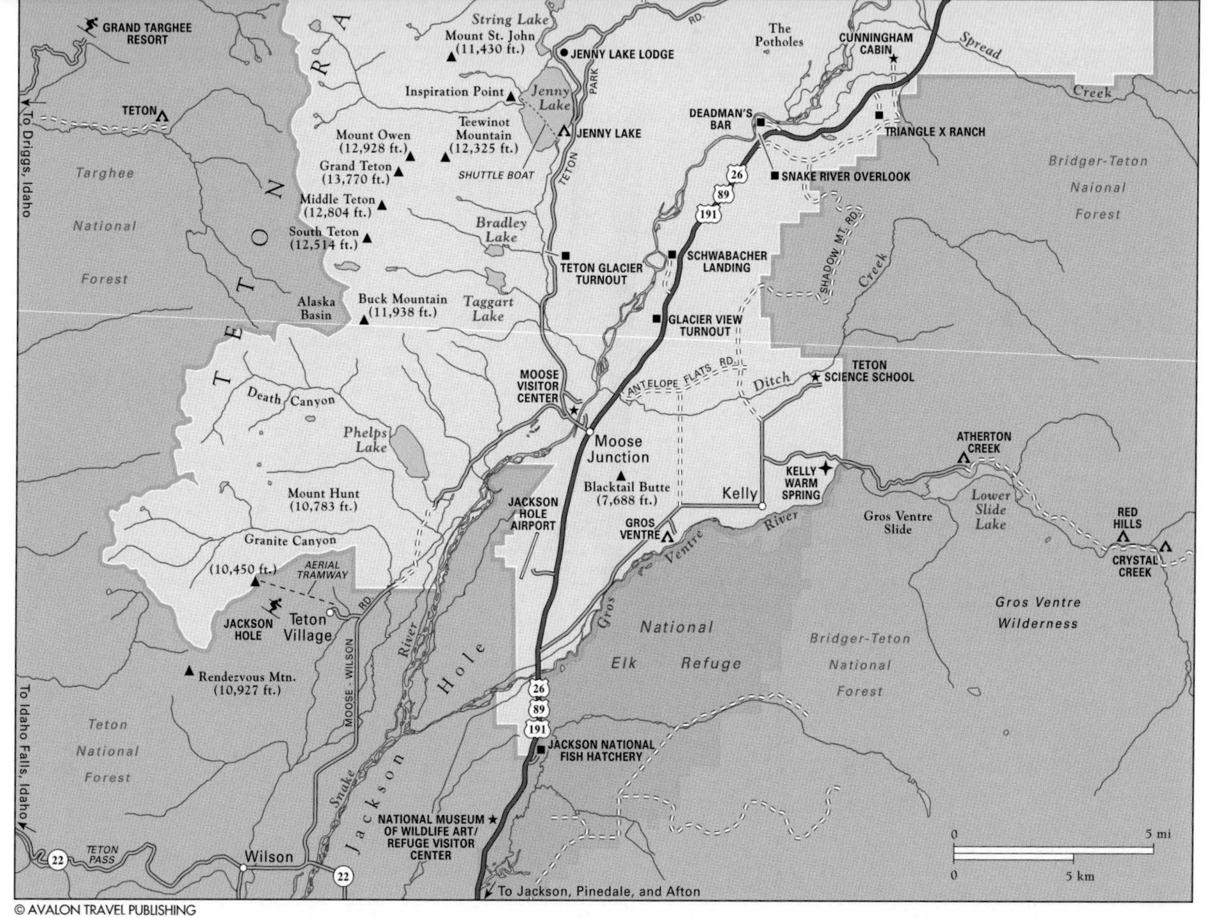

GRAND TARGHEE RESORT
String Lake
Mount St. John (11,430 ft.)
JENNY LAKE LODGE
RD.
The Potholes
CUNNINGHAM CABIN
Spread Creek
Inspiration Point
Jenny Lake
PARK
TETON
JENNY LAKE
TETON
To Driggs, Idaho
Teewinot Mountain (12,325 ft.)
Mount Owen (12,928 ft.)
Grand Teton (13,770 ft.)
SHUTTLE BOAT
Middle Teton (12,804 ft.)
South Teton (12,514 ft.)
Bradley Lake
TETON RANGE
DEADMAN'S BAR
TRIANGLE X RANCH
SNAKE RIVER OVERLOOK
26
89
191
Bridger-Teton Naional Forest
Targhee National Forest
TETON GLACIER TURNOUT
SCHWABACHER LANDING
SHADOW MT. RD.
Creek
Alaska Basin
Buck Mountain (11,938 ft.)
Taggart Lake
GLACIER VIEW TURNOUT
MOOSE VISITOR CENTER
ANTELOPE FLATS RD.
Ditch
TETON SCIENCE SCHOOL
Death Canyon
Phelps Lake
Moose Junction
Blacktail Butte (7,688 ft.)
ATHERTON CREEK
KELLY WARM SPRING
Kelly
Mount Hunt (10,783 ft.)
JACKSON HOLE AIRPORT
GROS VENTRE
Gros Ventre River
Lower Slide Lake
Gros Ventre Slide
RED HILLS
CRYSTAL CREEK
Granite Canyon
(10,450 ft.)
AERIAL TRAMWAY
JACKSON HOLE
Teton Village
MOOSE - WILSON RD
Snake River
Jackson Hole
National Elk Refuge
Gros Ventre Wilderness
Bridger-Teton National Forest
Rendezvous Mtn. (10,927 ft.)
Teton National Forest
To Idaho Falls, Idaho
JACKSON NATIONAL FISH HATCHERY
NATIONAL MUSEUM OF WILDLIFE ART/ REFUGE VISITOR CENTER
TETON PASS
22
Wilson
22
To Jackson, Pinedale, and Afton
0 5 mi
0 5 km
© AVALON TRAVEL PUBLISHING

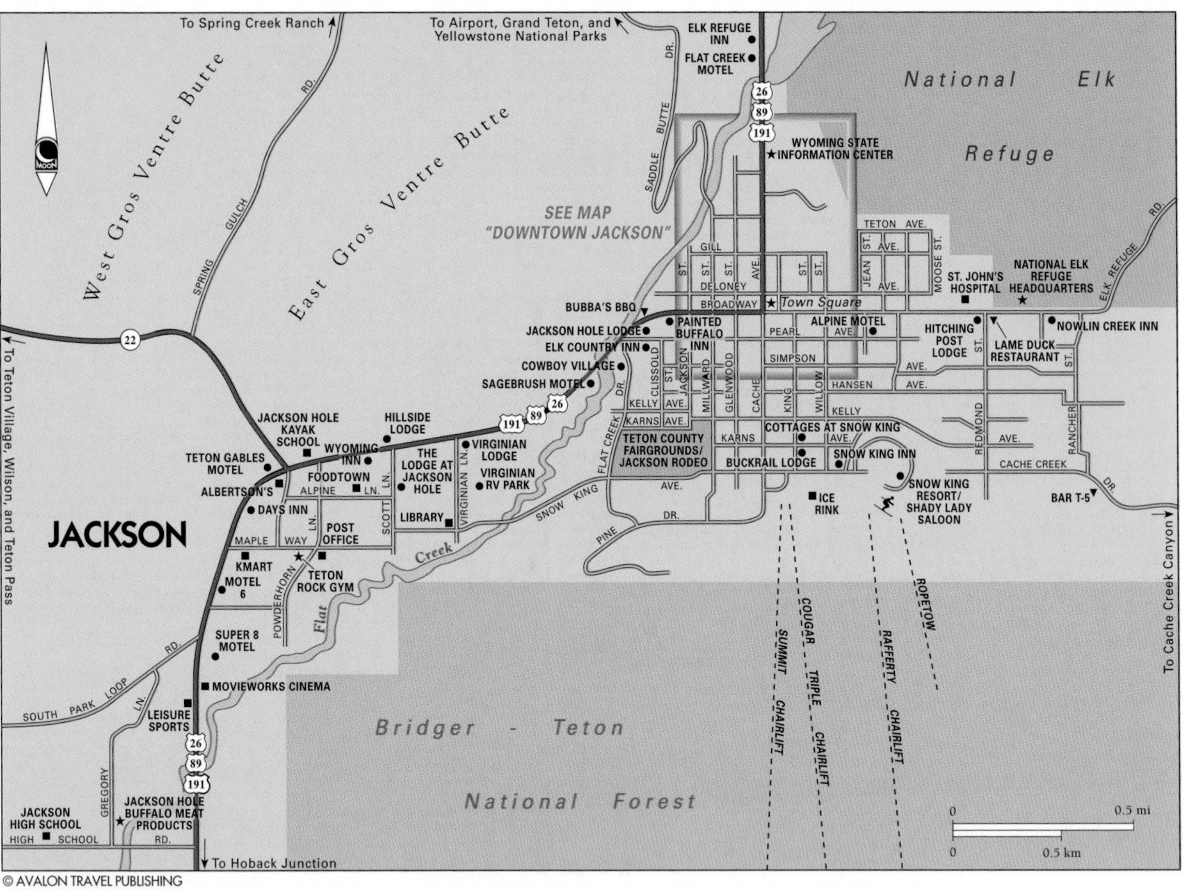

JACKSON
National Elk Refuge
Bridger - Teton National Forest
West Gros Ventre Butte
East Gros Ventre Butte
To Spring Creek Ranch
To Airport, Grand Teton, and Yellowstone National Parks
To Teton Village, Wilson, and Teton Pass
To Hoback Junction
To Cache Creek Canyon
SEE MAP "DOWNTOWN JACKSON"
ELK REFUGE INN
FLAT CREEK MOTEL
WYOMING STATE INFORMATION CENTER
ST. JOHN'S HOSPITAL
NATIONAL ELK REFUGE HEADQUARTERS
Town Square
BUBBA'S BBQ
PAINTED BUFFALO INN
ALPINE MOTEL
HITCHING POST LODGE
LAME DUCK RESTAURANT
NOWLIN CREEK INN
JACKSON HOLE LODGE
ELK COUNTRY INN
COWBOY VILLAGE
SAGEBRUSH MOTEL
TETON COUNTY FAIRGROUNDS/ JACKSON RODEO
COTTAGES AT SNOW KING
BUCKRAIL LODGE
SNOW KING INN
SNOW KING RESORT/ SHADY LADY SALOON
ICE RINK
BAR T-5
SUMMIT CHAIRLIFT
COUGAR TRIPLE CHAIRLIFT
RAFFERTY CHAIRLIFT
ROPETOW
JACKSON HOLE KAYAK SCHOOL
HILLSIDE LODGE
WYOMING INN
THE LODGE AT JACKSON HOLE
VIRGINIAN LODGE
VIRGINIAN RV PARK
TETON GABLES MOTEL
FOODTOWN
ALBERTSON'S
DAYS INN
LIBRARY
POST OFFICE
KMART
TETON ROCK GYM
MOTEL 6
SUPER 8 MOTEL
MOVIEWORKS CINEMA
LEISURE SPORTS
JACKSON HIGH SCHOOL
JACKSON HOLE BUFFALO MEAT PRODUCTS
Flat Creek
26
89
191
22
0 0.5 mi
0 0.5 km

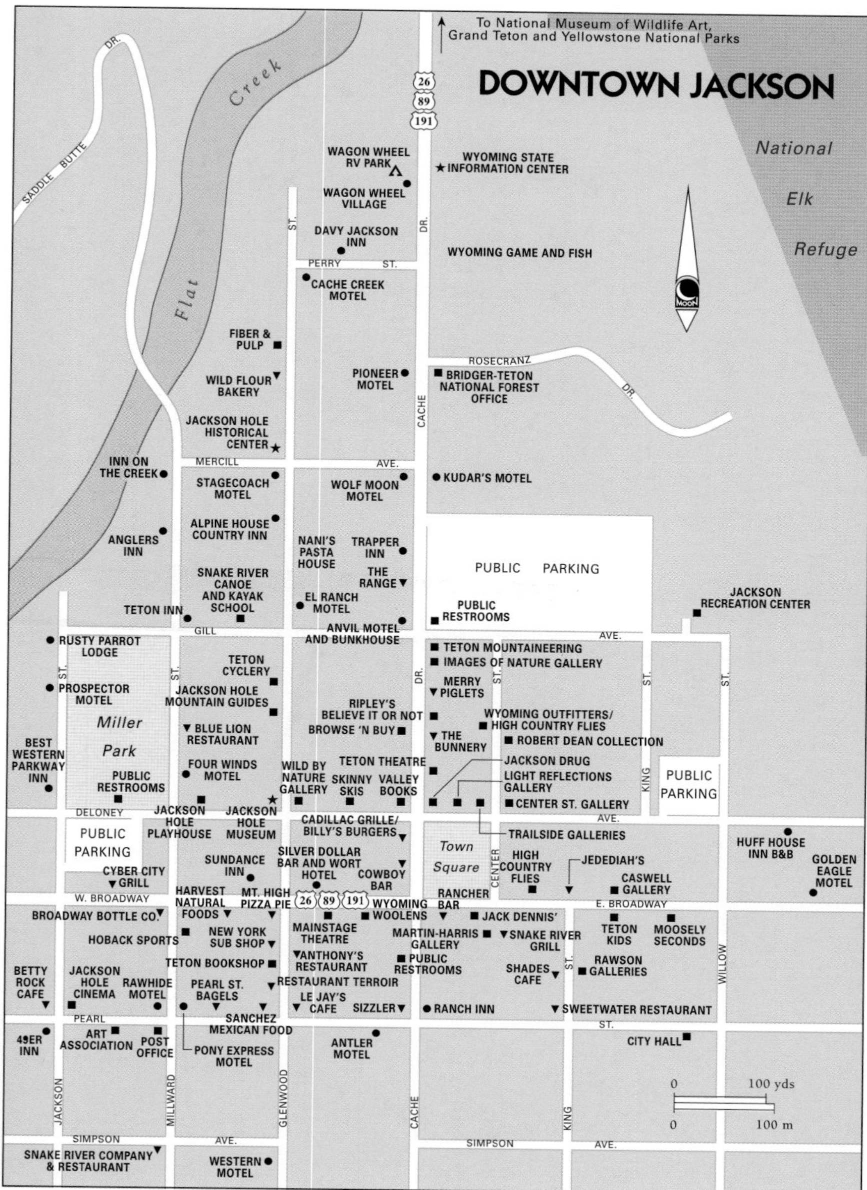
To National Museum of Wildlife Art, Grand Teton and Yellowstone National Parks
DOWNTOWN JACKSON
National Elk Refuge
Flat Creek
SADDLE BUTTE DR.
26 89 191
WAGON WHEEL RV PARK
WYOMING STATE INFORMATION CENTER
WAGON WHEEL VILLAGE
DAVY JACKSON INN
WYOMING GAME AND FISH
PERRY ST.
CACHE CREEK MOTEL
FIBER & PULP
WILD FLOUR BAKERY
PIONEER MOTEL
ROSECRANZ DR.
BRIDGER-TETON NATIONAL FOREST OFFICE
JACKSON HOLE HISTORICAL CENTER
CACHE DR.
INN ON THE CREEK
MERCILL AVE.
STAGECOACH MOTEL
WOLF MOON MOTEL
KUDAR'S MOTEL
ANGLERS INN
ALPINE HOUSE COUNTRY INN
NANI'S PASTA HOUSE
TRAPPER INN
PUBLIC PARKING
SNAKE RIVER CANOE AND KAYAK SCHOOL
THE RANGE
EL RANCH MOTEL
PUBLIC RESTROOMS
JACKSON RECREATION CENTER
TETON INN
ANVIL MOTEL AND BUNKHOUSE
GILL AVE.
RUSTY PARROT LODGE
TETON MOUNTAINEERING
IMAGES OF NATURE GALLERY
TETON CYCLERY
PROSPECTOR MOTEL
JACKSON HOLE MOUNTAIN GUIDES
MERRY PIGLETS
RIPLEY'S BELIEVE IT OR NOT
WYOMING OUTFITTERS/ HIGH COUNTRY FLIES
Miller Park
BLUE LION RESTAURANT
BROWSE 'N BUY
THE BUNNERY
ROBERT DEAN COLLECTION
BEST WESTERN PARKWAY INN
FOUR WINDS MOTEL
TETON THEATRE
JACKSON DRUG
LIGHT REFLECTIONS GALLERY
WILD BY NATURE GALLERY
SKINNY SKIS
VALLEY BOOKS
PUBLIC PARKING
CENTER ST. GALLERY
DELONEY AVE.
JACKSON HOLE PLAYHOUSE
JACKSON HOLE MUSEUM
CADILLAC GRILLE/ BILLY'S BURGERS
TRAILSIDE GALLERIES
Town Square
HUFF HOUSE INN B&B
GOLDEN EAGLE MOTEL
SUNDANCE INN
SILVER DOLLAR BAR AND WORT HOTEL
HIGH COUNTRY FLIES
JEDEDIAH'S
CASWELL GALLERY
CYBER CITY GRILL
COWBOY BAR
HARVEST NATURAL FOODS
MT. HIGH PIZZA PIE
RANCHER BAR
W. BROADWAY
WYOMING WOOLENS
E. BROADWAY
BROADWAY BOTTLE CO.
JACK DENNIS'
TETON KIDS
MOOSELY SECONDS
HOBACK SPORTS
NEW YORK SUB SHOP
MAINSTAGE THEATRE
MARTIN-HARRIS GALLERY
SNAKE RIVER GRILL
TETON BOOKSHOP
ANTHONY'S RESTAURANT
PUBLIC RESTROOMS
RAWSON GALLERIES
BETTY ROCK CAFE
JACKSON HOLE CINEMA
RAWHIDE MOTEL
PEARL ST. BAGELS
RESTAURANT TERROIR
SHADES CAFE
LE JAY'S CAFE
SIZZLER
RANCH INN
SWEETWATER RESTAURANT
PEARL ST.
SANCHEZ MEXICAN FOOD
49ER INN
ART ASSOCIATION
POST OFFICE
ANTLER MOTEL
CITY HALL
PONY EXPRESS MOTEL
JACKSON
MILLWARD
GLENWOOD
CACHE
KING
CENTER
WILLOW
0 100 yds
0 100 m
SIMPSON AVE.
SNAKE RIVER COMPANY & RESTAURANT
WESTERN MOTEL
© AVALON TRAVEL PUBLISHING

MOON HANDBOOKS

YELLOWSTONE ~GRAND TETON HANDBOOK

FIRST EDITION

DON PITCHER

AVALON TRAVEL publishing

**YELLOWSTONE~
GRAND TETON HANDBOOK
FIRST EDITION**

Published by
Avalon Travel Publishing, Inc.
5855 Beaudry St.
Emeryville, CA 94608, USA

Please send all comments, corrections, additions, amendments, and critiques to:
**MOON HANDBOOKS:
YELLOWSTONE-GRAND TETON HANDBOOK
AVALON TRAVEL PUBLISHING, INC.
5855 BEAUDRY ST.
EMERYVILLE, CA 94608, USA
e-mail: atpfeedback@avalonpub.com
www.travelmatters.com**

Printing History
1st edition—April 2000
5 4 3 2

ISBN: 1-56691-199-0
ISSN: 1534-5106

Editors: Valerie Sellers Blanton, Karen Gaynor Bleske, Don Root
Production & Design: Carey Wilson
Cartography: Brian Bardwell, Bob Race, Chris Folks, Mike Morgenfeld
Index: Sondra Nation

Front cover photo: The Tetons, © Don Pitcher, 2000

All photos by Don Pitcher unless otherwise noted.
All illustrations by Bob Race unless otherwise noted.

Distributed in the United States and Canada by Publishers Group West

Printed in U.S.A. by R.R. Donnelley

For Aziza Bali
Who discovered rainbows, bison, and chocolate cake in Jackson Hole
May you always chase rainbows and snowflakes
May you never lose your sense of wonder

CONTENTS

SPECIAL TOPICS

YELLOWSTONE GATEWAY TOWNS

SPECIAL TOPICS

THE BASICS

ACKNOWLEDGMENTS

This is the first edition of *Yellowstone-Grand Teton Handbook,* but the book is based upon my *Wyoming Handbook,* now in its fourth edition. Many people helped me in researching this book, but very special thanks are due the following individuals: Vicki Arundale (Jackson Hole Mountain Resort), Susie Barnett-Bushong (Grand Targhee Ski Resort), Megan Bogle (Targhee National Forest), Debbie Collins (Yellowstone Association), Ron Davler and Dawn Kent (Anne Kent Cabins), Harvey Harger (Shoshone National Forest), Myrna Hay (West Yellowstone Chamber of Commerce), Carrie-Lyn Hoffman (Gardiner Chamber of Commerce), Loretta Long (Cooke City-Silver Gate Chamber of Commerce), Jan Lynch (Grand Teton Natural History Association), John Mack (Yellowstone National Park), Sue Murphy (Yellowstone National Park), Dorothy Neckels (Bridger-Teton National Forest), Mitzi Voss (Dubois Chamber of Commerce), and Lee Whittlesey (Yellowstone National Park).

Four people deserve a Congressional Medal of Honor for their over-the-top assistance during my work on this book. Jesse O'Connor is the man travelers often encounter when they arrive at the visitor center in Jackson, and he is *the* font of all knowledge for the Jackson Hole-Grand Teton-Yellowstone area. But don't challenge him to race up Snow King; you'll lose. Claudia Wade of the Cody Country Chamber of Commerce was extraordinarily helpful, and her rich understanding of the Cody area proved invaluable. Also deserving a special commendation is Rick Hoeninghausen of Amfac Parks & Resorts, who provided last-minute assistance and helpful information within Yellowstone National Park. Freelance editor Beth Kaeding did a thorough reading of the Yellowstone chapter of this book, and her care prevented major errors from creeping into the final version of this book.

This book was put together by the staff at Avalon Travel Publishing, who saw it through the long process from computer screens to your hands. Thanks especially to my editor Karen Bleske, copy editors Valerie Sellers Blanton and Don Root, designer Carey Wilson, illustrations guru Bob Race, and mapmakers Brian Bardwell, Bob Race, Chris Folks, and Mike Morgenfeld for their hard work.

A very special thank you is reserved for my wife, Karen Shemet, and daughter, Aziza Bali, who helped me keep perspective while researching and writing this book.

MAPS

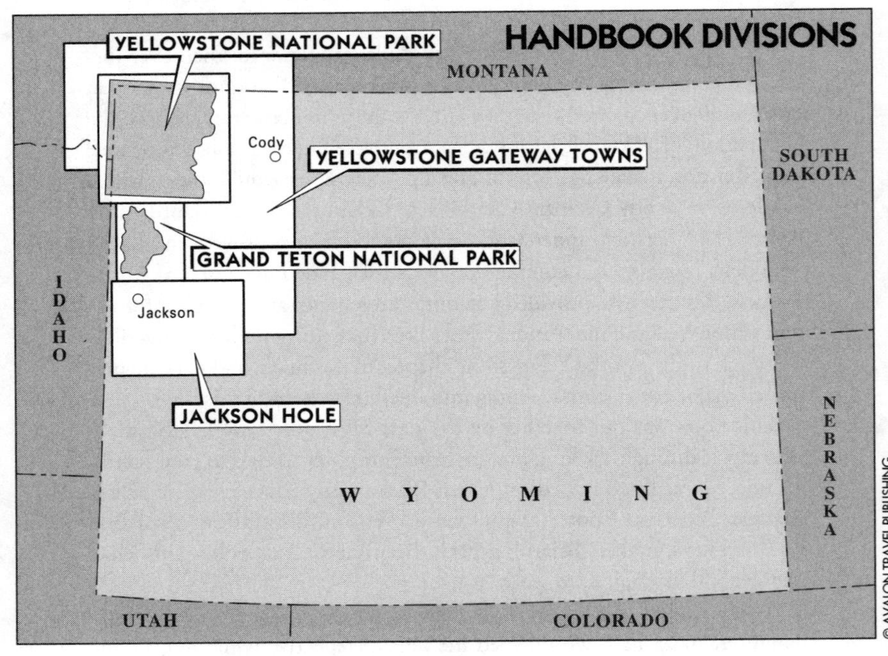

HANDBOOK DIVISIONS
YELLOWSTONE NATIONAL PARK
MONTANA
Cody
YELLOWSTONE GATEWAY TOWNS
SOUTH DAKOTA
GRAND TETON NATIONAL PARK
IDAHO
Jackson
JACKSON HOLE
NEBRASKA
WYOMING
UTAH
COLORADO
© AVALON TRAVEL PUBLISHING

HELP MAKE THIS A BETTER BOOK

This first edition of *Yellowstone-Grand Teton Handbook* offers a detailed look at one of the most fascinating parts of the United States. I have attempted to check all the information for accuracy, but errors are inevitable and places change constantly. So send those cards, letters, and e-mails, especially if you know something offbeat that I missed. I always appreciate any hot tips, criticisms, or compliments you may wish to contribute. Although I try to reply to all letters and messages, you may need to wait for a response since I'm often on the road.

To reach me via e-mail, put "Yellowstone-Grand Teton Handbook" in the subject heading and send messages to me at: info@travelmatters.com. Send snail-mail observations and comments to:

Don Pitcher
Moon Handbooks: Yellowstone-Grand Teton
c/o Avalon Travel Publishing
5855 Beaudry St.
Emeryville, CA 94608
USA

You may also want to visit www.donpitcher.com to send e-mails directly or to learn about my various books, photographic ventures, and other projects. The site contains links to a number of useful travel websites for Wyoming and other destinations.

ABBREVIATIONS

B&B—bed and breakfast
BLM—Bureau of Land Management
CCC—Civilian Conservation Corps
CG—campground (used on maps only)
d—double occupancy
F—Fahrenheit
4WD—four-wheel drive
I—interstate highway
km—kilometer
mph—miles per hour
RV—recreational vehicle
s—single occupancy

ACCOMMODATIONS RATINGS

In addition to including specific prices, all accommodations in this book are further rated by price category for comparison with other Moon Travel Handbooks. Categories are based on double-occupancy, high-season rates; the categories are:

Budget: under $35
Inexpensive: $35-60
Moderate: $60-85
Expensive: $85-110
Premium: $110-150
Luxury: $150 and up

INTRODUCTION

If ever a place deserved the term "Wonderland," it would have to be the northwest corner of Wyoming. In this spectacularly scenic region lies the nation's oldest and best-loved national park, Yellowstone, along with one of the most stunning mountainscapes on the planet, Grand Teton National Park. The valley beneath these peaks is Jackson Hole, recreation central for wintertime skiing and summertime whitewater rafting, horseback rides, day-hikes, mountain biking, gourmet dining, and even shopping; it's one of the most sought-after vacation destinations in North America. Beyond these three justifiably famous areas are a wealth of attractions to please anyone who loves the great outdoors and the West, including a world-class museum complex in Cody, gorgeous badlands topography near the Old-West town of Dubois, and several delightful mountain settlements in the areas surrounding Yellowstone National Park. This book provides an introduction to the Greater Yellowstone area, a region that attracts more than three million visitors each year from around the globe.

THE GREATER YELLOWSTONE ECOSYSTEM

The term Greater Yellowstone Ecosystem is broadly applied to the high plateau and mountain ranges inside and surrounding Yellowstone National Park. Covering approximately 18 million acres, this high-elevation country includes two national parks—Yellowstone and Grand Teton—along with portions of seven surrounding national forests—Beaverhead-Deerlodge, Bridger-Teton, Caribou, Custer, Gallatin, Shoshone, and Targhee—plus other public lands managed by the Bureau of Land Management and national wildlife refuges managed by the U.S. Fish & Wildlife Service. This vast landscape centers on the northwest corner of Wyoming, but also includes parts of Montana and Idaho. Much of the country within the Greater Yellowstone Ecosystem is forested, primarily with lodgepole pine, aspen, Douglas-fir, Engelmann spruce, subalpine fir, and whitebark pine. Intermountain valleys such as Jackson Hole are covered with grasses and sage, and once you get above treeline (approximately 10,000 feet) low-lying alpine tundra carpets the ground. All together, this is one of the largest relatively intact temperate-zone ecosystems on the planet.

GEOGRAPHY

The Greater Yellowstone Ecosystem is a very mountainous region, with a number of peaks topping 13,000 feet. The nation's Continental Divide cuts diagonally across the region from the southeast to the northwest. Wyoming's highest summit, 13,804-foot Gannett Peak is on the southern margin of the ecosystem in the Wind River Mountains, and the second-highest peak, Grand Teton (13,770 feet) forms the crown of the Tetons. Montana's tallest summit is 12,799-foot Granite Peak in the Absaroka-Beartooth Wilderness just northeast of Yellowstone. The little burgs of Cooke City and Silver Gate are not far away.

The heart of Yellowstone National Park is a high and rolling plateau that averages around 8,000 feet in elevation, but the eastern and northern portions of the park are considerably more rugged. The park's highest mountain is 11,358-foot Eagle Peak, on the southeastern border, and the lowest point (5,282 feet) is on the northwest corner near Gardiner, Montana. The eastern and northern borders of Yellowstone National Park front on the Absaroka Range, which contains many peaks topping 12,000 feet. To the west and northwest of the park are the lower-elevation Gallatin, Madison, and Centennial ranges and the town of West Yellowstone, while the Caribou Range lies to the southwest. The Yellowstone gateway town of Cody sits at the eastern margin of the Absarokas within Bighorn

Lamar Valley in northeastern Yellowstone National Park.

Basin, and another gateway town, Dubois, occupies the upper end of protected Wind River Valley.

Grand Teton National Park and Jackson Hole lie just south of Yellowstone. The Teton Range creates an incredible western skyline, and the less grandiose but still impressive Gros Ventre Range is to the east. Jackson Hole is a relatively flat intermountain basin through which the Snake River flows, with the town of Jackson on its southern margin. South of Jackson Hole are the Wyoming and Salt River ranges, while to the west of the Tetons lies Teton Valley, Idaho. The massive Wind River Mountains have many peaks over 13,000 feet and reach southeastward from Union Pass to South Pass, a distance of 100 miles. Areas south of Jackson Hole—including the Wind River Mountains—are beyond the scope of this book; for details see my *Wyoming Handbook* (Emeryville, CA: Avalon Travel Publishing, www.moon.com).

CLIMATE

The complex and mountainous nature of the Greater Yellowstone Ecosystem creates widely varying microclimatic conditions. It may be a beautiful sunny summer day in the town of Jackson, while backpackers 2,000 feet higher in the Tetons are getting drenched in a long and lightning-filled storm just a few miles away. The overall weather description below applies to Jackson Hole and the Yellowstone plateau (including the Old Faithful area). Temperatures may be a bit cooler along Yellowstone and Jackson Lakes and are often warmer in the lower-elevation towns of Gardiner, Cody, and Dubois. Killing frosts are possible in any month of the year; I've awakened to new snow on the ground in late June! Total precipitation also varies across the region, from a low of just 11 inches annually at Gardiner to an estimated 70 inches or more (mostly as snow) in the Lewis Lake area of Yellowstone National Park. Most of the precipitation falls in the winter as snow; summers are relatively dry. (An exception is the low elevation areas on the north side of Yellowstone, where spring and early summer rains are more common.)

Get detailed climate information from Western Regional Climate Center, on the web at www.wrcc.dri.edu/summary/climsmwy.html. To check daily weather forecasts, head to the National Weather Service's site for western and central Wyoming, riw.weather.wyoming.com. Most visitor centers inside and outside the parks have updated forecasts.

Summer

In general, summers are short but very pleasant throughout the region, with warm, sunny days and cool nights. Lower elevation hiking trails are usually free of snow from mid-June to mid-October, but some high areas may not melt until late July. You may need both shorts and a light jacket in the same day. Mid-summer daytime temperatures in Jackson Hole are typically in the upper 70s or low 80s F, with nighttime lows around 40° F. It's several degrees warmer in low-elevation places like Gardiner, and 5-10 degrees cooler in many road-accessible parts of Yellowstone. The warmest temperature recorded was 101° F for Jackson in 1934, and 103° F for Gardiner in 1960. Cody gets even hotter, and 90+° F summer days hit several times a month.

The air is generally dry, and most summer rain falls during afternoon thundershowers when the rain can come down in torrents for brief periods, particularly in the mountains. Average rainfall for July and August in Jackson Hole is just one inch each month. All this sunshine and showers make for an abundance of rainbows. Many days a late afternoon storm over the Tetons tapers off to a glorious display of colors arching into the sky.

Fall

Autumn provides a beautiful transition from the warm summer days to the surprisingly cold winters. Nights are crisp and chilly, sending many folks scurrying for warmer climes. In Jackson Hole during September you can expect daytime highs around 55-65° F and nighttime lows around 25-30° F. Temperatures are 5-10 degrees cooler in the central portions of Yellowstone, where nighttime lows may drop into the single digits by late fall.

The peak of fall colors takes place around the first week of October in Jackson Hole and Grand Teton National Park, where aspens and cottonwoods turn a bright yellow (with a few orange trees). Although most of Yellowstone is covered with evergreen trees, you will find colorful deciduous stands in some areas, primarily on the north side of the park. You can expect to find snow on the ground anytime after late October, and earlier at high elevations.

Winter

Winter brings snow and cold weather throughout the Greater Yellowstone Ecosystem, though again, local microclimatic conditions vary widely. You'll face the coldest conditions in January, when a typical Jackson Hole day is in the 20s, with nights dropping to around 0-5° F. When the

TROPICAL WYOMING

Sometimes I wish that Wyoming had more vegetation and less catarrh, more bloom and summer and fragrance and less Christmas and New Year's through the summer. I like the clear, bracing air of 7,500 feet above the civilized world, but I get weary of putting on and taking off my buffalo overcoat for meals all through dog days. I yearn for a land where a man can take off his ulster and overshoes while he delivers a Fourth of July oration, without flying into the face of Providence and dying of pneumonia. . . . As I write these lines I look out across the wide sweep of brownish gray plains dotted here and there with ranches and defunct buffalo craniums, and I see shutting down over the sides of the abrupt mountains, and meeting the foothills, a white mist which melts into the gray sky. It is a snow storm in the mountains.

I saw this with wonder and admiration for the first two or three million times. When it became a matter of daily occurrence as a wonder or curiosity, it was below mediocrity. Last July a snow storm gathered one afternoon and fell among the foothills and whitened the whole line to within four or five miles of town, and it certainly was a peculiar freak of nature, but it convinced me that whatever enterprises I might launch into here I would not try to raise oranges and figs until the isothermal lines should meet with a change of heart.

—19TH-CENTURY HUMORIST
BILL NYE

sky is clear, conditions can sometimes turn severely cold, with temperatures below zero for days at a time; the record low was recorded near West Yellowstone in 1933: -66° F. Fortunately, the relative humidity is quite low, making these temperatures easier to tolerate and creating fluffy powder snow conditions. The town of Jackson receives less summertime rain and wintertime snow than the nearby mountains. In a typical January you'll find a foot of snow on the ground, but nearby Jackson Hole Mountain Resort gets 38 feet of snow annually. Even more impressive is Grand Targhee Ski Resort on the west side of the Tetons, which gets an average of 42 feet of snow per year!

At Old Faithful in Yellowstone the snow is typically around 30-40 inches deep in mid-winter, but in Mammoth Hot Springs (park headquarters) you're likely to see just six to nine inches on the ground and much milder temperatures. At the other extreme, the Lewis Lake area may receive 50 feet of snow in a typical winter! Temperatures at Old Faithful average in the 20s in the day but often drop well below zero at night. At Mammoth Hot Springs, day temperatures approach 30° F, with nights dropping to around 10° F.

One surprising winter feature is the presence of temperature inversions in intermountain valleys such as Jackson Hole. These often occur on cold, clear nights when the cold air sinks into the valley floors. Skiers who leave the lodge bundled in down parkas and polypro longjohns are often surprised to find temperatures 20 degrees warmer at the top of the mountain.

Spring

Spring in the Greater Yellowstone Ecosystem is a transitional period as the snow gradually melts and the plants reappear after a long winter. For many locals this is the time to escape mud season for a week or two in southern Utah. Snow often remains on the ground until late April in Jackson Hole, and it doesn't melt from the higher mountains until late July. In addition, a few snowfields and glaciers remain year-round in the highest and most protected areas. Spring is the time when you'll meet the fewest travelers since the roads may not be plowed yet, snow blocks hiking trails, skiing gets worse by the day, and many summertime recreation operations haven't yet opened. Expect daytime temperatures in the 40s and 50s in early May, but warming up rapidly as the long days of June appear.

WILDLIFE

Watchable Wildlife

The Greater Yellowstone Ecosystem is famous as a place to view wildlife, particularly elk, bison, wolves, moose, and grizzlies. Because of its abundant animal populations, you'll sometimes hear the term "America's Serengeti" applied to Yellowstone, home of the largest concentration of free-ranging large mammals in the Lower 48. During the summer, the best times to see wildlife are from sunrise to early morning, or from late afternoon to early evening. At other times of the year they tend to be equally visible in the middle of the day. Bring a pair of binoculars for a close-up view, but make sure your behavior isn't disturbing the animal or causing it to move away. This is particularly true in mid-winter when any unnecessary movements lessen their chance of survival. Always stay at least 25 yards from wildlife and 100 yards from bears. See the Yellowstone chapter for additional wildlife information beyond that provided below, including details on bears, bighorn sheep, coyotes, deer, moose, and wolves.

Pronghorn Antelope

Antelope (biologists prefer the name pronghorn since they are not true antelopes) are sleek ungulates with beautiful reddish-brown and white coats accented by white throat patches and rumps. Antelope survive on grasses, forbs, and sagebrush—perhaps Wyoming's most abundant plant. They are almost never seen in wooded areas. Antelope are built for speed: oversized lungs and windpipes give them the ability to run for miles at 30 mph and they can accelerate to 45 mph for short bursts. Despite this speed, antelope have an innate inquisitiveness that makes them relatively easy to hunt, an attribute that nearly drove them to extinction by market hunting early in this century. One surprising trait in antelope is their inability to jump fences; instead they crawl under them. Fences that are too low will completely halt their migrations.

Both males and females grow horns, and those on the males typically have a prong (hence the name). Dominant males (bucks) gather

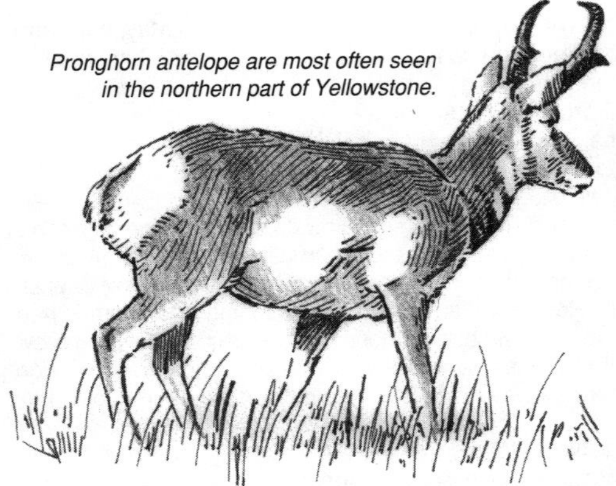

Pronghorn antelope are most often seen in the northern part of Yellowstone.

harems of females (does) and fawns, and fight off other bucks in the autumn rutting season. In May or June does give birth to one or two fawns.

Antelope are abundant in many parts of Wyoming, and more than 400,000 of them live in the state. They are not nearly as common in the northwest corner of Wyoming, where conditions are more marginal. You'll see small herds in open country within Grand Teton National Park, and on the north side of Yellowstone National Park, particularly near Mammoth and Gardiner.

Elk

A majestic member of the deer family, elk (many biologists prefer the term "wapiti") are a favorite with both tourists and hunters. In the summer months perhaps 100,000 elk can be found within the Greater Yellowstone Ecosystem. With bulls averaging 700 pounds and cows averaging 500 pounds, these are some of the largest antlered animals in the Americas.

Elk spend summers high in the mountains, feeding in alpine meadows and along forest edges. The young males and cows with their calves—generally born in late May and early June—group in large herds for protection. Meanwhile, the bachelor bulls hang out on their own, watching baseball games on TV while drinking Heineken (just kidding; they drink Teton Ale). When the fall rutting season arrives, bulls herd the cows and calves around, mating with cows when they come into estrus and defending their harems from other bulls. During this time of year the bugling of bull elk is a common sound in the mountains, a challenge to any bull within earshot. When a competitor appears, a dominance display often follows—complete with bugling, stomping, and thrashing of the ground—to show who is the baddest bull around. In a fight, bulls lock their massive antlers and try to push and twist until one finally gives in and retreats. These battles help ensure that the healthiest bulls produce the most offspring. Ironically, other bulls often wait in the wings for battles over harems to occur, then rush in to mate with the cows while the larger bulls are sparring. (When the cat's away. . . .) The snows of late fall push elk to lower-elevation winter ranges, notably at the National Elk Refuge in Jackson Hole. When spring comes, the bulls drop their antlers and immediately begin to grow new ones. The elk head back into the high country, following the melting snowline.

Elk and bison both can be infected with brucellosis, a bacterium causing spontaneous abortions. Brucellosis is potentially transmitted to other animals by contact with the dead fetus or birthing material and can cause undulant fever in humans. Though the evidence is circumstantial at best for this, ranchers worry that brucellosis can spread from elk and bison to cattle, particularly around elk feeding grounds in western Wyoming. To lessen the incidence of brucellosis, Wyoming state employees now routinely vaccinate elk at the feeding grounds, shooting them in the hindquarters with vaccine-loaded pellets.

Moose

The largest member of the deer family, moose are typically seen eating willow bushes in riparian areas. They are the loners of the deer world, and only during the fall mating season are you likely to see males (bulls) and females (cows) together or to see bulls jousting. Bulls can reach 1,300 pounds, while cows grow to 800 pounds and typically give birth to one or two calves. In addition to enormous racks, the bulls have a distinctive dewlap or "bell" that hangs below their throat, but apparently serves no physical purpose. Both Yellowstone and Grand Teton support moose; look for them along streams and other wet places in the summer.

BISON

The bison is the definitive frontier animal and Wyoming's state mammal—its outline graces the state flag. Weighing up to 2,000 pounds, these are the largest land mammals in the New World. Bison commonly live 12-15 years. The calves weigh 30 to 40 pounds at birth and within minutes are standing and able to nurse. Two races of bison exist: the plains bison, primarily east of the Rockies, and the mountain bison (sometimes called wood bison) in the higher elevations. Technically, these huge, hairy beasts are bison—the only true buffalo are the water buffalo of Southeast Asia—but the name buffalo is commonly used.

With their massive heads, huge shoulder humps, heavy coats of fur, and small posteriors, buffalo are some of the strangest animals in North America. They look so front-heavy as to seem unstable, ready to topple forward onto their snouts at any time. Despite this impression, buffalo are remarkably well adapted to life on the plains. A bison will use its strong sense of smell to find grass buried in a deep snowdrift and then sweep the snow away with a sideways motion of its head. The animals are also surprisingly fleet-footed, as careless Yellowstone photographers have discovered. In addition, the buffalo is one very tough critter. In 1907, a buffalo was pitted against four of the meanest Mexican bulls at a Juarez, Mexico, bullring. After knocking heads several times with the buffalo, the bulls fled and were saved only when bullfighters opened the chute gates to let them escape.

"Blackening the Plains"

When Europeans first reached the New World, they found massive herds of bison in the Appalachians and even more as they headed west. Daniel Boone hunted them in North Carolina in the 1750s; Pennsylvanians shot hundreds of buffalo that were invading their winter stores of hay. By 1820, settlers had nearly driven the buffalo to extinction in the east. But there were far more living to the west. As explorers, mountain men, and the first tentative settlers reached the "Great American Desert," they were awestruck by the numbers. Travelers told of slowly moving masses of buffalo blackening the plains and watched in astonishment as the herds stopped at rivers and nearly drank them dry. A fair estimate of the original population of buffalo in North America is 60 million. Even in the middle 1860s, travelers through Wyoming's Wind River Valley reported seeing 10,000 bison at one time. A pioneer Kansas settler named William D. Street recalled a trip in which a herd roared past his camp for an entire night. The next morning, he climbed a nearby butte and saw buffalo covering the plains below. According to Street:

The herd was not less than 20 miles in width—we never saw the other side—at least 60 miles in length, maybe much longer; two counties of buffaloes! There might have been 100,000, or 1,000,000, or 100,000,000. I don't know. In the cowboy days in western Kansas we saw 7,000 head of cattle in one roundup. After gazing at them a few moments our thoughts turned to that buffalo herd. For a comparison, imagine a large pail of water; take from it or add to it a drop, and there you have it. Seven thousand head of cattle was not a drop in the bucket as compared with that herd of buffalo.

Indians and Buffalo

The Plains Indians depended heavily upon the buffalo for food and—like the proverbial hot dog, which "contains everything but the moo"—they used every part of the animal. Hooves were carved into spoons, skins became buffalo robes and covers for boats and tepees, rawhide was used for drumheads, calf skins became storage sacks, hair was turned into earrings, and horns were formed into cups and arrow points. Everything that remained—including the muzzle, penis, eyes, and cartilage—was boiled down to use as glue for arrowheads. The buffalo's dried testicles and scrotum were used for rattles, and the ubiquitous buffalo chips became a cooking fuel on the treeless prairies.

Hunting techniques varied depending upon the terrain. When possible, the Indians drove herds of bison into arroyos with no exits, over cliffs, or into deep sand or snow, making them easier to kill. The arrival of Spanish horses in the 16th century made it far easier to hunt bison. In a surround, mounted hunters attacked from at least two sides, creating chaos in the herd and allowing buffalo to be shot with arrows or guns.

When whites first spread across the plains, they found the bison a plentiful food source, but also viewed the massive herds as a hindrance to agriculture and cattle raising. But these were not the only reasons whites wanted to destroy the buffalo. Killing off the bison would starve the Indians into submission and force them to take a more "civilized" way of life. General Philip Sheridan, commenting in support of white buffalo hunters, said

> *Instead of stopping the [white] hunters they ought to give them a hearty, unanimous vote of thanks, and appropriate a sufficient sum of money to strike and present to each one a medal of bronze, with a dead buffalo on one side and a discouraged Indian on the other. They are destroying the Indian's commissary, and it is a well-known fact that an army losing its base of supplies is placed at a great disadvantage. Send them powder and lead, if you will; for the sake of a lasting peace, let them kill, skin and sell until the buffaloes are exterminated.*

This reckless slaughter did indeed endanger the Indians, but it also had an unwanted side effect: the Indians went on the warpath. The loss of their primary food source helped convince many Indians that their own extinction was

A hunter finishes off a wounded animal.

next. The warriors who massacred Custer and his men at Little Bighorn had watched their people pushed to the brink of starvation by the destruction of the buffalo.

The Slaughter

Two factors propelled the slaughter to new heights in the 1870s: new railroads across the plains, and a sudden international demand for buffalo robes and hides. Buffalo meat proved to be a readily available food source for railway construction workers and hunters such as "Buffalo Bill" Cody, who provided a steady supply, generally taking just the hindquarters and hump and leaving the rest on the plains. Hundreds of thousands were killed. Once the railroads were completed in 1869, a new "sport" appeared—shooting buffalo from the moving railcars and leaving them to rot on the prairie. Wealthy gentry from the East Coast and Europe also discovered the joys of killing. One Irish nobleman had an entourage of 40 servants, with an entire wagon just for firearms; he killed 2,000 buffalo in a three-year carnage.

Conservationists tried to halt the buffalo slaughter through legislation in 1874, but President Ulysses S. Grant's corrupt Secretary of the Interior, Columbus Delano, said, "I would not seriously regret the total disappearance of the buffalo from our western prairies, in its effect upon the Indians. I would regard it rather as a means of hastening their sense of dependence upon the products of the soil and their own labors." The legislation was pocket-vetoed by Grant.

In 1872, thousands of hide hunters spread through Kansas, Nebraska, and Colorado in search of buffalo. Over the next three years, they brought in more than three million buffalo hides, with Indians killing another 400,000 bison for meat and robes. Good hide hunters could bring down 25 to 100 buffalo in a typical day, keeping five skinners busy from sunup to sundown. One hunter, Jim White, killed at least 16,000 buffalo in his career. Only the hides, cured hams, and buffalo tongues (which could be salted and shipped in barrels) were saved. When Gen. Grenville M. Dodge toured Kansas in the fall of 1873, he noted that "the air was foul with a sickening stench, and the vast plain, which only a short twelvemonth before teemed with animal life, was a dead, solitary, putrid desert." Buffalo carcasses dotted the plains in such numbers that in later years bone pickers would collect massive piles of bones for knife handles, combs, and buttons or to be ground up for sugar refining, fertilizer, or glue.

When the buffalo of the central states approached extinction, hunters turned their attention elsewhere, reaching Wyoming, Montana, and the Dakotas in 1880. In 1882, more than 200,000 hides were taken, and another 40,000 the following year. By 1884, only 300 hides were shipped. The slaughter was nearly over; only a few private herds and scattered individual bison remained. The Indians who had once depended so heavily on buffalo for all the necessities of life were reduced to eating muskrats, gophers, and even grass. Some killed their horses, others stole settlers' cattle, and the rest had to beg the government for food. In only a couple of years, an entire culture had been devastated.

But the slaughter ruined the lives not just of the buffalo or the Indians; hide hunters often spiked buffalo carcasses with strychnine, returning later to skin the wolves that had come to feed on the meat. Coyotes, kit foxes, badgers, vultures, eagles, ravens, and anything else that ate the meat were also killed. With both the buffalo and the "vermin" out of the way, the West was safe for domestic sheep and cattle.

Protection

It wasn't until 1894 that Congress passed legislation protecting bison, and this was only inside Yellowstone National Park. The following year, only 800 buffalo remained in all of North America, a little over one-thousandth of one percent of their original numbers. Despite this dismal picture, the population has rebounded dramatically; today an estimated 65,000 bison roam across America. A strong demand for buffalo meat has led some western ranchers to raise bison. Approximately 2,500 bison remain in Yellowstone (one of the few large wild populations in existence), with another 400 in Grand Teton National Park.

MOUNTAIN MEN

The era of the fur trapper is one of the most colorful slices of American history, a time when a rough and hardy breed of men took to the Rockies in search of furs and adventure. Romanticized in such films as *Jeremiah Johnson,* the trappers actually played but a brief role in history and numbered fewer than 1,000 individuals. Their real importance lay in acting as the opening wedge for the West, a vanguard for the settlers and gold miners who would follow their paths—often led by these same mountain men.

The Fur Business

Fashion sent men into the Rockies in the first place, since the waterproof underfur of a beaver could be used to create the beaver hat, all the rage in the early part of the 19th century. (It cost a month's wages for a man in England to buy a fine beaver hat in the 1820s!) Beavers in the eastern U.S. were soon trapped out, forcing trappers to head farther and farther west. Several companies competed for the lucrative fur market, but John Jacob Astor's American Fur Company proved the most successful. In 1811, Astor sent a party of men across the Rockies to the mouth of the Columbia to build a trading post and then set up a chain of posts across the West. The men—known as the Astorians—were probably the first whites to follow the route that would later become the Oregon Trail.

a well-outfitted participant in the Whiskey Mountain Buckskinners Wind River Rendezvous, held every August in Dubois

John Jacob Astor's trappers went head to head against the Rocky Mountain Fur Company, which was owned at various times by some of the most famous mountain men—Jedediah Smith, David Jackson, William and Milton Sublette, Jim Bridger, Thomas Fitzpatrick, and others. Competition for furs became so intense that Astor's men began following Jim Bridger and Tom Fitzpatrick to discover their trapping grounds. After trying unsuccessfully to shake the men tailing them, Bridger and Fitzpatrick deliberately headed into the heart of Blackfeet country, where Indians killed the leader of Astor's party and managed to leave Bridger with an arrowhead in his shoulder that was not removed until three years later.

A large number of Indians (particularly from the Flathead and Nez Percé tribes) were also involved in the fur trade, and a standard Indian trade value was 240 beaver pelts for a riding horse. In the mountains, anything from the world back east had considerable value: guns sold for $100 each, blankets for $40 apiece, tobacco for $3 a pound, and alcohol (often diluted) for up to $64 a gallon. After just two years of such trading, William Ashley retired with an $80,000 profit. Control of the fur market continued to change hands as the Rocky Mountain Fur Company and the American Fur Company competed with each other and with a mysterious company headed by Capt. Benjamin Bonneville, which some believe was a front for the U.S. Army to explore the West.

Most of the men who trapped in the Rockies were hired and outfitted by the fur companies, but others worked under contract and traded furs for overpriced supplies. Many men found themselves in debt to the company at the end of a season. At the top of the heap were the free trappers, men who worked either alone or with others but who sold their furs to whoever offered the highest prices. Some men—primarily those who brought trade goods to the rendezvous—became rich in the process. Others, such as John Colter, Jim Bridger, James Beckwourth, Jedediah Smith, Thomas Fitzpatrick, and Kit Carson, would achieve fame for their rich knowledge of the land and their ability to survive against insurmountable odds. Many trappers married Indian women, learned sign language and various Indian tongues, and lived in tepees.

Trappers worked through the winter months when the beaver pelts were their finest; most summers were spent hunting and fishing, or hanging out with fellow trappers or friendly Indians. In his *Journal of a Trapper 1834-1843,* Osborne Russell described a campfire scene among fellow mountain men:

> *A large fire was soon blazing encircled with sides of Elk ribs and meat cut in slices supported on sticks down which the grease ran in torrents The repast being over the jovial tale goes round the circle the peals of loud laughter break upon the stillness of the night which after being mimicked in the echo from rock to rock it dies away in the solitary. Every tale puts an auditor in mind of something similar to it but under different circumstances which being told the "laughing part" gives rise to increasing merriment and furnishes more subjects for good jokes and witty sayings such as Swift never dreamed of Thus the evening passed with eating drinking and stories enlivened with witty humor until near Midnight all being wrapped in their blankets lying around the fire gradually falling to sleep one by one until the last tale is "encored" by the snoring of the drowsy audience The Speaker takes the hint breaks off the subject and wrapping his blanket more closely about him soon joins the snoring party—The light of the fire being supersed by that of the Moon just rising from behind the Eastern Mountains a sullen gloom is cast over the remaining fragments of the feast and all is silent except the occasional howling of the solitary wolf on the neighboring mountain whose senses are attracted by the flavors of roasted meat but fearing to approach nearer he sits upon a rock and bewails his calamities in piteous moans which are re-echoed among the Mountains.*

A good trapper could take in upward of 150 beaver in a year, worth $4-6 apiece. It was an arduous job, and the constant threat of attacks by the Blackfeet Indians made it even more difficult. The great letting-go came with the summer rendezvous, an event anticipated for months ahead of time.

The Rendezvous

William H. Ashley, founder of the Rocky Mountain Fur Company, was one of the most important figures in the fur trade. In 1822, he ran an ad in a St. Louis paper that read:

> *To Enterprising Young Men. The subscriber wishes to engage ONE HUNDRED MEN, to ascend the river Missouri to its source, there to be employed for one, two or three years.—For particulars enquire of Major Andrew Henry, near the Lead Mines, in the County of Washington, (who will ascend with, and command the party) or to the subscriber at St. Louis.*
>
> —WM. H. ASHLEY.

Ashley's company of men—along with $10,000 in supplies—made it up into the Yellowstone River country, where he left them the following year, promising to resupply them in 1825 on the Henrys Fork near its confluence with the Green River, along the present-day Wyoming-Utah border. Thus began the first rendezvous. They would take place every summer until 1840. Ashley failed to bring booze that first summer and the rendezvous only lasted two days. In future years, however, the whiskey flowed freely and the festivities lasted for weeks.

The rendezvous—a French word meaning "ap-

(continued on next page)

MOUNTAIN MEN

(continued)

pointed place of meeting"—was a time when both white and Indian trappers could sell their furs, trade for needed supplies and Indian squaws (the women had little say in the matter but most took considerable pleasure in the arrangement), meet with old friends, get rip-roaring drunk, and engage in storytelling, gambling, gun duels, and contests of all sorts. Horse racing, wrestling bouts, and shooting contests were favorites—Kit Carson killed Shunar, a big French bully, in a duel during one of the Green River rendezvous. Debauchery reigned supreme in these three-week-long affairs, and by the time they were over, many of the trappers had lost their entire year's earnings.

During the heyday of the fur trade, a common saying was "all trails lead to the Seedskeedee [Green River]." Six rendezvous were held here in the 1830s, others were held in the Wind River/Popo Agie River area, on Ham's Fork of the Green River, and in Idaho and Utah. Sites were chosen where there was space for up to 500 mountain men and 3,000 Indians, plenty of game, ample grazing for the thousands of horses, and good water. Not coincidentally, all were held in Shoshone country rather than farther east or north, where the hostile Sioux, Blackfeet, and Crow held sway. Despite such precautions, over half of Ashley's men were scalped by Indians.

Changing Times

The end of the rendezvous system—and most of the Rocky Mountain fur trapping—came about for a variety of reasons: overtrapping, the financial panic of 1837, and the growing use of other materials—particularly the South American nutria and Chinese silk—for hats. In addition, permanent trading posts such as Fort Laramie drew Indians away from the mountains to trade for buffalo robes instead of beaver furs. By 1840, when the last rendezvous was held on the banks of the Green River near present-day Pinedale, it was obvious there would be no more. One of the longtime trappers, Robert Newell, said to his partner, Joseph Meek:

> *We are done with this life in the mountains—done with wading in beaver dams, and freezing or starving alternately—done with Indian trading and Indian fighting. The fur trade is dead in the Rocky Mountains, and it is no place for us now, if ever it was. We are young yet, and have life before us. We cannot waste it here; we cannot or will not return to the States. Let us go down to the Wallamet and take farms.*

REGIONAL BESTS~ OUTDOOR RECREATION

Northwest Wyoming is famous for its year-round recreational opportunities. In the summertime, hiking, camping, horseback rides, river rafting, mountain biking, and other adventures top the charts, and winter brings out the skis, snowboards, skates, snowshoes, and snowmobiles. Each part of the region has its own attractions, from whitewater rafting through Snake River Canyon to mountain climbing within Grand Teton National Park to family day-hikes in Yellowstone. If outdoor adventure is what you crave, you've come to the right place!

FISHING

Outstanding fishing opportunities abound throughout the Greater Yellowstone Ecosystem, and a number of rivers have achieved an almost mythical status among fly-fishers. Several good books provide detailed information for fishing enthusiasts. Try one of the following: *Yellowstone Fishes; Ecology, History, and Angling in the Park* by John Varley and Paul Schullery (Mechanicsburg, PA: Stackpole Books); *Yellowstone Fishing Guide* by Robert E. Charlton (Ketchum, ID: Lost River Press); *Fishing Yellowstone* by Richard Parks (Helena, MT: Falcon Publishing); *Fly Fishing the Yellowstone River: An Angler's Guide* by Rod Walinchus and Tom Travis (Boulder, CO: Pruett Publishing Company); and *Fishing the Beartooths* by Pat Marchuson (Helena, MT: Falcon Publishing). For broader coverage, see *Fishing Wyoming.* by Kenneth Graham (Helena, MT: Falcon Publishing Co.); or Ken Retallic's *Flyfisher's Guide to Wyoming,* (Gallatin Gateway, MT: Wilderness Adventures Press). A number of other books detail the multitude of fishing options on surrounding lands in Montana and Idaho. In Jackson, stop by Jack Dennis' Outdoor Shop, 50 E. Broadway, tel. (307) 733-3270 or (800) 570-3270, www.jackdennis.com, to pick up a copy of the free *Western Fishing Newsletter,* with descriptions of regional fishing areas and which lures to try.

Fishing Licenses

In Wyoming, nonresident fishing permits cost $6 for one day, or $70 for a season. Nonresident youths ages 14-19 pay $20 for the year. (These prices include mandatory $5 conservation stamps.) Kids under 14 don't need a license if they're with an adult who has a valid fishing license. Purchase permits at most sporting-goods stores or from Game and Fish offices. For more fishing information, contact the **Wyoming Game and Fish Department,** tel. (307) 777-4601 or (800) 842-1934, www.gf.state.wy.us.

Get Montana fishing information from the **Montana Fish, Wildlife and Parks Department,** tel. (406) 444-2535, http://fwp.mt.gov. Nonresident two-day licenses cost $15, and season licenses are $50; these prices include a mandatory $5 conservation license. No license is required for children under age 12 if accompanied by an adult with a Montana fishing license.

In Idaho, nonresident fishing licenses are $7.50 for one day plus $3 a day for additional days, or $51.50 for an annual license. Kids ages 14-18 pay $21.50 annually. Get details from the **Idaho Department of Fish and Game,** tel. (208) 334-3700 or (800) 635-7820, www.state.id.us/fishgame.

Separate regulations apply in Yellowstone National Park. You don't need a state fishing license, but you will need to purchase a park license from a visitor center or ranger station. The adult fishing fee is $10 for a 10-day permit or $20 for a season permit. Kids ages 12-15 get permits free, and younger children do not need a permit. Within Grand Teton National Park a Wyoming fishing license is required.

ON THE SNOW

Downhill Skiing and Snowboarding

Jackson Hole is the primary skiing and snowboarding area in Wyoming. It includes one of America's top winter destinations, Jackson Hole Mountain Resort, located in Teton Village, 12 miles from the town of Jackson. For ease of access, it's hard to beat the smaller (but surprisingly steep) Snow King Resort, located just seven blocks from downtown. On the other side of Teton Pass—44 miles from Jackson—is Grand Targhee Ski Resort, famous for its deep powder skiing. Sleeping Giant Ski Area is a family area 50 miles west of Cody near Yellowstone. See the appropriate chapters for descriptions of each of these. During the winter call the Wyoming Division of Tourism at (800) 225-5996 for the statewide ski report, or visit its website, www.wyomingtourism.org.

Many more ski resorts can be found in Montana, including ones at Red Lodge (northeast of Yellowstone) and Big Sky (south of Bozeman and west of Yellowstone). For details on Montana resorts, see *Montana Handbook* by W.C. McRae and Judy Jewell (Emeryville, CA: Avalon Travel Publishing, www.moon.com).

Cross-Country Skiing

Skinny-skiers have an overwhelming choice of places to ski in the Yellowstone-Grand Teton-Jackson Hole area. Developed Nordic areas are located in Jackson Hole, west of Cody, and at West Yellowstone, Montana. In addition, Yellowstone and Grand Teton National Parks have cross-country skiing with views to die for, though the trails are not groomed. Adjacent Forest Service lands provide deep snow and inexhaustible opportunities for those with backcountry skiing experience. See specific chapters for details on all these cross-country skiing places. The special topic Safety in Avalanche Country has precautions to take while cross-country skiing in the backcountry.

Snowmobiling

Snowmobiling is an exceptionally popular winter activity in the Yellowstone region, but it is also quite controversial. An extensive network of snowmobile trails leads through northwest Wyoming and nearby parts of Montana and Idaho. Best-known is the 365-mile **Continental Divide Snowmobile Trail,** stretching around the south end of the Wind River Mountains northward through Grand Teton National Park to Yellowstone. Yellowstone National Park is the focal point for most snowmobile travel in Northwest Wyoming, with the primary entry points from West Yellowstone and through the South Entrance. The Park Service is currently reviewing its winter use policy and has proposed to stop allowing snowmobile entry from West Yellowstone, so this could change quite dramatically.

Snowmobile trail maps and listings of snowmobile rental companies are available from local visitor centers. For trail conditions around Wyoming, call (307) 777-7777 or (800) 225-5996, and ask for the snowmobile hotline. Find more detailed snowmobile info and other snowmobile links on the web at http://commerce.state.wy.us/sphs/snow.

GETTING INTO THE WILDERNESS

To get a real feel for the Greater Yellowstone Ecosystem, you need to abandon your car, get away from the towns, and head out into the vast and undeveloped public lands. The region contains some of the most remote country in the Lower 48, and one of the largest intact temperate-zone ecosystems anywhere.

Many campers prefer to use horses for longer trips, but backpacking is very popular on the shorter trails, especially in the national parks. Backcountry permits are required only within Yellowstone and Grand Teton. It is, however, a good idea to check in at a local Forest Service ranger station to get a copy of the regulations, since each place is different in such specifics as how far your tent must be from lakes and trails and whether wood fires are allowed. Be sure to take insect repellent along on any summertime trip since mosquitoes, deerflies, and horseflies can be quite thick, especially early in the summer.

A number of hiking trips, mostly two- or three-day treks, are described for Yellowstone and Grand Teton national parks, along with nearby Forest Service wilderness areas. An excellent hiking guide for the Tetons and Jackson Hole is *Jackson Hole Hikes* by Rebecca Woods (Jackson, WY: White Willow Publishing). For Yellowstone, there are two fine guidebooks: *Yellowstone Trails* by Mark Marschall (Mammoth, WY: Yellowstone Association), and *Hiking Yellowstone National Park* by Bill Schneider (Helena, MT: Falcon Publishing). The Park Service and Forest Service can also provide specific trail information.

Horses

For many people, the highlight of a Western vacation is the chance to ride a horse into wild country. Although a few folks bring their own steeds, most visitors leave the driving to an expert local outfitter instead. (If you've ever worked around horses in the backcountry, you'll understand why.) Horse packing is an entirely different experience from backpacking. The trade requires years of experience in learning how to properly load horses and mules with panniers, which types of knots to use for different loads, how to keep the packstrings under control, which horses to picket and which to hobble, and how to awaken when the horses decide to head down the trail on hobbles at three in the morning. Add to this a knowledge of bear safety, an ability to keep guests entertained with campfire tales and ribald jokes, a complete vocabulary of horse-cussing terms, and a thorough knowledge of tobacco chewing, and you're still only about 10% of the way to becoming a packer.

Get a complete listing of local backcountry outfitters from **Wyoming Outfitters and Guides Association,** tel. (307) 527-7453, www.wyoga.org; **Montana Outfitters and Guides Association,** tel. (406) 449-3578, www.moga-montana.org; or **Idaho Outfitters and Guides Association,** tel. (800) 494-3246, www.ioga.org. Not all of these guides and outfitters may be permitted in a given backcountry area; contact the Park Service or Forest Service to see which ones are licensed to use the place you plan to visit.

Although horses are far more common, **llamas** are increasingly being seen in some backcountry areas. You can't ride them, but they're easier to control than horses and do not cause as much damage to trails and backcountry meadows. Llamas are perfect for folks who want to hike while letting a pack animal carry most of the weight. Contact local Forest Service and Park Service offices for permitted llama packers.

Trail Etiquette

Because horses are so commonly used in the Yellowstone region, hikers should follow a few rules of courtesy. Horses and mules are not the brightest critters on this planet, and they can spook at the most inane thing, even a bush blowing in the breeze or a brightly colored hat. Hikers meeting a pack string should move several feet off the trail and not speak loudly or make any sudden moves. If you've ever seen what happens when just one mule in a string decides to act up, you'll appreciate the chaos that can result from sudden noises or movements. Anyone hiking with a dog should keep it well away from the stock and not let it bark. Last of all, never walk close behind a horse, unless you don't mind spending time in a hospital. Their kick is *definitely* worse than their bite.

Backcountry Ethics

The wilderness areas of northwest Wyoming are places to escape the crowds, enjoy the beauty and peace of the countryside, and develop an understanding of nature. Unfortunately, as more and more people head into backcountry areas, these benefits are becoming endangered. To keep wild places wild, always practice "leave no trace" hiking and camping. This means using existing campsites and fire rings, locating your campsite well away from trails and streams, staying on designated trails, not cutting switchbacks, burning only dead and down wood, extinguishing all fires, washing dishes 200 feet from lakes and creeks, digging "catholes" at

BEAR COUNTRY

Bears seem to bring out conflicting emotions in people. The first is an almost gut reaction of fear and trepidation: What if the bear attacks me? But then comes that other urge: What will my friends say when they see these *great* bear photos? Both of these reactions can lead to a multitude of problems in bear country. "Bearanoia" is a justifiable fear but can easily be taken to such an extreme that one avoids going outdoors at all for fear of meeting a bear. The "I want to get close-up shots of that bear and her cubs" attitude can lead to a bear attack. The middle ground incorporates a knowledge of and respect for bears with a sense of caution that keeps you alert for danger without letting fear rule your wilderness travels. Nothing is ever completely safe in this world, but with care you can avoid most of the common pitfalls that lead to bear encounters.

Brown and Black Bears

Old-timers joke that bears are easy to differentiate: a black bear climbs up the tree after you, while a grizzly snaps the tree off at the base. Black bears live in forested areas throughout Wyoming, but grizzlies exist mainly in the northwest corner of the state, primarily within and around Yellowstone National Park. Both grizzlies and black bears pose potential threats to backcountry travelers, although you are considerably more likely to be involved in a car accident while driving to a wilderness area than to be attacked by a bear once you arrive.

Grizzlies once ranged across the entire Northern Hemisphere, from Europe across what is now Russia and through the western half of North America. When whites arrived, there were perhaps 50,000-100,000 grizzlies in what would become the Lower 48 states. Unfortunately, as white settlers arrived, they came to view these massive and powerful creatures (average adult males weigh 500 pounds) as a threat to themselves and their stock. The scientific name, *Ursus arctos horribilis,* says much about human attitudes toward grizzlies. Grizzlies still have healthy populations in Alaska and western Canada, but elsewhere they were shot, trapped, and poisoned nearly to the brink of extinction. In the Lower 48 states grizzlies survive in only a few of the most remote parts of Montana, Wyoming, Idaho, and Washington. By 1975, when the Fish & Wildlife Service listed them as threatened, fewer than 1,000 grizzlies survived south of Canada. Since that time the population appears to have recovered somewhat and includes approximately 300-600 grizzlies in Wyoming's Greater Yellowstone Ecosystem.

Avoiding Bear Hugs

Surprise bear encounters are rare but frightening experiences. There were just 22 bear-caused injuries in Yellowstone National Park between 1980 and 1997—one injury for every 2.1 million visitors. Avoid unexpected encounters with bears by letting them know you're there. Most bears hear or smell you long before you realize their presence, and hightail it away. Surprising a bear—especially a sow with cubs—is the last thing you want to do in the backcountry. Before heading out, check at a local ranger station to see whether there have been recent bear encounters. If you discover an animal carcass, be extremely alert since a bear may be nearby and may attack anything that appears to threaten its food. Get away from such areas. Do not hike at night or dusk, when bears can be especially active. Safety is also in numbers: the more of you hiking together, the more likely a bear is to sense you and stay away.

Make noise in areas of dense cover or when coming around blind spots on trails. If you're unable to see everything around you for at least 50 yards, warn any hidden animals by talking, singing, clapping your

hands, tapping a cup, or rattling a can of pebbles. Some people tie bells to their packs for this purpose, while others regard this as an annoyance to fellow hikers. In general, bells are probably of little value since the sound does not carry far, and they might actually serve to attract bears. If bears can't hear you coming, don't be shy—make a lot of noise! It might seem a bit foolish, but yelling may prevent an encounter of the furry kind. Unfortunately, it will probably scare off other animals, so you're not likely to see many critters, and other hikers may not appreciate the noise. Personally, I reserve yelling "Hey Bear!" for situations where I'm walking in brushy bear country with low visibility and I have to compete with other noises such as a nearby creek. I wouldn't recommend doing so while walking the paved path around Old Faithful Geyser; you might get carried off in a straitjacket.

Hunters and photographers are the main recipients of bear hugs. Never under any circumstances approach a bear, even if it appears to be asleep. Move away if you see bear cubs, especially if one comes toward you—mom is almost always close by. Dogs create dangerous situations by barking and exciting bears—leave yours at home (dogs are not allowed in the backcountry in national parks). And, of course, never leave food around for bears. Not only is this illegal, but it also trains the bears to associate people with free food. Fed bears become garbage bears, and that almost inevitably means that the bear gets killed. Remem-

(continued on next page)

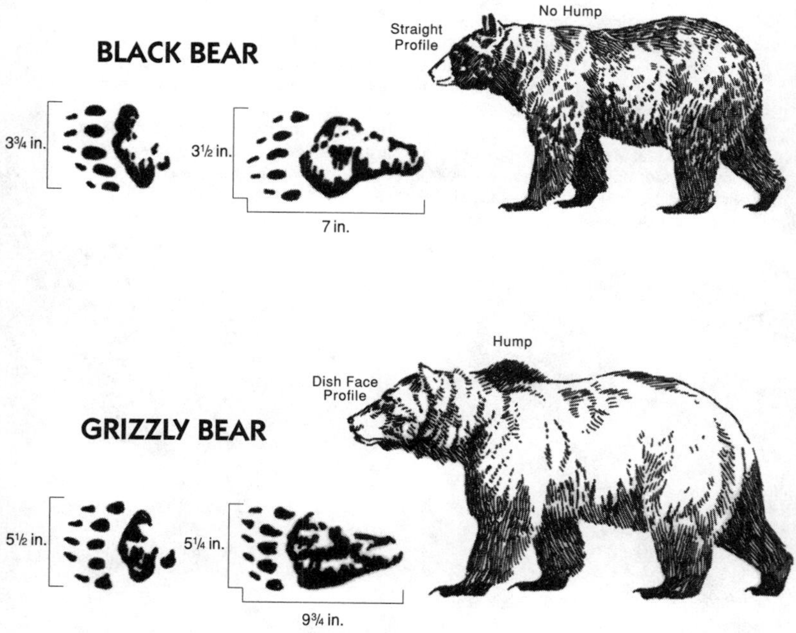

BLACK BEAR

Straight Profile

No Hump

3¾ in.

3½ in.

7 in.

GRIZZLY BEAR

Dish Face Profile

Hump

5½ in.

5¼ in.

9¾ in.

Note: Color can't be used for identification.

BEAR COUNTRY

(continued)

ber, bears are dangerous wild animals. This is *their* country, not a zoo. By going in you accept the risk—and thrill—of meeting a bear.

At the Campsite

Before camping, take a look around the area to see if there are recent bear tracks or scat and to make sure you're not on a game trail. Bears are attracted to odors of all sorts, including food, horse feed, soap, toothpaste, perfume, and deodorants. Your cooking, eating, and food storage area should be at least 50 yards away from your tent. Keep your campsite clean and avoid such smelly items as tuna, ham, sausage, and bacon; freeze-dried food is light and relatively odorless (though also relatively tasteless). Store food away from your sleeping area in airtight containers or several layers of plastic bags, and be sure to hang all food and other items that bears may smell at least 12 feet off the ground and four feet from tree trunks. Bring 50 feet of rope for this purpose. Tie two cups or pots to it so you will hear if it's moved. Some Forest Service and Park Service wilderness areas provide food storage poles at campsites. In the Teton and Bridger Wilderness Areas you can also rent bear-resistant backpacker food tubes or horse panniers from Forest Service offices. Camping stores in Jackson, Cody, and elsewhere sell similar containers.

Good news: researchers have reported no evidence that either sexual activity or menstrual odors precipitate bear attacks, despite reports to the contrary. The Park Service does recommend several common-sense precautions, including that menstruating women use tampons instead of pads and store soiled tampons in double ziplock bags above the reach of bears.

Encounters of the Furry Kind

If you do happen to suddenly encounter a bear and it sees you, try to stay calm and not make any sudden moves. Do not run, since you could not possibly outrun a bear; they can exceed 40 mph for short distances. Bear researchers now suggest that quickly climbing a tree is also not a wise way to escape bears and may actually incite an attack. Instead, make your-

self visible by moving into the open so the bear will (hopefully) identify you as a human and not something to eat. Do not stare directly at a bear. Sometimes dropping an item such as a hat or jacket will distract the bear, and talking calmly (easier said than done) also seems to have some value in convincing bears that you're a human. If the bear sniffs the air or stands on its hind legs it is probably trying to identify you. When it does, it will usually run away. If a bear woofs and postures, don't imitate it—this is a challenge. Keep retreating. Most bear charges are also bluffs; the bear will often stop short and amble off.

If a **grizzly bear** actually attacks, hold your ground and freeze. It may well be a bluff charge, with the bear halting at the last second. If the bear does not stop its attack, curl up face-down on the ground in a fetal position with your hands wrapped behind your neck and your elbows tucked over your face. Your backpack may help protect you somewhat. Remain still even if you are attacked, since sudden movements may incite further attacks. It takes an enormous amount of courage to do this, but often a bear will only sniff or nip you and leave. The injury you might sustain would be far less than if you tried to resist. After the attack, prevent further attacks by staying down on the ground till the grizzly has left the area.

Bear authorities now recommend not dropping to the ground if you are attacked by a **black bear,** as they tend to be more aggressive in such situations and are more likely to prey on humans. If a black bear attacks, fight back with whatever weapons are at hand; large rocks and branches can be surprisingly effective deterrents, as can yelling and shouting. (This, of course, assumes you can tell black bears from brown bears. If you can't, have someone who knows—such as a park ranger—explain the differences before you head into the backcountry.)

In the rare event of a night attack in your tent, defend yourself very aggressively. Do not play dead under such circumstances, since the bear probably views you as prey; it may give up if you make it a fight. Before you go to bed, try to plan escape routes should you be attacked in the night, and be sure to have a flashlight and pepper spray handy. Keeping your sleeping bag partly unzipped also allows the chance to escape should a bear attempt to drag you away. If someone is attacked in a tent near you, yelling and throwing rocks or sticks may drive the bear away.

Protecting Yourself

Recently, cayenne pepper sprays (sold in camping goods stores) have sometimes proven useful in fending off bear attacks. Note, however, that these "bear mace" sprays are only effective at close range. This is particularly true in open country where winds quickly disperse the mist or may blow it back in your own face. Another problem with bear mace is that you cannot carry it aboard commercial jets due to the obvious dangers should a canister explode. If you do carry a pepper spray, make sure it is readily available by carrying it in a holster on your belt or across your chest. Also be sure to test-fire it to see how the spray carries. Though they *are* better than nothing, pepper sprays are not a cure-all or a replacement for caution in bear country. It's far better to avoid bear confrontations in the first place. A few clueless individuals have sprayed themselves with the pepper spray thinking it would work like mosquito repellent. Needless to say, this isn't of much help, and there is some evidence it might even attract bears looking for a spicy meal!

A fine source for detailed bear safety information on the web is the Yellowstone Grizzly Foundation's site: http://home.wyoming.com/~ygf. Two good bear safety books are *Bear Attacks: Their Causes and Avoidance* by Stephen Herrero (New York, NY: Lyons Press) and *Bear Aware: Hiking and Camping in Bear Country* by Bill Schneider (Helena, MT: Falcon Publishing Company).

least 200 feet from lakes or streams, and hanging all food well above the reach of bears. Don't litter the ground with toilet paper; instead bury it deep or burn it in your campfire. (Do not, however, try to burn TP in the woods; more than one person has started a forest fire in this way.) Your tent site should be 100 yards from the food storage and cooking areas to reduce the likelihood of bear problems. Wood fires are not allowed in many areas, so be sure to bring along a portable gas stove. And, of course, haul your garbage out with you. Burning cans and tinfoil in the fire lessens their weight (and the odors that attract bears), but be sure to pick them out of the fire pit before you depart. And make sure that fire is completely out. For a detailed brochure on minimizing your impact and treating the land with respect, call (800) 332-4100, or visit the Leave no Trace website at www.lnt.org.

Backcountry Safety Tips

The most important part of enjoying—and surviving—the backcountry is to be prepared. Know where you're going; get maps, camping information, weather forecasts, and trail conditions from a ranger before setting out. Although I have often hiked alone, single hikers are at a greater risk of getting into trouble than those trekking with companions. Two are better than one, and three are better than two; if one gets hurt, one person can stay with the injured party and one can go for help. Bring more than enough food so hunger won't cause you to continue when weather conditions say stop. Tell a responsible person where you're going and when you'll be back. Dealing with bears is discussed in the Bear Country special topic within this chapter, and lightning is discussed in another special topic within the Grand Teton chapter. For additional precautions, see Health and Safety below.

Always carry the **10 essentials:** map, compass, water bottle, first-aid kit, flashlight, matches (or lighter) and fire starter, knife, extra clothing (a full set, in case you fall in a stream) including rain gear, extra food, and sunglasses—especially if you're hiking on snow.

Check your ego at the trailhead; stop for the night when the weather gets bad, even if it's 2 p.m., or head back, and don't press on when you're exhausted—tired hikers are sloppy hikers, and even a small injury can be disastrous in the woods.

JACKSON HOLE

Jackson Hole is one of the most-visited slices of wild country in North America, attracting well over three million travelers each year. They come here for a multitude of reasons: to camp under the stars in Grand Teton National Park, to play and shop in the New West town of Jackson, to hike flower-bedecked trails up forested valleys, to ride sleighs among thousands of elk, to raft down the Snake River, to ski or snowboard at one of the local resorts, or to simply stand in wonderment as the sun colors the sky behind the mountains. Many continue north to Yellowstone National Park, another place on everyone's must-see list. Drive north from Jackson toward Yellowstone and you'll quickly discover the biggest reason so many people are attracted to this place—its beauty. The Tetons act as a magnet, drawing your eyes away from the road and forcing you to stop and absorb some of their majesty. Welcome to one of the world's great wonderlands.

In the lingo of the mountain men, a "hole" was a large valley ringed by mountain ranges, and each was named for the trapper who based himself there. Jackson Hole, on Wyoming's far western border, is justifiably the most famous of all these intermountain valleys. Although Jackson Hole reaches an impressive 40 miles north to south and up to 10 miles across, the magnificent range of mountains to the west is what defines this valley. Shoshone Indians who wandered through this country called the peaks Teewinot ("Many Pinnacles"); later explorers would use such labels as Shark's Teeth or Pilot Knobs. But it was lonely French-Canadian trappers arriving in the early 1800s who provided the name that stuck: les Trois Tetons (literally, "the Three Tits").

Contrary to what you may have been told, Jackson Hole is *not* named for Michael Jackson. The valley, originally called Jackson's Hole, was instead named for likable trapper David E. Jackson, one of the men who helped establish the Rocky Mountain Fur Company. When Jackson and his partners sold out in 1830, they realized a profit of over $50,000. Jackson's presence remains in the names of both Jackson Hole and Jackson Lake. Eventually, more polite folks began calling the valley Jackson Hole, in an attempt to end the ribald stories associated with the name Jackson's Hole. (It's easy to imagine the jokes with both Jackson's Hole and the

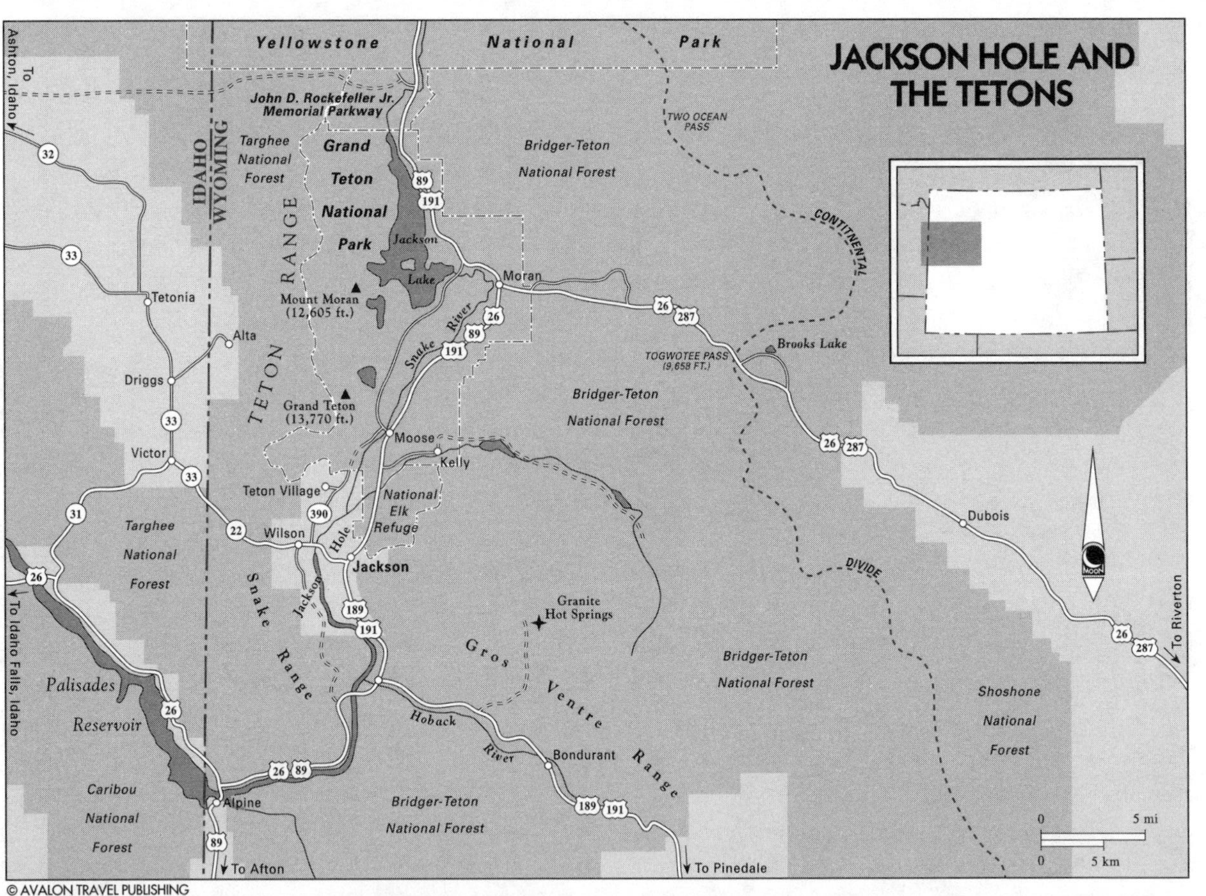
JACKSON HOLE AND THE TETONS
Yellowstone National Park
John D. Rockefeller Jr. Memorial Parkway
TWO OCEAN PASS
CONTINENTAL
DIVIDE
Bridger-Teton National Forest
Targhee National Forest
Grand Teton National Park
TETON RANGE
IDAHO
WYOMING
Jackson Lake
Moran
Mount Moran (12,605 ft.)
Grand Teton (13,770 ft.)
Snake River
TOGWOTEE PASS (9,658 FT.)
Brooks Lake
Tetonia
Alta
Driggs
Victor
Moose
Kelly
Teton Village
National Elk Refuge
Wilson
Jackson Hole
Jackson
Dubois
To Riverton
To Ashton, Idaho
Snake Range
Granite Hot Springs
Gros Ventre Range
Hoback River
Bondurant
Shoshone National Forest
Palisades Reservoir
To Idaho Falls, Idaho
Caribou National Forest
Alpine
To Afton
To Pinedale
0
5 mi
5 km

Tetons in the same place.) By the way, in 1991, a group calling itself the Committee to Restore Decency to Our National Parks created quite a stir by suggesting that Grand Teton National Park be renamed. A letter sent to the Park Service and various members of Congress noted: "Though a great many Americans may be oblivious to this vulgarity, hundreds of millions of French people around the world are not! How embarrassing that these spectacular, majestic mountains are reduced to a dirty joke overseas." After a flurry of letters in response, the hoax was revealed; it was a prank by staff members of *Spy* magazine.

HISTORY

The last major glaciation in the Jackson Hole area ended around 15,000 years ago, and the first peoples may have reached this valley while the ice was still retreating. Clovis stone arrowheads—a style used at least 11,000 years ago—have been found along the edges of the valley. These early peoples were replaced in the 16th and 17th centuries by the Shoshone, Bannock, Blackfeet, Crow, and Gros Ventre tribes, who hunted bison from horses. When the first fur trappers tramped into Jackson Hole, they found Indian paths throughout the valley.

John Colter

Transport yourself back to the early 19th century, a time when people from the new nation called America saw the world west of the Mississippi River as just a blank spot on the map. In 1803, Thomas Jefferson purchased the Louisiana Territory from France, and to learn more about this gigantic piece of real estate he sent Meriwether Lewis and William Clark on a military expedition to the Pacific coast, a trip that took nearly two and a half years. Although the expedition skirted around Wyoming—heading across Montana instead—it proved the opening wedge for the settlement of the West and, indirectly, the discovery of Jackson Hole. On the return trip, the party met two fur trappers en route to the upper Missouri River. One of Lewis and Clark's respected scouts, John Colter, was allowed to join the trappers, "provided no one of the party would ask or expect a Similar permission."

After a winter of trapping with his partners, Colter headed alone down the Platte River, but before he could get back to civilization he met up with a company of trappers led by Manuel Lisa. They were on their way to the Rockies, determined to cash in on the huge demand for beaver furs by trapping the rich beaver streams that Lewis and Clark had described. Wealth beckoned, and John Colter gladly turned around again, guiding Lisa's men up to the mouth of the Big Horn River, where they built a small fort. From there Colter was sent on a mission: contact Indians throughout the region, trading beads and other items for beaver furs.

His wanderings in the winter of 1807-08 were the first white exploration of this region. A map produced by William Clark in 1814 and based upon Colter's recollections shows an incredible midwinter journey around Yellowstone and Jack-

JACKSON HOLE IN 1835

This Valley is called "Jackson Hole" it is generally from 5 to 15 mls wide: the southern part where the river enters the mountain is hilly and uneven but the Northern portion is wide smooth and comparatively even the whole being covered with wild sage and Surrounded by high and rugged mountains upon whose summits the snow remains during the hottest months in Summer. The alluvial bottoms along the river and streams inter sect it thro. the valley produce a luxuriant groth of vegetation among which wild flax and a species of onion are abundant. The great altitude of this place however connected with the cold descending from the mountains at night I think would be a serious obstruction to growth of most Kinds of cultivated grains. This valley like all other parts of the country abounds with game.

—From *Journal of a Trapper 1834-1843*, by Osborne Russell

son Lakes, across the Tetons twice, and up through Jackson Hole. He did not get back to the fort until the following spring, telling tales of huge mountain ranges and a spectacular geothermal area that others quickly laughed off as "Colter's Hell."

Colter went on to become one of the most famous of all mountain men, and his later harrowing escape from the Blackfeet in Montana has become the stuff of legend. After being captured and stripped naked, he was forced to literally run for his life. Somehow he managed to outdistance his pursuers for six miles before hiding in a pile of logs until dark. He walked barefoot the 300 miles back to Manual Lisa's fort, surviving on roots and tree bark. Shortly thereafter, Colter was reported to have thrown his hat on the ground, declaring, "I'll be damned if I ever come into [this country] again." He returned to St. Louis, married, and established a farm near that of fellow explorer Daniel Boone. Colter lived long enough to give William Clark a description of the country he had visited, but he died from jaundice just three years later, in 1813.

Because of the abundance of beavers along tributaries of the Snake River, Jackson Hole became an important crossroads for the Rocky Mountain fur trade. Although no rendezvous was ever held in the valley, many of the most famous mountain men spent time here. They first trapped beavers in Jackson Hole in 1811, but it was not until the 1820s that fur trapping really came into its own as mountain men fanned through the wilderness in search of the "soft gold." It was a hazardous business, with the constant threat of Indian attacks and the many

THE WHITE SHOSHONE

The little Jackson Hole-area town of Wilson is named for one of Wyoming's most fascinating characters, "Uncle Nick" Wilson. Born in 1842, Wilson grew up in Utah, where he made friends with a fellow sheepherder, an Indian boy, and learned to speak his language. Then Nick's life suddenly took a strange twist. The mother of Chief Washakie (from Wyoming's Wind River Reservation) had recently lost a son, and in a dream she was told that a white boy would come to take his place. Unable to convince her otherwise, Washakie sent his men out to find the new son. They came across Nick and offered him a pinto pony and the chance to fish, hunt, and ride horses all he wanted. It didn't take much persuading, and for the next two years he lived as a Shoshone, learning to hunt buffalo, to use a bow and arrow, and to answer to his new name, Yagaiki. He became a favorite of Chief Washakie, but when word came (falsely) that Nick's father was threatening to attack the Shoshones with an army of men to retrieve his son, the chief reluctantly helped Nick return home.

At age 18, Nick Wilson became one of the first Pony Express riders, a job that nearly killed him when he was struck in the head during a Paiute Indian attack. A doctor managed to remove the arrow point, but Wilson remained in a coma for nearly two weeks. Thereafter, Wilson always wore a hat to cover the scar, even inside buildings. He went on to become an Army scout and a driver for the Overland Stage before returning to a more sedate life as a farmer. Many years later, in 1889, Nick Wilson led a party of five Mormon families over steep Teton Pass and down to the rich grazing lands in Jackson Hole. The town that grew up around them became Wilson. In later years, "Uncle Nick" recounted his adventures in *The White Indian Boy.*

JACKSON HOLE MUSEUM & TETON COUNTY HISTORICAL SOCIETY

SAVING JACKSON HOLE

The Jackson Hole economy has been stuck in permanent high gear for the last few decades as expensive homes spread across old ranchlands, retailers such as Kmart moved in, and the town of Jackson grew from a sleepy burg to a national focal point for outdoor fun. Today, development reaches for miles south from Jackson itself. Despite the fact that 97% of the land in Teton County is in the public domain, the 70,000 acres of private land that remain are rapidly being developed, and Jackson Hole is in grave danger of losing the wild beauty that has attracted visitors for more than a century. This is immediately obvious to anyone arriving in Jackson. Instead of the wide open spaces that remain protected by public land ownership, the edges of Jackson are falling under a proliferation of trophy homes, real-estate offices, chain motels, fast-food outlets, megamarts, gas stations, and elaborate banks, all competing beneath a thicket of signs. Summertime traffic jams are becoming all too common in this once-quiet place where more than 35,000 visitors can now be found on a summer afternoon.

In 1994, Jackson voters got fed up with the pace of development and voted to scrap the town's two-percent lodging tax, which had provided over a million dollars per year in funding to promote Jackson Hole around the world. Despite this lack of promotional effort, growth shows no signs of slowing down. A large new Albertson's grocery store went up in 1999, and an even bigger Smith's is expected to open by 2001. Housing costs continue to spiral upward, pushed by the arrival of a wealthy clientele willing to drop $1 million or more for a Jackson Hole home.

The **Jackson Hole Conservation Alliance,** tel. (307) 733-9417, www.jhalliance.com, is a 1,600-member environmental group that works to preserve the remaining natural areas of Jackson Hole. Membership starts at $25 a year and includes a bimonthly newsletter and a chance to help control the many developments that threaten this still-beautiful valley.

Another influential local group is the **Jackson Hole Land Trust,** tel. (307) 733-4707, www.jhlt.org, a nonprofit organization that obtains conservation easements to maintain ranches and other land threatened by development. They have protected more than 10,000 acres in the valley in this way, including the 1,740-acre Walton Ranch, visible along the highway between Jackson and Wilson.

natural hazards such as angry grizzlies, disease, and injuries. Help was hundreds of miles away. This quest continued for the next two decades, finally dying out when overtrapping made beavers harder to find and silk hats replaced fur hats. After the last rendezvous in 1840, most of the old trappers headed on to new adventures, the best becoming guides for those en route to Oregon and California. Because Jackson Hole was not near the Oregon Trail or other routes west, the area remained virtually deserted until the late 19th century.

Settlers

The first Jackson Hole homesteaders arrived in 1884, followed quickly by others coming to escape the law. The settlers survived by grazing cattle, harvesting hay, and acting as guides for rich hunters from Europe and eastern states. Gradually they filled the richest parts of the valley with homesteads. Conflicts soon arose between the Bannock Indians, who had been hunting in Jackson Hole for more than a hundred years, and the new settlers who made money guiding wealthy sportsmen.

By 1895, Wyoming had enacted game laws prohibiting hunting during 10 months of the year. Claiming that the Indians were taking elk out of season, Constable William Manning and 26 settlers arrested a group of 28 Indians (mostly women and children) who had been hunting in Hoback Canyon. When the Bannocks attempted to flee, an elderly Indian was shot four times in the back and died. Most of the others escaped. Settlers in Jackson Hole feared revenge and called in the cavalry, but the Indians who had been hunting in the area all returned peaceably to their Idaho reservation. Astoundingly, *The New York Times* headlined its report of the incident, "Settlers Massacred—Indians Kill Every One at Jackson's Hole—Courier Brings the News—Red Men Apply the Torch to All the

Houses in the Valley." Absolutely none of this was true, but the attack by whites succeeded in forcing the Indians off their traditional hunting grounds, an action eventually upheld in a landmark U.S. Supreme Court case.

Jackson Hole Comes of Age

By the turn of the 20th century, the Jackson Hole settlements of Jackson, Wilson, Kelly, and Moran had all been established. The towns grew slowly; people survived by ranching, guiding, and engaging in the strange new business of tending to wealthy "dudes" from back east. Eventually, tourism would vastly eclipse raising cattle in importance, but even today Teton County has nearly as many cattle as people.

Jackson, the largest town in Jackson Hole, was established in 1897 when Grace Miller (wife of a local banker known derisively as "Old Twelve Percent") bought a large plot of land and planned a townsite. In an event that should come as no surprise in "The Equality State," Jackson later became the first town in America to be entirely governed by women. The year was 1920, and not only was the mayor a woman (Grace Miller), but so were all four council members, the city clerk, the treasurer, and even the town marshal. They remained in office until 1923.

Over the years Jackson has grown, spurred on by the creation of Grand Teton National Park and the development of Jackson Hole Mountain Resort. In the last two decades Jackson Hole has seen almost continuous growth; tourists have flooded the region to play, investors have built golf courses and ostentatious hotels, and wealthy families have snatched up their own parcels of paradise. Although much of the area is public land and will remain undeveloped, rapid growth on private land is transforming Jackson Hole into the Wyoming version of Vail. The standard quip is that the billionaires are buying land so fast that they're driving the millionaires out of Jackson Hole. Even the formerly quiet town of Wilson has not managed to fight off the development onslaught, with a massive new grade school and a collection of modest new homes that locals call Whoville (after those in the Dr. Seuss book). As one who once lived in Wilson, I can appreciate the joke now going the rounds: How many Wilsonites does it take to change a light bulb? Seven. One to screw it in, and the other six to talk about how good the old one used to be.

JACKSON

The town of Jackson (pop. 8,000) lies near the southern end of Jackson Hole, hemmed in on three sides by Snow King Mountain, the Gros Ventre Range, and East Gros Ventre Butte. At 6,200 feet in elevation, Jackson experiences cold snowy winters, wet springs, delightfully warm and sunny summers, and crisp but color-filled falls. Jackson is quite unlike any other place in Wyoming; on a typical summer day more than 35,000 tourists flood the town. Sit on a bench in Town Square on a summer day and you're likely to see cars from every state in the Union. Tourists dart in and out of the many gift shops, art galleries, fine restaurants, Western-style saloons, and trendy boutiques. The cowboy hats all look as if the price tags just came off. This sure isn't Rock Springs!

In other parts of Wyoming, Jackson is viewed with a mixture of awe and disdain—awe over its booming economy, but disdain that Jackson is not a "real" town, just a false front put up to sell things to outsiders. Yes, Jackson is almost wholly dependent upon the almighty tourist dollar, but as a result it enjoys a cultural richness lacking in other parts of the state. Besides, if you don't like all the commercial foolishness, it's easy to escape to a campsite or remote trail in the wonderful countryside of nearby Grand Teton National Park or Bridger-Teton National Forest.

Keep your eyes open around Jackson and you're likely to see famous (or infamous, depending upon your perspective) residents such as actor Harrison Ford, former Secretary of the Interior James Watt (who resigned in disgrace in 1983), attorney Gerald Spence (of Karen Silkwood and Imelda Marcos notoriety), former Wyoming governor Clifford Hansen, Yvon Chouinard (mountaineer and founder of Patagonia), actress Connie Stevens, industrial heir Charles DuPont, and members of the extended Rockefeller family.

SIGHTS

Town Square

In 1932, the local Rotary Club planted trees in the center of Jackson, adding four picturesque arches made from hundreds of elk antlers. Today the trees offer summertime shade, and at any time of day or night you'll find visitors admiring or getting photos taken in front of the arches that mark the corners of Town Square. During the winter, the snow-covered arches and trees are draped with lights, giving the square a festive atmosphere. Surrounded by dozens of boardwalk-fronted galleries, bars, restaurants, factory outlets, and gift shops, the square is the focal

Jackson's elk antler arches are featured attractions at Town Square.

point of tourist activity in Jackson. During the summer, stagecoaches wait to transport you on a leisurely ride around town, and each evening "cowboys" put on a free **shoot-out** for throngs of camera-happy tourists. The shoot-out starts every summer night (except Sunday) at 6:30 p.m. They've been killing each other like this since 1955. With stereotypical players and questionable acting, the "mountain law" system seems in dire need of reform. Most folks love the sham; Kodak and Fuji love it even more. Warning: the sound of blanks is surprisingly loud and can be frightening for small children.

National Museum of Wildlife Art

Jackson is home to the magnificent National Museum of Wildlife Art, which lies two miles north of town along US Hwy. 26/89, directly across from the National Elk Refuge. Built from brown Arizona sandstone, the exterior blends in with nearby rock outcroppings. Step inside the doors of this 51,000-square-foot museum to discover a marvelous interior space. As visitors enter the main gallery, a larger-than-life bronze mountain lion crouches above, ready to pounce. Kids will enjoy the hands-on Children's Gallery. Adults will appreciate the artwork spread through a dozen galleries, along with the video theater, Rising Sage Cafe (delicious lunches), 200-seat auditorium, and gift shop.

The museum collection features pieces by Carl Rungius, George Catlin, Albert Bierstadt, Karl Bodmer, Alfred Jacob Miller, N.C. Wyeth, Conrad Schwiering, John Clymer, Charles Russell, Robert Bateman, and many others. Of particular interest are the reconstructed studio of John Clymer and the spacious Carl Rungius Gallery, where you'll find the most complete collection of his paintings in the nation. Also of note is the exhibit on the American bison, which documents these once vastly abundant animals and their slaughter. Six galleries contain changing exhibitions of photography, painting, and other art. Spotting scopes in the lobby and the cozy members' lounge (open to the public) are useful for watching residents of the adjacent National Elk Refuge. Call (307) 733-5771 for details on the museum, or check their website, www.wildlifeart.org.

Admission to the museum costs $6 for adults, $5 for seniors and students, $14 for families; kids under six get in free. It's open daily 8 a.m.-5 p.m. Memorial Day through Labor Day; daily 9

JACKSON HOLE AT A GLANCE

Jackson elevation 6,209 feet

Wyoming State Information Center, 532 N. Cache Dr., tel. (307) 733-3316, www.jacksonholechamber.com, open daily year-round

National Elk Refuge, tel. (307) 733-9212, www.r6.fws.gov/refuges/natlelk

National Museum of Wildlife Art, tel. (307) 733-5771, www.wildlifeart.org, open daily

Bridger-Teton National Forest Supervisor's Office, 340 N. Cache Dr., tel. (307) 739-5500, www.fs.fed.us/btnf

Targhee National Forest Teton Basin Ranger District, Driggs, Idaho, tel. (208) 354-2431, www.fs.fed.us/tnf

Grand Targhee Ski and Summer Resort, tel. (800) 827-4433, www.grandtarghee.com

Jackson Hole Mountain Resort, tel. (307) 733-2292 or (888) 333-7766, www.jacksonhole.com

Snow King Resort, tel. (307) 733-5200 or (800) 522-5464 (outside Wyoming), www.snowking.com

Jackson Hole Central Reservations, tel. (307) 733-4005 or (800) 443-6931, www.jacksonholeresort.com

Jackson Hole Bed & Breakfast, tel. (307) 734-1999 or (800) 542-2632, www.jacksonholebus.com

Jackson Hole Rodeo, tel. (307) 733-2805, Wednesday and Saturday nights from Memorial Day to Labor Day

Teton Valley Chamber of Commerce, Driggs, Idaho, tel. (208) 354-2500, www.tetonvalleychamber.com, open Mon.-Fri. year-round

a.m.-5 p.m. December to early April; and Mon.-Sat. 9 a.m.-5 p.m. and Sunday 1-5 p.m. in the fall and spring (Labor Day through November and early April through Memorial Day). Very informative 45-minute free museum tours are given daily at 11 a.m. or by request for groups.

Wildlife films, slide lectures, talks, concerts, kid programs, and other activities take place throughout the year in the auditorium and galleries; pick up a schedule of upcoming events at the entrance desk. One of the most popular events is the **Miniature Show and Sale** in mid-September; it attracts more than a hundred of the country's leading artists.

During the winter, come to the museum to purchase tickets for sleigh rides on the refuge. A combination museum entrance and Elk Refuge sleigh ride costs $15 for adults, $11 for ages 6-12, free for kids under six.

Historical Museums

The small **Jackson Hole Museum,** 105 N. Glenwood, tel. (307) 733-2414, has a surprising homespun charm. Inside are displays and collections illustrating the days when Indians, trappers, cattlemen, and dude ranchers made this magnificent valley their home. Check out the Paul Bunyan-size bear trap and the old postcards. Admission costs $3 for adults, $2 for seniors, $1 for students, and $6 for families. Hours are Mon.-Sat. 9:30 a.m.-6 p.m. and Sunday 10 a.m.-5 p.m. from Memorial Day to early October; closed the rest of the year. The museum sponsors hour-long **historical walking tours** of Jackson's downtown on Tuesday, Thursday, Friday, and Saturday at 10 a.m. Memorial Day through Labor Day. These cost $2 for adults, $1 for seniors and students, or $5 for families.

The **Jackson Hole Historical Center,** 105 Mercill Ave., tel. (307) 733-9605, is a small research facility housing photo archives, a library of old books from the area, a fine exhibit on the fur trade, and an impressive collection of Indian trade beads and mountain-man paraphernalia. A replica of the "Colter stone" is also on display, as are rotating exhibits through the year. Hours are Mon.-Fri. 8 a.m.-5 p.m. year-round; free admission.

Art in Jackson

Artists have long been attracted by the beauty of Jackson Hole and the Tetons. Mount Moran, the 12,805-foot summit behind Jackson Lake, is named for Thomas Moran, whose watercolors helped persuade Congress to set aside Yellowstone as the first national park. The late Conrad Schwiering's paintings of the Tetons have attained international fame—one was even used on the Postal Service's Wyoming Centennial stamp in 1990. Ansel Adams's photograph of the Tetons remains etched in the American consciousness as one of the archetypal wilderness images. A copy of the image was included in the payload of the *Voyager II* spacecraft currently en route out of our solar system. Today many artists live or work in Jackson Hole, and locals proclaim it "Art Center of the Rockies," ranking it with New York, San Francisco, Santa Fe, and Scottsdale.

More than 30 galleries crowd the center of Jackson, their collections covering the spectrum from Indian art of questionable authenticity to impressive photographic exhibits and shows by nationally acclaimed painters. Unfortunately, many of these galleries offer recycled ideas now manufactured in mass quantity with every possible cliché thrown in. Particularly egregious examples are the Southwestern-style pastel pottery, the glowing country scenes at Thomas Kinkade Gallery, and the prints of sexy Indian maidens with windblown hair and strategically torn garments. See the local free newspapers for a complete rundown of current exhibitions and displays, along with maps showing gallery locations, but don't believe everything the galleries say about themselves in their ads.

Several galleries are worth a visit, most notably the outstanding National Museum of Wildlife Art (described above). The nonprofit **Art Association,** 260 W. Pearl, tel. (307) 733-6379, has art classes of all types throughout the year and displays changing exhibitions by local artists in its **Artwest Gallery,** open Mon.-Fri. 9 a.m.-4:30 p.m. **Fiber & Pulp,** 365 N. Glenwood, tel. (307) 734-2599, has workshops in book and paper arts, including short training sessions on such topics as bookbinding, silk painting, Polaroid dye transfers, and mask making.

Just off Town Square at the corner of Center and Deloney, **Trailside Galleries,** tel. (307) 733-3186, www.trailsidegalleries.com, focuses on Western works, but you'll also find everything from impressionism to wildlife art here. More unusual is the nearby **Center Street**

Gallery, 110 Center St., tel. (307) 733-1115 or (888) 733-1115, where the emphasis is on brightly colored contemporary art and jewelry.

Jackson's finest gallery space is **Martin-Harris Gallery,** 60 E. Broadway (upstairs next to Snake River Grill), tel. (307) 733-0350 or (800) 366-7814, specializing in contemporary Western ("New West") paintings and sculptures by nationally known artists. Also of note here are the collectibles and one-of-a-kind pieces of handcrafted furniture. But bring plenty of cash or a big limit on your credit card. Last time I visited they were asking $21,000 for a desk—but it was probably worth every penny.

Also downtown, the **Caswell Gallery & Sculpture Garden,** 145 E. Broadway, tel. (307) 734-2660, is home to Jackson's only outdoor sculpture garden, with wildlife bronzes by Rip Caswell. Not my cup of tea (or espresso for that matter), but you may appreciate the innovative sculptures from other artisans displayed in this gallery. **Jack Dennis' Wyoming Gallery,** 50 E. Broadway, tel. (307) 733-7548, specializes in wildlife and traditional landscape paintings. **Rawson Galleries** features traditional (and a few avant-garde) watercolors, displayed in a crowded space at 50 King St., tel. (307) 733-7306.

The **Joanne Hennes Studio & Gallery,** 5850 N. Larkspur Dr. (off Spring Gulch Rd. near the Jackson Hole Golf and Tennis Club), tel. (307) 733-2593, features oil and watercolor paintings of the Tetons by Joanne Hennes. Two of her commissioned works hang in the Moose Visitor Center and Jenny Lake Lodge.

One of Jackson's largest private exhibition spaces is **Wilcox Gallery,** a mile north of town on US Hwy. 26/89, tel. (307) 733-6450. Inside are traditional oil paintings by Jim Wilcox, along with works by other prominent Western painters and sculptors.

For art from the natural world, head six miles south of town on US Hwy. 89 to **Fossil Works & Ulrich Studio.** Inside are beautifully prepared fish fossils from the Kemmerer area (where the Ulrich's have a fossil quarry), including tabletops, flooring tiles, wall pieces, and other prepared specimens. The gallery is open by appointment only; call (307) 733-1019 or (307) 733-3613.

For a different kind of art, head to **Dancer's Workshop,** downstairs in the Pink Garter Plaza at 49 W. Broadway, tel. (307) 733-6398, which offers country-and-western, modern, ballet, tap, and jazz dance classes throughout the year, with nationally known guest artists in the summer.

Photo Galleries

Many nationally known photographers live or work in Jackson Hole and exhibit their prints in Jackson galleries. Tom Mangelsen displays his outstanding wildlife and landscape photos at **Images of Nature Gallery,** 170 N. Cache Dr., tel. (307) 733-9752. Inside **Light Reflections,** 35 E. Deloney, tel. (307) 733-4016 or (800) 346-5223, are many of Fred Joy's large-format visions of the American West. Also well worth a visit is **Wild by Nature Gallery,** 95 W. Deloney, tel. (307) 733-8877, where photographer Henry H. Holdsworth offers prints of his striking wildlife and nature imagery.

Kitsch

If you're a fan of the *National Enquirer,* check out the weird and wacky collection at **Ripley's Believe It or Not,** 140 N. Cache, tel. (307) 734-0000. Here you'll discover a shrunken head, six-legged buffalo calf, six-foot long cigar, antique bedpan collection, and even art created from dryer lint. Who says art is only for the elite? Entrance costs a steep $8 for adults, $5 for ages 5-12; free for kids under five. The family rate is $30, a bargain price for families of 10 from Salt Lake City. Ripley's is open daily 9 a.m.-10 p.m. May-Oct., and daily 9 a.m.-6 p.m. the rest of the year.

Head a dozen miles south of Jackson to Hoback Junction for more weirdness at **Teton Mystery,** tel. (307) 733-4285. What is it? Pay your money and find out.

NATIONAL ELK REFUGE

Just two miles north of Jackson is the National Elk Refuge, winter home for thousands of these majestic animals. During the summer, the elk range up to 65 miles away to feed on grasses, shrubs, and forbs in alpine meadows. But as the snows descend each fall, the elk move downslope, wintering in Jackson Hole and the surrounding country. The chance to view elk up close from a horse-drawn sleigh makes a trip to the National Elk Refuge one of the most popular wintertime activities for Jackson Hole visitors.

History

When the first ranchers arrived in Jackson Hole in the late 19th century, they moved onto land that had long been an elk migration route and wintering ground. The ranchers soon found elk raiding their haystacks and competing with cattle for forage, particularly during severe winters. The conflicts reached a peak early in the 20th century when three consecutive severe winters killed thousands of elk, leading one settler to claim that he had "walked for a mile on dead elk lying from one to four deep."

Fortunately, local rancher and hunting guide Stephen N. Leek had been given a camera by one of the sportsmen he had guided, George Eastman (founder of Kodak). Leek's disturbing photos of starving and dead elk found a national audience and helped pressure the state of Wyoming to appropriate $5,000 to buy hay in 1909. Two years later the federal government began purchasing land for a permanent winter elk refuge, a refuge that would eventually cover nearly 25,000 acres. Today it's administered by the U.S. Fish & Wildlife Service. Famed biologist, illustrator, and conservationist Olaus Murie came to Jackson Hole in 1927 to begin his studies of the elk, remaining here until his death in 1963. Murie and his wife, Margaret "Mardie" Murie, chronicled their adventures in *Wapiti Wilderness* (Colorado Associated University Press). Conservationist Mardie Murie—now over 90—still lives in Moose, holding near-sainthood status among conservationists.

Today more than 10,000 elk (two-thirds of the local population) spend November through May on the refuge. Because development has reduced elk habitat in the valley to a quarter of its original size, refuge managers try to improve the remaining land by seeding, irrigation, and prescribed burning. In addition, during the most difficult foraging period, the elk are fed pelleted alfalfa paid for in part by sales of elk antlers collected on the refuge. During this time, each elk eats more than seven pounds of supplemental alfalfa a day, or 30 tons per day for the entire herd. Elk head back into the mountains with the melting of snow each April and May; during the summer months you'll only see a few on the refuge.

Visiting the Refuge

The National Elk Refuge, tel. (307) 733-9212, is primarily a winter attraction, although it's also an excellent place to watch birds and other wildlife in summer. Trumpeter swans nest and winter here. The refuge has staff members on duty year-round in the Wyoming State Information Center. Find them on the web at www.r6.fws.gov/refuges/natlelk.

The main winter attraction here is the chance to see thousands of elk up close from one of the **horse-drawn sleighs** that take visitors through the refuge. The elk are accustomed to these sleighs and pay little heed, but people on foot would scare them. A tour of the National Elk Refuge is always a highlight for wintertime visitors to Jackson Hole. In December and January the bulls have impressive antlers that they start to shed by the end of February. The months of January and February are good times to see sparring matches. You might also catch a glimpse of a wolf or two since a pack now resides in the area year-round and hunts elk in winter. Morning is the best time to look for wolves.

Begin your wintertime visit to the refuge at the National Museum of Wildlife Art, two miles north of Jackson on Hwy. 26/89. Purchase your sleigh ride tickets here; $12 for adults, $8 for ages 6-12, free for kids under age six. A better deal is the combination ticket that includes museum entrance and an Elk Refuge sleigh ride for $15 adults, $11 ages 6-12, and free for kids under six. For reservations, call Bar-T-Five (they run the sleighs) at (307) 733-5386 or (800) 772-5386. The museum shows an interpretive slide show about the refuge while you're waiting for a shuttle bus to take you downhill to the delightful sleighs. The sleighs run daily 10 a.m.-4 p.m. between mid-December and early April (closed Christmas), heading out as soon as enough folks show up for a ride—generally just long enough for the early-comers to finish watching the slide show. The rides last 45-60 minutes. Be sure to bring along warm clothes, as the wind can get bitterly cold.

Special START (Southern Teton Area Rapid Transit) buses connect Jackson with the Elk Refuge and the Museum of Wildlife Art for just $1 each way; call (307) 733-4521 for details. If you don't want to wait for a bus, call **All Star Taxi,** tel. (307) 733-2888 or (800) 378-2944, or **Buckboard Cab,** tel. (307) 733-1112, both of which offer shuttle service to the museum from Teton Village or downtown Jackson.

Four miles north of town and next to the elk refuge is the **Jackson National Fish Hatchery,** tel. (307) 733-2510, which rears a half million cutthroat and lake trout annually. It's open daily 8 a.m.-4 p.m. year-round.

ACCOMMODATIONS

As one of the premier centers for tourism in Wyoming, Jackson Hole is jam-packed with more than 70 different motels, hotels, and B&Bs, plus many more condominiums and guest ranches. Other lodging can be found just to the north within or near the park; these are detailed in Park Camping and Lodging in the Grand Teton National Park chapter. See Additional Jackson Hole Accommodations in the appendix for a listing of motels and hotels that are not described below.

Because of the town's popularity, lodgings in Jackson command premium prices—a marked contrast to rates in other parts of Wyoming. With a few exceptions, you can expect to pay a minimum of $85 s or d during the peak visitor seasons of July-Aug. and late December to early January. Rates can drop over 50% in the off-season, so if you can visit March-May or late September to mid-December, you'll save a lot of cash. (The same Super 8 Motel rooms that go for $140 in July cost just $52 in April!) In the town of Jackson, the highest rates are usually in July and August, while at Teton Village, skiers send lodging prices to their peak between mid-December and early January.

Reservations are highly recommended. For midsummer, make reservations at least two months ahead—longer if you really want to be certain of a place—and during the Christmas-to-New Year's period you should probably reserve six months in advance to ensure a spot. Summer weekends tend to be the most crowded, with many families driving up from Salt Lake City for a cooling break in the mountains.

Jackson hostels, motels, and hotels are arranged below by price, with the least expensive places first. Add a six percent tax to these rates.

Hostels

Jackson's least-expensive lodging option, the **Bunkhouse,** tel. (307) 733-3668 or (800) 234-4507, www.anvilmotel.com, is in the basement of the Anvil Motel at 215 N. Cache Drive. Right in town, it almost always has space. The hostel costs $22 per person and includes a TV room and a kitchen with a refrigerator and microwave (but no stove or dishes). The big sleeping room contains 30 bunk beds with linen and adjacent storage lockers; bring your own lock. Though men's and women's showers and restrooms are separate, the sleeping space is coed. It can get pretty noisy with all those snoring bodies in one room at night, so earplugs are a smart purchase. Check in after 3 p.m. and be out by 11 a.m. Alcohol is not allowed. Folks who aren't staying here can take showers for $5. Inexpensive.

Out in Teton Village, **Hostel X,** tel. (307) 733-3415, www.hostelx.com, provides a somewhat quieter alternative, with four-person dorms going for $19 per person (but you need to be an AYH member). They also have private rooms for $47 d. The lounge includes a TV, pay phones, a pool table, ping pong, a children's play area, fireplace, microwave, games, Internet access to check your e-mail, and a ski-waxing room. Inexpensive.

Easiest on the Wallet

The definition of "budget" lodging has to be stretched a bit in Jackson, where even fairly basic rooms with older furnishings go for $60 a night. The following lodgings have at least some of their rooms for under $90.

Hostel X features very small, plain-vanilla rooms (no TV or phones) and a central area for camaraderie. Rates are $47 s or d. Because of its Teton Village location at the foot of Jackson Hole Mountain Resort, it is very popular with skiers on a budget; reserve three months ahead for midwinter rooms. Inexpensive. See Hostels above for details on Hostel X.

In a quiet part of town but just a few blocks from Town Square is **Alpine Motel,** 70 S. Jean St., tel. (307) 739-3200. Most of the rooms contain old-fashioned furnishings (including tiny TVs), but they're clean and cost just $54 s or $58 d. Remodeled rooms with Motel 6-style furnishings are $68 s or $72 d. Add $8 to these rates for four people in a room. A small outdoor pool is on the premises, and some rooms include fridges and microwaves. Moderate.

Despite its name, **The Cottages at Snow King,** 470 King St., tel. (307) 733-3480 or (800) 483-8667, www.townsquareinns.com, doesn't have cottages, but it does rent out modest but comfortable motel rooms in a residential part of town. These range from modest rooms with one queen bed and a fridge for $64 d, up to full-kitchen units that sleep four for $102. Winter rates provide skiers with some of the best deals in Jackson: $125-200 d for seven days! Moderate.

Sagebrush Motel, 550 W. Broadway, tel. (307) 733-0336, has a variety of units. Motel rooms with older furnishings and kitchenettes cost a reasonable $65-84 s or d. Cabin units start at $70 s or d, but those with kitchens ($94 for up to four people) are much nicer. Sagebrush Motel is open May-Oct. only. Moderate.

Kudar's Motel, 260 N. Cache Dr., tel. (307) 733-2823, offers rather plain motel rooms with "antique" furnishings and microscopic televisions for reasonable prices: $65 d. Of more interest are their rustic log cabins that were built in 1938. These go for $75-90 d, and the larger ones can sleep six. Moderate-Expensive.

One of Jackson's better deals for standard motel rooms is—not surprisingly—**Motel 6,** 1370 W. Broadway, tel. (307) 733-1620 or (800) 466-8356, but even here peak summer rates are $70 s or $76 d. You'll find predictable rooms and an outdoor pool, but reserve six months in advance for July and August. The off-season rates ($34 s or $40 d) are a much better bargain. Moderate.

Twelve miles south of Jackson in Hoback Junction, **Hoback River Resort,** tel. (307) 733-5129, www.jacksonholenet.com/hrr, has large motel rooms and cabins for up to six people on attractive grounds facing the Hoback River. The rooms are very clean and well maintained. But the location—away from busy downtown Jackson—is the real draw here. Rates are $70-80 s or d in motel rooms with decks; $95 s or d in cabins with full kitchens (but no maid service). A three-night minimum stay is required in the cabins. Moderate-Expensive.

Another good place is **Anvil Motel,** 215 N. Cache Dr., tel. (307) 733-3668 or (800) 234-4507, www.anvilmotel.com, where the modern rooms are $90 d or $115 for two beds (four people). All rooms here have microwaves and small fridges. An outdoor jacuzzi is available. Expensive. Just around the corner at 240 N. Glenwood is **El Rancho Motel,** with the same owners and phone number as the Anvil. The small rooms here have older furnishings. Rooms with one bed cost $75 d; larger rooms with two beds are $105 for up to four people. Guests can use the Anvil Motel's jacuzzi. Moderate-Expensive.

Log Cabin Motels

Several local motels offer log cabin accommodations for a step back to the Old West while keeping such newer amenities as televisions and private baths.

Hitching Post Lodge, 460 E. Broadway, tel. (307) 733-2606 or (800) 821-8351, www.jacksonholenet.com/htchngp, is in a residential part of Jackson but within walking distance of downtown. The lovingly maintained cabins cluster around a central lodge built in 1931, and guests will appreciate the summertime outdoor pool and wintertime jacuzzi. A light breakfast is served in the lodge in winter. Cabins cost $78-136 s or d, while newer two-bedroom suites have kitchenettes and run $149-199 for up to four people. All units contain lodgepole beds, fridges, and microwaves. Moderate-Luxury.

Set amid tall cottonwood trees, **Wagon Wheel Village,** 435 N. Cache Dr., tel. (307) 733-2357 or

(800) 323-9279, www.wagonwheelvillage.com, has a number of well-maintained and cozy log cabins, along with log motel units. Rates are $87 s or $92-119 d, including access to two outside hot tubs. More luxurious are their modern log-style suites ($129 for four people), each with a fireplace, fridge, microwave, and small deck facing Flat Creek. Wagon Wheel Village is closed in April and November. Expensive-Premium.

Near a busy Jackson intersection, **Cowboy Village Log Cabin Resort,** 120 Flat Creek Dr., tel. (307) 733-3121 or (800) 962-4988, www.cowboyvillage.com, has 84 modern and jammed-together cabins with kitchenettes. Rates are $139 for up to three; $169 for up to six in two-bedroom units. Guests have access to two enclosed jacuzzis. Premium-Luxury.

Other places with log units include Sagebrush Motel, Hoback River Resort, and Kudar's Motel (described above), along with Antler Motel and Elk Country Inn (described below).

Costlier but Comfortable Lodging

Many Jackson motels fall in the $90-130 range, with pricing factors being location, type of room, quality of furnishings, and presence of amenities such as pools and hot tubs. A number of comfortable midrange motels are described below. These are not the corporate lodging giants, but they offer good value and down-home friendliness.

The rooms are a bit on the crowded side, but guests appreciate the friendly service and extra touches at **Sundance Inn,** 135 W. Broadway, tel. (307) 733-3444 or (888) 478-6326, www.sundanceinnjackson.com. The motel is close to Town Square and serves a light homemade breakfast plus evening cookies and lemonade. Guests can also use the outdoor jacuzzi (with alleyway ambience, alas). Standard rooms cost $79-99 s or d, while two-room suites are $139 d or $159 for four people. Moderate-Premium.

Rawhide Motel, 75 S. Millward, tel. (307) 733-1216 or (800) 835-2999, www.rawhidemotel.com, is a fine place with large rooms containing handmade lodgepole furniture. Rates are $88-108 s or $93-113 d. Expensive-Premium.

It's quite a distance from Jackson, but **Hatchet Motel,** tel. (307) 543-2413 or (877) 543-2413, www.hatchetmotel.com, has clean and friendly country accommodations in a great setting. The motel is in Buffalo Valley, 39 miles northeast of Jackson (eight miles east of Moran Junction) on US Hwy. 26/287, and is open year-round. Well-maintained rooms go for $90 s or d. A restaurant, general store, and gas station are also on the premises. Expensive.

Anglers Inn, 265 N. Millward St., tel. (307) 733-3682 or (800) 867-4667, www.anglersinn.net, has attractive rooms with Western fixtures, lodgepole beds and chairs, new carpets, and small baths. This cozy motel is right on Flat Creek, but just a couple of blocks from Town Square. Rates are $95-105 s or d, and the rooms contain fridges and microwaves. Expensive.

Antler Motel, 50 W. Pearl Ave., tel. (307) 733-2535 or (800) 522-2406, www.townsquareinns.com, is a large property with 100 recently remodeled rooms. Most contain two queen beds and cost $98 s or d, but also available are a dozen large family rooms/suites ($120 d) with three beds and space for up to 10 people. Some of these contain wood-burning fireplaces or jetted tubs. Rounding out the options here are some attractive Panabode log cabins starting at $88 d. All guests have access to an exercise room, sauna, and large indoor jacuzzi. Expensive-Premium.

One of the nicer moderately priced Jackson motels is **Wolf Moon Inn,** 285 N. Cache Dr., tel. (307) 733-2287 or (800) 964-2387, www.jak-biz.com/wolfmooninn. The clean and spacious rooms contain new furnishings, fridges, and ceiling fans. Rates are $85-95 s or d in standard rooms or $149 for six people in two-room suites. Expensive.

You'll find a quiet escape at **Western Motel,** 225 S. Glenwood, tel. (307) 733-3291 or (800) 845-7999, www.jak-biz.com/westernmotel. Standard rooms cost $99-109 for up to four people, and some have fridges and microwaves. Eight-person suites with two bedrooms, two baths, and a kitchen are $219. Also available is a two-bedroom house containing a fireplace and hot tub for $219. The motel has a seasonal outdoor pool. Expensive.

Buckrail Lodge, 110 E. Karns Ave., tel. (307) 733-2079, www.jacksonwy.com/buckrail, is in a quiet part of town six blocks from Town Square. The immaculate grounds include an outdoor jacuzzi, and the 12 motel rooms are all in faux-log-cabin style. The well-maintained rooms all have two queen beds and are decorated with Western-style furnishings. Rates are $100-110 d or $110-120 for four people. No phones in the rooms, and Buckrail is closed mid-October through April. Premium.

Elk Country Inn, 480 W. Pearl, tel. (307) 733-2364 or (800) 483-8667, www.townsquareinns.com, is popular with families and small groups of travelers. The spacious motel rooms (a bit old fashioned but nicely maintained) all have three beds and cost $112 for up to four people; add $6 for loft units that sleep six and include kitchenettes. Modern log cabins with kitchenettes and lodgepole furnishings go for $136 d. The inn also has a hot tub and ski-waxing room. Premium.

Top-end Accommodations

It should come as no surprise that tony Jackson Hole has a number of elaborate, pricey, and sumptuous places to stay, with rooms starting around $150 and hitting the stratosphere at more than $700 a night.

An excellent in-town choice is **Parkway Inn,** 125 N. Jackson St., tel. (307) 733-3143 or (800) 247-8390, www.parkwayinn.com. This midsize lodge has a delightful Victorian ambience with antique furniture and quilts in every room. The rooms are spacious and immaculate, and guests can also enjoy a small indoor lap pool, two jacuzzis, two saunas, and a big exercise gym. A light breakfast is served in the lobby each morning. Rates are $149 d for standard rooms with two queen beds or a king bed, or $174-184 d for two-room suites; $12 each for additional guests (maximum of four in a room). Premium-Luxury.

An excellent nine-room lodge just a few blocks from Town Square, **Inn on the Creek,** 295 N. Millwood, tel. (307) 739-1565 or (800) 669-9534, www.innonthecreek.com, has a peaceful location beside Flat Creek. Standard rooms ($169 s or d) feature designer furnishings, down comforters, and VCRs. The deluxe rooms ($209 s or d) also include balconies, fireplaces, and in-room jacuzzis. The gorgeous suite ($379) sleeps up to six and has a full kitchen, jacuzzi bath, and private patio. A light breakfast is served in the comfortable lounge, and all guests have access to the outdoor jacuzzi facing the creek. Luxury.

If you're looking for attractive accommodations in Teton Village instead of Jackson, your best bet is **Best Western Resort Hotel at Jackson Hole,** tel. (307) 733-3657 or (800) 445-4655, www.resorthotelatjh.com. The refurbished New West-style lobby is the primary focal point here, and the rooms continue the theme with attractive lamps, pine furniture, and prints. Facilities include a heated outdoor pool (open year-round), indoor and outdoor jacuzzis, a sauna, ski lockers, and concierge service. Be sure to check out the amusing bench out front. Rates are $169-199 s or d. Luxury.

A very attractive downtown lodging is **Davy Jackson Inn,** 85 Perry Ave., tel. (307) 739-2294 or (800) 584-0532, www.davyjackson.com, where the modern rooms come in a variety of styles, including some with old-fashioned clawfoot tubs.

Downtown's Wort Hotel, rebuilt after a disastrous fire, is better than ever.

Suites include steam showers, gas fireplaces, and king-size canopy beds. All guests are served a full breakfast and can relax in the outdoor hot tub. Rates are $179-229 s or d. Luxury.

Close to Town Square, the **Wort Hotel,** 50 N. Glenwood St., tel. (307) 733-2190 or (800) 322-2727, www.worthotel.com, has been a Jackson favorite since 1941 and is the only downtown hotel earning a four-diamond rating from AAA. A disastrous 1980 fire—started by a bird that built a nest too close to a neon sign—destroyed the roof and upper floor. The hotel was completely restored within a year, and today it's better than ever, with such modern amenities as a fitness center and two jacuzzis. The lobby, with its grand central staircase and stone fireplace with crackling fire, makes a fine place to meet friends. The SilverDollar Bar & Grille serves meals, or sidle up to the famous curving bar—inlaid with 2,032 uncirculated silver dollars from 1921. The hotel's spacious rooms are attractively decorated with a New West motif that includes lodgepole-pine beds, creative fixtures, and barbed-wire-patterned wallpaper. Rates are $194-210 d for standard rooms; junior suites cost $265, and luxury suites will set you back $450 d. Luxury.

Rusty Parrot Lodge, 175 N. Jackson, tel. (307) 733-2000 or (800) 458-2004, www.rustyparrot.com, offers outstanding lodging just two blocks from Town Square. The 31 rooms feature handcrafted furniture, original artwork, oversize tubs, and goose-down comforters; some also contain fireplaces and jacuzzi tubs. A gourmet breakfast (it's never the same) is served each morning in the luxurious dining room, and guests can relax in the jacuzzi on a deck overlooking Jackson, borrow a book from the library, or enjoy a massage, aromatherapy session, or facial from Body Sage Day Spa (extra charge). Rates are $250-275 s or d for standard rooms; $500 d for luxurious suites. No children under age 12. Luxury.

Some of the most dramatic vistas of the Tetons are from the luxurious **Spring Creek Ranch,** tel. (307) 733-8833 or (800) 443-6139, www.springcreekranch.com. Located on a thousand-acre estate, the resort sits high atop Gros Ventre Butte four miles west of Jackson and includes a wide range of lodging options. Hotel rooms are $250 s or d; suites, studios, and one-bedroom condos cost $295-375 s or d; while one- to three-bedroom condos are $475-1,200 and sleep four to six. Also available are executive homes that sleep eight and cost a mere $1,400 per night. All rooms contain fireplaces and lodgepole furnishings. Amenities at Spring Creek Ranch include a private pond, tennis courts, and an outdoor pool and jacuzzi. Luxury.

Teton Pines Resort & Country Club, tel. (307) 733-1005 or (800) 238-2223, www.tetonpines.com, is four miles south of Teton Village and features the amenities you'd expect in a year-round resort, including an 18-hole golf course, tennis center, and classy restaurant. The accommodations are varied, but all include a continental breakfast, access to the outdoor pool and jacuzzi, athletic-club privileges, concierge service, and airport shuttle. One-bedroom units (with separate his and hers baths) are $350 d, while two-bedroom and living-room suites cost $695 for four. Fully furnished three-bedroom townhouses sleep eight people and cost $895. Each townhouse has a kitchen, two decks, a fireplace, washer and dryer, and garage. Luxury.

Atop Gros Ventre Butte near Spring Creek Ranch is stunning **Amangani,** tel. (307) 734-7333 or (877) 734-7333, www.amanresorts.com, the only representative of Amanresorts in America. (Most of the company's other lavish resorts are in Southeast Asia.) Aman groupies and business travelers know to expect the utmost in luxury, and they will certainly not be disappointed here, starting with a knowledgeable DIB (dressed-in-black) staff and spare-no-expenses construction. The three-story sandstone-faced hotel contains 40 suites, each with a patined-metal fireplace, mountain-facing balcony, king-size bed, deep soaking tub (with a window view), minibar, and terrazzo dining table. Amangani's central lobby is particularly impressive, blending sandstone columns, redwood accents, custom furnishings, and soaring two-story windows. Outside, a whirlpool and heated 35-meter pool enjoy a remarkable view of the Tetons. Among other amenities are a complete health center (exercise facility, gym, steam rooms, yoga and meditation classes, and massage), a gourmet restaurant, and a lounge. Amangani's accommodations include suites ($550 d), deluxe suites ($650 d), and three luxury suites with two baths and spacious balconies ($750 d). Luxury.

Bed and Breakfasts

Jackson holds many fine B&Bs, where those who can afford it can relax in comfort at the homes of locals. Be sure to reserve space far ahead during the peak summer season, though you might get lucky at the last minute if someone cancels. **Jackson Hole Bed & Breakfast,** tel. (307) 734-1999 or (800) 542-2632, www.jacksonholebus.com, offers one-stop B&B shopping—call to make reservations at any of a dozen local B&Bs or to obtain the latest information on availability.

On the way to Teton Village, **Teton View B&B,** 2136 Coyote Loop, tel. (307) 733-7954, www.tetonview.com, features three guest rooms with shared or private baths for $99-120 s or d. Guests enjoy a full breakfast and a dramatic view of the Tetons from the outdoor jacuzzi. A five-night minimum stay is required in the winter months. Expensive-Premium.

Moose Meadows B&B, tel. (307) 733-9510, sits on five acres just east of Wilson. A major renovation in 1999 transformed this 4,200-square-foot ranch-style home into an elegant place to stay, with Teton vistas from the dining area, and a jacuzzi on the deck. There are five guest rooms (four with private bath), plus a barn and pasture for those who bring horses. A full breakfast is served each morning. Rates are $100-180 d, with a three-night minimum stay in the summer. Children are welcome. Expensive-Luxury.

You'll find outdoorsy owners at **Alpine House Country Inn,** 285 N. Glenwood, tel. (307) 739-1570 or (800) 753-1421, www.alpinehouse.com. Both Hans and Nancy Johnstone were skiers for U.S. Olympic teams. The modern timber-frame lodge is just two blocks from Jackson's Town Square. With an addition completed in 2000, Alpine House now has 21 guest rooms in two connected buildings. The buildings are bright and modern, accented by Swedish-style stenciling on the walls. All rooms have private baths and balconies, plus access to the jacuzzi. A healthy full breakfast is served, along with evening wine and cheese. Children are welcome. Rates are $130 s or d in the original rooms, and $160 s or d in the new building, which also features TVs, gas fireplaces, and jacuzzi tubs. Suites cost $265 d. Premium-Luxury.

For quiet close-to-downtown accommodations, another fine option is **The Huff House Inn,** 240 E. Deloney Ave., tel. (307) 733-4164, www.cruising-america.com/huff.html. Built in 1917, this was for many years the home of one of Jackson's first doctors, Charles Huff. Today it is a gracious place with a feminine sense of style. The five guest rooms ($133-174 s or d) are attractive, and all have private baths. Also available are four modern cottages with cathedral ceilings, king-size beds, sleeper-sofas, VCRs, and jacuzzi tubs. These go for $194 d. An outdoor jacuzzi is on the premises, and a creative full breakfast is served family-style each morning. Kids are welcome in the cottages. Premium-Luxury.

On the road to Teton Village, **The Painted Porch,** 3755 N. Moose-Wilson Rd., tel. (307) 733-1981, was built in 1901 in Idaho and moved here many years later. Located on three acres and surrounded by a white picket fence and tall aspen trees, this rambling red farmhouse contains four attractive guest rooms, each with its own personality—from frilly lace to cowboy culture. All also have private baths. Rates are $135-235 s or d, including a full breakfast. Children over age six are welcome, and a two-night minimum stay is required. Find them on the web at www.jacksonholenet.com/paintedporch. Premium-Luxury.

A personal favorite—it gets high marks from all who visit—is **Teton Treehouse B&B,** tel. (307) 733-3233, a gorgeous four-story hillside home in Wilson. This spacious open-beam B&B sits up 95 steps (needless to say, it's not accessible for disabled people) and contains six guest rooms with private baths. It really does offer the feeling of living in a treehouse, and it's a great place for birdwatchers. Decks provide impressive views across the valley below, and you can soak in the outdoor hot tub each evening and enjoy a healthy full breakfast each morning while the owners regale you with stories of Jackson Hole. Lodging costs $145-180 s or d. No young children, but kids age 10 and over are welcome. There's a four-night minimum stay in July and August. Find them on the web at www.cruising-america.com/tetontreehouse. Premium-Luxury.

Near the Aspens along the road to Teton Village, **The Sassy Moose Inn,** tel. (307) 733-1277 or (800) 356-1277, is a modest log house with five guest rooms, each with private bath, TV, and VCR. A full breakfast is served each morning, along with complimentary wine and fruit. An indoor jacuzzi is also available. Lodging rates are $149 s or d. Family rooms provide space for kids, and pets are welcome (a rarity for B&Bs). Get more information on the web at www.bbonline.com/wy/sassymoose. Premium.

Built in 1993, **Nowlin Creek Inn,** 660 E. Broadway, tel. (307) 733-0882 or (800) 533-0882, www.jackson-hole-lodging.com, has five spacious and brightly lit guest rooms for $160-195 d. All of these include private baths, and three also contain fireplaces. A full breakfast is served, and guests can use the jacuzzi in the small backyard. In addition, the inn has a 1920 two-bedroom log cabin with full kitchen and bath ($250 for up to six people; breakfast not included). From the front porch you can look across to the National Elk Refuge, but it's just six blocks to the center of Jackson. The Western decor—including a mix of old and new—reflects the owners' strong artistic sensibilities. A three-night minimum stay is required June-September. Children are welcome. Luxury.

A recommended place is **Wildflower Inn,** tel. (307) 733-4710, www.jacksonholenet.com/wildflower. This spacious log house sits on three acres of country land along Teton Village Rd. and contains five bright guest rooms. Four rooms have their own private decks, and all contain private baths and handcrafted lodgepole log beds. One of the rooms is actually a suite with a separate sitting room, jacuzzi tub, and gas fireplace. Wildflower's hot tub sits inside a plant-filled solarium. The owner/builders are an Exum climbing guide and a former ski instructor. Rates are $200 d ($280 d in the suite) including an earthy breakfast served family-style. Children are welcome. Luxury.

One of the most impressive local lodging options is **Bentwood B&B,** just north of the junction on the road to Teton Village, tel. (307) 739-1411. This 6,000-square-foot log home sits amid tall cottonwood trees and is a favorite place for weddings and receptions. The grand living room is centered around a three-story stone fireplace, and each of the five luxurious guest rooms has its own fireplace, deck or balcony, and jetted tub. The loft room is perfect for families. The interior is filled with Western styling and English antiques, not to mention gracious hosts and two gregarious dogs. Drinks and hors d'oeuvres are served each evening, and morning brings a creative breakfast. Rates are $235-325 s or d. Children are welcome in this very special place. Get the full scoop by visiting the website: www.bentwoodinn.com. Luxury.

Condominium Rentals

Condominiums provide one of the most popular lodging options for families and groups visiting Jackson Hole. These privately owned places are maintained by a number of local property-management companies and range from small studio apartments to spacious five-bedroom houses. All are completely furnished (including dishes) and have fireplaces, cable TV, phones, and midstay maid service. The nicest also include access to pools and jacuzzis and have balconies overlooking the spectacular Tetons. Many of the condominiums are in Teton Village (adjacent to the ski area) or just to the south in Teton Pines or the Aspens; others are scattered around Jackson Hole.

Condo prices vary widely, but during the winter holiday season, expect to pay $150-200 per night for studios (one or two people). Two-bedroom units (up to four people) cost $200-400 per night, and full four-bedroom condos (these sleep eight and also have a private jacuzzi and stone fireplace) are $700-800. The fanciest places at the base of the tram will set you back over $1,400 per night in the peak winter season! Summer and off-peak rates are 40-50% lower, with spring and fall rates 50-75% less than peak-season prices. In fall or spring, condos offer a real bargain for traveling families looking to stay several nights in the area. Minimum stays of between two and seven nights are required throughout the year.

If you have the luxury of time, do a little comparison shopping before renting a condo. Things to ask include whether you have access to a pool and jacuzzi, how close you are to the ski slopes, how frequent the maid service is, and whether the units include such amenities as VCRs and washing machines. Also be sure to find out what beds are in the rooms, since couples might not enjoy sleeping in twin bunk beds.

For condo rental information, including prices and available dates, you can go to www.jacksonholenet.com and click on lodging, which will give you connections to most of the larger condo companies. You can also contact the following rental companies directly:

Black Diamond Vacation Rentals, tel. (307) 733-6170 or (800) 325-8605, www.blackdiamondvrre.com

Ely & Associates, tel. (307) 733-8604 or (800) 735-8310, www.jackson-hole-vacations.com

Jackson Hole Lodge, tel. (307) 733-2992 or (800) 604-9404, www.jacksonholelodge.com

Jackson Hole Resort Lodging, tel. (307) 733-3990 or (800) 443-8613, www.jhresortlodging.com

Jackson Home Management, tel. (307) 739-3000 or (800) 739-3009, www.jhomemgmt.com

Mountain Property Management, tel. (307) 733-1684 or (800) 992-9948, www.jacksonholenet.com/mtnprop

MTA Resorts of Jackson Hole, tel. (307) 733-0613 or (800) 272-8824, www.mtaresorts.com

Rendezvous Mountain Rentals, tel. (307) 739-9050 or (800) 739-2565, www.rmrentals.com

Snow King Resort Condominiums, tel. (307) 733-5200 or (800) 522-5464, www.snowking.com.

The largest of these companies—and a good place to begin your search—is Jackson Hole Resort Lodging. Owned by Jackson Hole Mountain Resort, it manages 400 units, more than all the other companies combined. Among the largest of the other management companies on the list are Black Diamond Vacation Rentals, Jackson Hole Lodge, and Snow King Resort Condominiums. Additional condos are available at Spring Creek Ranch and at Teton Pines Resort & Country Club; see Top-end Accommodations, above.

Cabins

A number of Jackson Hole places offer log-cabin accommodations for a taste of old-time living. These small places are generally rented for several days or a week at a time and are favorites of families and groups. They may or may not have TVs and phones, and maid service may not be on a daily basis. See Log Cabin Motels above and Park Camping and Lodging in the Grand Teton National Park chapter for additional places with cabin-style accommodations in Jackson Hole.

Buffalo Valley Ranch, tel. (307) 543-2026 or (888) 543-2477, has six cabins with fine views of the Buffalo Valley and the Tetons. The cabins range from basic older units that share a bathhouse and cost $45 d, to modern log affairs with two bedrooms and kitchenettes that sleep six for $100. You'll find them next to Heart Six Ranch in Buffalo Valley, 45 miles northeast of Jackson. Buffalo Valley Ranch offers horseback rides in the summer. Inexpensive-Expensive.

Moulton Ranch on Historic Mormon Row, tel. (307) 733-3749, offers several cabins in one of Jackson Hole's most majestic locations. This is the only private property on Mormon Row inside Grand Teton National Park, and the much-photographed Moulton Barn—one of the prototypical Wyoming images—is just a few hundred feet away. The four cabins are cozy but not at all elaborate. Nevertheless, where else might you awake to a spectacular Teton vista with bison grazing outside your window? Rates start at just $50 for a two-person cabin with a separate bathhouse, up to $85 for a cabin that sleeps six and has a fridge and microwave. Inexpensive-Moderate.

Camp Creek Inn, 16 miles south of Jackson in quiet Hoback Canyon, tel. (307) 733-3099 or (877) 338-4868, www.camp-creek-inn.com, has nine A-frame cabins costing $75 for up to four people. No TVs or phones in the rooms, but a bar and restaurant are on the grounds. Camp Creek also offers horseback rides, pack trips, fishing trips, snowmobiling, and mountain-biking. Moderate.

Six miles south of Jackson along busy US Hwy. 89, **Old West Cabins,** tel. (307) 733-0333, has 14 modern log cabins with kitchenettes. The smallest one is $79 d, and the largest is a six-person cabin for $149. Moderate-Premium.

Snowking Inn, 35 Snow King Ave., tel. (307) 733-1007 or (800) 648-2602, www.snowkinginn.com, is a delightful and relaxing little place just six blocks from Town Square and right across from Snow King Resort. The two suites are nicely furnished and contain full kitchens and decks with barbecues. Rates are $95 d, including such amenities as CD players, a basket of fruit, and a fridge stocked with juices. Snowking Inn is open May-September. The proprietor also owns Jackson Hole Whitewater. Expensive.

Out in the quiet town of Kelly (12 miles northeast of Jackson), **Anne Kent Cabins,** tel. (307) 733-4773, offers rustic accommodations with an unbeatable view of the Tetons. These cabins are perfect for those who want a real taste of Wyoming from a family with a long local history. Two rental options are available. Your best bet is to request

The Anne Kent Cabins in Kelly offer great views of the Tetons and a taste of old-time Wyoming.

the very comfortable log house, which has bedrooms in the loft and basement, two baths, a complete kitchen, washer, and dryer. The home could sleep 10 people. Next door are two cabins that rent together. The front one (built in 1939) includes a bedroom and kitchen, while the back cabin contains a second bedroom plus bath. The Anne Kent Cabins feature handmade lodgepole furniture created by co-owner Ron Davler, who creates them next door at Jackson Hole Log & Rawhide Furniture. Rates for either the log house or cabins are $100 d, plus $25 per person for additional guests; kids free. Expensive.

Split Creek Ranch, tel. (307) 733-7522, www.splitcreekranch.com, is seven miles north of Jackson and right along the Snake River. The ranch covers 25 acres of land and is a good place to see elk, moose, and other animals. Nine rooms are available. Eight of these are attractive log motel-type units ($100-110 d; plus $8 for additional people), and one is a separate honeymoon cabin ($180 d) with a fireplace, full kitchen, and private jacuzzi. The other units contain either kitchenettes or microwaves and fridges. The ranch has a new barnlike building that contains a workout facility, jacuzzi, and sitting room with fireplace. Evening campfires are a favorite of guests, and other amenities include a stocked fishing pond, continental breakfasts, and chuck wagon barbecues in the summer. Split Creek Ranch is open all year; this is a good place for cross-country skiers in the winter. There's a two-night minimum stay. Expensive-Luxury.

Mad Dog Ranch Cabins, tel. (307) 733-3729 or (800) 992-2246, www.maddogranch.com, has nine modern duplex cottages along Teton Village Road. All cottages have two bedrooms, sleeping lofts, kitchens, and woodstoves. An outdoor jacuzzi is available year-round. The cabins start at $149 d and range up to $219 for six people. Premium.

You'll discover spectacular views of the Tetons from **Luton's Log Cabins,** 36 miles northeast of Jackson (five miles east of Moran Junction), tel. (307) 543-2489. The modern duplex cabins have full kitchens, private baths, and front porches facing the mountains. One-bedroom units cost $148 d or $158 for four people, and two-bedroom units are $230-260 for six people. They're open May-November. For more information, visit www.tetoncabins.com. Premium.

Budges' Slide Lake Cabins, tel. (307) 733-9061, www.jacksonholecabins.com, consists of four secluded but modern cabins along Slide Lake, six miles east of Kelly. Each has a woodstove, full kitchen, and phone. Rates are $215 d, plus $10 each for additional people. Luxury.

Home Rentals

Jackson Hole home rentals are available from **Absolute Heaven in the Tetons,** tel. (307) 733-4881; **Flying J Vacation Rentals,** tel. (307) 733-4245; **Harley Varley Lodge,** tel. (307) 733-7072 or (800) 342-0833; **Andrei Moskowitz Vacation Home,** tel. (212) 721-2280 or (800) 682-0180; and **Mountain Valley Properties,** tel.

(800) 993-0936, www.jacksonholenet.com/mvp.

Don't Fence Me Inn, tel. (307) 733-7979, is a 5,000-square-foot custom log home on six acres along Teton Village Road. The eight big bedrooms provide space for 20 people, but the $1,000-a-night price tag and three-night minimum stay will scare many folks off. The home is set back from the road, with a pond in the back and an active osprey nest nearby. Luxury.

Rancho Alegre Lodge, 3600 S. Park Loop Rd., tel. (307) 733-7988, www.ranchoalegre.com, offers Jackson's most expensive lodging. On a 50-acre spread facing the Tetons, this 10,000-square-foot structure houses seven bedrooms (each with its own TV, phone, feather bed, and fridge) and offers a hunting lodge decor and such amenities as a concierge, private chef (additional fee for meals), seven fireplaces, a jacuzzi, and pool table. Full house rentals are $2,000 per night with a two-night minimum stay. Up to 14 people can stay for this price, or, save money and rent it all month for only $40,000! At these prices, the lodge is primarily used for weddings, corporate retreats, large (and wealthy) families, and ski groups. In the off-season, individual suite rentals are available for $300-550 d per night. Luxury.

Guest Ranches

Jackson Hole is a natural place for dude ranches and is home to several of the best-known and most luxurious ones in the state. These are wonderful places for families looking to rough-it in style. A 15% gratuity is standard for the dude ranch staff and guides. In addition to the local places listed alphabetically below, many more guest ranches are just over Togwotee Pass in the Dubois area (see the Yellowstone Gateway Towns chapter) and to the south in the Pinedale area (see my *Wyoming Handbook*).

Built in 1927, **Crescent H Ranch,** tel. (307) 733-3674 or (888) 838-6671, www.crescenth.com, covers 1,300 acres south of Wilson. The ranch specializes in fishing packages ($6,200 for two people per week!) that include a fly-fishing school along with guided fishing trips. Also available are traditional ranch vacations with horseback riding, hiking, and fishing. These cost $4,900 for two people per week, all-inclusive. Meals at the Crescent H are a special treat, with gourmet food three times a day. The ranch has room for 25 guests in 10 cabins, and a seven-night minimum stay is required in midsummer.

Twelve miles east of Moran Junction in Buffalo Valley (43 miles northeast of Jackson), **Diamond D Ranch,** tel. (307) 543-2479 or (800) 233-6299, has modern cabins with great views of the Tetons. The ranch offers weekly stays June-Sept., with a variety of Western adventures, including horseback riding, kids' programs, hayrides, cookouts, fishing, overnight pack trips, and wildlife tours. All-inclusive weekly rates are $2,000 for two people. The ranch hosts a maximum of 36 people. In the fall, nightly rates are available at $100 d without meals. Get detailed information on the web at www.diamonddranch.com.

Looking for a wonderfully peaceful place to relax? Twenty miles up a dirt road in undeveloped Gros Ventre Valley (30 miles northeast of Jackson), **Goosewing Ranch,** tel. (307) 733-5251 or (888) 733-5251, is probably the most remote guest ranch in the Jackson Hole area. The well-appointed modern log cabins have fireplaces, private baths, and decks. Guests can use the outdoor jacuzzi all year and the outdoor heated pool in the summer. Popular summertime activities include horseback excursions, riding instruction, fishing, and hiking. All-inclusive weekly summertime rates are $2,960 for two people. There's a three-night minimum stay. When winter arrives, the ranch becomes a favorite destination for snowmobiling, with a variety of packages available. Get details on the ranch at www.goosewingranch.com.

Gros Ventre River Ranch, tel. (307) 733-4138, sits up undiscovered Gros Ventre River Valley, 18 miles northeast of Jackson near Slide Lake. This small ranch has accommodations for up to 34 guests in modern log cabins or a homestead house, and it serves delicious meals. The main activities are horseback riding, world-class fly-fishing, cookouts, canoeing, and mountain-biking. The lodge has a pool table, ping pong, and a large-screen television. A one-week minimum stay is required May-Oct., and weekly all-inclusive rates are $2,400-2,800 for two people. In the winter, the ranch becomes a base for cross-country skiing and snowmobiling, with four-person cabins costing $175 per night with a three-night minimum; no maid service or meals. Get details on the web at www.ranchweb.com/grosventre.

Heart Six Ranch, tel. (307) 543-2477 or (888) 543-2477, www.heartsix.com, is in Buffalo Valley, 12 miles east of Moran Junction (43 miles northeast of Jackson). It's a classic family dude ranch with log cabins, kids' programs, day trips to Yellowstone National Park and the Jackson Hole rodeo, and a range of evening activities including cookouts, nature programs, and country music. All-inclusive weekly rates are $2,500 for two people. The ranch takes in up to 50 guests at a time and is open year-round. Only weekly stays are available June-Aug., but at other times of the year the ranch offers nightly lodging for $50 s or $75 d, plus $25 if you want three meals a day. This is a favorite base for snowmobilers mid-December through March.

Wyoming's most elaborate—and expensive—guest ranch, **Lost Creek Ranch,** is 21 miles north of Jackson, tel. (307) 733-3435. This showplace resort emphasizes fitness, with a spa facility that includes exercise classes, a weight room, steam room, sauna, and jacuzzi, along with massage and facials (extra charge). Guests stay in modern duplex log cabins and enjoy gourmet meals in the main lodge's patio overlooking the Tetons. Amenities include such nontraditional items as a heated swimming pool, tennis courts, and a skeet range, in addition to more standard horseback riding, kids' programs, float trips, hiking, and fly-fishing. It's all a bit too Disneyesque for my tastes, and the prices are too Madison Avenue. Weekly all-inclusive rates are $5,240 for two people in a duplex cabin, or an astounding $12,064 for four people (even if two of these are children!) in a luxurious two-bedroom, two-bath cabin with a living room and fireplace. Some consider this a small price to pay for such pampering. The ranch hosts up to 60 guests at a time and is open late May to mid-October. A one-week minimum stay is required except after Labor Day, when it drops to a three-night minimum. Call for details or visit the place virtually at www.lostcreek.com.

You may get lucky and find a space at historic **Moose Head Ranch,** 13 miles north of Moose, tel. (307) 733-3141 in the summer, or (850) 877-1431 the rest of the year. This family ranch has space for 45 guests, and it receives so many repeat customers that it's almost always booked up. The ranch is entirely surrounded by Grand Teton National Park and features modern log cabins, horseback riding, private trout ponds, fly-fishing lessons, and excellent meals. There's a five-night minimum stay, and all-inclusive rates are $3,300 per week for two people. The ranch is open mid-June through August.

Another historic dude ranch is **R Lazy S Ranch,** 13 miles northeast of Jackson, tel. (307) 733-2655. The ranch has space for 45 guests who enjoy horseback rides, fishing, and other Western adventures. Tykes under age seven are not allowed, but older kids can take advantage of a special program just for them. A one-week minimum stay is required. All-inclusive rates are $2,114-2,870 for two people per week, and the ranch is open mid-June through September. For additional information, look on the web at www.rlazys.com.

Located along the rolling Gros Ventre River, **Red Rock Ranch,** tel. (307) 733-6288, faces spectacular orange-red badlands. The ranch is 32 miles northeast of Jackson, and the quiet location and drop-dead scenery are reason enough to stay here. Guests settle into comfortable log cabins with woodstoves, and they can take part in horseback riding, cattle drives, cookouts, and other activities. The ranch also features kids' programs, a fishing pond, swimming pool, and jacuzzi. There's space for a maximum of 30 guests, and a six-night minimum stay is required. Open June to mid-October. All-inclusive rates are $2,280 for two people for six nights. For more information, log onto the web at www.redrockranch.com.

Spotted Horse Ranch, tel. (307) 733-2097 or (800) 528-2084, lies on the banks of the Hoback River, 16 miles south of Jackson. The ranch exudes a comfortable rusticity; the main lodge and cabins contain lodgepole furniture, and guests stay in log cabins with modern conveniences. Activities include horseback riding (some Appaloosas), fly-fishing, and cookouts, and you can unwind in the jacuzzi or sauna. All-inclusive weekly rates are $2,680 for two people. A three-night minimum stay is required. For more details, stop by the website: www.spottedhorseranch.com.

At the base of the mountains in Wilson, **Trail Creek Ranch,** tel. (307) 733-2610, is an old-time 300-acre dude ranch with space for 25 guests. They specialize in horseback riding (of course), but also offer hiking, fishing, weekly cookouts, and a swimming pool. A one-week minimum stay is standard, and all-inclusive rates are $2,800 for two people per week. The ranch is open mid-June to Labor Day.

Located within Grand Teton National Park, 25 miles north of Jackson, **Triangle X Guest Ranch,** tel. (307) 733-2183, www.trianglex.com, is a classic family-oriented ranch with stunning Teton views. The ranch has been in the Turner family for more than six decades. Activities center around horseback riding, but also include kids' programs and nightly events such as Dutch-oven cookouts, naturalist presentations, square dancing, and campfire sing-alongs. All-inclusive weekly rates are $1,145 for two people. The ranch is open May-Oct. and Jan.-March. In the winter months Triangle X goes upscale, with fewer guests (maximum of 35 versus 80 in the summer), a jacuzzi, and three gourmet meals a day. The nightly winter rate is $200 d, including lodging, meals, and use of cross-country skis and snowshoes. There's a two-night minimum stay in winter and a one-week minimum stay in summer.

A longtime favorite—it began taking guests in the 1920s—is **Turpin Meadows Guest Ranch,** tel. (307) 543-2496 or (800) 743-2496, www.turpinmeadow.com. The ranch's Buffalo Valley location provides impressive Teton vistas, along with all the traditional ranch activities: horseback riding, cookouts, and pack trips. Turpin Meadows also has special kids' activities two days a week, as well as weekly natural history programs by Forest Service naturalists. Guests stay in modern cabins and have access to an indoor jacuzzi. Summertime all-inclusive rates are $252/day for two people, with a three-night minimum stay. The ranch is open year-round and is a favorite snowmobile spot in the winter months.

Mountain Resorts

Two noteworthy mountain resorts are east of Moran Junction off US Hwy. 26/287. At Togwotee Pass (9,658 feet) the highway tops the Continental Divide and then slides eastward towards Dubois and the Wind River Valley. The Togwotee Pass area is famous for luxuriously deep snow all winter and is a destination for snowmobilers, cross-country skiers, and dogsledding enthusiasts. Just north of the pass is Teton Wilderness, a place to discover what solitude means. Facing west from the pass, the Teton Range offers up a jagged horizon line. This entire area provides a delicious escape from hectic Jackson and is home to two attractive high-elevation resorts: Cowboy Village Resort at Togwotee and Brooks Lake Lodge. Additional Togwotee Pass resorts and dude ranches east of these are described in the Dubois section of the Yellowstone Gateway Towns chapter.

Forty-eight miles northeast of Jackson and just a few miles west of Togwotee Pass is **Cowboy Village Resort at Togwotee,** tel. (307) 733-8800 or (800) 543-2847, a pleasantly rustic place to spend a night or a week. The resort is a busy place, offering horseback rides, mountain-bike tours, fly-fishing, and backcountry pack trips in summer, along with snowmobiling (the primary winter activity), dogsledding, and cross-country skiing when the snow flies. Togwotee has a variety of accommodations, and guests will enjoy summertime naturalist programs, plus a sauna and four large jacuzzis. Summer rates are $109 d for rooms in the lodge, $129 d for mini-suites, and $159 d for cabins. The mini-suites and cabins sleep up to six people ($8 per person for more than two). In winter, the resort has package deals that include lodging, breakfast and dinner, snowmobile use, a guide, and free airport shuttle. There's a four-night minimum stay in the winter. The resort also houses a steak house, bar, gas station, and convenience store. Togwotee is closed from early April to early June, and from mid-October to mid-November. Get details on the web at www.cowboyvillage.com.

Brooks Lake Lodge, tel. (307) 455-2121, www.brookslake.com, has what may be the finest location of any lodge in Wyoming, with a placid lake in front and the cliffs of Pinnacle Buttes nearby. Built in 1922, the lodge has long served travelers en route to Yellowstone, and its enormous great hall contains big-game trophies from all over the world. The lodge was completely restored in the late 1980s and is now on the National Register of Historic Places. Six guest rooms are available in the main lodge, and six private cabins are hidden in the trees; all are furnished with handmade lodgepole furniture. Guests can ease into the jacuzzi or put on hiking or cowboy boots to explore the magnificent country nearby. The turnoff for Brooks Lake Lodge is 65 miles northeast of Jackson (34 miles east of Moran Junction or 23 miles west of

JACKSON HOLE/GRAND TETON PUBLIC CAMPGROUNDS

The following public campgrounds are available on a first-come basis with no reservations. They are listed by distance and direction from Jackson. Get details for each by calling Bridger-Teton National Forest (BTNF; tel. 307-739-5400), Grand Teton National Park (GTNP; tel. 307-739-3603), or Targhee National Forest (TNF; tel. 208-354-2312). See the text for private RV campgrounds in the area.

CAMPGROUNDS NORTH OF JACKSON

Curtis Canyon Campground; $10, BTNF; seven miles northeast of Jackson, open early June to mid-Sept., six miles of gravel road with fine view of the Tetons

Gros Ventre Campground; $12, GTNP; 10 miles northeast of Jackson, open May to early Oct., along Gros Ventre River, often fills by evening in mid-summer

Atherton Creek Campground; $10, BTNF; 18 miles northeast of Jackson, open early June-Oct., six miles up Gros Ventre Road near Gros Ventre River

Jenny Lake Campground; $12, GTNP; 20 miles north of Jackson, open mid-May to late Sept., tents only (no RVs), campground fills by 8 a.m. in mid-summer

Red Hills Campground; $8, BTNF; 22 miles northeast of Jackson, open early June-Oct., 12 miles up Gros Ventre Road (partly dirt) along Gros Ventre River

Crystal Creek Campground; $8, BTNF; 23 miles northeast of Jackson, open early June-Oct., five miles up Gros Ventre Road (dirt) along Gros Ventre River

Signal Mountain Campground; $12, GTNP; 32 miles north of Jackson, open early May to mid-Oct., on Jackson Lake, dump station, campground fills by 10 a.m. in mid-summer

Colter Bay Campground; $12, GTNP; 40 miles north of Jackson, open mid-May to late Sept., on Jackson Lake, coin-operated showers, dump station, campground fills by noon in mid-summer

Hatchet Campground; $10, BTNF; 40 miles northeast of Jackson, open late June to mid-Sept., in Buffalo Valley

Blackrock Bicycle Campground; free, BTNF; 40 miles northeast of Jackson, open mid-June to early Sept., bikes only, three miles off Hwy. 26/287 in Buffalo Valley, no potable water

Box Creek Campground; free, BTNF; 46 miles northeast of Jackson, open June-Sept., on Buffalo Valley Road, no potable water

Pacific Creek Campground; free, BTNF; 46 miles north of Jackson, open June to early Sept., 12 miles up Pacific Creek Road (enter through Grand Teton National Park)

Lizard Creek Campground; $12, GTNP; 48 miles north of Jackson, open early June to early Sept., on Jackson Lake, campground fills by 2 p.m. in mid-summer

Turpin Meadow Campground; $10, BTNF; 48 miles northeast of Jackson, open June to early Sept., in Buffalo Valley

Sheffield Creek Campground; free, BTNF; 55 miles north of Jackson, open mid-June to mid-Nov., small site off Hwy. 89/191/287 near Flagg Ranch Resort, poor road access until late summer

CAMPGROUNDS SOUTH OF JACKSON

Cabin Creek Campground; $12, BTNF; 19 miles south of Jackson, open late May to mid-Sept., along Snake River Canyon

Elbow Campground; $15, BTNF; 22 miles south of Jackson, open mid-June to mid-Oct., along Snake River Canyon, may be closed in 2000 due to highway construction

Hoback Campground; $12, BTNF; 22 miles southeast of Jackson, open early June to mid-Sept., along Hoback River eight miles east of Hoback Junction

East Table Creek Campground; $15, BTNF; 24 miles south of Jackson, open early June to mid-Oct., along Snake River, road construction may be nearby

Station Creek Campground; $15, BTNF; 25 miles south of Jackson, open mid-June to mid-Oct., along Snake River Canyon, road construction may be nearby

Kozy Campground; $10, BTNF; 30 miles southeast of Jackson, open early June to mid-Sept., along Hoback River 13 miles east of Hoback Junction

Granite Creek Campground; $12, BTNF; 35 miles southeast of Jackson, open late June to mid-Sept., near Granite Hot Springs, nine miles up Granite Creek Road (gravel), reservable only over 4th of July by calling (307) 734-7400

CAMPGROUNDS WEST OF JACKSON

Trail Creek Campground; $6, TNF; 20 miles west of Jackson, open mid-June to mid-Sept., on the west side of Teton Pass

Mike Harris Campground; $6, TNF; 21 miles west of Jackson, open mid-June to mid-Sept., on the west side of Teton Pass

Dubois) and another five miles off the highway via Brooks Lake Road. The lodge is open July-Sept. and late December to March. There's a three-night minimum stay in summer, when the rates are $390 d per day in the lodge or $430 d per day in the cabins. This includes all meals, horseback riding, canoeing, and fishing. Weekly rates are also available, but be sure to reserve far ahead. In winter Brooks Lake Lodge is a popular cross-country skiing and snowmobiling spot. Overnight winter accommodations are $300 d per night in the lodge or $350 d per night in the cabins, including breakfast, dinner, and use of skis. Couples can stay here midweek for $525-625 for two nights, including meals. Snowmobile rentals are available. The restaurant is open to the public for lunch in the winter months, but reservations are mandatory; call a week ahead to reserve a table.

CAMPING

Public Campgrounds

Both the National Park Service and the U.S. Forest Service maintain campgrounds around Jackson Hole. The Jackson Hole/Grand Teton Public Campgrounds chart shows 24 public campgrounds within 50 miles of Jackson. For more specifics on public sites, contact Bridger-Teton National Forest in Jackson at 340 N. Cache Dr., tel. (307) 739-5500, www.fs.fed.us/btnf, or Grand Teton National Park in Moose, tel. (307) 739-3603, www.nps.gov/grte. In addition to these sites, many people camp for free on dispersed sites on Forest Service lands; see the Forest Service for locations and restrictions.

RV Parks

Jackson has a number of RV parks scattered around town and in surrounding areas. Additional privately run campgrounds are located at Colter Bay and Flagg Ranch Resort inside Grand Teton National Park. For details on these, see Park Camping and Lodging in the Grand Teton National Park chapter.

None of the private RV parks in the town of Jackson is really noteworthy; "parking lots" would be a better term. They can also be surprisingly expensive—some places charge more for a tent space than it would cost to stay in a motel room in many Wyoming towns! Even more expensive is a ticket for parking RVs overnight on Jackson city streets. It's illegal to do so, and the ordinance is strictly enforced by local police.

Virginian RV Park, 750 W. Broadway, tel. (307) 733-7189 or (800) 321-6982 (summer) or (800) 262-4999 (winter), is the biggest RV parking lot in the area, with over 100 sites on the south end of town. Full hookups costs $34-42; no tents. Guests at the RV park can use the Virginian Lodge's outdoor pool and jacuzzi. It's open May to mid-October. Find the park and lodge on the web at www.virginianlodge.com.

Elk Country Inn, 480 W. Pearl, tel. (307) 733-2364 or (800) 483-8667, www.townsquareinns.com, has a cluster of graveled RV sites for $35, but tents are not allowed; open all year.

Wagon Wheel RV Park & Campground, 525 N. Cache, tel. (307) 733-4588, www.wagonwheelvillage.com, is along Flat Creek on the north end of town. Located behind the motel of the same name, it has both RV hookups ($32) and grassy tent spaces ($15) and is open May-September.

Teton Village KOA, tel. (307) 733-5354 or (800) 562-9043, www.koa.com, is five miles south of Teton Village and six miles from Jackson. The location is out of the way and quiet, with trees providing shade (lacking in other local RV parks). Full RV hookups cost $36, tent sites are $26, and basic camping cabins run $43 d. Also here are a game room and playground. It's open May to mid-October.

Grand Teton Park RV Park is 37 miles northeast of Jackson (six miles east of Moran Junction) along Hwy. 26/287, tel. (307) 733-1980 or (800) 563-6469, www.yellowstonerv.com. There are good views of the Tetons, and facilities include a hot tub, recreation room, and grocery store. The cost is $36 for RVs, $25 for tents. Simple camping cabins go for $44-48, and tepees run $35-39. Open year-round.

Three private campgrounds are in the Hoback Junction area, 12 miles south of Jackson. **Lazy J Corral,** tel. (307) 733-1554, is right on the highway at Hoback Junction and has RV sites for $20; no tent spaces. Open May-October. **Snake River Park KOA,** tel. (307) 733-7078 or (800) 562-1878, www.koa.com, is a mile north of Hoback Junction and has RV spaces for $36, tent sites for $27, and simple "kamping kabins" for $45 d. Open April to mid-October.

Lone Eagle Resort Campground, four miles southeast of Hoback Junction, tel. (307) 733-1090 or (800) 321-3800, www.loneeagleresort.com, sits on 20 acres of land and has a range of amenities including an outdoor pool, hot tub, playground, and game room, along with river trips (extra charge) and bike rentals. Full-hookup RV sites cost $36, and tent sites are $10; open mid-May through September. They also rent tent cabins for $29 and basic log cabins for $67.

FOOD

Jackson stands out from the rest of Wyoming on the culinary scene: chicken-fried steak may be available, but it certainly isn't the house specialty! You won't need to look far to find good food; in fact, the town seems to overflow with impressive (and even more impressively priced) eateries. If you stood in Town Square and walked in any direction for a block you would find at least one restaurant that would be a standout in any other Wyoming town. More than 70 local restaurants do business here—in a town that contains just 8,000 people. To get an idea of what to expect at local restaurants, pick up a copy of the free ***Jackson Hole Dining Guide*** at the visitor center or local restaurants. You'll find the same info online at www.focusproductions.com/jhdining. The guide includes sample menus and brief descriptions of most local establishments. If you don't find a place to your liking among those listed in the dining guide or below, be assured that all the major fast-food outlets line Jackson's streets, ready to grease your digestive tract. And if you just want to eat in, call **Mountain Express,** tel. (307) 734-0123, which will deliver meals from a dozen local restaurants to your motel room in Jackson or Teton Village.

Breakfast

The best breakfast place in Jackson isn't in Jackson, but in Wilson, where **Nora's Fish Creek Inn,** tel. (307) 733-8288, www.jacksonholenet.com/noras, attracts a full house each morning. The food is great, the atmosphere is authentically rustic, and the waitresses are always friendly and fast. Nora's also serves tried-and-true lunches and dinners at very good prices. Highly recommended, but you may have to contend with a smoky atmosphere at the counter in the morning.

Very popular for breakfast and lunch is **Jedediah's House of Sourdough,** 135 E. Broadway, tel. (307) 733-5671, where, as the name implies, sourdough pancakes are the morning specialty. Housed in a 1910 log cabin, the restaurant gets noisy and crowded in the morning, making it perfect for families with young kids. The lunch menu stars burgers, sandwiches, and salads.

Another longtime breakfast and lunch standout is **The Bunnery,** 130 N. Cache Dr., tel. (307) 733-5474. Good omelets, and delicious lunch sandwiches on freshly baked breads.

The old-time crowd heads to **LeJay's Sportsman's Cafe,** 72 S. Glenwood St., tel. (307) 733-3110, a greasy spoon open 24 hours a day. This is the place to go when no other restaurant is open and your stomach is demanding all-American grub. But be ready for clouds of cigarette smoke. Other local breakfast places are listed below under Espresso and Light Meals.

Lunch

One of the most popular noontime spots in Jackson is **Sweetwater Restaurant,** 85 King St., tel. (307) 733-3553, where the lunch menu includes dependably good salads, homemade soups, and a variety of earthy sandwiches. For dinner, try mesquite-grilled chicken or the spinach-and-feta vegetarian casserole. Dinner entrées $16-20. Recommended.

Pearl Street Bagels, 145 Pearl St., tel. (307) 739-1218, serves home-baked bagels (they're on the small side, however) along with espresso and juices. Open daily till 6 p.m. in the summer. They have a second shop in Wilson, tel. (307) 739-1261. The latter is *the* groovy place to be seen in Wilson (OK, so are Nora's and the 'Coach).

Get delicious sub sandwiches on tangy homemade bread at **New York City Sub Shop,** 25 S. Glenwood St., tel. (307) 733-4414. Fastest sandwich makers in the business and vastly better than Subway.

If you're in search of a substantial vegetarian breakfast or lunch, try the cafe at **Harvest Natural Foods,** 130 W. Broadway, tel. (307) 733-5418. The salad-and-soup bar in the back is a favorite lunch break for locals. Great sandwiches, fruit smoothies, and baked goods, too. You won't go wrong here.

Established in 1912 and in the same place since 1937, **Jackson Drug,** right off Town Square at 15 E. Deloney Ave., tel. (307) 733-2442, has an always-crowded soda fountain that serves homemade ice cream and shakes.

For lunches in the Teton Village area, stop by **Westside Store & Deli,** tel. (307) 733-6202, located in the Aspens. The deli will be glad to pack you a big picnic lunch, and it also sells such dinner entrées as lemon dijon chicken, lasagna, and ribs.

Espresso and Light Meals

The hip crowd heads for breakfast and lunch to two excellent local cafes: Betty Rock and Shades. **Betty Rock Cafe and Coffeehouse,** 325 W. Pearl, tel. (307) 733-0747, is a great and noisy place for lunch, with delectable homemade breads, paninis, salads, soups, and espresso. Highly recommended. You'll find similar food and service at the oft-crowded **Shades Cafe,** 82 S. King St., tel. (307) 733-2015. This tiny log cabin has a shady summer-only patio on the side. Breakfasts feature waffles, egg dishes, fruit, and yogurt, plus lattes, mochas, and other coffee drinks. At lunch, the standouts are salads, quiches, burritos, and paninis. Shades is a relaxing place to hang out with the latte habitués, though it does close early in the fall, winter, and spring.

Out in Teton Village across from the tram, **Village Cafe,** tel. (307) 733-5998, serves very good breakfasts, baked goods, sandwiches, lasagna, burritos, Starbucks espresso, and microbrewed beer. Open summers and winters only.

The National Museum of Wildlife Art, two miles north of Jackson on US Hwy. 26/89, houses a delightfully bright little restaurant with dramatic vistas across the National Elk Refuge. Called **Rising Sage Cafe,** tel. (307) 733-8649, the place has a lunch menu that includes panini, pita and hummus, homemade soups served in a bread bowl, salads, and espresso. It's open the same hours as the museum. **Charlie's Jackson Hole Coffee Company,** 49 W. Broadway (upstairs in Pink Garter Plaza), tel. (307) 733-9192 or (800) 771-9192, has espresso and sweets, along with a computer terminal for Internet access.

American

The most popular locals' eatery is **Bubba's Bar-B-Que Restaurant,** 515 W. Broadway, tel. (307) 733-2288. Each evening the parking lot out front is jammed with folks waiting patiently for a chance to gnaw on barbecued spare ribs, savor the spicy chicken wings, or fill up at the salad bar. Lunch is a real bargain, with specials under $5. They don't serve alcohol, but you can bring in your own beer or wine. Although based in Jackson, Bubba's now has restaurants in five other locations around Wyoming, Colorado, and Idaho.

Get great all-American burgers at the '50s-style **Billy's Burgers,** 55 N. Cache Dr., tel. (307) 733-3279. This is the same location as the more upscale Cadillac Grille. The Billy burger is a half-pound monster. Not on the menu, but recommended if you aren't absolutely famished, is the one-third-pound Betty burger. Ask for it.

Next door to Billy's and the Cadillac is the **Million Dollar Cowboy Steakhouse,** tel. (307) 733-4790, with "casual Western elegance" and great steaks, from porterhouse to filet mignon.

In addition, the menu includes salads, rack of lamb, seafood, pasta, and vegetarian specials. The bar features a dozen different single malt scotches. Also popular is **Gun Barrel Steakhouse,** 862 W. Broadway, tel. (307) 733-3287, www.gunbarrel.com, where the mesquite-grilled steaks, elk, and buffalo are served up in a hunting-lodge atmosphere with trophy game mounts; they came from a wildlife museum that previously occupied the site. You'll find lots of historic guns and other Old West paraphernalia around the Gun Barrel too, making this an interesting place to explore even if you aren't hungry. It's a bit on the pricey side, with dinner entrées for $15-25. The bar has a wide choice of beers on tap.

Head three miles south of town on US Hwy. 89 to find some of the finest steaks in Jackson Hole at the **Steak Pub,** tel. (307) 733-6977. Diners are served in a rustic log-cabin setting. Another recommended place is **Camp Creek Inn,** 16 miles south of Jackson in Hoback Canyon, tel. (307) 733-3099 or (800) 228-8460. The cozy fireplace and rustic setting make this a good place to escape the Jackson Hole crowds. Very good steaks and prime rib, and "no mercy" one-pound burgers enough to fill even Rush Limbaugh's lardbelly.

Housed within the classic Wort Hotel at 50 N. Glenwood St., **Silver Dollar Bar & Grill,** tel. (307) 733-2190, serves surprising and delicious dinners, including fresh Rocky Mountain trout, buffalo T-bones, and peppercorn-encrusted elk chops. Very good Caesar salads too. The bar next door is a fun place for an after-dinner drink.

Horse Creek Station, 10 miles south of Jackson, tel. (307) 733-0810, serves delicious smokehouse meats including pork chops, baby back ribs, chicken, prime rib, and brisket in a casual Old West atmosphere with stuffed animal heads on the walls. A very popular place with both locals and ski bums is the **Mangy Moose** in Teton Village, tel. (307) 733-4913, where you'll find a big salad bar and fair prices on steak, pasta, chicken, and seafood (dinner entrées $11-23). Downstairs is Rainbow Cafe, offering inexpensive burgers, pizza, sandwiches, corned-beef-hash omelets, and other breakfast and lunch fare.

Get chicken atchaflaya, seafood gumbo, crawfish and shrimp étouffée, fried catfish, and other Cajun specialties at **The Acadian House,** 180 N. Millward, tel. (307) 739-1269. Not everything here is Cajun; they also serve such diverse entrées as mahimahi and Thai curry vegetable sauté.

Wilson's **Stagecoach Bar,** tel. (307) 733-4407, makes delicious nachos, burgers, and other pub grub.

Pasta and Pizza

One of the tried-and-true local eateries is **Anthony's Italian Restaurant,** 62 S. Glenwood St., tel. (307) 733-3717. In business since 1977, Anthony's has built a reputation for simple food (a bit heavy for some tastes) and attentive, efficient service. Prices are very reasonable, and vegetarians will find several good menu items.

Billy's Burgers, home of the half-pound Billy burger

Dinners come with homemade soup, salad, and fresh-baked garlic bread—guaranteed to fill you up and then some.

Hidden away on the north end of town, **Nani's Genuine Pasta House,** 242 N. Glenwood, tel. (307) 733-3888, www.nanis.com, is Jackson's gourmet Italian restaurant. Meals are served in a charming little home with an old-country ambience and friendly service. Prices are surprisingly reasonable, with most entrées for $10-17. Many vegan dishes are also available. Be sure to ask about the nightly specials.

Several pizza places stand out in Jackson. You'll find **Calico Italian Restaurant & Bar,** tel. (307) 733-2460, in a garish red and white building three-quarters of a mile north on Teton Village Road. The menu has gone a bit upscale of late, but prices are still reasonable, with entrées for $8-17. During the summer, be sure to get a side salad, fresh from the big house garden; kids will love the two-and-a-half-acre lawn. The bar at Calico is a very popular locals' watering hole. **Mountain High Pizza Pie,** 120 W. Broadway, tel. (307) 733-3646, is a favorite downtown place offering free delivery in Jackson. From mid-October through April, Mountain High's under-$7 stuff-yourself lunchtime pizza buffet (Mon.-Fri. 11:30 a.m.-2 p.m.) is the best meal deal in Jackson. See Breweries below for two other notable pizza places in Jackson Hole.

Continental/Nouvelle Cuisine

If you want fine continental dining and aren't scared off by entrées costing $20 or more, Jackson has much to offer.

Just off Town Square, **Snake River Grill,** upstairs at 84 E. Broadway, tel. (307) 733-0557, is one of Jackson's finest gourmet restaurants—with prices to match (entrées $16-29). The meals are exquisite, and the seasonal menu typically contains a variety of seafood, free-range beef, and organic vegetables that are artfully presented. A few outside tables face the square. Reservations are a must; reserve a week in advance for prime-time seatings in the summer. Snake River Grill is a good place to watch for Jackson's best-known resident, Harrison Ford. Closed November and April.

The Range, 225 N. Cache Dr., tel. (307) 733-5481, serves acclaimed nouvelle-cuisine dinners, making this a favorite of out-on-the-town locals and visitors. The menu varies seasonally, the sauces are delectable, and there are always nightly fish and game specialties. Entrées are $16-27.

For views so spectacular they make it difficult to concentrate on your meal, don't miss **The Granary,** tel. (307) 733-8833, located atop East Gros Ventre Butte west of Jackson. This is also a very popular place for evening cocktails, and the Sunday brunch here is the best around. Dinner entrées run $15-28.

An excellent in-town continental restaurant is **The Blue Lion,** 160 N. Millward St., tel. (307) 733-3912. The front patio makes for delightful summertime dining. Try the Southwestern tempeh crepes or Sicilian chicken. Jackson's most popular nouvelle-cuisine restaurant is **Cadillac Grille,** 55 N. Cache (on the square), tel. (307) 733-3279. The food is artfully prepared and includes a changing menu of seafood, grilled meats, and game. The art-deco decor of the Cadillac helps make it one of the most crowded tourist hangouts in town. Portions tend toward the small side.

Jenny Lake Lodge, inside Grand Teton National Park, is famous for gourmet American cuisine served in an elegantly cozy log lodge. The Sunday dinner buffet is legendary. Open June-Sept. only; call (307) 733-4647 for reservations (required).

Restaurant Terroir, 45 S. Glenwood, tel. (307) 739-2500, is an exquisite little place with a handful of tables and a classy white-linen setting. The menu blends American, Asian, and French influences to create a memorable meal. Entrées are $18-20. The wine list is one of the best in Jackson, with over 200 choices. This isn't a place to bring the kids, but it's fine for a special romantic meal. Open for dinners only; call for reservations (highly recommended).

Inside the ultraluxurious Amangani Resort atop Gros Ventre Butte, **Amangani Grill,** tel. (307) 734-7333 or (877) 734-7333, is open to the public for three meals a day, with a menu that changes frequently. Reservations are advised, and this is decidedly *not* a place for T-shirts or shorts. Dinner entrées are typically $24-32.

Out in the Aspens on Teton Village Rd., **Stiegler's,** tel. (307) 733-1071, has a menu with names big enough to eat—you could start with leberknödel suppe, before a main course of veal sweetbreads forestiere, followed by a topfen palatschinken. The dense Austrian cuisine is outstanding, but the portions are small.

If you enjoy German cooking, particularly veal, lamb, and game, head to the **Alpenhof,** tel. (307) 733-3462, in Teton Village. The **Alpenhof Bistro** upstairs has a more casual setting and a less-expensive dinner menu. People come to the bistro for balcony dining with a close-up view of Teton Village.

South of the Border

For the fastest Mexican food in town (with the possible exception of Taco Bell), drop by **Sanchez Mexican Food,** 75 S. Glenwood, tel. (307) 732-2326, where burritos, tacos, and enchiladas are all under $7. They also have a few seats inside and picnic tables out front. **The Merry Piglets,** 160 N. Cache Dr., tel. (307) 733-2966, is an unpretentious little spot with very good Mexican meals, including the specialty, the cheese crisp. Excellent margaritas too. The restaurant has been here for over three decades.

Mama Inez, 380 W. Pearl, tel. (307) 739-9166, has fill-you-up servings of authentic Mexican cooking, including chimichangas, fajitas, and enchiladas. The largest and most popular Mexican restaurant is **Vista Grande,** tel. (307) 733-6964, on the road to Teton Village. The biggest drawing cards here are the pitchers of margaritas; the food itself is reasonably priced but nothing special.

Asian Food

Chinatown Restaurant, 850 W. Broadway, tel. (307) 733-8856, makes good Chinese dishes—particularly the mu shu vegetables, lemon chicken, and pot stickers—and offers bargain-priced lunch specials. Busy **Lame Duck Chinese Restaurant,** 600 E. Broadway, tel. (307) 733-4311, serves a mix of Asian specialties, including Chinese, Japanese, and even a few Thai specialties. The food is less traditional than Chinatown's. Service can be slow. Get freshly rolled sushi at **Masa Sushi,** tel. (307) 733-2311, located at the Inn at Jackson Hole in Teton Village. Hint to anyone who knows a Thai restaurant owner anywhere in America (or Thailand for that matter): tell them to move to Jackson where people are dying for good Thai food. It never ceases to amaze me that the town has no Thai restaurants.

Breweries

Before Prohibition in 1920, nearly every town in Wyoming had its own brewery, making such local favorites as Hillcrest, Schoenhofen, and Sweetwater. After repeal of "the noble experiment," breweries again popped up, but competition from industrial giants such as Anheuser-Busch and Coors forced the last Wyoming operation—Sheridan Brewing—out of business in 1954. It was another 34 years before commercial beermaking returned. In 1988, Charlie Otto started a tiny backyard operation in Wilson. His **Otto Brothers Brewing Company,** tel. (307) 733-9000, www.ottobrothers.com, now brews its beer just over Teton Pass in Victor, Idaho, but you can sample Teton Ale, Old Faithful Ale, Moose Juice Stout, Teton Golden Ale, Teton Huckleberry Wheat, and Teton Pass Porter at the company's old 1932 log cabin in Wilson. Sample the beers ($2 for a taste of all six), get a classy Teton Ale T-shirt, or order up savory pizzas, calzones, and salads. It's open daily 4-9 p.m. winter and summer, but call ahead in the fall and spring. You'll find Otto Brothers beers on tap at many Jackson-area bars and restaurants and for sale in six-pack bottles. Or take some home in a "growler," a half-gallon refillable bottle available from local liquor stores.

Snake River Brewing Co. & Restaurant, 265 S. Millward, tel. (307) 739-2337, is the opposite of low-key Otto Brothers. The brewery and restaurant are housed in a bright and spacious old warehouse that has been beautifully remodeled. It fills with a young and convivial crowd of outdoors enthusiasts most evenings, and it features nearly a dozen Snake River beers on tap. The award-winning Zonker Stout is always among these, along with Snake River Lager, and Snake River Pale Ale. The lunch and dinner cafe menu includes delicious thin-crust wood-fired pizzas and calzones, flavorful appetizers, daily pasta specials, sandwiches, and salads. Great food in a lively atmosphere. It's one of *the* places to be seen in Jackson.

Wine Shops

The most complete local wine and beer shops are **Westside Wine & Spirits,** in the Aspens along Teton Village Rd., tel. (307) 733-5038; **The Liquor Store,** next to Albertson's on W. Broadway, tel. (307) 733-4466; and **Dornan's** in

Moose, tel. (307) 733-2415, ext. 202. **Broadway Bottle Company,** 200 W. Broadway, tel. (307) 739-9463, also has a fine selection and offers free Friday afternoon wine tastings all summer long, featuring a different choice of wines each week. It's a great way to learn about various vintages from wine experts. You'll generally find the lowest wine prices from **Jackson's Original Discount Liquor Store at Sidewinders,** 802 W. Broadway, tel. (307) 734-5766.

Bakeries

The Bunnery, 130 N. Cache Dr., tel. (307) 733-5474, bakes a big variety of treats and sweets, but it's best known for its hearty-flavored OSM (oat, sunflower, and millet) bread—on the pricey side at around $4 a loaf. Another place for fresh baked goods is **Harvest Natural Foods,** 130 W. Broadway, tel. (307) 733-5418.

The location is a bit out of the way, but a visit to **Wild Flour Bakery,** 345 N. Glenwood, tel. (307) 734-2455, is a must if you're in search of French baguettes and other breads. You can also find the company's goods in several local grocers, and they bake the house bread for several of Jackson's gourmet restaurants. Wild Flour also bakes cookies and muffins.

Housed in the Stagecoach Bar in Wilson, **Patty-Cake West,** tel. (307) 733-7225, creates wonderful sweets and also serves burgers, sandwiches, Mexican food, and espresso.

Groceries

Get groceries from the new **Albertson's,** on the south end of town at the corner of Buffalo Way and Broadway, tel. (307) 733-5950. Inside you'll find a bakery, pharmacy, deli, one-hour photo lab, bank branch, and coffee bar. Meet the locals at the less ostentatious (and generally cheaper) **Food Town,** in the Powderhorn Mall at 970 W. Broadway, tel. (307) 733-0450. As this was written, a large new Smiths grocery store was in the planning stages for Jackson. It is expected to open in 2001 on the south end of town near the corner of High School Rd. and US Hwy. 89.

The best spot for fresh vegetables and fruit is the little **market stand** next to the Maverik gas station on the south end of town. It's open Thurs.-Sat. only in the summer, and it has better prices and higher quality than local grocers.

In business since 1947, **Jackson Hole Buffalo Meat,** 1655 Berger Lane, tel. (307) 733-8343 or (800) 543-6328, www.jhbuffalomeat.com, sells smoked buffalo salami, jerky, roast, and burgers, along with buffalo meat gift packs and New Zealand elk steaks.

For health foods, head downtown to **Harvest Natural Foods,** 130 W. Broadway, tel. (307) 733-5418, or to the smaller **Here & Now Natural Foods,** 1925 Moose-Wilson Rd., tel. (307) 733-2742.

ENTERTAINMENT AND THE ARTS

Nightlife

Barflies will keep buzzing in Jackson, especially during midsummer and midwinter, when vis-

Charlie Otto started Otto Brothers' Brewing Company in 1988 and now has brewpubs in Wilson and Victor.

itors pack local saloons every night of the week. At least one nightclub always seems to have live tunes; check Jackson's free newspapers to see what's where. Cover charges are generally $3-5 on the weekends, and most other times you'll get in free.

The famous **Million Dollar Cowboy Bar,** on the west side of Town Square, tel. (307) 733-2207, is a favorite of real cowboys and their wannabe cousins. Inside the Cowboy you'll discover burled lodgepole pine beams, four pool tables (nearly always in use), display cases with stuffed dead bears and other cuddly critters, bars inlaid with old silver dollars, and barstools made from old saddles. Until the 1950s, the Cowboy was Jackson's center for illegal gambling. Bartenders kept a close eye on Teton Pass, where messengers used mirrors to deliver warnings of coming federal revenuers, giving folks at the bar time to hide the gaming tables in a back room. Today the dance floor fills with honky-tonking couples as the bands croon lonesome cowboy tunes six nights a week. Looking to learn swing and two-step dancing? Every Thursday you can join an excellent free beginners' class at 7:30 p.m., then dance up a storm when the band comes on at 9.

Just across the square and up the stairs is **Rancher Spirits & Billiards,** where you'll find a room filled with a half dozen pool tables for billiards aficionados. **SilverDollar Bar & Grill,** in the Wort Hotel at 50 N. Glenwood St., tel. (307) 733-2190, offers a setting that might seem more fitting in Las Vegas: gaudy pink neon lights curve around a bar inlaid with 2,032 (count 'em!) silver dollars. It tends to attract an older crowd, and the music is generally of the piano or acoustic variety.

Right next to the tram in Teton Village is **Mangy Moose Saloon,** tel. (307) 733-4913, Jackson Hole's jumpingest pick-up spot and *the* place to rock out. The Moose attracts a hip skier/outdoorsy crowd with rock, blues, or world beat bands Wed.-Sat. both summer and winter. This is also where you'll hear nationally known acts.

Sidewinders Tavern & Sports Grill, 802 W. Broadway, tel. (307) 734-5766, is filled with big-screen TVs for sports enthusiasts. It also offers bands on Saturday nights and Latino dance tunes on Tuesday. Smokers head to the cigar bar, but there's also a big smoke-free section.

The **Shady Lady Saloon** at Snow King Resort, 400 E. Snow King Ave., tel. (307) 733-5200, typically serves up live rock, jazz, or bluegrass music on Wednesday nights. More popular are the Monday night **hootenannies** held in the lodge room of the Snow King Center, where local musicians get together to jam in an all-acoustic set. Join the onstage fun if you have musical talent, or can pretend.

Over in Wilson, **The Stagecoach Bar,** tel. (307) 733-4407, is *the* place to be on Sunday nights 5:30-10 p.m. (Wyoming bars close their doors at 10 p.m. on Sunday.) In the early '70s, when hippies risked getting their heads shaved by rednecks at Jackson's Cowboy Bar, they found the 'Coach a more tolerant place. Today tobacco-chewing cowpokes show their partners slick moves on the tiny dance floor as the Stagecoach Band runs through the country tunes one more time—the band has performed here every Sunday since February 16, 1969! On Thursday nights the 'Coach turns the clock back with disco fever as DJs spin the retro grooves for a polyester-dressed crowd. For more entertainment, try a game of pool. Or just chow down on a tasty buffalo burger. Outside you'll find picnic tables and a volleyball court for pickup games in the summer.

Other spots with occasional live music are the **Acadian House,** 180 N. Millward, tel. (307) 739-1269; the **Spur Bar,** at Dornan's in Moose, tel. (307) 733-2415, ext. 200; **The Granary,** atop East Gros Ventre Butte, tel. (307) 733-8833; **Leek's Marina Restaurant,** along Jackson Lake, tel. (307) 543-2494; and **Teton Pines,** on Teton Village Rd., tel. (307) 733-1005.

Classical Music

In existence since 1962, the **Grand Teton Music Festival** takes place at Walk Festival Hall in Teton Village, with performances of classical and modern works by a cast of 200 world-renowned symphony musicians. Concerts take place evenings late June to late August each year, with chamber music on Tuesday and Wednesday, small ensembles on Thursday, and festival orchestra concerts on Friday and Saturday. They also perform a free outdoor "Music in the Hole" concert on the Fourth of July, plus special young people's concerts later in July. The three-hour-long Friday morning rehearsals are just $5. Call (307) 733-3050 for a schedule of events and ticket prices, or get details on the web at www.gtmf.org.

Musicals and Movies

In addition to the bar scene, summers bring a number of lighthearted acting ventures to Jackson. For family musicals such as *Paint Your Wagon* or *The Unsinkable Molly Brown,* head to **Jackson Hole Playhouse,** 145 W. Deloney, tel. (307) 733-6994. Shows take place Mon.-Sat. evenings in a campy 1890s-style setting. A family saloon (no alcohol) and restaurant are next door.

Productions of Broadway and Western musical comedies play throughout the summer at **Mainstage Theatre,** in the newly remodeled Pink Garter Plaza at 50 W. Broadway, tel. (307) 733-3670. The rest of the year, the Mainstage puts on more serious plays and attracts national touring productions and comedians. Both Mainstage and Jackson Hole Playhouse are very popular with families, and reservations are strongly recommended.

Watch flicks at **Teton Theatre,** 120 N. Cache Dr., **Jackson Hole Twin Cinema,** 295 W. Pearl St., or **MovieWorks Cinema Four-plex,** 860 S. US Hwy. 89. All three of these have the same ownership and phone number: (307) 733-6744.

Rodeo

On Wednesday and Saturday nights in the summer you can watch bucking broncs, bull riders, rodeo clowns, and hard-riding cowboys at the **Jackson Hole Rodeo,** on the Teton County Fair Grounds. Kids get to join in the amusing calf scramble. The rodeo starts at 8 p.m. and costs $8-10 for adults, $6 for ages 4-12, free for kids under four, $25 for the whole family. Rodeos take place from Memorial Day to Labor Day; call (307) 733-2805 for details.

Chuck Wagon Cookouts

Jackson Hole is home to six different chuck wagon eateries offering all-you-can-eat barbecue cookouts and Western musical performances all summer long. Each has its own advantages such as professional musicians, wagon rides, horseback rides, or a particularly beautiful setting. Reservations are highly recommended at all of these.

Run by the Thomas family since 1973, **Bar-T-Five,** 790 Cache Creek Rd., tel. (307) 733-5386 or (800) 772-5386, www.bartfive.com, is one of the best chuck wagon feeds. Horse-drawn Conestoga-style wagons depart just east of Snow King, carrying visitors along Cache Creek past costumed mountain men, cowboys, and Indians. At the in-the-trees cookout site cowboys serenade your meal, tell stories, and crack corny jokes that aren't entirely politically correct. It's great fun for families and busloads of Japanese tourists. Rates are $28 for adults, $21 for ages 6-12, and free for kids under six. Open mid-May through September, with departures at 5:30 and 6:30 p.m. each evening. Recommended.

A/OK Corral, 10 miles south of Jackson near Hoback Junction, tel. (307) 733-6556, www.horsecreekranch.com, has 45-minute horseback

Bar-T-Five's chuck wagons carry hungry diners to a barbecue feast.

or wagon rides that end at an outdoor cookout. Big ranch breakfasts and steak suppers are on the menu. Breakfasts cost $30 for adults, $12 for kids; dinners are $40 for adults with the horseback ride, $28 with a covered-wagon ride. For kids, a covered-wagon ride and dinner are $16. Western musical entertainment is provided with the evening meals.

In beautiful Buffalo Valley, 40 miles northeast of Jackson, **Box K Ranch,** tel. (307) 543-2407 or (800) 729-1410, has two-hour covered-wagon rides into Bridger-Teton National Forest, with magnificent views of the Tetons along the way. The cowboy cookout features steak, barbecue beans, baked potatoes, dessert, and nonalcoholic drinks, all served amid tall aspen trees. Dinners are $25 for adults, $20 for kids 4-11. Breakfast cookouts cost $15 for adults, $12 for kids. Kids under age four are free. Closed Sunday.

Also in Buffalo Valley is **Diamond Cross Ranch,** tel. (307) 543-2015, where you get to watch a horse whisperer at work, listen to cowboy poetry, and enjoy a seven-course chuck wagon dinner for $25.

Along the Teton Village Rd. near Teton Pines, the **Bar J,** tel. (307) 733-3370 or (800) 905-2275, www.barjchuckwagon.com, seats 750 people and fills up many summer evenings. In existence for more than 40 years, Bar J is known for its first-rate musicians who fiddle, sing, yodel, tell jokes, and offer up cowboy poetry. The menu includes a choice of barbecued beef, chicken and beef, or rib-eye steak—each served with baked potatoes, beans, biscuits, applesauce, spice cake, and lemonade (no alcohol). Dinner and entertainment take place in a cavernous building and cost $14-19 for adults (depending upon your meal), $6 for kids under eight, and free for tots. Open Memorial Day to late September, with dinner at 7:30 each evening; many folks arrive earlier to get front-row seats for the show. The Bar J does not offer wagon or horseback rides.

Certainly the most unusual local offering is the **Pitchfork Fondue** at Lucas Lazy Double A Ranch, 5330 N. Spring Gulch Rd., tel. (307) 734-2541. Sirloin steak is cooked on a pitchfork in a cauldron of hot oil! I'm told it's better than it sounds. The meal also includes salads, potatoes, rolls, lemonade, and dessert. The price is $17 for adults, $9 for kids. Open Memorial Day through September.

Green River Outfitters, tel. (307) 733-1044, offers combination trail rides and cookouts in the Gros Ventre Mountains 35 miles south of Jackson. These cost $120 per person, including guided horseback rides, roundtrip transport from Jackson, and a barbecued-steak lunch. Overnight rides and multiday pack trips are also available.

EVENTS

Jackson Hole is packed with entertaining events almost every day of the year. Some of these are little homegrown affairs such as the county fair, while others attract people from near and far. Of particular note are the International Rocky Mountain Stage Stop Sled Dog Race, the Pole-Peddle-Paddle Race, the Elk Antler Auction, the Grand Teton Music Festival, and the Jackson Hole Fall Arts Festival. (In addition to the events listed below, see Grand Targhee Ski Resort later in this chapter for a year-round calendar of events on the other side of the Tetons.)

Winter

December is a particularly beautiful time in downtown Jackson. Lights decorate the elk-antler arches, and a variety of events take place. Buy arts and crafts during the **Christmas Bazaar** early in the month, or take the kids to visit Saint Nick and his elves on Town Square starting in mid-December; they're there daily 5-7 p.m.

Kick the year off by watching (or participating in) the annual **torchlight ski parades** at all three local ski areas. They take place on Christmas evening and New Year's Eve at both Jackson Hole Mountain Resort and Grand Targhee Ski Resort, and on New Year's Eve at Snow King.

Each February, local Shriners hold horse-drawn **cutter races**—essentially a wild chariot race on a quarter mile of ice—at Melody Ranch, six miles south of Jackson. Call (307) 733-1938 for more info.

In existence since 1996, the **International Rocky Mountain Stage Stop Sled Dog Race** (IRMSSSDR) is the largest sled dog race in the lower 48 states. Unlike the Iditarod and most other mushing events, this one is run in short 30- to 80-mile stages totaling 400 miles, with teams ending in a new town each night. As with the Tour de France, it's the total time that counts in this stage race. The race is the creation of Iditarod musher Frank Teasley and nurse Jayne Ottman, who came up with the idea as a way to raise awareness of the need to immunize children; it's unofficially called "The Race to Immunize." The IRMSSSDR (try saying that fast!) starts in Jackson and travels through Moran, Dubois, Pinedale, Lander, Atlantic City, Mountain View, Lyman, Evanston, Kemmerer, Afton, Box Y Guest Ranch (Greys River area), and Alpine before ending in Jackson. Each town has its own activities associated with the event. The race boasts a $100,000 purse and has attracted some of the top names in dog mushing. It's held over 12 days in late January and early February, and it may be linked to the 2002 Salt Lake City Winter Olympics as an exhibition event. Call (307) 734-1163 for details, or check the website: www.wyomingstagestop.org.

Also in February, the **Cowboy Ski Challenge** provides a different kind of race, with skiers pulled behind a horse and rider at speeds of up to 40 miles an hour. The race takes place at the base of Jackson Hole Mountain Resort.

Ski races take place all winter long, ranging from elegant "Powder Eight" Championships in early March to blazingly fast downhill races. (Volunteer to work one of the gates at a downhill race and you get to ski free the rest of the day.) In mid-March, the **Connie Stevens Celebrity Extravaganza** attracts Hollywood types for a weekend of skiing, indoor tennis, and ice hockey to support people with disabilities.

One of the most popular (and dumbest) Jackson events is the **World Championship Snowmobile Hillclimb,** in which man (or woman) and machine churn up the slopes at Snow King Resort. The event takes place in late March.

The ski season ends the first weekend of April with the **Pole-Pedal-Paddle Race,** combining alpine skiing, cross-country skiing, cycling, and canoeing in a wild, tough competition. It's the largest such event in the West and great fun for spectators and contestants—many of whom dress up in goofy costumes. Call (307) 733-6433 for details.

Spring

Spring in Jackson Hole is the least favorite time of the year for many locals. The snow is going, leaving behind brown grass and trees; biking and hiking trails aren't yet passable; and the river is too cold to enjoy. For many folks, this is the time to load up the car and head to Utah for a desert hike in Canyonlands. Despite this, April and May can be a good time to visit, especially if you want to avoid the crowds, need to save money on lodging, or are planning to stay for the summer and need a job and a place to live. (Housing gets progressively more difficult to find after April.)

On the third Saturday in May, the world's only public **elk antler auction** takes place at Town Square, attracting hundreds of buyers from all over the globe. Local Boy Scouts collect five tons of antlers from the nearby National Elk Refuge each spring, with 80% of the proceeds helping to fund feeding of the elk. This may sound like an odd event, but the take is over $100,000! Prices average $10 per pound and the bidding gets highly competitive; perfectly matched pairs can go for over $2,000. The antlers are used in taxidermy, belt buckles, furniture, and most important to satisfy the high demand for antlers in the insatiable (pun intended) South Korean and Chinese aphrodisiac markets. There's more than a touch of irony in the Boy Scouts making money from the sale of sexual stimulants! Call (307) 733-5935 for more info.

Summer

Memorial Day weekend brings **Old West Days,** complete with a parade, Indian dancing, street dance, barbecue dinner, blacksmithing demonstrations, children's rodeo, music, and **mountain-man rendezvous.** Call (307) 733-3316 for details. The **Fourth of July** is another big event in Jackson, with a parade, rodeo, barbecue, and an impressive fireworks show from Snow King Mountain. Another very popular Fourth of July event is the free **Music in the Hole** outdoor classical concert by the Grand Teton Music Festival orchestra; call (307) 733-1128.

All summer long, the **Jackson Hole Rodeo** brings spills and thrills to town every Wednesday and Saturday night. See Entertainment and the Arts above for the full scoop on this must-see event. Another ongoing event is the **Grand Teton Music Festival,** providing summertime classical music at Teton Village. See Entertainment and the Arts above for details.

The last week of July brings an always-fun **Teton County Fair,** tel. (307) 733-5289, with 4-H exhibits, pig wrestling in the mud, free pony rides and a petting zoo, live music and comedy acts, a carnival, rodeos, and everyone's favorite: a bang-up demolition derby on the final Sunday night.

In early September, the invitation-only **Jackson Hole One-Fly Contest** attracts anglers from all over, including a number of celebrity competitors. For details, call (307) 733-3270 or (800) 570-3270.

Fall

Jackson Hole is at its most glorious in the fall, as aspens and cottonwoods turn a fire of yellow and orange against the Teton backdrop. Most tourists have fled back home, leaving locals and hardier visitors to savor the cool autumn nights. The peak time for **fall colors** is generally the first week of October—considerably later than most people expect. The primary autumn event is the **Jackson Hole Fall Arts Festival,** featuring exhibits at the National Museum of Wildlife Art and local galleries, a miniature art show, art demonstrations, silent auctions, live music, and other events over a 10-day period from mid- to late September. Also fun is a "quick draw" in which artists paint, draw, and sculpt while you watch; the pieces are then auctioned off. For more info and a schedule of the many events, call (307) 733-3316. The festival's **Arts for the Parks National Art Competition** attracts thousands of paintings representing scenes from America's national parks. This isn't for amateurs; the purse is $50,000. The banquet and silent auction seats fill by mid-August; call (307) 733-2787 or (800) 553-2787 for reservations. In early October, **Quilting in the Tetons** brings a week of exhibits, classes, workshops, and quilting demonstrations. Call (307) 733-3087 for details, or point your browser to www.quiltthetetons.org.

RIVER RAFTING

Jackson Hole's most popular summertime recreational activity is running Wyoming's largest river, the Snake. Each year more than 150,000 people climb aboard rafts, canoes, and kayaks to float down placid reaches of the Snake or to blast through the boiling rapids of Snake River Canyon. (As an aside, the name "Snake" comes from the Shoshone Indians, who used serpentine hand movements as sign language for their tribal name—a motion trappers misinterpreted as a snake and applied to the river flowing through Shoshone land.)

Almost 20 different rafting companies offer dozens of different raft trips each day of the summer. Although you may be able to walk up and get a raft trip the same day, it's a good idea to reserve ahead for any river trip in July and August. In general, try to book a trip three or four days in advance if possible, and at least one week ahead if you need a specific time, prefer an overnight float trip, or are traveling with a larger group. One or two people are more likely to get onboard at the last minute.

You may want to ask around to determine the advantages of each company. Some are cheaper but require you to drive a good distance from town; others offer more experienced crews; still others provide various perks such as fancy meals, U-paddle trips, overnight camps along the river, interpretive trips, or boats with fewer (or more) people. A number of operators also lead seven-hour combination trips that include a lazy float followed by a meal break and a wild whitewater run.

The rafting companies generally operate from mid-May to late September, and river conditions change through the season. Highest flows—and the wildest rides—are generally in May and June. Get a complete listing of floating and boating outfits, along with descriptive brochures, from the Wyoming State Information Center in Jackson.

Float Trips

The gentlest way to see the Snake is by taking one of the many commercial float trips. Along the way, you'll be treated to stunning views of the Tetons and glimpses of eagles, ospreys, beavers, and perhaps moose or other wildlife along the riverbanks. A number of companies—Fort Jackson, Grand Teton Lodge Co., Heart Six Ranch, Signal Mountain, Solitude, and Triangle X—offer five- or 10-mile scenic float trips along the quiet stretch within Grand Teton National Park, generally putting in at Deadman's Bar or Schwabacher Landing and taking out in Moose. Flagg Ranch Resort has float and whitewater rafting on the Snake River above Jackson Lake.

Several other rafting operations offer 13-mile float trips outside the park (these typically include a lunch), putting in at the bridge near Wilson and taking out above Hoback Junction. These companies include Barker-Ewing, Dave Hansen, Flagg Ranch/O.A.R.S., Lewis & Clark, Lone Eagle, Sands, and Teton Expeditions.

Prices run $32-40 for adults and $22-30 for children. Age limits vary, but kids must generally be at least eight to float the river. Roundtrip transportation from Jackson is included by most (but not all) companies. A wide variety of special voyages are also available, including overnight camping, and fish-and-float trips.

Call one of the following raft companies for details, or pick up their slick brochures at the visitor center or from their offices scattered around town: **Barker-Ewing Float Trips,** tel. (307) 733-1000 or (800) 448-4202, www.barker-ewing.com; **Dave Hansen Whitewater,** tel. (307) 733-6295 or (800) 732-6295, www.davehansenwhitewater.com; **Fort Jackson Scenic Snake River Float Trips,** tel. (307) 733-2583 or (800) 735-8430; **Grand Teton Lodge Float Trips,** tel. (307) 543-2811 or (800)

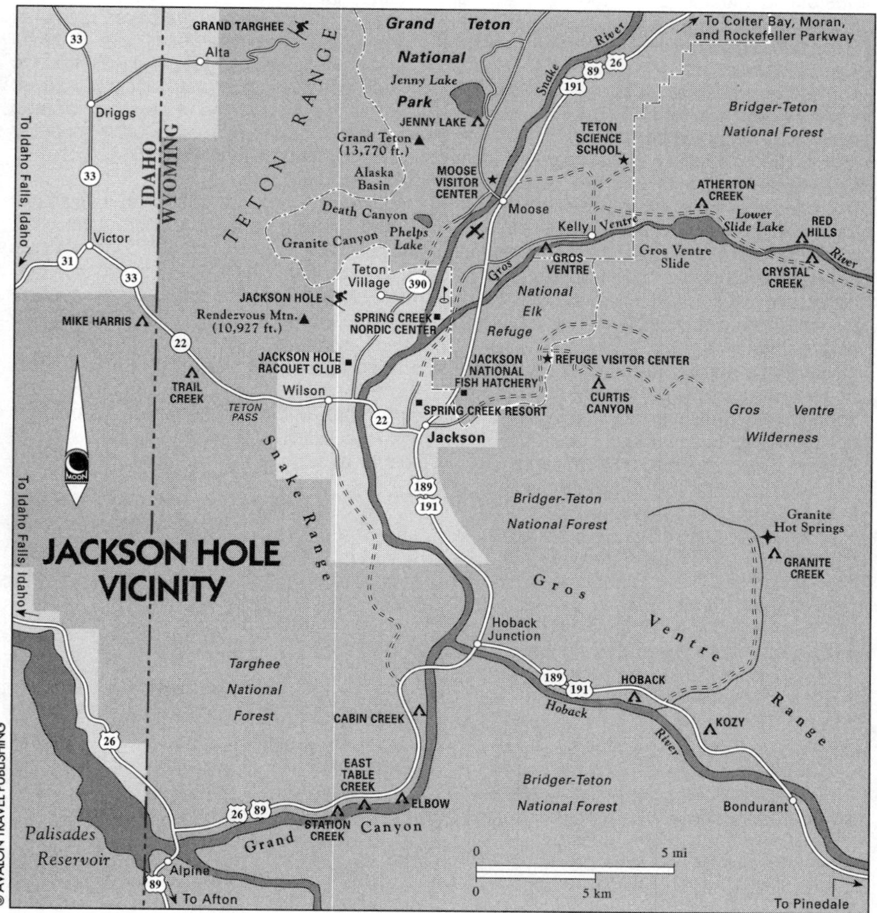

628-9988, www.gtlc.com; **Heart Six Ranch,** tel. (307) 543-2477 or (888) 543-2477, www.heartsix.com; **Lewis & Clark Expeditions,** tel. (307) 733-4022 or (800) 824-5375, www.lewisandclarkexped.com; **Lone Eagle Whitewater,** tel. (307) 733-1090 or (800) 321-3800, www.loneeagleresort.com; **Mad River Boat Trips,** tel. (307) 733-6203 or (800) 458-7238, www.mad-river.com; **Sands Wild Water,** tel. (307) 733-4410 or (800) 358-8184, www.sandswhitewater.com; **Signal Mountain Lodge & Marina,** tel. (307) 733-5470 or (307) 543-2831, www.signalmtnlodge.com; **Solitude Scenic Float Trips,** tel. (307) 733-2871 or (888) 704-2800, www.jacksonwy.com/solitude; **Teton Expeditions** (the same folks run Jackson Hole Whitewater), tel. (307) 733-1007 or (888) 700-7238, www.tetonexpeditions.com; and **Triangle X Float Trips,** tel. (307) 733-5500, www.trianglex.com. **Flagg Ranch Rafting,** tel. (307) 543-2861 or (800) 443-2311, www.flaggranch. com, leads 10-mile float trips down the upper Snake River, starting at Flagg Ranch Resort and heading downriver to Jackson Lake. These trips are actually run using O.A.R.S. boats and guides. O.A.R.S. also leads one- to five-day sea kayaking trips around Jackson Lake; see Other Park Recreation within the Grand Teton National Park chapter for details.

Note that a few of these operators are regarded as "training grounds" for other companies; recommended rafting outfits with good records include Barker-Ewing, Flagg Ranch/O.A.R.S., Solitude, Teton Expeditions, and Triangle X.

Whitewater Trips

Below Jackson, the Snake enters the wild Snake River Canyon, a stretch early explorers labeled "the accursed mad river." The usual put-in point for whitewater "rapid transit" trips is West Table Creek Campground, 26 miles south of Jackson. The take-out point is Sheep Gulch, eight miles downstream. In between the two, the river rocks and rolls through the narrow canyon, pumping past waterfalls and eagle nests and then over the two biggest rapids, Big Kahuna and Lunch Counter, followed by the smaller Rope and Champagne Rapids. For a look at the action from the highway, stop at the paved turnout at milepost 124, where a trail leads down to Lunch Counter. The river changes greatly through the season, with the highest water and wildest rides in June. By August the water has warmed enough for a quick dip. Be sure to ask your river guide about the Jeep that sits in 60 feet of water below Lunch Counter!

Whitewater trips last around three and a half hours (including transportation from Jackson) and cost $30-40 for adults, $29-34 for children (age limits vary). Seven-hour combination trips that include a float trip, meal, and whitewater run are $55-60 for adults or $50 for kids. Overnight trips (same river distance as the combination trips) cost approximately $112 for adults and $85 for kids. You'll find discounted rates early or late in the summer and with operators who use Titanic-size 16-person rafts. The U-paddle versions are more fun than letting the

Every summer more than 150,000 adventurers float the Snake River.

guide do all the work in an oar raft, and the smaller eight-person rafts provide the most challenging (and wettest) runs. Most companies include roundtrip transportation from Jackson.

Expect to get wet, so wear lightweight clothes and bring a jacket for the return ride. Most rafting companies provide wetsuits and booties. Note that this is not exactly a wilderness experience, especially in mid-July, when stretches of the river look like a Los Angeles freeway with traffic jams of rafts, kayaks, inner tubes, and other flotsam and jetsam. The river isn't as crowded on weekdays and early in the morning; take an 8 a.m. run for the fewest people.

Don't take your own camera along unless it's waterproof; bankside float-tographers are positioned along the biggest rapids to shoot both commercial and private rafters. Stop by Float-O-Graphs at 130 W. Broadway, tel. (307) 733-6453 or (888) 478-7427, www.floatographs.com, for a photo from your run. Another company with a similar service is **Whitewater Photos & Video,** 140 N. Cache Dr., tel. (307) 733-7015 or (800) 948-3426.

For details on whitewater raft trips, contact one of the following companies: **Barker-Ewing Whitewater,** tel. (307) 733-1000 or (800) 448-4202, www.barker-ewing.com; **Dave Hansen Whitewater,** tel. (307) 733-6295 or (800) 732-6295, www.davehansenwhitewater.com; **Jackson Hole Whitewater,** tel. (307) 733-1007 or (800) 700-7238, www.jhwhitewater.com; **Lewis & Clark Expeditions,** tel. (307) 733-4022 or (800) 824-5375, www.lewisandclarkexped.com; **Lone Eagle Whitewater,** tel. (307) 733-1090 or (800) 321-3800, www.loneeagleresort.com; **Mad River Boat Trips,** tel. (307) 733-6203 or (800) 458-7238, www.mad-river.com; **Sands Wild Water,** tel. (307) 733-4410 or (800) 358-8184, www.sandswhitewater.com; or **Snake River Park Whitewater,** tel. (307) 733-7078 or (800) 562-1878, www.srpkoa.com.

Recommended companies with good safety records and well-trained staff include Barker-Ewing, Dave Hansen, Jackson Hole Whitewater, and Sands. The largest local rafting company, Mad River, has a reputation as a proving ground for novice guides. It's your choice, but I also would personally not raft with either Lone Eagle Whitewater or Snake River Park Whitewater.

Float It Yourself

Grand Teton National Park in Moose, tel. (307) 739-3602, has useful information on running the park portions of the river; ask for a copy of *Floating the Snake River.* Note that life jackets, boat permits ($5 for a seven-day permit), and registration are required to run the river through the park, and that inner tubes and air mattresses are prohibited. Floating the gentler parts (between Jackson Lake Dam and Pacific Creek) is generally easy for even novice boaters and canoeists, but below that point things get more dicey. The water averages two or three feet deep, but it sometimes exceeds 10 feet and flow rates are often more than 8,000 cubic feet per second, creating logjams, braided channels, strong currents, and dangerous sweepers. Peak flows are between mid-June and early July. Inexperienced rafters or anglers die nearly every year in the river. Flow-rate signs are posted at most river landings, the Moose Visitor Center, and the Buffalo Ranger Station in Moran. If you're planning to raft or kayak on the whitewater parts of the Snake River, be sure to contact the Bridger-Teton National Forest office in Jackson, tel. (307) 739-5500, for additional information.

Excellent waterproof maps of the Grand Canyon of the Snake River are sold at the Forest Service office at 340 N. Cache. In addition to showing the rapids, these maps describe local geology and other features.

Rent rafts from **Riding & Rafts** in Alpine, tel. (307) 654-9900; **Rent-A-Raft** in Hoback Junction, tel. (307) 733-2728 or (800) 321-7328; or **Leisure Sports** in Jackson at 1075 S. US Hwy. 89, tel. (307) 733-3040. Call local taxi companies for rafting shuttle services.

FISHING AND BOATING

Fishing

Jackson Hole has some of the finest angling in Wyoming, with native Snake River cutthroat (a distinct subspecies) and brook trout in the river, along with Mackinaw (lake trout), cutthroat, and brown trout in the lakes. The Snake is a particular favorite of beginning fly-fishing enthusiasts; popular shoreside fishing spots are just below Jackson Lake Dam and near the Wilson Bridge. (I've heard complaints from some readers that they had no luck fishing in Jackson Hole, but others pull in fish every time they go out.) Jackson Lake may provide higher odds for catching a fish, but you'll need to rent a boat from one of the marinas. This is the place parents take kids to increase their odds of catching a fish. Another very popular fishing hole is just below the dam on Jackson Lake. Flat Creek on the National Elk Refuge is an acclaimed spot for fly-fishing. Note that Wyoming fishing licenses are valid within Grand Teton National Park but not in Yellowstone, where you'll need a separate permit.

Many local companies offer guided fly-fishing float trips down the Snake River and other area waterways. Two people (same price for one person) should expect to pay $325-350 a day for a guide, rods and reels, lunch, and boat. Your fishing license and flies are extra. The visitor center has a listing of local fishing guides and outfitters, and its racks are filled with their brochures.

If you'd rather do it yourself, pick up a copy of the free ***Western Fishing Newsletter,*** which offers descriptions of regional fishing areas and advice on which lures to try. Find it at **Jack Dennis' Outdoor Shop,** 50 E. Broadway, tel. (307) 733-3270 or (800) 570-3270, www.jackdennis.com. While there, you may want to buy a regional guide to fishing such as *Flyfisher's Guide to Wyoming* by Ken Retallic (Gallatin Gateway, MT: Wilderness Adventures Press) or *Fishing Wyoming* by Kenneth Lee Graham (Helena, MT: Falcon Publishing Co.).

Jackson has several excellent fly-fishing shops, including the aforementioned Jack Dennis' Outdoor Shop. **Westbank Anglers,** 3670 Teton Village Rd., tel. (307) 733-6483 or (800) 922-3474, www.westbank.com, is a nationally known fly-fishing dealer with a slick mail-order catalog, excellent fishing clinics, and float trips. Both **High Country Flies,** 185 N. Center St., tel. (307) 733-7210, www.highcountryflies.com, and **Orvis Jackson Hole,** 485 W. Broadway, tel. (307) 733-5407, offer fly-fishing classes and sell quality gear. Rent fishing rods, fly rods, float tubes, and waders from Jack Dennis, High Country Flies, or **Leisure Sports,** 1075 S. US Hwy. 89, tel. (307) 733-3040.

Somewhere at the eastern base of the Tetons did those hoofprints disappear into a mountain sanctuary where many crooked paths have led. He that took another man's possession, or he that took another man's life, could always run here if the law or popular justice were too hot at his heels. Steep ranges and forests walled him in from the world on all four sides, almost without a break; and every entrance lay through intricate solitudes. Snake River came into the place through canyons and mournful pines and marshes, to the north, and went out at the south between formidable chasms. Every tributary to this stream rose among high peaks and ridges, and descended into the valley by well-nigh impenetrable courses. . . . Down in the bottom was a spread of level land, broad, and beautiful, with the blue and silver Tetons rising from its chain of lakes to the west and other heights residing over its other sides.

—FROM OWEN WISTER'S *THE VIRGINIAN*

Kayaking and Canoeing

Snake River Kayak & Canoe School, 155 W. Gill St., tel. (307) 733-3127 or (800) 529-2501, www.snakeriverkayak.com, offers sea kayaking and canoeing classes. Full-day private lessons—including transportation, boats, paddles, wetsuit, rubber booties, and lifejackets—cost $230 per person; with two students they are $130 per person. Beginners may want to start out with one of the three-hour "rubber duckie" inflatable kayak river trips for $45. In addition, the school has sea kayak tours of Yellowstone Lake. **Teton Aquatics,** at the same address and phone, rents practically anything that floats: canoes, sea kayaks, whitewater kayaks, inflatable kayaks, rowboats, and rafts, all with paddles and roof racks included. Also available for rent are scuba equipment, water skis, dry bags, and life jackets.

The folks at **Rendezvous River Sports** (a.k.a. Jackson Hole Kayak School), 1033 W. Broadway, tel. (307) 733-2471 or (800) 733-2471, www.jhkayakschool.com, teach a wide range of kayaking courses from the absolute beginner level to advanced "hairboating" for experts. Classes include kayak roll clinics ($75), river rescue ($120), and special women's and kids' classes. Two-day introductory classes cost $235; four days of instruction is $450. Private lessons are available, and the company rents sea kayaks and whitewater kayaks.

Leisure Sports, 1075 South US Hwy. 89, tel. (307) 733-3040, rents rafts, canoes, kayaks, inflatable kayaks, water skis, wet suits, dry bags, life jackets, and all sorts of other outdoor equipment (including jet skis). They can also provide a shuttle service for rafters. **Adventure Sports** in Moose, tel. (307) 733-3307, also rents canoes and kayaks.

Windsurfing

Jackson Lake is a popular sailboarding place with moderate winds (perfect for beginners) and an impressive Teton backdrop. Advanced windsurfers looking for stronger wind conditions head to Slide Lake east of Kelly or to blow-me-down Yellowstone Lake. Equipment rentals are not available locally.

OTHER SUMMER RECREATION

Horsin' Around

Think of the Wild West and one animal always comes to mind—the horse. A ride on Old Paint gives city slickers a chance to saunter back in time to a simpler era and to simultaneously learn how ornery and opinionated horses can be. If it rains, you'll also learn why cowboys are so enthralled with cowboy hats. In Jackson Hole you can choose from brief half-day trail rides in Grand Teton National Park all the way up to weeklong pack trips into the rugged Teton Wilderness. The visitor center has a brochure listing more than a dozen local outfitters and stables that provide trail rides and pack trips.

For rides by the hour or day (approximately $20 for a one-hour ride or $75 for all day), try **Scott's Jackson Hole Trail Rides** in Teton Village, tel. (307) 733-6992; **Snow King Stables,** behind Snow King Resort, tel. (307) 733-5781, www.snowking.com; **Spring Creek Ranch,** atop Gros Ventre Butte off Spring Gulch Rd., tel. (307) 733-8833 or (800) 443-6139, www.springcreekranch.com; **A/OK Corral,** in Hoback Junction, tel. (307) 733-6556, www.horsecreekranch.com; **Mill Iron Ranch,** 10 miles south of Jackson, tel. (307) 733-6390 or (888) 808-6390, www.jacksonwy.com/millironranch; or **Goosewing Ranch,** 25 miles east of Kelly near the Gros Ventre Wilderness, tel. (307) 733-5251 or (888) 733-5251, www.goosewingranch.com. Of these, Scott's Jackson Hole Trail Rides, Spring Creek Ranch, and Mill Iron Ranch are very well liked, but you probably won't go wrong with any of these companies. Farther afield are a number of companies offering trail rides, including four that operate out of Buffalo Valley (45 miles northeast of Jackson): **Buffalo**

getting ready to hit the trail

Valley Ranch, tel. (307) 543-2026 or (888) 543-2477; **Two Ocean Pass Ranch & Outfitting,** tel. (307) 543-2309 or (800) 726-2409; **Turpin Meadow Ranch,** tel. (307) 543-2496 or (800) 743-2496, www.turpinmeadow.com; and **Yellowstone Outfitters/Wagons West,** tel. (800) 447-4711. More trail rides are offered at **Cowboy Village Resort at Togwotee,** tel. (307) 733-8800 or (800) 543-2847, www.cowboyvillage.com, 48 miles northeast of Jackson on the way to Togwotee Pass. The minimum age for horseback riding is typically five or six; these young children typically ride while the horse is being led around by a parent. Many of the companies above also offer combination horseback rides and cookouts for an extra fee.

Rides of all sorts are available in Grand Teton National Park at **Jackson Lake Lodge** and **Colter Bay Corral;** call (307) 733-2811 or (800) 628-9988 for specifics. In Alpine (35 miles southwest of Jackson), **Riding & Rafts,** tel. (307) 654-9900, offers unguided horse rentals for $15 for the first hour and $12 for subsequent hours; it's the only place for do-it-yourselfers in the area.

Experienced riders head out Spring Creek Rd. to **Spring Creek Equestrian Center,** tel. (307) 739-9062. The center (not connected with Spring Creek Ranch) emphasizes English riding, with lessons in dressage, cross-country, and jumping. Facilities include a heated indoor arena, three outdoor arenas, a cross-country course, and a small tack store. The equestrian center is open to the public, but is primarily for those looking to enroll in extended lessons, particularly people with their own horses.

Jackson Hole Llamas, tel. (307) 739-9582 or (800) 830-7316, www.jhllamas.com, offers backcountry treks with these fascinating and gentle animals.

Wagon Trains

Two local companies lead overnight wagon-train rides (in wagons with rubber tires) into the country around Jackson Hole. **Wagons West,** tel. (307) 886-9693 or (800) 447-4711, charges $595 for four days (bring your sleeping bag) and also has one-night and five-night packages. **Double H Bar,** tel. (307) 734-6101 or (888) 734-6101, www.jacksonholenet.com/tetonwagon, charges $745 for a three-night package that includes horseback and wagon riding, meals, and camping gear.

Mountain-biking

Jackson Hole offers all sorts of adventures for cyclists, particularly those with mountain bikes. **Teton Cycle Works,** 175 N. Glenwood St., tel. (307) 733-4386; **Hoback Sports,** 40 S. Millward St., tel. (307) 733-5335, www.hobacksports.com; **The Edge Sports,** 490 W. Broadway, tel. (307) 734-3916; **Leisure Sports,** 1075 S. US Hwy. 89, tel. (307) 733-3040; **Wilson Backcountry Sports,** in Teton Village, tel. (307) 733-5228; **Teton Village Sports,** in Teton Village, tel. (307) 733-2181 or (800) 874-4224; and **Adventure Sports** in Moose, tel. (307) 733-3307, all rent mountain bikes and helmets for around $25 per day, $15 per half day. Several of these also rent hybrid bikes, bike trailers, car racks, and kids' bikes, and most sell and repair bikes.

The easiest places to ride are the **Jackson Hole Community Pathways,** a series of several paved paths. A four-mile section starts behind the main post office on Maple Way, crosses US Hwy. 89, and continues past the high school before turning north to meet the road to Wilson (State 22). Another six-mile portion heads south of town, paralleling the highway almost to the Snake River bridge. It provides a connection to the very popular Game Creek Trail, which meets the Cache Creek Trail, circling back to Jackson behind Snow King. In addition, two shorter trails are in the Wilson and Teton Pines areas. Get details from the Friends of Pathways, tel. (307) 733-4534, www.jhpathways.org.

Most bike shops provide maps of local mountain-bike routes, or you can purchase a waterproof Jackson Hole mountain-biking map. Note that mountain bikes are not allowed on hiking trails in Grand Teton National Park or in Forest Service wilderness areas. If you visit Jackson early in the season, check out the Jenny Lake road inside the park; in April it's plowed but closed to cars. Great for an easy and very scenic mountain-bike ride.

Half-day mountain-bike tours are available for $40-50 per day from **Fat Tire Tours/Hoback Sports,** tel. (307) 733-5335, www.hobacksports.com; one of the tours includes a chairlift ride to the top of Snow King. **Teton Mountain Bike Tours,** tel. (307) 733-0712 or (800) 733-

0788, www.tetonmtbike.com, offers scenic half- or all-day bike trips through Grand Teton and Yellowstone National Parks as well as Bridger-Teton National Forest and the National Elk Refuge. These are for all levels of ability, with prices starting at $30 for a three-hour ride.

Scenic Rides

Take a fast and very scenic ride to the top of Rendezvous Mountain (10,450 feet) aboard the **aerial tram** at Teton Village. The tram ride takes 10 minutes, gains more than 4,000 feet in elevation, and costs $16 for adults, $13 for seniors, $6 for ages 6-17, free for kids under six. Call (307) 733-2753 or (800) 450-0477 for details. Open daily late May to late September, this is a sensational way to reach the alpine. On top is a small snack shop, but you should bring a lunch since the choices are limited and pricey. Several trails provide enjoyable hikes from the top, and naturalists lead free two-hour walks at 9:30 a.m. and 12:30 p.m. daily. You can rent hiking boots at Nick Wilson's Cafe and Gift Shop, at the base of the mountain. Be sure to pack drinking water and a warm jacket. The summit of Rendezvous Mountain is a favorite place for paragliders to launch. Tandem paragliding flights ($175) are available from **Two Can Fly Paragliding,** tel. (307) 739-2626. No experience is needed for these half-hour flights.

At Snow King Mountain right on the edge of Jackson, the resort's main **chairlift** operates during the summer, taking folks for a 20-minute ride to the summit of the 7,751-foot mountain for $7 ($5 for kids under 13, $6 for seniors). The chairlift runs daily 9 a.m.-6 p.m. On top you'll find a short nature trail and panoramic views of the Tetons. Call (307) 733-5200 for details. Also at Snow King is the 2,500-foot-long **Alpine Slide,** a favorite of kids. For adults and teens, the cost is $8 for one ride or $19 for three rides; for ages 6-12, it's $7 for one ride or $16 for three; and for children under six (riding with an adult) it's $1 per ride. Call (307) 733-7680 for details.

On the other side of the Tetons at **Grand Targhee Ski Resort,** you can ride the chairlift for $8 ($5 for kids) to the 10,200-foot summit of Fred's Mountain, where Grand Teton stands just seven miles away. The lift operates Wednesday, Saturday, and Sunday in June, and Wed.-Sun. in July and August.

Swimming

Jackson is home to the marvelous **Teton County/ Jackson Recreation Center,** 155 E. Gill St., tel. (307) 739-9025, which includes an indoor aquatics complex with a lap pool, corkscrew water slide, and hot tub, plus a wading pool featuring a waterfall, slide, and water geyser. After your workout, relax in the sauna and steam room. Nonresident prices are a steep $6 for adults, $4.75 for seniors and ages 13-17, $3.50 for ages 3-12, and $16 for families. The rec center also offers a variety of courses and activities, including yoga, toddler swimming, basketball, volleyball, and aerobics. It's open Mon.-Fri. 6 a.m.-9 p.m., Saturday noon-9 p.m., and Sunday noon-7 p.m.

Out of the way is the wonderful hot mineral pool (93-112° F) at **Granite Hot Springs,** tel. (307) 733-6318. Head south 12 miles to Hoback Junction and then 12 miles east on US Hwy. 189 to the turnoff for Granite. The pool is another 10 miles out a well-maintained gravel road—a total of 35 miles from Jackson. Entrance is $5.50 for adults, $3.50 for ages 3-12, free for infants; open daily 10 a.m. till dusk in the summer.

Golf and Tennis

Jackson Hole Golf & Tennis Club, a mile north of town, tel. (307) 733-3111, has an 18-hole golf course (rated one of the 10 best in America), a private swimming pool, and tennis courts. Also here is The Strutting Grouse Restaurant and Lounge, the perfect place for outdoor dining on the patio.

The **Teton Pines Country Club,** on Teton Village Rd., tel. (307) 733-1773 or (800) 238-2223, www.tetonpines.com, is Jackson Hole's other golf spot. Its Arnold Palmer-designed 18-hole championship course is very challenging; 14 of the holes require over-water shots. The club also features a grand clubhouse, tennis courts, a large (and private) outdoor pool, and fine dining at The Pines restaurant. Both Teton Pines and Jackson Hole Golf & Tennis Club have rentals and lessons for golfers and tennis aficionados. And for the truly serious professional golfer, **Alpine Miniature Golf,** tel. (307) 733-5200, offers a Lilliputian 18-hole course next to the Alpine Slide at Snow King Resort.

More Sports

Teton Rock Gym, 1116 Maple Way, tel. (307) 733-0707, offers large indoor climbing walls, a weight room, climbing instruction, and gear rentals. See Mountain Climbing in the Grand Teton National Park chapter for other mountain-climbing options.

If you're feeling flush with cash, call **Rainbow Balloon Flights,** tel. (307) 733-0470 or (800) 378-0470, or **Wyoming Balloon Co.,** tel. (307) 739-0900, both of which offer one-hour hot-air balloon flights for $175 per person. Wyoming Balloon Co. takes off from the Jackson Hole side of the mountains. Rainbow picks people up in Jackson and transports them over the mountains to Teton Valley, Idaho, for the flight.

For something a bit less exciting, there's always the local bowling alley, **Jackson Bowl,** at 1110 Maple Way, tel. (307) 733-2695.

Take exercise classes at **Jackson Hole Athletic Club,** 875 W. Broadway, tel. (307) 733-8830, which has a gymnasium with Nautilus and other equipment.

Hikes, Historical Walks, and Photo Treks

During June, July, and August, the **Teton County Parks and Recreation Department,** inside the Teton County/Jackson Recreation Center at 155 E. Gill St., tel. (307) 739-9025, sponsors various outings, including hikes for adults every Tuesday and Thursday ($7); senior walks on Monday morning (free); and kids outings with swimming, hiking, and more on Wednesday and Friday ($5). The office also rents out volleyballs, horseshoes, and croquet sets.

The Jackson Hole Museum, 105 N. Glenwood, tel. (307) 733-2414, leads hour-long **historical walking tours** of Jackson's downtown at 11 a.m. on Tuesday, Thursday, Friday, and some Saturdays, Memorial Day-September. The cost is $2 for adults, $1 for seniors and students, and $5 for families.

Educational nature walks into the mountains around Jackson are offered by **The Hole Hiking Experience,** tel. (307) 690-4453, www.holehike.com. Rates start at $45 ($32 for kids) for a four-hour hike. For a free version, Grand Teton National Park offers its own guided walks and nature talks throughout the year (see the Grand Teton National Park chapter for details). **Great Plains Wildlife Institute,** tel. (307) 733-2623, www.wildlifesafari.com, specializes in wildlife safaris and photography expeditions within Grand Teton and Yellowstone National Parks. The most unusual local tours are offered by Walt Farmer, a.k.a. the **Movie Tours of Jackson's Hole.** His day-long tours provide a fun visit to the setting for such films as *Shane* and *The Big Trail,* not to mention *Son of Lassie, Rocky IV,* and other forgettable flicks. Call (307) 690-6909 to schedule a tour, or visit www.jhinet.com/astrocowboy. The website has all sorts of Jackson Hole movie trivia and links.

WINTER RECREATION

For details on the many skiing and snowboarding opportunities in and around Jackson Hole, see the Downhill Skiing and Snowboarding and Cross-country Skiing sections later in this chapter.

Ice Skating

Each winter, the town of Wilson floods a hockey-rink-size part of the town park for skating, hockey, and broomball. A warming hut stands next to the rink. Jackson maintains a smaller ice rink at 155 E. Gill Ave., plus a rink in Snow King Ballpark which is used for hockey and broomball. All three of these are free to the public and are lighted 6-10 p.m. Call (307) 733-5056 for details.

All three local ski resorts have ice skating and skate rentals. You'll find skating ponds in Teton Village at the base of **Jackson Hole Mountain Resort** and across the Tetons in Alta at **Grand Targhee Ski Resort.** For the out-of-the-elements version, skate over to **Snow King Resort,** tel. (307) 733-3000 or (800) 522-5464, where the indoor ice-skating rink is open in the winter and offers skate rentals and lessons.

Snowshoeing

Snowshoeing began as a way to get around in the winter, and the old-fashioned wood-and-rawhide snowshoes were bulky and heavy. In recent years snowshoeing has become a popular form of recreation, as new technology created lightweight and easily maneuverable snowshoes. Snowshoeing requires no real training—just strap on the 'shoes, grab a pair of poles, and start walking. But be careful where you walk; see the special topic Safety in Avalanche Country for tips.

Grand Teton National Park has excellent naturalist-led **snowshoe hikes** several times each week during the winter months. Snowshoes are

A sleigh ride through the National Elk Refuge is a great way to see elk up close.

provided at no charge, and no experience is necessary. These generally depart at 2 p.m. from the visitor center in Moose, but for specifics call (307) 739-3399. Reservations are required; no kids under eight.

Snowshoe walks into the mountains around Jackson are also offered by **The Hole Hiking Experience,** tel. (307) 690-4453, www.holehike.com, the only company permitted to guide snowshoeing trips in Bridger-Teton and Targhee National Forests. The company's most popular trips go to Shadow Mountain north of Kelly.

All three local ski resorts offer snowshoeing. Guided snowshoe tours at **Snow King Resort** depart from the top of the Summit Lift. These are perfect for those looking for a break from skiing and snowboarding; call (307) 734-8077 for reservations and details. At **Jackson Hole Mountain Resort,** naturalist-led snowshoe hikes are included in the price of your lift ticket; call (307) 739-2753 for details. For information on snowshoe tours at **Grand Targhee Ski Resort,** call (800) 827-4433. Snowshoe trails and tours are also available at **Spring Creek Ranch Nordic Center,** three miles north of State 22 on Spring Gulch Rd., tel. (307) 733-1004 or (800) 443-6139. Spring Creek specializes in moonlight tours that climb East Gros Ventre Butte.

Rent snowshoes from **Skinny Skis,** 65 W. Deloney Ave., tel. (307) 733-6094 or (888) 733-7205, www.skinnyskis.com; **Teton Mountaineering,** 170 N. Cache Dr., tel. (307) 733-3595 or (800) 850-3595, www.tetonmtn.com; **Jack Dennis' Outdoor Shop,** 50 E. Broadway, tel. (307) 733-3270 or (800) 570-3270, www.jackdennis.com; **Gart Sports,** 485 W. Broadway, tel. (307) 733-4449; **Wilson Backcountry Sports,** Wilson, tel. (307) 733-5228; **Leisure Sports,** 1055 S. US Hwy. 89, tel. (307) 733-3040; and **Grand Targhee Ski Resort** in Alta, tel. (307) 353-2300 or (800) 827-4433.

Sleigh Rides

Several companies offer romantic dinner horse-drawn sleigh rides in the Jackson Hole area mid-December through March. Make reservations well in advance for these popular trips. If you don't have the cash for one of these, take a daytime sleigh ride at the National Elk Refuge (described earlier in this chapter).

Jackson Hole Mountain Resort picks up Teton Village guests for a romantic 30-minute ride to a rustic log cabin where they are served a four-course roast prime-rib or broiled salmon dinner. Prices are $50 for adults, $31 for children under 11. Call (307) 739-2603 for reservations (advised).

Spring Creek Ranch, tel. (307) 733-8833 or (800) 443-6139, www.springcreekranch.com, transports guests on an hour-long sleigh ride to the top of Gros Ventre Butte for dinner at the Granary restaurant. The cost is $48 for adults, $30 for kids under 12. They also offer a one-hour afternoon sleigh ride (no dinner) for $12 per person. No sleigh rides on Monday.

Dinner sleigh rides are also offered at **Grand Targhee Ski Resort,** tel. (800) 827-4433, where a horse-drawn sleigh transports you to a remote yurt for a Western-style meal; $30 for adults, $15 for kids.

Tubing

Two local ski areas have sliding parks with customized inner tubes and rope tows. At Snow King Resort it's called **King Tubes,** tel. (307) 734-8823, and is available during ski hours as well as in the evenings. Rates are $6/hour for adults, $5/hour for kids. The **Grand Targhee Ski Resort** tube park is open for après-ski fun only (after 5 p.m.) and costs $5 per hour; call (800) 827-4433 for details.

Dogsledding

Founded by Iditarod musher Frank Teasley, **Jackson Hole Iditarod Sled Dog Tours,** tel. (307) 733-7388 or (800) 554-7388, www.jhsledog.com, offers half-day trips ($135 per person including lunch) and all-day trips ($225 per person including a big dinner) up Shadow Mountain, along the Gros Ventre River, and out to Granite Hot Springs. Overnight trips to remote lodges are also available.

Washakie Outfitting, tel. (307) 733-3602 or (800) 249-0662, www.dogsledwashakie.com, leads a variety of dogsled tours in the Jackson Hole area, including one-and-a-half hour rides out of Teton Village for $60 ($40 for kids). For a more remote experience join their trips from Cowboy Village Resort at Togwotee (48 miles north of Jackson) or Brooks Lake Lodge (65 miles northeast of Jackson). On these, Iditarod veteran Billy Snodgrass offers half-day ($131), full-day ($175), overnight ($325), and extended trips with Alaskan husky racing dogs.

Geyser Creek Dog Sled Adventures, tel. (307) 739-0165 or (800) 531-6874, www.dogsledadv.com, also leads dogsled tours of the Brooks Lake area and offers longer trips as well, including a three-day sled adventure that makes overnight stops at a tepee and a yurt. All-day rates are $195 for adults, $95 for kids under age 10.

Grand Targhee Ski Resort, tel. (800) 827-4433, www.sharplink.com/dogsled, offers dogsled trips on the west side of the Tetons. Half-day rates are $115 for one or $200 for two people on a sled. They also lead moonlight dogsled tours where you can join the dogs in howling at the moon.

Snowmobiling

One of Jackson Hole's most popular—and controversial—wintertime activities is snowmobiling. Hundreds of miles of packed and groomed snowmobile trails head into Bridger-Teton National Forest as well as Yellowstone and Grand Teton National Parks. Some of the most popular places include the Togwotee Pass area 48 miles north of Jackson, Cache Creek Rd. east of town, and Granite Hot Springs Rd. 25 miles southeast. More than a dozen different Jackson companies offer guided all-day snowmobile trips into Yellowstone and elsewhere. Yellowstone tours typically cost $155-180 for one rider or $245-270 for two riders (including breakfast and lunch). Tours to other areas are usually less expensive, and some motels offer package deals. You can also rent machines for self-guided trips for around $120 per day. The visitor center has a complete listing of local snowmobile-rental companies and maps of snowmobile trails.

The controversial 365-mile-long **Continental Divide Snowmobile Trail** passes through the heart of Grand Teton National Park, connecting the Yellowstone road network with snowmobile trails that reach all the way to Atlantic City at the southern end of the Wind River Mountains. Unfortunately, this means that snowmobiles now roar into two of America's great national parks. Don't be a part of this desecration; instead, enjoy these parks in quieter, less hurried ways such as on snowshoes or cross-country skis.

SHOPPING

If you have the money, Jackson is a great place to buy everything from artwork to mountain bikes. Even if you just hitchhiked in and have no cash to spare, it's always fun to wander through the shops and galleries surrounding Town Square. The corporate chains and factory outlets have moved into Jackson, with a number of the standards to choose from: The Gap, Eddie Bauer, Pendleton, Ralph Lauren Polo, Häagen-Dazs, Big Dogs, and Scandia Down.

Outdoor Gear

Outdoor enthusiasts will discover several excellent shops in Jackson. Climbers, backpackers, and cross-country skiers head to **Teton Moun-**

Thousands of tourists flood downtown Jackson during the summer.

taineering, 170 N. Cache Dr., tel. (307) 733-3595 or (800) 850-3595, www.tetonmtn.com, for quality equipment, maps, and travel guides. This is America's oldest climbing shop. They also rent tents, sleeping bags, backpacks, cookstoves, climbing shoes, ice axes, cross-country skis, and even climbing and skiing videos. Check the bulletin board for used items.

Jack Dennis' Outdoor Shop, 50 E. Broadway, tel. (307) 733-3270 or (800) 570-3270, www.jackdennis.com, is a large upscale store that sells fly-fishing and camping gear in the summer and skis and warm clothes during the winter. They also rent almost anything: tents, stoves, lanterns, cookware, sleeping bags, fishing poles, fly rods, waders, float tubes, backpacks, skis, snowshoes, and more.

Skinny Skis, 65 W. Deloney Ave., tel. (307) 733-6094 or (888) 733-7205, www.skinnyskis.com, has more in the way of high-quality clothing and supplies, especially cross-country ski gear. Rent sleeping bags, tents, climbing shoes, ice axes, rollerblades, baby carriers, and backpacks here. Another place to rent outdoor gear of all types—including volleyball sets, fishing gear, float tubes, tarps, tents, sleeping bags, backpacks, campstoves, and lanterns—is **Leisure Sports,** 1075 S. US Hwy. 89, tel. (307) 733-3040. **Moosely Seconds,** 150 E. Broadway, tel. (307) 733-7176, has outdoor gear at good prices, including seconds from Patagonia, Grammici, Lowe, and other companies. A second Moosely Seconds out in Moose (tel. 307-739-1801) sells climbing and outdoor gear and rents trekking poles, ice axes, crampons, rock shoes, approach shoes, plastic boots, day packs, and snowshoes. The Moose store is open summers only.

Gart Sports, 485 W. Broadway, tel. (307) 733-4449, is a large store with a variety of outdoor and sports gear. Purchase used outdoor gear of all types from **Gear Revival,** 854 W. Broadway, tel. (307) 739-8699. The least expensive place to buy rugged outdoor wear, cowboy boots, and cowboy hats is **Corral West Ranchwear,** 840 W. Broadway, tel. (307) 733-0247.

Wyoming Wear, an Afton-based local manufacturer of colorful high-quality outdoor clothing, operates a retail shop near the square at 20 W. Broadway, tel. (307) 733-2991. Despite the name, nearly everything here is made from high-tech fabrics such as Polartec fleece. Wyoming Wear also produces a mail-order catalog; call (800) 732-2991 for a copy, or visit them on the web at www.wyomingwear.com. You can purchase many of the company's items (but not their famous fleece socks) online from www.rei.com.

Bargain Shopping

Buy used clothing and other items at **Browse 'N Buy Thrift Shop,** 139 N. Cache Dr., tel. (307) 733-7524, or the more chaotic **Orville's,** 285 W. Pearl, tel. (307) 733-3165. Hint: Browse 'N Buy puts out new items on Wednesday, attracting a queue of discount shoppers for their 1 p.m. opening. Get there early for the real deals! Orville's sometimes sells old Wyoming license plates—a big hit with European tourists. You can also find Wyoming license plates at the little country store in the town of Kelly, 15 miles north of Jackson.

INFORMATION AND SERVICES

Information Sources

Anyone new to Jackson Hole should be sure to visit the spacious **Wyoming State Information Center** on the north end of town at 532 N. Cache Dr., tel. (307) 733-3316, www.jacksonholechamber.com. Hours are daily 8 a.m.-7 p.m. between Memorial Day and Labor Day, and daily 8 a.m.-5 p.m. the rest of the year. (The phone is answered only on weekdays, but on weekends you can leave a message and they will send you an information packet.) The information center is a two-level, sod-roofed wooden building with natural history displays, a blizzard of free leaflets extolling the merits of local businesses, a gift shop selling books and maps, and an upstairs rear deck overlooking the National Elk Refuge. Ducks and trumpeter swans are visible on the marsh in the summer, and elk can be seen in the winter. The information center is staffed by the Jackson Hole Chamber of Commerce, along with Fish & Wildlife Service and Forest Service personnel in the summer. In addition to the main information center, you'll find racks of brochures at the airport, outside the Pink Garter Plaza on the corner of W. Broadway and Glenwood, at the stagecoach stop on Town Square, and at the Mangy Moose in Teton Village.

The **Bridger-Teton National Forest** supervisor's office is at 340 N. Cache Dr., tel. (307) 739-5500, www.fs.fed.us/btnf. It's open Mon.-Fri. 8 a.m.-4:30 p.m. Get information and Forest Service maps from the Wyoming State Information Center.

Find **National Public Radio** on your dial at 90.3 FM. The locals' station is **KMTN** at 96.9 FM. Other Jackson radio stations are KZJH 95.3 FM and KSGT 1340 AM.

Jackson Hole on the Web

I have attempted to incorporate Internet addresses for most Jackson Hole businesses, but these change constantly as more and more businesses go online and get their own domain name. By the time you read this virtually all Jackson Hole businesses may be on the web. If they aren't listed in the text, try one of the Internet search engines. A great place to begin your web tour is the chamber of commerce site: www.jacksonholechamber.com. Also very useful are www.jackson-hole.com, from Circumerro Publishing; and www.jacksonholenet.com, sponsored by *Jackson Hole Magazine.* All three of these contain links to dozens of local businesses of all types. You may also want to check out another local site, www.jacksonnetwork.com, which includes links to other communities throughout Wyoming and even a joke of the day. Federal government websites for the local area include Grand Teton National Park at www.nps.gov/grte, Yellowstone National Park at www.nps.gov/yell, Bridger-Teton National Forest at www.fs.fed.us/btnf, and Targhee National Forest at www.fs.fed.us/tnf.

Trip Planning

A number of local travel agencies offer reservation services for those who prefer to leave the planning to someone else. They can set up airline tickets, rental cars, lodging, horseback riding, fishing trips, whitewater rafting, ski vacations, and all sorts of other packages. The biggest is **Jackson Hole Central Reservations,** tel. (307) 733-4005 or (800) 443-6931. Find them on the web at www.jacksonholeresort.com (primarily summer info) or www.jhsnow.com (geared to winter use). Central Reservations will also send out big glossy brochures describing local ski areas and lodging. Also helpful for trip planning is the smaller **Resort Reservations,** tel. (307) 733-6331 or (800) 329-9205, www.jacksonholeres.com.

Post Offices

Jackson's main post office is at 1070 Maple Way, near Powderhorn Lane, tel. (307) 733-3650; open Mon.-Fri. 8:30 a.m.-5 p.m., Saturday 10 a.m.-1 p.m. Other post offices are downtown at 220 W. Pearl Ave., tel. (307) 739-1740; in Teton Village, tel. (307) 733-3575; in Wilson, tel. (307) 733-3335; and in Kelly, tel. (307) 733-8884.

Recycling

Just because you're on vacation doesn't mean you should just throw everything away. Jackson has a good recycling program and accepts newspaper, aluminum cans, glass, tin cans, plastic milk jugs, magazines, catalogs, cardboard, and white office paper. The recycling center, tel. (307) 733-7678, is the big brown building two miles south of the high school on US Hwy. 89. Bins are accessible 24 hours a day.

Medical Help

Because of the abundance of ski and snowboard accidents, orthopaedic specialists are in high demand in Jackson and are some of the best around. Physicians at Orthopaedics of Jackson Hole also tend to the U.S. and French national ski teams! For emergency medical attention, head to **St. John's Hospital,** 625 E. Broadway, tel. (307) 733-3636. Medical service by appointment or on a walk-in basis is available at several local clinics, including: **InstaCare of Jackson,** 545 W. Broadway, tel. (307) 733-7003; **Emerg-A-Care,** 975 W. Broadway (Powderhorn Mall), tel. (307) 733-8002; and **Jackson Hole Medical Clinic,** 988 S. US Hwy. 89, tel. (307) 739-8999. Unfortunately, none of these will bill your insurance company; you'll have to fork out the $75-80 and hope for a refund later.

Banking

Get fast cash from **ATMs** in more than a dozen locations around town—in banks, Albertson's, downtown in front of Sirk Shirts, at the airport, and in Teton Village and the Aspens. Note that most if not all local ATMs charge an extra $1.50 "service charge." Jackson has four different banks, several with ludicrously ostentatious structures (probably paid for in part by these service charges). You can escape this rip-off by making a purchase with your ATM card at one of the grocery stores and simultaneously withdrawing extra cash.

International travelers will appreciate the **currency exchange** at three Jackson State Bank locations: 112 Center St., 50 Buffalo Way, and in the Aspens on Teton Village Road. Call (307) 733-3737 for details.

Library

The spacious **Teton County Library,** 125 Virginian Lane, tel. (307) 733-2164, is the kind of library every town should have. Inside this new building is a large collection of books about Wyoming and the West, plus a great kids' section (complete with a fenced-in children's garden with a tepee). Computers provide **Internet access** and are available by reservation (call the library a day in advance) or on a walk-up-and-wait basis. Library hours are Mon.-Thurs. 10 a.m.-9 p.m., Friday 10 a.m.-5:30 p.m., Saturday 10 a.m.-5 p.m., and Sunday 1-5 p.m.

If you plan to be in the Jackson area for a week or more, it may be worth your while to get a visitor's library card. For a one-time fee of $5 you can check out up to four books at a time.

Books

Unlike many Wyoming towns where the book selection consists of a few bodice-buster romance novels in the local pharmacy, Jackson is blessed with several fine bookstores. **Teton Bookshop,** 25 S. Glenwood, tel. (307) 733-9220, is a small downtown shop with a knowledgeable staff. The larger **Valley Bookstore,** 125 N. Cache Dr., tel. (307) 733-4533, www.valleybook.com, sometimes has author signings and readings. **Main Event,** in the Powderhorn Mall at 980 W. Broadway, tel. (307) 733-7112, sells new books and CDs and rents a wide choice of videos. A few doors away in the mall is **Jackson Hole Book Traders,** tel. (307) 734-6001, where you'll find a surprising selection of used and rare books. **The Open Door,** 65 E. Pearl Ave., tel. (307) 734-9101, sells New Age titles.

Up in Grand Teton National Park, find natural history books and maps at the **Moose Visitor Center,** tel. (307) 739-3399, and **Colter Bay Indian Arts Museum,** tel. (307) 543-2467.

Newspapers

Jackson has not just one but two thick local newspapers, each produced in tabloid format. The ***Jackson Hole News*** (www.jacksonholenews.com) and the ***Jackson Hole Guide*** (www.jhguide.com) both publish weekly editions with local news for 50 cents, as well as weekday freebies found in shops in Jackson, Wilson, and Teton Village. The *Guide* typically represents more traditional Wyoming views (i.e., it's basically Republican) while the *News* has more liberal leanings. Despite any leanings, both are excellent sources of information and strive for balanced coverage of news.

Children in Jackson

Those traveling with children will find an abundance of kid-friendly options in Jackson Hole. A few noteworthy examples include: the hands-on Children's Gallery at the National Museum of Wildlife Art; playgrounds at Mike Yokel Jr. Park

(Kelly and Hall Sts.) and Miller Park (Powderhorn Lane and Maple Way); the excellent swimming pool and corkscrew water slide at the Teton County Recreation Center; the fine children's section of the library; chuck wagon dinners at Bar-T-Five or Bar J; comedies and melodramas at Jackson Hole Playhouse or Mainstage Theatre; the aerial tram up Rendezvous Mountain at Jackson Hole Resort; the evening shoot-outs at Town Square; horseback or wagon rides; and a boat ride and hike at Jenny Lake inside Grand Teton National Park. During the summer, older kids will also enjoy hiking, mountain-biking, Snake River float and whitewater trips, the Alpine Slide at Snow King Resort, and the putting course at Alpine Miniature Golf. In winter, snowboarding and skiing are favorites of older kids, but sleigh rides, dogsledding, ice skating, and snowshoeing are also fun.

For those traveling with tots, **Baby's Away,** tel. (307) 733-0387, rents all sorts of handy baby supplies, including car seats, cribs, gates, backpacks, swings, and high chairs. They have a similar operation at Grand Targhee Ski Resort, tel. (307) 787-2182, and will deliver locally. You'll find more stroller and backpack rentals—along with kids' clothing—at **Teton Kids,** 130 E. Broadway, tel. (307) 739-2176. Just down the street is a large toy shop, **Broadway Toys and Togs,** 48 E. Broadway, tel. (307) 733-3918. **Second Helpings,** 141 E. Pearl Ave., tel. (307) 733-9466, has a big selection of quality used baby and children's clothes. Call **Babysitting by the Tetons,** tel. (307) 733-0754, for child care.

Dog Kennels

Thinking of bringing a dog to Jackson but not sure what to do if the hotel won't allow pets? Several local kennels will keep an eye on Fido for you. Try **Kindness Kennels,** 1225 S. Gregory Lane, tel. (307) 733-2633; **Jackson Hole Veterinary Clinic,** Rafter J Subdivision, tel. (307) 733-4279; or **Spring Creek Kennels,** 1035 W. Broadway, tel. (307) 733-1606.

Other Services

Wash clothes at **Soap Opera Laundry,** 850 W. Broadway, tel. (307) 733-5584, or **Ryan Cleaners,** 545 N. Cache Dr., tel. (307) 733-2938. You'll find public lockers at Jackson Hole Mountain Resort during the winter.

To keep in touch with folks via e-mail, use the free terminals in the library (see above) or go to **Cyber City Grill,** 265 W. Broadway, tel. (307) 734-2582, where Internet access costs $5 for a half hour.

Amy Haggart of **Valley Valet,** tel. (307) 734-4116, offers a variety of services for those who would rather enjoy the scenery than run around on errands. For a fee, she'll shop for your groceries or other items, and she can also provide child care and arrange rental of a cellular phone.

LIVING IN JACKSON HOLE

Jackson Hole is an increasingly popular place to live and work—a fact that angers many longtime residents who themselves came here to escape crowds elsewhere. The surrounding country is grand, with many things to do and places to explore, the weather is delightful, and you're likely to meet others with similar interests. Jobs such as waiting tables, operating ski lifts, driving tour buses, cleaning hotels and condos, and doing construction work are plentiful. The unemployment rate generally hovers around two percent, and housing is so scarce—and jobs so plentiful—that the local rescue mission kicks folks out after a week if they don't find work. Wages are not high, but have improved with the rising demand for workers. Get to Jackson in mid-May and you'll find the papers filled with half a dozen pages of

employment ads, and Help Wanted signs at virtually every shop. Even in midsummer, many places are still looking for help.

Finding Work

The best jobs are those that either offer such perks as housing or free ski passes, or give you lots of free time to explore the area. To get an idea of available jobs, check local classified ads or stop by the Wyoming Job Service Center, 545 N. Cache Dr., tel. (307) 733-4091. You can also search for jobs on the state's Job Bank homepage: http://wyjobs.state.wy.us. Another good place to check is www.jacksonholejobs.com.

Navigating the Housing Maze

Unfortunately, because of Jackson Hole's popularity, finding a place to live is extremely difficult, especially during the peak summer and winter tourist seasons. As the moneyed class has moved in, those who work in service jobs find it tougher and tougher to obtain affordable housing. Reports of workers living out of their cars or commuting from Idaho are not uncommon. Land prices (and consequently housing costs) have been rising an average of 15% per year over the past decade. Because of this, the median home price is now twice what the median household income will buy! One-bedroom apartments rent for $700-900 per month, and buying a two-bedroom tract home will probably set you back at least $250,000. The median single-family home costs almost $400,000. More prestigious local homes sell for $1-3 million, and the very finest log mansions ("log cabins on steroids") fetch well over $5 million each. The inflation of real estate has attracted the major players: both Christie's and Sotheby's (the auction folks) have offices in Jackson.

A few Jackson-area businesses include housing as a way to lure workers, but this is the exception; many employees are forced to live under less-than-ideal conditions such as sleeping in tents during the summer or jamming into too-small apartments. The best times to look for a place to live are in April and November. Check the papers as well as local laundromat and grocery-store bulletin boards for apartments or cabins. The "Trash and Treasure" morning program on radio station KMTN (96.9 FM) is another place to try.

TRANSPORTATION

Access to Jackson Hole has become easier in recent years, with several airlines and daily buses now serving the city. Most summer visitors arrive by car, though a few more adventurous souls pedal in on bikes. If you're looking for or offering a ride, KMTN (96.9 FM), tel. (307) 733-4500, has daily ride-finder announcements during its "Trash and Treasure" radio program. Tune in weekdays 9:30-9:50 a.m.

By Air

Jackson Hole Airport is eight miles north of Jackson inside Grand Teton National Park. It's the only commercial airport within any national park. The airport is small and cozy, but has daily jet service to several American cities. The tarmac is often crowded with Lear jets and other transportation symbols of the elite. Those who don't have the bucks for their own private jet can choose **Delta/Delta Skywest,** tel. (800) 221-1212, www.delta-air.com (service through Salt Lake City); **American,** tel. (800) 433-7300, www.aa.com (flights from Dallas in the summer and Chicago in the winter); and **United/United Express,** tel. (800) 241-6522, www.unitedairlines.com (year-round service from Denver and winter service out of Los Angeles). **Jackson Hole Aviation,** tel. (307) 733-4767 or (800) 437-5387, offers scenic flights over the valley and charter air service.

Airport Shuttles

Alltrans/Gray Line, tel. (307) 733-4325 or (800) 443-6133, www.jacksonholenet.com/grayline, provides airport shuttle service to and from motels in Jackson ($12 one-way or $19 roundtrip per person) and Teton Village ($19 one-way or $29 roundtrip per person). The shuttles meet most commercial airline flights in the summer and winter months, but you should make advance reservations to be sure of an airport pick-up. Make outgoing reservations for motel pick-up a day in advance.

Taxicabs

Local taxis provide direct service from the airport to Jackson; $18 for one or two people. To Teton Village you're best off getting a roundtrip ticket for $27 per person. The taxi companies are: **Airport Taxi/Alltrans,** tel. (307) 733-1700 or (800) 443-6133; **All Star Taxi,** tel. (307) 733-2888 or (800) 378-2944; **Buckboard Cab,** tel. (307) 733-1112; **Cowboy Cab,** tel. (307) 734-8188; and **Teton Taxi & Backcountry Shuttle,** tel. (307) 733-1506. **Downhill Express,** tel. (307) 734-9525 or (877) 943-3574, may have lower rates than the other taxis, and it also provides service to Idaho Falls, West Yellowstone, and other destinations.

Car Rentals

Most of the national and regional chains offer rental cars in town or at the airport. Rent cars from **Alamo,** tel. (307) 733-0671 or (800) 327-9633, www.freeways.com; **Aspen Rent-A-Car,** tel. (307) 733-9224 or (877) 222-7736, www.aspenrentacar.com; **Avis,** tel. (307) 733-3422 or (800) 831-2847, www.avis.com; **Budget,** tel. (307) 733-2206 or (800) 527-0700, www.drivebudget.com; **Eagle Rent-A-Car,** tel. (307) 739-9999 or (800) 582-2128; **Hertz,** tel. (307) 733-2272 or (800) 654-3131, www.hertz.com; **Leisure Sports,** 1075 S. US Hwy. 89, tel. (307) 733-3040; **National,** tel. (307) 733-0735 or (800) 227-7368, www.nationalcar.com; **Rent-A-Wreck,** tel. (307) 733-5014 or (800) 637-7147, www.rent-a-wreck.com; **Rent Rite,** tel. (307) 739-9999; and **Thrifty,** tel. (307) 739-9300 or (800) 367-2277, www.thrifty.com. Of these, Alamo, Avis, Budget, and Hertz all have counters at the airport; most others provide a shuttle bus to town. You may be better off getting a car in town where you don't have to pay the additional taxes imposed at the airport.

Most Jackson Hole rental companies also offer 4WD cars and minivans. The best deals (if you don't mind used cars) are generally from Rent-A-Wreck. Note that peak-season car rental rates in Jackson are on the high side; expect to pay around $55 a day for a midsize car. Reserve cars at least a month ahead during the summer and two months ahead for midsummer or Christmas to New Year's.

START Buses

Local buses are operated by Southern Teton Area Rapid Transit and serve Jackson and Teton Village all year. START fares are 50 cents within town and $2 to Teton Village (cheaper for seniors and children). Discount coupons are available for multiple rides in the winter. Hours of operation are generally 7:30 a.m.-10 p.m. During the summer, buses run seven days a week, with in-town service every 15 minutes after 10 a.m. Service to Teton Village is eight times a day in the summer and more often in the winter. Reduced bus service is available in the fall and spring. Get bus schedules and route maps in the visitor center. Buses stop near most Jackson hotels and motels and are equipped to carry skis (in winter) and bikes (in summer) on outside racks. Wintertime service is also offered to the National Museum of Wildlife Art. Unfortunately, START buses do not run to the airport, Kelly, Moose, or Wilson. Call (307) 733-4521 for more information.

Buses and Tours

Greyhound buses don't come even close to Jackson; the nearest stopping places are Evanston, West Yellowstone, Idaho Falls, and the regional hub at Salt Lake City. **Jackson Hole Express,** tel. (307) 733-1719 or (800) 652-9510, www.jacksonholebus.com, provides daily bus or van connections between Salt Lake City ($45 one-way) or Idaho Falls ($20 one-way) and Jackson.

Community and Rural Transportation (CART), tel. (208) 354-2240 or (800) 657-7439, www.cyberhighway.net/~cartbus, has twice-daily bus service between Idaho Falls and Jackson for $19 one-way.

Wind River Transportation Authority (WRTA), tel. (307) 856-7118 or (800) 439-7118, provides on-demand service in western and southwestern Wyoming. You can call them for service between Salt Lake City and Jackson, or to other Wyoming towns, including Pinedale, Dubois, Evanston, Rock Springs, Lander, and Riverton.

Grand Teton Lodge Company, tel. (307) 733-2811 or (800) 628-9988, www.gtlc.com, has twice-daily summer shuttle buses between Jackson and Jackson Lake Lodge for $15 one-way (plus a $10 park entrance fee), and on to Colter Bay Village for an additional $2.75 one-way. Buses depart from the Homewood parking lot on the corner of Gill and Cache. Transportation from the airport to Jackson Lake Lodge is $20 one-way. They also lead narrated bus tours of Grand Teton National Park on Monday, Wednesday, and Friday for $20 ($10 for kids under 12) and of Yellowstone National Park on Tuesday,

Thursday, and Saturday for $44 ($26 for kids). Tours depart from Jackson Lake Lodge at 8:30 each summer morning.

Daily summertime bus tours of Grand Teton and Yellowstone National Parks are available from **Gray Line,** tel. (307) 733-4325 or (800) 443-6133, www.jacksonholenet.com/grayline. Yellowstone tours last 11 hours and cost $48 plus park entrance fees. Eight-hour Grand Teton tours are $45 plus the park entrance. Those without vehicles can use these tours for access to the parks; reserve ahead to schedule a pick-up in Jackson, Grand Teton, or Yellowstone. In Yellowstone, travelers can connect with other buses to West Yellowstone (Montana), Gardiner (Montana), or Cody. Gray Line's four-day tours of the Yellowstone and Grand Teton areas start at $654 for one person or $830 for two, including lodging (but only one meal). During the winter, Gray Line has daily bus runs to Flagg Ranch Resort for $35 one-way ($50 roundtrip), arriving in time to meet the snowcoach departures for Yellowstone. Reservations are required. Both **Buckboard Cab,** tel. (307) 733-1112, and **All Star Taxi,** tel. (307) 733-2888 or (800) 378-2944, also offer shuttles to Flagg Ranch Resort in the winter months ($75 for one to three people), as well as guided van tours of Jackson Hole and surrounding areas.

Other companies offering guided van tours of the area include: **Callowishus Park Touring Company,** tel. (307) 733-9521, www.ulster.net/~heberle; **Jackson's Hole Adventure,** tel. (307) 654-7849 or (800) 392-3165; **Rocky Mountain Outdoor Adventures,** tel. (307) 739-1001 or (888) 557-6465; and **Upstream Anglers/Outdoor Adventures,** tel. (307) 739-9443 or (800) 642-8979.

COURTESY AISLINN RACE

DOWNHILL SKIING AND SNOWBOARDING

Jackson Hole is fast gaining an international reputation as a winter destination. As access has become easier and the facilities more developed, many people have discovered the wonders of a Jackson Hole winter, especially one centered around a week of skiing or snowboarding. Three very different ski resorts attract the crowds: Grand Targhee for down-home, powder-to-the-butt conditions; Snow King for steep, inexpensive, edge-of-town slopes; and Jackson Hole for flashy and challenging world-class skiing. All three places have rental equipment, ski schools, and special programs for kids. Snowboarders and telemarkers are welcome on the slopes. These resorts combine with an incredible abundance of developed and wild places to ski cross-country to make Jackson Hole one of the premier ski destinations in America.

See your travel agent for package trips to any of the Jackson-area resorts. For daily ski reports—including information on both downhill and Nordic areas and the backcountry—listen to KMTN (FM 96.9) in the morning. Hot tip: If you plan to spend more than a couple of days in the area, it is probably worth your while to join the **Jackson Hole Ski Club,** tel. (307) 733-6433. In return for a $30 annual membership, you receive an impressive number of premiums, including discounted rates for lift tickets, lodging, meals, drinks, snowmobile trips, and shopping at dozens of local stores. Join up at any local ski shop.

Ski and Snowboard Rentals

Rent or buy downhill skis and snowboards from: **Hoback Sports,** 40 S. Millward St., tel. (307) 733-5335, www.hobacksports.com; **The Edge Sports,** 490 W. Broadway, tel. (307) 734-3916; **Gart Sports,** 485 W. Broadway, tel. (307) 733-4449; **Jack Dennis' Outdoor Shop,** 50 E. Broadway, tel. (307) 733-3270 or (800) 570-3270, www.jackdennis.com, and in Teton Village, tel. (307) 733-6838; **Pepi Stiegler Sports** in Teton Village, tel. (307) 733-4505; **Wildernest Sports,** Teton Village, tel. (307) 733-4297; **Teton Village Sports,** tel. (307) 733-2181 or (800) 874-4224; or **Leisure Sports,** 1055 S. US Hwy. 89, tel. (307) 733-3040. Rentals are also available at all three ski areas.

Snowboarders will find the latest gear at **Boardroom of Jackson Hole,** 245 W. Pearl, tel. (307) 733-8327; **Hole in the Wall Snowboard Shop,** tel. (307) 739-2689; **Lowrider Board Shop,** at Pepi Stiegler Sports in Teton

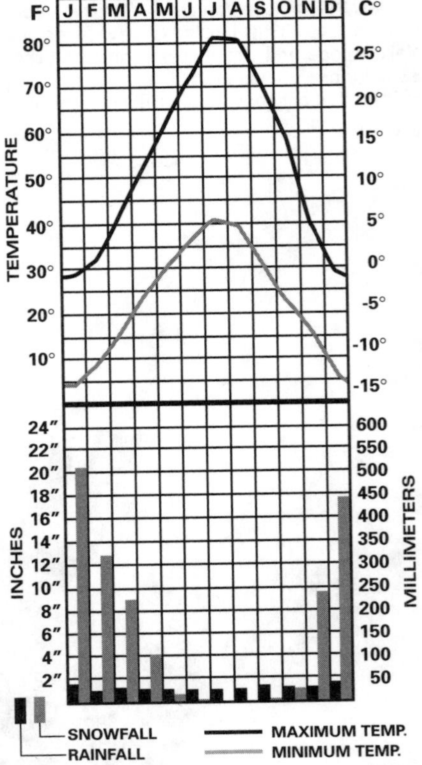

Average Maximum Temp.	53.8°F
Average Minimum Temp.	22.9°F
Annual Rainfall	15.98"
Annual Snowfall	74.8"

Village, tel. (307) 733-4505; and **Village Board Shop,** at Teton Village Sports, tel. (307) 733-2181 or (800) 874-4224. Over at Grand Targhee, rent or buy boards from **Phat Fred's,** tel. (307) 353-2300 or (800) 827-4433.

GRAND TARGHEE SKI RESORT

On the west side of the Tetons 44 miles from Jackson, Grand Targhee Ski Resort offers the friendliness of a small resort with the amenities and snow you'd expect at a major one. To get here you'll need to drive into Idaho and turn east at Driggs. The resort sits at the end of the road 12 miles east of Driggs and just six miles inside Wyoming. Their motto says it all: "Snow from heaven, not from hoses." With an annual snowfall topping 500 inches (42 feet!)—most of which is champagne powder—Targhee became the secret spot where powderhounds got all they could ever want. Ski magazines consistently rank it as having North America's best snow. In fact, the resort guarantees its snow: if you find conditions not to your liking, you can turn in your ticket within an hour of purchase and get a "snow check" good for another day of skiing.

Now owned by Booth Creek Resorts—one of the largest ski resort management companies in the nation—Grand Targhee has seen a number of changes in recent years, including remodeled lodging facilities and the addition of a tube park and ice skating rink for après-ski fun. The most significant change is a new quad chairlift that opens in 2000 on adjacent Peaked Mountain, providing access to 500 acres of intermediate skiing terrain. In addition, Grand Targhee is negotiating a land swap with the Forest Service to gain ownership of the public land on which the resort sits. If this happens (and it is very controversial), it may lead to a number of major developments at Targhee. But some things won't change: the beautifully groomed slopes, the uncrowded and relaxed setting, the dramatic Teton backdrop, and the friendly staff, including a number of cowboy-hatted potato farmers who double as lift operators.

The biggest drawback to Grand Targhee is the same thing that makes it so great—the weather. Lots of snow means lots of clouds and storms, and because it snows so much there are many days when the name cynics apply—"Grand Foghee"—seems more appropriate. Many folks who have returned to Targhee year after year have still not seen the magnificent Grand Teton backdrop behind the ski area! Be sure to bring your goggles. The new quad lift up adjacent Peaked Mountain will provide intermediate skiing on slopes that are more protected and suffer less wind and fog.

Skiing and Snowboarding

Call (800) 827-4433 for details on Grand Targhee, or find them on the web at www.grandtarghee.com. As of the 2000-01 winter season, the resort will offer up two quads, one double chairlift, and a surface lift on Fred's Mountain, plus a quad on adjacent Peaked Mountain. The top elevation is 10,200 feet, with the longest run dropping 2,200 feet over almost three miles. Although only 300 acres are groomed, that means you'll always find track-free skiing on the remaining 1,200 acres of ungroomed powder (bring your snorkel). In addition, snowcat skiing ($240 per day including lunch and guide) will continue to be offered on Peaked Mountain.

Lift tickets at Grand Targhee cost $42 a day ($30 a half day) for adults and $25 per day for children ages 14 and under and seniors (free under age six). Discounts are offered for multiday lift tickets or lodging-and-ski packages.

Fully 70% of Targhee's groomed runs are intermediate to advanced-intermediate, but advanced skiers will find an extraordinary number of deep-powder faces to explore. Snowboarders can play at the half-pipe. The ski school offers lessons for all abilities, and children's programs make it possible for parents to leave their kids behind. Cross-country skiers enjoy the Nordic center (see Cross-country Skiing below). Rental skis and snowboards are available at the base of the mountain. The ski area usually opens in mid-November and closes in late April, though some years you may be able to ski even into July. Lifts operate 9:30 a.m.-4 p.m. daily.

Other Winter Activities

Moon Mountain Ranch (www.sharplink.com/dogsled) leads **dogsled tours** from the lodge in the winter months, starting with a half-day trip for $115 per adult for single riders, or $100 per adult with two riders. Lunch trips and moonlight rides are also available. Guided **snowshoe wildlife tours** ($28) will appeal to amateur naturalists, and on the **sleigh ride dinner** ($30 for adults; $15 for kids), you'll ride in a horse-drawn sleigh to a yurt where a Western-style meal is served. Targhee's **tubing park** ($5/hour) is a fun place for kids to slide down a snowy hill, and Targhee also has an outdoor **skating pond** and skate rentals. Child care is available, and a **Kid's Club** at Targhee provides supervised activities.

Summer Activities

Not far from Grand Targhee are several popular summertime hiking trails (see Jedediah Smith Wilderness later in this chapter). The resort itself is a popular place to relax in the summer and offers many activities. The quad chairlift ($8 for adults, $5 for ages 6-14) takes you up the 10,200-foot summit of Fred's Mountain for strikingly close views of the Tetons. The lift operates Wednesday, Saturday, and Sunday in June, and Wed.-Sun. in July and August. A Forest Service naturalist leads mountaintop **guided walks** on weekends, or by request Wed.-Friday. The resort rents mountain bikes and lets you take them up the chairlift for a fast downhill run; guided mountain-bike tours are available.

Horseback rides and lessons are a favorite Targhee summertime activity; one-hour rides are $22. The climbing wall is open to all abilities and is a good place to learn some basic (or advanced) rock-climbing moves. Even more challenging is the adventure ropes course, for those who've always wanted to walk the high wire. Other summer activities/facilities at Targhee include Dutch oven dinners, basketball, an outdoor swimming pool and hot tub, a fitness center, tetherball, paragliding, tennis, and volleyball. The nine-hole **Targhee Village Golf Course** is just down the road. After all this, you'll probably

LOCALS DISCOUNT

By Tom Bie

It's seven o'clock on a frigid February morning and the alarm is buzzing you out of an especially cozy slumber.

If it were waking you for work, you'd hit that little button and crumple back under the covers for 10 more minutes in snoozeville.

But this is different. It has snowed all night and you're meeting your buddies in 30 minutes. You know they won't wait.

You climb off your mattress, step over your roommate and make your way up to the kitchen, where two cold pizzas have been waiting for five house since your other roommate left them after she got off work delivering them. The pepperoni and sausage is all the breakfast needed and you thank her silently for the offering.

You grab enough skis, boots, poles and warm clothing to make a complete outfit from the stockpile in the corner and you head out the door, wondering where you can get the quickest latté in town.

This is a winter morning for Jackson Hole locals, people who've often left real lives elsewhere for real skiing here. But there's more to being a local than being first in line at the tram dock. Being a citizen of a ski town carries with it certain benefits, but also certain responsibilities.

Yet the benefits are often all the visitor sees while sharing a 10-minute lift ride up the mountain.

Yes, we ski hard and ski often at one of the finest and most challenging resorts in the country. And yes, we know which bars to go to on which nights. We know which runs to ski on which days and we know which apres ski scene offers the best deal and that if our friends are working we may not have to pay at all.

But we do pay. We pay everytime we clock out at 2 a.m. the night before a powder day. We pay every time we write a $400 rent check for a room the size and temperature of a refrigerator's insides. We pay with every nail-pounding, boat rowing, table-serving, retail-working day of summer, when we put in six or seven 10-hour days a week in order to earn that ski pass.

A family on vacation may chat with the hired help at dinner in an attempt to gain some understanding of what it's like to be a local.

The group of young, nine-to-fiver city types out from Ohio to ski Corbet's may want desperately to know where that guy with the dreadlocks goes after he gets done serving them drinks. But the brief conversation between a waitress and her table guests rarely provides true insight.

want to relax with a massage, aromatherapy, facial, or steam bath from the on-site spa.

The **Targhee Institute** offers four-day science programs for children in the summer, including a range of fun classes. The institute also directs weeklong elderhostel programs April to early December. Call (307) 353-2233 for details.

Targhee Lodging

Call Targhee at (307) 353-2300 or (800) 827-4433 for details on lodging options at or near the resort, or visit the website: www.grandtarghee.com. The three lodges at the base of the mountain—Targhee Lodge, Teewinot Lodge, and Sioux Lodge (all in the Luxury price category)—offer ski-in, ski-out access, a large heated outdoor pool, hot tub, and workout room. Rates quoted below are for the winter holiday season; they're approximately 40% lower in the summertime. Most lodging places are closed from early September to mid-November, and from mid-April to mid-June.

Get standard motel accommodations at **Targhee Lodge** for $154 d. Deluxe hotel rooms with lodgepole furnishings and access to an indoor hot tub are $200 d at **Teewinot Lodge.** The lobby here is a fine place to relax in front of the fire on winter evenings. **Sioux Lodge** continues the Western theme with lodgepole furnishings, but also has kitchenettes, adobe-style fireplaces, and small balconies. Studio units are $269 d, loft units $364 d, and two-bedroom units $478 d. Rates are higher for more than two people in a room. The two-bedroom units can sleep eight for $557 per night. A wide variety of ski-and-lodging package deals are also available for stays over three nights. A package that provides seven nights lodging and six days of skiing costs $1,560 for two people during the holiday season at Targhee Lodge; rates are considerably higher in Teewinot or Sioux Lodge.

If you want to see what being a local in a ski town is really like, then you must enter the often squalid netherworld of a ski-tuning room at midnight, when the waxy scent of a hundred pairs of demo skis drips into your subconscience like a spilled bottle of cheap perfume.

You must waltz through a dishroom after the dinner bell rings and see the collective anguish of the night crew build like the 10-pound pile of pasta they've scraped into a nearby slag heap.

Then there are the "natives"—the truest locals in my book. Many tourists will joke that there must not be any natives left in Jackson Hole because they never meet any. But they're here. Plenty of them.

They may have just picked you up from the airport or taken you on a guided snowmobile trip but you would probably never know it because they are often the most unassuming people you'll meet.

They'll simply answer the questions politely that they've heard a thousand times and then go on knowing much more than you or I ever will.

With natives at the top, the caste system of localness drifts down through a twisted hierarchy of 90-day wonders, trust-funded voyagers, second-home owners and southerners, arriving finally at the subterranean world of the true skid, who owns little and wants less, knows of every cheap buffet and happy hour in town, has never held a winter day job and splits sleep time between van, borrowed couch space and the occasional significant other until the hospitality runs out.

They are the kings and queens of the "poverty with a view" set and often constitute not only the underbelly of an industry but also the strongest skiers on the mountain.

"So how long do they think they can do this?" is an oft-heard question during a chairlift ride with a resident of reality. "What'll they do when they're done skiing?"

But what the askers don't get, what they'll never get, is that the purest ski bums rarely look beyond skiing because they can't imagine life without it.

Skiing isn't an escape from reality, it's simply the only reality these people have ever wanted or cared for and no amount of money or power or family life is likely to change that.

These are the locals for whom a deep powder day is paradise found, and they will never smile a bigger, more meaningful smile than the one produced as a result of diving into a stash of bottomless snow.

It may be fleeting, but it is genuine and, crazy as it sounds, I've seen it be a stronger producer of happiness than anything, even love, often is for the rest of us.

The resort also has off-site condo lodging available approximately 10 miles down the hill at **Teton Creek Resort** and **Powder Valley Condominiums** (also Luxury price category). Choose from one-, two-, and three-bedroom condominiums, each with fireplace, kitchen, private patio, and VCR. Outdoor jacuzzis are also available. Nightly holiday-season rates start at $155 for the one-bedroom units up to $345 for eight people in a three-bedroom unit. Most people rent these condos on a weekly basis; four people can stay in a two-bedroom unit for $657 per week during the winter holiday season.

In addition to the places at the base of the resort, lodging is available just down the hill in Alta, Wyoming, and in the nearby Idaho towns of Driggs, Victor, and Tetonia. For details on these, see Teton Valley, Idaho, at the end of this chapter.

Food and Entertainment

At the base of Grand Targhee is a compact cluster of shops and lodging places. You won't have to walk far to find a cafeteria, pizza place, and burger joint. The nicest place is **Skadi's,** serving hearty breakfasts and lunches, along with cozy dinners. Grand Targhee's social center is the **Trap Bar,** with live music on winter weekends, and pub grub on the menu all the time. Guests at Targhee can also take a horse-drawn sleigh on a 15-minute ride to a Mongolian-style yurt for a home-cooked steak or chicken dinner. The price is $30 ($15 for kids ages 14 and under), and reservations are required. Other shops here sell groceries, ski and snowboard gear, clothing, and gifts.

Lost Horizon Dinner Club, tel. (307) 353-8226, is five miles below the resort in the town of Alta and is highly recommended for a relaxing formal dinner. See Alta, Wyoming, at the end of this chapter, for details.

Getting There

Grand Targhee is 42 miles northwest of Jackson on the western side of the Tetons in Alta, Wyoming. Get there by driving over Teton Pass (occasionally closed by winter storms), north through Victor and Driggs, Idaho, and then east back into Wyoming.

The **Targhee Express** bus makes daily wintertime trips (90 minutes each way) to Grand Targhee from Jackson and Teton Village. Buses leave from several Jackson motels around 7:30 a.m. and return from Targhee at 4:30 p.m. for a roundtrip fare of $51, including a full-day lift ticket. (Roundtrip bus fare alone costs $13.) Reservations are required; make them before 9 p.m. on the night before by calling (307) 733-3101 or (307) 734-9754. You can also pick up tickets from the company's Jackson offices at 110 W. Broadway or inside the Mangy Moose Building at Teton Village. Van service is also available year-round to airports in Jackson or Idaho Falls, Idaho. Call the resort for details; tel. (307) 353-2300 or (800) 827-4433.

Downhill Express, tel. (307) 734-9525 or (877) 943-3574, has a similar over-the-Tetons bus service for skiers.

Events

End the year—and start the new one—with **Torchlight Parades** at Grand Targhee on the evenings of December 25 and 31. Also on New Year's Eve is a fireworks display over the mountain. Each March, the resort celebrates telemark skiing with **Nordic Fest.** Ski races of all sorts take place, including the potato race and Elvis jumping contest.

Grand Targhee is home to two very popular outdoor music festivals during the summer. **Rockin' the Tetons Music & Microbrew Festival** comes on the second weekend of July and features well-known rock and blues musicians. It's also a good time to sample some of the region's best microbrews. The equally popular **Targhee Bluegrass Festival** appears in mid-August, again featuring national acts. Bring your dancin' shoes! Both of these attract hundreds of people, so call the resort well ahead of time for camping or lodging reservations.

JACKSON HOLE MOUNTAIN RESORT

Just 12 miles northwest of Jackson is Jackson Hole Mountain Resort, the largest and best-known Wyoming ski area. A true skiers' and snowboarders' mountain, Jackson Hole is considered the most varied and challenging of any American ski area. The powder is usually deep (average snowfall is 38 feet), lift lines are short, the slopes are relatively uncrowded, and the vis-

tas are unbelievable. First opened in 1965, Jackson Hole Mountain Resort has become one of the nation's favorite ski areas.

The resort has invested many millions of dollars over the last several years, upgrading facilities, adding lifts, expanding snowmaking, completing a spacious children's center, and building an ice rink and snowboarding half-pipe. These improvements have helped expand the resort's reputation as an expert's paradise to also include facilities more friendly to families and intermediate skiers. The mountain has one unusual feature that occurs in midwinter: a temperature inversion frequently develops over the valley, meaning that when it's bitterly cold at the base of the mountain, the top is 15-20° F warmer. Skiers often remain on the upper slopes all day to enjoy these warmer temperatures.

Reach Jackson Hole Mountain Resort at tel. (307) 733-2292 or (888) 333-7766, or on the web at www.jacksonhole.com.

Superlatives

With an unsurpassed 4,139-foot vertical drop (longest in the U.S.), 2,500 acres of terrain spread over two adjacent mountains, runs that exceed four miles in length, and 24 miles of groomed trails, Jackson Hole Mountain Resort is truly a place of superlatives. Half the resort's 60 runs are in the advanced category—including several of the notorious double-diamonds—but it is so large that even rank beginners will find plenty of bunny slopes on which to practice.

The only way to the summit of 10,450-foot Rendezvous Mountain is aboard one of the 63-passenger aerial tram cars. Powered by 500-horsepower engines, they climb nearly two and a half miles in 10 minutes, offering jaw-dropping views across Jackson Hole. Rendezvous Mountain is where experts strut their stuff on these steep and fast slopes, and if you're not at least close to the expert status you'll find your blood pressure rising as the tram heads up the mountain. More than a few skiers and boarders have taken the tram back down after seeing what lies below. And yes, those death-defying cliff-jumping shots are real; from the tram, check out infamous Corbet's Couloir, a rocky gully that requires a leap of faith and suicidal urges.

Fortunately, intermediate skiers and boarders are not given short shrift at Jackson Hole Mountain Resort, particularly on the friendlier slopes of 8,481-foot Apres Vous Mountain. Intermediate (and advanced) downhillers could spend all day playing on these slopes, and the 1999/2000-season addition of a high-speed quad here means that riders can blast to the summit of Apres Vous in just five minutes. Because of the speed of this and other new lifts, the wait at the base is now usually just a few minutes.

In addition to these lifts, you can ride a gondola, three other quad chairs, a triple chair, double chair, and poma lift. Snowboarders will appreciate the half-pipe and boarders' terrain trail. The resort's Kids Ranch provides supervised day care, including a spacious play area. Not far away is a special "magic carpet" (a conveyer belt of sorts) for children learning to ski or snowboard.

Rates and Services

Get to Teton Village from the town of Jackson by hopping on the START bus ($2 each way). This is the only inexpensive part of a visit to Jackson Hole Resort, since prices for lift tickets approach the stratosphere. Single-day tickets for all lifts (including the tram) are $54 for adults ($40 per half day) and $27 ($20 per half day) for kids under 14 and seniors. Multiday all-lift tickets—the most common kind bought—are $240 a week (five days of skiing) for adults or $120 a week for kids. Lifts are open 9 a.m.-4 p.m. daily (last tram departs at 3:30 p.m.) from around Thanksgiving till early April.

Skis and snowboards can be rented at shops in Jackson or Teton Village. The ski school offers a special Kinderschule program for children, and beginning snowboarders can learn from the pros. Jackson Hole Resort even has special steep snowboarding and skiing camps, where you learn from extreme downhill fanatics. Tommy Moe—gold and silver medalist at the 1994 Lillehammer Winter Olympics—teaches a four-day ski camp at the resort in January and is a ski ambassador for the resort; he also owns a home in the area. Jackson Hole's director of skiing (he headed the ski school here for 30 years) is Pepi Stiegler, the Austrian winner of a silver medal in the 1960 Olympics and a gold medal in the 1964 Olympics. You can get two hours of instruction from Pepi on weekday mornings; call (307) 739-2663 for reservations and Olympic-class prices.

Ski hosts are scattered around the mountain, ready to provide information and free hourly tours of the slopes from the top of Rendezvous Mountain. Racers and spectators will enjoy NASTAR events each Sunday, Tuesday, and Thursday, along with various other competitions throughout the winter.

If you're looking for untracked powder, call **Jackson Hole Guide Service,** tel. (307) 739-2663, which leads small groups of folks to parts of the mountain off-limits to mere mortals. Powder-hound skiers with a ton of cash will find unparalleled outback conditions accessed via **High Mountain Heli-Skiing,** tel. (307) 733-3274, www.skitvs.com. Note, however, that the areas where the choppers land are under consideration for wilderness status, and heli-skiing in these backcountry areas is not supported by some local environmental groups.

For more information on Jackson Hole Mountain Resort, call (307) 733-2292 or (888) 333-7766. Get recorded snow conditions by calling (307) 733-2291; the messages are changed each morning before 5 a.m. Find them on the Internet at www.jacksonhole.com.

Teton Village

At the base of the mountain is the Swiss-style Teton Village—alias "the Vill." Everything skiers and boarders need is crowded together here: lodges, a hostel, condominiums, espresso stands, restaurants, après-ski bars, gift shops, groceries, booze, ski and snowboard rentals, storage lockers, car rentals, a skating pond, child care, and even a travel agency for escapes to Hawaii.

On-the-mountain facilities include Casper Restaurant at the bottom of Casper Bowl, and snack bars at the top of the tram, the base of Thunder chairlift, and the top of Apres Vous chairlift. Casper Restaurant serves a barbecue picnic most days and is a popular place to meet up with friends for lunch.

SNOW KING RESORT

Snow King Resort has three things that other local ski areas lack: location, location, and location. The resort sits directly behind town and just seven blocks from Town Square. This is the locals' place, Jackson's "town hill," but it also offers surprisingly challenging runs. It may not be the largest or fanciest place around, but the King's ski runs make up in difficulty what they lack in size. From below, the mountain (7,871 feet tall) looks impossibly steep and narrow. High atop the big chairlift, the vista provides a panoramic tour of Jackson Hole and the Tetons.

Snow King was the first ski area in Wyoming—it opened in 1939—and one of the first in North America. The original chapter of the National Ski Patrol was established here in 1941. The mountain has a 1,571-foot vertical drop. You'll find more than 400 acres of skiable terrain at Snow King, with the longest run stretching nearly a mile. A triple chair, two double chairs, and a Poma lift climb the mountainside. Other features include snowmaking, a tubing park, and a very popular 300-foot half-pipe and terrain park for snowboarders. It's the only local resort with lights for nighttime skiing.

Rates and Services

Prices for lift tickets at Snow King are well below those at other Jackson Hole resorts: $30 a day ($20 per half day) for adults and $20 a day ($12 per half day) for kids under 15 and seniors. Hours of operation are 9:30 a.m.-4:30 p.m., with **night skiing** (Mon.-Sat. 4:30-8:30 p.m.) available on the lower sections of Snow King for an additional $14 for adults or $9 for kids and seniors. In addition, the King has hourly rates for lift tickets ($9/hour for adults, $5/hour for kids and seniors), perfect for skiers and boarders who arrive late in the afternoon and want to hit the slopes for an hour. With some of the best snowmaking in Wyoming, the resort usually opens by Thanksgiving and remains in operation till early April.

At the base of Snow King you'll discover a lodge with reasonable ski-and-stay packages. A plethora of lodging options are scattered around the adjacent town of Jackson. Also at Snow King are two restaurants, the Shady Lady Saloon, ski and snowboard rentals and lessons, plus a variety of other facilities, including an indoor ice rink and mountaintop snack-shack. Guided snowshoe tours are available; call (307) 734-8077 for details. Jackson's START buses offer frequent service to town (50 cents) or Teton Village ($2). For more info on Snow King Resort, call (307) 733-5200 or (800) 522-5464 (outside Wyoming), or find them on the Internet at www.snowking.com.

CROSS-COUNTRY SKIING

For many Jackson Hole residents the word "skiing" means heading across frozen Jenny Lake or telemarking down the bowls of Teton Pass rather than sliding down the slopes of the local resorts. Jackson Hole has become a center for cross-country enthusiasts and offers an impressive range of conditions—from flat-tracking along summertime golf courses where a gourmet restaurant awaits, to remote wilderness settings where a complete knowledge of snowpack structure, avalanche hazards, and winter survival techniques is essential. Beginners will probably want to start out at a Nordic center, progressing to local paths and the more gentle lift-serviced ski runs with experience. More advanced skiers will quickly discover incredible snow in the surrounding mountains.

Ski Rentals

Rent or buy cross-country skis from: **Skinny Skis,** 65 W. Deloney Ave., tel. (307) 733-6094 or (888) 733-7205, www.skinnyskis.com; **Teton Mountaineering,** 170 N. Cache Dr., tel. (307) 733-3595 or (800) 850-3595, www.tetonmtn.com; **Jack Dennis' Outdoor Shop,** 50 E. Broadway, tel. (307) 733-3270 or (800) 570-3270, www.jackdennis.com; **Wilson Backcountry Sports,** Wilson, tel. (307) 733-5228; or **Leisure Sports,** 1055 S. US Hwy. 89, tel. (307) 733-3040. All the local Nordic centers also rent equipment. Most places rent both classical cross-country skis and skate skis (much faster and a better workout), along with telemarking equipment. In addition, randonnée (alpine touring) skis are available from Wilson Backcountry Sports, Teton Mountaineering, and Skinny Skis.

NORDIC CENTERS

Jackson Hole Nordic Center

Nordic skiing enthusiasts will find three different developed facilities near Jackson and others at Grand Targhee Ski Resort and near Togwotee Pass. Largest is Jackson Hole Nordic Center, tel. (307) 739-2629, with 17 km of groomed trails—both set track and skating lanes that cover a wide range of conditions. Call (307) 733-2291 for the snow report. Located in Teton Village, this is the best place to learn cross-country skiing. Daily trail passes are $8 a day for adults or $5 a day for children and seniors. Traditional cross-country skis, skate skis, and telemarking equipment are available for rent, along with lessons. Hours are daily 8:30 a.m.-4:30 p.m. After 12:30 p.m., you can exchange your alpine lift ticket at Jackson Hole Mountain Resort for one at the Nordic center (but, hey, it better be for no extra charge since you already dropped $54!). The center offers a wide spectrum of lessons and tours.

Teton Pines Cross-Country Ski Center

Located along Teton Village Rd., Teton Pines features 14 km of groomed track (both classical and skating) on a summertime golf course. Daily trail passes cost $8 for adults or $5 for children, and ski rentals and lessons are avail-

able. Hours are daily 9 a.m.-5 p.m. The clubhouse here has a pricey restaurant for gourmet après-ski lunches and dinners. Get details by calling (307) 733-1005 or (800) 238-2223, or on the web at www.tetonpines.com.

Spring Creek Ranch Nordic Center
Three miles north of State Hwy. 22 on Spring Gulch Rd., Spring Creek, tel. (307) 733-1004 or (800) 443-6139, www.springcreekranch.com, is open 9:30 a.m.-4:30 p.m. daily. If you're staying in town, you can catch the free shuttle bus at the Wort Hotel; call the Nordic center for specifics. Guests of the Spring Creek Ranch ski free here. The center has 15 km of gentle groomed trails with skating lanes, making this perfect for beginners. Trail passes are $8 a day for adults or $5 a day for seniors or kids. Ski rentals and lessons are available. Half-day guided ski tours cost $45, and guided snowshoe tours are $30 for a half day (including snowshoe rental). There's a two-person minimum on ski and snowshoe tours. The center also has separate snowshoe trails ($5) available if you want to head out on your own.

Brooks Lake Lodge
Considerably farther afield, but worth the drive, is Brooks Lake Lodge, 65 miles northeast of Jackson near Togwotee Pass. The lodge has some of the most incredible scenery and cross-country skiing in the West, and it's five miles off the highway on a machine-packed road, making it a perfect destination for overnight trips. Once there, you'll find another five km of groomed trails plus access to the nearby Teton Wilderness, where skiers can escape the snowmobiles. Get details by calling (307) 455-2121 or visting the website, www.brookslake.com. See Accommodations above for more on Brooks Lake Lodge.

Grand Targhee Nordic Center
On the west side of the Tetons 44 miles out of Jackson, Grand Targhee Nordic Center, tel. (307) 353-2300 or (800) 827-4433, www.grandtarghee.com, has 15 km of groomed cross-country ski trails covering rolling terrain. Trail passes are $8 for adults and $5 for seniors and kids. Lessons, ski rentals, and a variety of tours are also available. Hours are daily 9:30 a.m.-4 p.m. Guests with Targhee lodging packages can ski free on the cross-country tracks.

ON YOUR OWN

Nordic skiers who would rather explore Jackson Hole and the mountains that surround it on their own will discover an extraordinary range of options, from beginner-level treks along old roads to places where only the most advanced skiers dare venture. Because Jackson has so many cross-country fanatics (and visiting enthusiasts), tracks are quickly broken along the more popular routes, making it easier for those who follow. For complete coverage of all these options, pick up a copy of the helpful free winter outdoors guide ***Trailhead*** at Skinny Skis, 65 W. Deloney Ave., tel. (307) 733-6094 or (888) 733-7205, www.skinnyskis.com. The store also rents cross-country, skating, and telemark skis, and snowshoes. If you're heading out on your own, be prepared for deep snow (four feet in the valley) and temperatures that often plummet below zero at night.

The **Teton County Parks and Recreation Department,** inside the recreation center at 155 E. Gill, tel. (307) 739-9025, leads a variety of all-day cross-country ski outings every Tuesday from mid-December to mid-March for $7-10 per person. Bring your own skis and a lunch—they provide the guide and transportation. The department also offers a full-moon ski tour once each winter.

Ski Tours
Jackson Hole Mountain Guides, tel. (307) 733-4979 or (800) 239-7642, www.jhmg.com, runs wintertime ski tours, avalanche courses, and ski mountaineering outings, along with rock- and ice-climbing classes. Longer winter trips, including a six-day Teton Crest tour, are also available.

Over on the western slopes of the Tetons, **Rendezvous Ski Tours** maintains three Mongolian-style yurts in the Jedediah Smith Wilderness, each located several hours of skiing (or hiking) from the next. The huts can sleep up to eight and have kitchens, bunks, sleeping bags, and woodstoves. Rates are $165 per night, but you need to be experienced in backcountry skiing and have the necessary safety equipment and avalanche training. If you don't quite measure up, they can provide guided backcountry ski tours to the huts ($360/day for two people). A good base for these trips is the company's modern three-bedroom guest house at the mouth of Fox Creek Canyon, eight miles north of Victor. The home comes complete with all the amenities, including a hot tub. You can rent the entire place for $300, or $75 d if you're willing to share with other folks, including a make-it-yourself breakfast. For details on the various options, call Rendezvous at (208) 787-2906, or look them up on the web at www.skithetetons.com.

Jackson Area

Even rank beginners will enjoy exploring several local spots. Get to **Moose-Wilson Road** by heading a mile north of Teton Village to where the plowing ends. The nearly level road continues for two scenic miles across a creek and through groves of aspen. For more adventure, turn off at the **Granite Canyon Trailhead** (a mile up the unplowed Moose-Wilson Rd.) and follow the trail along the moraine, which offers a range of skiing conditions. Just don't ski into the canyon, where avalanches are a hazard.

The closest place to Jackson for on-your-own cross-country skiing is **Cache Creek Canyon.** The trailhead is at the east end of Cache Creek Dr., where the plowing ends at a parking lot. Snowmobiles and skiers have packed the route. For a longer trip, take the Rafferty ski lift at Snow King and then ski west through the trees and down to Cache Creek, returning via the road. Ask at Snow King Resort for specifics. Another popular local place is along the **Snake River dikes,** where State Hwy. 22 crosses the river a mile east of Wilson. The dikes extend along both sides of the river for several miles, making for easy skiing. This is also a good place to watch ducks, moose, and other critters or to listen to the river rolling over the rocks.

Grand Teton National Park Area

A bit farther afield, but well worth the detour, are several trails in Grand Teton National Park. Orange markers denote the paths, but these are not machine-groomed, just tracks laid down by other skiers. Park at the Cottonwood Creek bridge (the road isn't plowed beyond this) and head out for **Jenny Lake** (nine miles roundtrip) or **Taggart Lake** (three miles roundtrip). Just three miles south of Moose on Moose-Wilson Rd., you may also want to try the trail to **Phelps Lake** (five miles roundtrip). Or, if you have more ambition and skill (along with avalanche beacons and other gear), longer routes could take you far up into the canyons of the Tetons. Be sure to stop at the Moose Visitor Center for current conditions and a copy of their trail map. Overnight ski tourers must also register here.

For unsurpassed vistas of the Tetons, try skiing to the top of 8,252-foot **Shadow Mountain,** 14 miles northeast of Jackson. From the town of Kelly, drive another five miles north to a parking area—the road isn't plowed beyond this—and then ski up the nearby Forest Service road that snakes up the mountain. It's fairly steep in places and seven miles roundtrip. Snowmobilers also use this road, so be ready to move out of the way quickly.

Granite Hot Springs

One of the most popular ski- and snowmobile-in sites is Granite Hot Springs, tel. (307) 734-7400, a delightful hot-spring-fed pool on Forest Service land. Get there by driving 25 miles southeast of Jackson into Hoback Canyon and then skiing 10 miles in from the signed parking area. The route is not difficult, but due to the distance it isn't recommended for beginners unless they are prepared for a 20-mile roundtrip trek. The pool costs $5.50 for adults, $3.50 for ages 3-12, and free for infants. It's open 10 a.m. to dusk. Bring your swimsuit or rent a suit and towel here. Ask the attendant about places to snow camp nearby.

Teton Pass

Locals head to 8,429-foot Teton Pass when they really want to test their abilities. The summit parking area fills with cars on fresh-snow mornings as everyone from advanced beginners to world-class ski mountaineers heads out for a day in the powder or a week of wilderness trekking in the Tetons. Snow depths of eight feet or more are not uncommon in midwinter. (The snow once became so deep on the pass that it

SAFETY IN AVALANCHE COUNTRY

Backcountry skiing is becoming increasingly popular in the mountains surrounding Jackson Hole. Unfortunately, many skiers fail to take the necessary precautions. Given the enormous snowfalls that occur, the steep slopes the snow piles up on, and the high winds that accompany many storms, it should come as no surprise that avalanches are a real danger.

Nearly all avalanches are triggered by the victims. If you really want to avoid avalanches, ski only on groomed ski trails or "bombproof" slopes, which, because of aspect, shape, and slope angle, never seem to slide. Unfortunately, this isn't always possible, so an understanding of the conditions that lead to avalanches is imperative for backcountry skiers. The Forest Service produces a useful booklet called ***Basic Guidelines for Winter Recreation,*** available in many of its offices around Wyoming. The best way to learn about backcountry safety is through an avalanche class. These are offered in the Jackson area by **American Avalanche Institute,** tel. (307) 733-3315, www.avalanchecourse.com; **Skinny Skis,** tel. (307) 733-6094 or (888) 733-7205, www.skinnyskis.com; **Teton Mountaineering,** tel. (307) 733-3595 or (800) 850-3595, www.tetonmtn.com; and **Jackson Hole Mountain Guides,** tel. (307) 733-4979 or (800) 239-7642, www.jhmg.com. Failing that, you can help protect yourself by following these precautions when you head into the backcountry:

- Before leaving, get up-to-date avalanche information. On the web, you can visit www.avalanche.org for links to avalanche forecasting sites throughout the Western states. For the Jackson Hole area, contact the 24-hour Forest Service's **Backcountry Avalanche Hazard & Weather Forecast,** tel. (307) 733-2664, www.untracked.com/forecast. For areas around Yellowstone—including West Yellowstone and Cooke City on the margins and the Washburn Range inside the park—contact the **Avalanche Advisory Hotline** in Bozeman, tel. (406) 587-6981, www.gomontana.com/avalanche. If they say the avalanche danger is high, ski on the flats instead.
- Be sure to carry extra warm clothes, water, high-energy snacks, a dual-frequency avalanche transceiver (make sure it's turned on and you know how to use it!), a lightweight snow shovel (for digging snow pits or excavating avalanche victims), an emergency snow shelter, first-aid supplies, a Swiss Army or Leatherman knife, topographic map, an extra plastic ski tip, flashlight, matches, and compass. Many skiers also carry that cure-all, duct tape, wrapped around a ski pole. Let a responsible person know exactly where you are going and when you expect to return. It's also a good idea to carry special ski poles that extend into probes in case of an avalanche. Check with local ski shops, or talk to Forest Service or Park Service folks for details on specific areas.
- Check the angle of an area before you ski through it; slopes of 30-45 degrees are the most dangerous; lesser slopes do not slide as frequently.
- Watch the weather; winds over 15 mph can pile snow much more deeply on lee slopes, causing dangerous loading on the snowpack. Especially avoid skiing on or below cornices.
- Avoid the leeward side of ridges, where snow loading can be greatest.
- Be aware of gullies and bowls; they're more likely to slip than flat open slopes or ridgetops. Stay out of gullies at the bottom of wide bowls; these are natural avalanche chutes.
- Look out for cracks in the snow, and listen for hollow snow underfoot. These are strong signs of dangerous conditions.
- Look at the trees. Smaller trees may indicate that avalanches rip through an area frequently, knocking over the larger ones. Avalanches can, however, also run through forested areas.
- Know how much new snow has fallen recently. Heavy new snow over older weak snow layers is a sure sign of extreme danger on potential avalanche slopes. Most avalanches slip during or immediately after a storm.
- Learn how to dig a snow pit and how to read the various snow layers. Particularly important are the very weak layers of depth hoar or surface hoar that have been buried under heavy new snow.

took plows two weeks to clear the road!) The slopes around Teton Pass cover the full spectrum, but be sure you know your own ability and how to avoid avalanches. Check the abovementioned Skinny Skis *Trailhead Guide* for specifics on Teton Pass, or talk to folks at Skinny Skis or Teton Mountaineering. This is the backcountry, so you won't see any signs at the various bowls; ask other skiers if you aren't sure which is which. Avalanches do occur in some of these bowls, and it's possible to get lost up here during a storm, so come prepared.

Those without backcountry experience should contact **Rendezvous Ski Tours,** tel. (208) 787-2906; **Jackson Hole Mountain Guides,** tel. (307) 733-4979 or (800) 239-7642, www.jhmg.com; or **Jackson Hole Nordic Center,** tel. (307) 739-2629, for guided ski tours at Teton Pass and elsewhere. Expect to pay around $175 for one person or $215 for two people.

BRIDGER-TETON NATIONAL FOREST

Bridger-Teton ("the B-T") National Forest is the second-largest national forest in the Lower 48, stretching southward for 135 miles from the Yellowstone border and covering 3.4 million acres. In Jackson Hole, the two areas of most interest for recreation are the Teton Wilderness and the Gros Ventre Wilderness. Because of its extensive wilderness areas, the B-T has more outfitters than any other national forest in the nation. Much of the remaining nonwilderness land managed by the Forest Service is multiple-use, meaning lots of logging, cattle grazing, and oil and gas leasing.

The Bridger-Teton National Forest **supervisor's office** is at 340 N. Cache Dr. in Jackson, tel. (307) 739-5500, www.fs.fed.us/btnf. It's open Mon.-Fri. 8 a.m.-4:30 p.m. The Wyoming State Information Center, a block or so north on Cache, usually has a Forest Service worker who can provide recreation information. The center also sells Bridger-Teton maps and has a good choice of books. Local ranger stations are the **Jackson Ranger District,** also at 340 N. Cache Dr., tel. (307) 739-5400, and the **Blackrock Ranger Station,** nine miles east of Moran Junction, tel. (307) 543-2386.

TETON WILDERNESS

The Teton Wilderness covers 585,468 acres of mountain country, bordered to the north by Yellowstone National Park, to the west by Grand Teton National Park, and to the east by the Washakie Wilderness. Established as a primitive area in 1934, it was declared one of the nation's first wilderness areas upon passage of the 1964 Wilderness Act. The Teton Wilderness offers a diverse mixture of rolling lands carpeted with lodgepole pine, spacious grassy meadows, roaring rivers, and dramatic mountains. Elevations range from 7,500 feet to the 12,165-foot summit of Younts Peak. The Continental Divide slices across the wilderness, with headwaters of the Yellowstone River draining the eastern half and headwaters of the Buffalo and Snake Rivers flowing down the western side.

One of the most unusual places within Teton Wilderness is **Two Ocean Creek,** where a creek abruptly splits at a rock and the two branches never rejoin. One branch becomes Atlantic Creek, and its waters eventually reach the Atlantic Ocean, while the other becomes Pacific Creek and its waters flow to the Snake River, the Columbia River, and thence into the Pacific Ocean! Mountain man Osborne Russell described this phenomenon in 1835:

> *On the South side about midway of the prairie stands a high snowy peak from whence issues a Stream of water which after entering the plain it divides equally one half running West and other East thus bidding adieu to each other one bound for the Pacific and the other for the Atlantic ocean. Here a trout of 12 inches in length may cross the mountains in safety. Poets have sung of the "meeting of the waters" and fish climbing cataracts but the "parting of the waters and fish crossing mountains" I believe remains unsung yet by all except the solitary Trapper who sits under the shade of a spreading pine whistling blank-verse and*

beating time to the tune with a whip on his trap sack whilst musing on the parting advice of these waters.

Two natural events have had a major effect on the Teton Wilderness. On July 21, 1987, a world-record high-elevation tornado created a massive blowdown of trees around the Enos Lake area. The blowdown covered 10,000 acres, and trails are only now being rebuilt through this incredible jackstraw pile (since this is a wilderness area, chainsaws cannot be used). In 1988, extreme drought conditions led to a series of major fires in Yellowstone and surrounding areas. Within the Teton Wilderness, the Huck and Mink Creek Fires burned (in varying degrees of severity) approximately 200,000 acres. Over half of the wilderness remained untouched. Don't let these incidents dissuade you from visiting; this is still a marvelous and little-used area. Herds of elk graze in alpine areas, and many consider the Thorofare country abutting Yellowstone National Park the most remote place in the Lower 48. This is prime grizzly habitat, so be very cautious at all times. Poles for hanging food have been placed at most campsites, as have bear-resistant boxes or barrels. Local Forest Service offices have brochures showing the locations of these poles. You can rent bear-resistant backpacker food tubes or horse panniers from the Blackrock Ranger District, tel. (307) 543-2386. It's a good idea to make reservations for these before your trip.

Access

Three primary trailheads provide access to the Teton Wilderness: Pacific Creek on the southwestern end, Turpin Meadow on the Buffalo Fork River, and Brooks Lake just east of the Continental Divide. Campgrounds are at each of these trailheads. Teton Wilderness is a favorite of Wyoming people, particularly those with horses, and in the fall elk hunters come here from across the nation. Distances are so great that few backpackers head into this wilderness area. No permits are needed, but it's a good idea to stop in at the Blackrock Ranger District, tel. (307) 543-2386, nine miles east of Moran Junction on US Hwy. 26/287, for topographic maps and info on current trail conditions, bear problems, regulations, and a list of permitted outfitters offering horse or llama trips.

For a shorter trip, you could take a guided horseback ride with one of two companies based at the Turpin Meadow Trailhead: **Two Ocean Pass Ranch & Outfitting,** tel. (307) 543-2309 or (800) 726-2409; and **Yellowstone Outfitters,** tel. (307) 543-2418 or (800) 447-4711. Additional rides are available from nearby **Turpin Meadow Ranch,** tel. (307) 543-2496 or (800) 743-2496, www.turpinmeadow.com, and **Buffalo Valley Ranch,** tel. (307) 543-2026 or (888) 543-2477. All four of these have horses available for hourly or all-day rides into the Teton Wilderness. **Teton Horseback Adventures,** tel. (307) 543-9119, www.horsebackadv.com, has horseback rides out of the Pacific Creek Trailhead.

taking a water break in North Fork Meadow within the Teton wilderness

Unfortunately, the USGS maps fail to show the many Teton Wilderness trails built and maintained (or not maintained) by private outfitters. These can make hiking confusing. A few of the many possible hikes are described below.

Whetstone Creek

Whetstone Creek Trail begins at the Pacific Creek Trailhead, on the southwest side of Teton Wilderness. An enjoyable 20-mile roundtrip hike leaves the trailhead and follows Pacific Creek for 1.5 miles before splitting left to follow Whetstone Creek. Bear left when the trail splits again another three miles upstream and continue through a series of small meadows to the junction with Pilgrim Creek Trail. Turn right here and follow this two more miles to Coulter Creek Trail, climbing up Coulter Creek to scenic Coulter Basin and then dropping down along the East Fork of Whetstone Creek. This rejoins the Whetstone Creek Trail and returns you to the trailhead, passing many attractive small meadows along the way. The upper half of this loop hike was burned in 1988; some areas were heavily scorched, while others are quite patchy. Flowers are abundant in the burned areas, and this is important elk habitat.

South Fork to Soda Fork

A fine loop hike leaves Turpin Meadow and follows South Buffalo Fork River to South Fork Falls. Just above this, a trail splits off and climbs to Nowlin Meadow (excellent views of Smokehouse Mountain) and then down to Soda Fork River, where it joins the Soda Fork Trail. Follow this trail back downstream to huge Soda Fork Meadow (a good place to see moose and occasionally grizzlies) and then back to Turpin Meadow, a distance of approximately 23 miles roundtrip. For a fascinating side trip from this route, head up the Soda Fork into the alpine at Crater Lake, a six-mile hike above the Nowlin Meadow-Soda Fork Trail junction. The outlet stream at Crater Lake disappears into a gaping hole, emerging as a large creek two miles below at Big Springs. It's an incredible sight.

Cub Creek Area

The Brooks Lake area just east of Togwotee Pass is a very popular summertime camping and fishing place with magnificent views. Brooks Lake Trail follows the western shore of Brooks Lake and continues past Upper Brooks Lakes to Bear Cub Pass. From here, the trail drops down to Cub Creek, where you'll find several good campsites. You can make a long and very scenic loop by following the trail up Cub Creek into the alpine country and then back down along the South Buffalo Fork River to Lower Pendergraft Meadow. From here, take Cub Creek Trail back up along Cub Creek to Bear Cub Pass and back out to Brooks Lake. Get a topographic map before heading into this remote country. Total distance is approximately 33 miles roundtrip.

GROS VENTRE WILDERNESS

The 287,000-acre Gros Ventre Wilderness was established in 1984 and covers the mountain country just east of Jackson Hole. This range trends mainly in a northwest-southeast direction and is probably best known for Sleeping Indian Mountain (maps now call it Sheep Mountain but locals never use that appellation), the distinctive rocky summit visible from Jackson Hole. Although there are densely forested areas at lower elevations, the central portion of the wilderness lies above timberline, and many peaks top 10,000 feet. Tallest is Doubletop Peak at 11,682 feet. The Tetons are visible from almost any high point in the Gros Ventre, and meadows line the lower-elevation streams. Elk, mule deer, bighorn sheep, moose, and black bears are found here, and a few grizzlies have been reported. The Forest Service office in Jackson has more info on the wilderness, including brief trail descriptions and maps.

Access and Trails

A number of roads provide good access to the Gros Ventre Wilderness: Gros Ventre River Rd. on the northern border; Flat Creek, Curtis Canyon, and Cache Creek Rds. on the western margin; and Granite Creek Rd. to the south. Note that hikes beginning or ending in the Granite Creek area have the added advantage of nearby Granite Hot Springs, a great place to soak tired muscles.

An enjoyable two-day trip begins at **Jackpine Creek Trailhead** on Granite Creek Rd., 35 miles southeast of Jackson. Follow Jackpine Creek Trail up to Shoal Lake and then loop back down via the Swift Creek Trail. The distance is approximately 16 miles roundtrip but involves gaining and then losing 4,000 feet of elevation. Another good hike is to follow **Highline Trail** from the Granite Creek area across to Cache Creek, a distance of 16 miles. This route passes just below a row of high and rugged mountains, but since it isn't a loop route, you'll need to hitchhike or arrange a car shuttle back. Plan on three days for this scenic hike. A third hike begins at the **Goosewing Ranger Station,** 12 miles east of Slide Lake on Gros Ventre River Road. Take the trail from here to Two Echo Park (a fine camping spot) and then continue up to Six Lakes. You can return via the same trail or take the Crystal Creek Trail back to Red Rock Ranch and hitch back to Goosewing. The trail distance is approximately 23 miles roundtrip.

TARGHEE NATIONAL FOREST

The 1.8 million-acre Targhee National Forest extends along the western face of the Tetons and then south and west into Idaho. Much of the forest is heavily logged, but two wilderness areas protect most of the Wyoming portion of the Targhee. Also note that cattle and sheep graze many backcountry areas. Check with the Forest Service office in Driggs, Idaho (tel. 208-354-2312), for areas you can go to avoid running into livestock. Get additional details on Targhee National Forest on the web at www.fs.fed.us/tnf.

JEDEDIAH SMITH WILDERNESS

The 123,451-acre Jedediah Smith Wilderness lies on the west side of the Teton Range, facing Idaho but lying entirely within Wyoming. Access is primarily from the Idaho side, although trails breach the mountain passes at various points, making it possible to enter from Grand Teton National Park. This area was not declared a wilderness until 1984. A second wilderness area, the 10,820-acre **Winegar Hole Wilderness** (pronounced "WINE-a-gur"), lies along the southern border of Yellowstone National Park. Grizzlies love this country, but hikers will find it uninteresting and without trails. In contrast, the Jedediah Smith Wilderness contains nearly 300 miles of paths and some incredible high-mountain scenery.

A number of mostly gravel roads lead up from the Driggs and Victor areas into the Tetons. Get a map ($4) showing wilderness trails and access points from the Targhee National Forest ranger station in Driggs, Idaho, tel. (208) 354-2312, or from the Forest Service offices in Jackson. Be sure to camp at least 200 feet from lakes and 100 feet from streams. If you plan to cross into Grand Teton National Park from the west side, you will need to get a camping permit in advance. Both grizzly and black bears are present throughout the Tetons, so all food must be either hung out of their reach or stored in bear-resistant containers. As this was written, the Forest Service was considering instituting backcountry user fees in the Jedediah Smith Wilderness; contact the Driggs office for the latest.

Hidden Corral Basin

At the northern end of the wilderness, Hidden Corral Basin provides a fine loop hike. Locals (primarily those on horseback) crowd this area on late-summer weekends. Get to the trailhead by driving north from Tetonia on Idaho 32 to Lamont, then turn north on a gravel road. Follow it a mile and then turn right (east) onto Coyote Meadows Road. The trailhead is approximately 10 miles up, where the road dead-ends. An eight-mile trail parallels South Bitch Creek (the name Bitch Creek comes from the French word for a female deer, *biche*) to Hidden Corral, where you may see moose. Be sure to bring a fishing pole to try for the cutthroats.

Above Hidden Corral you can make a pleasant loop back by turning north onto the trail to Nord Pass and then dropping down along the Carrot Ridge and Conant Basin Trails to Bitch Creek Trail and then on to Coyote Meadows, a distance of 21 miles roundtrip. Note that this is grizzly and black bear country, and bear resistant containers are required. By the way, Hidden Corral received its name in the outlaw days, when rustlers would steal horses in Idaho, change the brands, and then hold them in this natural corral until the branding wounds healed. The horses were then sold to Wyoming ranchers. Owen Wister's *The Virginian* describes a pursuit of horse thieves through Bitch Creek country.

Alaska Basin

The most popular hiking trail in the Jedediah Smith begins near the **Teton Canyon Campground** ($8; open mid-May to mid-September) and leads through flower-bedecked meadows to mountain-rimmed Alaska Basin. It's great country, but don't expect a true wilderness experience since many other hikers will also be hiking and camping here. Get to the campground by following the Grand Targhee Ski Resort signs east from Driggs, Idaho. A gravel road splits off to the right approximately three miles beyond the little settlement of Alta. Follow it to the campground. (If you miss the turn, you'll end up at the ski area.) For an enjoyable loop, follow Alaska Basin Trail up the canyon to Basin Lakes and

hiking Alaska Basin in the Jedediah Smith Wilderness

then head southwest along the Teton Crest Trail to the Teton Shelf Trail. Follow this back to its junction with the Alaska Basin Trail, dropping down the Devils Stairs—a series of very steep switchbacks. You can then take the Alaska Basin Trail back to Teton Campground, a roundtrip distance of approximately 19 miles. You could also use these trails to access the high peaks of the Tetons or to cross the mountains into Death Canyon within Grand Teton National Park (camping permit required). Campfires and horse camping are not allowed in Alaska Basin.

Moose Meadows

For a somewhat less crowded hiking experience, check out the Moose Meadows area on the southern end of the Jedediah Smith Wilderness. Get to the trailhead by going three miles southeast of Victor on Idaho State Hwy. 33. Turn north (left) on Moose Creek Rd. and follow it to the trailhead. The trail parallels Moose Creek to Moose Meadows, a good place to camp. You'll need to ford the creek twice, so this is best hiked in late summer. At the meadows, the trail deadends into Teton Crest Trail, providing access to Grand Teton National Park through some gorgeous alpine country. A nice loop can be made by heading south along this trail to flower-covered Coal Creek Meadows. A trail leads from here past 10,068-foot Taylor Mountain (an easy side trip with magnificent views), down to Taylor Basin, through lodgepole forests, and then back to your starting point. This loop hike will take you 15 miles roundtrip.

TETON VALLEY, IDAHO

The west side of the Tetons is dramatically different from the Jackson Hole side. As the road descends from Teton Pass into Teton Valley, Idaho (a.k.a. Pierre's Hole), the lush farming country spreads out before you, reaching 30 miles long and 15 miles across. This, the "quiet side" of the Tetons offers a slower pace than bustling Jackson, but the Teton Range vistas are equally dramatic.

In recent years the growth in Jackson Hole has spilled across the mountains. The potato farms, horse pastures, and country towns are now starting to undergo the same transformation that first hit Jackson in the 1970s. As land prices soar and affordable housing becomes more difficult to find in Jackson, more and more people have opted to move over the pass and commute to jobs from the Idaho side. Glossy ads now fill *Teton Valley Magazine,* offering ranchland with a view, luxurious log homes, cozy second homes, balloon flights, espresso coffee, mountain-bike rentals, and handmade lodgepole furniture. Despite these changes, Teton Valley remains a laid-back place, and spud farming is still a part of the local economy. The primary town here—it's the county seat—is Driggs, with tiny Victor nine miles south, and even more insignificant Tetonia eight miles north.

See Don Root's *Idaho Handbook* (Moon Travel Handbooks, www.moon.com) for excellent coverage of eastern Idaho, including the Swan Valley to the south and the Island Park area to the north.

HISTORY

The area now known as Teton Valley was used for centuries by various Indian tribes, including the Bannock, Blackfeet, Crow, Gros Ventre, Shoshone, and Nez Percé. John Colter—a member of the Lewis and Clark expedition—was the first white man to reach this area, wandering through in the winter of 1807-08. In 1931, an Idaho farmer claimed to have plowed up a stone carved into the shape of a human face, with "John Colter 1808" etched into the sides. The rock later turned out to be a hoax created by a man anxious to obtain a horse concession with Grand Teton National Park. He got the concession after donating the rock to the park museum.

Vieux Pierre, an Iroquois fur trapper for the Hudson's Bay Company, made this area his base in the 1820s, but was later killed by Blackfeet Indians in Montana. Many people still call the valley Pierre's Hole. Two fur trapper rendezvous took place in Pierre's Hole, but the 1832 event proved pivotal. Some 1,000 Indians, trappers, and traders gathered for an annual orgy of trading, imbibing, and general partying. When a column of men on horseback appeared, two white trappers headed out for a meeting. The column turned out to be a group of Gros Ventre Indians, and the meeting quickly turned sour. One trapper shot the Gros Ventre chief point-blank, killing him. A battle quickly ensued that left 38 people dead on both sides and forced rendezvous participants to scatter. Later rendezvous were held in valleys where the animosities were not as high. For the next 50 years, virtually the only whites in Pierre's Hole were horse thieves and outlaws. Hiram C. Lapham was the first to try his hand at ranching in the valley, but his cattle were rustled by three outlaws, including Ed Harrington, alias Ed Trafton; see the special topic Lone Highwayman of Yellowstone for more on the area's most notorious scoundrel.

In 1888, a lawyer from Salt Lake City, B.W. Driggs, came to the valley and liked what he found. With his encouragement, a flood of Mormon settlers arrived over the next few years, establishing farms the entire length of Teton Valley. By the 1940s the valley was home to a cheese factory, sawmills, a railroad line, and numerous sprawling ranches. Teton Valley's population plummeted in the 1960s, but in 1969 development began at Grand Targhee Ski Resort, and the economy started to turn around. Recent years have seen the area come into its own as tourism-related businesses began to eclipse farming and ranching. By the late 1990s, the valley was positively booming, and Teton County, Idaho, was one of the fastest-growing counties (on a percentage basis) in the nation.

VICTOR

Twenty-four miles west of Jackson, the town of Victor, Idaho, is little more than the proverbial wide spot in the road. It does, however, have several places that make it worth visiting.

Pierre's Playhouse, on Main St. in Victor, tel. (208) 787-2249, www.pierresplayhouse.com, offers up old-fashioned melodramas twice weekly from mid-June to early September. A Dutch-oven chicken dinner is served before the show. You know you're in for a serious production when the villian is named Gustavo Scumsuckler.

Accommodations

Built in the 1940s, **Timberline Inn,** 38 W. Center St., tel. (208) 787-2772 or (800) 711-4667, has a log-cabin exterior, with standard motel rooms for $50 s or d. Open June-October. Inexpensive.

Four miles southeast of Victor at the foot of Teton Pass, **Moose Creek Ranch,** tel. (208) 787-2784 or (800) 676-0075, has guest ranch accommodations on a weekly basis; $2,190 for two people. The rate includes lodging, meals, horseback lessons and rides, children's programs, whitewater float trips, chuck wagon dinners, and other ranch activities. Accommodations are cozy cabins with private baths, and the ranch also has an outdoor pool and jacuzzi. Get additional information by visiting the website, www.webfactor.com/mooscrk. Luxury.

Camping

The Forest Service's pleasant **Trail Creek Campground** ($6; open mid-May to mid-September) is six miles southeast of Victor and just across the Wyoming state line. **Teton Valley Campground,** one mile west of Victor on Idaho Hwy. 31, tel. (208) 787-2647, www.jacksonholenet.com/tvc, has RV hookups ($27), tent sites ($19), basic cabins ($36), and a small outdoor pool. The campground also rents canoes, mountain bikes, and fishing gear.

Food

For the finest meals in Teton Valley, make dinner reservations at **The Old Dewey House Restaurant,** 37 S. Main St., tel. (208) 787-2092, www.odh.com. Everything is made from scratch by the owners, and the entrées are accompanied by freshly baked breads, salads with homemade dressings, fresh vegetables, and spicy appetizers. Entrées ($14-31) change frequently at this eight-table restaurant, but house favorites include blackened chicken and jalapeño cream sauce, charbroiled rack of lamb, and Mexican-style baked fish. Delectable desserts, too. The menu warns: "undisciplined children will be impounded and sold into slavery, or fed to the Yellowstone wolves!" Closed Tuesday. The same characters also run tiny Grumpy's Goat Shack next door, with wines, beers, and appetizers, including wonderful roasted garlic with homemade goat cheese from their own goats.

Victor Emporium, tel. (208) 787-2221, houses an old-fashioned soda fountain with good fish tacos and famous shakes—especially their huckleberry shakes in season. They've been in business for over 50 years, and also sell fishing supplies and Idaho souvenirs.

Also in Victor is **Knotty Pine Restaurant,** tel. (208) 787-2866, considered one of the better local places for ribs and steaks, but be ready for clouds of cigarette smoke with your meal.

Brewpub

The **Otto Brothers' Brewing Company,** tel. (208) 787-9000, www.ottobrothers.com, is on the east side of Victor at 430 Old Jackson Highway. Drop by for a free tour or to sample Teton Ale, Old Faithful Ale, Moose Juice Stout, Teton Huckleberry Wheat, Teton Golden Ale, and/or Teton Pass Porter. The pub also serves up brick-oven pizzas, calzones, and salads, and sells attractive T-shirts and glasses. Hours are Tues.-Sat. 4-9 p.m., with tours available by request before 6 p.m.

Recreation

A paved path parallels Hwy. 33 between Victor and Driggs, providing a pleasant biking or rollerblading opportunity. The route may eventually continue over Teton Pass to Wilson.

Rendezvous Ski Tours, tel. (208) 787-2906, www.skithetetons.com, maintains three Mongolian-style yurts in the backcountry, each located several hours of skiing (or hiking) apart from the next. The huts can sleep up to eight and have kitchens, bunks, sleeping bags, and woodstoves. Rates are $165 per night, but you need to be experienced in backcountry skiing and have the necessary safety equipment and avalanche training. If you don't quite measure up, they also offer guided backcountry ski tours to the huts ($360/day for two people). A good base for these trips is the company's modern three-bedroom guest house at the mouth of Fox Creek Canyon, eight miles north of Victor. The home comes complete with all the amenities, including a hot tub. You can rent the entire place for $300, or get just a room for $75 d if you're willing to share with other folks. Rates include a make-it-yourself breakfast.

DRIGGS

Driggs (pop. 850) is an odd conglomeration of a town, mixing an old-time farming settlement and newfangled recreation mecca. There isn't much to the town itself, so it's pretty easy to find your way around

Sights

Driggs is perhaps best known as home to the delightfully amusing **Spud Drive-In,** here since 1953. You can't miss the big truck out front with a flatbed-sized "potato" on the back. The drive-in even attracts folks from Jackson, who cross the pass for an evening of fun beneath the stars. Call (208) 354-2727 or (800) 799-7783 for upcoming flicks. For the in-house version, head to **Spud Too The-**

LONE HIGHWAYMAN OF YELLOWSTONE

Because of its remote location, Teton Valley became a rendezvous place for rustlers and outlaws in the 1880s. Horses stolen from the soldiers at Fort Hall, along with cattle "liberated" from Wyoming and Montana ranches, made their way through Pierre's Hole to the railroads. Hiram C. Lapham was the first to try his hand at ranching in the valley, but his cattle quickly disappeared. With the help of a posse from Rexburg, Lapham tracked down the culprits, one of whom was killed in the ensuing gunfight. The others surrendered, but they escaped from jail when the wife of bandit Ed Harrington smuggled a gun to him in clothing worn by his baby. Harrington and partner Lum Nickerson were eventually tracked down and sent to jail.

Although Harrington was sentenced to 25 years, the governor pardoned him after just three. Harrington went on to become Teton Valley's first postman, but his criminal activity continued. Using the alias Ed Trafton, Harrington went on to rob stores throughout Teton Valley, and eventually spent another two years behind bars. After getting out, he turned his attention to the tourism business in Yellowstone, but not in the standard way. Though it was never proven, he was suspected of being behind a string of stagecoach robberies in 1908 in which cash and jewelry were taken from tourists at gunpoint. Harrington's most brazen feat came on July 29, 1914, when he single-handedly robbed 15 stages, earning the nickname "the lone highwayman of Yellowstone." The tourists were particularly impressed with his gentlemanly manner as he asked them to "please" hand over all their cash and jewelry. Harrington made off with $915.35 in cash and $130 in jewelry, but he made the mistake of posing for photos in the process. He was caught the following year and spent five years in Leavenworth Prison.

When Harrington died, a letter in his pocket claimed that he had been Owen Wister's model for the Virginian in his famous novel. Others suspected that he was more likely to have been Wister's model for the villain, Trampas.

atre, 190 N. Main St., tel. (208) 354-2718. Both places are locally famous for their Gladys burger and Spud buds—served by carhops at the drive-in or right to your seat at the theater.

A tiny one-room museum sits behind the American Legion building in Driggs, but it has no set hours; call (208) 354-2282 or (208) 354-2200 for a visit. A new museum building just north of Driggs is expected to open in 2001.

Accommodations

For a town this small, Driggs offers a surprising number of places to stay. In addition to those listed below, you'll find others just east in Alta, Wyoming (described below).

The Pines Motel-Guest Haus, 105 S. Main St., tel. (208) 354-2774 or (800) 354-2778, is a delightful European-style guest house built in 1900. Run by the Nielson family, the home has eight-rooms, each different but all nicely appointed with tasteful touches such as handmade quilts. A jacuzzi is available outside. Rates are very reasonable: $35 d or $40 d, and children are welcome. Breakfasts cost $10 per person. Inexpensive.

Super 8 Motel, on the north side of Driggs at 133 Hwy. 33, tel. (208) 354-8888 or (800) 800-8000, has standard rooms for $40 s or $50 d, including a continental breakfast and jacuzzi. Inexpensive.

Intermountain Lodge, 34 Ski Hill Rd. (a mile east of Driggs), tel. (208) 354-8153, offers modern log cabin lodging with an outdoor jacuzzi. All rooms include kitchenettes. Rates are $49-59 s or d. Inexpensive.

Best Western Teton West, 476 N. Main St., tel. (208) 354-2363 or (800) 252-2363, features a continental breakfast, indoor pool, and jacuzzi. Rates are $46 s or $60 d in standard rooms, or $100 for kitchenettes. It may be closed in the fall. Moderate-Expensive.

Teton Ranch, tel. (208) 456-2010 or (888) 456-2012, www.tetonranch.com, offers three log homes on a working ranch. Each contains two bedrooms, a fireplace, and kitchen and costs $150-225 for four people. The cabins are six miles northeast of Driggs; reserve three to six months ahead for the peak summer season. There's a two-night minimum stay. Moderate-Expensive.

Short-term bookings for townhouses, homes, cabins, and condos in the area are provided by two property management companies: **Grand Valley Lodging,** tel. (208) 354-8890 or (800) 746-5518, www.tetonvalley.net/gvlodge; and **Teton Valley Property Management,** tel. (208) 354-8881 or (888) 354-8881, www.tetonvalley-idaho.com. Rates range from $120 to $400 per night. These are popular with families and ski groups heading to Grand Targhee.

Bed and Breakfasts

On the southern edge of Driggs, **Three Peaks Inn B&B,** tel. (208) 354-8912, boasts Teton Range views and an outdoor hot tub. The five spacious guest rooms have private or shared baths and are furnished with lodgepole pieces. Rates are $65-85 s or d, including a hearty breakfast. Kids are welcome. Moderate.

Locanda di Fiori (The Inn of Flowers), tel. (208) 456-0909, is a modern log cabin seven miles north of Driggs. You'll find masses of wildflowers nearby (hence the name) and stunning views of the Tetons to the east. Two comfortable guest rooms are available, both with private baths and entrances, plus access to an outdoor jacuzzi. A full breakfast is served each morning, along with wine and cheese in the evening. Rates are $95 d. The inn is open June-Oct.; no kids under age 15. Expensive.

Willowpine B&B Guest Home, 136 E. Little Ave., tel. (208) 354-2735, has three guest rooms with shared baths in a refurbished 1940s home. It's right in town. Rates are $65 s or d, including a full breakfast. No kids. Moderate.

Teton Creek B&B, 41 S. Baseline Rd., tel. (208) 354-2584, has four guest rooms and a jacuzzi; $55-65 d. Inexpensive-Moderate.

Teton Sunrise Inn, tel. (208) 456-2777 or (888) 456-2777, www.tetonsunriseinn.com, is a newly built B&B halfway between Driggs and Tetonia (three miles in either direction). The lodge-style home contains five large guest rooms, each with a private bath. An enclosed jacuzzi faces the Tetons, and a full breakfast is served, along with evening snacks. Rates are $80 d, and children are welcome. Moderate.

Camping

The nearest public campsites are at **Teton Canyon Campground** ($8; open mid-May to mid-September), 11 miles east of Driggs in the Tetons. This is a delightful camping spot, and the trailhead into beautiful (and very popular) Alaska Basin is nearby. Park RVs at **Larsen's Mobile Park,** 97 S. Main St., tel. (208) 354-2205, for $15 per night; no showers.

Food

One benefit of Teton Valley's rapid growth is a dramatic improvement in the local restaurant scene. Driggs now has several good dining places. (The best local meals, however, are Dewey's in Victor and Lost Horizon in Alta.)

Start your day at **The Breakfast Shoppe,** 95 S. Main St., tel. (208) 354-8294, where the specialties are delicious eggs Benedict (six types!), huevos rancheros, and Belgian waffles. Everything is made from scratch, but don't ask for a recipe; the sauces are a family secret. They also serve light lunches, including a tasty Cajun club sandwich. Recommended.

Main Street Grill, 68 N. Main St., tel. (208) 354-3303, is another lunch place with good sandwiches.

Inside Outfitters Mall at 189 N. Main St., **Auntie M's Sweet Shoppe & Coffee,** tel. (208) 354-2010, serves espresso, teas, cookies, homemade pies, and tasty lunches in a bright and classy setting.

For fast eats in a '50s-style diner, try **Mike's Eats,** on Main St., tel. (208) 354-2797. The menu includes Navajo fry bread, buffalo burgers, and smoked rainbow trout, along with malts and homemade pies. Open summers only.

Bunk House Bistro, 285 N. Main St., tel. (208) 354-3770, emphasizes "cowboy" breakfasts and lunches all week, with Friday and Saturday dinners starring pasta, seafood, and prime rib. The kitchen is small, so you may need to wait for your meal, but the servings are substantial. Reservations recommended.

In the evening, you might want to stop by the attractive **O'Rourke's Sports Bar & Grille,** 42 E. Little Ave., tel. (208) 354-8115, where you can watch sports on the tube while you munch delicious pizzas, sandwiches, and burgers.

Inside a 1916 home off the main drag, **Royal Wolf,** tel. (208) 354-8365, is another place with a big choice of beers on tap, plus a diverse dinner menu. A pool table, dartboards, and sports on the TVs provide for extraculinary fun.

Tony's Pizza & Pasta, 364 N. Main St., tel. (208) 354-8829, serves hand-tossed New York-style pizzas, plus focaccia, calzone, and Italian meals. Choose from a big choice of microbrewed beers, with many on draught. Tony's flavorful "Avalanche" pizza comes with ricotta, mozzarella, and garlic—but no tomato sauce. No smoking here.

Get malts, shakes, and hot fudge sundaes at the old soda fountain inside **Corner Drug,** 10 S. Main St., tel. (208) 354-2334. Lime freezes are their claim to fame. For fruit smoothies and espresso, along with light breakfasts and lunches, squeeze into **Squeeze to Please,** tel. (208) 354-2801, east of town at the Teton Valley Fitness Center, 50 Ski Hill Road. This is also one of the few places in North America where you'll find that Argentinian favorite, *yerba matte.*

The main place for groceries is **Broulim's,** 52 S. Main St., tel. (208) 354-2350. Right next door is tiny **Barrels and Bins,** tel. (208) 354-2307, selling health foods and freeze-dried backcountry meals.

Teton Valley Events

The main summer event comes on **Fourth of July** weekend and is highlighted by the **Teton Valley Balloon Festival,** with sunrise launches, tethered balloon rides for the kids, and live bands in the evening. Also in Driggs that weekend are an arts-and-crafts fair, old-time-fiddle contest, antique-car show, and fireworks. Victor offers up a small-town Independence Day parade and breakfast feed, while Grand Targhee Ski Resort puts on a cross-country bike race that attracts everyone from beginners to pros.

Grand Targhee Ski Resort is home to two very popular outdoor music festivals each summer: **Rockin' the Tetons Music & Microbrew Festival** on the second weekend of July, and the mellower **Targhee Bluegrass Festival** in mid-August. Call the resort for details, tel. (800) 827-4433.

Heritage Days in late July celebrates the area's Mormon settlers; featured attractions are a parade through the center of Driggs, art shows, and a theatrical production. **Taste of the Tetons** arrives in early August, with local restaurants showing off their fare to raise funds for the nonprofit Teton Regional Land Trust. Call (208) 354-8939 for information on the event or this organization.

In mid-August, the **Teton County Fair** brings down-home fun with livestock judging, arts and crafts, quilts, pies, jams, and other fare on display. Call (208) 354-2961 for details.

Teton Valley Recreation

Outdoor enthusiasts will discover an array of activities at all times of the year in the Driggs area. The Teton River runs the entire length of Teton Valley and is justifiably renowned among fly-fishing enthusiasts. A plethora of hikes can be found both to the east in the Tetons and to the west in the Big Hole Mountains. See Targhee National Forest earlier in this chapter for details on Alaska Basin; it's one of the most popular day (or multinight) hikes in the area. The Forest Service office in Driggs has details on other hiking options if you're looking for a less crowded experience.

The **National Outdoor Leadership School** (NOLS) has an office off the main road south of Driggs at 166 E. 200 S., tel. (208) 354-8443. This is one of nine regional NOLS offices scattered around the globe; headquarters is in Lander, Wyoming. The Driggs office runs summertime backpacking and whitewater training, plus backcountry skiing classes in the winter. Classes last two weeks to three months. Find NOLS on the web at www.nols.edu.

A paved path parallels Hwy. 33 between Victor and Driggs, providing an easy biking and rollerblading opportunity. The path will eventually continue north all the way to Ashton along an old railroad right-of-way.

One block up the road to Grand Targhee Ski Resort, **Peaked Sports,** 70 E. Little Ave., tel. (208) 354-2354 or (800) 705-2354, rents mountain bikes, bike trailers, and rollerblades. **Big Hole Mountain Sports,** 99 S. Main St., tel. (208) 354-2209 or (877) 574-3377, www.boardsnbikes.com, is for the real biking enthusiast. The store rents high-quality mountain bikes in the summer and snowboards in winter. Ask at Big Hole for their guide to local biking trails. On Thursday afternoons you can join locals for a ride out local trails, but this is for advanced riders only—unless you want to get left in the dust.

Rainbow Balloon Flights, tel. (307) 733-0470 or (800) 378-0470, offers one-hour hot-air balloon flights over Teton Valley, and **Teton Aviation Center,** tel. (208) 354-3100 or (800) 472-

6382, www.tetonaviation.com, offers scenic glider and airplane rides during the summer.

In the winter months, **Basin Auto,** 180 N. Main St., tel. (208) 354-2297, has snowmobile rentals and guided tours.

Shopping

For a unique shopping experience at "the cultural hub of the universe," drop by **Mountaineering Outfitters,** 62 N. Main St., tel. (208) 354-2222 or (800) 359-2410. Inside the jam-packed aisles are hiking boots, sleeping bags, Patagonia clothing (good prices), army-surplus wool pants, and maps. Owner Fred Mugler opened his shop in 1971 and has been cramming it with supplies ever since. Stop for a chat and a laugh.

Considerably more organized is **Yöstmark Mountain Equipment,** 12 E. Little Ave., tel. (208) 354-2828, www.yostmark.com, which sells a wide range of outdoor equipment. They also rent fishing gear, drift boats, backpacks, tents, sleeping bags, boots, inflatable kayaks, rafts, rollerblades, and all sorts of other outdoor gear, along with snowshoes, cross-country skis, skate skis, and alpine touring skis in the winter. Open every (!) day of the year 8 a.m.-7 p.m. Ask them about backcountry ski tours.

You'll find an excellent and eclectic selection of regional books at the friendly **Dark Horse Books,** 76 N. Main St., tel. (208) 354-8882. In the back is Big Hole Music, selling CDs. Kids will love the great selection of toys and travel games at **Dragonfly Toys,** 24 E. Little Ave., tel. (208) 354-3458. **Bergmeyer Manufacturing Co.,** 229 N. Hwy. 33, tel. (208) 354-8611 or (800) 348-3356, creates quality log furniture in traditional styles.

Information and Services

The **Teton Valley Chamber of Commerce,** tel. (208) 354-2500, www.tetonvalleychamber.com, has an office inside Aspen Artworks downtown on Main Street. Their hours are officially Mon.-Fri. 10 a.m.-3 p.m., but call first to make sure someone is there. Another source for information—with links to local businesses—is on the web at www.tetonguide.com.

Get Targhee National Forest information from the **Teton Basin Ranger District Office,** just south of town at 525 S. Main St., tel. (208) 354-2312.

Teton Valley Hospital is at 283 N. 1st East, tel. (208) 354-2383. Also here is **Teton Valley Medical Center,** tel. (208) 354-2302, for non-emergency care.

Transportation

Community and Rural Transportation (CART), tel. (208) 354-2240 or (800) 657-7439, www.cyberhighway.net/~cartbus, has bus service between Driggs and Rexburg five days a week.

Downhill Express, tel. (307) 734-9525 or (877) 943-3574, provides a daily shuttle service from Driggs and Victor to Teton Village (Jackson Hole Mountain Resort) and Jackson (Snow King Resort) in the winter.

Rent cars from **Aspen Rent-A-Car,** tel. (208) 354-3386 or (877) 882-7736, at Grand Teton Motors on the north end of Driggs.

TETONIA

Tiny Tetonia is eight miles north of Driggs. The town is surrounded by farming country and grand old barns; it's a good place to see kids riding horseback. The crest of the tourist wave is just starting to lap at the shores of Tetonia, and at last check no local place sold espresso, focaccia, or cell phones.

Accommodations

The newest Teton Valley motel, **Teton Mountain View Lodge,** tel. (208) 456-2741 or (800) 625-2232, www.tetonmountainlodge.com, has large rooms with rustic furnishings; some also have fireplaces. Other amenities include a continental breakfast and enclosed jacuzzi. Rates are $60-110 s or d. Moderate-Expensive.

Occupying a 4,000-acre spread five miles northeast of Tetonia, **Teton Ridge Ranch,** 200 Valley View Rd., tel. (208) 456-2650, provides guest ranch accommodations. The modern 10,000-square-foot log lodge forms a central focal point, but a cottage is also available for guests. Rates are $550 d per day including excellent meals, horseback riding, and fishing in their stocked ponds. A three-night minimum stay is required, and the ranch has space for 14 guests. During the winter months they provide groomed cross-country ski trails. Winter rates are $450 d per day, including lodging, meals, and guided skiing. Open mid-June through October, and mid-December to mid-March. Luxury.

East of Tetonia in the Teton foothills inside Wyoming, **Beard's Mountain Ranch,** tel. (307) 576-2694, has a two-bedroom cabin with kitchenette. Rates are $85 d, and the cabin can sleep up to six. The ranch also offers horseback riding and guided fishing trips. Moderate.

Food

Trail's End Cafe, tel. (208) 456-2202, attracts local farmers and ranchers from all around for home-cooked meals of turkey, gravy, mashed Idaho potatoes, burgers, and other hearty fare. The homemade pies are worth the visit. This is where you'll meet the hardworking good ole boys. Open at 6 a.m. daily.

Recreation

Teton Stage Co. has horseback rides in the Tetonia area; call (208) 465-3075 for reservations (required). **Robson Snowmobile Outfitters,** tel. (208) 456-2805, guides snowmobile tours into nearby mountains.

Shopping

A Tetonia company called **Drawknife** creates one-of-a-kind billiard tables using hand-carved lodgepole bases and top-quality tabletops. Find them at 516 N. Hwy. 33, tel. (800) 320-0527, or on the web at www.drawknife.com.

ALTA, WYOMING

The tiny place called Alta sits right along the Wyoming border and just six miles northeast of Driggs, Idaho. There are no stores in Alta, but the settlement does have a stellar restaurant and several places to stay. East from Alta, the road climbs through heavily timbered country, with periodic views of the Big Hole Mountains to the west and up-close looks at the Teton Range. Also in Alta is the nine-hole **Targhee Village Golf Course,** tel. (208) 354-8577.

Well-known **Grand Targhee Ski Resort,** tel. (800) 827-4433, www.grandtarghee.com, is only five miles above Alta and is the main attraction for the entire Teton Valley area. The resort offers excellent skiing and snowboarding in winter, along with a wide range of summer activities. Get the complete scoop, including details for on-mountain lodging and meals in Downhill Skiing and Snowboarding above.

Accommodations

Alta Lodge B&B, tel. (307) 353-2582 or (800) 707-2582, www.pdt.net/altalodge, is a large modern home with tall picture windows framing the Tetons. Four guest rooms are here (two with private baths), and a jacuzzi is available. Rates are $65-85 d, including a full breakfast. No kids. Moderate.

Teton Teepee Lodge, 470 W. Alta Rd., tel. (307) 353-8176 or (800) 353-8176, contains a spacious common area at the center of a tepee-shaped building. Twenty-one guest rooms (no TV or phones in rooms) surround it, and two large dorm rooms—primarily used by kids—occupy a lower level. The lodge is a favorite of skiers and snowboarders, with a large central stone fireplace, dining area, pool table, game room, TV room, and outdoor jacuzzi. In the winter, the rooms are rented on a package basis only: $816 for three days for two people, including private room, breakfast, dinner, drinks, transportation to Grand Targhee, and lift tickets. For five days, the all-inclusive rate is $1,240 for two people. In summer the lodge is a popular place for family reunions and weddings, but they also rent individual rooms for $60 per night and dorm beds for $25 per person for adults, $20 for ages 15-18, and $15 for ages 6-14. Summertime rates include a full breakfast and drinks. Get the complete story at www.tetonteepee.com. Moderate-Luxury.

Also in Alta is **Wilson Creekside Inn B&B,** 130 Alta North Rd., tel. (307) 353-2409, where you'll find a century-old home on a 200-acre sheep farm. Four guest rooms are available and all contain family heirlooms. One costs $80 d and includes a king-size bed and private bath; the others share a bath and run $70 d. An outdoor jacuzzi is available, and guests are served an ample country breakfast. Kids are welcome, but no credit cards. The owner's son raises some 150 ewes on the ranch. Moderate.

Call **Grand Targhee Vacation Rentals** at (887) 667-4663 for one-, two-, and three-bedroom condo rentals at Teton Creek Resort, 8.5 miles below Grand Targhee Ski Resort, or at Powder Valley Condominiums, 10 miles away.

Guests at either place may use the fitness center, outdoor pool, and two jacuzzis at Teton Creek Resort. Rates are $250 per night in the winter holiday season, with a three-night minimum. Luxury.

Food

Lost Horizon Dinner Club, tel. (307) 353-8226, is one of two standout places in the Teton Valley area (the other being the Dewey Restaurant in Victor). The restaurant/home has room for just a dozen guests, who sit down to a memorable 10-course Japanese and Chinese meal ($40) prepared by co-owner and chef Shigako Irwin. This isn't for vegetarians, or for those in a hurry; expect to be here for over three leisurely hours. Dinners are served Fri.-Sun. nights, and reservations are required. Formal dress isn't necessary, but don't come in shorts, sandals, or T-shirts. Recommended.

GRAND TETON NATIONAL PARK

Grand Teton National Park remains one of the preeminent symbols of American wilderness. The Tetons rise abruptly from the valley floor, their bare triangular ridges looking like broken shards of glass from some cosmic accident of creation. With six different summits topping 12,000 feet, plus some of the finest climbing and hiking in Wyoming, the Tetons are a paradise for lovers of the outdoors. They have long been a favorite of photographers and sightseers and once even appeared in an ad promoting Colorado tourism! The Tetons change character with the seasons. In summer the sagebrush flats are a garden of flowers set against the mountain backdrop. When autumn arrives, the cottonwoods and aspens become swaths of yellow and orange. Winter turns everything a glorious, sparkling white, set against the fluorescent blue sky.

GEOLOGY

Building a Mountain Range

The precipitous Teton Range contains perhaps the most complex geologic history in North America. Although the Tetons are ancient by any human scale, they are the youngest mountains in the Rockies, less than 10 million years old (versus 60 million years for the nearby Wind River Mountains). The Tetons are a fault-block range, formed when the earth's crust cracked along an angled fault. Forces within the earth have pushed the western

GRAND TETON NATIONAL PARK AT A GLANCE

Park Headquarters in Moose, tel. (307) 739-3600, www.nps.gov/grte

Entrance: $20 per vehicle or $40 for annual pass to Grand Teton and Yellowstone

VISITOR CENTERS

Moose Visitor Center, tel. (307) 739-3399, open daily (except Christmas) year-round

Jenny Lake Visitor Center, open daily June-September

Colter Bay Visitor Center, tel. (307) 739-3594, open daily early June to early October

Flagg Ranch Information Station (in John D. Rockefeller Jr. Memorial Parkway), open daily early June to early September; reduced winter hours

PARK CONCESSIONERS

Grand Teton Lodge Company, tel. (307) 543-3100 or (800) 628-9988, www.gtlc.com

Dornan's, tel. (307) 733-2522, www.dornans.com

Signal Mountain Lodge, tel. (307) 733-5470 or (307) 543-2831, www.signalmtnlodge.com

Flagg Ranch Resort, tel. (307) 543-2861 or (800) 443-2311, www.flaggranch.com

side (the Tetons) up, while the eastern portion (Jackson Hole) dropped down like a trapdoor. Geologists believe the fault could slip up to 10 feet at a time, producing a violent earthquake. All this shifting has created one of the most dramatic and asymmetric mountain faces on earth.

Unlike typical mountain ranges, the highest parts are not at the center of the range but along the eastern edge, where uplifting continues. The western slope, which drops gently into Idaho, is much less dramatic, though the views are still very impressive. This tilting-and-subsidence process is still going on today, pushed by the movement of a plume of magma beneath Yellowstone as the continental plate slides over the top. Because of this subsidence, the town of Wilson in Jackson Hole now lies 10 feet below the level of the nearby Snake River; only riverside dikes protect the town from flooding.

As the mountains rose along this fault, millennia of overlying deposits were stripped away by erosion, leaving three-million-year-old Precambrian rock jutting into the air above the more recent sedimentary deposits in the valley. Because of this shifting and erosion, sandstone deposits atop Mt. Moran match those 24,000 feet below Jackson Hole. Although the most recent major earthquake on the Teton Fault was at least 2,000 years ago, geologists are convinced that Jackson Hole could experience a major temblor at any time.

Rivers of Ice

In counterpoint to the uplifting actions that created the general outline of the Tetons, erosional

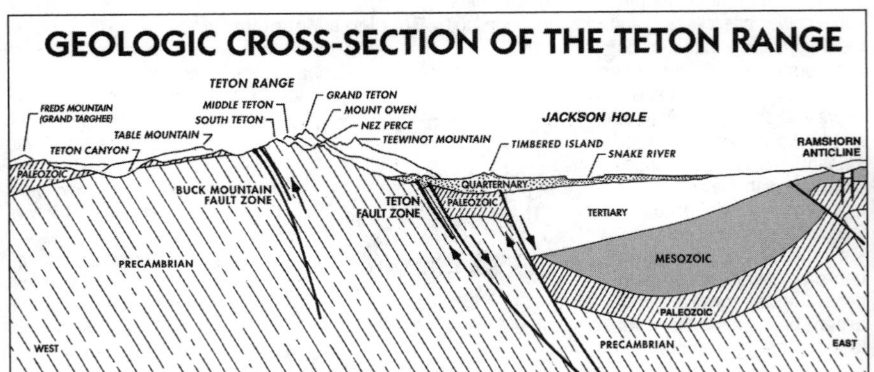

REDRAWN FROM U.S.G.S. MAP OF

CUTAWAY VIEW OF A TYPICAL VALLEY GLACIER

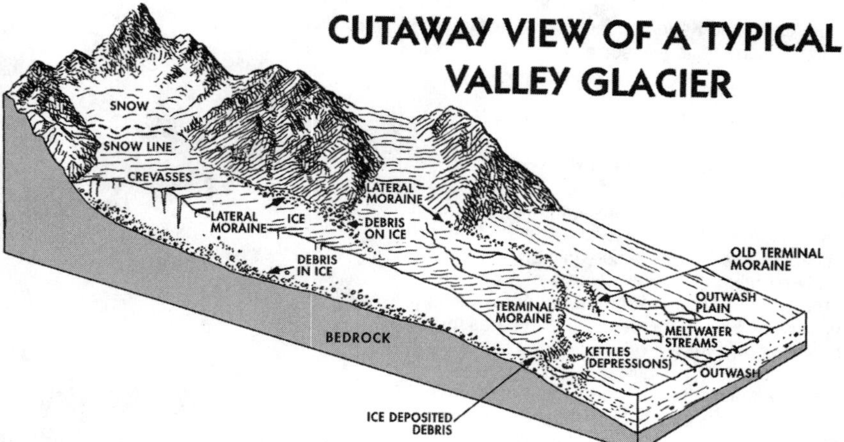

REDRAWN FROM CREATION OF THE TETON LANDSCAPE BY J.D. LOVE AND JOHN C. REED, JR.

forces have been wearing them down again. Glaciers—created when more snow falls than melts off—have proven one of the most important of these erosional processes. After a period of several years and under the weight of additional snow, the accumulated snow crystals change into ice. Gravity pulls this ice slowly downhill, creating what is essentially a frozen river that grinds against whatever lies in the way, plucking loose rocks and soil and polishing hard bedrock. This debris moves slowly down the glacier as if on a conveyer belt, eventually reaching the glacier's terminus.

When a glacier remains the same size for a long period, large piles of glacial debris accumulate at its end, creating what glaciologists call a terminal moraine. One of these created Jackson Lake, when a huge glacier dumped tons of rock at its snout. After the glacier melted back, this terminal moraine became a natural dam for the waters of the Snake River. Similar mounds of glacial debris dammed the creeks that formed Jenny, Leigh, Bradley, Taggart, and Phelps Lakes within Grand Teton National Park.

The earth has experienced cyclical periods of glaciation for hundreds of thousands of years, probably due to changes in the earth's orbit around the sun. During the colder portions of these cycles, glaciers appear and advance. The entire Yellowstone region has undergone a series of massive glaciations, the last of which is called the Pinedale Glaciation. It began around 70,000 years ago and had essentially disappeared by 15,000 years ago. At its peak, the Pinedale Glaciation covered all of Yellowstone and reached well into Jackson Hole.

Streams flowed from the ends of these glaciers, carrying along gravel, sand, silt, and clay. The cobbles and sands from these streams were dropped on the flat valley below, while the finer silts and clays continued downstream, leaving behind soils too rocky and nutrient-poor to support trees. Only sagebrush grows on this plain today, while the surrounding hills and mountain slopes (which were spared this rocky deposition) are covered with lodgepole and subalpine fir forests. Trees can also be found covering the silty terminal moraines that ring the lakes.

Other reminders of the glacial past are the "potholes" (more accurately termed "kettles") that dot the plain south of Signal Mountain. These depressions were created when large blocks of ice were buried under glacial outwash. When the ice melted, it left a kettle-shaped pond surrounded by glacial debris. Only a dozen or so small glaciers remain in the Tetons; the largest is the 3,500-foot-long Teton Glacier, visible on the northeastern face of Grand Teton. For a far more detailed picture of Teton geology, read *Interpreting the Landscape: Recent and Ongoing Geology of*

Grand Teton & Yellowstone National Parks, by John Good and Kenneth Pierce (Moose: Grand Teton Natural History Association).

WILDLIFE

Grand Teton National Park is an excellent place to look for wildlife. Moose are often seen in the willow meadows along Jackson Lake, south of the settlement of Moose, and along the Snake River. The best times to see animals are in the early morning or at dusk. Herds of pronghorn antelope are common on the sagebrush flats near Kelly. Elk are frequent sights in fall as they migrate down from the high country to the elk refuge near Jackson, but smaller numbers are in the park during the summer. (Grand Teton is the only national park outside Alaska that allows hunting. The rules are pretty strange, however, requiring elk hunters to become temporarily deputized park rangers before they head out!) Grizzlies are currently found only on the park's northern margins, but black bears are present in wooded canyons and riverbeds, so be sure to use caution when hiking or camping in the park. Moose are often seen along the Snake River, at Oxbow Bend, and at Willow Flats. Other animals to look for are bald eagles and ospreys along the Snake River and trumpeter swans and Canada geese in ponds and lakes. Look for mule deer in meadow areas and at forest edges, such as those near Colter Bay.

Bison

Herds of bison (buffalo) are commonly seen in the Moran Junction area and in the Mormon Row area. They were present historically (hence the name Buffalo River) but had been extinct for perhaps a century when eight bison were released into Grand Teton National Park in 1969. The population grew slowly for the first decade until they discovered the free alfalfa handout at the elk refuge north of Jackson. Partly because of this winter feeding, the population has grown to almost 400 animals—much to the chagrin of the elk-refuge managers. A small number of bison are hunted outside the park to control their numbers.

About 400 bison live in Grand Teton National Park.

Wolves

Wolves were reintroduced to Yellowstone National Park starting in 1995, and they continue to spread into new territory. By the winter of 1998-99, they had moved into Grand Teton National Park and are now denning in the park. They're most easily seen in the winter, particularly on the adjacent National Elk Refuge where they prey on elk, but they may sometimes be seen during the summer inside the park.

PARK HISTORY

Once the wonders of Yellowstone came to widespread public attention, it took only a few months for Congress to declare that area a national park. But the magnificent mountain range to the south proved an entirely different story. Early on, there were suggestions that Yellowstone be expanded to include the Tetons, but it would take decades of wrangling before Jackson Hole would finally be preserved.

"DAMNING" JACKSON LAKE

Jackson Lake represents one of the sadder chapters in the history of northwestern Wyoming. Jackson Lake Dam was built in the winter of 1910-11 to supply water for Idaho potato and beet farmers. The town of Moran was built to house construction workers for Jackson Lake Dam and at one time included more than a hundred ramshackle structures. Virtually nothing remains of the town. The 70-foot-tall dam increased the size of the natural lake, flooding out more than 7,200 acres of trees and creating a tangle of floating and submerged trunks and stumps. To some, the dam seemed like the serpent in the Garden of Eden, a symbol of the development that would destroy the valley if not stopped. The trees remained in Jackson Lake for many years, creating an eyesore until the Park Service and the CCC finally launched a massive cleanup project in the 1930s. The dam was completely rebuilt in 1988-89, and while the lake now looks quite attractive, it remains yet another example of how Wyoming provides water for farmers in surrounding states. Late in the fall—especially in dry years—the lake can drop to a large puddle with long stretches of exposed bottom at the upper end. Fortunately, Idaho irrigators did not succeed in their planned dams on Jenny, Leigh, and Taggart Lakes in what is now Grand Teton National Park.

DUDES AND DEVELOPMENT

Because of the rocky soils and long winters, Jackson Hole has always been a marginal place for cattle ranching, and only in the southern end of the valley are the soils rich enough to support a decent crop of hay. It was this poor soil and harsh climate that saved Jackson Hole from early development and forced the ranchers to bring in dudes to supplement their income. (One old-timer noted, "Dudes winter better than cattle.")

The first Jackson Hole dude ranch, the JY, was established in 1908 along Phelps Lake by Louis Joy. It was followed a few years later by the Bar BC Ranch of Struthers Burt, an acclaimed East Coast author who had come west as a dude but learned enough to go into the business for himself. The dude ranchers were some of the first to realize the value of Jackson Hole and to support its preservation. Burt proposed that the valley and mountains be saved not as a traditional park but as a "museum on the hoof," where ranching and tourism would join hands to stave off commercial developments. The roads would remain unpaved, all homes would be log, and Jackson would stay a frontier town. Needless to say, that didn't happen.

The movement to save Jackson Hole coalesced in a 1923 meeting at the cabin of Maude Noble. Horace Albright, superintendent of Yellowstone National Park, was there, along with local dude ranchers, businessmen, and cattlemen eager to save the remote valley from exploitation. To accomplish this goal, they proposed finding a wealthy philanthropist who might be willing to invest the two million dollars that would be needed to buy the land. Fortunately, one of Struthers Burt's friends happened to be Kenneth Chorley, an assistant to John D. Rockefeller Jr. Burt used this contact to get Rockefeller interested in the project.

ROCKY TO THE RESCUE

In 1926, Rockefeller traveled west for a 12-day trip to Yellowstone. Horace Albright used the chance to take him on a side trip into Jackson Hole and to proselytize for protection of the valley. What they saw portended badly for the future: the Jenny Lake dance hall, roadside tourist camps and hot dog stands, rusting abandoned cars, and a place that billboards proclaimed "Home of the Hollywood Cowboy." Rockefeller was angered by the prospect of crass commercial developments blanketing Jackson Hole and quickly signed on to the idea of purchasing the land and giving it to the Park Service.

To cover his tracks as he bought the land, Rockefeller formed the Snake River Land Company—if ranchers had known that the Rockefeller clan was behind the scheme, they would have either refused to sell or jacked up the price. Only a few residents—mostly supporters—knew of the plan. The local banker, Robert Miller, served as land-purchasing agent, although even he opposed letting the Park Service gain control of the valley. Miller used his position to buy out ranches with delinquent mortgages at his Jackson State Bank and then resigned, claiming the whole thing was part of a sinister plot to run the ranchers out and halt "progress." In 1929, Congress voted to establish a small Grand Teton National Park that would encompass the mountains themselves—which stood little chance of development—but not much else. Conservationists knew that without preservation of the valley below, the wonderful vistas would be lost.

A NATIONAL BATTLEGROUND

Rockefeller and Albright finally went public with their land-purchasing scheme in 1930, releasing a tidal wave of outrage. Antipark forces led by Sen. Milward Simpson (father of recently retired Sen. Alan Simpson) spent the next decade fighting the park tooth and nail, charging that it would destroy the economy of Jackson Hole and that ranchers would lose their livelihood. Rockefeller's agents were falsely accused of trying to intimidate holdouts with strong-arm tactics. Congress refused to accept Rockefeller's gift, and local opposition blocked the bill for more than a decade.

Finally, in 1943, President Roosevelt made an end run around the antipark forces; he accepted the 32,000 acres purchased by Rockefeller, added 130,000 acres of Forest Service land, and declared it the Jackson Hole National Monument. The move outraged those in the valley, prompting more hearings and bills to abolish the new national monument. Wyoming's politicians attacked Roosevelt's actions. A bill overturning the decision was pocket-vetoed by the president, but for the next several years, the Wyoming delegation kept reintroducing the measure.

Things came to a head when Wallace Beery—a Reaganesque Hollywood actor—threatened to "shoot to kill" park officials. Beery—who had to use a stepladder to climb on his horse—organized a cattle drive across the monument. Unable to find anyone to fire on in the new monument, his cadres sat on a creek bank and drank a case of beer, cussing out the damn bureaucrats. So much for the Wild West.

By 1947, the tide had turned as increasing postwar tourism revitalized the local economy. Finally, in 1950, a compromise was reached granting ranchers lifetime grazing rights and the right to trail their cattle across the park en route to summer grazing lands. The new-and-improved Grand Teton National Park had finally come to fruition.

POSTMORTEM

Some of the early fears that Rockefeller would use the new park for his own gain seem at least partly justified. His descendants still own the old JY Ranch and use Phelps Lake as something of a semiprivate playground, while most of the other dude ranches have long since been taken over by the Park Service. Rockefeller also built the enormous Grand Teton Lodge along Jackson Lake and facilities at Colter Bay Village and Jenny Lake, leading some to accuse the family of attempting to monopolize services within the park. The company, Rockresorts, was sold in 1986 to CSX Corporation, which now manages Jackson Lake Lodge, Jenny Lake Lodge, and Colter Bay Village, along with Jackson Hole Golf & Tennis Club (near Jackson).

Looking back on the controversial creation of Grand Teton National Park, it's easy to see how wrong park opponents were. Teton County has Wyoming's most vibrant economy, and millions of people arrive each year to enjoy the beauty of the undeveloped Tetons. As writer Nathaniel Burt noted, "The old enemies of the park are riding the profitable bandwagon of unlimited tourism with high hearts and open palms." Park opponents' claims that the Park Service would "lock up" the land ring as hollow as similar anti-wilderness claims today by descendants of the same politicians who opposed Grand Teton half a century ago. Without inclusion of the land purchased by Rockefeller, it is easy to imagine the valley covered with all sorts of summer-home developments, RV campgrounds, souvenir shops, motels, billboards, and neon signs. Take a look at the town of Jackson to see what might have been.

TOURING GRAND TETON

Grand Teton National Park has fewer "attractions" than Yellowstone—its big sister to the north—and an easy day's drive takes you past the road-accessible portions of Grand Teton. The real attractions are the mountains and the incomparable views one gets of them from Jackson Hole. This is one backdrop you will never tire of seeing.

PARK ROADS

Grand Teton is bisected by the main north-south highway (US Hwy. 26/89/191) and by the road heading east over Togwotee Pass (US Hwy. 26/287). Both of these routes are kept open year-round, although wintertime plowing ends at Flagg Ranch Resort, just south of the Yellowstone boundary. In addition, a paved park road cuts south from Jackson Lake Dam to Jenny Lake and Moose. Only the southern end of this is plowed in winter; the remainder becomes a snowmobile and cross-country ski route. South of Moose, a narrow, winding road (Moose-Wilson Road) connects the park to Teton Village, nine miles away. It is rough dirt in places (no trailers or RVs) and is closed in winter.

The following tour takes you past points of interest along the main roads. The route follows a general clockwise direction beginning at the **Moose Visitor Center,** tel. (307) 739-3399. Before heading out, step inside the center (open daily) for an introduction to the park and a look at the natural history videos, books, and oil paintings. A large three-dimensional map here reveals the lay of the land.

MENOR'S FERRY AREA

Just inside the South Entrance to Grand Teton National Park, a side road leads to **Chapel of the Transfiguration** and Menor's Ferry. The rustic log church (built in 1925) is most notable for its dramatic setting. The back window faces directly toward the Tetons, providing ample distractions for worshippers. The bell out front was cast in 1842. Nearby **Menor's Ferry** is named for William D. Menor, who first homesteaded here in 1894 and later built a cable ferry to make it easier to cross the river. His old whitewashed store still stands. You can cross the river in a reconstructed version of the old ferry when the water level is low enough; check out the ingenious propulsion mechanism that uses the current to pull it across. For many years, Menor's ferry served as the primary means of crossing the river in the central part of Jackson Hole. Wagons were charged 50 cents, while those on horseback paid 25 cents. (William Menor's brother, Holiday, lived on the opposite side of the river, but the two often feuded, yelling insults across the water at each other and refusing to acknowledge one another for years at a time.) Also here is the half-mile **Menor's Ferry Trail;** a brochure describes historic points of interest along the path. Bill Menor's cabin houses a small country store that sells the old-fashioned supplies he stocked at the turn of the 20th century. It is open daily 9 a.m.-4:30 p.m. from Memorial Day to late September; closed the remainder of the year.

Menor sold out to Maude Noble in 1918, and she ran the ferry until 1927, when a bridge was built near the present one in Moose. Her cabin now houses an excellent collection of historical photos from Jackson Hole. Maude Noble gained a measure of fame in 1923 when she hosted the gathering of residents to save Jackson Hole from development (see above for park history).

TAGGART AND BRADLEY LAKES

Heading northwest beyond the Menor's Ferry area, the main road climbs up an old river bench,

BEAVER DICK LEIGH

Around 1863, Richard "Beaver Dick" Leigh became the first white man to attempt a permanent life in Jackson Hole. An Englishman by birth, Beaver Dick lived in a log cabin with his Shoshone wife, Jenny, and their four children, scraping out the barest existence by hunting, trapping, and guiding. As guide for the 1872 Hayden Survey of the Jackson Hole area, Beaver Dick gained the respect of the surveyors, who named Leigh Lake for him and Jenny Lake for his wife. Today a local bar denigrates this remarkable man by calling itself Beaver Dick's and using a cartoonish image of him in its ads. The real man was nothing like this, and reading his diaries and letters is a lesson in how difficult life was for early Wyoming settlers. On one terrible Christmas in 1876, Beaver Dick watched his entire family—Jenny, their newborn baby, and the four other children—all slowly die from smallpox. Their deaths left him badly shaken, as he related in a letter to a friend:

i got Dick in the house and to bed and Tom went over to get Mr. Anes. Wile Tom and Anes was sounding the ice to see if a horse could cross my wife was struck with Death. she rased up and looked me streaght in the face and then she got excited . . . and she sade she was going to die and all our childron wold die and maby i wold die . . . she was laying very quiet now for about 2 hours when she asked for a drink of water. i was laying downe with one of my daughters on eatch arme keeping them quiet because of the fevor. i told Anes what she wanted and he gave hur a drink and 10 minuts more she was ded . . . i can not wright one hundreth part that pased thrue my mind at this time as i thaught deth was on me. i sade Jinny i will sone be with you and fell asleep. Tom sade i ad beene a sleep a half hour when i woke up everything was wet with presperation i was very weak. i lade for 10 or 15 minuts and saw William and Anne Jane had to be taken up to ease themselves every 5 minuts and Dick Juner very restlas . . . Anne Jane died about 8 o clock about the time every year i used to give them a candy puling and thay menchond about the candy puling many times wile sick . . . William died on the 25 about 9 or 10 o clock in the evening

YELLOWSTONE NATIONAL PARK

Beaver Dick and Jenny Leigh with their children

. . . on the 26th Dick Juner died . . . Elizabeth was over all danger but this, and she caught cold and sweled up agane and died on the 28 of Dec about 2 o clock in the morning. this was the hardist blow of all . . . i shall improve the place and live and die near my famley but i shall not be able to do enything for a few months for my mind is disturbed at the sights that i see around me and [the] work that my famley as done wile thay were liveing.

But the human spirit is remarkably resilient. Beaver Dick later married a Bannock girl, raised another family, and guided for others, even meeting Theodore Roosevelt on one of his hunting trips. Beaver Dick Leigh died in 1899 and was buried on a ridge overlooking Idaho's Teton Basin.

created by flooding from the rapid melting of the glaciers, and passes the trailhead to the turquoise waters of Taggart Lake. The land around here was burned in the 1,028-acre Beaver Creek lightning fire of 1985, and summers find a riot of wildflowers. A very popular day-hike leads from the parking lot at the trailhead to Taggart Lake and then back via the Beaver Creek Trail, a distance of 4.4 miles roundtrip. A side loop to Bradley Lake adds about two miles to this. These trails provide a fine way to explore the damlike glacial moraines that created these lakes. You can also continue beyond Bradley Lake on a trail that climbs to beautiful Amphitheater Lake, the primary access point for climbs up Grand Teton. (Climbers generally begin from Jenny Lake, however.)

JENNY LAKE AREA

The most loved of all Grand Teton lakes is Jenny Lake, nestled at the foot of Cascade Canyon and surrounded by a luxuriant forest of Engelmann spruce, subalpine fir, and lodgepole pine. Jenny Lake is named for Jenny Leigh, the Shoshone wife of Beaver Dick Leigh (see special topic). A one-way loop road leads south past Jenny and String Lakes, providing excellent views of the **Cathedral Group:** Teewinot, Grand Teton, and Mt. Owen. This is the most popular part of the park, and day-hikers will find a plethora of trails to sample, along with crowds of fellow hikers. Paths lead around both Jenny and String Lakes, while another nearly level trail follows the east shore of Leigh Lake to several pleasant sandy beaches. String Lake is narrow but very pretty and makes a fine place for canoeing or swimming. Get supplies from the small store at Jenny Lake, and info or guidebooks from the **Jenny Lake Ranger Station.** Coin-operated storage lockers are next to the store.

Beautiful **Jenny Lake Lodge** sits on the northeast end of the lake and is one of the finest lodging places in Jackson Hole. The gourmet meals—especially the Sunday evening buffet—are legendary, but be sure to make advance reservations by calling (307) 733-4647.

Inspiration Point and Cascade Canyon

One of the most popular attractions in the area is Inspiration Point, on the west side of Jenny Lake. It's 2.4 miles by trail from the Jenny Lake Ranger Station on the east side, or you can ride one of the summertime shuttle boats that cross the lake every 20 minutes or so for $5 roundtrip. In midsummer, the shuttle boat lines lengthen around 11 a.m., so get here early in the morning to avoid the crush and to better your odds at finding a parking spot. Afternoon thunderstorms frequently build up over the Tetons; another good reason to start your hike early. Boat tickets are not available in advance. Scenic boat cruises and fishing-boat rentals are also available at Jenny Lake; call (307) 733-2703.

From the boat dock on the west side, the trail climbs a half mile to picturesque **Hidden Falls,** then continues steeply another half mile to Inspiration Point, which overlooks Jackson Hole from 400 feet above Jenny Lake. Avoid the crowds on the way down from Inspiration Point by following a second trail back to Jenny Lake. If you miss the last boat at 6 p.m., it's a 2.4-mile hike around the lake to the parking area.

Many day-hikers continue at least part of the way up Cascade Canyon from Inspiration Point.

taking in the view of Jenny Lake from Inspiration Point

The trail climbs gradually, gaining 640 feet in the next 3.6 miles, and provides a good chance to fish for trout or watch for moose and other animals along Cascade Creek. Those with strong legs can make a *very* long day-hike all the way up to Lake Solitude (18.4 miles roundtrip) or even Hurricane Pass (23.2 miles roundtrip and gaining almost 3,600 feet on the way up). If you're into hiking that far, it probably makes more sense to reserve a backcountry campsite and take things a bit more leisurely. See Backcountry Hiking below for details.

SIGNAL MOUNTAIN AREA

As the road approaches Jackson Lake, a paved but narrow side road (no RVs or trailers) turns east and leads to the summit of Signal Mountain, 800 feet above Jackson Hole. On top are panoramic views of the Tetons, Jackson Lake, the Snake River, and the long valley below. To the south lies **The Potholes,** a hummocky area created when huge blocks of ice were left behind by retreating glaciers. The melting ice created depressions, some of which are still filled with water. Signal Mountain was burned by a massive 1879 fire and offers a good opportunity to see how Yellowstone may look in a century.

Hugging the southeast shore of Jackson Lake, **Signal Mountain Lodge,** tel. (307) 733-5470 or (307) 543-2831, www.signalmtnlodge.com, includes cabins and campsites, plus a gift shop, convenience store, gas station, marina with boat rentals, restaurant, and bar. Just east of the lodge is **Chapel of the Sacred Heart,** a small Roman Catholic church. The road then crosses **Jackson Lake Dam,** which raises the water level by 39 feet, alters the river's natural flow, and inundates a large area upstream. Many conservationists fought to have Jackson Lake excluded from the park, concerned that it would establish a bad precedent for allowing reservoirs in other parks. Nevertheless, once you get away from the dam, the lake appears relatively natural today.

ALONG JACKSON LAKE

A turnout near Jackson Lake Junction provides views over **Willow Flats,** where moose are frequently seen, especially in the morning. Topping a bluff overlooking the flats is **Jackson Lake Lodge,** built in the 1950s with the $5 million financial backing of John D. Rockefeller Jr. Architects are not thrilled about the design (one author termed it "the ugliest building in Western Wyoming"), but the 60-foot-tall back windows frame an unbelievable view of the Tetons and Jackson Lake. Immediately across from the lodge is a trail leading to **Emma Matilda** and **Two Ocean** Lakes. It is 14 miles roundtrip around both lakes, with lots of wildlife along the way, including moose, trumpeter swans, pelicans, and ducks. You may have to contend with large groups on horseback.

COLTER BAY

Colter Bay Village is one of the most developed parts of Grand Teton National Park, with a full marina, stores, a gas station, cabins, a campground, restaurants, and acres of parking. The main attraction here is the visitor center, which houses the **Colter Bay Indian Arts Museum,** tel. (307) 739-3594. It's open daily 8 a.m.-5 p.m. mid-May to Memorial Day; daily 8 a.m.-8 p.m. from early June to Labor Day; and daily 8 a.m.-5 p.m. from Labor Day to mid-October. The museum is closed the rest of the year. Admission is free. Inside you will find the extraordinary David T. Vernon collection of Indian pieces, the finest of its kind in any national park and one of the best anywhere in Wyoming. The collection spreads through several rooms on two floors and includes exquisitely beaded buckskin dresses, moccasins, kachina dolls, masks, ceremonial pipes, warbonnets, shields, bows, a blanket that belonged to Chief Sitting Bull, and other decorated items. Indian craft-making demonstrations are given daily Memorial Day to Labor Day. This museum should not be missed! Step out back to join the shoreside fun or to rent a canoe or boat from the nearby marina.

A mostly level trail leads from the marina out to **Hermitage Point** before looping back again, a distance of nine miles roundtrip. Along the way you pass beaver ponds and willow patches where trumpeter swans, moose, and ducks are commonly seen. Get a map of Colter Bay trails from the visitor center. Shorter loop paths include the two-mile **Lakeshore Trail** and the three-mile **Swan Lake-Heron Pond Trail.**

ROCKEFELLER MEMORIAL PARKWAY

North of Colter Bay, the highway cruises along the shore of Jackson Lake for the next nine miles, providing a number of fine vantage points of the Tetons. The burned area on the opposite shore was ignited by lightning in the 1974 Waterfalls Canyon Fire, which consumed 3,700 acres. By late fall each year, Idaho spud farmers have drawn down water in the lake, leaving a long, barren shoreline at the upper end.

Shortly after the road departs from the upper end of Jackson Lake, a signboard announces your entrance into **John D. Rockefeller Jr. Memorial Parkway.** This 24,000-acre parcel of land was transferred to the National Park Service in 1972 in commemoration of Rockefeller's unstinting work in establishing Grand Teton National Park. The land forms a connection between Grand Teton and Yellowstone and is managed by Grand Teton National Park. Much of this area was severely burned by the catastrophic 1988 Huck Fire, which began when strong winds blew a tree into power lines. Despite immediate efforts to control the blaze, it consumed 4,000 acres in the first two hours and later grew to cover nearly 200,000 acres, primarily within the Forest Service's Teton Wilderness. Dense young lodgepole pines now carpet much of the land.

Flagg Ranch Resort

On the northern end of Rockefeller Parkway is Flagg Ranch Resort, tel. (307) 543-2861 or (800) 443-2311, www.flaggranch.com, where recently built facilities include a store, gas station, cabins, restaurant, and campground. During the winter, this is the jumping-off point for snowcoach and snowmobile trips into Yellowstone, and snowmobiles are available for rent.

Two nearby trails provide easy day-hikes. The nearly level **Polecat Creek Loop Trail** is 2.3 miles roundtrip and follows a ridge overlooking a marsh and through conifer forests. **Flagg Canyon Trail** is five miles roundtrip and provides views of a rocky canyon cut through by the Snake River.

Grassy Lake Road

Grassy Lake Rd. takes off just north of Flagg Ranch Resort and continues 52 miles westward to Ashton, Idaho. It's a scenic drive, but don't attempt this narrow and rough dirt road with a trailer or RV. This route provides a shortcut to the Bechler River area of Yellowstone National Park and is a popular wintertime snowmobile route. Huckleberry Hot Springs, a short hike north from the Grassy Lake Rd. bridge over the Snake River, was the site of a public swimming pool until 1983, when the facility was razed by the Park Service. The hot springs are accessible via an unmaintained trail, but you'll need to wade Polecat Creek to reach them. Although they remain popular with hikers and cross-country skiers, it's worth noting that the springs may pose a risk from dangerously high radiation levels.

A few miles east of the Idaho/Wyoming border on Grassy Lake Rd. is **Squirrel Meadows,** where Targhee National Forest has a guard station that is available for rent. It sleeps six and costs $40; call (208) 652-7442 for details. During the winter, access is via snowmobile or skis for the last 12 miles to the cabin from the Idaho side. Lodging is also available just across the Idaho border in cabins at **Squirrel Creek Elk Ranch,** tel. (208) 652-3972.

JACKSON LAKE TO MORAN JUNCTION

Heading east and south from Jackson Lake, the road immediately passes **Oxbow Bend,** where the turnout is almost always filled with folks looking for geese, ducks, moose, and other animals. The oxbow was formed when the meandering river cut off an old loop. The calm water here is a delightful place for canoes, though the mosquitoes can be a major annoyance in midsummer. Come fall, photographers line the shoulder of the road for classic shots of flaming aspen trees with Grand Teton and **Mt. Moran** in the background. Mt. Moran is the massive peak with a flattened summit, a skillet-shaped glacier across its front, and a distinctive black vertical diabase dike that looks like a scar from some ancient battle. It rises 12,605 feet above sea level and is named for Thomas Moran, whose beautiful paintings of Yellowstone helped persuade Congress to set aside that area as the world's first national park.

At **Moran Junction** you pass the park's Buffalo Entrance Station and meet the road to Togwotee Pass and Dubois. A post office and school are the only developments remaining here. The epic Western *The Big Trail* was filmed nearby in 1930, starring an actor named John Wayne in his first speaking role. (Wayne had never ridden a horse before this.) An interesting side trip is to head east from Moran on US Hwy. 26/287 for three miles to **Buffalo Valley Road.** This narrow and scenic road leads to Turpin Meadow, a major entryway into the Teton Wilderness (see Bridger-Teton National Forest in the Jackson Hole chapter). It is very pretty—especially in early summer when flowers carpet the fields. Buck-and-rail fences line the road, and the pastures are filled with horses and cattle. Beyond Turpin Meadow, the road turns to gravel and climbs sharply uphill, rejoining the main highway a couple of miles below Cowboy Village Resort at Togwotee. The Blackrock Ranger Station of Bridger-Teton National Forest is eight miles east of Moran Junction on US Hwy. 26/287. Nearby is historic **Rosie's Cabin,** built early in the 20th century by Rudolph Rosencrans, an Austrian emigrant who was the first forest ranger in this part of the Tetons.

MORAN JUNCTION TO MOOSE

Heading south from Moran, US Hwy. 26/89/191 immediately crosses the Buffalo River (a.k.a. Buffalo Fork of the Snake River), where bison were once abundant. With a little help from humans, bison have been reestablished and are now often seen just south of here along the road. The turnoff to the **Cunningham Cabin** is six miles south of Moran Junction. The structure actually consists of two sod-roofed log cabins connected by a covered walkway called a "dogtrot." Built around 1890, it served first as living quarters and later as a barn and smithy. A park brochure describes the locations of other structures on the property.

Pierce Cunningham came here as a homesteader and with his wife Margaret settled to raise cattle. Although this was some of the better land in this part of the valley, the soil was still so rocky that they had a hard time digging fencepost holes. Instead, they opted to build the buck-and-rail fences that have become a hallmark of Jackson Hole ranches. Cunningham Ranch gained notoriety in 1893 when a posse surrounded two suspected horse thieves who were wintering at Cunningham's place while he was away. Vigilantes shot and killed George Spencer and Mike Burnett in an example of "mountain justice." Later, however, suspicions arose that hired killers working for wealthy cattle barons had led the posse and that the murdered men may have been innocent. **Spread Creek** is just north of the Cunningham cabin; it gained its name by having two mouths, separated by a distance of three miles.

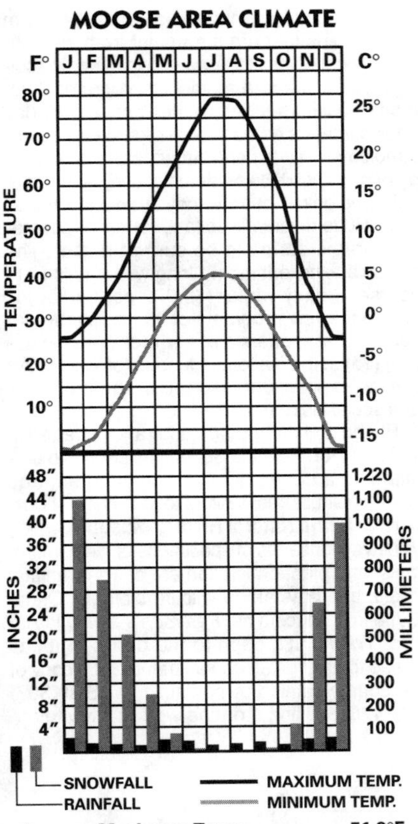

The highway next rolls past **Triangle X Ranch,** one of the most famous dude ranches in Jackson Hole. Although it's on park land, the Turner family has managed Triangle X for over 60 years. (One of the owners, John Turner, was director of the U.S. Fish & Wildlife Service under President Bush.) Stop by just after sunup to watch wranglers driving 120 head of horses to the corrals. It's a scene straight out of an old Marlboro ad.

Southwest from Triangle X, the road climbs along an ancient river terrace and passes **Hedrick Pond,** where the 1963 Henry Fonda movie *Spencer's Mountain* was filmed. Although the book on which it was based was set in Virginia, the producers found the Tetons a considerably more impressive location. Trumpeter swans are often seen on the pond. Hedrick Pond isn't really visible from the road and there are no signs pointing it out, but you can get there by parking near the S-curve road sign 1.4 miles south of Triangle X. The pond is a good example of a kettle pond, created when retreating glaciers left behind a block of ice covered with gravel and other deposits. The ice melted, leaving behind a depression that filled to become Hedrick Pond.

Several turnouts provide very popular photo-opportunity spots, the most famous being **Snake River Overlook.** Ansel Adams's famous shot of the Tetons was taken here and has been repeated with less success by generations of photographers. Throughout the summer, a progression of different flowers blooms in the open sagebrush flats along the road, adding brilliant slashes of color. They're prettiest in late June; in the high country, the peak comes a month or more later than elsewhere.

Just north of Snake River Overlook is the turnoff to **Deadman's Bar.** A steep partially dirt road (not for RVs) drops down to one of the primary river-access points used by river rafters. The river bar received its name from an incident in 1886. Four German prospectors entered the area, but only one—John Tonnar—emerged. Bodies of the other three were found along the Snake River, and Tonnar was charged with murder. The jury in Evanston believed his claim of self-defense, and he was set free, an act that so angered locals that they vowed to take care of future Jackson Hole criminals with a shotgun. A skull from one of the victims is on display in the Jackson Hole Museum.

Another popular put-in for river runners is **Schwabacher Landing,** at the end of a one-mile gravel road that splits off just north of the Glacier View Turnout. This is a pleasant place for riverside picnics. Some of the most famous Teton Range photos—the ones you see in local galleries—were taken just a few hundred yards upstream from the parking area.

BLACKTAIL BUTTE AND MORMON ROW

A mile north of the turnoff to Moose, Antelope Flats Rd. heads east along Ditch Creek. Just south of here lies Blacktail Butte, a timbered knoll rising over the surrounding sagebrush plains. It's a favorite of rock climbers and has a hiking trail up the back (east) side. You will want to stop at the much-photographed old farm buildings known as Mormon Row. The farmland here was homesteaded by predominantly Mormon settlers in the early 1900s but was later purchased by Rockefeller's Snake River Land Company and transferred to the Park Service. Only one set of buildings—an acre of the Moulton Ranch—is still in private hands. The other buildings were allowed to decay until the 1990s when the Park Service recognized their value and stepped in to preserve the structures. Herds of bison often wander past the old farmsteads in the summer months, providing one of the best places to view them. Also keep your eyes open for small groups of pronghorn antelope in the vicinity.

Teton Science School

Hidden away in a valley along upper Ditch Creek is Teton Science School, a fine hands-on school for both young and old. Founded in 1967 as a summer field-biology program for high-school kids, it has grown into a year-round program with classes that run the gamut from elementary-school level all the way up to intensive college courses and a residency program. Summertime visitors will enjoy their one- to four-day adult seminars on such diverse subjects as entomology for fly-fishers, birdwatching, the biology of bugs, wildflower identification, river channels, and grizzly bear biology. These are limited to 12 students and fill up fast, so make reservations in the spring to be sure of a spot. The school's excellent month-long wilderness EMT course in early winter ($2,000 per person) is one of the few programs of its kind in the nation. TSS also offers a fine **winter speaker series** ($5) at the National Museum of Wildlife Art covering a spectrum of scientific, environmental, and social issues.

Based at the old Elbo dude ranch (started in 1932), Teton Science School includes two dormitories, a central kitchen, dining area, and other log structures. Visitors to the school should visit the **Murie Natural History Museum,** which displays thousands of specimens of birds, mammals, and plants. Included are casts of animal tracks used by famed wildlife biologist Olaus Murie in producing his *Peterson's Guide to Animal Tracks.* It's open to the public, but call ahead to arrange an appointment. Get a copy of the course catalog by contacting TSS at (307) 733-4765, or find it on the web at www.tetonscience.org.

The Tetons frame an old farm building along Mormon Row.

SHADOW MOUNTAIN AREA

North from the Teton Science School turnoff, the paved road splits. Turn left (west) on Antelope Flats Rd. to head back to Mormon Row and the main highway, or continue straight ahead to climb up Shadow Mountain (8,252 feet). The name comes from the shadows of the Tetons that fall across the mountain's face each evening. The road is paved for the first mile or so, but turns to gravel as it snakes rather steeply up the mountain. The road is definitely not recommended for RVs or trailers, or for any vehicles after rains when some sections turn to slippery mud. The views from the top of Shadow Mountain are truly amazing, with the Tetons in all their glory. A number of dispersed campsites can be found along this route.

KELLY AND GROS VENTRE VALLEY

The small settlement of Kelly borders on the southeastern end of Grand Teton National Park and has log homes and a cluster of Mongolian-style yurts—certainly the most unusual dwellings in Wyoming. Folks living in the yurts share a common bathhouse and rent the land. The town has a shoebox-size post office and a small store that sells snacks, gifts, and old Wyoming license plates. The Park Service's **Gros Ventre Campground** is three miles west of here.

Gros Ventre Rd. leads east from the Kelly area, passing **Kelly Warm Spring** on the right. Its shallow and warm waters are a favorite place for local kayakers to practice their rolls or for families to swim on a summer afternoon. A short distance up the road and off to the north (left) are the collapsing remains of the ***Shane*** **cabin,** where a scene from the classic 1951 Western was filmed. Beyond this, the road enters Bridger-Teton National Forest and the Slide Lake area, where there is a Forest Service campground.

Gros Ventre Slide

One of the most extraordinary geologic events in recent Wyoming history took place in the Gros Ventre (pronounced "GROW-vont"—"Big Belly" in French trapper lingo) Canyon, named for the Gros Ventre Indians of this area. Sheep Mountain, on the south side of the canyon, consists of sandstone underlain by a layer of shale that becomes slippery when wet. Melting snow and heavy rains in the spring of 1925 lubricated this layer of shale, and on June 23 the entire north end of the mountain—a section 2,000 feet wide and a mile long—suddenly slid a mile and a half downslope, instantly damming the river below and creating Slide Lake. A rancher in the valley, Guil Huff, watched in amazement as the mountain began to move, but he managed to gallop his horse out of the way as the slide roared within 30 feet. Huff's ranch floated away on the new lake several days later.

For two years folks kept a wary eye on the makeshift dam of rock and mud. Then, on May 18, 1927, the dam suddenly gave way, pushing an enormous wall of water through the downstream town of Kelly. Six people perished in the flood, and when the water reached Snake River Canyon nine hours later it filled the canyon to the rim with boiling water, trees, houses, and debris. Today a smaller Slide Lake still exists, and the massive landslide that created it more than 75 years ago remains an exposed gouge visible for miles around. Geologists say that, under the right conditions, more of Sheep Mountain could slide. Dead trees still stand in the upper end of Slide Lake.

Gros Ventre River Valley

Above Slide Lake (six miles up), the road turns to gravel, becoming quite rutted in places. Surprising scenery makes the sometimes bone-jarring route easier to take. The landscape here is far different from that of the Tetons, with brilliant red-orange badlands hills rising sharply above the Gros Ventre River. Two more Forest Service campgrounds (Red Hills and Crystal Creek) are four miles above Slide Lake, or you can camp in dispersed sites off the road. The road continues another 15 beautiful miles along the river, getting rougher at the upper end. Several remote guest ranches are up here. Beyond Cow Creek Trailhead (29 miles from Kelly) the route is virtually impassable unless you have a high-clearance 4WD and are ready to get stuck. Hardcore mountain-bikers sometimes continue up this road/trail and then drop down into the Green River watershed north of Pinedale. Cow Creek Trail and other paths lead into the Gros Ventre

Wilderness, which borders the south side of the road. On the drive back down the Gros Ventre River valley you will discover some fine views across to the Tetons.

MOOSE-WILSON ROAD

This narrow and winding road heads south from park headquarters in Moose, continuing nine miles to Teton Village. It is paved most of the way, but a sometimes bone-jarring middle section is dirt. Keep your speed down to reduce the amount of dust in the air. No trailers or RVs are allowed, and the road is not plowed in the winter. It is especially pretty in the fall when the aspens are turning, and it's a good place to watch for moose and other animals in summer or for easy cross-country ski adventures on a sunny winter day. Two backcountry trailheads—Death Canyon Trailhead and Granite Canyon Trailhead—are accessed from the Moose-Wilson Road.

A long loop hike up Death Canyon is described as an overnight hike below. For something less challenging, start from Death Canyon Trailhead (three miles south of Moose) and hike about a mile to **Phelps Lake Overlook,** where you get a view across this beautiful mountain lake 600 feet below. The historic JY Ranch (built in 1908) sits back from Phelps Lake and still belongs to the Rockefeller family; any motorboats you see are probably theirs. This is one of the only remaining private inholdings within Grand Teton National Park. From Phelps Lake Overlook you can hike steeply down for a lakeside picnic on the sandy beach (four miles roundtrip from the trailhead). An alternative dayhiking option is to continue from the overlook to **Death Canyon Patrol Cabin.** Getting to the cabin requires losing 400 feet in elevation and then climbing 1,000 feet higher. The small log cabin was built by the Civilian Conservation Corps in the 1930s and is still used by trail maintenance crews. Continue a half mile beyond the cabin up the trail to Fox Creek Pass for a dramatic vista into Death Canyon. It's a bit over eight miles roundtrip between this viewpoint and Death Canyon Trailhead.

BACKCOUNTRY HIKING

The precipitous Tetons that look so dramatic from the roads are even more impressive up close and personal. Grand Teton National Park is laced with 200 miles of trails, and hikers can choose anything from simple day-treks to week-long trips along the crest of the range. Unlike nearby Yellowstone, where most of the country is forested, the Tetons contain extensive Alpine scenery. This means, however, that many of the high passes won't be free of snow until late July and may require ice axes before then. Check at the visitor centers or Jenny Lake Ranger Sta-

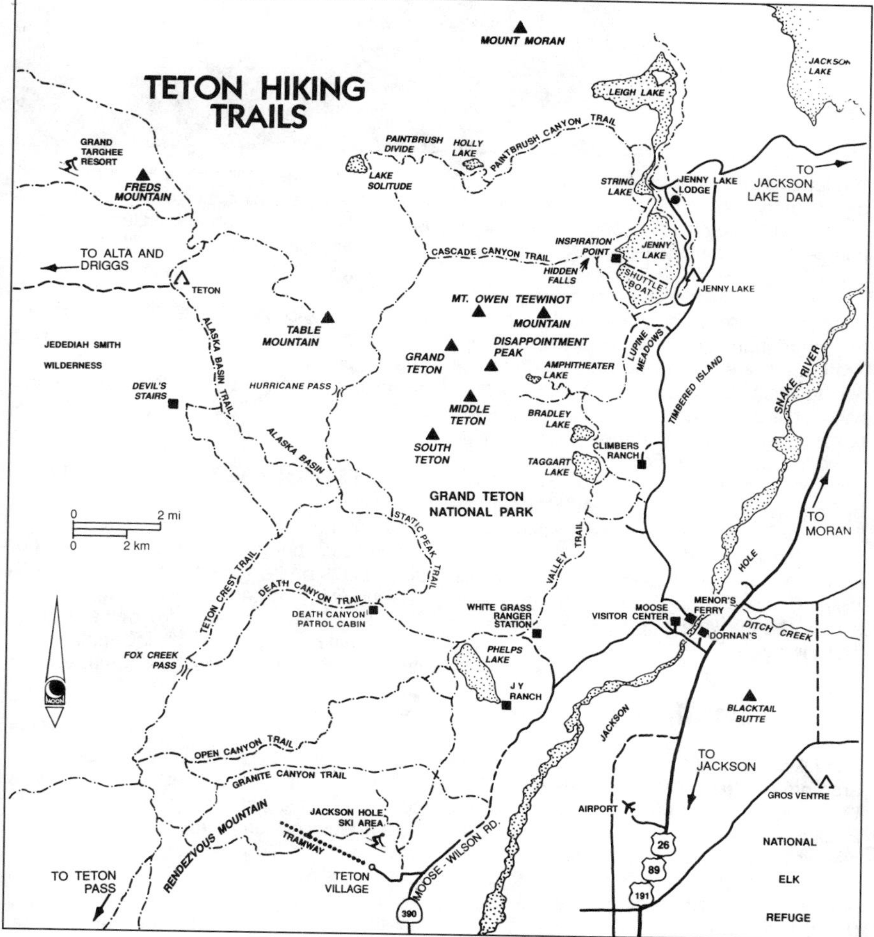

Grand Teton National Park offers some of the finest hiking in Wyoming.

tion for current trail conditions. In addition, this high country can be dangerous when the frequent thunderstorms roll through in summer. A number of people have been killed by lightning strikes in the Tetons.

The most popular hiking area centers on the crest of the Tetons and the lakes that lie at its feet, most notably Jenny Lake. **Teton Crest Trail** stretches from Teton Pass north all the way to Cascade Canyon, with numerous connecting paths from both sides of the range. Three relatively short (two- to three-day) loop hikes are described below. For more complete descriptions of park trails, see *Jackson Hole Hikes* by Rebecca Woods (Jackson: White Willow Publishing) or *Teton Trails* by Katy Duffy and Darwin Wile (Moose: Grand Teton Natural History Association). Get topographic maps at the Moose Visitor Center or Teton Mountaineering in Jackson. Best is the waterproof version produced by Trails Illustrated.

REGULATIONS AND PERMITS

The hiking trails of Grand Teton National Park are some of the most heavily used paths in Wyoming, and strict regulations are enforced. Backcountry-use permits are required of all overnight hikers, and you'll need to specify a particular camping zone or site for each night of your trip. Get permits and detailed backcountry brochures from the visitor centers in Moose or Colter Bay or the Jenny Lake Ranger Station. Get there early in the morning during the summer for permits to popular trails. A limited number of backcountry permits can be reserved in advance from January 1 to May 15 by writing the Permits Office, Grand Teton National Park, P.O. Drawer 170, Moose, WY 83012. For faster service, send a fax to (307) 739-3438. You'll need to pick the permit up in person. Get more information on permits and reservations by calling (307) 739-3309 or (307) 739-3397.

SAFETY IN THE BACKCOUNTRY

Grizzlies are only found in the northern end of Grand Teton, but you still need to hang all food, since black bears roam throughout the park, particularly in the forested areas along the lakes. Special boxes are provided for food storage at some backcountry campsites. Campfires are not allowed at higher elevations, so be sure to bring a cooking stove. Bikes are not permitted on trails anywhere in the park.

Backcountry hikers (and day-hikers for that matter) need to be aware of the dangers from summertime thunderstorms in the Tetons. A common weather pattern is for clear mornings to build to blustery thunderstorms in late afternoon, followed by gradual clearing as evening arrives. Lightning is a major threat in the park's exposed alpine country, and rain showers can be surprisingly heavy at times. Make sure all your gear

LIGHTNING SAFETY

Lightning is a significant hazard for travelers on foot or horseback in Wyoming, particularly in the high mountains such as the Tetons, Wind River Range, Snowy Range, or the Big Horns. Three people were killed by lightning strikes in 1998 and 1999 in the Snowy Range west of Laramie, and others are struck almost every year around the state. Perhaps the most famous incident came in the 1990s when acclaimed writer Gretel Ehrlich was struck while riding a horse on her ranch at the foot of the Big Horns. Her long and excruciating recovery is detailed in *A Match to the Heart* (New York: Pantheon Books).

Creating a Thunderhead

Thunderstorms are created by a combination of convective forces, moisture, and unstable air. On sunny days as the ground warms, heat begins to rise convectively. When the air above is unstable (much cooler at higher altitudes than closer to the ground), the warm air rises rapidly. As it rises, the air cools enough that tiny droplets of moisture precipitate out, forming clouds that may grow into thunderheads if there is enough moisture and atmospheric instability. The rapid development of thunderheads generates enormous amounts of energy that is released as lighting, wind, hail, and rain. During a lightning strike, an electrical charge reaches toward the ground and is met by an opposite charge rising from the earth. They connect in a brilliant flash of light, heat, and noise as 35,000 amperes of charge are released.

Protecting Yourself

Nearly 100 people die each year from lightning strikes in the United States, and hundreds of others are injured. Statistically speaking, golfers are the most likely to get zapped because they are often in open areas carrying metal golf clubs when a storm rolls in. Others at risk include softball and soccer players, mountain climbers, horseback riders, swimmers, and hikers.

Several factors are important in protecting yourself from lighting. One defense is to pay attention to building storms, even distant ones, and especially those that build quickly. Mountain thunderstorms—created when winds push air masses upslope against a mountain range—are five times more likely than storms over adjacent valleys. The color of thunderheads is another factor to watch; black bases means that they contain significant amounts of moisture and may create a more violent thunderstorm.

The most dangerous times are—surprisingly—before a thunderstorm comes directly overhead. Strikes can hit up to five miles in front of a fast moving thunderstorm. In 1999, a Boy Scout was struck in the Tetons while watching a distant thunderstorm; overhead it was mostly blue sky! To determine your distance from an approaching storm, count the number of seconds between a lightning strike and the subsequent thunderclap, and divide by five to get the approximate distance in miles. If thunder arrives within five seconds, the storm is dangerously close, just a mile away.

If you see a storm approaching, get off ridgetops and other high places, move out of open fields, away from single trees or other tall objects, and out of the water. Lightning follows the path of least resistance, and that usually means taller objects or those containing metal. Safer places are inside a car or house, or in a stand of even-sized trees. If those options aren't possible, lie down and stay as low as possible—preferably in a *dry* ditch (stay away from wet areas). If you're caught on an open ridge, sit on an insulated pad or a backpack. Metallic objects attract lightning, so stay away from fenceposts, golf clubs, climbing gear, or metal objects in your backpack. Don't stand in a group of people. If you're indoors when a storm hits, move away from windows, doors, appliances, pipes, and telephones.

Lightning strikes are sometimes preceded by a tingling sensation and your hair may stand on end. If this happens, immediately crouch down (but don't lie down or put your hands on the ground) and cover your ears. If someone near you is struck by lightning, get immediate help, and be ready to perform CPR. For additional lightning safety information, contact the **Lightning Protection Institute,** tel. (800) 488-6864, www.lightning.org.

is wrapped in plastic (garbage bags work well), and carry a rain poncho or other rainwear.

CASCADE CANYON TO PAINTBRUSH CANYON

One of the most popular hikes in Grand Teton is this 19-mile loop trip up Cascade Canyon, over Paintbrush Divide, and down Paintbrush Canyon (or vice versa). The trip offers a little of everything: dense forests, alpine lakes, flower-covered meadows, and magnificent views of Grand Teton. This trip is best done in late summer, since a cornice of snow typically blocks Paintbrush Divide until the latter part of July. Most folks do it as an overnight trip, but it's possible to do the entire loop in a single very long day if you're in good shape and have a masochistic streak. Be sure to bring plenty of water along.

Begin at the String Lake Trailhead and head south around Jenny Lake, stopping to enjoy the views (and crowds) at Inspiration Point before heading up along Cascade Creek. The trail splits at the upper end of this canyon; turning left takes you to Hurricane Pass and the Teton Crest Trail where you'll discover wonderful views of the back side of Grand Teton. Instead, turn right (north) and head up to beautiful Lake Solitude. Behind you, Teewinot, Mt. Owen, and Grand Teton are framed by the glacially carved valley walls. Above Lake Solitude, the trail climbs sharply to Paintbrush Divide and then switchbacks even more quickly down into Paintbrush Canyon. The trail eventually leads back to String Lake. Be sure to stop at beautiful Holly Lake on the way down.

DEATH CANYON LOOP

Another fine loop trip departs from the Death Canyon Trailhead, approximately three miles south of park headquarters on the Moose-Wilson Road. Many hiking options are available here, with trails leading to Phelps Lake, up Open Canyon, or into Death Canyon. (The name came about when a survey party was in the area in 1899 and one of the men disappeared. He was never seen again.) Despite the name, Death Canyon provides a wonderful 26-mile loop hike that takes you over three high passes and into spectacular alpine country. From the trailhead, hike to Phelps Lake Overlook before dropping down to a junction where you turn right to hike up Death Canyon. Bear left at a patrol cabin built in the 1930s, and continue climbing all the way to Fox Creek Pass (9,520 feet). After this the going is fairly easy for the next three miles along Death Canyon Shelf to Mt. Meek Pass, where you drop into famous Alaska Basin (described under Targhee National Forest in the Jackson Hole chapter). Return to your starting point by climbing east from Alaska Basin over Static Peak Divide (10,800 feet) and then switchbacking downhill to the CCC cabin and the trailhead. This is a late-season trek since snow often blocks the passes till July; get snow conditions at the Jenny Lake Ranger Station.

AMPHITHEATER LAKE

A relatively short but very steep hike begins at the Lupine Meadows Trailhead just south of Jenny Lake. Amphitheater Lake is only five miles up the trail but is 3,000 feet higher, making this the quickest climb to the Teton treeline. Many folks day-hike this trail to savor the wonderful vistas across Jackson Hole along the way. Camping is available at Surprise Lake, a half mile below Amphitheater Lake. More adventurous folks may want to climb **Disappointment Peak,** the 11,618-foot summit directly in front of Grand Teton. (It was named by climbers who mistakenly thought they were on the east face of Grand Teton.) If you plan to do so, first talk to the climbing rangers at Jenny Lake—and only attempt it if you're able to handle a few areas of Class 3 moves.

RENDEZVOUS MOUNTAIN TO DEATH CANYON

This 23-mile-long loop hike is different in that much of the way is downhill. Begin at the Jackson Hole tram in Teton Village, where a $16 ticket takes you to the top of Rendezvous Mountain. From the summit, the trail leads down to a saddle, across the South Fork of Granite Creek, and up to Teton Crest Trail. Head north on this trail to Marion Lake—a popular camping site—and then over Fox Creek Pass. The trail splits, and the right fork drops sharply down into scenic Death Canyon, named when a member of a survey party disappeared here in 1903. At the lower end of Death Canyon, cliffs rise nearly 3,000 feet on both sides. The trail forks at Phelps Lake, and from here you can either hike back to Teton Village via the Valley Trail or head to the trailhead at White Grass Ranger Station, 1.5 miles northeast of Phelps Lake. Note: If you reverse the direction of this hike you can save your money, since there is no charge for riding the tram down to Teton Village.

MOUNTAIN CLIMBING

The Tetons are considered some of the premier mountaineering country in the nation, with solid rock, good access, and a wide range of climbing conditions. Hundreds of climbing routes have been described for the main peaks, but the goal of many climbers is Grand Teton, better known as "the Grand." At 13,770 feet, this is Wyoming's second-highest summit, exceeded only by 13,804-foot Gannett Peak in the Wind River Mountains.

FIRST TO THE TOP

In the climbing trade, first ascents always rate highly, but the identity of the first climbers to have scaled Grand Teton has long been a matter of debate. The official record belongs to the party of William Owen (as in nearby Mt. Owen), Bishop Spalding (as in nearby Spalding Peak), John Shive, and Frank Petersen, who reached the summit in 1898. Today, however, it appears that they were preceded by two members of the 1872 Hayden Expedition: Nathaniel P. Langford (first superintendent of Yellowstone National Park) and John Stevenson. In addition, another party made it to the top in 1893. Owen made a big deal out of his climb and spent 30 years trying to work himself into the record books by claiming the Langford party never reached the top. The whole thing got quite nasty, with Owen even accusing Langford of bribing the author of a history book to gain top honors. In 1929, Owen convinced the Wyoming Legislature to declare his group the first on top. Few people believe it today, and the whole thing looks pretty foolish since even seven-year-old kids have made it up the Grand. Several thousand people climb the mountain each summer, many with no previous climbing experience (but with excellent guides and a couple days of training). And just to prove that it could be done, in 1971 one fanatic actually skied the Grand (he's the ski-school director at Snow King Resort), followed in 1989 by a snowboarder. Both lived to tell the tale.

GETTING THERE

Most climbing takes place after the snow has melted back (mid-July) and before conditions again deteriorate (late September). Overnight mountain climbing or off-trail hiking requires a special permit available from the **Jenny Lake Ranger Station** which is staffed daily June to mid-September. There's no need to register if you're climbing or doing off-trail hiking for the day only, just for overnight trips. (Still, it's a good idea to leave a detailed trip itinerary with a responsible person in case of an emergency.) In the winter months, register at the Moose Visitor Center. The climbing rangers—one of the most prestigious and hazardous jobs in the park—are all highly experienced mountaineers and can provide specific route information for the various summits. Call (307) 739-3604 for recorded climbing info, or talk to folks at the Jenny Lake Ranger Station, tel. (307) 739-3343, for weather conditions, route information, and permits.

Many climbers who scale Grand Teton follow the Amphitheater Lake Trail from Lupine Meadows to its junction with the Garnet Canyon Trail. This leads to the **Lower Saddle,** which separates Grand Teton and Middle Teton. Exum and the Park Service have base-camp huts and steel storage boxes here, along with an outhouse. Other folks pitch tents behind boulders in this extraordinarily windy mountain gap. See Park Service handouts for camping restrictions and recommendations in this fragile alpine area where heavy use by 4,000 climbers each year has caused considerable damage. The final assault on the summit of Grand Teton requires technical equipment and expertise. No motorized drills are allowed for the placement of climbing bolts. Mountaineers can stay at **Climbers' Ranch,** near Taggart Lake, for $7 a night including bunk accommodations with showers and covered cooking areas; bring your own sleeping bag and food. The ranch is open mid-June to mid-September only. Call (307) 733-7271 for reservations.

CLIMBING SCHOOLS

Jackson Hole is blessed with two of the finest climbing schools in North America: **Jackson Hole Mountain Guides,** 165 N. Glenwood, tel. (307) 733-4979 or (800) 239-7642, www.jhmg.com; and **Exum Mountain Guides,** tel. (307) 733-2297, www.exumguides.com, with a summertime office at the south end of Jenny Lake near the boat dock. Both are authorized concessions of the National Park Service and the U.S. Forest Service and offer a wide range of classes, snow training, and climbs in the Tetons and elsewhere—even as far away as Alaska and the Himalayas. Exum has been around since 1931, when Glenn Exum pioneered the first solo climb of what has become the most popular route to the top of the Grand, the Exum Route. It's the only company permitted to guide all Teton peaks and routes throughout the year. Exum's base camp is in the busy Lower Saddle area, while Jackson Hole Mountain Guides' base camp is 450 feet lower in elevation in a more secluded location (it takes an extra hour of climbing on the day of your ascent). Exum has some of the most experienced guides in the world, but they take up to four clients in a group, while Jackson Hole limits its Grand Teton ascent parties to three clients.

During midsummer, you'll pay around $330-520 (depending upon the number of people in the group) for an ascent of Grand Teton; this includes two days of basic and intermediate training followed by a two-day climb up the Grand and back. Food, gear, and shelter are also included. If you're planning to climb the Grand during the peak summer season, be sure to make reservations several months in advance to be assured of a spot. For July and August, make Grand Teton climbing reservations before the end of March.

One-day basic and intermediate climbing schools cost $75-110, but reservations are not generally needed for these. Also available are climbs of other faces such as Baxter's Pinnacle, Symmetry Spire, and Cube Point, along with more advanced classes and climbs in the Wind River Mountains and up Devils Tower and other precipices throughout the western states. In addition, both companies offer many winter classes, such as avalanche safety and ski or snowboard mountaineering.

ON YOUR OWN

If you already have the experience and want to do your own climbing, the most accessible local spot is **Blacktail Butte,** just north of Moose near Ditch Creek. The parking lot here fills on warm summer afternoons as hang-dogging enthusiasts try their moves on the rock face. Get climbing gear at **Moosely Seconds Mountaineering** in Moose, tel. (307) 739-1801, or in Jackson at **Teton Mountaineering,** 170 N. Cache Dr., tel. (307) 733-3595 or (800) 850-3595, www.tetonmtn.com. Both stores rent climbing shoes and other gear. **Teton Rock Gym,** 1116 Maple Way, tel. (307) 733-0707, has challenging indoor climbing walls where you can practice your moves. They also offer classes for beginners and rent climbing gear.

For complete details on local climbing, see Ortenburger and Jackson's *A Complete Guide to the Teton Range* (Seattle, WA: The Mountaineers Books) or the smaller but well-written *Teton Classics,* by Richard Rossiter (Evergreen, CO: Chockstone Press).

OTHER PARK RECREATION

BOATING AND FISHING

Canoeists will discover several excellent places to paddle within Grand Teton, particularly the Snake River Oxbow Bend, String Lake, and Leigh Lake. Boaters within Grand Teton will need to purchase a permit; seven-day permits cost $10 for motorboats, $5 for nonmotorized craft. Motorboats are only allowed on Jackson Lake, Jenny Lake (7.5-horsepower max), and Phelps Lake. Sailboarding, water-skiing, and sailing are permitted on Jackson Lake. For info on floating the Snake River through the park, see River Rafting in the Jackson Hole chapter.

Jackson Lake has three marinas. At **Signal Mountain Lodge Marina,** tel. (307) 733-5470 or (307) 543-2831, www.signalmtnlodge.com, you can rent water-ski boats and skis, life jackets, deck cruisers, fishing boats, pontoon boats, and canoes. **Colter Bay Marina,** tel. (307) 543-2811 or (800) 628-9988, www.gtlc.com, is near a Park Service campground, cabins, and the Colter Bay Indian Arts Museum. It's an exceptionally busy place in the summer, with motorboat, pontoon boat, and canoe rentals, along with guides to take you to the hot fishing spots. Scenic boat cruises ($12 for adults, $6 for kids under 12) are also available from Colter Bay Marina, as are breakfast or evening cruise-and-dine trips ($24 for breakfast; $39 for dinner). A short distance north of Colter Bay is **Leek's Marina,** tel. (307) 543-2494, a simple place with a couple of docks, a pizza restaurant, and gas pumps.

Grand Teton National Park anglers must have a valid Wyoming state fishing license ($6 for one day). Pick up a handout describing fishing creel and size limits from park visitor centers. For more on fishing and river rafting within the park, see the appropriate sections in the Jackson Hole chapter.

SEA KAYAKING

O.A.R.S., tel. (209) 736-4677 or (800) 346-6277, www.oars.com, offers one- to five-day sea kayaking trips around Jackson Lake—perfect for beginning kayakers and families. You don't need any paddling experience for these trips, which are supported by a motorized skiff. One-night overnight trips cost $205 for adults or $165 for youths; five-day kayak trips will set you back $680 for adults or $585 for kids. O.A.R.S. also has combination trips that include kayaking on the lake and rafting down the Snake River. Their two-day combo trips cost $345 for adults or $285 for youths; four-day trips run $500 for adults or $515 for kids. Tents and sleeping bags are available for rent on O.A.R.S. overnight trips, or bring your own. Reserve ahead for these popular trips.

TRAIL RIDES

Horseback and wagon rides—including popular breakfast and dinner rides—take place at **Jackson Lake Lodge Corral** and **Colter Bay Village Corral.** Get details from Grand Teton Lodge Company, tel. (307) 733-2811 or (800) 628-9988, www.gtlc.com. In the Rockefeller Parkway between Grand Teton and Yellowstone, **Flagg Ranch Resort,** tel. (307) 543-2861 or (800) 443-2311, www.flaggranch.com, offers hour-long horseback trail rides in the summer.

WINTER RECREATION

The snow-covered landscape of Grand Teton National Park draws cross-country skiers, snowshoers, and snowmobilers throughout the winter. **Cross-country skiing** is possible on a number of trails within the lower reaches of the park, but the high country is dangerous due to extreme avalanche hazards. Park ski trails are not machine-groomed but are generally well packed by other skiers. After a new snowfall you'll need to break trail as you follow the orange markers. See Cross-country Skiing in the Jackson Hole chapter for information on Nordic skiing in the park, or pick up a brochure describing ski trails from the Moose Visitor Center. If you're planning to camp overnight in the park, you'll need to get a free permit here as well. Skiers and snowshoers are not allowed on the Continental Divide Snowmobile Trail for safety reasons. Unfortunately, snowmobiles ride on Teton Park Rd., so your peace and solitude may be broken by the roar of distant machines.

Park naturalists lead two-hour **snowshoe hikes** from late December through March and provide snowshoes at no charge. No experience necessary. The hikes generally depart from the Moose Visitor Center at 2 p.m. several times a week. Reservations are required; no kids under age eight. Call (307) 739-3399 for details on these and other winter activities in the park.

The controversial 365-mile-long **Continental Divide Snowmobile Trail** now cuts through 33 miles of Grand Teton National Park, providing a link between the Wind River Mountains and Yellowstone National Park. Within Grand Teton it is generally open from early January to mid-March and essentially parallels US Hwy. 26/287 from the east park boundary to Moran Junction and then along US Hwy. 89 north to Yellowstone. A spur trail connects the trail with other snowmobile routes along the Teton Park Rd. and up Signal Mountain. Snowmobiles are only allowed on designated routes, and specific regulations are enforced within the park. Get a copy of the park snowmobiling handout from the Moose Lake Visitor Center, or call (307) 739-3612 for recorded info on the Continental Divide Snowmobile Trail. For details on snowmobile rentals and tours in the Jackson area, see Winter Recreation in the Jackson Hole chapter.

During the winter, **Gray Line,** tel. (307) 733-4325 or (800) 443-6133, www.jacksonholenet.com/grayline, has daily bus runs between Jackson and Flagg Ranch Resort for $35 one-way or $50 roundtrip, arriving in time to meet the snowcoach departures for Yellowstone. Reservations are required. Both **Buckboard Cab,** tel. (307) 733-1112, and **All Star Taxi,** tel. (307) 733-2888 or (800) 378-2944, also offer shuttles to Flagg Ranch Resort in the winter; $75 for one to three people.

PARK CAMPING AND LODGING

CAMPGROUNDS

Grand Teton National Park has five places to camp: Colter Bay Campground, Lizard Creek Campground, Gros Ventre Campground, Signal Mountain Campground, and Jenny Lake Campground. See the Jackson Hole/Grand Teton Public Campgrounds chart for details of these and nearby Forest Service campgrounds. Accommodations at all park campgrounds cost $12 and are on a first-come, first-served basis with no reservations. By midafternoon in the peak summer season all park campgrounds may well be full. The largest—and last to fill—is Gros Ventre Campground, near the town of Kelly. The most scenic—and quickest to fill—is Jenny Lake Campground. Showers and a laundromat are available in Colter Bay Village. All Grand Teton National Park campgrounds are closed in the winter, but limited tent camping and RV parking ($5; restrooms and water but no hookups) is available near the Colter Bay Visitor Center. Call (307) 739-3603 for additional park campground information.

In addition to the public campgrounds, park concessioners maintain two seasonal RV parks. **Flagg Ranch Resort** in Rockefeller Parkway, tel. (307) 543-2861 or (800) 443-2311, www.flaggranch.com, has RV sites with full hookups for $31, and tent sites for $20. It's open early to mid-May till early October; reservations are highly recommended. On the south shore of Jackson Lake, **Colter Bay RV Park,** tel. (307) 543-3100 or (800) 628-9988, www.gtlc.com, charges $30-32 for RVs and is open late May to early October. No tent spaces available here. Evening nature programs are offered in the summer.

GRAND TETON LODGING

Several places provide concessioner lodging inside Grand Teton National Park. As in all national parks, none of the lodge rooms contain TVs or radios. See Accommodations in the Jack-

The Tetons loom over Jackson Lake and the marina at Colter Bay Village.

son Hole chapter for dozens of other lodging places south and east of the park.

Jackson Lake Lodge

Built on a grand scale, the 385-room Jackson Lake Lodge, tel. (307) 543-3100 or (800) 628-9988, www.gtlc.com, occupies a bluff above Willow Flats on the southeast side of Jackson Lake. Sixty-foot-high windows look across to the Tetons, and the spacious central hall is flanked by fireplaces. Outside are two large swimming pools, and the building houses restaurants, a cocktail lounge, gift shop, newsstand, clothing shop, and an ATM. All rooms contain two double beds. Cottages are $135-198 d, rooms in the main lodge cost $115-198 d, and the luxury suite will set you back $500 d. The lodge is open mid-May to mid-October. Premium-Luxury.

Jenny Lake Lodge

For four-star accommodations right at the base of the Tetons, stay at Jenny Lake Lodge, tel. (307) 733-4647 or (800) 628-9988, www.gtlc.com, where 37 comfortably appointed cabins surround a cozy Old West main lodge. This is a marvelous honeymoon or big-splurge place, and the $318 s or $398 d price (or go for one of the luxurious suites at $540-560 d) includes horseback rides, bikes, breakfast, and a six-course dinner. (Note, however, that the meals are only served at specific times, so you'll need to adjust your schedule accordingly; some find the regimented schedule too confining.) The big Sunday night buffet is a special treat that attracts folks from Jackson. Jenny Lake Lodge is open early June to early October. Luxury.

Colter Bay Village

Family-oriented Colter Bay Village, tel. (307) 543-3100 or (800) 628-9988, www.gtlc.com, has 166 rustic cabins of varying sizes and types, some of which sleep six people. The most basic are simple canvas-and-log tent cabins with outdoor grills and picnic tables, woodstoves, and bring-your-own-bedding bunks. These cost just $31 d ($3 for each additional person). Restrooms are nearby, and the showers are coin-operated. Guests at the tent cabins can rent sleeping bags and other camping supplies. The experience isn't even remotely like staying at Jenny Lake Lodge! Step up to basic log units that share a bath for $32 d, or get one with a private bath for $66-94 d. Two-room cabins with a connecting bath are $120 for up to four people. Colter Bay Village is open late May to late September. Budget-Expensive.

Dornan's

Near park headquarters in Moose, Dornan's Spur Ranch Cabins, tel. (307) 733-2522, www.dornans.com, has a dozen modern log cabins filled with handcrafted lodgepole pine furniture. One-bedroom cabins are $140 d or $170 for up to four people, and two-bedroom cabins cost $200 and can sleep up to six. There's a three-night minimum stay in the summer. All cabins have full kitchens and are open year-round. Premium.

Signal Mountain Lodge
Set on the south shore of Jackson Lake, Signal Mountain Lodge, tel. (307) 733-5470 or (307) 543-2831, www.signalmtnlodge.com, offers a variety of accommodation options that range from simple log cabins starting at $80 to two-room lakefront bungalows with kitchenettes for $170. It's open early May to mid-October. Moderate-Luxury.

Flagg Ranch Resort
In Rockefeller Parkway just three miles south of Yellowstone, Flagg Ranch Resort, tel. (307) 543-2861 or (800) 443-2311, www.flaggranch.com, has modern fourplex cabins with patios for $131 d in the summer, or $99 d in winter; kids stay free. It's open mid-May to mid-October and mid-December to mid-March. The main lodge contains a restaurant, gift shop, and large fireplace. Premium.

GRAND TETON PRACTICALITIES

GETTING IN

Entrance to Grand Teton National Park is $20 per vehicle, or $10 for individuals entering by bicycle, foot, or as a bus passenger. Motorcycles and snowmobiles are $15. The pass covers entrance to both Yellowstone and Grand Teton National Parks and is good for seven days. If you're planning to be here longer or to make additional visits, get an annual pass covering both parks for $40, or the Golden Eagle Passport—good for all national parks—for $50 a year. A Golden Age Passport for all national parks is available to anyone over 62 for a one-time fee of $10, and people with disabilities can get a free Golden Access Passport. Both of these also give the holders 50% reductions in most camping fees. Call (307) 739-3600 for additional park information, or visit the park on the web at www.nps.gov/grte.

At the entrance stations, park visitors receive a copy of ***Teewinot,*** the park newspaper. It lists park facilities and services, along with interpretive programs, nature walks, and other activities. Family favorites for generations are the evening campfire programs held at campground amphitheaters throughout the summer.

VISITOR CENTERS

Grand Teton National Park headquarters is in the settlement of Moose near the southern end of the park. **Moose Visitor Center,** tel. (307) 739-3399, is open daily 8 a.m.-7 p.m. from early June to early September, and daily (except Christmas) 8 a.m.-5 p.m. the rest of the year. **Jenny Lake Visitor Center** is open daily 8 a.m.-7 p.m. from early June to early September, and daily 8 a.m.-5 p.m. the rest of September; closed the remainder of the year.

On the east side of Jackson Lake, **Colter Bay Visitor Center,** tel. (307) 739-3594, is open daily 8 a.m.-8 p.m. from early June to early September, and daily 8 a.m.-5 p.m. from early September to early October; closed in winter.

Just north of Grand Teton inside John D. Rockefeller Jr. Memorial Parkway is **Flagg Ranch Information Station,** open daily 9 a.m.-6 p.m. between early June and early September, and with varying hours from mid-December to mid-March.

Support Organizations
The **Grand Teton Natural History Association** operates bookstores in the visitor centers and the store at Menor's Ferry. The association also provides a mail-order service for books about the park. For a free catalog, call (307) 739-3403, or visit the website: www.grandteton.com/gtnha.

The **Grand Teton National Park Foundation,** tel. (307) 739-3410, provides support for park projects that would not otherwise be funded, and all contributions are tax-deductible.

FOOD

Summertime restaurants and other eateries are located at Colter Bay Village, Signal Mountain, Flagg Ranch Resort, Jenny Lake, Jackson Lake Lodge, and Leek's Marina (with a pizzeria that has open mike for musicians on Monday nights). At **Jackson Lake Lodge,** the Pool Grill and BBQ features poolside dining on summer nights, and the Mural Room offers 60-foot windows fronting the Tetons (reservations are required in the summertime). Marvelous old **Jenny Lake Lodge** has impeccable service, windows that face the mountains, and a cozy setting. Six-course dinners and sumptuous Sunday night buffets are the featured attractions, and the wine list is extensive. Lunch is à la carte, but breakfast and dinner are fixed price (and pricey). Jenny Lake Lodge is open June to mid-October, and reservations are required; call (307) 733-4647. This is a dress-up place, so a jacket is recommended for dinner.

An old favorite with a more egalitarian setting is **Dornan's Chuck Wagon Restaurant,** tel. (307) 733-2415, www.dornans.com, offering very reasonable meals every summer since 1948. These include all-you-can-eat pancake breakfasts ($6.25), lunchtime sandwiches, and old-fashioned chuck wagon dinners ($12) of barbecued ribs, beef stew, mashed potatoes, and other filling fare. Across the street—and open all year—is Dornan's **Spur Bar/Moose Pizza & Pasta Co.,** tel. (307) 733-2415, offering a wide range of superb homemade pizzas, sandwiches, calzones, and pastas. Dining is available on two outside decks facing the Tetons, and folk music is offered once or twice a month year-round. The bar puts on monthly wine tastings ($5-15) on the first Monday of the month, Oct.-May.

SERVICES

The little settlement of Moose has several businesses in addition to Dornan's Restaurant. **Adventure Sports,** tel. (307) 733-3307, rents mountain bikes, canoes, and kayaks. Next door is **Moosely Seconds,** tel. (307) 739-1801, with good deals on outdoor clothing and climbing gear; open mid-May through September. They also rent ice axes, crampons, rock shoes, trekking poles, approach shoes, plastic boots, day packs, and snowshoes. **Snake River Anglers,** tel. (307) 733-3699, sells and rents fishing supplies and camping equipment.

Across the road are several more Dornan's operations; tel. (307) 733-2415. **The Trading Post** is open all year, selling groceries, tasty deli sandwiches, fresh baked goods, and camping supplies. **Dornan's Wine Shoppe** has the biggest selection of fine wine and beer in Jackson Hole, including over 1,700 different wines. Also at Dornan's are the Spur Bar/Moose Pizza & Pasta (described above), a gift shop, and an **ATM** for cash. The gift shop rents cross-country skis, snowshoes, and pull-behind sleds in the winter months. You'll find additional ATMs at Jackson Lake Lodge and Colter Bay Village.

Colter Bay General Store, tel. (307) 733-2811, has a good choice of groceries and supplies, and in summer, smaller general stores and convenience stores operate at Signal Mountain, Flagg Ranch Resort, and Jenny Lake. The store at Flagg Ranch Resort is open in both summer and winter seasons (mid-May to mid-October, and mid-December to mid-March).

Gas is available year-round at Moose and Flagg Ranch Resort and summers only at Colter Bay Village and Jackson Lake Lodge. You'll find gift shops at Signal Mountain, Flagg Ranch Resort, Jackson Lake Lodge, Moose, and Colter Bay. **Post offices** are located at Colter Bay Village (summer only), and year-round at Moran, Moose Junction, and Kelly.

Get emergency medical assistance at the **Grand Teton Medical Clinic,** tel. (307) 543-2514, near the Chevron station at Jackson Lake Lodge. It's open daily 10 a.m.-6 p.m. mid-May to mid-October. The nearest hospital is in Jackson.

TRANSPORTATION AND TOURS

Grand Teton Lodge Company, tel. (307) 733-2811 or (800) 628-9988, www.gtlc.com, has three-times-daily summer shuttle buses connecting Jackson with Jackson Lake Lodge for $15 one-way, and on to Colter Bay Village for an additional $2.75 one-way. Transportation to the airport is $20 one-way. In Jackson, the buses depart from the Homewood parking lot on the corner of Gill St. and N. Cache Drive. The company also offers three-hour bus tours of Grand Teton National Park on Monday, Wednesday, and Friday for $20 ($10 for kids under 12) and eight-hour tours of Yellowstone National Park on Tuesday, Thursday, and Saturday for $44 ($26 for kids). Tours depart from Jackson Lake Lodge at 8:30 in the morning.

Daily summertime bus tours of Grand Teton and Yellowstone National Parks are available from **Gray Line,** tel. (307) 733-4325 or (800) 443-6133, www.jacksonholenet.com/grayline. Yellowstone tours last 11 hours and cost $48 plus park entrance fees. Eight-hour Grand Teton tours are $45 plus the park entrance. Those without vehicles can use these tours for access to the parks; reserve ahead to schedule a pick-up in Jackson, Grand Teton, or Yellowstone. In Yellowstone, travelers can connect with other buses to West Yellowstone, Gardiner, or Cody. Gray Line's four-day tours of Yellowstone and Grand Teton start at $654 for one person or $830 for two, including lodging. See Transportation in the Jackson Hole chapter for other transportation and tours in the Jackson Hole area.

Based in Jackson, **Great Plains Wildlife Institute,** tel. (307) 733-2623, www.wildlife-safari.com, leads a range of wildlife-viewing safaris in Grand Teton and Yellowstone.

YELLOWSTONE NATIONAL PARK

The words "national park" seem to stimulate an almost Pavlovian response: Yellowstone. The geysers, canyons, and bears of Yellowstone National Park are so intertwined in our collective consciousness that even 1960s' American cartoons used the park as a model—Jellystone Park, where Yogi Bear and Boo Boo were constantly out to thwart the rangers. One source estimated that nearly a third of the U.S. population has visited the park, and each year three million people roll through its gates.

Yellowstone has always been a place of wonder. There is considerable evidence that the Indians who first lived in this area viewed it as a place of great spiritual power and treated it with reverence. Yellowstone was to later become the birthplace for the national-park movement, and Americans today still love the park, though they don't always treat it with reverence.

There is something about Yellowstone National Park that calls people back again and again, something more than simply the chance to see the curiosities of the natural world. Generation after generation of parents have brought their children to see the place that they recall from their own childhood visits. Other cultures have the Ganges River, Rome, or Mecca as places with deep spiritual meaning. In America, our national parks have become places for similar renewal, and as the nation's first national park, Yellowstone remains one of our most valued treasures.

So, into the park we come in our cars with our crying babies in the back—babies who suddenly quiet down at the sight of a bison or elk. I recall bringing relatives to Yellowstone after I had worked in the vicinity all summer and had become a bit jaded. Their emotional reaction surprised me, and more than a decade later they still tell stories of the bison calves, the astounding geysers, the rush of the waterfalls, and the night they spent at Old Faithful Inn. Yellowstone is a collective religious experience that sends us back to our roots in the natural

YELLOWSTONE NATIONAL PARK AT A GLANCE

Park Headquarters, Mammoth Hot Springs, tel. (307) 344-7381, www.nps.gov/yell

Recorded camping or road information, tel. (307) 344-2114

Entrance: $20 per vehicle or $40 for annual pass to Yellowstone and Grand Teton

VISITOR CENTERS

Albright Visitor Center, tel. (307) 344-2263, open daily year-round

Old Faithful Visitor Center, tel. (307) 545-2750, open daily mid-April to early November, and mid-December to mid-March

Canyon Visitor Center, tel. (307) 242-2550, open daily Memorial Day to mid-October

Grant Village Visitor Center, tel. (307) 242-2650, open daily Memorial Day to early October

Fishing Bridge Visitor Center, tel. (307) 242-2450, open daily Memorial Day to mid-October

PARK CONCESSIONERS

Amfac Parks & Resorts (lodging, restaurants, and activities), tel. (307) 344-7311, www.travelyellowstone.com

Hamilton Stores, tel. (406) 646-7325, www.hamiltonstores.com

world. The smell of wood smoke from a campfire, the picnic lunch on the shore of Lake Yellowstone, the backcountry horseback ride, the hike down to the lip of Lower Falls, the quick strike of a trout on the line, the gasp of the crowd as the first spurt of Old Faithful jets upward, the campfire program where a park ranger talks about the lives of grizzlies, the herds of bison wading Firehole River, the evening piano tunes drifting through the air at Lake Hotel, the howl of a distant wolf, and even the infamous rubber tomahawks—all of these things combine to leave an indelible mark on visitors to Yellowstone National Park.

The Setting

On a map, Yellowstone appears as a gigantic box wedged so tightly against the northwest corner of Wyoming that it squeezes over into Montana and Idaho. The park measures 63 by 54 miles and covers 2.2 million acres, making it one of the largest national parks in the Lower 48 (though it is dwarfed by Alaska's Wrangell-St. Elias National Park and Preserve, which covers almost six times as much land). The United Nations has declared Yellowstone both a World Biosphere Reserve and a World Heritage Site.

The park is accessible from all four sides, and a loop road provides easy access to all the best-known sights. Because of its popularity as a destination, tourist towns have grown up on all sides of Yellowstone: Jackson to the south, Cody to the east, Gardiner and Cooke City on the northern margin, and West Yellowstone on the western border. Also because so many people visit the park, there is a well-developed network of facilities inside the park, including campgrounds, hotels, restaurants, gift shops, ATMs, one-hour photo shops, espresso stands, and other supposed necessities of modern life. Although less than two percent of the park is developed, Yellowstone contains more than 2,000 buildings of various types. In some spots (most egregiously around Old Faithful), these developments have grown to the point that the natural world seems simply a backdrop for the human world that pulls visitors in to buy T-shirts or to watch park slide shows on wildlife or geysers while missing the real thing just outside the door.

More than any other national park, Yellowstone seems to provide the oddities of nature, creating, as historian Aubrey L. Haines noted, "a false impression that the park is only a colossal, steam-operated freak show." Yellowstone is a mix of the real and the unreal, a place where our fantasies of what nature should be blend with the reality of crowds of fellow travelers and the impact we have on the place we love so much. During midsummer, a trip into Yellowstone can be something less than a natural experience. Long lines of cars back up behind RVs creeping up the too-narrow roads, and throngs of visitors crowd the benches around Old Faithful Geyser waiting for an eruption, while dozens of others cluster around bewildered elk to get photos for their scrapbooks. But despite this—or perhaps because most folks prefer to stay on paved paths—many parts of the park remain virtually uninhabited. In the Yellowstone backcountry, one can still walk for days without seeing more than a handful of other hardy hikers.

A Place of Controversy

Yellowstone National Park evokes a torrent of emotions in anyone with a knowledge of and concern for the natural world. Perhaps more than any other wild place in America, the park seems to be in a perpetual state of controversy, be it over fire policies, geothermal bioprospecting, bison management, winter use, or some other issue—there's always something getting folks stirred up. Perhaps it is because so many Americans have visited the park that we feel a vested interest in what it means to us. Writer Paul Schullery in his wonderful book *Searching for Yellowstone* put it best when he noted, "Caring for Yellowstone National Park brings to mind all the metaphors of growth and change; it is a process more organic than political; a crucible of ideas, ambitions, dreams, and belief systems; a cultural, intellectual, and spiritual crossroads at which we are forever debating which way to turn." As visitation has risen in recent years, more and more folks have begun to suggest some sort of limits on numbers to preserve the experience and protect the park. Don't-tread-on-me Westerners consider the idea of limits an example of environmental extremism for the elite, but as visitation increases, conflicts and controversies are a natural outcome.

GEOLOGY

Yellowstone is, without a doubt, the most geologically fascinating place on this planet. Here the forces that elsewhere lie deep within the earth seem close enough to touch. They're palpable not only in the geysers and hot springs but also in the lake that fills part of an enormous caldera, the earthquakes that shake this land, the evidence of massive glaciations, and the deeply eroded Grand Canyon of the Yellowstone.

FIRE AND ICE

The Yellowstone Hotspot

When geologists began to study the Yellowstone area in depth they found a surprising pattern. Extending far to the southwest was a chain of volcanic fields, the most ancient of which—16 million years old—lay in northern Nevada. In addition, geologic fault lines created a hundred-mile-wide semicircle around the Yellowstone area, as if some deep-seated force were pushing the land outward and upward the way a ripple moves across a pond.

Both the volcanic activity and the wavelike pattern of faults are due to the same source: a plume of superheated material moving up from the core of the planet through a narrow tube, creating a hotspot beneath the earth's crust. As the North American continent has slid to the southwest over the eons, this plume has traced a line of volcanoes across the West, and as the land continues to move, the plume causes massive deformations in the crust that show up as mountain ranges, fault lines, and earthquakes. It's a little like somebody tugging a piece of cloth across a candle. Approximately 40 such hotspots are known to exist around the globe, but most are beneath the seas. Other than Yellowstone, the best-known example is the chain of Hawaiian Islands. The earth has been moving over the Yellowstone hotspot at the rate of 15 miles per million years for the last 10 million years, and on the present track, the spot might eventually end up in around Hudson Bay in a 100 million years or so. Don't hold your breath.

Tambora on Steroids

The volcanic activity revealed by Yellowstone's geysers, hot springs, and fumaroles is not always benign. Within the last two million years there have been three stupendous volcanic eruptions in the area, the most recent taking place 650,000 years ago. The largest of these eruptions took place two million years ago and created an event beyond the realm of imagination: 600 cubic miles of ash were blasted into the atmosphere! This eruption—probably one of the largest to ever occur on earth—ejected 17 times more material than the massive Tambora erup-

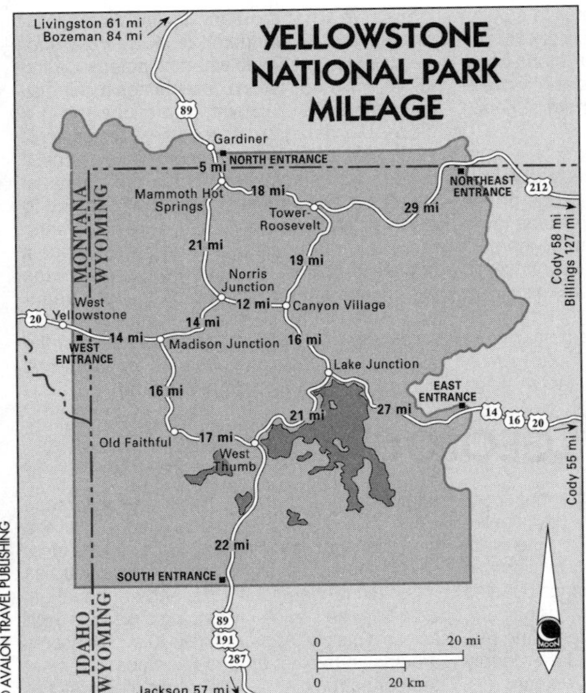

tion of 1815, an explosion that was heard 1,600 miles away. And, compared to an explosion that is better known to Americans, the 1980 eruption of Mt. St. Helens, the first Yellowstone event was 2,400 times as large. Ash from this first Yellowstone eruption carried east to Iowa, north to Saskatchewan, south to the Gulf of Mexico, and west to California. This titanic infusion of ash into the atmosphere undoubtedly affected the global climate for years to follow.

The process that creates these explosions starts when molten rock pushes up from the center of the earth, bulging the land upward into an enormous dome. Eventually the pressure becomes too great and fractures develop around the dome's margins, sending hot gases, ash, and rock blasting into the atmosphere. After the most recent eruption (650,000 years ago), the magma chamber collapsed into a gigantic, smoldering pit reaching 28 by 47 miles in surface area and perhaps several thousand feet deep. Over time, additional molten rock pushed up from underneath and flowed as thick lava over the land. The most recent of these lava flows was 70,000 years ago.

Two resurgent domes—one near Old Faithful and the other just north of Yellowstone Lake near LeHardy Rapids—have been discovered by geologists. Measurements at LeHardy Rapids showed that the land rose almost three feet from 1923 to 1985, though it has since been subsiding. This upsurge raised the outlet of Yellowstone Lake, causing the water level to increase and flooding trees along the lake's margins. Obviously, Yellowstone's volcanism is far from dead, and scientists believe another eruption is possible or even likely, though nobody knows when it might occur.

Glaciation

Not everything in Yellowstone is the result of volcanic activity. The entire Yellowstone region has undergone a series of at least eight major glaciations over the last million years, the last of which—the Pinedale Glaciation—began around 70,000 years ago. At its peak, the Pinedale Glaciation covered almost all of Yellowstone and reached southward into Jackson Hole and north much of the way to Livingston, Montana. Over Yellowstone Lake the icefield was 4,000 feet thick and covered 10,000-foot mountains. This period of glaciation ended about 15,000 years ago, but trees did not appear in the Yellowstone area until 11,500 years ago, and it wasn't till around 5,000 years ago that the landscape began to appear as it does today.

GEYSERS

Yellowstone is famous for geysers, and geyser-gazers will not be disappointed. At least 60% of the world's geysers are in the park, making this easily the largest and most diverse collection in existence. Yellowstone's more than 300 geysers are spread over nine different basins, with half of these in Upper Geyser Basin, the home of Old Faithful.

Geysers need three essentials to exist: water, heat, and fractured rock. The water comes from snow and rain falling on this high plateau, while the heat comes from molten rock close to the earth's surface. Massive pressures from below have created a ring of fractures around the edge of Yellowstone's caldera. This is one of the hottest places on the planet, with heat flows more than 60 times the global average.

How They Work

Geysers operate because cold water is dense and sinks, while hot water is less dense and rises. The periodic eruption of geysers is due to constrictions in the underground channels that prevent an adequate heat exchange with the surface. Precipitation slowly moves into the earth, eventually contacting the molten rock. Because of high pressures at these depths, water can reach extreme temperatures without vaporizing (as in a pressure cooker). As this superheated water rises back toward the surface, it emerges in hot springs, fumaroles, mud pots, and geysers. The most spectacular of these phenomena are geysers. Two general types of geysers exist in Yellowstone. Fountain geysers (such as Great Fountain Geyser) explode from pools of water and tend to spray water more widely, while cone-type geysers (such as Old Faithful) jet out of nozzlelike formations.

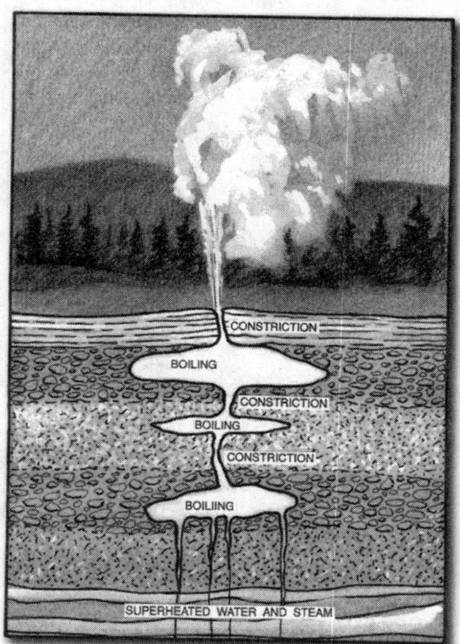

In a geyser, steam bubbles upward from the superheated source of water and expands as it rises. These bubbles block the plumbing system, keeping hot water from reaching the surface. Eventually, however, pressure from the bubbles begins to force the cooler water above out of the vent. This initial release triggers a more violent reaction as the sudden lessening of pressure allows the entire column to begin boiling, explosively expelling steam and water to produce a geyser. Once the eruption has emptied the plumbing system, water gradually seeps back into the chambers to begin the process anew. Some of Yellowstone's geysers have enormous underground caverns that fill with water; in its rare eruptions, massive Steamboat Geyser can blast a million gallons of water into the air!

As an aside, the term geyser is one of the few Icelandic terms in the English language; it means to "gush forth." There are probably 30 active geysers in Iceland, many more on Russia's Kamchatka Peninsula, and a few in New Zealand, where geothermal development has greatly lessened geyser activity.

Preserving the Geysers

Unfortunately, some of Yellowstone's geysers have been lost because of human stupidity or vandalism. At one time, it was considered great sport to stuff logs, rocks, and even chairs into the geysers for a little added show. Others poured chemicals into them to make them play. As a result of such actions, some geysers have been severely damaged or destroyed, and a number of hot springs have become collection points for coins, rocks, sticks, and trash. It shouldn't be necessary to point out that such actions ruin these thermal areas for everyone and destroy something that may have been going on for hundreds of years.

OTHER GEOTHERMAL ACTIVITY

Although geysers are Yellowstone's best-known features, they make up only a tiny fraction of perhaps 10,000 thermal features in the park. **Hot springs** appear where water can reach the ground surface relatively easily, allowing for a dissipation of the heat that builds up in the chambers of geysers. When less groundwater is present, you may find **fumaroles,** vents that shoot steam, carbon dioxide, and even hydrogen sulfide gas. **Mud pots** (also called paint pots) are essentially wet fumaroles. Hydrogen sulfide gas comines with water to produce hydrosulfuric acid. This acid breaks down surrounding rocks to form clay, and the clay combines with water to create mud. As gas passes through the mud it creates the bubbling mud pots. Probably the best examples of these different forms are at Fountain Paint Pot in Lower Geyser Basin, where geysers and hot springs are found in the wetter areas below, while mud pots and fumaroles sit atop a small hill.

The colors in Yellowstone's hot springs come from a variety of sources, including algae and bacteria as well as various minerals, particularly sulfur, iron oxides, and arsenic sulfide. The algae and bacteria are highly temperature-specific and help to create the distinct bands of colors around many hot springs. Interestingly, many of these algal species are found only in hot springs, though they exist around the world. The bacteria have proven of considerable interest to science because of their ability to survive such high temperatures. One such organism, *Thermus aquaticus,* was discovered in a Yellowstone hot springs in 1967, and scientists extracted an enzyme that was later used to develop the increasingly important technique of DNA fingerprinting. Above 190° F, even these hot-water bacteria and algae cannot survive, so the hottest springs may appear a deep blue due to the water's ability to absorb all wavelengths of light except blue, which is reflected back into our eyes.

More Terminology

A couple of other terms are worth learning before heading out to see the sights of Yellowstone. **Sinter** (also called "geyserite") is a deposit composed primarily of silica. The silica is dissolved by hot water deep underground and brought to the surface in geysers or hot springs. At the surface the water evaporates, leaving behind the light gray sinter, which can create large mounds (up to 30 feet high) around the older geysers. The rate of accumulation is very slow, and some of the park's geysers have obviously been active for many thousands of years. The other precipitate that is sometimes deposited around Yellowstone's hot springs and geysers is **travertine,** consisting of calcium carbonate that has been dissolved underground. (See Mammoth Hot Springs below for more on this process.)

A Note of Warning

The surface around many of the hot springs and geysers is surprisingly thin, and people have been killed or seriously injured by falling through into the boiling water. Stay on the boardwalks in developed areas, and use extreme caution around backcountry thermal features. If in doubt, stay away!

travertine terraces at Mammoth Hot Springs

THE GREATER YELLOWSTONE ECOSYSTEM

One of the largest intact temperate-zone ecosystems on the planet, Yellowstone was for decades viewed as an island of nature surrounded by a world of human development. Unfortunately, this attitude has led to a host of problems. Despite its size, Yellowstone alone is not large enough to support a viable population of all the animals that once existed within its borders, and developments outside the park pose threats within. In recent years, there have been increasing calls to treat the park as part of the larger Greater Yellowstone Ecosystem—18 million acres of land at the juncture of Wyoming, Montana, and Idaho covering both public and private lands. With each year that passes it has become more obvious that Yellowstone can never be simply an island. Most of the issues that have made headlines in the last decade or so—from fisheries problems to snowmobile use—have been ones that spread beyond the artificial park boundaries.

Within surrounding lands, conflicts between development and preservation are even more obvious than within the park itself. Logging is one of the most apparent of these, and along the park's western border aerial photos reveal a perfectly straight line, with lodgepole pines on the park side and old clearcuts on the Forest Service side. One of these was the largest timber sale ever made outside of Alaska! Near the park boundaries, housing developments, the massive growth of the tourism industry, oil and gas drilling, mining, a grizzly bear and wolf theme park and other activities all create potential problems within the park and for the Yellowstone ecosystem as a whole.

The way everything is tied together is perhaps best exemplified by two seemingly unrelated issues that have been on the front burner in recent years: bison and snowmobiles. I talk more about both later, but needless to say environmentalists think there are far too many snowmobiles heading into the park, and Montana ranchers think there are far too many bison coming out of the park about the same time of year. As a result, bison are being sent to slaughter, sometimes in large numbers. But these two problems are partially linked; some bison exit the park on roads kept smooth for the snowmobiles. If the roads were not groomed it is possible that more of the bison would remain inside the park in heavy snow years. The point here is not that we should immediately ban all snowmobiles in Yellowstone, but that our actions can have unforeseen ramifications both outside and inside the park.

PLANTS

Yellowstone National Park is primarily a series of high plateaus ranging from 7,500 to 8,500 feet in elevation. Surrounding this gently rolling expanse are the Absaroka Mountains along the east and north sides and the Gallatin Range in the northwestern corner. Elevations are lowest along the northern end of the park, where the Yellowstone River and other streams cut through. Here one

> *At this place there is also large numbers of hot Springs some of which have formed cones of limestone 20 feet high of a Snowy whiteness which make a splendid appearance standing among the ever green pines Some of the lower peaks are very serviceable to the hunter in preparing his dinner when hungry for here his kettle is always ready and boiling his meat being suspended in the water by a string is soon prepared for his meal without further trouble. . . . Standing upon an eminence and superficially viewing these natural monuments one is half inclined to believe himself in the neighborhood of the ruins of some ancients City whose temples had been constructed of the whitest marble.*
>
> —MOUNTAIN MAN OSBORNE RUSSELL, DESCRIBING THE FIREHOLE RIVER AREA IN 1839

finds open country with sagebrush, grasses, and shrubs, along with patches of aspen and Douglas-fir. Farther south on the central plateaus are the extensive lodgepole pine forests that cover more than half the park.

At higher and cooler elevations, lodgepole pine forests give way to groves of Engelmann spruce and subalpine fir, which in turn leave the highest elevations to stands of whitebark pine—an important food source for grizzlies. At timberline (approximately 10,000 feet), even these trees give way and only low-growing forbs, grasses, and shrubs survive. Not all areas follow this simple elevational gradient, however. The park contains extensive wet meadow areas in the Bechler and upper Yellowstone River areas. Other broad openings are found along the Gardner River, in Pelican Valley, and in Hayden Valley.

WILDLIFE

Yellowstone is world-famous for its wildlife and provides a marvelous natural setting in which to view bison, elk, moose, wolves, coyotes, pronghorn antelope, bighorn sheep, and other critters. One of the easiest ways to find wildlife is simply by watching for the brake lights, the cars pulled half off the road, and the cameras all pointed in one direction. Inevitably, you'll find an elk or a bison placidly munching away, trying to remain oblivious to the chaos that surrounds it. Be sure to bring binoculars for your trip to Yellowstone. A spotting scope is also very helpful in searching for distant bears and wolves.

The Park Service has a free brochure showing where you're most likely to see wildlife in Yellowstone. Pick one up at any visitor center. During the summer, the best wildlife-viewing hours are early in the morning and in the late afternoon to early evening. Because of the constant parade of visitors and the lack of hunting, many of Yellowstone's animals appear to almost ignore the presence of people, and it isn't uncommon to see visitors approach an animal without respecting its need for space. Although they may appear tame, Yellowstone's animals really are wild, and attacks are not uncommon. Those quiet bison can suddenly erupt with an enormous ferocity if provoked by photographers who come too close. Between 1983 and 1994, four people were killed by bison in Yellowstone and Grand Teton National Parks. **Stay at least 25 yards away from bison and elk and at least 100 yards away from bears.** (Those with a perverse sense of humor will want to visit the Park Service's website for a short video showing a bison throwing a too-close visitor into a tree; find it under wildlife viewing at www.nps.gov/yell.) Do not under any circumstances feed the park's animals. This creates an unnatural dependency, is unhealthy for the animal, and may even lead to its death.

The park contains some 60 different species of resident mammals, ranging from shrews and bats to bison and grizzlies. Some 309 species of birds have been recorded, along with 18 species of fish (five of which are nonnative), four amphibians, and six reptiles. The only poisonous animal is the prairie rattlesnake, found at low elevations in the northern end of Yellowstone. Oh yes, countless insect species, too. Some Yellowstone critters are more friendly than others, most notably the mosquitoes that show up in large numbers early in the summer. By mid-August they're much less of a hassle, and winter visitors will have no problems at all with mosquitoes!

Trumpeter swans—beautiful white birds with seven-foot wingspans—are a fairly common sight in Yellowstone, particularly on the Madison and Yellowstone Rivers and on Yellowstone Lake. Many trumpeter swans winter in hot spring areas. These are some of the largest birds in America, weighing 20-30 pounds. Another large white bird here is the ungainly-looking and bulbous-billed white pelican, a common sight on Yellowstone Lake and near Fishing Bridge. Upward of 350 pairs of pelicans nest on the Molly Islands in Yellowstone Lake; this is one of the largest white-pelican breeding colonies in the Rockies. Bald eagles—America's national bird—and ospreys have managed comebacks in recent years and are frequently seen along the Yellowstone River and above Yellowstone Lake. Look for golden eagles flying over the open grasslands of Lamar Valley or Hayden Valley.

Killing the Predators

Wildlife has always been one of the big drawing cards at Yellowstone, and early on there were constant charges of mass slaughter by poachers and market hunters. It was not until 1894 that

Congress passed the Lacey Act, finally making it illegal to hunt within the park. Unfortunately, predators such as wolves, coyotes, mountain lions, and wolverines were regarded as despoilers of the elk, deer, and moose and became fair targets for poisoning and shooting by early park managers. (This happened throughout the West, not just in the park.) The campaign proved all too successful, devastating the wolf and mountain lion populations. In recent years, wolves have returned in a spectacular way, though mountain lion numbers remain low.

Controversy on the Northern Range

A recurring area of strife in Yellowstone has been the suggestion that elk and bison are overgrazing and destroying the Lamar and Yellowstone River basins, an area known as the northern range. The issue periodically flares up, fed in part by the efforts of Montana ranchers and others who suffer from bison and elk that migrate out of Yellowstone onto their land each winter. They—and some researchers—believe that the Park Service has allowed too many animals to survive and that the land is being damaged by overgrazing. Most research, however, points in the opposite direction—that the land is not overgrazed, and that ecological processes are working fine in a system termed "natural regulation." The populations of elk and bison fluctuate over time; some years numbers are up, and other years they drop due to harsh winters, predation, hunting outside the park, or other factors.

Bears

During Yellowstone's early years, bears were commonly viewed as either pets or nuisances. Cubs were tethered to poles in front of the hotels, and other bears fed on the garbage piles that grew up around the camps and hotels. Older folks still recall the bear-feeding grounds at the garbage dumps, where visitors might see 50 bears pawing through the refuse. These feeding shows continued until 1941, but it wasn't until 1970 that the park's open-pit dumps were finally sealed off and the garbage cans bear-proofed. Closure of the dumps helped create confrontations between "garbage bears" and humans; the bears nearly always lost. Between 1970 and 1972 dozens of grizzlies died in showdowns with humans in the park or surrounding areas. Fortunately, careful management in the intervening years has helped the population to rebound. Today there are believed to be at least 300-350 grizzlies in the Greater Yellowstone Ecosystem, and their numbers have been increasing fairly steadily since the 1980s. (Some scientists believe there are more than 600 grizzlies.)

Both black and grizzly bears are found throughout Yellowstone, but the days of bear jams along the park roads are long past, since rangers actively work to prevent bears from becoming habituated to people. Most bears have returned to their more natural ways of living, although problems still crop up with individuals wandering through campgrounds in search of food. You're more likely to encounter a bear in the backcountry areas, and some places are closed to hiking for extended periods each year for this reason. The best places to watch for grizzlies along the road system are in the Hayden and Lamar Valleys, near Mt. Washburn, and in the Antelope Creek drainage.

One unusual aspect of the Yellowstone grizzlies was just discovered in recent years: the importance of moths as a food source in the grizzly diet. Millions of army cutworm moths congregate on Yellowstone's high alpine slopes during the summer, where they feed on nectar from the abundant flowers. Bears are attracted to this food source because of the insect's abundance and high fat content. Researchers have sometimes seen two dozen bears feeding on a single slope!

Safety in grizzly country is always a concern, but statistically you are considerably more likely to be hurt in a traffic accident than to be mauled by a bear. There were just 22 bear-caused injuries in the park between 1980 and 1997—one injury for every 2.1 million visitors! Most of these injuries took place in backcountry areas and involved female bears with cubs or yearlings, and nearly all attacks took place following a surprise encounter with a bear. Three people were killed by Yellowstone bears in the last three decades of the 20th century, the most recent being a 1986 fatality caused when a photographer approached an adult female grizzly too closely. For details on staying safe around bears, see the special topic Bear Country in the Introduction chapter.

The **Yellowstone Grizzly Foundation,** tel. (307) 734-8643, http://home.wyoming.com/~ygf, is an excellent nonprofit organization dedicated to conserving grizzlies within the Greater Yellowstone Ecosystem. Established by Steve and Marilynn French—who have been studying grizzly bears since 1983—the foundation emphasizes nonintrusive observations. One of their groundbreaking projects collected hair samples as bears crawled under barbed wire. DNA analysis of these hairs led to a new understanding of how grizzly bears in Yellowstone are related to other bears. It turns out that more than 90% of Yellowstone grizzlies originated from the same maternal lineage, a fact that may have important ramifications for management. The research also showed that the grizzlies of Yellowstone differ markedly from Alaskan grizzlies such as those found at the wildlife park in West Yellowstone.

Bighorn Sheep

These stocky mountain dwellers are named for the massive curling horns of the males (rams) and can be seen in several parts of Yellowstone. They have a tan-colored coat with a white rump patch. Bighorns were once abundant throughout the western U.S., and early trappers in the mountains east of Yellowstone reported finding thousands of sheep in and around the present-day park. They were also an important source of food for the Sheepeater Indians who lived in Yellowstone before the arrival of whites. Bighorn sheep were virtually wiped out by hunters in the late 19th century, and domestic sheep overran their lands and brought deadly diseases. Within a few decades, the millions of sheep that had roamed the West were reduced to a few hundred survivors.

Both the rams and ewes (females) have horns that remain for life, but only the rams get the massive curl for which bighorn sheep are known. Rams are 125-275 pounds in size, with ewes 75-150 pounds. During the mating season in November and December you're likely to see the original head-bangers in action as rams clash to establish dominance. The clashes can be surprisingly violent, and to protect the brain, bighorns have a double cranium that absorbs much of the shock. Those with the larger horns are typically the dominant bighorns and the primary breeders. The young lambs are born in May and June. In the summer months the sexes separate, with the ewes and lambs remaining lower while the bachelor herds climb higher into the mountains. Bighorns use their ability to climb steep and rocky terrain as protection from predators such as coyotes, wolves, and mountain lions. Winter often finds bighorns in mixed herds at lower elevations. Around 250 bighorns live within Yellowstone National Park, with much larger populations in the surrounding national forests.

Look for bighorn sheep on cliffs in the Gardner River Canyon between Mammoth Hot Springs and the town of Gardiner. Ewes and lambs are also frequently seen just off the road on Dunraven Pass north of Canyon, and day-hikers commonly encounter rams up-close on the slopes of Mt. Washburn. Another place where bighorns may be seen is along Specimen Ridge.

Bison

Before their virtual annihilation in the 19th century, 60 million bison were spread across America. When Yellowstone was established in 1872, hundreds of mountain bison (also called wood bison) still ranged across this high plateau. Sport and meat hunting—legal until 1894—and later poaching reduced the population so that by 1902 perhaps fewer than 25 remained. That year, 21 plains bison were brought in from private ranches in Montana and Texas to help restore the Yellowstone herd, and today there are approximately 2,500 in the park, making this the largest free-ranging herd of bison anywhere on earth. Unfortunately, interbreeding between the mountain and plains bison means that the animals in Yellowstone today are genetically different from the original inhabitants.

Bison are typically found in open country throughout the park, including Hayden, Lamar, and Pelican Valleys, along with the Firehole River Basin (including Old Faithful). A favorite time to see bison in Yellowstone is late May, just after the new calves have been born. The calves' antics are always good for laughs. Be sure to use caution around bison; many people have been gored when they've come too close. Always stay at least 25 yards away, preferably farther.

Bison are carriers of brucellosis, a disease that causes cows to abort calves and is the source of undulant fever in humans. Brucellosis can be spread when a contaminated fetus or birthing material is licked by other animals, a situation that is unlikely given the timing of bison movements. In 1985, Yellowstone's bison began wandering north into the Gardiner area for the winter. Montana and Wyoming are certified as "brucellosis-free" states, and although there is absolutely no evidence that wild bison have ever transmitted the disease to cattle, ranchers feared that the bison might threaten Montana's brucellosis-free status. If cattle become infected with brucellosis, ranchers might potentially be prohibited from shipping livestock out of state. (Ironically, the park's far more numerous elk also carry brucellosis. Although they are hunted outside Yellowstone, you won't ever hear Montana authorities talking about slaughtering all elk that wander across Yellowstone's borders.) The state of Wyoming has managed to keep its brucellosis-free status despite the presence of both cattle and bison in Jackson Hole. There, most ranchers vaccinate their cattle and work with the Park Service to keep bison and elk separate from livestock. Why won't it work in Montana? The answer probably has far more to do with Montana politics than biology.

A highly controversial "hunt" during the late 1980s let hunters shoot bison when they wandered outside the park. After a public outcry, the job was turned over to the Montana state Division of Livestock, an agency accustomed to dealing with cattle, not wildlife. Bison that wander out of the park—primarily in the Gardiner and West Yellowstone areas—are hazed in an attempt to push them back in. If this fails, they are typically captured in pens and tested for brucellosis (the blood test is notoriously inaccurate), and those that test positive are usually killed.

Things came to a head in the heavy-snow winter of 1996-97 when nearly 1,100 Yellowstone bison were sent to slaughter, cutting the park bison herd by a third. It was one of the largest killings of bison anywhere since their destruction on the Great Plains in the 1880s. Only a small number of bison were killed in the milder winters of 1997-99, and as this was written the Park Service and Montana were continuing to operate under the controversial bison management plan while putting together a final environmental impact statement on bison management to be released in 2000. You can find out more at the Yellowstone website, www.nps.gov/yell. In the meantime, a number of environmental organizations are pushing for an alternate plan that would put wildlife professionals in charge instead of the Department of Livestock, encourage vaccination of livestock, alter cattle-grazing practices to prevent them from intermingling with bison, and compensate landowners for damage caused to fences and other property.

Coyotes

Although wolves get the media attention, visitors to Yellowstone are probably more likely to see another native of the dog family: the coyote. Keep your eyes open for coyotes anywhere in Yellowstone but especially in open grassy areas where they are more easily spotted. During the summer, they're often seen in small packs or alone as they hunt small mammals such as mice, voles, and pocket gophers. At other times of the year they prey on larger animals, including the calves of elk and pronghorn antelope, and scavenge carrion.

Differentiating coyotes from wolves can be a bit tricky, especially from a distance without binoculars. Coyotes are considerably smaller animals; adult male coyotes weigh around 30 pounds, while wolves are far more massive, with many weighing 100 pounds or more. The wolf has a large head, short and rounded ears, and a broad and blocky muzzle, while the coyote has a small head, large and pointy ears, and a narrow, pointy nose. From a distance coyotes are more delicate in appearance, with smaller feet and thin legs.

The coyotes within Yellowstone generally live in packs containing six or seven animals led by a dominant pair called the alpha male and female. Most packs have a long family lineage and a well-defined territory; some coyote packs have been using the same denning areas for at least 50 years! The average coyote lives around six years. The alphas mate in early February, and pups are born in early April. Other members of the pack guard the den from wolves and other predators and regurgitate food to feed the pups.

Before the reintroduction of wolves, coyotes were the big dogs (so to speak) in northern Yellowstone and the primary predators of elk calves, killing about 1,200 each year. Wolves occupy a similar ecological niche to coyotes, and their return has led to a 50% reduction in coyote numbers in northern Yellowstone. Some of this comes from outright killing of coyotes by the far larger wolves, particularly the killing of alpha coyotes. The ever-resourceful coyotes have responded by banding together in larger packs, denning in rocky areas, becoming more wary, and staying on the margins of wolf territories. Despite the competition, coyotes remain common and are certainly in no danger of being displaced from Yellowstone; after all, both species were here for thousands of years before the extermination of wolves in the 20th century. Good places to look for coyotes are in the Blacktail Plateau area and Lamar Valley, along with the Upper and Lower Geyser Basins near Old Faithful.

Deer

Mule deer (also known as black-tailed deer) are common in many parts of Yellowstone during the summer months, but most migrate to lower elevations when winter comes. They are typically found in open areas containing sagebrush or grass. Mule deer are named for their long, mulelike ears. They also have black-tipped tails and a peculiar way of pogoing away when frightened. Adult males (bucks) grow antlers each summer, and mating season arrives in November and December. Fawns are born in May or June.

The smaller **white-tailed deer** are occasionally seen within Yellowstone but are far less common. You are most likely to find them along rivers or in brushy areas at low elevations, such as around Mammoth Hot Springs or in Lamar Valley. Other places to watch for them are along Yellowstone Lake and in the Upper Geyser Basin.

Elk

One animal virtually every visitor to Yellowstone sees is elk. About 30,000 of these regal animals summer in the park, and approximately 15,000 remain through the winter, primarily on the north end of Yellowstone. In summer, look for elk in Mammoth Hot Springs, Elk Park, and Gibbon Meadows, but you're certain to also see them elsewhere in Yellowstone. Bull elk can top 700 pounds, while the cows (females) weigh around 500-525 pounds, making elk the second-largest members of the deer family after moose. Each summer, adult bulls grow massive antlers that can weigh 30 pounds or more, and these antlers prove useful in the fall mating season as bulls spar with each other. Dominant bulls herd females into harems during the rut and may sometimes control 25 or so cows, mating with those that come into estrus and battling with rivals intent upon taking over their harems. The bugling of bull elk is a common autumn sound in Yellowstone, as anyone who visits Mammoth Hot Springs at that time of year can attest. It's a strange sound that starts out low, followed by a trumpetlike call and then a series of odd grunts. Approximately 90% of the elk cows become pregnant each year.

The mating season ends by mid- to late November, and winter snows push the elk to lower elevations on the north side of Yellowstone or out of the park into surrounding areas. With the arrival of spring, bulls lose their antlers, and elk start moving back toward the high country. Calves are born in late May or early June (sometimes during the migration) and weigh 25-40 pounds at birth. Elk—particularly young calves—are an important food source for predators in Yellowstone; almost a third of the calves are killed each year by wolves, grizzly and black bears, coyotes, and golden eagles.

Moose

The largest members of the deer family, moose are typically seen eating willow bushes in riparian areas inside Yellowstone National Park. During the winter, these moose migrate into high-elevation forests where the snow isn't as deep (tree branches hold the snow) or as crusty as in the open. In these forests they browse on subalpine fir and Douglas-fir. The fires of 1988 burned through many of these forests, and the loss of cover has hurt the Yellowstone moose population. The best places to look for moose are Hayden Valley, around Yellowstone Lake, the Willow Park area north of Norris, the southwestern corner along the Bechler and Falls Rivers, and along the Gallatin, Lamar, and Lewis River drainages.

Pronghorn Antelope

These speedy and colorful ungulates (hoofed mammals) are common sights on the plains of Wyoming, but most of Yellowstone doesn't provide adequate habitat. Pronghorn antelope are only found in sagebrush and grassy areas on the northern end of the park from Lamar Valley to the Gardiner area. Their populations declined sharply in the 1990s within the park, and as of 1999 pronghorn numbered around 200. Coyotes and other predators take many newborn fawns each spring and may be a significant factor in the decline, combined with a number of other factors such as inbreeding due to the small population; changes in vegetation; loss of habitat to development in their Paradise Valley wintering area north of the park; increasing numbers of fences across their range; and hunting.

Wolves

The wolves are back! One of the most exciting developments for visitors to Yellowstone has been the reintroduction of wolves to the park, making this one of the few places in the Lower 48 where they can be viewed in the wild. Wolves once ranged across nearly all of North America, but white settlers regarded them—along with mountain lions, grizzly bears, and coyotes—as threats to livestock and unwanted predators upon game animals. Even in Yellowstone wolves were hunted and poisoned by both the army and the Park Service. By 1940, the wolf was probably gone from the park, though a few lone animals turned up briefly again in the early 1970s.

In the U.S., until 1995 wolves could only be found in Alaska, in northern Minnesota, and in Isle Royale and Glacier National Parks. With the more enlightened public attitude evident in recent years, ecologists and conservationists began pushing for the reintroduction of wolves to Yellowstone, considered one of the few remaining areas in the Lower 48 that could support a viable wolf population.

The proposal to return wolves to Yellowstone set off a firestorm from ranchers (with the ardent support of Wyoming's Republican senators) who feared that they would wander outside the park to destroy sheep and cattle. Opponents said hundreds of livestock would be killed each year around the park and that the reintroduction cost might reach $1.8 million per wolf, a figure that proved grossly inflated. Despite these dire predictions, the U.S. Fish & Wildlife Service began reintroducing wolves to Yellowstone in 1995, initially releasing 14 gray wolves that had been captured in British Columbia. Additional wolves were set free the following spring. During the next six years things went far better than anyone had predicted. By 1999 biologists estimated that 12 groups of wolves totaling 167 individuals inhabited the Greater Yellowstone Ecosystem from north of Yellowstone to the Jackson area.

The return of the wolf to Yellowstone has created a buzz of excitement as visitors gather to watch for wolves. The best place to look is the open terrain of Lamar Valley, where the **Druid Peak and Rose Creek Packs** have taken up residence and are visible at many times of the year. The best time to go looking is early in the morning or near dusk. And, yes, you may well hear their plaintive cry from your campground late at night. Binoculars or spotting scopes are very helpful for roadside wolf watching; do not follow the wolves around since this may disturb them and affect their survival. Denning activity typically takes place early April to early May, with active denning areas closed to humans; check with the Park Service for currently closed areas.

Wolves are the largest members of the canids (dog family), with males averaging 70-120 pounds and stretching up to six feet long from head to tail. They are much more massive than coyotes, though the two are sometimes confused. Wolves live in packs of two to eight, led by an alpha male and alpha female, and establish territories to exclude other wolf packs. Most pack members are from an extended family, but they may include outside members. The alphas are the only ones that generally mate, and a litter of six or so pups is born in early spring. Once they are weaned, the pack feeds pups regurgitated meat until they are large enough to join the hunt. Wolves hunt primarily in the evening and morning hours when their prey—elk, deer, moose, bison, and pronghorn—are feeding.

PARK HISTORY

Yellowstone National Park has a rich and fascinating history that reaches back through thousands of years of settlement. The most thorough source for history is *The Yellowstone Story* (Boulder: University Press of Colorado), an excellent two-volume set by former park historian Aubrey L. Haines. For an engaging and personal journey through the past, read *Searching for Yellowstone* by Paul Schullery (New York: Houghton Mifflin).

SHEEPEATER INDIANS

The last major glaciation ended around 15,000 years ago, and the first peoples may have reached Yellowstone while the ice was still retreating. There is good evidence that the country was occupied for at least 10,000 years, though the tribes apparently changed over time. By the mid-19th century, the country was surrounded by

THE NEZ PERCÉ WAR

One of the saddest episodes in the history of Yellowstone took place in 1877 and involved the Nez Percé Indians of Oregon's Wallowa Valley. When the government tried to force the people of Chief White Bird and Chief Joseph onto an Idaho reservation so that white ranchers could have their lands, they stubbornly refused. A few drunken young men killed four whites, and subsequent raids led to the deaths of at least 14 more. The Army retaliated but was turned back by the Nez Percé. Rather than face government reinforcements, more than 1,000 Nez Percé began a 1,800-mile flight in a desperate bid to reach Canada. A series of running battles followed as the Indians managed to confound the inept Army using their geographic knowledge and battle skills. The Nez Percé entered Yellowstone from the west, and a few hotheads immediately attacked vacationing tourists and prospectors. Two whites were killed in the park, others were kidnapped, and another man nearly died from his wounds.

The Nez Percé exited Yellowstone two weeks after they arrived, narrowly missing an encounter with their implacable foe, Gen. William T. Sherman, who just happened to be vacationing in Yellowstone at the time. East of the park, the Indians plotted a masterful escape from two columns of Army forces, feinting a move down the Shoshone River and then heading north along a route that left their pursuers gasping in amazement—straight up the narrow Clarks Fork Canyon, "where rocks on each side came so near together that two horses abreast could hardly pass." Finally, less than 40 miles from the international border with Canada, the Army caught up with the Nez Percé, and after a fierce battle the tribe was forced to surrender (although 300 did make good their escape).

Chief Joseph in October 1887 immediately after his surrender at Bear Paw

Chief Joseph's haunting words still echo through the years: "Hear me, my chiefs, I am tired; my heart is sick and sad. From where the sun now stands, I will fight no more forever." Despite promises that they would be allowed to return to their traditional home, the Nez Percé were instead hustled onto reservations in Oklahoma and Washington while whites remained on their ancestral lands. Chief Joseph spent the rest of his life on Washington's Colville Reservation and died in 1904, reportedly of a broken heart. Yellowstone's Nez Percé Creek, which feeds the Firehole River, is named for this desperate bid for freedom.

YELLOWSTONE NATIONAL PARK

Sheepeater Indian in wickiup

Blackfeet to the north, Crow to the east, and Shoshone and Bannock to the south and west. These tribes all traveled through and hunted in Yellowstone, building temporary shelters, called wickiups, made of aspen poles covered with pine boughs; a few of these still exist in the park. The primary inhabitants of this high plateau were the Sheepeater Indians, who may have been here for over 2,000 years. Of Shoshone stock, the Sheepeaters hunted bighorn sheep (hence the name) and made bows from the sheep horns, but their diet also included other animals, fish, roots, and berries. Because they did not have horses, the Sheepeaters used dog-pulled travois to carry their few possessions from camp to camp. Summers were spent in high alpine meadows and along passes, where they hunted migrating game animals or gathered roots and berries. They wintered in protected canyons.

The Sheepeaters were smaller than other Indians and have achieved an aura of mystery since so little is known of their way of living. Yellowstone was at the heart of their territory, but with the arrival of whites came devastating diseases, particularly smallpox. The survivors joined their Shoshone brothers on the Wind River Reservation or the Bannock Reservation in Idaho. The last of the tribe left Yellowstone in the 1870s.

FUR TRAPPERS

The word "Yellowstone" appears to have come from the Minnetaree Indians, who called the river "Mi tse a-da-zi," a word French-Canadian trappers translated into "Rive des Roche Jaunes"—literally, "Yellow Rock River." The Indians apparently called it this because of the yellowish bluffs along the river near Billings, Montana (not because of the colorful Grand Canyon of the Yellowstone). The term "Yellow Stone" was first used on a map made in 1797. When the Lewis and Clark Expedition traveled through the country north of Yellowstone in 1805-06, the Indians told them tales of this mysterious place: "There is frequently heard a loud noise like thunder, which makes the earth tremble, they state that they seldom go there because children Cannot sleep—and Conceive it possessed of spirits, who were adverse that men Should be near them." (This certainly was not the attitude of all the native peoples, for the park had long been inhabited.) The first white man to come through Yellowstone is believed to be John Colter, a former member of the Lewis and Clark Expedition who wandered through the region in the winter of 1807-08. A map based on Colter's recollections shows Yellowstone Lake ("Eustis Lake"), along with an area of "Hot Spring Brimstone."

As fur trappers spread through the Rockies in the 1820s and '30s, many discovered the geysers and hot springs of Yellowstone, and stories quickly spread around the rendezvous fires. The word of the trappers was passed on to later settlers and explorers but not entirely believed. After all, mountain man Jim Bridger described not just petrified trees, but petrified birds singing petrified songs! His tales of a river that "ran so fast that it became hot on the bottom" could well have referred to the Firehole River. When Bridger tried to lead a party of military explorers into Yellowstone, they were stymied by deep snows. Still, the word gradually got out that something very strange could be found in this part of the mountains. Little remains today from the mountain-man era, although in 1880 the letters "J.O.R. Aug. 19, 1819" were found carved in a tree near the Upper Falls of the Yellowstone, and later a cache of iron beaver traps similar to those used by the Hudson's Bay Company was discovered near Obsidian Cliff.

EXPEDITIONS

National attention finally came to Yellowstone with a series of three expeditions to check out the wild claims of local prospectors. In 1869, David E. Folsom, Charles W. Cook, and William Peterson headed south from Bozeman, finding the Grand Canyon, Lake Yellowstone, and the geyser basins. When a friend pressured them to submit a description of their travels for publication, the *New York Tribune* refused to publish it, noting that the paper "had a reputation that they could not risk with such unreliable material."

The adventures of this first expedition led another group of explorers into Yellowstone the following year, but this time money was the motive. Jay Cooke's Northern Pacific Railroad needed investors for a planned route across Montana. A good public-relations campaign was the first step, and it happened to coincide with the visit of a former Montana tax collector named Nathaniel P. Langford, who had heard of the discoveries of Folsom, Cook, and Peterson. The party of 19 soldiers and civilians, including Langford, headed out in August of 1870 under Gen. Henry D. Washburn. They were thrilled by what they discovered and proceeded to give the geysers names—Old Faithful, Castle, Giant, Grotto, Giantess—which became permanently attached to the features. The joy of the trip was marred when one man—Truman Everts—became separated from the others and then lost his horse. He was not found until 37 days later, by which time he weighed just 50 pounds. His rescuer did not even recognize him as human. Amazingly, Everts survived and recovered.

With the return of the Washburn Expedition, national newspapers and magazines finally began to pay attention to Yellowstone, and Langford began lecturing in the East on what they had found. One of those listening was Dr. Ferdinand V. Hayden, director of the U.S. Geological Survey. Hayden asked Congress to fund an official investigation. With the help of Representatives James G. Blaine (coincidentally a supporter of the Northern Pacific Railroad) and conservationist Henry M. Dawes, Congress appropriated $40,000 for an exploration of "the sources of the Missouri and Yellowstone Rivers." Thus began the most famous and influential trip into Yellowstone, the 1871 Hayden Expedition. The troop included 34 men, an escort of cavalry, painter Thomas Moran, and photographer William H. Jackson.

ESTABLISHING THE PARK

When Hayden returned to Washington to prepare his report, he found a letter from railroad promoter Jay Cooke. In the letter, Cooke proposed that "Congress pass a bill reserving the Great Geyser Basin as a public park forever—just as it has reserved that far inferior wonder the Yosemite valley and big trees." (Abraham Lincoln had established Yosemite earlier as a state park.) In an amazingly short time, a bill was introduced to set aside the land, and Hayden rushed to arrange a display in the Capitol rotunda of geological specimens, sketches by Moran, and photos by Jackson. The bill easily passed both houses of Congress and was signed into law on March 1, 1872, by Pres. Ulysses S. Grant. The first national park had come into existence, a culmination not just of the discoveries in Yellowstone but also of a growing appreciation for preserving the wonders of the natural world.

Congress saw no need to set aside money for this new creation, since it seemed to be doing fine already. Besides, it was thought that Jay Cooke's new railroad would soon arrive, making it easy for thousands of vacationers to explore Yellowstone. In turn, concessioners would build roads and hotels and pay the government franchise fees. The park was placed under the control of the secretary of the interior, with Nathaniel P. Langford as its unpaid superintendent. Meanwhile, the planned railroad fizzled when Jay Cooke & Co. declared bankruptcy, precipitating the panic of 1873.

ROADS AND RAILROADS

Because of the difficult access, fewer than 500 people visited in each of Yellowstone's first few years as a park, most to soak in tubs at Mammoth Hot Springs. Not a few decided to take home souvenirs, bringing pickaxes and shovels for that purpose. Meanwhile, hunters—including some working for the Mammoth Hotel—began shooting the park's abundant game. Two brothers who had a ranch just north of the park killed 2,000 elk in a single year. Superintendent Langford did little to stop the slaughter and only bothered to visit the park twice. Finally, in 1877, the secretary of the interior fired him, putting Philetus W. Norris in charge instead. Norris proved a good choice, despite a knack for applying his name to everything in sight. (Most of his attempts at immortality have been replaced by other titles, but Norris Geyser Basin, Norris Road, and even the town of Norris, Michigan, remain.)

Norris oversaw construction of the first major road in Yellowstone, a rough 60-mile route built in just 30 days to connect Upper Geyser Basin with Mammoth and the western entrance. All of this was precipitated by the raids of the Nez Percé Indians earlier that summer and threats that the Bannock Indians would strike next. In addition, Norris began, but never completed, the Queen's Laundry, a bathhouse that is considered the first government building built for the public in any national park. The log walls are still visible in a meadow near Lower Geyser Basin.

By 1882, Norris had managed to alienate the company that helped found the park, the Northern Pacific Railroad. The company announced plans to build a railroad line to the geysers and construct a large hotel, "being assured by the Government of a monopoly therein." Norris's opposition led to his being fired and replaced by railroad man Patrick H. Conger. Soon, however, the scheme began to unravel. The Yellowstone Park Improvement Company—whose vice-president happened to be construction superintendent for the Northern Pacific's branch line into Gardiner—had planned not just a lodging monopoly but also a monopoly on all transportation, timber rights, and ranching privileges in the park. Later it was discovered that the company had contracted for 20,000 pounds of venison (killed in the park) to feed the construction crews. As one newspaper writer commented, "It is a 'Park Improvement Company' doing this, and I suppose they consider it an improvement to rid the park, as far as possible, of game."

Finally, in 1884 Congress acted by limiting the land that could be leased—thus effectively ending the railroad's plans—and adding funding to hire 10 assistants to patrol Yellowstone. Unfortunately, they neglected to include any penalties for the poachers and despoilers other than expulsion, so even the few assistants who did decent work found the culprits quickly returning. The problems were myriad. Cooke City miners were fishing with spears, seine nets, and even dynamite. Guides were throwing rocks into the geysers, squatters had ensconced themselves on prime land in Lamar Valley, and visitors were leaving fires unattended and breaking off specimens from the geysers.

Superintendent Conger was later replaced by Robert E. Carpenter, a man about whom historian Hiram Chittenden noted, "In his opinion, the Park was created to be an instrument of profit to those who were shrewd enough to grasp the opportunity." Carpenter lobbied Congress to remove lands from the park so that the Northern Pacific could construct a railroad along the Yellowstone and Lamar Rivers to Cooke City. In return, friends promised to locate claims in his name along the route so that he too might profit from the venture. The landgrab fell apart when the Senate vetoed the move, and Carpenter was summarily removed from office. Not long thereafter, Congress flatly refused to fund the civilian administration of Yellowstone, and the Secretary of the Interior was forced to request the aid of the military in 1886. It proved a fortuitous step.

THE ARMY YEARS

The U.S. Army finally brought a semblance of order to Yellowstone, eliminating the political appointees who viewed the park as a place to get rich. That first year, a temporary fort—Camp Sheridan—was thrown up and a troop of soldiers arrived, but it wasn't until 1891 that work began on a permanent Fort Yellowstone at Mammoth. By 1904, the fort consisted of some 26 buildings housing 120 men. The soldiers had clear objectives—protecting wildlife (or at least bison and elk) from poachers, fighting fires, stopping vandalism, and generally achieving order out of chaos. These goals were accomplished with a fervor that gained widespread respect, and in a way that would later influence the organization of the National Park Service. One of the major accomplishments of the soldiers was completion of the Grand Loop Road, which passes most of Yellowstone's attractions. The basic pattern was completed by 1905.

Fort Yellowstone was a favorite station for soldiers, and it was considered something of an honor to be sent to such a setting. The life of the soldiers was not always easy, however, and a number died in the bitter winters or in accidents. A series of 16 soldier stations—actually little more than large cabins—was established around the park, and each was manned year-round, usually by four soldiers.

Before the arrival of cars, many visitors to Yellowstone were wealthy people from the East Coast or Europe intent upon doing the grand tour of the West. The railroads (Northern Pacific to the north, Union Pacific to the west, and the Burlington to the east) deposited them near park borders, where they were met by carriages, Tallyhos (26-passenger stagecoaches), and surreys. In 1915, some 3,000 horses were in use within the park! Most "dudes" paid approximately $50 for a six-day tour that included transportation, meals, and lodging at the hotels. They paid another $2.50 for the privilege of sailing across Lake Yellowstone on the steamship *Zillah.* By contrast, another group, the "sagebrushers," came to Yellowstone in smaller numbers, arriving in their own wagons or hiring a coach to transport them between the "Wylie Way" campgrounds. These seasonal tent camps were scattered around the park, providing an inexpensive ($35 for a seven-day tour) way to see the sights. Even as early as 1908, Yellowstone was being seen by 18,000 visitors a year.

The Northern Pacific was still intent upon carving Yellowstone into a moneymaking resort, even going so far as to propose an electric railroad, to be powered by a dam at the falls of the Yellowstone River. Fortunately, equally powerful forces—notably Gen. Philip Sheridan and naturalist Joseph Bird Grinnell—saw through their designs and thwarted each attempt to bring railroads into Yellowstone. Still, the Northern Pacific's interests were represented by its indirect control of many of Yellowstone's hotels, stagecoaches, wagons, and other vehicles used to transport tourists.

All this changed when the first car was allowed through the gate on August 1, 1915. (Entrance fees were a surprisingly stiff $5 for single-seat vehicles and $7.50 for five-passenger cars.) Almost immediately, it became clear that horses and cars could not mix, and motor buses replaced the old coaches. From then on, the park would be increasingly a place for "autoists." Interestingly, within a year the park would come under the jurisdiction of the newly created National Park Service.

THE PARK SERVICE TAKES OVER

After years of army control, supporters of a separate National Park Service finally had their way in 1916. The congressional act created a dual role for the new park system: to "conserve the scenery" and to "provide for the enjoyment of the same," a contradictory mandate that would later lead to all sorts of conflicts. The first couple of years were tenuous, as management flip-flopped between the army and civilians; the final changeover came in 1918 and ended three decades of military supervision. The management of Yellowstone fell on the shoulders of two men, Horace M. Albright and his mentor, Stephen Mather, both of whom had been heavily involved in lobbying to create the new agency. Mather became the Park Service's first director, while Albright served as superintendent at Yellowstone and later stepped into Mather's shoes to head the agency.

Albright quickly upgraded facilities to meet the influx of motorists who demanded more camping facilities but also cabins, lodges, cafeterias, and bathhouses. Forty-six camps of one sort or another were constructed (only 12 survive today), fulfilling Albright's dream of "a motorist's paradise." The focus of the new Park Service was clearly visitation rather than preservation. Albright assembled a first-rate force of park rangers and instituted the environmental-education programs that have been the agency's hallmark ever since.

As the automobile took over Yellowstone, the railroads gradually lost their sway, and the final passenger train to the park's gateway towns stopped in 1960. In the 1950s, the Park Service initiated "Mission 66," a decade-long project to

THE YELLOWSTONE FIRES OF 1988

Many will long remember the summer of 1988 as the year that fires seared Yellowstone National Park. TV reporters flocked to the park, pronouncing the destruction of America's most famous national wonder as they stood before trees turned into towering torches and 27,000-foot clouds of black smoke. Newspaper headlines screamed, "Park Sizzles," "Winds Whip Fiery Frenzy Out of Control," and "Firestorms Blacken Yellowstone." Residents of nearby towns complained of lost tourism dollars, choking smoke, and intentionally lit backfires that threatened their homes and businesses. Wyoming politicians berated the Park Service's "Let Burn" policy; President Reagan expressed astonishment that fires were ever allowed to burn in the national parks, though the policy had been in place for 16 years. Perhaps the most enduring image is from a forest that had been blown down by tornado-force winds in 1984 and then burned by the wind-whipped fires of 1988. The media ate it up, with one headline reading, "Total Destruction: Intense Heat and Flames from the Fires in Yellowstone Left Nothing but Powdered Ash and Charcoal Near Norris Junction." Unfortunately, the real story behind the fires of '88 was lost in this media feeding frenzy.

A Century of Change

In reality, these fires were not unprecedented; we were just fortunate enough to witness a spectacle of nature that may not occur for another 300 years. When Yellowstone National Park was established in 1872, most of the land was carpeted with a mixture of variously aged lodgepole-pine stands established after a series of large fires. Fewer large fires, partly due to a fire-suppression policy in effect until 1972, meant that by the 1980s a third of the park's lodgepole stands were more than 200 years old. Yellowstone was ripe to burn.

Since the early 1950s, Smokey the Bear had drummed an incessant message: "Only You Can Prevent Forest Fires." Forest fires were viewed as dangerous, destructive forces that had to be stopped to protect our valuable public lands. Unfortunately, this immensely effective and generally valid ad campaign convinced the public that *all* fires were bad. Ecological research has shown not only that this is wrong, but that putting out all fires can sometimes create conditions far more dangerous than if fires had been allowed to burn in the first place. Fire, like the other processes that have affected Yellowstone—cataclysmic volcanic explosions, geothermal activity, and massive glaciation—is neither good nor evil. It is simply a part of the natural world that national parks are attempting to preserve. Unfortunately, national parks are no longer surrounded by similarly undeveloped land, so when fires burned in Yellowstone and adjacent Forest Service lands they also affected nearby towns and the people who made a living from tourism or logging.

Fire in Lodgepole Forests

Fire has played an important role in lodgepole-pine forests for thousands if not millions of years, and as a result the trees have evolved an unusual adaptation. Some of the cones are sealed with a resin that melts in a fire, thus releasing the seeds. The parent trees are killed, but a new generation is guaranteed by the thousands of pine seeds released to

(continued on next page)

THE YELLOWSTONE FIRES OF 1988

(continued)

the bare, nutrient-rich soil underneath the blackened overstory. Within five years the landscape is dotted with thousands of young pines, competing with a verdant cover of grasses and flowers.

Although some animals are killed in the wildfires (including, in 1988, 269 of Yellowstone's 30,000 elk), and others die from severe winter weather or a lack of food immediately after the fire, the decades immediately following major fires create conditions that are unusually rich for many animals. Wildlife diversity in lodgepole forests reaches a peak within the first 25 years after a fire as woodpeckers, mountain bluebirds, and other birds feed on insects in the dead trees, and elk and bears graze on the lush grasses.

As the forest ages, a dense thicket of trees develops, keeping light from reaching the forest floor and making it difficult for understory plants to survive. These trees are eventually thinned by disease and windthrow, creating openings in the forest, but after 200-300 years without fire, lodgepole forests become a tangle of fallen trees that are difficult to walk through, are of lesser value to many animals, and burn easily. They also become susceptible to attacks by bark beetles, such as those that killed thousands of acres of trees in Yellowstone starting in the 1960s and continuing through the 1980s. These beetle-killed trees added to the fuel available to burn once a fire started.

Yellowstone in 1988

Yellowstone's 1988 fires were due not just to the heavy fuel loading from aging forests but also to weather conditions that were the driest and windiest on record. The winter of 1987-88 had been a mild one, and by spring there was a moderate to severe drought in the park, lessened only by above-normal rainfall in April and May. Since 1972, when Yellowstone Park officials first began allowing certain lightning fires to burn in backcountry areas, the acreage burned had totaled less than two percent of the park. (Mistakenly called a "let burn" policy, the natural fire program actually involved close monitoring of these lightning-ignited fires to determine when and if a fire should be suppressed. All human-caused fires were immediately suppressed, as were any that threatened property or life.)

When the first lightning fires of the 1988 season began in late May, those in the backcountry areas were allowed to burn, as fire management officials anticipated normal summer weather conditions. Many went out on their own, but when June and July came and the rains failed to materialize, the fires began to spread rapidly. Alarmed park officials declared them wildfires and sent crews to put them out. (Ironically, the largest fire, the North Fork/Wolf Lake Complex, was started by a logger outside the park who tossed a lit cigarette to the ground. Although firefighters immediately attacked the blaze, it consumed more than 500,000 acres.) As the summer progressed, more and more firefighters were called in, eventually totaling over 25,000 personnel, at a cost exceeding $120 million. Firefighters managed to protect most park buildings but had little effect on the forest fires themselves. Experts say that conditions in the summer of 1988 were so severe that even if firefighters had immediately responded to all the natural fires, it would likely have made little difference. Yellowstone has experienced these massive fires in the past and will again in the future, no matter what humans do.

Out of Control

August brought worsening conditions with each passing day. Winds blew steadily at 20-40 miles an hour, and gusts to 70 mph threw firebrands two miles in beyond the firefront, across fire lines, roads, and even over the Lewis River Canyon. The amount of moisture in the large logs was less than that in kiln-dried wood. By mid-August, more than 25 fires were burning simultaneously across the park and in surrounding national forests, with many joining together to create massive complexes such as the Clover-Mist Fire, the Snake River Complex, and the North Fork/Wolf Lake Complex. On a single day-September 7-more than 100,000 acres burned. Also torched that day were 20 cabins and outbuildings in the vicinity of Old Faithful (out of the more than 400 structures there). Fortunately, all the major historical buildings were spared. The fires seemed poised to consume the remainder of Yellowstone, but four days later the season's first snow carpeted the park. Within a few days firefighters had the upper hand.

A Transformed Landscape

The fires had burned nearly 800,000 acres—more than a third of the park—plus another 600,000 acres on adjacent Forest Service lands. Of the park total, 41% were canopy fires in which all the trees were killed, and another 35% were a mixture of ground fires and canopy fires. The remainder were lighter burns. Less than a tenth of one percent of the land was burned hot enough to sterilize the soil. The fires killed countless small mammals, along with at least 269 elk, nine bison, six black bears, four deer, and two moose. The drought of 1988 followed by the severe winter of 1988-89 led to a large die-off of elk and bison, but their carcasses provided food for predators. Since then, wildlife populations have rebounded and may even exceed levels before the fires.

It's been over a decade since the last of the massive fires were put out, and much has changed, including the park's natural-fire program. It was replaced by a somewhat more conservative version that requires managers to provide daily certifications that fires are controllable and that they will remain "in prescription" for another 24 hours. Visitors to Yellowstone today will find dense thickets of young lodgepole pines in many areas that burned, and the first seedlings of other evergreen species starting to emerge. In other places, grasses, colorful wildflowers, forbs, and other plants dominate. Not everything burned, of course, so you'll also see many green older forests next to burned stands, creating a complex mosaic of habitats that supports a higher diversity of animal life. Once you grow accustomed to the burned areas and understand that they are a part of the natural process, they actually add interest to the park and help you appreciate Yellowstone as a functioning ecosystem rather than a static collection of plants and animals.

Take a hike through one of the burned areas to discover the wealth of new life within Yellowstone. Vistas that were long blocked by forests are now more open and will gradually become more so; by 2008 most of the standing dead trees will have fallen. The Park Service has placed informative signboards at sites around Yellowstone describing the fires and the changes they brought about. Stop by the Grant Village Visitor Center for an informative exhibit and to watch a film on the fires of 1988 and the transformations they brought about.

upgrade facilities and add more lodging. By the late '60s, a growing appreciation for the natural world was shifting public opinion away from such developments, and the 1973 master plan scaled back proposed developments. From day one, Yellowstone National Park had been set up for what Edward Abbey called "industrial tourism." The park had come into existence in part because of a railroad promoter who hoped to gain from its development, and it grew to maturity on a diet of roads, hotels, and curio shops. In recent years, Americans have taken a second look at this heritage and have begun to wonder which matters more: providing a public playground or preserving an area that is unique on this planet. The inherent conflict between the need for public facilities and services in Yellowstone and the survival of a functioning ecosystem will continue to create a tug-of-war between various factions. Writer Paul Schullery's description of Yellowstone hits home: "The pro-development moguls of the Yellowstone Park Improvement Company of the 1880s have their modern equivalents in a tourism industry whose most aggressive members see the park as a huge tree-covered goose that is capable of laying a bigger golden egg every year; these people can think of nothing more pleasing than the prospect of Yellowstone with 4 or 5 million visitors instead of 3 million."

Certainly the most famous recent event was the series of massive fires that swept across nearly half of Yellowstone in 1988. The land has recovered surprisingly well since then, and in recent years other issues came to the fore: wolf reintroduction, bison being killed on the park boundaries, snowmobile and other winter use, and problems caused by exotic species and fish disease. There's always something stewing in the mud pots of Yellowstone! Some things have been improving in recent years, including efforts to repair aging roads and to replace outdated buildings in the park. Despite any problems and controversies, the park is just as fascinating as ever. The geysers never cease to amaze, the scenery remains majestic, Grand Canyon of the Yellowstone is still just as stunning, and the superb wildlife-viewing continues to make this the Serengeti of America.

TOURING YELLOWSTONE

Yellowstone is perhaps the most accessible national park in America. Nearly all the famous sights are within a couple hundred feet of the Grand Loop Road, a 142-mile figure-eight through the middle of the park. The speed limit on all park roads is a vigilantly enforced 45 mph (or less); exceed the limit and you're likely to get a ticket! Whatever you do, *don't* see Yellowstone at 45 miles an hour; that's like seeing the Louvre from a passing train.

For all too many visitors, Yellowstone becomes a checklist of places to visit, geysers to watch, and animals to see. This tends to inspire an attitude that treats this great national treasure as a drive-through theme park, where the animals come out to perform and the geyser eruptions are predicted so everyone can be there on time. If you're one of this crowd, give yourself a giant kick in the rear and take a walk, even if it is just around Upper Geyser Basin where you see something beyond Old Faithful.

The following loop tour of Yellowstone begins in the south and traces a clockwise path around the Grand Loop with a number of side trips. Although it is possible to follow this sequence (or some variation) the entire distance, a far better way to learn about Yellowstone is to stop for a while in the places that are the most interesting to you and really explore them, rather than trying to see everything in a cursory way. If you have the time, the entire park is well worth visiting, but if you only have a day or two, pick a couple of spots and see them right. And don't just check out the views everyone else sees; find a nearby trail and do a little exploring on your own. If you are planning a trip to the area, try to set aside a bare minimum of three days in Yellowstone.

Most roads in Yellowstone close with the first heavy snows of early November and usually open again by mid-May. The roads connecting Mammoth to West Yellowstone open first, and Dunraven Pass is plowed last. Only the road between Mammoth and Cooke City is kept open all year. If you're planning a trip early or late in the season, call the park for current road conditions; tel. (307) 344-7381, ext. 5, and then ext. 2. The same information can be found on the park webpage: www.nps.gov/yell.

SOUTH ENTRANCE ROAD

The South Entrance Station consists of several log structures right along the Snake River. Just 1.5 miles beyond the entrance is an easily missed turnout where you can walk down to 30-foot-high **Moose Falls.** Beyond this, the road climbs up a long, gentle ramp to Pitchstone Plateau, passing green forests of lodgepole pine. Stop at a turnout to look back at the majestic Tetons. Abruptly, this gentle country is broken by the edge of **Lewis River Canyon,** with rhyolite walls that up to 600 feet. The fires of 1988 burned hot through much of this area, and dead trees line both sides of the canyon in all directions, though young trees are now carpeting many areas.

The road parallels the river for the next seven miles. Nearly everyone stops for a look at 29-foot-high **Lewis Falls.** Camping is available at the south end of **Lewis Lake,** which, like the lake, falls, river, and canyon are all named for the Lewis and Clark expedition's Meriwether Lewis. Lewis Lake is the park's third-largest body of water (after Yellowstone Lake and Shoshone Lake) and is popular with canoeists, kayakers, and anglers. The clear waters contain brown trout and Mackinaw (lake trout). Approximately four miles north of Lewis Lake, the highway tops the Continental Divide, 7,988 feet above sea level. This is one of three such crossings that roads make within Yellowstone.

Day-hikes in the Lewis Lake Area

Two trailheads a mile north of Lewis Lake provide access west to Shoshone Lake and east to Heart Lake. At the Dogshead Trailhead you can choose between two trails to Shoshone Lake, both of which cross land burned in the 1988 fires. The four-mile-long **Dogshead Trail** is more direct, while the seven-mile **Lewis Channel Trail** takes a much more scenic trek via the channel that connects Shoshone and Lewis

Lakes. This slow-flowing channel is popular with anglers who come to fish for brown and cutthroat trout during the fall spawning season, and it's also used by canoeists and kayakers heading into Shoshone Lake. Once you reach Shoshone Lake, follow Delacy Creek Trail northward along the shore for fine vistas. The area gets considerable overnight use, and campsites are scattered around the lake.

Heart Lake Trailhead is on the opposite side of the road and south a few hundred feet from Dogshead Trailhead. Heart Lake is a scenic and interesting area that gets considerable day-use, but it's probably best visited on a backpacking trip of several days or longer since it's an eight-mile (one-way) hike to the lake. Be sure to bring water with you. Hardcore hikers may want to attempt a day-trip all the way to the summit of Mt. Sheridan, but this is 22 miles roundtrip, and you gain (and lose) 2,700 feet in elevation along the way. The Heart Lake area is closed to access before July because of grizzly activity. For details on longer hikes in the Heart Lake and Shoshone Lake areas, see Into the Backcountry later in this chapter.

Grant Village

Named for American president Ulysses S. Grant, who established Yellowstone, Grant Village was built in the 1980s to replace facilities at Fishing Bridge, an area of important grizzly habitat. Unfortunately, instead of one bad development, Yellowstone now has two—a number of the buildings at Fishing Bridge still stand. Unlike some of the more historic places in Yellowstone where a natural rusticity prevailed, Grant Village has less charm than most Kmarts. A steak house restaurant juts out along the shore of Yellowstone Lake, and the lodging at Grant Village forms a chintzy condo backdrop. Other facilities include a campground, store, gas station, and post office. Much of the area around here was consumed in the 1988 Snake River Fire; unfortunately, the fire missed this scar on the Yellowstone landscape.

Grant Village Visitor Center, tel. (307) 242-2650, houses an interesting exhibit and film on the fires of 1988. These provide a good background to help understand the changes taking place as the burned areas recover. (See the special topic The Yellowstone Fires of 1988 for an overview.) The visitor center is open daily 8 a.m.-7 p.m. Memorial Day to Labor Day, and daily 9 a.m.-5 p.m. in September. It's closed from early October to Memorial Day. (Hours may vary depending upon park budgets and staffing.)

West Thumb

If you look at a map of Yellowstone Lake, it's possible to imagine the lake as a giant hand with three mangled fingers heading south and a gnarled thumb hitching west. Hence the name West Thumb. This portion of Yellowstone Lake is the deepest (to 390 feet) and is actually a caldera that filled with water after erupting 150,000 years ago. There is still considerable heat just below the surface, as revealed by **West Thumb Geyser Basin.** A short loop trail leads through steaming hot springs and pools. Right on the shore is **Fishing Cone,** where tourists once caught fish and then plopped them in the cone to be cooked; after a number of clowning tourists were injured, the Park Service put a stop to this stunt. The **West Thumb Information Station** is open daily 9 a.m.-5 p.m. from Memorial Day through late September and has a small bookstore. (Hours may vary depending upon park budgets and staffing.) In wintertime the station is used as a warming hut.

WEST THUMB TO UPPER GEYSER BASIN

Heading west from West Thumb, the highway climbs over the Continental Divide twice. Most of these forests escaped the 1988 fires. A few miles beyond the eastern crossing of the divide is a turnout at **Shoshone Point,** where you catch glimpses of Shoshone Lake and the Tetons. In 1914, highwayman Ed Trafton (his real name was Ed Harrington) held up 15 stagecoaches as they passed by this point carrying tourists. He got away with $915.35 in cash and $130 in jewelry but made the rather obvious mistake of posing for photos. He was caught the following year and spent five years in Leavenworth. When he died, a letter in his pocket claimed that he had been Owen Wister's model for the Virginian. Others suspected that he was more likely to have been Wister's model for the villain, Trampas.

DeLacy Creek Trail provides access to Shoshone Lake—Yellowstone's largest backcountry lake—and begins at the picnic area between the two passes. It's three miles to the lake, which is circled by more trails. Keep your eyes open for moose and other animals in the meadows along the way. The western crossing of the Continental Divide is at **Craig Pass,** where a tiny pond (Isa Lake) empties into both the Atlantic and Pacific Oceans through its two outlet streams.

Approximately 14 miles beyond West Thumb, pull off to see the Firehole River as it drops over **Kepler Cascades.** Just to the east, a wide and partly paved trail (actually an old road) leads five miles roundtrip to **Lone Star Geyser.** This is a popular route for bicyclists in the summer and skiers in the winter. Bikes are not allowed beyond the geyser. Lone Star Geyser erupts every three hours from a distinctive nine-foot-high cone, with eruptions generally reaching 45 feet and lasting for 30 minutes. Hikers can also get to Lone Star via the Howard Eaton Trail out of Old Faithful. For a longer hike, you can continue south from Lone Star on **Shoshone Lake Trail** to Shoshone Lake, eight fairly easy miles from the main road. (See Into the Backcountry later in this chapter for other Shoshone Lake hikes.)

OLD FAITHFUL AREA CLIMATE

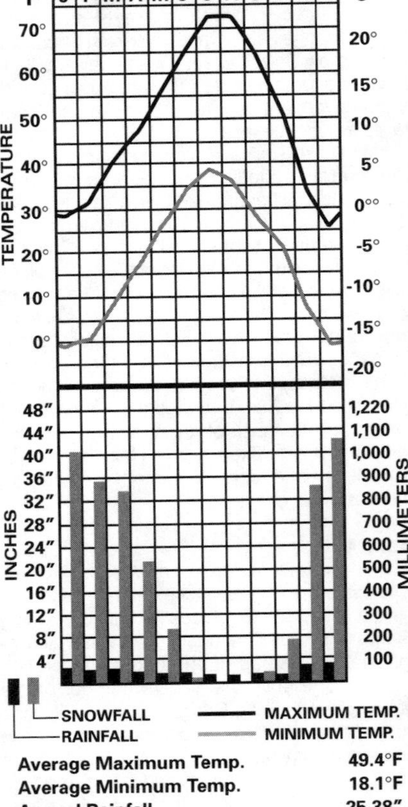

Average Maximum Temp.	**49.4°F**
Average Minimum Temp.	**18.1°F**
Annual Rainfall	**25.38″**
Annual Snowfall	**228.3″**

UPPER GEYSER BASIN

As you approach Old Faithful from either direction, the two-lane road suddenly widens into four, and a cloverleaf exit takes you to Yellowstone's most fabulous sight. Welcome to Upper Geyser Basin, home of Old Faithful, some 400 buildings of all sizes, and a small town's worth of people. For many folks, this is the heart of Yellowstone, and a visit to the park without seeing Old Faithful is like a baseball game without the national anthem. If you came to Yellowstone to see the wonders of nature, you're going to see more than your share here, but you'll probably have to share your share with hundreds of other folks. On busy summer days more than 25,000 visitors come through the Old Faithful area! Fortunately, the Upper Geyser Basin contains the largest concentration of geysers in the world, and the adventurous will even discover places almost nobody ever visits. But be very careful—the crust can be dangerously thin around some of the hot springs and geysers, and people have been badly scalded and even killed by missteps. Stay on the boardwalks and trails.

Old Faithful

The one sight seen by virtually everyone who comes to Yellowstone is Old Faithful Geyser, easily the most visited geyser in the world. Old Faithful is neither the tallest nor the most frequently erupting geyser in Yellowstone, but it always provides a

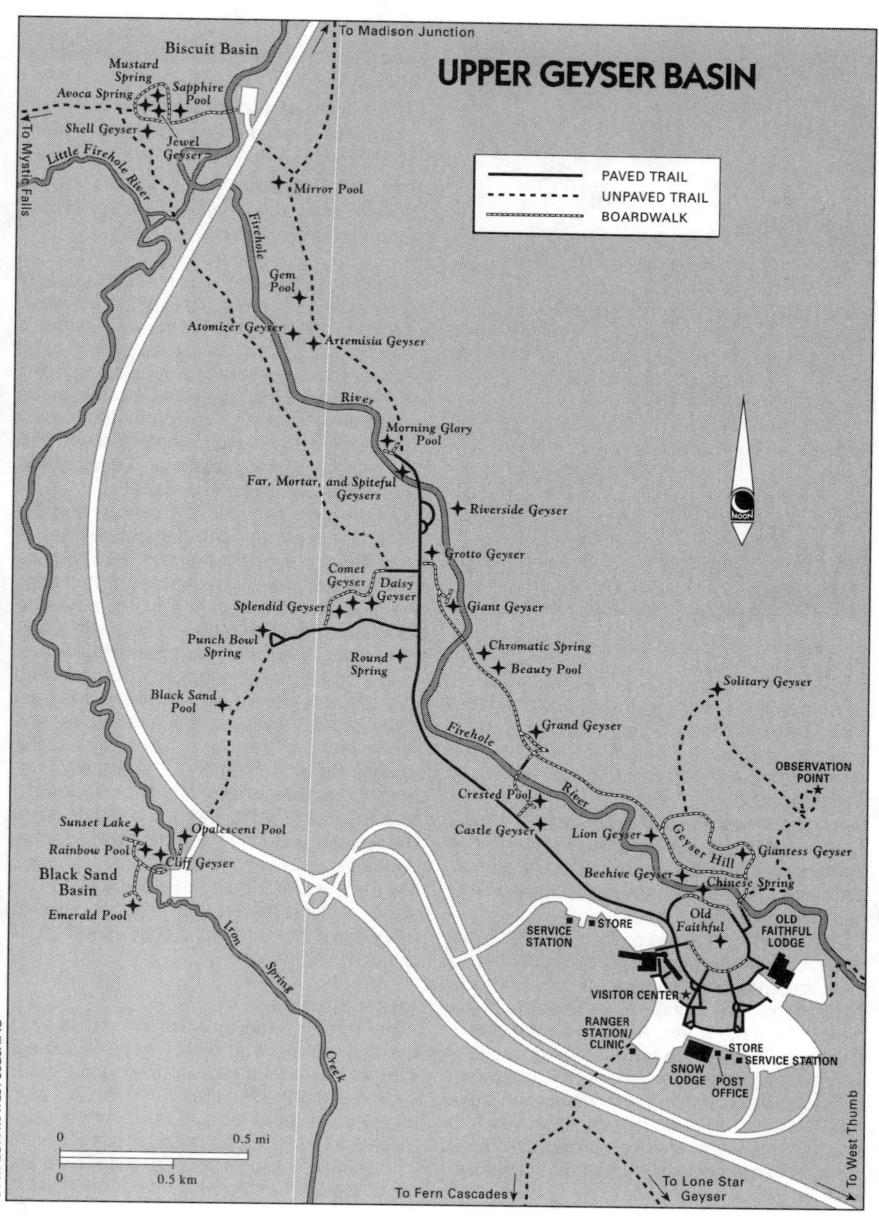
UPPER GEYSER BASIN
PAVED TRAIL
UNPAVED TRAIL
BOARDWALK
To Madison Junction
Biscuit Basin
Mustard Spring
Avoca Spring
Sapphire Pool
Shell Geyser
Jewel Geyser
To Mystic Falls
Little Firehole River
Mirror Pool
Firehole
Gem Pool
Atomizer Geyser
Artemisia Geyser
River
Morning Glory Pool
Far, Mortar, and Spiteful Geysers
Riverside Geyser
Grotto Geyser
Comet Geyser
Daisy Geyser
Splendid Geyser
Giant Geyser
Punch Bowl Spring
Round Spring
Chromatic Spring
Beauty Pool
Black Sand Pool
Solitary Geyser
Grand Geyser
Firehole
OBSERVATION POINT
Crested Pool
River
Castle Geyser
Lion Geyser
Geyser Hill
Giantess Geyser
Beehive Geyser
Chinese Spring
Sunset Lake
Opalescent Pool
Rainbow Pool
Cliff Geyser
Black Sand Basin
Emerald Pool
Iron Spring Creek
SERVICE STATION
STORE
Old Faithful
OLD FAITHFUL LODGE
VISITOR CENTER
RANGER STATION/ CLINIC
STORE
SERVICE STATION
SNOW LODGE
POST OFFICE
MOON
0
0.5 mi
0
0.5 km
To Fern Cascades
To Lone Star Geyser
To West Thumb

Yellowstone's most famous geyser erupts about once every 80 minutes.

good show and is both highly accessible and fairly predictable. Contrary to the rumors, Old Faithful never erupted "every hour on the hour," but for many years its period was a little over an hour. It has slowed down in recent years and is now averaging around 80 minutes per cycle. In general, the longer the length of the eruption, the longer the interval till the next eruption. Check at the visitor center for the latest prognostications on this and other geysers in the basin.

An almost level paved path circles Old Faithful, providing many different angles from which to view the eruptions, although none of these is particularly close to the geyser because of the danger from hot water. Along the north side is **Chinese Spring,** named in 1885 for a short-lived laundry operation. Apparently, the washman had filled the spring with clothes and soap, not knowing that soap can cause geysers to erupt. One newspaper correspondent claimed—though the tale obviously suffered from embellishment and racism—that,

> *The soap awakened the imprisoned giant; with a roar that made the earth tremble, and a shriek of a steam whistle, a cloud of steam and a column of boiling water shot up into the air a hundred feet, carrying soap, raiment, tent and Chinaman along with the rush, and dropping them at various intervals along the way.*

Old Faithful provides a textbook example of geyser activity. The first signs of life are when water begins to splash out of the vent in what is called preplay. This splashing can last up to 20 minutes, but it's generally only a few minutes before the real thing. The water quickly spears into the sky, reaching 100-180 feet for two to five minutes before rapidly dropping down. During a typical eruption, between 3,700 and 8,400 gallons of water are sent skyward.

On any given summer day, the scene at Old Faithful is almost comical. Just before the predicted eruption time, the benches encircling the south and east sides are jammed with hundreds of people waiting expectantly for the geyser to erupt, and with each tentative spray the camera shutters begin to click. Listen closely and you'll hear half the languages of Europe and Asia. Once the action is over, there is a mad rush back into the visitor center, the stores, and Old Faithful Inn, and within a few minutes the benches are virtually empty. A tale is told of two concessioner employees who once decided to have fun at Old Faithful by placing a large crank atop a box and putting the contraption near the geyser. When they knew it was ready to erupt, they ran out and turned the crank just as Old Faithful shot into the air. Their employer failed to find humor in the prank, and both were fired, or so the story claims.

Geyser Hill Area

Upper Geyser Basin is laced with paved trails that lead to dozens of nearby geysers and hot springs. The easiest path loops around Geyser Hill, just across the Firehole River from Old Faithful. Here are more than 40 different geysers. Check at the visitor center to get an idea of current activity and predicted eruptions, and while there pick up the excellent Upper Geyser Basin map (50 cents), which describes some of them. Several geysers are particularly noteworthy. When it plays, **Beehive Geyser** (it has a tall, beehive-shaped cone) vents water as high as 180 feet into the air. These spectacular eruptions vary in frequency; one time you visit they may be 10 days apart, while the next time you come they may be happening twice every 24 hours or so. **Lion Geyser Group** consists of four different interconnected geysers with varying periods of activity. Listen for the roaring sound when Lion is ready to erupt. **Giantess Geyser** may not be active for years at a time—or may erupt several times a year—but the eruptions are sensationally powerful, sending water 100-200 feet skyward. **Doublet Pool** is a beautiful deep-blue pool that is a favorite of photographers. Not far away is **Sponge Geyser,** which rockets water 2.29 billion angstroms into the air (that's nine inches for the nonscientific crowd).

> *From the surface of a rocky plain or table, burst forth columns of water of various dimensions, projected high in the air, accompanied by loud explosions, and sulphurous vapors, which were highly disagreeable to the smell. . . . The largest of these wonderful fountains, projects a column of boiling water several feet in diameter, to the height of more than one hundred and fifty feet. . . . After having witnessed three of them, I ventured near enough to put my hand into the water of its basin, but withdrew it instantly, for the heat of the water in this immense couldron, was altogether to great for comfort, and the agitation of the water, disagreeable effluvium continually exuding, and the hollow unearthly rumbling under the rock on which I stood, so ill accorded with my notions of personal safety, that I retreated back precipitately to a respectful distance.*
>
> —YELLOWSTONE'S FIRST "TOURIST,"
> ANGUS FERRIS, IN 1833

It's considered the smallest named geyser in Yellowstone and gets its title by sending up a spurt of water big enough to be mopped up with a sponge.

Observation Point Loop Trail splits off shortly after you cross the bridge on the way to Geyser Hill and climbs to an excellent overlook where you can watch eruptions of Old Faithful. This is also a good place to view the effects of, and recovery from, the 1988 North Fork Fire. It's two miles rountrip to Observatin Point from the visitor center. Another easy trail splits off from this path to **Solitary Geyser**—actually just a pool that periodically burps four-foot splashes of hot water. This is not a natural geyser. In 1915, the hot spring here was tapped to provide water for Old Faithful Geyser Bath, a concession that lasted until 1948. The lowering of the water level in the pool completely changed the plumbing system of the hot springs and turned it into a geyser that at one time shot 25 feet in the air. The system still hasn't recovered, although water levels have been restored for more than 40 years.

More Geyser Gazing

Another easy, paved path follows the Firehole River downstream, looping back along the other side for a total distance of three miles. Other trails head off from this loop to the Fairy Falls Trailhead, Biscuit Basin, and Black Sand Basin. The loop is a very popular wintertime ski path, and portions are open to bikes in the summer. Twelve-foot-high **Castle Geyser** does indeed resemble a ruined old castle. Because of its size and the slow accretion of sinter (silica) to form this cone, it is believed to be somewhere between 5,000 and 50,000 years old. Castle sends up a column of water and steam 90 feet into the air and usually erupts every 10-12 hours. Check at the visitor center for current activity.

Daisy Geyser is farther down the path and off to the left. It is usually one of the most predictable of the geysers, erupting to 75 feet approximately every 90-115 minutes. The water shoots out at a sharp angle and is visible all over the basin, making this a real crowd pleaser. Just east of Daisy is **Radiator Geyser,** which isn't much to look at—eruptions to two feet—but was named when this area was a parking lot and the sudden eruption under a car led people to think its radiator was overheating. A personal favorite, **Grotto Geyser** is certainly the weirdest of all the geysers, having formed around a tangle of long-petrified tree stumps. It is in eruption a third of the time, but most eruptions only reach 10 feet.

Look for **Riverside Geyser** across the Firehole from the path and not far below Grotto. This picturesque geyser arches spray 75 feet over the river and is one of the most predictable, with 20-minute-long eruptions approximately every six hours. The paved trail crosses the river and ends at **Morning Glory Pool.** For many years, the main road passed this colorful pool, which became something of a wishing well for not just coins but trash, rocks, logs, and other debris. Because of this junk, the pool began to cool, and the beautiful blue color is now tinged by brown and green algae, despite efforts to remove the debris.

Turning back at Morning Glory, recross the bridge and head left where the path splits at Grotto Geyser. **Giant Geyser** is on the left along the river. Years may pass between eruptions of Giant (or it might erupt every week or so), but when it does go, the name rings true, since the water often tops 200 feet. Cross the river again and pass **Beauty Pool** and **Chromatic Pool,** which are connected below the ground so that one declines as the other rises. Very pretty. **Grand Geyser** is a wonderful sight. The water column erupts in a towering burst every 7-15 hours, with a series of bursts lasting 10 minutes or so and sometimes reaching 200 feet. It's the tallest predictable geyser on the planet. When Grand isn't playing, watch for smaller eruptions from nearby **Turban** and **Sawmill** Geysers. Cross the river again just beyond Grand Geyser and pass **Crested Pool** on your way back to Castle Geyser. The pool contains deep-blue water that is constantly boiling, preventing the survival of algae.

Black Sand Basin

Just a mile west of Old Faithful is Black Sand Basin, a small cluster of geysers and hot springs. Most enjoyable is unpredictable **Cliff Geyser,** which often sends a spray of hot water 25-30 feet over Iron Spring Creek. Three colorful pools are quite interesting in the basin: **Emerald Pool, Rainbow Pool,** and **Sunset Lake. Handkerchief Pool** is now just a small spouter but was famous for many years as a place where visitors could drop a handkerchief in one end and then recover it later at another vent. In 1929, vandals jammed logs in the pool, destroying this little game. The pool was covered with gravel in subsequent eruptions of Rainbow Pool.

Biscuit Basin and Mystic Falls

Three miles north of Old Faithful, this basin is named for biscuitlike formations that were found in one of the pools; they were destroyed in an eruption following the 1959 Hebgen Lake earthquake. From the parking lot, the trail leads across the Firehole River to **Sapphire Pool** and then past **Jewel Geyser,** which typically erupts every 10 minutes to a height of 15-20 feet. The boardwalk follows a short loop through the other sights of Biscuit Basin.

From the west end of the boardwalk, a one-mile trail leads to where the Little Firehole River cascades 100 feet over **Mystic Falls.** You can switchback farther up the trail to the top of the falls and then connect with another trail for the loop back to Biscuit Basin (three miles roundtrip). This is a very nice short hike and can be lengthened into a trip to **Little Firehole Meadows** (10 miles roundtrip), where bison are often seen in the summer.

Old Faithful Inn

Matching one of the great sights of the natural world is one of America's grandest hotels, Old Faithful Inn. Said to be the largest log structure of its kind in existence, the inn has delighted generations of visitors and continues to enthrall all who enter. The building was designed by Robert Reamer and built in the winter of 1903-04. Its steeply angled roofline reaches seven stories high, with gables jutting out from the sides and flags flying from the roof. Surprisingly, the hotel does not face the geyser. Instead, it was built facing sideways to allow newly arriving visitors the opportunity to view the geyser as they stepped from carriages. As you open the rustic split-log front doors with their handwrought hardware, you enter a world of the past. The central lobby towers more than 75 feet overhead and is dominated by a massive four-sided stone fireplace that required 500 tons of stone from a nearby quarry. Four overhanging balconies extend above, each bordered by posts made from gnarled lodgepole burls found within the park. Above the fireplace is an enormous clock designed by Reamer and built on the site by a

Historic Old Faithful Inn is one of the most fascinating buildings in any national park.

blacksmith. Reamer also designed the two wings that were added in 1913 and 1928.

On warm summer evenings, visitors stand out on the porch where they can watch Old Faithful erupting or sit inside at the handcrafted tables to write letters as music spills from the grand piano. It's enough to warm the heart of even the most cynical curmudgeon. A good restaurant is on the premises, along with a rustic but comfortable bar, a gift shop, fast-food eatery, ice cream shop, and ATM. Free 45-minute **tours** of Old Faithful Inn are given daily at 9:30 a.m., 11 a.m., 2 p.m., and 3:30 p.m. from mid-May to late September. Meet at the fireplace in the lobby. Old Faithful Inn closes during the winter months; it would be hard to imagine trying to heat such a cavern when it's 30° below zero outside!

Another nearby building of interest is **Old Faithful Lodge.** Built in 1928, this is the large stone-and-log building just south of the geyser of the same name. The giant fireplace inside is a joy on frosty evenings, and cafeteria windows face the geyser. Much newer, but an instant classic, is the award-winning **Old Faithful Snow Lodge,** which opened in 1999. This large building offers a sense of rustic elegance, with heavy timbers, a window-lined main entrance, a large stone fireplace, overstuffed couches, and handmade wrought-iron light fixtures and accents. It is one of just two places (the other being Mammoth Hot Springs Hotel) open in the winter months. The new Snow Lodge replaces a dowdy utilitarian structure that was torn down in 1998.

Old Faithful Services

The Park Service's **Old Faithful Visitor Center,** tel. (307) 545-2750, is generally open mid-April to early November and mid-December to mid-March. It's open daily 8 a.m.-7 p.m. from Memorial Day to Labor Day, daily 8 a.m.-6 p.m. the rest of September, and daily 9 a.m.-5 p.m. at other times. (Hours may vary depending upon park budgets and staffing.) Among the films about Yellowstone shown throughout the day here is a fascinating new production (narrated by Walter Cronkite) on the lifeforms that survive in Yellowstone's hot springs. The center has a fine selection of books, maps, and other Yellowstone publications, and it also posts predictions for six of the major geysers (including Old Faithful) during the summer. The rangers can provide you with all sorts of other info, from where to see bighorn sheep to where to find the restrooms. A much-needed new visitor center is in the planning stages for Old Faithful, but don't expect to see it till 2005 or so, since the Park Service needs to raise $15 million for its construction.

Backcountry permits are available from the ranger station; food, supplies, and postcards can be purchased at either of the two Hamilton Stores. Old Faithful Inn has a gift shop, restaurant, snack bar, ice cream parlor, lounge, and ATM. Cafeteria meals, espresso, and baked goods are available at Old Faithful Lodge, and Old Faithful Snow Lodge houses a restaurant and snack bar. Both of these also have gift shops. In addition, the Old Faithful area has two gas stations, a post office, photo shop, and medical clinic. See Yellowstone Camping and Lodging later in this chapter for lodging details. Note that camping is *not* available in the Old Faithful area, and it's illegal to stay overnight in the parking lots. The closest campgrounds are in Madison (16 miles north) and Grant Village (19 miles southeast).

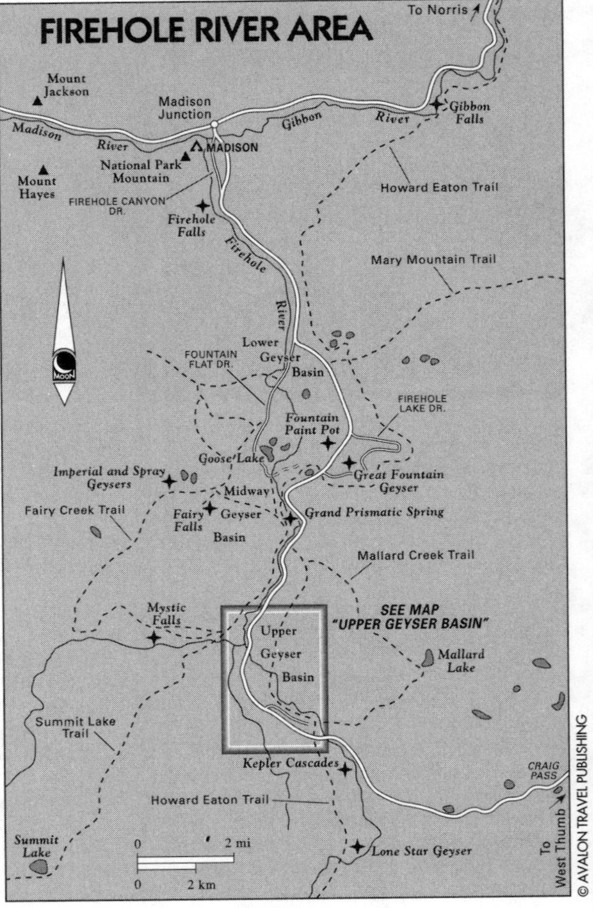

MIDWAY AND LOWER GEYSER BASINS

Heading north from Upper Geyser Basin, the road follows the Firehole River past Midway and Lower Geyser Basins, both of which are quite interesting. This stretch of the river is very popular with fly-fishing enthusiasts, and several side roads provide access to a variety of hot springs and other sights.

Fairy Falls

Just south of Midway Geyser Basin (or 4.5 miles north of the Old Faithful Interchange) is a turnoff that leads to the southern end of Fountain Freight Road. This four-mile-long trail is closed to cars, but it's a great place for mountain-bikers and those out for a relatively level walk. A steel bridge crosses the Firehole River at the trailhead, and the road soon passes the west side of Grand Prismatic Spring; rough trails lead up the hillside for a better view. A mile up from the trailhead you'll come to **Fairy Falls Trail** on your left. It's an easy 1.5-mile walk to the falls, a 200-foot ribbon of water that cascades into a large pool. The hike to Fairy Falls can be combined with longer treks to Little Firehole Meadow and Mystic Falls (both described above) or to a pair of small peaks called Twin Buttes. A half mile beyond Fairy Falls is **Imperial Geyser,** which was active in the 1920s and from 1966-84, but is now just a boiling pool. Nearby **Spray Geyser** erupts frequently, sending water six feet in the air. For a longer version of the hike to Fairy Falls (10 miles roundtrip), start from the north end, where Fountain Flat Drive ends.

Midway Geyser Basin

Midway is a large and readily accessible geyser basin with a loop path leading to most of the sights. **Excelsior Geyser** is actually an enormous hot spring that pours 4,000 gallons per minute of steaming water into the Firehole River. The water is a deep turquoise-blue. During the 1880s, this was a truly stupendous geyser, with explosions that reached 380 feet in the air and were almost as wide. These violent eruptions apparently damaged the plumbing system that fed them, and the geyser was dormant for nearly a century until smaller eruptions took place in 1985. At 370 feet across, **Grand Prismatic Spring** is Yellowstone's largest hot spring. The brilliant reds and yellows around the edges of the blue pool are from algae and bacteria that can tolerate temperatures of 170° F. It's difficult to get a good perspective on this spring from the ground; see aerial photos to really appreciate its pulchritude.

At length we came to a boiling Lake about 300 ft in diameter forming nearly a complete circle as we approached on the south side The steam which arose from it was of three distinct Colors from the west side for one third of the diameter it was white, in the middle it was pale red, and the remaining third on the east light sky blue Whether it was something peculiar in the state of the atmosphere the day being cloudy or whether it was some Chemical properties contained in the water which produced this phenomenon I am unable to say and shall leave the explanation to some scientific tourist who may have the Curiosity to visit this place at some future period—The water was of deep indigo blue boiling like an imense caldron running over the white rock which had formed the edges to the height of 4 or 5 feet from the surface of the earth sloping gradually for 60 or 70 feet. What a field of speculation this presents for chemist and geologist.

—MOUNTAIN MAN OSBORNE RUSSELL DESCRIBING GRAND PRISMATIC SPRING IN 1839

Firehole Lake Drive

This road (one-way heading north) goes three miles through Lower Geyser Basin, the park's most extensive geyser basin. **Great Fountain Geyser** is truly one of the most spectacular geysers in Yellowstone. Charles Cook, of the 1869 Cook-Folsom-Peterson Expedition, recalled his impression of the geyser: "We could not contain our enthusiasm; with one accord we all took off our hats and yelled with all our might." Modern-day visitors would not be faulted for reacting similarly.

Great Fountain erupts every 8-12 hours (although it can be irregular) and usually reaches 100 feet, but has been known to blast over 200 feet. Eruptions begin approximately an hour after water starts to overflow from the crater and last for 45-60 minutes in a series of decreasingly active eruptive cycles; but don't leave too early or you may miss the real show! Eruption predictions are posted at the geyser. While you're waiting, watch the periodic eruptions of **White Dome Geyser** just a hundred yards down the road. Because of its massive 30-foot cone, this is believed to be one of the oldest geysers in the park. Eruptions occur every 10 minutes to three hours and spray 30 feet into the air.

Another mile ahead, the road literally cuts into the mound of **Pink Cone Geyser,** which now erupts every 6-15 hours and reaches a height of 25 feet. The pink color comes from manganese oxide. Just up from here at the bend in the road is **Firehole Lake,** which discharges 3,500 gallons of water per minute into Tangled Creek, which in turn drains across the road into **Hot Lake. Steady Geyser** is unusual in that it forms both sinter (silica) and travertine (calcium carbonate) deposits. The geyser is along the edge of Hot Lake and, true to its name, erupts almost continuously, though the height is only five feet. Firehole Lake Dr. continues another mile to its junction with the main road right across from the parking area for Fountain Paint Pot. (In the winter, Firehole Lake Dr. is popular with skiers but is closed to snowmobiles.)

Fountain Paint Pot

Always a favorite of visitors, Fountain Paint Pot seems to have a playfulness about it that belies the immense power just below the surface. Pick up a trail guide as you head up the walkway.

Silex Spring, off to the right as you walk up the small hill, is colored by different kinds of algae and bacteria. The spring has been known to erupt as a geyser (to 20 feet) but is currently dormant. The famous Fountain Paint Pot is a few steps up the boardwalk and consists of colorful muds that change in consistency throughout the season depending upon soil moisture. The pressure from steam and gases under the Paint Pot can throw gobs of mud up to 20 feet into the air. Just north of here are fumaroles that spray steam, carbon dioxide, and hydrogen sulfide into the air. Continuing down the boardwalk, you come upon an impressive overlook above a multitude of geysers that change constantly in activity, including **Morning Geyser,** which erupts to over 150 feet. The most active is **Clepsydra Geyser,** in eruption much of the time. **Fountain Geyser** is usually active every 11 hours or so and can occasionally reach 80 feet. Very impressive, particularly at sunset. The rest of the loop trail passes dead lodgepole pines that are being petrified as the silica is absorbed, creating a bobby-socks appearance.

The 8,235-foot Mt. Haynes is named for early park photographer F.J. Haynes.

COURTESY AISLINN RACE

Fountain Flat

Fountain Flat Dr. provides access to meadows along the Firehole River and is a good place to see bison and elk. The paved road ends after a mile at a parking area, but hikers and cyclists (or skiers in winter) can continue another four miles on Old Fountain Freight Road to its junction with the main road again near Midway Geyser Basin. The road ends in a parking area near **Ojo Caliente**—a small hot springs with a big odor—right along the river. Several more hot springs are upstream from here, and the **Fairy Falls Trail** starts three miles south of the parking area. See Midway Geyser Basin above for details on this very scenic and popular day-hike.

Firehole Canyon Drive

This one-way road (south only) curves for two miles through Firehole Canyon, where dark rhyolite cliffs rise hundreds of feet above the river. The road begins just south of Madison Junction and was intensely burned in the 1988 North Fork Fire, giving the canyon's name a dual meaning. **Firehole Falls,** a 40-foot drop, is worth stopping to see, as is **Firehole Cascades** a bit farther up. Kids of all ages enjoy the very popular hot-springs-warmed swimming hole a short distance up the road. It's one of the few places along the Yellowstone road system where swimming is openly allowed (albeit not encouraged). No lifeguard, of course.

MADISON JUNCTION TO WEST YELLOWSTONE

At Madison Junction, the Gibbon and Firehole Rivers join to form the Madison River, a major tributary of the Missouri River. The 14-mile drive from Madison Junction to the West Entrance closely parallels this scenic river, in which geese, ducks, and trumpeter swans are commonly seen. Bison and elk are other critters to watch for in the open meadows. The 406,359-acre North Fork Fire of 1988 ripped through most of the Madison River country, so be ready for many blackened trees, but also expect to see many flowers in midsummer. The river is open only to fly-fishing and is considered one of the finest places in the nation to catch trout (though they can be a real challenge to fool). On warm summer evenings, you're likely to see dozens of anglers casting for wily rainbow and brown trout and mountain whitefish. **West Entrance** is the busiest of all the park entry stations, handling more than a third of the more than 3 million people who enter Yellowstone each year. The tourist town of West Yellowstone, Montana (see the Yellowstone Gateway Towns chapter), is right outside the boundary.

Madison Canyon is flanked by mountains named for two photographers who had a marked influence on Yellowstone. To the north is 8,257-foot **Mt. Jackson** (as in William H. Jackson, whose photos helped bring the area to national attention), and to the south is distinctive, 8,235-foot **Mt. Haynes,** named for the man who held the park photo concession for nearly four decades. These mountains and the surrounding slopes were created by rhyolite lava flows.

THE NORTHWEST CORNER

Highway 191 heads north from West Yellowstone, Montana, to Bozeman, passing through a small corner of Yellowstone National Park en route. There are no entrance stations or developed facilities here, but the area provides backcountry access for hikers and horsepackers from several trailheads. The drive itself is quite scenic, and the road is wide and smooth. The road enters the park approximately 10 miles north of West Yellowstone and gradually climbs through stretches that were burned in the fires of 1988 before emerging into unburned alpine meadows near tiny Divide Lake. North of here, US Hwy. 191 follows the growing Gallatin River downhill through a pretty mix of meadows, sagebrush, rocky outcrops, and forested hillsides with grassy carpets beneath. Approximately 31 miles north of West Yellowstone, the road exits Yellowstone and enters Gallatin National Forest. It's another 17 miles from here to the turnoff for Big Sky Resort or 60 miles from the park boundary to Bozeman.

Bighorn Peak Hike

If you're up for a long and challenging day-hike, climb Bighorn Peak on the northern boundary of Yellowstone. Start from the Black Butte Creek Trailhead just south of milepost 29 on US Hwy. 191. The hike is steep, rising 3,100 feet in just seven miles and providing spectacular views. Look for pieces of petrified wood along the way, but leave them in place; it's illegal to take them from the park. As an added bonus, this country was untouched by the 1988 fires. Be sure to bring plenty of water since it is nonexistent on the upper portion of this hike. It is possible to do an overnight loop trip (21 miles roundtrip) by continuing north from Bighorn Peak along the beautiful **Sky Rim Trail** and dropping back down Dailey Creek Trail to Black Butte Cutoff Trail. (A backcountry permit is required for this, however.) This connects to Black Butte Trail and your starting point. See one of the Yellowstone hiking guides for details on this hike.

MADISON JUNCTION TO NORRIS

The **Madison Information Station,** near Madison Junction, is open daily 8 a.m.-7 p.m. Memorial Day to Labor Day and daily 9 a.m.-5 p.m. from Labor Day to mid-October. Closed in winter. (Hours may vary depending upon park budgets and staffing.) A small bookstore is also here. Directly behind Madison Junction Campground is 7,500-foot **National Park Mountain,** named in honor of a fabled incident in 1870. Three explorers were gathered around the campfire, discussing the wonders that they had found in this area, when one suggested that rather than letting all these wonders pass into private hands, they should be set aside as a national park. Thus was born the concept that led to the world's first national park. The tale was passed on as the gospel truth for so long that the mountain was named in honor of this evening. Unfortunately, the story was a complete fabrication. Cynics may read something into the fact that National Park Mountain was torched by the fires of 1988.

North of Madison Junction, the road (in very poor condition when this was written) follows the Gibbon River nearly all of the 14 miles to Norris. It crosses the river five times and hangs right on the edge through Gibbon Canyon. The pretty, 84-foot-high **Gibbon Falls** is approximately five miles up the road and situated right at the edge of the enormous caldera that fills the center of Yellowstone. The 1988 fires consumed most of the trees around the falls. Another five miles beyond this, the road emerges from the canyon into grassy **Gibbon Meadows,** where elk and bison are commonly seen. The prominent peak visible to the north is 10,336-foot Mt. Holmes. On the west end of Gibbon Meadows is a barren area that contains **Sylvan Springs Geyser Basin.** No maintained trail leads to this small collection of pools and springs, but hikers sometimes head across the north end of the meadows at the Gibbon River Picnic Area. The path is wet most of the summer.

An easy half-mile trail leads to **Artist Paint Pots,** filled with colorful plopping and steaming mud pots and hot springs. Although it's a short hike, the paint pots see far fewer visitors than roadside sites, making it a nice place to escape the crowds. The forest was burned in the North Fork Fire, so it's also a good place to see how the lodgepole pines are regenerating. Just south of the parking area for Artist Paint Pots is a trail to **Monument Geyser Basin,** where there isn't much activity, but the tall sinter cones form all sorts of bizarre shapes, including Thermos Bottle Geyser. The mile-long hike climbs 500 feet and provides views of the surrounding country. Another attraction is **Chocolate Pots,** found along the highway just north of Gibbon Meadows. The reddish-brown color comes from iron, aluminum, and manganese oxides. Just before you reach Norris, the road crosses through the appropriately named **Elk Park.**

NORRIS GEYSER BASIN

Although Old Faithful and the Upper Geyser Basin are more famous, many visitors to Yellowstone find Norris Geyser Basin equally interesting. Norris sits atop the junction of several major fault lines, providing conduits for heat from the molten lava below. Because of this, it is apparently the hottest geyser basin in North America, if not the world; a scientific team found temperatures of 459° F at 1,087 feet underground and was forced to quit drilling when the pressure threatened to destroy the drilling rig! Because of considerable sulfur (and hence sulfuric acid) in the springs and geysers, the water at Norris is quite acidic; a majority of the world's acid geysers are here. The acidic water kills lodgepole trees in the basin, creating an open, nearly barren place. Norris Basin has been around at least 115,000 years, making it the oldest of any of Yellowstone's active geyser basins. It is a constantly changing place, with small geysers seeming to come and go on an almost daily basis.

The paved trail from the oft-crowded parking area leads to **Norris Museum,** tel. (307) 344-2812, built of stone in 1929-30. The small museum houses exhibit panels on hot springs and geothermal activity and is generally open daily 8 a.m.-7 p.m. from Memorial Day to Labor Day, and daily 9 a.m.-5 p.m. from Labor Day to mid-October. (Hours may vary due to park budgets and staffing.) Pick up a detailed brochure describing the various features at Norris. Ranger-led walks are given several times a day in the summer. From the museum, the Norris Basin spreads both north and south, with two rather different trails to hike. Take the time to walk along both. The Norris Campground is only a quarter mile from the geyser basin.

Porcelain Basin

Just behind the museum is an overlook that provides an impressive view across Porcelain Basin. The path descends into the basin, along the way passing hissing steam vents, bubbling hot pools, and small geysers, including **Dark Cavern Geyser,** which erupts several times an hour to 20 feet. **Whirligig Geyser** is another one that is often active, spraying a fan of water. (Watch your glasses and camera lenses in the steam; silica deposits can be very hard to remove.) For an enjoyable short walk, follow the boardwalk around the mile-long loop. Stop to admire the bright colors in the steaming water, indicators of iron, arsenic, and other elements, along with algae and cyanobacteria.

Back Basin

A mile-long loop trail takes you to the sights within the Back Basin south of the museum. Before heading out, check at the museum for the latest on geyser activity. Most people follow the path in a clockwise direction, coming first to **Emerald Spring,** a beautiful green pool with acidic water just below boiling. A little ways farther down the path is **Steamboat Geyser.** Wait a few minutes and you're likely to see one of its minor eruptions, which may reach 40 feet. On rare occasions, Steamboat erupts with a fury that is hard to believe, blasting over 300 feet into the air—more than twice the height of Old Faithful—making this the world's tallest geyser. Eruptions can last up to 20 minutes, enough time to pour out a million gallons of water, and the explosions have been heard up to 14 miles away. Steamboat's unforgettable eruptions cannot be predicted; a 50-year span once passed between eruptions, while at other times several eruptions may occur in one year.

The path splits just below Steamboat; on the right is **Cistern Spring,** whose deep blue waters are constantly building deposits of sinter and have flooded the nearby lodgepole-pine forests, killing the trees. If you turn left where the trail splits, you come to **Echinus Geyser,** a personal favorite. (The name—Greek for "spiny"—comes from the pebbles that lie around the geyser; resembling sea urchins, they are a result of sinter accumulation.) In the recent past Echinus erupted every hour or so and was one of the most dependable and enjoyable geysers in the park. At last check it was far less regular, and you may have to wait several hours for an eruption. When it does erupt, the geyser sends explosions of acidic steam and water (pH 3.5) 40-60 feet. These generally last 6-14 minutes but sometimes continue for up to an hour or more. Unlike Old Faithful, this is one geyser where you can get up close and personal. Bench-sitters may get splashed, although the water is not hot enough to burn.

Continue along this trail beyond Echinus to see many more hot springs and steam vents. **Porkchop Geyser** was in continuous eruption for several years, but in 1989 it self-destructed in an explosion that threw rocks more than 200 feet, leaving behind a bubbling hot spring.

NORRIS JUNCTION TO CANYON

From Norris Geyser Basin to Canyon, the road cuts across the center of the park on the high Solfatara Plateau. This dozen-mile stretch of road is best known for what looks like a scene from an atomic blast, with the blackened remains of a forest seemingly blown down by the ferocity of the 1988 North Fork Fire. This is the place the news media focused on after the fires, making it appear as if it were typical of the park as a whole. In reality, the lodgepole pines were all uprooted in a wild 1984 windstorm that flattened many miles of forest both here and farther south in the Teton Wilderness. The dead trees dried out over the next four years, and when the wind-whipped fires arrived, the trees went up in a holocaust. In 50 years, this may well be a meadow. **Virginia Cascades Road** is a 2.5-mile-long, one-way road that circles around this blow-down area and provides a view of the 60-foot-tall Virginia Cascade of the Gibbon River. Back on the main highway heading east, keep your eyes open for elk and bison as the road approaches Canyon. Also note the thick young forest of lodgepole pines that was established after a fire burned through in 1955.

NORRIS JUNCTION TO MAMMOTH

The park road between Norris and Mammoth Hot Springs provides a number of interesting sights, although much of this country burned in the 1988 North Fork Fire. Just beyond the highway junction is the **Norris Soldier Station.** Built by the army in 1897 and modified in 1908, it is one of just three still standing in the park. The attractive log building now houses the small **Museum of the National Park Ranger,** tel. (307) 344-7353, with displays and a video on the history of park rangers. It is open daily 9 a.m.-6 p.m. from Memorial Day to Labor Day, and daily 9 a.m.-5 p.m. the rest of September. (Hours may vary depending upon park budgets and staffing.) Closed in winter.

Just up the road is **Frying Pan Spring** (named for its shape), where the water is actually not that hot. The bubbles are from pungent-smelling hydrogen-sulfide gas. **Roaring Mountain** is a bleak, steaming mountainside four miles north of Norris. In 1902, the mountain erupted into activity with fumaroles that made a roar audible at great distances. It is far less active today and is best seen in winter, when the temperature difference results in much more steam.

Obsidian Cliff

Stop at Obsidian Cliff to see the black glassy rocks formed when lava cooled very rapidly. One mountain man (not, as many sources claim, Jim Bridger) told tall tales of "Glass Mountain," where his shots at an elk kept missing. When he got closer, he found he had actually been firing at a clear mountain of glass. The elk was

25 miles away, but the mountain was acting as a telescope to make the animal appear close. Obsidian Cliff was an important source of rock Indians used in making fine arrowheads and other tools. The obsidian from here was of such value that Indians traded it extensively; obsidian points made from this rock have even been found in Ohio and Ontario. (It is illegal to remove obsidian; leave it for future generations to enjoy.) North of here the countryside opens up along Obsidian Creek at **Willow Park,** one of the best places to see moose, especially in the fall.

Sheepeater Cliff and Golden Gate

Approximately 13 miles north of Norris, the road passes Indian Creek Campground and the basalt columns of Sheepeater Cliff, named for the Indian inhabitants of these mountains. North of this, the country opens into Swan Lake Flats, where you get a fine gander at 10,992-foot Electric Peak nine miles to the northwest.

At Golden Gate the road suddenly enters a narrow defile, through which flows Glen Creek. Stop to look over the edge of **Rustic Falls** and to note how the road is cantilevered over the cliff edge. Acrophobics should *not* stop here. Instead, have someone else drive, close your eyes, and say three Hail Marys.

Bunsen Peak

Just south of Mammoth is Bunsen Peak, an 8,564-foot inactive volcanic cone. Any chemistry student will recognize the name, for Robert Wilhelm Eberhard von Bunsen not only first explained the action of geysers but also invented the Bunsen burner. Parts of Bunsen Peak look like a chemistry experiment run amok. The North Fork Fire of 1988 swept through this area in a patchy mosaic, leaving long strips of unburned trees next to those that are now just blackened telephone poles.

Bunsen Peak Road is a dirt track open to hikers and mountain-bikers but closed to cars. Starting approximately five miles south of Mammoth and just beyond the Golden Gate, it circles the east side of the mountain, connecting with the main road six miles later. Approximately four miles in on the road is a side trail to **Osprey Falls.** This steep trail drops 800 feet in less than a mile to the base of a stunning 150-foot waterfall, but you'll need to climb back out the same way, so don't get too late of a start. Trails also lead to the summit of Bunsen Peak from both the east and west sides. Most folks choose the west trail (four miles roundtrip with an elevation difference of 1,300 feet), which begins a short way up the road from the Golden Gate entrance. From the mountaintop you can drop down the east side and hike back along the road, making a total of nine miles roundtrip.

The Hoodoos

North of Golden Gate, the main road soon passes the Hoodoos, a fascinating jumble of travertine boulders leaning in all directions. The rocks were created by hot springs thousands of years ago

the Golden Gate, circa 1898. Note the cantilevered section of the road.

COURTESY AISLINN RACE

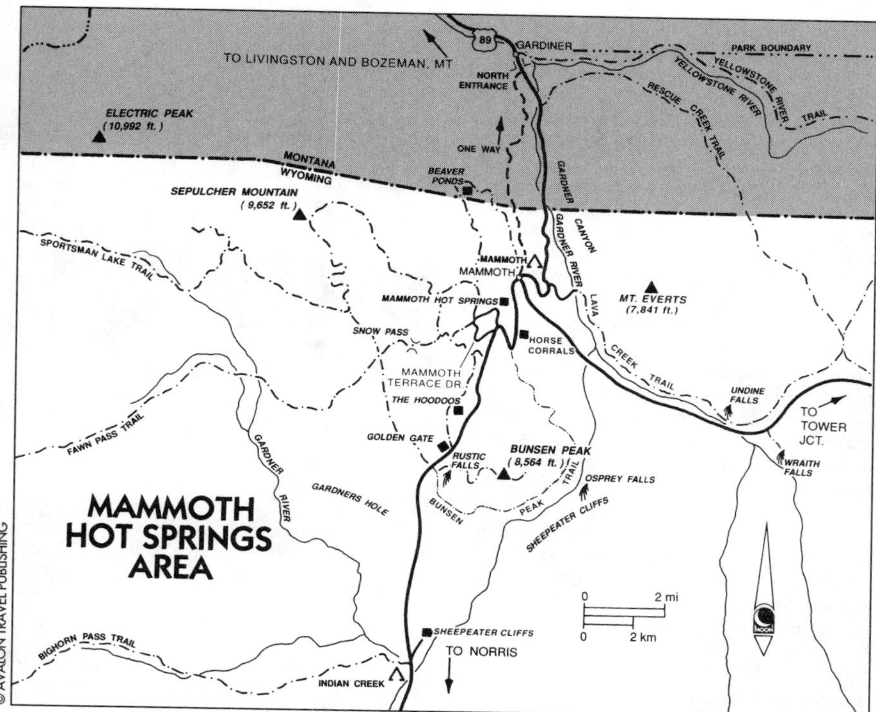

and toppled from the east face of Terrace Mountain. Just before Mammoth, turn left onto Upper Terrace Dr., a half-mile loop road providing access to the upper end of Mammoth Hot Springs. (No trailers or large RVs.)

MAMMOTH HOT SPRINGS VICINITY

Mammoth Hot Springs lies at an elevation of 6,239 feet near the northern border of Yellowstone, just five miles from the town of Gardiner, Montana. Here you'll find park headquarters, a variety of other facilities, and delightfully colorful hot springs. The Mammoth area is an important wintering spot for elk, pronghorn antelope, deer, and bison. During the fall, at least one bull elk and his harem can be seen wandering across the green lawns, while lesser males bugle challenges from behind the buildings or over the hill. The bugling may even keep you awake at night if you're staying in the Mammoth Hotel.

Origins

Mammoth Hot Springs consists of a series of multihued terraces down which hot, mineral-laden water trickles. This water originates as snow and rain that falls on the surrounding country, although some is believed to come from the Norris area, 20 miles to the south. As it passes through the earth, the water comes into contact with volcanic magma containing massive amounts of carbon dioxide, creating carbonic acid. The now-acidic water passes through and dissolves the region's sedimentary limestone, and the calcium carbonate remains in solution until it reaches the surface at Mammoth. Once at the surface, the carbon dioxide begins to escape into the atmosphere, reducing the acidity and causing the lime to precipitate out, forming the travertine terraces that are so prominent here. As the water flows over small obstructions, more carbon dioxide is released, causing accumulations that eventually grow into the lips that surround the terrace pools. The rate of accumulation of travertine (calcium carbonate) is astounding: more than two tons a day at Mammoth Hot Springs. Some terraces grow by eight inches a year. The first explorers were fascinated by these terraces; mountain man Jim Bridger noted that they made for delightful baths. A later operation—long since ended—coated knick-knacks by dipping them in the hot springs!

The springs are constantly changing as underground passages are blocked by limestone deposits, forcing the water in new directions. As a result, old dried-out terraces stand on all sides, while new ones grow each day. Areas that were active just a few years ago may now be simply gray masses of crumbling travertine rock, and new areas may appear and spread in a matter of days. Mammoth is guaranteed to be different every time you visit. One of the most interesting aspects of the hot springs here is the variety of colors, results of the many different species of algae and bacteria that live in the water. Various factors, including temperature and acidity, affect the survival of different species; bright yellow algae live in the hottest areas, while cooler waters are colored orange and brown by other algae.

the Liberty Cap

Visiting the Springs

Mammoth Hot Springs covers a steep hillside and consists of a series of colorful springs in various stages of accretion or decay. The area is accessible by road from below or above (Upper Terrace Dr.), and a boardwalk/staircase connects the two. At the bottom of Mammoth Hot Springs and off to the right is a 37-foot-tall mass of travertine known as **Liberty Cap** for its faint similarity to the caps worn in the French Revolution. The spring that created this no longer flows. (You may well find the Liberty Cap shows a more striking similarity to a certain anatomical feature found only on males.)

Because of their continuously changing nature, I won't attempt to describe the springs at Mammoth, but do pick up the Park Service's very informative brochure from the box at the parking area. Across the road is **Opal Terrace,** one of the more active springs. It began flowing in 1926 and has continued to expand over the years; it now is heading toward a house built in 1907 and designed by Robert Reamer (the architect of Old Faithful Inn).

All the water flowing out of Mammoth terraces quickly disappears into underground caverns. In front of the Mammoth Hotel are two sinkholes from which steam often rises. Caverns above the terraces were once open to the public but later were closed when it became apparent that they contained poisonous gases. Dead birds are sometimes found around one of the small pools in this area appropriately named Poison Spring.

Buildings

Albright Visitor Center, tel. (307) 344-2263, is named for Horace Albright, the first National Park Service superintendent at Yellowstone. The center is housed in the army's old bachelor officers' quarters and is open daily 8 a.m.-7 p.m. from Memorial Day to Labor Day, daily 9 a.m.-5 p.m. the rest of the year. Spread over the two floors are exhibits on park wildlife and history, but the real treats are the works of two artists who helped bring Yellowstone's magnificent scenery to public attention. Twenty-three of painter Thomas Moran's famous Yellowstone watercolors line the walls, and his studio has been re-created in one corner. Equally impressive are 26 classic photographs—including one of Thomas Moran at Mammoth Hot Springs—taken by William H. Jackson during the 1871 Hayden Survey. The paintings and photos are must-sees for anyone with an artistic bent. (By the way, you can check out a gallery of paintings by Moran and photos by Jackson on the web at www.cr.nps.gov/csd/exhibits/moran.) The center also has an information desk, racks of books, and films about the park and Moran. Check at the information desk for schedules of wildlife talks and frequent ranger-led walks to surrounding sights in the summer.

Mammoth contains a number of other historic structures built during the army's tenure at Fort Yellowstone. The most distinctive are the six buildings (all in a row) constructed between 1891 and 1909 as quarters for the officers and captains. Most of the grunt soldiers lived just behind here in barracks, one of which is now the park administration building. The U.S. Engineers Department was housed in an odd stone building with obvious Asian influences; it's right across from the visitor center.

Although one wing survives from a hotel built in 1911, most of the **Mammoth Hot Springs Hotel** was constructed in 1937. Step inside to view the large map of the United States built from 15 different types of wood. Mammoth also features a Hamilton Store, post office, gas station, restaurant, fast-food eatery, medical clinic, and horseback rides. Mammoth Campground is just down the road.

North to Montana

The main road north from Mammoth Hot Springs follows the Gardner River, dropping nearly 1,000 feet in elevation before reaching the town of Gardiner, Montana. (Both the river and the misspelled town are named for Johnson Gardner, a ruthless trapper from the 1820s.) The river is a favorite of fly-fishing enthusiasts. A turnout near the Wyoming/Montana border notes the "boiling river" section of the Gardner River; it's well worth a stop. Sometimes during the winter you can spot bighorn sheep on the mountain slopes just north of the river as you head down to Gardiner.

The "back way" to Gardiner is the Old Gardiner Rd., a five-mile gravel road (great for mountain bikes, but not for RVs or trailers) that starts behind Mammoth Hot Springs Hotel. Traffic is downhill only, so you'll need to take the main road for your return into the park; mountain bikes can go in both directions. This is one of the best places to spot pronghorn antelope in the park, and it also provides a fine escape from the crowds at Mammoth.

Day-hikes

For a relatively easy loop hike, try the five-mile (roundtrip) **Beaver Ponds Trail,** which begins between Liberty Cap and the stone house. It gains 500 feet in elevation, passing through spruce and fir forests along the way and ending at several small beaver ponds. The path then drops down to join Old Gardiner Rd., which you can follow back to Mammoth. This trail provides a good opportunity to see mule deer, elk, pronghorn antelope, and moose, but is best hiked in the spring or fall when temperatures are cooler. Black bears are sometimes seen along the way, so be sure to make noise while you walk.

A longer (12 miles roundtrip) hike is the **Sepulcher Mountain Trail,** which climbs to the top of this 9,652-foot peak just northwest of Mammoth. There are several possible routes to the top, and any of them can be combined into a very nice loop hike. One begins at the same place as the Beaver Ponds Trail. You'll find many flowers in the expansive meadows on the south side of Sepulcher Mountain (named for several strange rocks at its summit). From Mammoth, it is a 3,400-foot elevation gain, so be ready to sweat. Before heading out, check at the visitor center to see if there are any major bear problems in the area and to get a topographic map and hiking tips.

MAMMOTH TO TOWER JUNCTION

The 18-mile drive from Mammoth to Tower Junction takes visitors through some of the driest and most open country in Yellowstone. Two waterfalls provide stopping places along the way.

Beautiful **Undine Falls** is a 60-foot-high double falls immediately north of the road. Just up the road is a gentle half-mile path to the base of **Wraith Falls,** where Lupine Creek cascades 90 feet. Look for ducks and trumpeter swans in **Blacktail Pond,** a couple of miles farther east.

Blacktail Plateau Drive, approximately nine miles east of Mammoth, turns off from the main road. The rough seven-mile dirt road is a one-way route that loosely follows the Bannock Trail, a path used by the Bannock tribe on their way to buffalo-hunting grounds east of here. Their travois trails are still visible. The Bannocks used this route from 1838 to 1878, but it had probably been used for hundreds or thousands of years by various tribes crossing the high plateau. Much of Blacktail Plateau Dr. is through open sagebrush, grass, and aspen country, where you're likely to see deer and pronghorn antelope. The trees are very pretty in the fall. On the east end, the road drops back into a forest burned by a severe crown fire in 1988 but now containing young aspen and lodgepole trees and abundant summertime flowers.

The Park Service has developed a two-thirds-mile boardwalk **Forces of the Northern Range Self-Guiding Trail** approximately six miles east of Mammoth Hot Springs. Trailside exhibits describe the natural world. A half mile beyond where Blacktail Plateau Dr. rejoins the main road is the turnoff to the **petrified tree.** The 20-foot-tall stump of an ancient redwood tree (50 million years old) stands behind iron bars; a second petrified tree that used to stand nearby was stolen piece by piece over the years by thoughtless tourists. The **Tower Ranger Station,** originally occupied by the U.S. Army, is just before Tower Junction where the road splits, leading to either Northeast Entrance Rd. or Canyon.

NORTHEAST ENTRANCE ROAD

Of the five primary entryways into Yellowstone, Northeast Entrance is the least traveled, making this a great place to escape the hordes in midsummer. It is also one of the best places to see tall mountains in Yellowstone. The road heads east from Tower Junction and immediately enters **Lamar Valley,** an area of grass and sage along the sinuous Lamar River. Osborne Russell, who trapped this country in the 1830s, described it with affection:

> *We descended the stream about 15 mls thro. the dense forest and at length came to a beautiful valley about 8 Mls. long and 3 or 4 wide surrounded by dark and lofty mountains. The stream after running thro. the center in a NW direction rushed down a tremendous canyon of basaltic rock apparently just wide enough to admit its waters. The banks of the stream in the valley were low and skirted in many places with beautiful Cotton wood groves. Here we found a few Snake indians comprising 6 men 7 women and 8 or 10 children who were the only Inhabitants of this lonely and secluded spot. They were all neatly clothed in dressed deer and Sheep skins of the best quality and seemed to be perfectly contented and happy. . . . We stopped at this place and for my own part I almost wished I could spend the remainder of my days in a place like this where happiness and contentment seemed to rein in wild romantic splendor surrounded by majestic battlements which seemed to support the heavens and shut out all hostile intruders. . . . There is something in the wild romantic scenery of this valley which I cannot . . . describe; but the impressions made upon my mind while gazing from a high eminence on the surrounding landscape one evening as the sun was gently gliding behind the western mountain and casting its gigantic shadows across the vale were such as time can never efface from my memory.*

This is still one of the best places in Yellowstone to view bison. Elk and mule deer are also commonly seen, and the reintroduction of wolves has added another dimension to wildlife viewing. The valley contains a number of small ponds created when the retreating glaciers left large blocks of ice that formed "kettles." Erratic glacial boulders are scattered along the way. There are campgrounds at Slough Creek and

Pebble Creek, and very good fishing in Slough Creek, too.

Yellowstone River Picnic Area

Picnic areas don't generally merit a mention, but this one—1.5 miles east of Tower Junction on the Northeast Entrance Rd.—is an exception because of its proximity to a grand view. A two-mile trail takes off from here for Grand Canyon of the Yellowstone River. The hike is easy and provides a good chance to see bighorn sheep, but be careful to stay away from the canyon rim. For a loop hike (four miles roundtrip), continue to the Specimen Ridge Trail where you turn left and follow it back to your starting point.

Slough Creek Area

Slough Creek Campground is a favorite of fly-fishers who come here to try for the area's acclaimed cutthroat trout. The **Slough Creek Trail** starts at the campground and is one of the more distinctive in the park. The trail—actually a wagon road—makes for a delightful and gentle day-hike through Douglas-fir forests and open meadows. It continues all the way to the park boundary, 11 miles north of the campground, and is used for access to Silver Tip Ranch. This is the only way into the ranch, and because no motor vehicles are allowed you may meet folks on a horse-drawn wagon during your hike. Day-hikers often go up the road as far as the first meadow, a distance of eight miles roundtrip.

Yellowstone Association Institute

The nonprofit Yellowstone Association Institute (see the special topic Yellowstone Association) teaches many classes out of Lamar Valley's historic Buffalo Ranch, approximately 10 miles east of Tower Junction. To augment the park's small wild herd, bison were brought here in 1902 from private ranches. The bison stayed in pens at night and were herded during the day. After 1915, they were allowed to roam freely in summer, although all the park's bison were rounded up and driven here for the winter months. After 1938, the roundups ended, but the bison were fed hay every winter in Lamar Valley. Finally in 1952, even this was halted and the bison were allowed to roam throughout the park. The historic buildings are worth a look, or better still, take one of the institute's excellent classes.

Specimen Ridge

Just east of the historic Buffalo Ranch is a turnout across from Specimen Ridge, where explorers discovered the standing trunks of petrified trees that had been buried in volcanic ash and mudflows some 50 million years ago. Over the centuries, the trunks literally turned to stone as silica entered the wood. The process was repeated again and again over the centuries as new forests gradually developed atop the volcanic deposits, only to be buried by later flows. Scientists have found 27 different forests on top of each other, containing walnut, magnolia, oak, redwood, and maple—evidence that the climate was once more like that of today's midwestern states. Erosion eventually revealed the trees, many of which are still standing. This is one of the largest areas of petrified trees known to exist.

There is no trail to the petrified forest, but during the summer rangers lead hikes into the area. Check at the Mammoth Visitor Center for upcoming treks. Mark Marschall's *Yellowstone Trails* provides a description of the 1.5-mile route if you want to try it on your own. A lesser-known petrified forest in the northwest corner of Yellowstone is accessible via US Hwy. 191.

Wolf Watching

Between the Slough Creek and Pebble Creek Campgrounds, wolf aficionados fill roadside turnouts each morning and evening, waiting patiently for members of the Druid Peak or Rose Creek Packs to appear. Bring your binoculars or spotting scope! During the wolf denning season, the Park Service prohibits parking or walking along certain stretches of the road, but two turnouts are available.

Northeast Entrance

At the east end of Lamar Valley, the road continues northeast up Soda Butte Creek and between the steep rocky cliffs of Barronette Peak (10,404 feet) and Abiathar Peak (10,928 feet). Stop at **Soda Butte,** where you'll find a small travertine mound similar to those at Mammoth. Although the springs are no longer very active, the air still reeks of hydrogen sulfide, the "rotten egg" gas. South of Soda Butte and several miles up a backcountry trail is **Wahb Springs,** found within Death Gulch. Here poisonous gases are emitted from the ground, killing animals in the vicinity. Early explorers reported finding dead bears that had been overcome by the fumes.

North of Pebble Creek Campground, the road squeezes through chilly **Icebox Canyon** and into the lodgepole pine forests. It follows the creek all the way to the edge of the park, crossing into Montana two miles before the park border. The **Northeast Entrance Station** is a classic log building built in 1935 and now designated a National Historic Landmark. The twin towns of Silver Gate and Cooke City (see the Yellowstone Gateway Towns chapter) are just up the road.

A fine day-hike starts from the Warm Creek Picnic Area, 1.5 miles west of the entrance station. The trail climbs 1,100 feet in 1.5 miles before dropping into flower-filled mountain meadows along Pebble Creek. If you continue more than two miles you'll need to ford the creek, which can be deep before late summer. Backpackers use this trail for longer trips into the area; see Into the Backcountry below for details.

TOWER JUNCTION TO CANYON

Roosevelt Lodge

Lying at the junction of the roads to Canyon, Mammoth, and Lamar Valley, Roosevelt Lodge was built in 1920 and named for Pres. Theodore Roosevelt, who camped a few miles to the south during his 1903 visit. Roosevelt, a lifelong supporter of Yellowstone, helped push through legislation that clamped down upon the rampant destruction of park wildlife early in the 20th century.

The Roosevelt area is a favorite of families, many of whom return year after year. The lodge building has the rough-edged flavor of a hunting lodge and a peacefulness that you won't find at Old Faithful, Canyon, or Mammoth. Inside the lodge are two giant stone fireplaces, and the porch out front has comfortable rocking chairs. Rustic cabins, a restaurant, and gift shop are here, along with horseback and wagon rides. The location is a great base for wolf-watchers and anglers.

Stop at the overlook to **Calcite Springs,** two miles southeast of the junction, where a walkway provides dramatic views into the canyon of the Yellowstone River, with steaming geothermal activity far below. The cliff faces contain a wide strip of columnar basalt, some of which overhangs the highway just to the south.

> *Here is your country. Cherish these natural wonders, cherish the natural resources, cherish the History and Romance as a sacred heritage, for your children and your children's children. Do not let selfish men or greedy interests skin your country of its beauty, its riches or its romance.*
>
> —THEODORE ROOSEVELT IN 1903

Tower Fall

On summer afternoons the parking lot at Tower Fall fills with cars as folks stop to see Tower Creek plummeting 132 feet before joining the Yellowstone River. The towerlike black rocks of the area are made of volcanic basalt. Nearby are a campground and a Hamilton Store. Tower Fall overlook is just a couple hundred paved feet from the parking area, or you can follow the path a half mile down the switchbacks to the canyon bottom, where the vista is far more impressive and a rainbow is sometimes visible. Be prepared to get wet in the spray! A ford of the Yellowstone River—used by Bannock Indians in the 19th century—is just a quarter mile away. For more than a hundred years, a huge boulder stood atop Tower Fall; the water and gravity finally won in 1986.

Dunraven Pass and Mt. Washburn

Continuing southward, the road climbs along Antelope Creek and eventually switchbacks up the aptly named Mae West Curve. The North Fork Fire swept through this country in 1988, but the area is now verdant with new trees, grasses, and flowers. **Dunraven Pass** (8,859 feet) is named for the Earl of Dunraven, who visited the park in 1874 and whose widely read book *The Great Divide* brought Yellowstone to the attention of wealthy European travelers. This is the highest point along any park road, even higher than the three other places where the road crosses the Continental Divide! Look for whitebark pines near the road, and be sure to stop just south of here for a view across to the distant Grand Canyon of the Yellowstone.

For an outstanding day-hike, climb **Mt. Washburn,** a 10,243-foot peak with commanding vistas in all directions. The two trails up the mountain both gain about the same elevation (1,400 feet) and are around six miles roundtrip. The most popular route begins from the often-full parking lot at Dunraven Pass and heads up from the south side. A few miles north of the pass, the old Chittenden Rd. turns off and leads to another access point; drive the first mile up this road to a large parking area and then hike—or mountain-bike—to the summit of Washburn from the north side. Many wildflowers bloom in midsummer, and bighorn sheep may be seen right along the trail. Bring warm clothes and rain gear, since conditions on top may be much cooler and windier than below.

GRAND CANYON OF THE YELLOWSTONE

Yellowstone is best known for its geysers and animals, but for many visitors the Grand Canyon is its most memorable feature. This 20-mile-long canyon ranges from 1,500 to 4,000 feet across and has colorful yellow, pink, orange, and buff cliffs that drop as much as 1,200 feet on either side. The river itself tumbles abruptly over two massive waterfalls, sending up a roar audible for miles along the rims. Grand Canyon is accessible by road from both the north and south sides, with equally amazing views. The lodgepole pine forests around here escaped the fires of 1988.

Carving a Canyon

After the massive volcanic eruptions some 650,000 years ago, rhyolite lava flows came through what is now the Grand Canyon. The flows eventually cooled, but geothermal activity within the rhyolite weakened the rock with hot steam and gasses, making it susceptible to erosion. Over the centuries, a series of glaciers blocked water upstream, each time creating a lake. As each glacier retreated it undammed the stream, allowing the water in the lake to empty suddenly. The weakened rhyolite was easily eroded by these periodic floods of water and glacial debris, thus revealing pastel yellow and red canyon walls

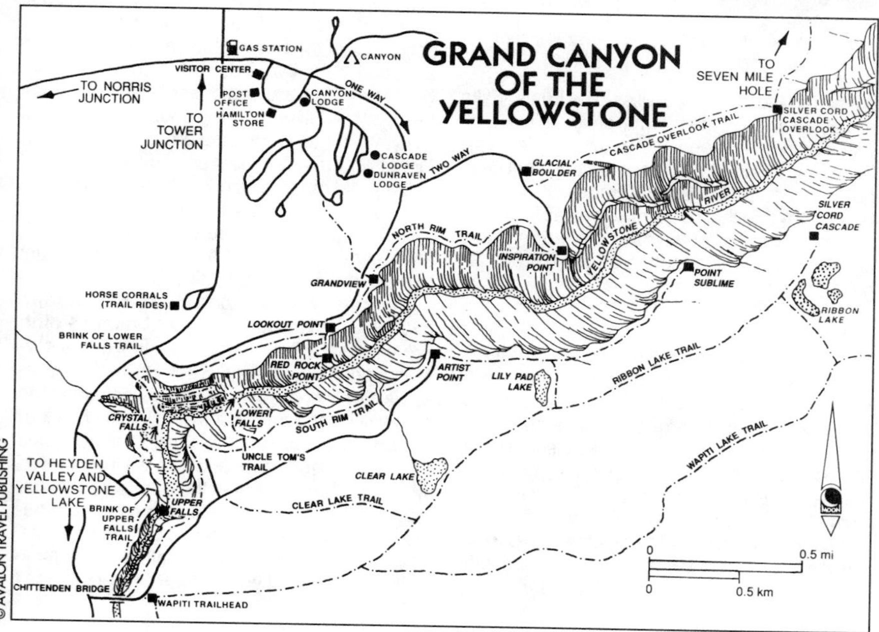

Lower Falls of the Yellowstone River plummet more than 300 feet.

colored by the thermal activities. The **Lower Falls** are at the edge of the thermal basin, above rock that was not weakened by geothermal activity. The **Upper Falls** are at a contact point between hard rhyolite that does not erode easily and a band of rhyolite that contains more easily eroded volcanic glass. Today, the canyon is eroding more slowly, having increased in depth just 50 feet over the last 10,000 years.

Canyon Village

Canyon Village on the north rim is a forgettable shopping mall in the wilderness, complete with various stores and eating places, a post office, gas station, cabins, lodges, and a campground. It's a good place to come on a rainy summer afternoon when the kids are starting to scream for ice cream. Horseback rides are available less than a mile south of here. Step into **Canyon Visitor Center,** tel. (307) 242-2550, for park information or to see the natural history exhibits. Hours are daily 8 a.m.-7 p.m. Memorial Day to mid-September, and daily 9 a.m.-6 p.m. till mid-October. (Hours may vary depending upon park budgets and staffing.) Closed in winter. A new and much improved visitor center is in the works and should open by 2004.

North Rim Vistas

A one-way road takes visitors to a series of extremely popular overlooks along the north rim of Grand Canyon of the Yellowstone. Farthest east is **Inspiration Point,** where the views of the canyon and Lower Falls are, well, inspirational. **North Rim Trail** leads along the rim from Inspiration Point up to Chittenden Bridge, three miles away. Some sections of this scenic and nearly level path are paved. Just a couple hundred feet up from Inspiration Point, be sure to look for a 500-ton boulder deposited by a glacier during the glaciation that ended 15,000 years ago. It originated in the Beartooth Mountains at least 30 miles north of here and was carried south atop a moving river of ice.

The five-mile-long **Seven Mile Hole Trail** takes off near this boulder, providing fantastic views for the first mile or so, minus the crowds at Inspiration Point. Look for **Silver Cord Cascade,** a thin ribbon of water dropping over the opposite wall of the canyon, but be careful not to go too close to the very loose edge. It's a very long way down! The trail switchbacks steeply to the Yellowstone River, passing odoriferous thermal areas en route. Many anglers come to Seven Mile Hole (it's seven miles downriver from Lower Falls) while other folks come to relax along the river. Save your energy for the strenuous 1,400-foot climb back up. Three campsites are available near the base of the trail for those who want to make this an overnight hike (permit required).

The one-way road continues westward to overlooks at **Grandview** and **Lookout Point.** From Lookout Point, a half-mile trail drops several hundred feet to **Red Rock Point** for a closer view of Lower Falls. Farthest west along the one-way North Rim Rd. is the trail to the **Brink of the Lower Falls.** The trail is half a mile long and paved, descending 600 feet to a viewing area where you can peer over the edge as the water plummets in a thunderous roar over the 308-foot precipice (twice the height of Niagara Falls). This is probably the most breathtaking sight in Yellowstone, but if you suffer from vertigo don't even think about looking over the brink! Just south of where the one-way road rejoins the main highway is a turnoff to the **Brink of the Upper Falls,** where a short walk takes you to a less dramatic but still beautiful view of the 109-foot-high Upper Falls.

A party of prospectors wandered north into this country in 1867, following the Yellowstone River downstream without suspecting the canyon below. A. Bart Henderson wrote in his diary of strolling down the river and being

> *very much surprised to see the water disappear from my sight. I walked out on a rock & made two steps at the same time, one forward, the other backward, for I had unawares as it were, looked down into the depth or bowels of the earth, into which the Yellow plunged as if to cool the infernal region that lay under all this wonderful country of lava and boiling springs.*

South Rim Vistas

The south rim is lined with additional dramatic views into Grand Canyon. Cross the Chittenden Bridge over the Yellowstone River (otters are sometimes seen playing in the river below) and continue a half mile to Uncle Tom's parking area, where a short trail leads to views of the Upper Falls and Crystal Falls. More unusual is **Uncle Tom's Trail,** which descends 500 feet to Lower Falls. The trail is partly paved, but it's steep and includes 328 metal steps before you get to the bottom. Good exercise if you're in shape. It was named for "Uncle" Tom Richardson who, with the help of wooden ladders and ropes, led paying tourists to the base of the falls around the turn of the 20th century. Because there was no bridge, Uncle Tom also rowed his guests across the river near the present Chittenden Bridge. After his permit was revoked in 1903, visitors had to make do on their own.

A mile beyond Uncle Tom's parking area, the road ends at the parking area for **Artist Point,** the most famous of all Grand Canyon viewpoints. A short paved path leads to an astoundingly beautiful point where one can look upriver to the Lower Falls or down the opposite direction into the canyon. Look for thermal activity far below. The point is apparently where artist Thomas Moran painted a number of his famous watercolors. **South Rim Trail** begins at the Chittenden Bridge and follows along the rim to Artist Point (two miles), providing more viewpoints along the way. The least-traveled part of this trail continues eastward from Artist Point another 1.5 miles to **Point Sublime,** with many fine looks into and across the canyon. This path provides an escape from the throngs at Artist Point, as well as a chance to see the kaleidoscopically colored canyon, hear the roar of the river from far below, and watch for squirrels and birds. But be careful to stay away from the edge where the rocks are loose—I doubt that anyone could survive such a fall.

For a longer day-hike, take **Ribbon Lake Trail,** which branches off the South Rim Trail a half mile east of Artist Point. This path takes you to a pair of lakes, and a spur trail leads to a hill that provides a wonderful view of the canyon and Silver Cord Cascade. With a drop of 1,200 feet, Silver Cord is the highest falls in Yellowstone. Also nearby are two campsites for those wanting to spend a night on the rim of the canyon; see Into the Backcountry below for camping details. From Artist Point parking area to Ribbon Lake, it's four miles roundtrip. A variety of other trails on the South Rim provide alternate starting points and possible loop hikes to the Ribbon Lake area.

CANYON TO LAKE JUNCTION

Hayden Valley

Just a few miles south of Canyon, the country abruptly opens into beautiful Hayden Valley, named for Dr. Ferdinand V. Hayden, leader of the 1871 expedition into Yellowstone. Reaching eight miles across, this relatively level part of the park was once occupied by an arm of Yellowstone Lake. The sediments left behind by the lake, along with glacial till, do not hold sufficient water to support trees. As a result, the area is occupied primarily by grasses, forbs, and sage. This is one of the best areas in the park to see wildlife, especially bison and elk. The Yellowstone River wanders across Hayden Valley, and streams enter from various sides. The waterways are excellent places to look for Canada geese, trumpeter swans, pelicans, and many kinds of ducks. Although they are less common, grizzly bears sometimes can be found feeding in the eastern end of the valley. Because of the bears, hikers need to be especially cautious when tramping through the grasses and shrubs, where it is easy to surprise a bear or to be likewise surprised. On the north end of Hayden Valley, the road crosses **Alum Creek,** named for its highly alkaline water, which could make anything shrink. In the horse-and-buggy days, Yellowstone wags claimed that a man had forded the creek with a team of horses and a wagon, but came out the other side with four Shetland ponies pulling a basket!

Mud Volcano Area

Shortly after the road climbs south out of Hayden Valley, it passes one of the most interesting of Yellowstone's many thermal basins. On the east side of the road, a turnout overlooks **Sulphur Caldron,** where a highly acidic pool is filled with sulfur-tinted waters and the air is filled with the odor of hydrogen-sulfide gas. Directly across the road is the Mud Volcano area, where a two-thirds-mile loop trail provides what could be a tour through a very bad case of heartburn. Pick up a Park Service brochure from the box for descriptions of all the bizarre features. The area is in a constant state of flux as springs dry up or begin overflowing, killing trees in their path. One of the most interesting features is **Black Dragons Caldron,** where an explosive spring blasts constantly through a mass of boiling black mud. The wildest place at Mud Volcano is **Dragon's Mouth,** which the Park Service notes is named for "the rhythmic belching of steam and the flashing tongue of water shooting out from the cavernous opening." It's easy to imagine the fires of hell not far below this. The waters are 180° F. During the winter months, the Mud Volcano area is a good place to see elk or bison.

Along the Yellowstone

South of Mud Volcano, the road parallels the Yellowstone River. At **LeHardy Rapids** a boardwalk provides an overlook where early summer visitors see blush-red spawning cutthroats. In late summer, this part of the Yellowstone River is a very popular fly-fishing spot—some call it the finest stream cutthroat fishing in the world—and a good place to view ducks and swans. Earlier in the year, it's open only to the bears that gorge on the cutthroats. By the way, the Yellowstone River, which begins at Yellowstone Lake, is the longest free-flowing (undammed) river in the Lower 48.

YELLOWSTONE LAKE

When first-time visitors see Yellowstone Lake, they are stunned by its magnitude. The statistics are impressive: 110 miles of shoreline, 20 miles north to south and 14 miles east to west, with an average depth of 139 feet and a maximum depth of 390 feet. Yellowstone Lake can seem a sheet of glass laid to the horizon at one moment and just a half hour later be a roiling ocean of whitecaps and wind-whipped waves. These changeable waters can be dangerous to those in canoes or small boats; a number of people have drowned, including experienced park rangers. The water is covered by ice at least half of the year, and breakup does not come until late May or early June. Even in summer, water temperatures are often only in the 40s. David Folsom, who was part of an exploration party traveling through the area in 1869, described Yellowstone Lake as an

> *inland sea, its crystal waves dancing and sparkling in the sunlight as if laughing with joy for their wild freedom. It is a scene of transcendent beauty which has been viewed by few white men, and we felt glad to have looked upon it before its primeval solitude should be broken by the crowds of pleasure seekers which at no distant day will throng its shores.*

Fishing Bridge

The area around famous Fishing Bridge (built in 1937) was for many years a favorite place to catch cutthroat trout. Unfortunately, these same fish are a major food source for grizzlies, and this area is considered some of the most important bear habitat in Yellowstone. Conflicts between bears and humans led to the death of 16 grizzlies here. To help restore trout populations and to proved food for the grizzlies, the Park Service banned fishing from Fishing Bridge in 1973 and tried to move the developments to the

Grant Village area. Lobbying by folks from Cody (worried lest they lose some of the tourist traffic) kept some of the facilities at Fishing Bridge from closing. Remaining facilities include an RV park, Hamilton Store, and gas station. **Fishing Bridge Visitor Center,** tel. (307) 242-2450, houses exhibits of birds, animals, and geology. It's open daily 8 a.m.-7 p.m. Memorial Day to mid-September, and daily 9 a.m.-6 p.m. from mid-September to mid-October. (Hours may vary depending upon park budgets and staffing.) Closed the remainder of the year. The bridge itself is still a very popular stopping point and a good place to see large cutthroat trout in the shallows. For a nice loop hike, take **Elephant Back Mountain Trail,** which begins a mile south of Fishing Bridge Junction. This three-mile (roundtrip) trail climbs 800 feet in elevation through dense lodgepole forests to panoramic views across Yellowstone Lake and into Pelican Valley.

Lake Yellowstone Hotel

Lake Yellowstone Hotel, the oldest extant park hostelry, was built in 1889-91 by the Northern Pacific Railroad and originally consisted of a simple boxlike structure facing Yellowstone Lake. The hotel was sold to Harry Child in 1901, and two years later Robert Reamer—the architect who designed Old Faithful Inn—was given free rein to transform this into a more attractive place. Hard to believe that the same architect could create a grand log masterpiece and a sprawling Southern colonial mansion with distinctive Ionic columns in the same park! Lake Yellowstone Hotel is the second-largest wood-framed building in North America and requires 500 gallons of paint each year to keep it in shape. During the 1960s and '70s the hotel fell into disrepair under the management of General Host Corporation, and in disgust, the Park Service bought out the concession and leased it to another company. Major renovations in the 1980s transformed the dowdy old structure into a luxurious grand hotel with much of the charm it had when Pres. Calvin Coolidge stayed here in the 1920s. Today, Lake Yellowstone Hotel is one of the nicest lodging places in the park, with fine vistas out over the lake and comfortable quarters. Relax with a drink in the sunlit Sun Room; string quartets play here many summer evenings. Free 45-minute **tours** of historic Lake Yellowstone Hotel are given each evening at 6:15 p.m. from early June to late September. The hotel also houses a gift shop and snack bar.

Be sure to take a walk along the lakeshore out front of the hotel, where the Absaroka Range forms a backdrop far to the east. The highest mountain is Avalanche Peak (10,566 feet). Almost due south is the 10,308-foot summit of Mt. Sheridan, named for Gen. Philip Sheridan, a longtime supporter of expanding the park to include the Tetons. Watch for the big white peli-

COURTESY AISLINN RACE

the original hotel at Yellowstone Lake circa 1898, built by the Northern Pacific Railroad.

The rambling Lake Yellowstone Hotel is the second-largest wood-framed building in North America.

cans catching fish on the lake. Just east of Lake Yellowstone Hotel is the **Lake Ranger Station,** built in 1922-23 and now on the National Register of Historic Places. Inside the octagonal main room you will find a massive central fireplace, exposed log rafters, and rustic light fixtures. Not far away is **Lake Lodge,** another rustic log structure that houses a reasonably priced cafeteria fronting the lake. A Hamilton Store stands nearby, and dozens of very plain cabins are behind.

To West Thumb

The highway south from Lake Junction to West Thumb follows the lakeshore nearly the entire distance. A campground and boat harbor are at **Bridge Bay,** along with a ranger station, marina, and store. Stop here for hour-long boat tours of Yellowstone Lake, offered several times a day throughout the summer, or for guided fishing trips and boat rentals.

For an enjoyable day-hike, visit **Natural Bridge,** a 51-foot-high span of rock that was carved by the waters of Bridge Creek. The three-mile (roundtrip) trail starts from the marina parking lot. The last part of the way into Natural Bridge is along a paved road that was until recently open to cars. Cyclists can ride bikes to Natural Bridge on a separate trail that starts south of the marina.

Back on the main road, keep your eyes open for Canada geese and trumpeter swans as you drive south. **Gull Point Dr.,** a two-mile-long side road, offers views of **Stevenson Island** just offshore; farther south, **Frank Island** and tiny **Dot Island** become visible. The small **Potts Hot Springs Basin,** just north of West Thumb, is named for fur trapper Daniel T. Potts, one of the first white men to explore the Yellowstone country. His travels here in 1826 were described the following year in a Philadelphia newspaper article. It was perhaps the first published mention of Yellowstone Lake and the hot springs.

EAST ENTRANCE ROAD

Heading east from Fishing Bridge, the road follows the shore of Yellowstone Lake past country that escaped the fires of 1988. Three miles east of the bridge are Indian Pond—popular with birders—and the trailhead for **Storm Point Trail.** This pleasant three-mile (roundtrip) loop trail is essentially level and goes past a large colony of yellow-bellied marmots before reaching Storm Point, where waves often pound against the rocks. The trail is often closed in spring and early summer because of grizzlies, and mosquitoes may make a June or July trip less enjoyable. North of here, Pelican Valley is considered important grizzly habitat and is closed to all overnight camping year-round. Even daytime use is not allowed until July 4, and then only between 9 a.m. and 7 p.m. Before venturing out on the Storm Point Trail or into Pelican Valley, check at the Lake Ranger Station for current bear info. The half-mile-long **Pelican Creek Na-**

ture Trail starts a mile east of Fishing Bridge and provides an easy hike to a beach along Yellowstone Lake. Much of the way is on boardwalk over a marshy area.

At **Steamboat Point** the road swings out along the shore, providing excellent views across the lake and of a noisy fumarole. For an even better view (don't miss this one!), take the **Lake Butte Overlook** road, which continues one mile to a small parking area a thousand feet above the lake. This is a fine place to watch sunsets and to get a feeling for the enormity of Yellowstone Lake. Back on the main highway and heading east, Yellowstone Lake is soon behind you and visible in only a few spots as the road climbs gradually, passing scenic **Sylvan Lake,** a nice place for picnics. Just up the road is tiny Eleanor Lake (little more than a puddle) and the trail to 10,566-foot **Avalanche Peak.** This two-mile-long unmarked trail begins across the road on the east side of the creek and climbs steeply. It emerges from the forest halfway up, with the top gained via a scree slope. At the summit, you can see most of the peaks in the Absarokas and in the Tetons 70 miles away, but snow is present on top till mid-July.

Immediately east of Eleanor Lake, the main road climbs to 8,530-foot **Sylvan Pass,** flanked by Hoyt Peak on the north and Top Notch Peak to the south. Steep scree slopes drop down both sides. East of Sylvan Pass, the road descends quickly along Middle Creek (a tributary of the Shoshone River), providing good views to the south of Mt. Langford and Mt. Doane. **East Entrance Ranger Station** was built by the army in 1904. For many years, the road leading up to Sylvan Pass from the east took drivers across Corkscrew Bridge, a bridge that literally looped over itself as the road climbed steeply up the narrow valley. The road continues eastward to Cody through beautiful Wapiti Valley; see the Yellowstone Gateway Towns chapter for details.

COURTESY AISLINN RACE

YELLOWSTONE CAMPING AND LODGING

PARK CAMPGROUNDS

Tent camping in Yellowstone's early days left a bit to be desired. One 1884 tourist noted that during the height of the summer season, "the principle upon which the beds are populated is said to be the addition of visitors so long as they may arrive, or until the occupants 'go for their guns.' The plan is simple, and relieves the authorities of responsibility." It's still crowded in the park, but at least guns are prohibited in the park today!

Camping is available at a dozen sites scattered along the road network; see the Yellowstone National Park Campgrounds chart for specifics, or call the Park Service at (307) 344-2114 for recorded campground information. Reservations are available for five concessioner-managed campgrounds: Bridge Bay Campground, Canyon Campground, Grant Village Campground, Madison Campground, and Fishing Bridge RV Park. Call Amfac Parks & Resorts at (307) 344-7311 for reservations (no extra charge), or find them on the web at www.travelyellowstone.com. The other seven (Park Service-managed) campgrounds inside Yellowstone are available on a first-come, first-camped basis with no reservations. You can pay with cash, checks, or credit cards. Only Mammoth Campground remains open year-round. Roadside or parking-lot camping is not allowed, and rangers *do* enforce this prohibition.

During July and August, virtually all campsites in Yellowstone fill *before noon,* so get there early! The busiest weekends are—not surprisingly—around July 4 and Labor Day. Yellowstone's most popular campgrounds fill up even in late fall and early summer.

Other Camping Options

When everything else is packed, folks head to campgrounds on surrounding Forest Service lands or to motels in the gateway towns. See Shoshone National Forest in the Yellowstone Gateway Towns chapter for areas east of Yellowstone, and see Jackson Hole/Grand Teton Public Campgrounds for areas to the south. Other campgrounds, both public and private, are described under the various park gateways—Cody, Jackson, Dubois, West Yellowstone, Gardiner, Cooke City, and Silver Gate. The farther you get from Yellowstone, the more likely you are to find space. If you reach Nebraska, you should have no trouble at all. Campers can take showers (fee charged) at Old Faithful Lodge, Grant Village, Fishing Bridge RV Park, and Canyon Village Campground.

PARK ACCOMMODATIONS

Yellowstone accommodations range from extremely basic cabins with four thin walls starting at $34 d, up to luxury suites that cost more than $400. Following a fine old Park Service tradition, none of the rooms has TVs or radios and only a few contain phones. What they do offer is the chance to relax in comfortable accommodations and explore the magical world outside. Most are open early June to mid-September. During the winter months, only Mammoth Hot Springs Hotel and the Old Faithful Snow Lodge remain open inside the park. Several hundred more motels and other lodging places operate outside park boundaries in the towns of Jackson, Cody, West Yellowstone, Gardiner, Cooke City, and elsewhere. See appropriate sections of this book for details.

Amfac Parks & Resorts is Yellowstone's official lodging concessioner. For reservations, call (307) 344-7311, or visit the website: www.travelyellowstone.com. **Make Yellowstone lodging reservations six months ahead** for the park's prime hotels, or you may find that the only rooms available are in Grant Village, the laughing stock of park lodges. Those traveling with small children should also request cribs when making reservations.

Hotels and Cabins

At the turn of the 20th century, most visitors to Yellowstone stayed in park hotels rather than roughing it on the ground. Three of these won-

YELLOWSTONE NATIONAL PARK CAMPGROUNDS

Bridge Bay Campground; $15; fills early, flush toilets, dump station, generators permitted, open mid-May to late September, call (303) 297-2757 for reservations

Canyon Campground; $15; fills early, laundry facilities, showers for $3 extra per person, flush toilets, dump station, generators permitted, open early June to mid-September, call (303) 297-2757 for reservations

Fishing Bridge RV Park; $27; fills early, hard-sided RVs only, full hookups, laundry facilities, showers $3 extra per person, flush toilets, sewer system, generators permitted, open mid-May to mid-September; call (303) 297-2757 for reservations

Grant Village Campground; $15; fills early, showers nearby for $3 per person, flush toilets, dump station, generators permitted, open late June to early October, call (303) 297-2757 for reservations

Indian Creek Campground; $10; vault toilets, open mid-June to mid-September

Lewis Lake Campground; $10; vault toilets, fills early, open mid-June to early November

Madison Campground; $15; fills early; flush toilets, dump station, generators permitted, open May to early November; call (303) 297-2757 for reservations

Mammoth Campground; $12; near a residential area and along the park road, flush toilets, generators permitted, open year-round

Norris Campground; $12; fills early, flush toilets, generators permitted, open mid-May to late September

Pebble Creek Campground; $10; vault toilets, open early June to late September

Slough Creek Campground; $10; vault toilets, open late May through October

Tower Fall Campground; $10; fills early, vault toilets, open mid-May to late September

derful old lodging places remain: Old Faithful Inn, Lake Yellowstone Hotel, and Mammoth Hot Springs Hotel. In addition, the new Old Faithful Snow Lodge joins the list as a modern classic. Not all lodging options inside the park are nearly as pleasant, however. Hundreds of simple boxes are clustered in the Lake, Mammoth, Old Faithful, and Roosevelt areas. Most of these cabins offer basic accommodations, a roof over your head, and communal showers, but the more expensive cabins are considerably nicer. A few of these even include private jacuzzis. Fortunately, prices are fairly reasonable for all of the cabins. In addition, two attractive and modern lodges are available at Canyon, along with standard motel rooms at Grant Village. All told, more than 2,200 rooms and cabins provide overnight accommodations in Yellowstone.

Lodging rates are listed below for two people; children under age 12 stay free. Add an extra $10 per person for additional older kids or adults in the hotel rooms or cabins. Prices may be lower in May when snow still covers much of the park. Call Amfac Parks & Resorts at (307) 344-7311 for reservations at any of these, or find them on the web at www.travelyellowstone.com. Rates listed below are without tax, which is six percent on the south half of the park (inside Teton County—including Old Faithful, Grant Village, and Lake Village) and eight percent on the north half (inside Park County—including Roosevelt, Mammoth Hot Springs, and Canyon Village).

Canyon Village

The centrally located **Canyon Lodge** is just a half mile from Grand Canyon of the Yellowstone, one of the park's premier attractions. The main lodge is part of a late-1950s' complex of ugly structures built around a large parking lot. The area has all the charm of an aging shopping mall from an era when bigger meant better. The lodge itself covers the space of a football field and houses a dining room, cafeteria, lounge, and snack shop, but no guest rooms. Behind the lodge in the trees (at least the setting is peaceful), the road circles past three sprawling clusters of cabins, all with private baths. You'll find 540 cabins here. The most basic "pioneer" units start at $54 d and aren't much to look at outside but are actually fairly roomy and comfortable inside. Two newer types of cabins are available at Canyon:

the "frontier" units for $82 d and the "western" cabins for $107 d. Providing far better accommodations are two 1990s additions: **Dunraven Lodge** and **Cascade Lodge.** Rooms at both of these attractive log- and rock-trimmed structures are furnished with rustic lodgepole pieces and have two double beds and private baths. Rooms in the lodges cost $111 d. The cabins and lodges at Canyon are open from early June to mid-September. Inexpensive-Expensive.

Grant Village

The southernmost lodging in Yellowstone, **Grant Village** offers accommodations in cramped condo-type units from the 1980s, with exceptional parking-lot views from the rooms. The buildings would be completely out of place in *any* national park, especially Yellowstone. Six lodge buildings contain motel-type units for $88 d, and recently redecorated rooms are $102 d. All rooms have two double beds and private baths. Nearby concessioner facilities include a restaurant, lounge, snack shop, and gift shop. Grant Village is open from late May through September. Expensive.

Lake Village

The Lake Village area has a variety of lodging options for travelers. **Lake Yellowstone Hotel** is a fascinating classic building with a magnificent view across Yellowstone Lake. Begun in 1889, the building expanded and changed over the decades to yield its current configuration of 158 guest rooms. The hotel has been lovingly restored and exudes a grandeur and charm rarely found today. It's the sort of place where Fred Astaire and Ginger Rogers would feel comfortable dancing—if they were still alive. The inviting hotel rooms all contain updated furnishings and range from standard units ($140 d on the backside or $152 d facing the lake) to spacious suites ($401 d). Out back (no view and modest furnishings) is an annex where rooms cost $102 d. Downstairs is a good restaurant (reservations required for dinner), along with a fast-food eatery; the cafeteria at Lake Lodge is only a short walk away. Free tours of the hotel are given each evening from early June to late September. The real treat at Lake Yellowstone Hotel is the Sun Room, where rows of windows front the lake. The room's ambience is further enhanced by period wicker furnishings and evening chamber music or classical piano. It's a great place to sip a martini or write a postcard. The hotel is open mid-May through September. Expensive-Luxury.

Behind Lake Yellowstone Hotel more than a hundred rather dingy old boxes have been jammed together in row after identical row to create the **Lake Yellowstone Hotel Cabins.** Fortunately, they're fairly reasonable ($82 d), and cabin guests can pretend they're traveling on a more ample budget by spending time in the hotel dining room and the Sun Room. Lake Yellowstone Hotel Cabins all contain two double beds and private baths, and they're open mid-May through September. Moderate.

A short distance east of Lake Yellowstone Hotel is **Lake Lodge.** Built in the 1920s, this archetypal log building has a gracious lobby containing two stone fireplaces, rustic furnishings, and an open ceiling where the supporting log trusses and beams are visible. One end of the building houses a large and reasonably priced cafeteria with picture windows framing Lake Yellowstone, and the other end contains a recreation hall for employees. Lodging options here are not nearly as gracious, consisting of plain-vanilla "pioneer" cabins from the 1920s and '30s, each with a double bed and private bath for $51 d, and a bit more comfortable "western" cabins built in the 1950s and '60s that include two double beds and private baths with showers for $107 d. The 186 cabins at Lake Lodge are open mid-June to mid-September. Guests here often walk over to the nearby Lake Yellowstone Hotel for fine dining and the chance to relax in the Sun Room. Inexpensive-Expensive.

Mammoth Hot Springs

The rambling **Mammoth Hot Springs Hotel** sits in the northwest corner of Yellowstone near park headquarters in the settlement of Mammoth. Built in 1937 (okay, one wing was constructed in 1911 and the original hotel was built even earlier), the hotel has 222 rooms in a variety of configurations. Elk are common sights on the hotel grounds, and in the fall the bulls' bugling may well wake you in the morning. There's live piano music downstairs in the map room most summer evenings as a counterpoint to the elk songs. Also just off the lobby is a gift shop. Just steps away are Park Service headquarters, the fine Albright Visitor Center and other historical build-

COURTESY AISLINN RACE

the original Mammoth Hot Springs Hotel, circa 1898

ings, along with places to eat, buy groceries, gas, and trinkets. Hotel rooms are comfortable but modest at Mammoth. Several rooms on each floor provide low-cost accommodations ($54 d) with communal baths, but most have two beds and private baths ($88 d); ask for a corner room with windows if available. The hotel also houses two luxury suites ($267 d). Behind the hotel are 116 cabins, including budget units without bath ($51 d) and very attractive duplex "frontier" cottages (from $82 d). Four units also have private outdoor jacuzzis and are the nicest cabins in the park ($122 d). The hotel and cabins are open from early May to mid-October. In addition, this hotel is one of two in the park (the other being Old Faithful Snow Lodge) that opens when the snow flies; the winter season runs mid-December to early March. In winter, the hot tubs are available on an hourly basis, offering a great way to relax after a day of cross-country skiing. Inexpensive-Luxury.

Old Faithful

The Old Faithful area contains a plethora of lodging options, including two large hotels—Old Faithful Inn and Old Faithful Snow Lodge—and several dozen cabins.

Built in 1903-04, the timeless **Old Faithful Inn** (described in Touring Yellowstone above) is easily the most delightful place to stay inside Yellowstone—if not in all of America. I wouldn't trade it for a thousand Hiltons. If you're able to get a room here during your visit to the park, do so; you certainly won't regret it! The hotel contains 327 guest rooms to suit all budgets. Even those staying in the most basic rooms here will enjoy the five-star lobby with its towering stone fireplace that always has a fire going, the old-fashioned writing tables, cushy overstuffed chairs, classy bar and restaurant, and evening piano music. Most rooms in the original section of the hotel are cramped spaces with in-room sinks, bare bulb lighting, old carpets, log walls, and communal baths down the hall; these go for $55 d. Of the cheap rooms, the best ones (these are often reserved a year ahead) are the dormer rooms on the second floor, but those who stay there must walk past folks in the lobby to take a shower! Many other types of rooms are available throughout this sprawling hotel. The nicely appointed midrange rooms ($89 d) are very comfortable and contain two double beds and tub baths. Premium rooms vary in price from $111 to $151 d depending upon whether or not they face the geyser, but personally I don't think they are much better than the midrange units. If you have the money, rent a suite ($345 d); suites 176 and 177 have the finest views of Old Faithful. Old Faithful Inn is open early May to mid-October. Inexpensive-Luxury.

Although it is an attractively rustic building that would be a major focal point almost anywhere else, **Old Faithful Lodge** is overshadowed by its grand neighbor, Old Faithful Inn.

The lodge does not contain guest rooms but houses a large cafeteria (open for lunch and dinner only), recreation hall, gift shop, bake shop, ice cream stand, espresso cart, and showers. Unlike the inn, Old Faithful Lodge has enormous windows that face the geyser, providing those eating in the cafeteria with dramatic views of the eruptions. The lodge was built from massive fir logs, and stone pillars add to a feeling of permanence. Behind and beside Old Faithful Lodge are approximately 130 moderately priced duplex cabins. The simplest share communal bathhouses and start for just $34 d; these are the cheapest rooms in Yellowstone. Somewhat nicer cabins have one or two beds and private baths. The older ones ("pioneers") cost $45 d, while newer units run $61 d. The cabins at Old Faithful Lodge open around mid-May and close in mid-September. Inexpensive-Moderate.

The 100-room **Old Faithful Snow Lodge** opened in 1999 to widespread acclaim, providing accommodations in both summer and winter (Mammoth Hot Springs Hotel is Yellowstone's only other wintertime hotel). Both inside and out, Snow Lodge evokes the spirit of "parkitecture" from the early 1900s. The building blends the past and present, with timbers (recycled from old buildings), hardwood floors, a central stone fireplace, custom-designed overstuffed couches, and wrought-iron accents, along with all the modern conveniences you expect from a fine hotel (unless you're expecting TVs or radios, which no park hotels contain). Rooms are beautifully appointed and comfortable, and all have private baths. The hotel also houses a restaurant, snack shop, lounge, and gift shop, along with a ski shop and snowmobile rentals in winter. Lodging costs $128 d. In addition, 34 fourplex Snow Lodge Cabins are available behind the building, costing $107 d. These are relatively new (built in 1990) but are quite plain. Each contains two beds and a bath. The Snow Lodge and Cabins are open early May to mid-October, and mid-December to early March. Expensive-Premium.

Roosevelt

Roosevelt Lodge is decidedly off the beaten path to the major Yellowstone sights, and that suits folks who stay here just fine. Located at the junction of the roads to Canyon, Mammoth, and Lamar Valley, this is the place to escape the crowds and return to a quieter and simpler era. Named for Pres. Theodore Roosevelt—perhaps the most conservation-minded president ever—the lodge has the well-worn feeling of an old dude ranch, and many families treat it as such. More than a few folks book cabins for several weeks at a stretch, enjoying the wolf-watching, fly-fishing, horseback and wagon rides, and barbecue cookout dinners. The main lodge features two large stone fireplaces, a family-style restaurant, lounge, gift shop, and big front porch with rocking chairs. Surrounding it are 82 utilitarian cabins. Most basic—and just a step up from camping—are the "Roughrider" cabins, each with two beds, a writing table, and woodstove (the only ones in any Yellowstone lodging places). These cabins share a communal bathhouse, cost $42 d, and fill very quickly. Call far ahead to reserve one of these classics! A bit nicer (but still no private bath) are the economy cabins for $54 d, and you'll also find "frontier" cabins with showers for $82 d. The Roosevelt Lodge and cabins are open mid-June to mid-September. Inexpensive-Moderate.

INTO THE BACKCOUNTRY

The vast majority of Yellowstone visitors act as though they were chained to their cars with a hundred-yard tether—as if by getting away from their vehicles they might miss some other sight down the road. For the two percent or so who *do* abandon their cars, Yellowstone has much to offer beyond the spectacular geysers and canyons for which it is famous. Although many parts of the Yellowstone backcountry are heavily visited, regulations keep the sense of wildness intact by separating campsites and limiting the number of hikers. And if you head out early or late in the season, you'll discover solitude just a few miles from the traffic jams.

Much of Yellowstone consists of rolling lodgepole (or burned lodgepole) forests. With a few exceptions, anyone looking for dramatic alpine scenery would probably be better off heading to Grand Teton National Park, the Beartooth Mountains, or the Wind River Mountains. Despite this, the Yellowstone backcountry is enjoyable to walk through, and many trails lead past waterfalls, geysers, and hot springs. Besides, this is one of the finest places in America to view wildlife—including bison, elk, grizzlies, and wolves—in a setting other than a zoo.

Before August, when they start to die down, you should also be ready for the ubiquitous mosquitoes. Ticks are a nuisance from mid-March to mid-July in lower elevation parts of Yellowstone. The fires of 1988 created some problems for backcountry hikers, but trails have all been cleared and hikers will get a good chance to see how the land is recovering.

Rules and Regulations

The Park Service maintains more than 300 campsites in the Yellowstone backcountry, most of which have pit toilets, fire rings, and storage poles to keep food from bears. Hikers may stay only at designated campsites. Wood fires are not allowed in many areas and are discouraged elsewhere, so be sure to have a gas stove for cooking. Bear-management areas have special regulations; they may be for day-use only, include seasonal restrictions, or specify minimum group sizes. Pets are not allowed on the trails within Yellowstone, and special rules apply for those coming in with horses, mules, burros, and llamas. Because of wet conditions and the lack of forage, no stock animals are permitted before July.

A free backcountry-use permit is required of each overnight party and is available in person from various Yellowstone ranger stations and visitor centers within 48 hours of your hike. Because of the popularity of backcountry trips, it is a very good idea to make reservations before your arrival in the park. Reservations cost $15 per trip, and the reservation forms are available from the Backcountry Office, P.O. Box 168, Yellowstone National Park, WY 82190, tel. (307) 344-2160. Campsite reservation requests must be mailed in, using these forms; reservations are not accepted by phone, fax, or over the web (though this might possibly change). You'll receive a confirmation notice by return mail and will exchange the notice for a permit when you get there; the permit must be obtained in person at a ranger station within 48 hours of your first camping date. Before receiving your permit, you will be given a lengthy rundown on what to expect and what precautions to take, and you'll be shown a bear-safety video. The ranger stations are open seven days a week June-Aug., generally from 8 a.m. to 4:30 p.m.

For a description of backcountry rules, bear safety, and suggestions for hiking and horsepacking, pick up (or request to have it sent to you) Yellowstone's ***Backcountry Trip Planner,*** which shows locations of campsites throughout the park and provides detailed information on wilderness access and precautions. You may want to also pick up or request the free park pamphlet *Beyond Road's End.*

Those interested in horsepacking or llama trips should call the park at (307) 344-7381 and ask for a list of outfitters authorized to operate in Yellowstone. The outfitters offer everything from daytrips to weeklong adventures deep into the backcountry. You can also find a list of outfitters on the Park Service website, www.nps.gov/yell.

More Info

I have described below a few two- to four-day backcountry hikes covering various parts of Yellowstone. The park has more than 1,000 miles of trails, so this is obviously a tiny sampling of the various hiking options. In addition, quite a few day-hikes are described above in the Touring Yellowstone section.

Before you head out you will probably want to look over your hiking options. Two excellent source books are *Yellowstone Trails,* by Mark Marschall (Mammoth, WY: Yellowstone Association), and *Hiking Yellowstone National Park,* by Bill Schneider (Helena, MT: Falcon Publishing). Get them from park gift shops or visitor centers, which also sell topographic park maps. The best maps are those produced by Trails Illustrated; these feature all the major trails and show the severity of burn from the 1988 fires—a considerable help when planning hiking trips.

NORTH YELLOWSTONE TRAILS

Sportsman Lake Trail and Electric Peak

The land west of Mammoth is some of the most rugged in Yellowstone, with a number of peaks topping 10,000 feet. Several trails cut westward across this country, one of the most interesting being the 24-mile-long Sportsman Lake Trail. The route begins at Glen Creek Trailhead five miles south of Mammoth and follows Glen Creek (a good place to see elk in autumn) for four miles before crossing into the Gardner River drainage. Along the way, a short spur trail leads to pretty Cache Lake. Considerably more challenging is a second side trip, the climb up 10,992-foot **Electric Peak,** tallest mountain in this corner of Yellowstone. Many folks camp near Electric Peak and spend a day climbing. It's eight miles roundtrip and you gain 3,000 feet on the way up, but the trail becomes harder to follow the higher you climb. See a park trail guidebook for details and precautions on this hike. It is possible to day-hike to the top of Electric Peak from the Glen Creek Trailhead, but it's not recommended unless you have a masochistic streak, have done a lot of hiking, and are in great shape.

Beyond the side trail to Electric Peak, Sportsman Lake Trail crosses the Gardner River twice, and there are no bridges. The water can be dangerously deep early in the summer, so this hike is generally done in August or September. After the river fords, the trail climbs to Electric Divide (watch for bighorn sheep) and then drops steeply to Sportsman Lake and down along pretty Fan Creek to the Fawn Pass Trailhead on US Hwy. 191. Because this is a one-way hike you will need to set up some sort of vehicle shuttle. Another problem is bears. This country overflows with grizzly activity, and a party size of four or more is recommended for travel here. Off-trail travel is prohibited in some areas; see the Park Service for details.

This photo of 10,992-foot Electric Peak, tallest mountain in this corner of Yellowstone, was taken about 1898.

COURTESY AISLINN RACE

Black Canyon of the Yellowstone

For an early-summer backpacking trip, it's hard to beat this 19-mile trek along the northern edge of Yellowstone. Start at the Hellroaring Trailhead, 3.5 miles west of Tower, and follow the Yellowstone River Trail in a steep descent to the river, 600 feet below. A suspension bridge crosses the river and from here on you remain on the north side all the way to Gardiner. One ford at Hellroaring Creek can be dangerous before August, but it can be avoided if you hike a mile or so upstream to a stock bridge crossing. After this, the hike alternates between high ridges overlooking Black Canyon of the Yellowstone and quieter stretches where the trail drops down along the edge of the water. Dramatic Knowles Falls is a highlight. The trail is in good condition, but you may find it very hot and dry in midsummer.

Pebble Creek and Bliss Pass Trails

Pebble Creek Trail cuts through a section of Yellowstone that is far away from the geysers and canyons for which the park is famous. The crowds don't come here, but the country is some of the nicest mountain scenery to be found. The trail connects with the Northeast Entrance road at both ends, making access easy. You can start from either end, but if you begin at Warm Creek Picnic Area (1.5 miles west of the entrance station) you get to the high meadows quicker. From the picnic area the trail climbs 1,100 feet in the first mile and a half, but beyond this it's all downhill. Best time to hike this trail is in late summer, when the water levels are lower (there are four fords) and the mosquitoes have abated. Hikers are treated to abundant alpine flowers and grand mountain scenery along the way, with the chance to see moose or elk in the meadows.

For a longer alternative hike, follow Pebble Creek Trail 5.5 miles from the picnic area and then turn west onto **Bliss Pass Trail.** The path crosses Pebble Creek (quite deep till late summer) before climbing 1,400 feet over Bliss Pass and then dropping down 2,700 feet to Slough Creek Trail. From here it is an easy walk to Slough Creek Campground. Total distance from the Warm Creek Picnic Area to Slough Creek Campground is 20 miles. The easy Slough Creek Trail is described as a day-hike in the Northeast Entrance Road section above.

SOUTH YELLOWSTONE TRAILS

Shoshone Lake

The largest lake in the Lower 48 without direct road access, Shoshone Lake is probably the most visited part of Yellowstone's backcountry. Its shoreline is dotted with more than two dozen campsites, but most of these fill on midsummer nights with hikers, canoeists, and kayakers. Because of the lake's popularity, reserve well ahead for a summertime campsite. On-water access is via Lewis Lake and the Lewis River Channel. Anglers come to fish in the channel or lakes; Shoshone Lake has good numbers of brown, lake, and brook trout, all of which were planted here. Hikers access Shoshone Lake primarily from the DeLacy Creek Trailhead on the north side between West Thumb and Old Faithful, or from the east side via Dogshead Trailhead. A 22-mile trail circles Shoshone Lake, although it is away from the shoreline much of the distance. You may see moose or elk and are certain to meet clouds of mosquitoes before August. The finest lake vistas come from the east side, where the trail follows the lakeshore for four miles. On the west end of the lake, hikers will find **Shoshone Geyser Basin,** an area filled with small geysers, beautiful pools, and bubbling mud pots. Most of the lake escaped the 1988 fires, but trails from the east side (via Dogshead Trailhead) traverse burned stands of lodgepole.

Heart Lake

The Heart Lake area is another extremely popular backcountry and day-hiking area, offering easy access, a pretty lake, hot springs, and impressive mountain vistas. **Heart Lake Trail** begins just north of Lewis Lake (six miles south of Grant Village). The trail is fairly easy, climbing slowly through unburned forests for the first five miles and then following Witch Creek down past burned forests to Heart Lake, eight miles from the trailhead. Witch Creek is fed almost entirely by the hot springs and geysers scattered along it.

Near the Heart Lake patrol cabin the trail splits. Continue straight ahead another 26 miles to eventually reach the isolated and challenging Thorofare Trail on the southeast end of Yellowstone Lake; getting there requires fording the Yellowstone River, which may be waist deep even in late summer. For something a bit less remote, turn right and hike a half mile to the **Mt. Sheridan Trail,** which heads west and climbs 2,800 vertical feet in three miles. Reaching the 10,308-foot summit will certainly leave you winded. A fire lookout at the top provides views across Yellowstone Lake and south to the Tetons.

At the base of Mt. Sheridan and just to the north is a small thermal area that contains **Rustic Geyser** (eruptions to 50 feet, but irregular) and **Columbia Pool,** among other attractions. Be very careful when walking here due to the overhanging rim at the pool edge.

Although many people simply hike to Heart Lake for an overnight trip, there are many longer hikes one could take out of here, including into the remote Thorofare (described below). A complete loop around the lake is approximately 34 miles roundtrip but requires two Snake River fords that are at least to your knees in late July; check with the rangers for flow levels. The Heart Lake area is prime grizzly habitat and is closed until the first of July. Do not take chances in this country!

Bechler River Area

The southwest portion of Yellowstone is known as Cascade Corner, a reference to its many tall waterfalls; more than half of the park's falls are here. This scenic and wild country escaped the fires of 1988 and is popular with anglers. Primary access is from either the Bechler Ranger Station (pronounced "BECK-ler") or the Cave Falls Trailhead, both of which are well off the beaten path and must be reached via Cave Falls Rd. from the Idaho side. It's 22 miles in from Ashton, Idaho, the last 10 on a gravel road. As an alternative, **Grassy Lake Road** provides a narrow and rough gravel connection to Cave Falls Road. Grassy Lake Rd. begins at Flagg Ranch Resort near Yellowstone's South Entrance; see a good map for the exact route.

All hikers must register at the Bechler Ranger Station, even if they are heading out from Cave Falls Trailhead, three miles farther down the road. Cave Falls itself is a very wide but not particularly tall drop along the Falls River. It's named for a cave on the west end of the waterfall. The Forest Service's **Cave Falls Campground** ($8) is open mid-May through August.

A spiderweb of trails cuts across the Bechler country, leading to many waterfalls and past a number of hot springs. One very popular hike goes from Bechler Ranger Station to the Old Faithful area, a distance of 30 miles; its downhill much of the way if you do this in reverse by starting at Old Faithful. From Bechler Ranger Station the trail cuts across expansive Bechler Meadows and then up narrow Bechler Canyon, passing Colonnade, Ouzel, and Iris Falls along the way. Many people stop overnight at Three River Junction to enjoy the hot springs-warmed water. Beyond this, the trail punches over the Continental Divide and then runs west of Shoshone Lake to Lone Star Geyser and the trailhead at Kepler Cascades. It's best to hike this route in August or September after the Bechler River drops enough to be more safely forded. This also allows time for the meadows to dry out a bit (watch out for leeches) and for the mosquitoes to quiet to a dull roar. For the long trek between Bechler Ranger Station and Old Faithful you will need to set up some sort of vehicle shuttle, but shorter in-and-out loop trips could be created by reading the various Yellowstone hiking guides and studying topographic maps.

The Thorofare

If any part of Yellowstone deserves the title untamed wilderness, it has to be the Thorofare. Situated along Two Ocean Plateau and cut through by the upper Yellowstone River, this broad expanse of unroaded country reaches from Yellowstone Lake into the Teton Wilderness south of the park. This is *the* most remote country anywhere in the Lower 48; at its heart you'd need to hike 30 miles in any direction to reach a road. Because of the distances involved, many people choose to traverse the Thorofare via horseback. There is considerable grizzly activity in this area, so various restrictions are in place. In addition, a number of major river crossings are impassable until late summer. Access to the Thorofare is via Heart Lake Trail (described above), the Thorofare Trail, or through Teton Wilderness within Bridger-Teton National Forest.

The **Thorofare Trail** begins at Nine Mile Trailhead on the East Entrance Rd. and hugs the shore of Yellowstone Lake for the first 17 miles. This stretch was spared from the fires of 1988 and provides some incredible opportunities to watch sunsets over the lake, particularly from campsites near Park Point. The trail continues along Southeast Arm and then follows the broad Thorofare Valley upstream beside the Yellowstone River (great fishing). There are several difficult creek and river crossings before you reach the Thorofare Ranger Station at mile 32. But this is not even the halfway point! Civilization is another 36 miles away. To get there, the often muddy South Boundary Trail heads west over the Continental Divide, through four difficult creek or river fords, through forests burned in the 1988 fires, and past Snake Hot Springs before finally ending at the South Entrance Station.

Needless to say, trips into the Thorofare are only for those with a lot of stamina and extensive backcountry experience. Shorter variations are possible, of course, but most involve hiking in and out the same way. Check at the Lake Ranger Station for conditions in the Thorofare and study Yellowstone hiking guides before even considering a big trip here. It's spectacular and remote country, but that means you're on your own much of the time.

One way to cut nine miles off your hike into the Thorofare is by a boat ride across Yellowstone Lake. The Amfac folks at Bridge Bay Marina (tel. 307-344-7311) can drop you off at a few campsites on the east side, but the cost is over $100 each way. They can carry up to six people for this price. Contact the Park Service's Backcountry Office (tel. 307-344-2160) to find out which campsites are accessible by motorboat. These sites tend to fill up fast so you'll need to reserve well ahead.

OTHER SUMMER RECREATION

FISHING AND BOATING

Catching the Big Ones

In the early years of the park, fish from Yellowstone Lake were a specialty at the various hotels, and because there was no limit on the take, up to 7,500 pounds of fish were caught each year. After commercial fishing was halted, park policy shifted to planting nonnative species. But by the 1970s, Yellowstone Lake had been devastated by overfishing, and new regulations were needed. Beginning in 1973, bait fishing was banned, Fishing Bridge was closed to anglers, and catch-and-release rules were put into place. Increased fish populations have been a boon for wildlife, especially grizzlies, bald eagles, and osprey. Because of these regulations, Yellowstone National Park has achieved an almost mythical status when it comes to fishing. Each year some half a million visitors spend time fishing in the park. The most commonly caught fish in Yellowstone are cutthroat, rainbow, brown, lake, and brook trout, along with mountain whitefish. Grayling are catch-and-release only and are found at only a few small lakes within the park, most notably Grebe Lake. Fishing regulations are quite complex and are described in a pamphlet available at park visitor centers or on the web at www.nps.gov/yell/fishing.htm.

The Yellowstone River is still considered one of the best places in the world to catch cutthroat trout, and the Madison River is a justifiably famous fly-fishing river with a wide range of conditions. Yellowstone Lake is where the lure anglers go to catch cutthroats and lake trout. Beginners may have luck in the Gallatin River, but they're less likely to do well in the Firehole River, where the fish are smart and wary. Peaceful Slough Creek in the northeast corner of Yellowstone is filled with fat rainbows and cutthroats, attracting fly-fishers from around the globe.

Several good books—available in local stores and visitor centers—provide tips on fishing Yellowstone waters. Try one of the following: *Yellowstone Fishes; Ecology, History, and Angling in the Park,* by John Varley and Paul Schullery (Mechanicsburg, PA: Stackpole Books); *Yellowstone Fishing Guide,* by Robert E. Charlton (Ketchum, ID: Lost River Press); or *Fishing Yellowstone,* by Richard Parks (Helena, MT: Falcon Publishing).

Trouble in Paradise

The 1990s were not at all kind to aquatic ecosystems in Yellowstone as a series of diseases and nonnative threats appeared. Per-

Fly-fishing for trout is a favorite activity in Yellowstone.

haps the greatest threat comes from lake trout (Mackinaw), a species that had been illegally planted either accidentally or intentionally in the 1980s or earlier. Lake trout were first discovered in Lake Yellowstone in 1994, and studies have since revealed that many thousands of them now inhabit the lake. A highly aggressive and long-lived species, lake trout feed upon and compete with the prized native cutthroat, threatening to devastate the population. (The average lake trout eats 80-90 cutthroat trout per year in Yellowstone.) Cutthroat spawn in the shallow waters of the lake's tributary streams, where they are caught by grizzly bears, bald eagles, and other animals. Lake trout spawn in deeper waters inaccessible to predators, and because of this, fewer cutthroat and more lake trout could have an impact on grizzlies and eagles. Eradication of the lake trout is virtually impossible, but the Park Service has used gill nets to catch thousands of them. There are no size or possession limits on lake trout caught in Yellowstone Lake or Heart Lake, but any lake trout you catch in these lakes must be kept and shown to rangers to help in determining the population size.

Another problem is threatening trout, especially rainbow trout, throughout the Rockies. Whirling disease, a devastating parasite-caused disease, has seriously hurt populations of rainbow trout in parts of the Madison River outside Yellowstone. The disease was discovered in Lake Yellowstone cutthroats in 1998, and there are fears that it could spread to other lakes and rivers in the park. It is spread in part when mud or water is brought in from contaminated areas on waders, boats, and boots. Be sure to clean up thoroughly before entering or leaving an area. Get details on whirling disease on the web at http://whirlingdisease.org.

As if the other problems weren't enough, the New Zealand mud snail was discovered in park waters in 1995. These miniscule snails (natives of New Zealand) are now in the Firehole, Gibbon, Madison, and Snake Rivers, where they can form dense colonies on aquatic plants and streambed rocks, crowding out native aquatic insects that are a food source for fish.

Fishing Regulations

In most parts of Yellowstone, the fishing season extends from Memorial Day weekend to the first Sunday of November, but check the regulations for specifics. Hayden Valley and certain other waters are entirely closed to fishing. Only artificial lures are allowed, lead is not allowed, and a catch-and-release policy (with exceptions) is in effect for cutthroat and rainbow trout and grayling. Some rivers, including the Madison River, the Firehole River, and the Gibbon River (downstream from Gibbon Falls) are open only to fly-fishing. Barbless hooks are preferable for catch-and-release fishing since they cause less damage and are easier to remove. Anglers don't need a state fishing license but must obtain a special Yellowstone National Park permit, available from visitor centers, ranger stations, and Hamilton Stores, plus fishing shops in surrounding towns. The adult fishing fee is $10 for a 10-day permit or $20 for a season permit. Kids ages 12-15 get permits for free, and younger children do not need a permit. Park visitor centers and ranger stations have copies of current fishing regulations.

Boating

Bridge Bay Marina runs hour-long scenic **boat tours** of Yellowstone Lake ($8.75 for adults, $4.75 for ages 2-11) several times a day in the summer, providing a fine introduction to the area. Also available at the marina are **guided fishing trips** ($52 an hour for up to six people) and **boat rentals** ($6 an hour for a 16-foot rowboat; $29 an hour for a motorboat).

The best Yellowstone Lake fishing is from boats rather than from the shoreline. If you're bringing your own boat or canoe to Yellowstone, pick up a park permit at the Lake Ranger Station or Grant Village Visitor Center. Boat slips are available at Bridge Bay Marina for $9 a night. All streams are closed to watercraft with the exception of the Lewis River Channel between Shoshone and Lewis Lakes. Motorboats are allowed only on Lewis Lake and parts of Yellowstone Lake.

Sea Kayaking

Several companies offer guided sea kayak trips on Yellowstone lakes. **Snake River Kayak & Canoe School,** tel. (307) 733-3127 or (800) 529-2501, www.snakeriverkayak.com, charges $145 per person/day for multiday sea kayak tours around Yellowstone Lake. **Jackson Hole Kayak School,** tel. (307) 733-2471 or (800) 733-2471, www.jhkayakschool.com, has day-tours of Lewis Lake for $130 per person. They also offer three-day tours of Yellowstone Lake for $605 per person, and three-day tours of Lewis and Shoshone Lakes for $550 per person. The overnight trip prices include transportation from Jackson, kayaking and camping gear, supplies, and all meals.

Each September, **O.A.R.S.,** tel. (209) 736-4677 or (800) 346-6277, www.oars.com, offers sea kayaking trips to the quiet south and southeast arms of Yellowstone Lake. Rates are $495 for three days, or $730 for five days. Tents and sleeping bags are available for rent, or bring your own.

BICYCLING

Cycling provides a unique way to see Yellowstone up close. Unfortunately, park roads tend to be narrow and have little or no shoulders, and some are filled with potholes, making for dangerous conditions. These problems are exacerbated early in the year by high snowbanks, so bikes are not allowed on certain roads. Call (307) 344-7381 for current road conditions. If you're planning a cycling trip through Yellowstone, be sure to wear a helmet and high-visibility clothing. A bike mirror also helps. If you want to avoid some of the hassles and don't mind spring conditions, visit the park between late March and the third Friday in April, when motorized vehicles are usually prohibited from entering the park (except for park administrative vehicles). During this period, cyclists are allowed to ride only on the stretch between the West Entrance and Mammoth Hot Springs; other roads are closed to cycling (they're being plowed). Fall is also a good time to ride, since traffic is much lighter than in the summer months. In the summer, the best times to ride are in the morning before traffic thickens or late in the afternoon before the light begins to fade and you become less visible to motorists.

Where to Ride

The best main park roads to ride (less traffic or better visibility and shoulders) are the following sections: Mammoth to Tower, Tower to Cooke City, Canyon to Lake, and Lake to Grant Village. Bikes are not allowed on backcountry trails or boardwalks inside Yellowstone. A number of relatively short but fun mountain-bike rides are available around the park, including the paved trail from Old Faithful to Morning Glory Pool (two miles), the partly paved trail to Lone Star Geyser in the Old Faithful area (two miles), Fountain Flat Dr. (six miles) to the vicinity of Midway Geyser Basin, the old Chittenden Rd. up Mt. Washburn (three miles each way, but gaining 1,400 feet on the way up), Bunsen Peak Rd. near Mammoth (six miles and steep in places), the Old Gardiner Rd. from Mammoth to Gardiner (five miles), and Blacktail Plateau Dr. (seven miles) east of Mammoth. Of these routes, cars are allowed only on the Old Gardiner Rd. and Blacktail Plateau Dr., but traffic is light on these two.

Bike Rentals and Tours

Unfortunately, there are no bike rentals inside Yellowstone or Gardiner, but they are available in the towns of West Yellowstone, Jackson, and Cody. **Backroads** has six-day cycling tours of

Yellowstone during the summer. These are offered as either camping trips ($1,198 per person including meals) or trips where you stay at local inns ($1,898 per person including meals). A sag wagon carries your gear, bike rentals are available, and you can choose your own pace. For details call (800) 462-2848 or visit the company's website at www.backroads.com. Contact the Park Service for a list of other permitted bicycle-tour operators.

OTHER RECREATION

Trail Rides and Cookouts

Horseback trail rides are available at Mammoth Hot Springs, Canyon Village, and Roosevelt Lodge and cost $20 for one hour, or $32 for a two-hour ride. Roosevelt also has **stagecoach rides** ($6 for adults or $5.25 for kids) several times a day in the summer, along with **Old West dinner cookouts.** Access to the latter is by either horseback ($50 for a two-hour ride and dinner) or in a wagon ($32 with dinner). Advance reservations are required for the cookouts; get tickets from any hotel or lodge in the park, or contact Amfac Parks & Resorts, tel. (307) 344-7311, www.travelyellowstone.com. A number of outfitters provide backcountry pack trips inside Yellowstone; get a list from Park Service visitor centers or on the web at www.nps.gov/yell, or call the park at (307) 344-7381.

Hot Springs Bathing

Many people are disappointed to discover that there are no places in Yellowstone where you can soak in the hot springs. Not only is it illegal, but it can also be dangerous, since temperatures often approach boiling and bathers can cause severe damage to these surprisingly fragile natural wonders. Legal bathing pools are found in cold-water streams that have hot springs feeding into them. You're not allowed to enter the source pool or stream itself. Families often stop for a swim in the Firehole River along Firehole Canyon Dr. near Madison. The Park Service doesn't encourage this, and there are no lifeguards, so parents need to watch children closely.

Thirty miles north of Yellowstone in the little burg of Pray, Montana, is **Chico Hot Springs.** If you're staying in the Mammoth Hot Springs area of Yellowstone, a side trip to Chico may be worthwhile. The large outdoor pool is a great place to relax, the gourmet restaurant serves some of the best dinners anywhere around, and the classic old hotel is a favorite. For more information, call (406) 333-4933 or (800) 468-9232, or visit the website: www.chicohotsprings.com.

WINTER IN YELLOWSTONE

Winter transforms Yellowstone into an extraordinarily beautiful place where the fires and brimstone of hell meet the bitter cold and snow of winter. The snow often averages four feet in depth but can exceed 10 feet on mountain passes. The snow is usually quite dry, although late in the season conditions deteriorate as temperatures rise. Early in the winter or after major storms, backcountry skiing can be very difficult due to the deep powder. Temperatures are generally in the 10-25° F range during the day, while nights frequently dip below zero. (The record is -66° F, recorded on Feb. 9, 1933.) Winds can make these temperatures feel even colder, so visitors should come prepared for extreme conditions.

The thermal basins are a real wintertime treat. Hot springs that are simply colorful pools in summer send up billows of steam in the winter, coating nearby trees with thick layers of ice and turning them into "ghost trees." The geysers put on astounding displays as boiling water meets frigid air; steam from Old Faithful can tower 1,000 feet into the air! Bison and elk gather around the hot springs, soaking up the heat and searching for dried grasses, and bald eagles are often seen flying over the heated waters of Firehole River. The bison are perhaps the most interesting to watch as they swing their enormous heads from side to side to shovel snow off the grass. Grand Canyon of the Yellowstone is another place transformed by the snow and cold. Although the water still flows, the falls are surrounded by tall cones of ice, and the canyon walls lie under deep snow. A good resource on winter access to Yellowstone is *Yellowstone Winter Guide* by Jeff Henry (Boulder, CO: Roberts Rinehart Publishers).

HISTORICAL WINTER USE

During Yellowstone's first 75 years as a park, winter visitation was almost unknown. The only people in the park were caretakers who spent months at a time with no contact with the world outside. This began to change in 1949, when snow-plane tours were first offered from the West Entrance. The planes skimmed over the surface and could only hold two people—the driver and a passenger—so visitation barely topped 30 people that winter. In 1955, snowcoaches were permitted to come into Yellowstone, and more than 500 people visited, though few stayed overnight.

Snowmobiling Changes Everything

The first snowmobilers arrived in 1963, when the machines were still a novelty. As snowmobiling became increasingly more popular, communities around Yellowstone benefited economically and began promoting the park as a winter wonderland. In the winter of 1971-72 the Park Service began encouraging the use by grooming the roads and opening Old Faithful Snow Lodge (it has since been replaced by a much nicer building of the same name). By the end of that winter, more than 25,000 people had visited. Since then, winter use has rocketed; today, upwards of 140,000 people visit Yellowstone each winter, and the park admits more snowmobiles than all other national parks combined. On a typical day 1,000 snowmobiles roar through the West Yellowstone gate, spewing choking blue smoke that sometimes creates localized pollution that sickens park employees working at entrance stations. (The two-cycle engines used in snowmobiles emit up to a third of their fuel as exhaust, and the haze comes from unburned lube oils.) While these numbers pale in comparison to summer visitation, some worry that snowmobilers and skiers could adversely affect the park's wildlife at a time when the animals are already under great stress.

In the heavy snow winter of 1996-97 large numbers of bison moved out of Yellowstone, some of them along the groomed snowmobile road out the west side of the park. Nearly 1,100 bison were killed that year as part of Montana's effort to protect cattle from brucellosis. The slaughter precipitated a lawsuit by the Fund for Animals that forced the Park Service to rethink its winter use policies. To address the effects of snowmobiles and other uses, in 1999 Yellowstone released a draft environmental impact statement in which the preferred alternative was to plow the road from West Yellowstone to Old Faithful all winter, allowing bus and shuttle van traffic only. Snowmobile use would still be allowed on most other road corridors in the park. The proposal has met with little support. A number of environmental groups are pushing for a complete closure to snowmobiling, while the snowmobile lobby is striving to keep the status quo. The verdict is far from in, but even if the Park Service's preferred option actually goes into effect it won't happen till the winter of 2001-02 at the earliest. In the meantime, snowmobiling will continue to reign supreme, particularly out of West Yellowstone. Get details from the Yellowstone National Park website, www.nps.gov/yell. For the environmentalists' take on winter use issues visit www.saveyellowstone.org; for the snowmobilers' version, head to www.mtsnow.org.

WINTER ROADS

Most of Yellowstone's roads officially close to cars on the Monday after the first Sunday in November and remain shut down all over except for the 56 miles between Mammoth and Cooke City. Roads don't open for cars again until sometime between mid-May and early June. The roads are groomed for snowmobiles and snowcoaches from mid-December to mid-March. The rest of the winter you'll only find skiers and park personnel on the roads. During the winter, the most popular (and crowded) times to visit Yellowstone are around Christmas and New Year's and over the Presidents' Day weekend in February. If you plan to arrive at these times, make lodging reservations six months to a year in advance. The rest of the winter, you should probably reserve at least three months ahead.

WINTER ACCOMMODATIONS

During the winter only two places offer lodging inside the park. **Mammoth Hot Springs Hotel,** on the north end of the park, is the only one accessible by road and has ski and snowshoe trails nearby, but the newly built **Old Faithful Snow Lodge and Cabins** puts you close to the geysers and many miles of ski trails. Each has a restaurant, lounge, gift shop, and rentals of skis and snowshoes. For a fee, Mammoth also offers Sunday breakfast buffets and special dinners and dancing, along with ice-skate and hot-tub rentals. In the winter months, both of these places have two-night discount packages that include lodging, a snowcoach trip, ski rentals, and other specials. For more information on winter lodging options in the park, contact Amfac, tel. (307) 344-7311, www.travelyellowstone.com.

Just south of Yellowstone in the Rockefeller Parkway is **Flagg Ranch Resort,** tel. (307) 543-2861 or (800) 443-2311, www.flaggranch.com, where you'll find newly built cabins that are open in the winter months. See the Grand Teton National Park chapter for specifics on Flagg Ranch. It's another 55 miles from Flagg Ranch to Jackson, a wintertime base for many Yellowstone visitors. On the east side of Yellowstone, lodging is available just outside the park at Pahaska Teepee and other lodges in the Wapiti Valley/North Fork area; see the Yellowstone Gateway Towns chapter for details. Other lodging places (described below) can be found just outside the park in the towns of West Yellowstone, Gardiner, Cooke City, and Silver Gate; these are also described in the Yellowstone Gateway Towns chapter.

The only wintertime camping place is Mammoth Campground, where temperatures are milder and the snow lighter.

WINTER SERVICES

Only the Mammoth and Old Faithful visitor centers are open during the winter season. Free ranger-led activities include evening programs at Mammoth and Old Faithful. Check the winter edition of *Yellowstone Today* for details, or find it on the web at www.nps.gov/yell.

Amfac Parks & Resorts, tel. (307) 344-7311, www.travelyellowstone.com, offers a variety of guided ski and snowmobile tours and provides wildlife bus or van tours; call for details. In addition, the Yellowstone Association Institute (see the special topic on Yellowstone Association) has a number of outstanding winter classes.

The Mammoth Clinic, tel. (307) 344-7965, is open weekdays (except Wednesday afternoons) in the winter for medical emergencies.

Supplies and Warming Huts

The Mammoth general store is open for groceries and supplies year-round, but only meals and gas are available at Old Faithful. Warming huts are located at Old Faithful, Madison Junction, Canyon, West Thumb, Fishing Bridge, and Indian Creek (south of Mammoth Hot Springs). All contain restrooms and snack machines (except Indian Creek and West Thumb), and all are open 24 hours (except for Old Faithful, where other facilities are available). The huts at Madison and Canyon also have snack bars selling hot chili or soup. Park rangers are often at the warming huts during the middle of the day.

SNOWCOACHES

The easiest and most enjoyable way to get into Yellowstone in the winter is on the ungainly snowcoaches—machines that look like something the Norwegian Army might have used during WW II. Most were actually built by a Canadian company, Bombidier. They can be noisy, and the windows fog up (hence the spray bottles of antifreeze). But despite their ancient condition and spartan interiors, these beasts still work well and can carry 10 passengers, gear (two suitcases per person), and skis. You will also see (or ride in) a number of other over-snow vehicles, including vans on tracks.

Snowcoach Tours

A variety of snowcoach tours are provided by Amfac Parks & Resorts, tel. (307) 344-7311, www.travelyellowstone.com. Rates to Old Faithful are $88 roundtrip from Flagg Ranch (where the plowing ends just south of Yellowstone), $79 roundtrip from West Yellowstone, and $84 roundtrip from Mammoth. They also provide tours from Mammoth to Canyon for $79 roundtrip, and Old Faithful to Canyon for $84 roundtrip. Snowcoach tours depart twice a week from Old Faithful for the Firehole River/Fountain Flats area (two and a half hours; $18 roundtrip) and West Thumb Geyser Basin (two

and a half hours; $18). All snowcoach tours and transportation are half price for kids ages 2-11 and free for toddlers. Three-hour winter wildlife bus tours to the Lamar Valley ($17-19) depart from Mammoth, providing a good opportunity to see wolves. See below for combination snowcoach and cross-country skiing trips. For any of these trips, be sure to make reservations well in advance.

During the winter, **Gray Line,** tel. (307) 733-4325 or (800) 443-6133, www.jacksonholenet.com/grayline, has daily bus runs from Jackson to Flagg Ranch for $35 one-way, arriving in time to meet the snowcoach departures for Yellowstone.

Based in West Yellowstone, **Yellowstone Alpen Guides,** 555 Yellowstone Ave., tel. (406) 646-9591 or (800) 858-3502, leads skiing tours inside the park, with access via one of their snowcoaches. All-day trips are $99 per person, and they also offer skier drop-offs and multinight trips. Their three-night trip includes two nights in West Yellowstone, a night at Old Faithful Snow Lodge, and two days of wildlife tours for $425 per person. Call for details, or visit them on the web at www.yellowstoneguides.com.

Also based in West Yellowstone, **Yellowstone Expeditions,** tel. (406) 646-9333 or (800) 728-9333, www.yellowstoneexpeditions.com, runs converted vans jacked up above tracks and skis. They offer day-tours from West Yellowstone to Old Faithful ($65 for adults or $45 for kids), as well as to the Canyon area ($75 for adults or $50 for kids) throughout the winter. Skiers can get dropped at Biscuit Basin and ski to Old Faithful where they meet the rest of the group for the return trip. In addition to day-trips, Yellowstone Expeditions has a remote base camp near Canyon that is perfect for those who want to really explore Yellowstone in winter. Guests stay in eight heated tent cabins, with two yurts providing a central kitchen and dining/social area. These overnight trips start at $1,220 for two people for three nights and four days, up to $2,000 for two people for seven nights and eight days. The price includes lodging, food, bedding, roundtrip transportation from West Yellowstone to the base camp near Canyon, and backcountry ski guides. Ski and snowshoe rentals are extra. Days are spent skiing or snowshoeing in the Canyon area or along trails around Hayden Valley, Norris, or Mt. Washburn. The camp sauna is perfect after a long day in the backcountry. This is the only overnight accommodation at the Canyon area in the winter. Recommended.

SKIING AND SNOWSHOEING

Cross-country skis and snowshoes provide the finest ways to see Yellowstone in the winter. Rent them from Old Faithful Snow Lodge or Mammoth Hot Springs Hotel. Both places also provide lessons and guided tours for groups or individuals. The towns surrounding Yellowstone also have shops that rent skis and snowshoes. The Old Faithful area is the center for skiing within Yellowstone, with trails circling the Upper Geyser Basin and leading to nearby sights. You'll find similar ski trails (marked but not groomed) in the Tower Fall, Canyon, Northeast, and Mammoth areas. Get free ski-trail maps at the visitor centers. Old Faithful Snow Lodge is open in the winter, providing an excellent base for day-trips into nearby areas or for a snowcoach tour of the park.

Skiers and snowshoers sometimes assume that they can't possibly cause problems for Yellowstone's wildlife, but studies show that elk and bison often move away from skiers, which forces the animals to expend energy they need to survive through the bitterly cold winters. It's best to stay on the trails and to keep from skiing into areas where elk or bison may be disturbed by your presence. For more on skiing and winter visitation in the park, see Jeff Henry's *Yellowstone Winter Guide* (Boulder, CO: Roberts Rinehart Publishers), or *Winter Tales and Trails: Skiing, Snowshoeing and Snowboarding in Idaho, the Grand Tetons and Yellowstone National Park* by Ron Watters (Pocatello, ID: Great Rift Press).

Skier and Snowshoe Shuttles

Amfac Parks & Resorts, tel. (307) 344-7311, www.travelyellowstone.com, operates **skier shuttles** ($10.50-11.50 roundtrip) from Mammoth eastward by van to Blacktail Plateau and Tower Junction, or southward by snowcoach to Golden Gate and Indian Creek. From these last two many folks choose to ski back to Mammoth, since it's mostly downhill. A similar snowcoach shuttle is available from Old Faithful to Fairy Falls Trailhead or the Continental Divide area for $9.50. In these last two trips you ski back to the Snow Lodge on your own; the Continental Divide run is eight miles long and primarily downhill.

Skiers will also appreciate the van service offered between Mammoth and Cooke City ($53 roundtrip) where you're given all day to ski into the beautiful Absaroka Mountains. In addition, Amfac has all-day Grand Canyon snowcoach-and-guided-ski tours that depart from Mammoth ($89 roundtrip) or Old Faithful ($92 roundtrip). Guided snowshoe tours (around $27 with snowshoes provided) are offered from Old Faithful and Mammoth twice a week; they last three hours and are a great way to explore the country. Besides these concessioner-run tours, park naturalists sometimes lead ski trips from Old Faithful to nearby sights. Stop by the visitor center for details.

Safety on Skis

Yellowstone's roads are heavily traveled by snowmobiles and snowcoaches, making for all sorts of potential conflicts. Be sure to keep to the right while skiing. Most trails are identified by orange metal markers on the trees. If you're planning a backcountry trip, pick up a use permit from one of the ranger stations. A thorough understanding of winter camping and survival is imperative before you head out on any overnight trip, and avalanche safety classes are a wise investment of your time.

Before heading into backcountry areas, get avalanche-safety information from the **Avalanche Advisory Hotline** in Bozeman, tel. (406) 587-6981, or on the web from www.gomontana.com/avalanche. The recording does not cover all of the park, but does include the Washburn Range and areas near Cooke City and West Yellowstone.

SNOWMOBILES

Winter snowmobile use in Yellowstone has risen rapidly in recent years, with almost three-quarters of winter visitors arriving aboard them. It's not uncommon to meet long lines of machines ripping down the roads at any time of the day, disrupting Yellowstone's pristine winter silence with their noise and choking blue smoke. Despite the fact that the five national forests surrounding Yellowstone have many hundreds of miles of groomed trails and thousands of square miles of terrain open to the machines, Yellowstone's 180 miles of roads have become the focus of this mechanized winter onslaught.

Practicalities

If you really *must* come into Yellowstone by snowmobile, please show a few courtesies and precautions. In particular, stay on the roads and stay well away from the bison and elk commonly found along or on the roads. This is a highly stressful time of the year for them already, without being harassed by a steady stream of machines. If they stop in the middle of the road, wait for them to move, don't try to make them move. Also, if skiers are on the road, slow down and give them a wide berth as you pass. The speed limit (45 mph) is enforced, and one of the most bizarre Yellowstone sights is a park ranger waiting in a speed trap with his radar gun, ready to catch speeding sleds. Snowmobilers can cut down on pollution from their machines by tuning their engines for high altitudes and using low smoke or biodegradable lubricants along with oxygenated fuels such as gasohol. If you're renting a machine, call around to find a company that uses these lubricants and fuel.

Snowmobiles are available for rent from all four sides of the park, with the majority of 'bilers coming in from West Yellowstone where prices are usually a bit lower. Expect to pay around $120 per day including clothing and helmet for a machine, or $130-180 for a guided tour. The machines can also be rented at Mammoth and Old Faithful inside the park. You'll need a valid driver's license to drive snowmobiles into Yellowstone. Contact chamber of commerce offices in West Yellowstone, Jackson, or Cody for a listing of snowmobile rental companies. You can purchase gas inside the park at Mammoth Hot Springs, Canyon, Fishing Bridge, and Old Faithful.

YELLOWSTONE PRACTICALITIES

THE BASICS

Entrance to Yellowstone costs $20 per vehicle, or $10 for individuals entering by bicycle, foot, or as a bus passenger. Motorcycles and snowmobiles are $15. The pass covers both Yellowstone and Grand Teton National Parks and is good for seven days. If you're planning to be here longer or to make additional visits, get an annual pass covering both parks for $40, or the Golden Eagle Passport—good for all national parks—for $50 a year. A Golden Age Passport for all national parks is available to anyone over 62 for a one-time fee of $10, and people with disabilities can get a free Golden Access Passport. Both of these also give you 50% reductions in most camping fees.

Upon entering the park, you'll receive a Yellowstone map and a copy of ***Yellowstone Today,*** a quarterly newspaper that describes facilities and services and provides camping, fishing, and backcountry information. This is the best source for up-to-date park information. It's also packed with enough warnings to scare off a platoon of Marines. Examples include cautions against falling trees, bathing in thermal pools (infections and/or amoebic meningitis), unpredictable wildlife, improper food storage, health problems from the altitude, steep roads, overexertion, and scalding water. And, oh yes, "swim at your own risk."

Planning a Yellowstone Vacation

If you're planning a trip to Yellowstone, call the park at (307) 344-7381 to request a copy of another free publication, ***Yellowstone Guide.*** It provides detailed up-to-date information on hiking and camping, fishing, services, road construction, safety issues, park highlights, and lots more.

Several print and online sources provide unofficial information on Yellowstone. One of the best private sources is the Lander-based ***Yellowstone Journal,*** tel. (307) 332-2323 or (800) 656-8762, www.yellowstonepark.com. The publication comes out five times a year and is sold in stores inside and around the park.

Visitor Centers

The Park Service maintains visitor centers in six different places: Mammoth Hot Springs, Norris, Old Faithful, Canyon, Fishing Bridge, and Grant Village. All of these sell maps and natural-history books covering the park and surrounding areas. You'll also find smaller information stations at Madison and West Thumb; hours and seasons are listed in **Touring Yellowstone** above. Get additional information from the Park Service website: www.nps.gov/yell.

Ranger-Naturalist Programs

Park naturalists offer slide shows, films, guided walks, kids' programs, campfire talks, and other activities at the campgrounds and visitor centers. These are always favorites of visitors, and on summer days you can choose from more than two dozen different Yellowstone activities. Get a complete listing in the *Yellowstone Today* paper you receive upon entering the park.

Evening slide programs are also offered in the winter months at Mammoth and Old Faithful.

Children in Yellowstone

Yellowstone is a major family destination in the summer months, and visiting the park has become something of a rite of passage for middle-class American families (along with thousands of European and Japanese families). Families will especially appreciate the woodsy campgrounds, the inexpensive but simple cabins, and the reasonable cafeteria meals that are available around the park. Most lodges and hotels have cribs for those traveling with infants. Of special interest to kids ages 5-12 is the **Junior Ranger Program,** in which children attend a nature program, hike a trail, and complete other activities. They're rewarded with an official Junior Ranger patch and are sworn in. It's always a big hit, but your kids may later try to arrest you if you get too close to an elk.

YELLOWSTONE ASSOCIATION

Founded in 1933, the nonprofit Yellowstone Association assists in educational, historical, and scientific programs. It publishes a number of natural history publications and provides funds to the Park Service to produce trail leaflets and park newspapers, along with the excellent *Yellowstone Science* magazine. The association also manages book sales at visitor centers, funds park exhibits and research, and otherwise assists the park in educating the public. It is probably best known for the **Yellowstone Association Institute,** which teaches many of its classes out of the historic Buffalo Ranch in Lamar Valley.

Instructors at the institute lead more than 100 different natural history and humanities classes in the summer months along with a number of others in the winter. Most of these last two to five days and typically cost $50-60 per day. Courses cover the spectrum from fly-fishing to horsepacking, and they provide a great way to learn about this wonderful wild place. Class size is small; most classes contain 10-15 students. Class participants typically stay at the Buffalo Ranch in comfortable log cabins ($15 per person per night) and cook meals in the shared kitchen.

Membership in the Yellowstone Association starts at $25 per year and is tax-deductible. Members get discounts on classes taught by the Yellowstone Association Institute and can sign up earlier than the general populace. Members also receive discounts on purchases of items sold by the Association and quarterly newsletters. For details, and a listing of books on the park, call the Yellowstone Association Institute at (307) 344-2294, or find it on the web at www.yellowstoneassociation.org.

Accessible Yellowstone

Disabled visitors to Yellowstone will find that the park is making a concerted effort to provide accessible facilities, though they also have a long way to go. Most of the major tourist areas have at least some paths that are paved (including at Old Faithful), and accessible accommodations can be found at Canyon, Grant Village, Old Faithful, and Lake. For details, call (307) 344-2018 to request a copy of the *Visitors Guide to Accessible Features in Yellowstone National Park,* or find the same information on the web at www.nps.gov/yell.

Supporting the Park

The **Yellowstone Association** is a nonprofit organization that assists with education, research, publishing, and book sales inside the park. The organization also teaches classes through the Yellowstone Association Institute; see the special topic on Yellowstone Association for details.

The **Yellowstone Park Foundation,** tel. (406) 586-6303, www.ypf.org, is another nonprofit group that works with the National Park Service by providing funds for projects and programs that would not be otherwise supported. All funding comes from individuals and corporations, not from the government. Contact the foundation for more details.

GETTING AROUND

By Car

Yellowstone's roads have long been a source of irritation to travelers. Much of the roadbed was built at the turn of the 20th century, when horses and carriages were the primary means of travel. Increasing traffic and larger vehicles contributed to the rapid deterioration of park roads, as did stretched-thin park maintenance budgets. By the early 1990s many miles of park roads were pockmarked with bone-jarring potholes. Yellowstone is now in the midst of a massive 20-year road reconstruction program, and each summer you'll find a different section undergoing rebuilding, so be ready for delays somewhere during your journey. Despite the ongoing work, you are certain to find several long stretches of bad—and sometimes unbelievably bad—roads. Check with the park for the latest on the road situation and this year's construction delays.

The speed limit on all park roads is a strictly enforced 45 mph, although during the summer you're not likely to approach this speed, since long lines of traffic form behind monstrous RVs. Gas stations are located at Old Faithful, Canyon Village, Mammoth Hot Springs, Fishing Bridge, Grant Village, and Tower Junction, while repair services are available at all of these except Mammoth Hot Springs and Tower Junction.

Most roads in Yellowstone close on the Monday after the first Sunday in November and usually open again by mid-May. Plowing begins in early March and the roads reopen in sections. The roads connecting Mammoth to West Yellowstone open first, and Dunraven Pass is plowed last. Note that spring storms may cause closures or restrictions on some park roads; get the latest from entrance stations or visitor centers. Only the road between Mammoth and Cooke City is kept plowed all winter long. The roads are groomed for snowmobiles (snow conditions permitting) by mid-December. If you're planning a trip early or late in the season, call the park for current road conditions; tel. (307) 344-7381 ext. 5, and then ext. 2.

Bus Tours

During the summer, most people come into Yellowstone in private cars or RVs, but there *are* other ways of getting around. For many people, a bus tour provides a quick overview of the park while leaving the driving to an expert. This is especially true for RVers who can park at Fishing Bridge RV Park and don't need to worry about driving on narrow park roads.

From mid-May to late September, **Amfac Parks & Resorts,** tel. (307) 344-7311, www.travelyellowstone.com, offers full-day bus tours from Canyon Lodge, Lake Hotel, Old Faithful Inn, Fishing Bridge RV Park, and Grant Village. Tours of either the upper or lower loops are $23-28 for adults or $12-15 for kids (free for children under age 12). A longer Grand Loop tour (not recommended unless you're into sensory overload and more than 10 hours of riding around) costs $33 for adults or $17 for kids. The Grand Loop tour is only available from Mammoth or Gardiner. Amfac also offers **Lamar Valley wildlife excursions** that originate from Canyon Lodge, Bridge Bay, Lake Yellowstone Hotel, or Fishing Bridge RV Park and cost $18-22 for adults or $9-11 for kids. These last three or four hours and provide a great opportunity to catch a glimpse of wolves. In addition, amateur photographers may want to join a professionally taught **Photo Safari** provided several times a week out of Old Faithful Inn and Lake Hotel; $32 for four hours.

Upper or lower loop tours ($35-38) are available out of West Yellowstone from **Buffalo Bus Lines,** tel. (406) 646-9564 or (800) 426-7669, www.yellowstonevacations.com, and **Gray Line,** tel. (406) 646-9374 or (800) 523-3102, www.grayline.com. Additional Yellowstone tours leave out of Cody ($50) aboard **Powder River Coach USA/Grub Steak Expeditions,** tel. (307) 527-6316 or (800) 527-6316, and from Jackson ($48) aboard **Gray Line,** tel. (307) 733-4325 or (800) 443-6133, www.jacksonholenet.com/grayline. Those without vehicles can use Gray Line tours for access to the parks; the bus can pick you up at many places along the road system, but you'll need to schedule this in advance. This is not a separate service from the Gray Line tours; instead the regular tour bus stops, meaning that you get a portion of the tour at the same time.

Based in Bozeman, **4x4 Stage,** tel. (406) 848-2224 or (800) 517-8243, offers by-request connections around the park and to surrounding communities. Call 24 hours ahead for reservations.

For a listing of licensed tour operators offering wildlife, natural history, and photography tours in the park, call the Park Service at (307) 344-7381 or check the official Yellowstone website: www.nps.gov/yell.

FOOD

You'll find restaurants at Mammoth Hot Springs, Lake Yellowstone Hotel, Old Faithful Inn, Old Faithful Snow Lodge, Grant Village, Roosevelt

Lodge, and Canyon Lodge. The enormous dining room at Old Faithful Inn is easily the best of these, and also here is a fine lounge backdropped by etched glass windows. Meals throughout the park are reasonably priced and quite good. Typical menus include steak, burgers, seafood, pasta, chicken, and vegetarian dishes. The chocolate pecan pie at Mammoth Hot Springs is noteworthy, as are the breakfast buffet and lunchtime soup-and-salad bar at Old Faithful Inn.

Dinner reservations are *required* in the summer at Old Faithful Inn (tel. 307-545-4999), Lake Yellowstone Hotel (tel. 307-242-3899), and Grant Village (tel. 307-242-3499), and they should be made before your arrival. For a dinner table at Old Faithful Inn, reserve a week ahead if you want a choice of seating times. Alternative dining options exist at all of these locations, but they generally aren't nearly as good. Run-of-the-mill cafeterias can be found at Lake Lodge, Old Faithful Lodge, and Canyon Lodge, and they'll provide box lunches. Not so bland are the Old West cookouts at Roosevelt Lodge, but you'll need to make advance reservations. In addition to these, you'll find smaller places selling burgers, sandwiches, espresso, and ice cream in Mammoth, Old Faithful, Lake, and Canyon. General stores carrying groceries (the choice may be limited) are available at Mammoth, Canyon, Old Faithful, Grant Village, and Lake; the biggest selection is at Canyon.

FACILITIES AND SERVICES

Shopping and Gifts

Nearly every road junction in Yellowstone has some sort of general store, gas station, gift shop, or other facility. **Hamilton Stores** are the most interesting, since they tend to be in rustic old log structures and staffed by friendly retired folks and fresh college kids. Here you'll find all the standard tourist supplies and paraphernalia, groceries, camping equipment, books, and fishing supplies. Old Faithful Lodge usually has an artist in residence working on a new piece (for sale, of course).

Money

You'll discover **ATMs** inside Old Faithful Inn, Lake Yellowstone Hotel, and Canyon Lodge. Both Cirrus- and Plus-system cards are accepted in these machines. Park lodges and hotels are able to provide **currency exchange** (US$50 max) for international travelers Mon.-Fri. 8 a.m.-5 p.m.

Medical Services

For medical emergencies, the park manages **Lake Hospital,** tel. (307) 242-7241, open late May to mid-September; also here are a clinic and pharmacy. The two other medical facilities in the park are: **Old Faithful Clinic,** tel. (307) 545-7325, open May through mid-October; and **Mammoth Hot Springs Clinic,** tel. (307) 344-7965, open year-round. Call 911 for emergencies.

Laundry and Showers

In the summer, find coin-operated washers and dryers at Fishing Bridge RV Park, Canyon Village

GREATER YELLOWSTONE COALITION

The primary environmental group involved with protecting Yellowstone and the surrounding public lands is the Greater Yellowstone Coalition, based in Bozeman, Montana. This private nonprofit organization is involved in all sorts of environmental issues within the 10-million-acre Greater Yellowstone Ecosystem, including such hot-button issues as logging, mining, winter use, and bison management. It represents some 8,000 members and publishes a quarterly newsletter detailing various issues. Annual membership costs $25; contact the organization by calling (406) 586-1593, or find it on the web at www.greateryellowstone.org.

Campground, and Grant Village Campground. Public showers are at Fishing Bridge RV Park, Lake Lodge, Old Faithful Lodge, Grant Village, and Canyon Village Campground.

Other Services

For a complete directory of the many other Yellowstone visitor services, see *Yellowstone Today,* which you receive upon entering the park. You can also download a copy off the web from the Yellowstone site, www.nps.gov/yell. **Post offices** are at Old Faithful, Lake Village, Canyon Village, and Grant Village. Check at any visitor center for a schedule of **church services.** Process film (prints only) at **film labs** at Old Faithful, Canyon, and Mammoth. At Mammoth and Old Faithful they will process your film in an hour or less. Trail rides, boat rentals, bus tours, and other services are detailed below.

WORKING IN YELLOWSTONE

During the summer months, both the National Park Service and private concessioners provide several thousand jobs in Yellowstone. These positions rarely last more than six months. You can find much more about Yellowstone jobs—both public and private—by heading to www.nps.gov/yell/technical/jobs on the web.

Park Service Jobs

Yellowstone National Park hires approximately 400 seasonal employees each year, but many more people apply, so the competition is stiff for new hires. Most seasonals start out as a park ranger (leading naturalist walks, working in entrance stations, etc.) or laborer (building trails, cleaning campgrounds and restrooms, etc.), but more specialized positions are available in the fields of natural resources or law enforcement. Seasonals typically make $6-11 per hour, with housing taken out of this. You must be a U.S. citizen to be employed by the Park Service. Although there is a national register for seasonal rangers, specific vacancy announcements come out when jobs are available, and you will need to apply within the specified time frame and meet all qualifications. For details and application forms, call Yellowstone's personnel office at (307) 344-2052, or head to www.usajobs.opm.gov for a listing of every federal job in the nation, or visit the Department of Interior's site: www.doi.gov/hrm/jobs.html. Get information on law enforcement or interpretive positions at www.sep.nps.gov.

Volunteer Positions

Unpaid volunteers do many jobs in Yellowstone and other national parks, and it isn't necessary to be a U.S. citizen to do volunteer work. The Park Service operates a **Volunteers in Parks** (VIP) program at Yellowstone that includes over 300 people each year. To join the ranks of the employed but unpaid, call the park's VIP coordinator at (307) 344-2039, or visit the volunteer website: www.nps.gov/volunteer.

A national nonprofit organization, the New Hampshire-based **Student Conservation Association** (SCA), tel. (603) 543-1700, www.sca-inc.org, provides workers for Yellowstone who do a wide range of activities, from trail maintenance to answering visitors' questions. Volunteers get most expenses paid. Contact SCA for details.

Concessioner Jobs

The park has two primary concessioners, Amfac Parks & Resorts and Hamilton Stores, along with the smaller Yellowstone Park Service Stations. Most employees of these companies are college students (who live in dorm-style accommodations), retired folks (who live in their RVs), or young people from other countries (including quite a few Eastern Europeans). Don't expect high pay; entry positions start at a little over $5 an hour, with meals and lodging deducted from this. A good overall website for concessioner jobs inside Yellowstone is www.coolworks.com/yell.htm.

Amfac Parks & Resorts is in charge of lodging, restaurants, bus tours, boat rentals, horse rides, and similar services within the park. They are also the largest park and resort management company in the nation, with concessioners in such diverse spots as Everglades National Park and Grand Canyon National Park. The company hires more than 3,000 people each summer in Yellowstone. For more info and an application, call (307) 344-5324, or head to their website: www.ynpjobs.com. It's best to apply early in the year (December and January) for summer jobs. The more competitive winter positions often go to those with previous work experience in the park.

Hamilton Stores is the oldest privately owned concession in the entire national park system, having been around since 1915. The company employs 1,000 folks annually. If you can start in April or May you're more likely to be hired. To receive an application form, call (800) 385-4979, or find details on the Internet at www.hamiltonstores.com/employment. You can contact the Hamilton Stores personnel department directly in the winter months (Nov.-March) at tel. (406) 587-2208, or in summer at tel. (406) 646-7325.

The third concessioner is **Yellowstone Park Service Stations,** the folks who pump Conoco gas and wash your windshield. Get hiring info by calling (406) 848-7333, or on the web at www.coolworks.com/ypss.

YELLOWSTONE GATEWAY TOWNS

Yellowstone National Park is most commonly entered via one of several Wyoming or Montana towns. From the south, people generally arrive from the energetic town of Jackson, detailed in an earlier chapter. Described below are four Montana towns that act as park gateways: West Yellowstone, which predictably enough is immediately west of Yellowstone; Gardiner, at the northwest gate just a few miles from Mammoth Hot Springs; and the twin towns of Cooke City and Silver Gate just beyond the Northeast Entrance to Yellowstone. Also described below are two Wyoming towns: Cody, which provides access through Wapiti Valley to Yellowstone's East Entrance, and the Wind River Valley town of Dubois on the east side of Togwotee Pass.

For points to the east and south—including the towns of Lander, Pinedale, Alpine, and Afton, see my *Wyoming Handbook.* Nearby towns in Montana, including Red Lodge, Bozeman, Billings, and Livingston, are fully covered in *Montana Handbook,* by W.C. McRae and Judy Jewell. See Don Root's *Idaho Handbook* for coverage of Island Park and Swan Valley, and the full scoop on the tater state. All three of these books are published by Avalon Travel Publishing (Emeryville, CA, www.moon.com).

WEST YELLOWSTONE

West Yellowstone, Montana, is the definitive Western tourist town. With a year-round population of only 1,000 (three times that in the summer) but more than 50 motels, it's pretty easy to see what makes the cash registers ring. The West Entrance gate—most popular of all Yellowstone entrances—lies just a couple hundred feet away. "West," as the town is known locally, isn't particularly attractive, and in the 1990s a major development added several corporate hotels and other ugly structures to an already crowded mix of restaurants, motels, T-shirt stores, and gift shops.

West Yellowstone may be decidedly middlebrow, but the surrounding land is anything but, with Gallatin (GAL-a-tin) National Forest lying north and west, Targhee National Forest just a few miles to the south, and Yellowstone National Park just a few feet to the east. It's just a couple of miles east from West Yellowstone to the Wyoming border, and the Idaho border lies only nine miles west. Hamilton Stores—one of the primary Yellowstone concessioners—has its summer offices in West Yellowstone.

WEST YELLOWSTONE AT A GLANCE

Elevation 6,650 feet

West Yellowstone Chamber of Commerce, 30 Yellowstone Ave., tel. (406) 646-7701, open daily, www.westyellowstonechamber.com

Gallatin National Forest Hebgen Lake Ranger District, just north of town on US Hwy. 191/287, tel. (406) 646-7369, www.fs.fed.us/r1/gallatin

West Yellowstone Central Reservations, tel. (406) 646-7077 or (888) 646-7077, www.yellowstone.reservations.net

COURTESY AISLINN RACE

entrance road to the park, circa 1898

HISTORY

In 1907, the Union Pacific Railroad completed laying tracks for its Oregon Short Line to the western border of Yellowstone. The following summer, Yellowstone Special trains began rolling in from Salt Lake City, dropping tourists for their stagecoach tours of the park. A small town—West Yellowstone—quickly developed on the margins of the park, providing lodging, meals, and tourist trinkets. After World War II, interest in rail travel dropped as more and more people came to Yellowstone by automobile. Although the last passengers stepped off the train in 1960, the Union Pacific's historic stone depot and neighboring buildings still stand; they now house a museum, library, police station, jail, medical clinic, and other offices.

The West Yellowstone area was rocked by a devastating magnitude-7.5 earthquake on August 17, 1959. One of the most powerful temblors ever recorded in the Lower 48 states, the quake cracked Hebgen Dam and caused a massive landslide (estimated at over 80 million tons of debris!) that caused a 20-foot-high tsunami and created Earthquake Lake. Twenty-eight people died, and the geysers and hot springs of Yellowstone were dramatically affected for years to come.

SIGHTS

Historical Sights

Museum of the Yellowstone, 124 Yellowstone Ave., tel. (406) 646-7814 or (800) 500-6923, is a stone-and-log structure from the railroad days. It's right along the main highway into the park. Entrance is $6 for adults; $5 for seniors, students, and kids; and $18 for families. Kids under eight get in free. The museum is open daily 8 a.m.-6 p.m. (until 10 p.m. in mid-summer) from mid-May to mid-Oct., and it also has a good collection of regional books for sale. Closed at other times of the year. Inside are exhibits on how the railroads helped establish Yellowstone National Park, the 1959 Hebgen Lake earthquake, the Yellowstone fires of 1988, "Old Snaggletooth" the grizzly (and other wildlife), mountain men, and the U.S. cavalry. Videos and movies about Yellowstone are shown in the theater. The Plains Indian collection includes artifacts rarely seen in museums today, including a Blackfeet medicine bundle and other sacred items. The grand old park bus parked out front was last used in 1959.

Right next door is another wonderful stone structure (built in 1925) that served until the late 1950s as an elegant Union Pacific Dining Lodge. The building has a spacious dining hall containing an enormous fireplace, a 45-foot-tall vaulted ceiling, and handmade light fixtures. Also worth a look-see is an **Oregon Short Line Railroad car** housed at the Holiday Inn Sunspree Resort, 315 Yellowstone Avenue. Built in 1903, the railroad cas has been beautifully restored with antiques.

Family-run **Eagle's Store,** on the corner of Canyon and Yellowstone, tel. (406) 646-9300, is definitely worth a stop. Built in the 1920s, this historic log building contains all the standard tourist knickknacks, along with quality Western clothing, jewelry, fishing tackle, and a delightful old-fashioned soda fountain in the summer months.

Not Officially a Zoo

In the early 1990s, a massive $50 million project covering 67 acres transformed (some might use the term decimated) the town of West Yellowstone. Included are a grizzly and wolf theme park, an IMAX theatre, three major hotels, cabins, a restaurant, fast-food joints, an RV park, and a post office. The centerpiece is the **Grizzly Discovery Center,** 201 S. Canyon St., home to eight Alaskan and Canadian grizzlies and 10 captive-born gray wolves. Not all the bears are visible at any given time, but visitors are bound to see at least one in the pseudo-natural habitat. The center is open daily all year 8:30 a.m.-8:30 p.m., with wildlife viewing until dusk. Entrance costs $7.50 for adults, $6.50 for seniors, $3 for ages 5-16, free for kids under five. This for-profit center attracts throngs of visitors and photographers who might otherwise never see a grizzly or wolf, and there's always a staff member out to answer any questions. It remains controversial, however. Scientists note that the bears here are genetically quite distinct from those in Yellowstone, and anyone who has spent time around grizzlies in the wild will be dismayed to see them in captivity, even in a facility less oppressive than traditional zoos. The folks at Grizzly Discovery Center counter that all these bears were either raised in captivity or were "problem" bears that would almost certainly have been killed had they not been moved here. In addition to the bears and wolves, the center has wildlife exhibits (including a walk-in bear den), bear safety tips (I recommend not entering bear dens), a 40-minute video on bears, plus the obligatory gift shop. Get more info about the center by calling (406) 646-7001 or (800) 257-2570, or visiting on the web at www.grizzlydiscoveryctr.com.

Yellowstone on the Big Screen

Directly in front of Grizzly Discovery Center is **Yellowstone IMAX Theatre,** tel. (406) 646-4100 or (888) 854-5862, where you can watch the big-budget production of *Yellowstone* on the 60- by 80-foot screen; other movies typically are on wolves and Alaska. The theatre is open daily 9 a.m.-9 p.m. May to mid-October, with reduced hours the rest of the year. Admission costs $7.50 for adults, $5.50 for ages 3-11, and free for younger children. The featured attraction is a 35-minute movie that presents Yellowstone history and geology complete with stirring music and a cast of dozens. If you haven't seen IMAX flicks before, hold onto your seat—lots of jaw-dropping scenes here. The movie packs in the crowds on summer days, but the film seems like a Disneylandish version of reality, ignoring many of the things you're likely to see in the park—such as burned forests, crowds of visitors, and potholed roads—and putting history into a pretty little box. Reality wasn't—and isn't—quite like this. Even more disconcerting is that this glorification of the park stands right next to the park. To me it symbolizes the make-a-buck attitude that holds Yellowstone up as an attraction while developing a massive complex on its very margin.

Rock and Roll

Evidence of the massive 1959 earthquake is still visible north of West Yellowstone along Hebgen Lake. The Forest Service has an **Earthquake Visitor Center;** get there by heading eight miles north on US Hwy. 191, and turning left on US Hwy. 287. Continue another 17 miles west to the center, open daily 8:30 a.m.-6 p.m. from Memorial Day to late September only.

ACCOMMODATIONS

Hostels

Budget travelers will be happy to discover the West Yellowstone International Hostel (not affiliated with AYH) in the historic **Madison Hotel,** 139 Yellowstone Ave., tel. (406) 646-7745 or (800) 838-7745, www.madisonhotel@wyellowstone.com/madisonhotel. Now on the National Register of Historic Places, the hotel has friendly owners and a delightfully rustic lobby crowded with deer and moose heads. Presidents Harding and Hoover stayed here, though it certainly wasn't a hostel at the time. Travelers today stay in comfortable bedrooms (three or four beds in each) that have been furnished with handmade lodgepole furniture. The classic hotel rooms are a delightful mix of old and new, providing the ambience of a place that has been here since 1912. No televisions or phones in the rooms, but they do have a small fridge for hostelers in the back. Rates are $18 per person in dorm rooms (three or four beds), or $27-52 d for a private hotel room. They also have standard motel accommodations behind the hotel for $49-79 d. Make hostel reservations a few days ahead in midsummer or get here before evening to be sure of a space in the dorms. It's open Memorial Day to early October only. Budget-Moderate.

The **Madison Winter Hostel** may or may not be in business when you read this. Housed in the log cabin directly behind the Madison Hotel, this is an inexpensive option for single folks in the winter months; beds are $20 per person. The facilities are rustic, but include a full kitchen, washer, and dryer. Call (406) 646-7100 for details. Inexpensive.

Motels

The proximity to Yellowstone makes the town of West Yellowstone, with more than 2,000 rooms available, an extremely popular stopping place for vacationers in both summer and winter. It is also a pricey place to stay; only a few places have rooms for less than $65 during the peak seasons. The streets are lined with more than three dozen motels, so I won't try to list all of them, but if you're a member of AAA, check its *TourBook,* which includes 20 of the better places. (Rates are usually lower for AAA members, too.) Be aware that during the summertime, everything in West Yellowstone fills up by early afternoon, so get there early or make advance bookings. Motels can even be full on weekends in late September. Reserve a room in March or April for the peak summer season. Add a 4% lodging tax to the rates listed below.

West Yellowstone Central Reservations, tel. (406) 646-7077 or (888) 646-7077, makes reservations for a dozen local motels and RV parks and can set up wintertime snowcoach tours and snowmobile rentals. Find it on the web at www.yellowstone.reservations.net.

Two recommended economy-end places (no phones in the rooms, however) are **Al's Westward Ho Motel,** 16 Boundary St., tel. (406) 646-7331 or (888) 646-7331, where rooms are $40-48 s or d (kitchenettes $3 more); and **Alpine Motel,** 120 Madison Ave., tel. (406) 646-7544, where rooms go for $45-53 s or d. Both of these are open May-Oct. only. Inexpensive.

For similarly priced lodging available all year, stay at **Lazy G Motel,** 123 Hayden, tel. (406) 646-7586, where the clean and cozy rooms cost $43-53 s or d. All contain fridges and phones; kitchenettes are $10 extra. Inexpensive.

Pony Express Motel, 4 Firehole Ave., tel. (406) 646-7644 or (800) 323-9708, www.yellowstonevacations.com, has a quiet location; $49 for one bed or $64 for two beds. A kitchenette is $75 for up to four people. Inexpensive-Moderate. **Golden West Motel,** 429 Madison Ave., tel. (406) 646-7778, www.wyellowstone.com/goldenwest, is a small motel with a dozen remodeled rooms costing $50 s or d. Open May to mid-October and January to mid-March. Inexpensive.

Three Bear Lodge, 217 Yellowstone Ave., tel. (406) 646-7353 or (800) 646-7353, is probably best known for its popular restaurant of the same name. The 74-room motel features contemporary-styled rooms, plus four indoor jacuzzis and an outdoor pool. Rates start at $73 s or d, up to $108 d for rooms with jetted tubs and $148 for full suites. Get more information by visiting the website: www.three-bear-lodge.com. Moderate-Premium.

Wagon Wheel Cabins and Campground, 408 Gibbon, tel. (406) 646-7872, www.w-yellowstone.com/wagonwheel, has a collection of 10 very attractive cabins, most containing full kitchens. The cabins are on large lots surrounded by trees, and each has a barbecue grill and picnic table. A one-bedroom unit starts at $75 d; the largest unit has three bedrooms and a fireplace, and sleeps six for $174. There's a three-night summertime minimum on the larger cabins, and a five-night minimum in winter. The cabins at Wagon Wheel fill early, so book well ahead. Moderate.

Hibernation Station, 212 Gray Wolf Ave., tel. (406) 646-4200 or (800) 580-3557, www.hibernationstation.com, is quite different from the more homey Wagon Wheel. Here you'll find 35 modern cabins—each a bit different inside—with handmade log furniture and down comforters. Some also contain kitchenettes. Rates start at $99 d for a cabin with a queen bed, or $169 for one that sleeps four and contains a queen-size bunk bed, fireplace, and kitchenette. Families will appreciate the large condo unit with room for eight, a full kitchen and dining area, fireplace and jetted tubs for $269. A big indoor jacuzzi is available for all guests. Moderate-Expensive.

You'll find very good accommodations at **Brandin' Iron Motel,** 201 Canyon St., tel. (406) 646-9411 or (800) 217-4613, www.brandin-iron.com. Rooms cost $80 s or $90 d, including fridges, a continental breakfast, and two jacuzzis. Expensive.

One of the nicer lodging places in West Yellowstone is **Stage Coach Inn,** filling an entire block at 209 Madison Ave., tel. (406) 646-7381 or (800) 842-2882, www.yellowstoneinn.com. Rooms go for $109-139 s or d and include access to a sauna and two jacuzzis. The hotel features an impressive Western-style lobby with fireplace, plus a restaurant, coffee shop, and heated underground parking. Premium.

Seven miles west of town, **Lionshead Super 8 Lodge,** tel. (406) 646-9584 or (800) 843-1991, has quality rooms, a country setting, plus a sauna and hot tub. Rooms are $90 s or d. It's very popular with the retirement crowd, who park RVs in the adjacent "campground." Expensive.

The motel chains have moved into West Yellowstone in a big way. One of the nicest of these new motels is **Comfort Inn,** 638 Madison Ave., tel. (406) 646-4212 or (888) 264-2466, www.w-yellowstone.com/comfortinn. The featured attraction here is the biggest indoor pool in town, but the motel also has a small exercise room, jacuzzi, and continental breakfast. Rates are $129 s or d in standard rooms, or $189 for six-person suites. Moderate-Premium.

Days Inn, 118 Electric St., tel. (406) 646-7656 or (800) 548-9551, www.wyellowstone.com/loomis, is another large and modern motel with standard rooms ($110 s or d), along with deluxe suites containing king beds and in-room jacuzzis ($155 d). The motel also has a hot tub, saunas, and a small indoor pool that features the star attraction: a 90-foot water slide. Premium-Luxury.

Best Western Desert Inn, 133 Canyon St., tel. (406) 646-7376 or (800) 528-1234, has an indoor pool and jacuzzi, and serves continental breakfast each morning. Prices fluctuate through the summer and may be higher on weekends and lower on weekdays, but expect to pay around $149 s or d. Premium-Luxury.

Several block-long lodging monstrosities have recently opened on the south side of town. Best of these is probably **Gray Wolf Inn & Suites,**

250 S. Canyon, tel. (406) 646-0000 or (800) 852-8602, www.graywolf-inn.com. The motel features a jacuzzi, sauna, and small indoor pool, plus a breakfast buffet. An added attraction—especially in the winter—is the heated underground parking garage. Rates are $139 s or d in standard rooms, or $189-289 for six-person suites that contain a living room and full kitchen. Premium-Luxury.

The most elaborate place in town is the ludicrously named **West Yellowstone Conference Hotel Holiday Inn Sunspree Resort,** 315 Yellowstone Ave., tel. (406) 646-7365 or (800) 646-7365, with spacious rooms, an indoor pool, exercise room, sauna, and jacuzzi. Standard rooms cost $125 d, two-room family suites are $179 and sleep six, and luxurious executive suites (king bed, jetted tub, and wet bar) run $200. Moderate-Premium.

Guest Houses

There are no B&Bs in West Yellowstone; the last one was driven out of business in 1999 after all the new chain motels flooded the local lodging market. Out in the country eight miles west of town, **Sportsman's High Vacation Rentals,** tel. (406) 646-7865, has six vacation homes and cabins for rent. These range from a luxurious carriage house (perfect for a romantic getaway) that sleeps four for $175 per night, up to a spacious two-story home with five bedrooms and five baths that sleeps eight for $310. All of these contain knotty pine interiors, country-style appointments, and full kitchens. A three-night minimum stay is required in the summer. Moderate-Expensive.

Local companies renting condos include: **Yellowstone Townhouses,** tel. (406) 646-9331; **Yellowstone Village Rental Condos** (near Hebgen Lake), tel. (406) 646-7335 or (800) 276-7335; and **Lodgepole Townhouse,** tel. (406) 646-9253. A three-night minimum stay is required for all of these.

CAMPING AND RV PARKS

Public Campgrounds

The nearest Park Service camping area is inside Yellowstone at **Madison Campground,** 14 miles east of West Yellowstone. The cost is $15, and it's open May to early November. Get here early since Madison fills quickly and doesn't take reservations. Gallatin National Forest has a number of campgrounds in the West Yellowstone area. Closest is **Baker's Hole Campground** ($10; open Memorial Day mid-Sept.) three miles north of West Yellowstone, but it is open for RVs and other hard-sided vehicles only because of bear problems. Tent campers will need to go north of town to **Hebgen Lake,** where five different tenting areas are strung westward along the lake; the closest is the **Lonesomehurst Campground** ($10; open Memorial Day to mid-Sept.), located 12 miles from West Yellowstone. No reservations are taken at any of these Forest Service sites.

The Forest Service maintains four public-use cabins ($25 a night for four people) in the country around West Yellowstone. Three of these are open year-round. The closest is **Basin Station Cabin,** approximately nine miles west of town. Get details on all four cabins by calling (406) 823-6961, or on the web at www.fs.fed.us/r1/gallatin/recreation.

RV Parks

West Yellowstone has six private campgrounds right in town, plus six more west or north of town. Most of the in-town places are just RV parking lots. Far nicer are two places with shady trees and quiet sites: **Rustic RV Campground,** 634 US Hwy. 20, tel. (406) 646-7387, www.w-yellowstone.com/rusticwagon, ($22 for tents or $32-34 for RVs); and **Wagon Wheel Cabins and Campground,** 408 Gibbon Ave., tel. (406) 646-7872, www.w-yellowstone.com/wagonwheel, ($20 for tents or $30-32 for RVs). Noncampers can shower at either of these for $5. Rustic is open mid-April to mid-October, and Wagon Wheel is open Memorial Day-September. **Canyon Street Laundromat,** 312 Canyon, tel. (406) 646-9733, also has hot showers.

The other in-town RV parks are **Brandin' Iron Inn,** 201 Canyon, tel. (406) 646-9411 or (800) 217-4613 (no tents, but it has a hot tub); **Hideaway RV Campground,** 310 Electric St., tel. (406) 646-9049; **Yellowstone Cabins & RV Park,** 504 US Hwy. 20 West, tel. (406) 646-9350; and **Yellowstone Grizzly RV Park,** 210 South Electric St., tel. (406) 646-4466. Two places are west of town on US Hwy. 20: **Yel-**

lowstone Park KOA, tel. (406) 646-7606 or (800) 562-7591; and **Lionshead Resort/Super 8 Motel,** tel. (406) 646-9584 or (800) 800-8000. The KOA has an outdoor pool. **Campfire Lodge Resort,** tel. (406) 646-7258, and **Yellowstone Holiday Resort,** tel. (406) 646-4242 or (800) 643-4227, both have RV campgrounds along Hebgen Lake north of West Yellowstone.

FOOD

West Yellowstone has quite a number of good eateries, but prices are generally higher than in Wyoming towns and the menu is plebeian. Expect to pay $10-20 for dinner entrées.

Breakfast and Lunch

For breakfast, run on over to **Running Bear Pancake House,** 538 Madison Ave., tel. (406) 646-7703, but be ready for a long wait in midsummer. Good for lunch, too; open 7 a.m.-2 p.m. only.

Get espressos and fresh baked goods—including monster cinnamon rolls—at **Nancy P's,** 29 Canyon St., tel. (406) 646-9737. Open summers only. Stop by **Freeheel & Wheel,** 40 Yellowstone Ave., tel. (406) 646-7744, for a latte or a light lunch and pizza by the slice. Another good espresso destination is **The Book Peddler,** 106 Canyon St., tel. (406) 646-9358 or (800) 253-2855, where you'll find several tables in the back for bagels and coffee. It's a good place to hang out on a cold winter day.

Ernie's Bighorn Deli, 406 Highway Ave., tel. (406) 646-9467, is the local doughnut shop in the morning and makes unbeatable sandwiches for lunch. They'll put together a big box lunch if you're heading into the park and want to leave the sandwiches to the experts.

American Eats

If you're searching for a down-home greasy spoon serving three meals a day, your hunt will end at **Old Town Cafe,** 18 Madison, tel. (406) 646-9633. Chicken fried steaks, biscuits and gravy, buffalo burgers, and hot open-faced sandwiches grace the menu, and pine paneling decorates the walls. Those who love '50s diners will appreciate the simple and filling meals here.

Pig out cheaply at tiny **Mountain Mike's Cafe,** 38 Canyon St., tel. (406) 646-9462, where they serve all-American faves: burgers, sandwiches, barbecued ribs, steak, and chicken, plus freshly baked cream pies for dessert.

Justifiably popular for both lunch and dinner, **Bullwinkles,** 19 Madison Ave. W, tel. (406) 646-7974, cranks out steaks, burgers, pork chops, salads, and homemade pastries. Big portions, too.

Pizza and Chinese

Pete's Rocky Mountain Pizza, 104 Canyon St., tel. (406) 646-7820, has the most creative local pizzas, plus Italian and even Mexican specialties. Free delivery is handy if you just want to eat a pizza in your motel room. **Gusher Pizza and Sandwich Shoppe,** Madison and Dunraven, tel. (406) 646-9050, is a family place with fast service, the best reubens in these parts, and tolerable pizzas (frozen crust, alas). Wednesday is all-you-can-eat spaghetti night. **Wild West Pizza,** 20 Madison Ave., tel. (406) 646-4400, has pizza by the slice or pie. **Chinatown,** 100 Madison Ave., tel. (406) 646-7088, serves surprisingly authentic Chinese meals.

Dinner

Three Bear Restaurant, 205 Yellowstone Ave., tel. (406) 646-7811, is a friendly place with an upmarket dinner menu of shrimp, halibut, trout, chicken, and steaks. It has the best salad-and-soup bar in town, and desserts are a specialty, particularly the famous apple brown betty. Open three meals a day, and entirely non-smoking.

Coachman Restaurant, downstairs in the Stage Coach Inn, 209 Madison Ave., tel. (406) 646-7381, serves three meals a day, including big traditional breakfasts (great omelets), along with steak, seafood, and pasta for dinner. It also features a salad bar and substantial wine list.

If gourmet meals are your goal, you're probably out of luck in pedestrian West Yellowstone. Best bet? Drive to Big Sky (57 miles north) for the acclaimed **Lone Mountain Ranch,** tel. (406) 995-4644 or (800) 514-4644, www.lmranch.com.

The most unusual local eatery is **Eino's Bar,** tel. (406) 646-9344, located nine miles north of town on US Hwy. 191. It's a fun cook-your-own steak, burger, and chicken place with a big indoor grill. Other accoutrements include fresh baked breads, a delicious potato dish, and salads.

Open for lunch and dinner year-round. The patio features a view across Hebgen Lake, and the bar has a big-screen TV and pool tables.

Groceries and Sweets

Market Place, 22 Madison Ave., tel. (406) 646-9600, and **Food Roundup Supermarket,** on the corner of Madison and Dunraven, tel. (406) 646-7501, are the local grocery stores. Market Place also contains a deli and bakery. For sweet treats, head to **Arrowleaf Ice Cream Parlor,** 29 Canyon St., tel. (406) 646-9776. In addition to shakes, banana splits, and waffle cones, Arrowleaf serves burgers, chili dogs, and surprisingly good homemade soups.

ENTERTAINMENT AND EVENTS

Entertainment

During the summer, **Playmill Theatre,** 124 Madison Ave., offers lighthearted comedies and musicals for the whole family. Get details at (406) 646-7757 or www.playmill.com. Watch flicks at **Bears Den Cinema,** 15 Electric St., tel. (406) 646-7777. In addition to the IMAX films described above, **Yellowstone IMAX Theatre,** tel. (406) 646-4100 or (888) 854-5862, shows Hollywood's latest efforts most evenings.

For live bands try **Stage Coach Inn,** 209 Madison Ave., tel. (406) 646-7381, or **Iron Horse Saloon,** inside the West Yellowstone Conference Hotel at 315 Yellowstone Ave., tel. (406) 646-7365. **Lionshead Super 8 Lodge,** seven miles west of town, tel. (406) 646-9584, has square dancing in the summer.

Events

On the second weekend of March the **Rendezvous Ski Race,** a nationally known Nordic ski race, attracts hundreds of participants. The following weekend brings a very different event, the **World Snowmobile Expo,** with races, demos, and other activities. There's a fun parade, live music, and a fireworks display on the **4th of July.** The **Yellowstone Rod Run** happens on the first full weekend of August, bringing vintage cars of all types; it is the oldest such event in the Pacific Northwest. **Burnt Hole Mountain Man Rendezvous** takes place the third weekend of August and includes arts and crafts, traditional games, tall tale competitions, and other old-time events.

RECREATION

Summer Recreation

Horseback trail rides and Western cookouts are available from **Parade Rest Guest Ranch,** seven miles north of town, tel. (406) 646-7217, and **Diamond P Ranch,** seven miles to the west, tel. (406) 646-7246. Several other ranches farther afield also offer horseback rides; contact the chamber of commerce for details.

The 30-km Rendezvous Trail System becomes mountain bike central when summer rolls around. It starts from the southern edge of town; get a map at the chamber of commerce. A small trail fee is charged. Rent mountain bikes from **Yellowstone Bicycles,** 132 Madison Ave., tel. (406) 646-7815; or **Freeheel & Wheel,** 40 Yellowstone Ave., tel. (406) 646-7744. Freeheel also rents bike trailers and baby joggers; ask about the free daily rides. Both shops have full repair facilities.

Yellowstone Rental & Sports, tel. (406) 646-9377 or (888) 646-9377, rents a wide range of outdoor gear, including tents, sleeping bags, cookstoves, fishing boats, canoes, mountain bikes, baby strollers and car seats, snowshoes, and even backhoes for those who want to dig things up a bit. It's located eight miles west of West Yellowstone along US Hwy. 20.

You'll find five different **fly-fishing shops** in town, a reflection of the sport's importance in the Yellowstone area: **Arrick's Fishing Flies,** 125 Madison Ave., tel. (406) 646-7290; **Bud Lilly's Trout Shop,** 39 Madison Ave., tel. (406) 646-7801 or (800) 854-9559; **Eagle's Tackle Shop,** 3 Canyon St., tel. (406) 646-7521; **Jacklin's Fly Shop,** 105 Yellowstone Ave., tel. (406) 646-7336; and **Madison River Outfitters,** 117 Canyon St., tel. (406) 646-9644. All of these offer guided fishing and equipment.

Three rafting companies run all-day and half-day whitewater trips down the Gallatin River approximately 50 miles north of West Yellowstone (near Big Sky). The rafting season is generally late May-Sept., and you'll pay around $80 for all day or $40 for a half-day trip. The companies are: **Geyser Whitewater Expeditions,** tel.

(406) 995-4989 or (800) 914-9031, www.raftmontana.com; **Montana Whitewater,** tel. (307) 763-4465 or (800) 799-4465, www.montanawhitewater.com; and **Yellowstone Raft Company,** tel. (406) 995-4613 or (800) 348-4376, www.yellowstoneraft.com. Yellowstone Raft Company also leads trips down the challenging Madison River northwest of West Yellowstone, and Geyser Whitewater has scenic float trips for those who'd rather relax.

Winter Recreation

West Yellowstone is infamous for its bitterly cold winters, when the thermometer can drop to 50 degrees below zero. Fortunately, it doesn't always stay there, and by March the days have often warmed to a balmy 20 degrees above. In November, West becomes a national center for cross-country skiers, with the U.S. Nordic and biathlon ski teams training here.

Two trail systems provide a wide variety of Nordic skiing conditions. The 30-km Rendezvous Trail system is groomed with both classical and skating tracks from early November through April; it takes off from the southern edge of town. The nine-km Riverside Trail begins on the east side of town and leads to the Madison River within Yellowstone National Park. This trail is partially groomed and provides a good opportunity to see bison, elk, and possibly moose; it's closed to skate skiing. You can also ski the snow-packed streets in winter. Find many more places for flat tracking or telemarking in adjacent Yellowstone National Park and the Gallatin and Targhee National Forests. Before heading out, get recorded avalanche safety information from the **Avalanche Advisory Hotline,** tel. (406) 587-6981, or on the web from www.gomontana.com/avalanche.

Rent skinny skis from **Bud Lilly's Trout Shop,** 39 Madison Ave., tel. (406) 646-7801 or (800) 854-9559, or **Freeheel & Wheel,** 40 Yellowstone Ave., tel. (406) 646-7744. Freeheel also rents snowshoes, as does **Yellowstone Rental & Sports,** eight miles west of town on US Hwy. 20, tel. (406) 646-9377 or (888) 646-9377.

Yellowstone Alpen Guides, 555 Yellowstone Ave., leads skiing tours inside Yellowstone, with access via one of its snowcoaches. All-day trips are $99 per person, and it also offers skier dropoffs and multi-night trips into the park. For details, call (406) 646-9591 or (800) 858-3502, or visit on the web at www.yellowstoneguides.com.

The closest downhill ski and snowboard area is the world-class **Big Sky Resort,** located 57 miles north of West Yellowstone. The resort features 15 lifts and more than 3,500 acres of terrain; call (800) 548-4486 for details, or visit its website, www.bigskyresort.com. You will find excellent cross-country trails at Lone Mountain Ranch near Big Sky.

The chamber of commerce trumpets West as the "snowmobile capital of the world," and each day between November and late March hundreds (and sometimes thousands) of 'bilers show up to roar through Yellowstone's West Entrance or across thousands of acres of adjacent Forest Service lands. On busy days long lines of snowmobiles belch blue smoke into the air while waiting to enter the park.

Nearly 20 different tour and snowmobile rental companies operate out of West Yellowstone. Rentals run around $85-150 per day depending upon the type of machine; guided Yellowstone tours are more expensive—around $180 per person per day. Hundreds more folks bring in their own "crotch rockets" to ride on park roads or national forest lands, and many local motels offer snowmobile/lodging packages. The West Yellowstone Chamber of Commerce, tel. (406) 646-7701, can provide current snow and trail conditions, a detailed map of local trails, and a listing of companies that rent snowmobiles.

A less polluting and quieter option is to take a snowcoach tour of Yellowstone from **Yellowstone Alpen Guides,** 555 Yellowstone Ave., tel. (406) 646-9591 or (800) 858-3502, www.yellowstoneguides.com; or **Yellowstone Expeditions,** tel. (406) 646-9333 or (800) 728-9333. Tours cost $65-99 per day, and both companies also have multi-night trips.

INFORMATION AND SERVICES

The **West Yellowstone Chamber of Commerce office** at 30 Yellowstone Ave., tel. (406) 646-7701, is open daily 8 a.m.-8 p.m. Memorial Day to Labor Day, and Mon.-Fri. 8 a.m.-5 p.m. the rest of the year. The office is staffed during the summer and winter months by Forest Service and Park Service employees who can provide info on the great outdoors. Find the chamber on the web at www.westyellowstonechamber.com. Another useful site is www.westyellowstone.com, maintained by Circumerro Publishing. Check your e-mail at **West Yellowstone Web Works,** 27 Geyser St., tel. (406) 646-7006, www.wyellowstone.com.

The **Hebgen Lake Ranger District Office** is just north of town on US Hwy. 191/287, tel. (406) 646-7369. Pick up maps of Gallatin National Forest (www.fs.fed.us/r1/gallatin) here, along with an interesting brochure on the Madison River Canyon Earthquake Area.

West Yellowstone's **post office** is at 209 Grizzly Ave., tel. (406) 646-7704. You'll find **ATMs** in several local banks, hotels, and other businesses.

Wash clothes at **Canyon Street Laundromat,** 312 Canyon St., tel. (406) 646-9733; **Econo-Mart Laundromat,** 307 Firehole Ave., tel. (406) 646-7887; or **Swan Cleaners & Laundromat,** 520 Madison Ave., tel. (406) 646-7892. Canyon Street Laundromat also has shower facilities.

Books

The Book Peddler, 106 Canyon St., tel. (406) 646-9358 or (800) 253-2855, is a large and attractive bookstore with many Montana, Wyoming, and Yellowstone titles. In back is a pleasant cafe selling espresso, bagels, and pastries. This is a great place to hang with the locals. **Bookworm Books,** 14 Canyon, tel. (406) 646-9736, is another good shop with both new and used titles including many first editions; it's open nightly until midnight all summer! The small local **library** is housed in the railroad's old stone dining lodge at 200 Yellowstone Ave., tel. (406) 646-9017.

TRANSPORTATION AND TOURS

Bus Service

Community Bus Service, tel. (406) 646-7600, provides bus service between West Yellowstone and Bozeman on Tuesdays and Thursdays in the summer, and Thursdays only the rest of the year. There is no charge for this community-sponsored service (!) but a $10 donation is requested. The bus stops in the chamber of commerce parking lot. **Greyhound Bus,** tel. (800) 231-2222, www.greyhound.com, has daily summer-only runs between Bozeman and Salt Lake City, with a stop in West Yellowstone in front of West Yellowstone Office Services at 132 Electric Street.

By Air

Sky West/Delta, tel. (406) 646-7351 or (800) 453-9417, has service to West Yellowstone airport (just north of town) from Salt Lake City in the summer months. Note that these only operate June-Sept.; the rest of the year the closest airport is in Bozeman or Jackson Hole. In the winter months **4x4 Stage,** tel. (406) 848-2224 or (800) 517-8243, provides shuttle vans between West Yellowstone and Bozeman airport for $57, with a minimum of four people. Although 4x4 Stage is based in Bozeman, it provides taxi service throughout the area, including into West Yellowstone year-round. Call 24 hours ahead for taxi reservations.

Car Rentals

Rental cars are available through **Budget** (at the airport), tel. (406) 646-7882 or (800) 527-0700; **Big Sky Car Rentals,** tel. (406) 646-9564 or (800) 426-7669, www.yellowstonevacations.com; and **Travelers Station Car Rentals** (summer only), tel. (406) 646-9332 or (800) 548-9551. Big Sky has the cheapest rates, starting around $35 a day for a compact car. By the way, West Yellowstone has some of the highest gas prices anywhere around; fill up before you get here!

Park Tours

Several companies offer all-day tours of Yellowstone from June through September. **Gray Line,** 633 Madison Ave., tel. (406) 646-9374 or (800) 523-3102, www.grayline.com, has daily "lower loop" park tours and "upper loop" tours three times a week for $38 plus park entrance fees. They also offer Quake Lake ($38) and Jackson Hole ($49) tours from West Yellowstone as well as several other regional tours. **Buffalo Bus Lines,** 429 Yellowstone Ave., tel. (406) 646-9564 or (800) 426-7669, www.yellowstonevacations.com, has narrated loop tours of Yellowstone for $35 per person (plus the park entrance fee). On odd days the tour circles the park's upper loop; on even days it takes you to sights along the lower loop road. 4x4 Stage (described above) leads all-day park tours in the summer for $50 per person.

Yellowstone Alpen Guides, 555 Yellowstone Ave., leads more personalized park tours, from day-trips to multi-day excursions. The company provides the naturalist guide, and you can choose to travel in either their van or your own car for getting around in the park. For details, call (406) 646-9591 or (800) 858-3502, or visit www.yellowstoneguides.com.

GARDINER

The little tourist town of Gardiner, Montana (pop. 800), lies barely outside the northwest entrance to Yellowstone, and three miles from the Wyoming line. The Yellowstone River slices right through town. Park headquarters at Mammoth Hot Springs is just five miles away, and the large warehouses of park concessioner Amfac Parks & Resorts dominate the vicinity. Gardiner is the only year-round entrance to Yellowstone, and the Absaroka-Beartooth Wilderness lies just north of here. The town sits at an elevation of 5,300 feet—some 900 feet lower than Mammoth—and has warm, dry summers and relatively mild winters.

Gardiner was founded in 1883 when the Northern Pacific Railroad extended a line to the edge of Yellowstone, making it the first major entryway into the park. A reporter of that era described Gardiner as having "200 hardy souls, with 6 restaurants, 1 billiard hall, 2 dance halls, 4 houses of ill-fame, 1 milk man and 21 saloons." Today, the most distinctive structure in town is the monumental stone park entryway—similar to France's Arc de Triomphe—which was for many years the primary entry point into Yellowstone. Built in 1903, **Roosevelt Arch** was dedicated by President Theodore Roosevelt, a man regarded by many as Yellowstone's patron saint. A tablet above the keystone is inscribed, "For the Benefit and Enjoyment of the People." (The arch was actually built to offset the park visitors' initial disappointment at finding the rather ordinary country in this part of Yellowstone!)

ACCOMMODATIONS

Gardiner has many lodging places, but be sure to reserve ahead in the summer; rooms may be hard to find even in mid-September. Rates plummet after (and before) the gold rush of seasonal tourists; $75 summertime rooms suddenly go for $30! Accommodations are listed below from least to most expensive. Add a 4% tax to these rates.

Motels and Cottages

Inexpensive-Moderate: Yellowstone River Motel, tel. (406) 848-7303 or (888) 797-4837, is open May-October. Economy rooms in the older

Roosevelt Arch in Gardiner, Montana, marks the northwest entrance to Yellowstone.

GARDINER AT A GLANCE

Elevation 5,260 feet

Gardiner Chamber of Commerce, on Park at 3rd, tel. (406) 848-7971, open Mon.-Sat. May-Sept., and Tues.-Thurs. the rest of the year, www.gardinerchamber.com

Gallatin National Forest Gardiner Ranger District, on the north side of town, tel. (406) 848-7375, www.fs.fed.us/r1/gallatin

building are $55 s or d, while rooms in the new addition run $75 s or d. A garden patio overlooks the river, and a family unit with kitchenette is also available.

Moderate: Jim Bridger Court, tel. (406) 848-7371 or (888) 858-7508, is a classic western place with clean and well-kept log cabins built in 1937. Rates are $60 d to $75 for four people; open mid-May to mid-October.

Originally built in the 1950s but updated with newer furnishings, **Hillcrest Cottages,** 200 Scott St., tel. (406) 848-7353 or (800) 970-7353, has 15 units, all with kitchenettes. Most have showers, but a few contain tubs. No phones. Rates are $60 s or $82 d; open May-November.

Riverside Cottages is a small place with four motel units ($69 s or d), plus four cottages ($89 d or $99 for four people) with full kitchens. Everything here has been recently refurbished, and guests will enjoy the deck out back that contains a hot tub overlooking the Yellowstone River. Get details by calling (406) 848-7719 or (877) 774-2836, or by visiting Riverside's website: www.riversidecottages.com.

Yellowstone Village Inn, tel. (406) 848-7417 or (800) 228-8158, has modern rooms for $69-79 s or d, including an indoor pool, sauna, and light breakfast.

The three-story **Motel 6,** tel. (406) 848-7520 or (800) 466-8356, has predictable rooms and a view of the parking lot. Summer rates are $70 s or $78 d.

Westernaire Motel, tel. (406) 848-7397 or (888) 273-0358, has clean rooms for $70 s or $75 d, but the furnishings are somewhat dated.

Expensive-Luxury: The modern **Best Western by Mammoth Hot Springs,** tel. (406) 848-7311 or (800) 829-9080, has an indoor pool, saunas, and a jacuzzi. Room rates are $84-94 s or d. **Super 8 Motel,** tel. (406) 848-7401 or (800) 800-8000, charges $89 s or d, including an indoor pool and continental breakfast.

Absaroka Lodge, tel. (406) 848-7414 or (800) 755-7414, is a modern motel with immaculate rooms for $90 s or d, and suites with kitchenettes that cost $100 s or d, or $110 for four people. All rooms have balconies overlooking the Yellowstone River.

Located out in the country five miles northwest of Gardiner, **Maiden Basin Inn** is a modern eight-room lodge with a variety of accommodations. Built by the owner/architect, the inn exudes country charm. Rooms start for $95 with two queens or a king bed, up to $185 for a two-bedroom townhouse with a full kitchen, living room, and loft. The latter sleeps seven people. All rooms have private decks where you can sit on a rocking chair with a view of Electric Peak inside Yellowstone. An outdoor hot tub is available, and a continental breakfast is served in the lobby. Maiden Basin Inn is open mid-May to mid-October. Get details at www.maidenbasininn.com, or by calling (406) 848-7080 or (800) 624-3364.

Comfort Inn, tel. (406) 848-7536 or (800) 228-5150, charges $129 s or d for contemporary rooms; suites and jacuzzi rooms are $169. A light breakfast is available in the lobby, and the motel has three indoor jacuzzis.

The most basic local accommodations are at **Gardiner Town Motel;** call (406) 848-7322 for rates.

Bed and Breakfasts

One of the nicest local lodging places is **Yellowstone Inn B&B,** tel. (406) 848-7000, consisting of a beautifully restored stone house (built in 1903) that has been furnished in a new-west style. The four guest rooms cost $74-94 d and have shared or private baths. Out back is a private cottage for $124 d. A full breakfast is served, and guests will enjoy the outdoor jacuzzi. Well-behaved kids are welcome. Find it on the web at www.westerntravel.com/ye. Moderate-Premium.

Also of note is **Yellowstone Suites B&B,** 506 4th St., another stone house that's nearly a century old. Features include Victorian antique furnishings, hardwood floors, a veranda, jacuzzi, and full breakfasts. The four guest rooms have shared or private baths and cost $59-98 s or d; one contains a kitchenette. Kids are welcome. Contact Yellowstone Suites at (406) 848-7937 or (800) 948-7937, or on the web at www.gomontana.com/ys.html. Moderate-Expensive.

Guest Houses

Arch House, tel. (406) 848-2205, is an historic rock home just two blocks from the arch entryway into Yellowstone. The two-bedroom guest house sleeps up to six and includes a full kitchen, bath, living room with stone fireplace, and dining room. The house rents for $125 d, plus $10 each for additional guests. The owners run Electric Peak Espresso next door, a good place to start your morning with a jolt of caffeine. Moderate-Premium.

Above the Rest Lodge has four modern and well-appointed cabins less than two miles north of Gardiner up Jardine Road. Smallest is a one-bedroom unit with a spiral staircase and full kitchen, which goes for $125 for four people. Largest is a spacious three-bedroom home that sleeps 10 people for $250 per night. All of these have full kitchens and decks facing Yellowstone. Get details at (406) 848-7747 or (800) 406-7748, www.ablodge.qpg.com. Inexpensive-Moderate.

Out of Town Lodging

Mountain Retreat, tel. (406) 848-7272 or (800) 727-0798, has a fully equipped two-bedroom house ($140 for up to five people), along with a two-bedroom cabin ($110 for four people). Both are out in the country 10 miles north of Gardiner; no TV or phones. Inexpensive-Moderate.

Slip and Slide Ranch, tel. (406) 848-7648, sits in the country 12 miles north of Gardiner. Bed and breakfast accommodations are available in the contemporary home, which has three guest rooms, two baths, and a private entrance. Rates are $65 d, including a full breakfast. The B&B rooms are available from mid-May to mid-September. If you really want to escape, the company also has a spacious and modern log lodge two and a half miles into the hills (4WD required). The lodge sleeps five for $150, or up to 12 for $200. A three-night minimum is required, and it is open mid-February to mid-October. The owners are outfitters, and they use this lodge for hunters in the fall and winter. Inexpensive-Moderate.

Besides lodging in Gardiner, a number of places are available in Paradise Valley, 20 miles to the north. A good one is **Dome Mountain Cabins and Guest Houses,** tel. (406) 333-4361 or (800) 313-4868, www.domemountainranch.com, which has B&B cabin accommodations for $75 d, and full-house rentals for $300-700 per night (the largest sleeps 12). Moderate-Premium.

Farther afield but worth a visit if you're heading north is **Chico Hot Springs,** located 30 miles north of Gardiner in Pray, Montana. This classic old hotel sits adjacent to a hot springs-fed pool ($4.75), and the restaurant is an attraction in its own right. Dinner reservations are required. Rooms in the main and lower lodge cost $45-107. They also have a variety of cabins and houses, all the way up to a five-bedroom log home that sleeps 20 for $315 per night. Call (406) 333-4933 or (800) 468-9232 for more information, or visit www.chicohotsprings.com. Horseback rides and fly-fishing are available in the summer, and the saloon swings to country tunes on Friday and Saturday nights year-round. Inexpensive-Expensive.

CAMPING

Public Campgrounds

Yellowstone National Park's **Mammoth Campground** is five miles up the hill at Mammoth Hot Springs and costs $12. The campground is open year-round, but it sits close to a busy road. No reservations. Closer—and more peaceful—is the small **Eagle Creek Campground** ($6; open mid-June through October), less than two miles northeast of Gardiner up the gravel road on the way to Jardine. This Gallatin National Forest campground is approximately 500 feet higher than Gardiner, and you will need to bring water from town or treat water from the creek here. Two other Forest Service campgrounds (free; open mid-June through October) are a few miles up Jardine Road.

RV Parks

Park RVs at **Rocky Mountain Campground,** tel. (406) 848-7251, for $23 ($18 for tents), open mid-May to mid-October. Showers for non-campers cost $4, and a public laundromat is on the site. Campsites are also available in crowded, along-the-river sites at **Yellowstone RV Park,** tel. (406) 848-7496, open May-Oct. on the northwest end of town. Rates are $22-28 for RVs, or $17 for tents.

FOOD

Bear Country Restaurant, tel. (406) 848-7188, has a popular breakfast buffet. **K Bar Club,** tel. (406) 848-9995, doesn't look like much either outside or inside, but the from-scratch pizzas are very good in this locals' hangout (not for kids since this is a bar). Families head to **Outlaw's Pizza** in the Outpost Mall on the northwest end of town, tel. (307) 848-7733, for standard pizzas, pasta, calzones, and a small salad bar.

Town Cafe, tel. (406) 848-7322, has sandwiches, burgers, and a big salad bar. Better food is upstairs in the Town Loft (summer only), where you can enjoy the vistas while you eat. Also downtown is **Sawtooth Deli,** tel. (406) 848-7600, with cold and hot subs, grilled sandwiches, soups, salads, and espresso. The covered deck is a favorite local hangout. Closed Nov.-April.

Yellowstone Mine Restaurant inside the Best Western on the northwest side of town, tel. (406) 848-7336, offers very good but overpriced meals, served in an old-timey mine atmosphere. Best steaks around. At **Corral Drive Inn,** tel. (406) 848-7627, Helen and her sons serve up the biggest, juiciest, and messiest (get a handful of napkins) hamburgers anywhere around.

Park Street Grill & Café, tel. (406) 848-7989, seems out of place in down-home Gardiner. Most of the menu isn't your standard Old West fare, though it does serve steaks and prime rib. Instead, it's Italian food with flair, including such delights as shrimp fra diavolo (large shrimp sautéed with garlic, peppers, and tomatoes and served over linguine), or penne arribiata (fiery peppers, macaroni, red pepper, garlic, and plum tomato sauce). Meals come with a big house salad, and the atmosphere is rustic elegance. Park Street Grill is open for dinners only ($8-14 entrées) but also has a lunchtime pizza-by-the-slice cafe next door. Open all year.

Shop for groceries, fresh baked goods, and deli items at **Food Farm,** tel. (406) 848-7524, on the northwest end of town.

EVENTS AND ENTERTAINMENT

The big annual event in town is the **Gardiner Rodeo,** which comes around the third weekend of June. The **Art in the Park** craft bazaar takes place in Arch Park on the first weekend of August. End summer with a blast at **Buffalo Days,** held the Friday before Labor Day, featuring an arts and crafts fair, live music and dancing, and plenty of barbecued buffalo, beef, and pork.

Look for live bands some weekends at the **Two Bit Saloon,** tel. (406) 848-7743.

RECREATION

River Rafting

During the summer, three rafting companies offer whitewater trips from Gardiner down the Yellowstone River. **Yellowstone Raft Company,** tel. (406) 848-7777 or (800) 858-7781, www.yellowstoneraft.com, has been running trips since 1978. Other good companies are **Montana Whitewater,** tel. (307) 763-4465 or (800) 799-4465, www.montanawhitewater.com; and **Wild West Rafting,** tel. (406) 848-2252 or (800) 862-0557, www.wildwestrafting.com.

The rapids in this stretch of the Yellowstone River are relatively gentle, in the Class II-III range, and the featured attractions are half-day eight-mile trips or all-day 17-mile trips. Expect to pay around $30 for adults, $20 for kids for three-hour trips, or $68 for adults, $48 for kids for a full-day voyage. Yellowstone Raft Company also has sit-on-top kayaks and guided fly-fishing trips, and Wild West offers scenic float trips in Paradise Valley north of Gardiner (same prices). In addition to the legit companies listed above, a number of two-bit operators also run whitewater trips each summer, but ask around to get an idea of their reputations before signing up.

More Outdoor Fun

Wilderness Connection, tel. (406) 848-7287, has horseback trips into Yellowstone. In winter, rent cross-country skis from **Park's Fly Shop,** tel. (406) 848-7314. No local companies rent mountain bikes, but if you bring your own there are a pair of fine biking options. The Old Gardiner

Road to Mammoth gains 900 feet in a distance of five miles and makes for a fun ride back down. Also worth a ride is the old road to Livingston, a gravel road that follows the west side of the Yellowstone River out of Gardiner. It starts near the arch and passes an interesting old cemetery with century-old graves a few miles up.

INFORMATION AND SERVICES

The **Gardiner Chamber of Commerce,** on Park St. at 3rd (near Bear Country Restaurant), tel. (406) 848-7971, has local info and is open Mon.-Sat. 9 a.m.-7 p.m. May-Sept.; and Tues.-Thurs. 10 a.m.-4 p.m. the rest of the year. Find it on the web at www.gardinerchamber.com. If the office is closed, check the bulletin board in the center of town.

The **Gardiner District Office** of Gallatin National Forest, tel. (406) 848-7375, www.fs.fed.us/r1/gallatin, has maps and info on the 930,584-acre **Absaroka-Beartooth Wilderness.** The portion around Gardiner is lower in elevation and covered with forests, while farther east are the alpine peaks of the Beartooth Mountains.

The **post office** is on the north end of town along US Hwy. 89, tel. (406) 848-7579. Get fast cash at the **ATM** inside the Exxon station just north of the river, or from the First Interstate Bank on the northwest end of town. Wash clothes at **Arch Laundrette,** just downhill from Cecil's Restaurant on Park Street.

Shopping

High Country Books and Gifts, on Park St. next to Cecil's Restaurant, tel. (406) 848-7707, has a choice of Western books, along with espresso coffee. **Yellowstone Gallery & Frameworks,** tel. (406) 848-7306, is an excellent place for quality pottery, jewelry, paintings, and photography. Also worth a look downtown is **Off the Wall Gallery,** tel. (406) 848-7775. **Flying Pig Pawn Shop,** tel. (406) 848-7510, has a variety of used outdoor gear for sale. Stop here for Internet access, too; open daily.

Transportation and Tours

Based in Bozeman, **4x4 Stage** offers taxi service throughout the Yellowstone area, including into Gardiner. Call 24 hours ahead for reservations, tel. (406) 848-2224 or (800) 517-8243.

From mid-May through September, **Amfac Parks & Resorts,** tel. (307) 344-7311, www.travelyellowstone.com, operates full-day bus tours of Yellowstone out of Gardiner. Rates are $33 for adults, $17 for ages 12-16, and free for kids under 12 (park entrance fees are extra). These are a bit grueling, since you leave at 8:30 a.m. and don't get back until 6:15 p.m.

COOKE CITY AND SILVER GATE

Shortly after you exit Yellowstone's northeast corner along US Hwy. 212, the road widens slightly as it passes through two settlements: Silver Gate and the larger Cooke City, Montana. The towns are just three miles apart and almost within spitting distance of the Wyoming line. The area code—406—is larger than the combined population of both settlements! Although they depend upon tourism, these quiet, homespun places lack the hustle and bustle of West Yellowstone and have a more authentic feel. No leash laws here, so you're likely to see dogs sleeping on the sidewalks or wandering lazily down the middle of the road. Most establishments are built of log, befitting the mining heritage of this area. Silver Gate even has a building code that requires all structures to be of log or rustic architecture—it's the only municipality in the country with such a code. Pilot and Index Peaks are the prominent rocky spires visible along the highway east of Cooke City. Dramatic Amphitheater Peak juts out just south of Silver Gate.

During the winter, the road is plowed all the way from Gardiner through the northern part of Yellowstone and into Cooke City, making this a popular staging area for snowmobilers and skiers heading into the Beartooth Mountains. East of Cooke City, the Beartooth Highway across 10,947-foot Beartooth Pass is closed by the first of November (often earlier) and doesn't open again until late May.

HISTORY

The town of Cooke City was first called Shoo-Fly, but the name was changed in honor of Jay Cooke, Jr., a promoter of the Northern Pacific Railroad. The promised railroad never materialized, but the name stuck. Cooke City had its start in 1882 when the boundaries of the Crow Reservation were shifted to the east, opening this area to mining. A small gold rush ensued, and by the following summer, Cooke City had grown to several hundred miners, along with two smelters, two sawmills, and a cluster of businesses. At its peak, the town was also home to 13 saloons. As with many 19th-century mining towns, the population of Cooke City had wild swings, with up to 1,000 people at one time, but just 20 souls a few years later. The isolation, modest gold and silver strikes, and high transportation costs (no railroad was ever built into the settlement) kept mining from ever really booming here. Today less than a hundred people live in Cooke City year-round, but the population triples with the arrival of summer residents.

The town of Silver Gate has a briefer history. The land here was first homesteaded in the 1890s, but the town didn't appear until 1932 when John Taylor and J.J. White founded it as a haven for summer residents looking for a home close to Yellowstone. Only a handful of folks live here in the winter, but that population swells to 100 or so when the long days of summer return.

The country around Silver Gate and Cooke City was torched in the Storm Creek Fire of 1988, leaving charred hills just a couple hundred feet to the north and prompting alterations in the road signs to read "Cooked City." Today, tourism is the ticket to ride for both Cooke City and Silver Gate. In summer the towns are crowded with folks en route to (or from) Yellowstone. Both Soda Butte Lodge and Miners Saloon in Cooke City have one-armed bandits, video poker, and keno gambling. In the fall, hunters head into the surrounding mountains, and when the snow flies, the snowmobiles come out of hibernation.

COOKE CITY AND SILVER GATE AT A GLANCE

Elevation 7,550 feet

Cooke City-Silver Gate Chamber of Commerce, tel. (406) 838-2495 (summers) or (406) 838-2272 (winters), open daily June through mid-September

SIGHTS

It's hard to miss the red **Cooke City General Store,** tel. (406) 838-2234, one of the oldest buildings in the area. Built in 1886, this classic country market sells groceries, quality T-shirts, and gifts that include Indian jewelry and imported items from all over the globe. Open summers only. Across the street is another summertime place that is well worth a look, **Blain Gallery,** tel. (406) 939-2474. The gallery features original watercolors by Mary Blain, along with pottery, baskets, and beautiful photographs taken in the northeast corner of Yellowstone.

ACCOMMODATIONS

Cooke City and Silver Gate have quite a few old-fashioned cabins that provide a delightful Old West feeling. As with other towns surrounding Yellowstone, advance reservations are always a good idea in mid-summer. Add a 4% lodging tax to the rates below; they're arranged by price, with the least expensive first.

Cooke City Lodging

Budget: The least-expensive and funkiest local lodging option is **Yellowstone Yurt Hostel,** tel. (406) 838-2349, where you'll pay just $12 per person for space in a cozy yurt. Nothing at all fancy here, just six bunk beds in a Tibetan-style yurt heated by a woodstove. It's a few steps to the shower, toilet, and full kitchen. You should bring a sleeping bag, though a couple of old cotton ones are here. Reservations are always a good idea, but necessary in the winter months. There's no hot water in winter. The yurt is available mid-May through September and mid-November through March.

Inexpensive-Moderate: Three miles east of Cooke City, **Big Moose Resort,** tel. (406) 838-2393, has simple cabins, gas, and a small store that are open June-October. The seven cabins contain older furnishings and private baths; two include kitchenettes. Rates start at $45 d, up to $65 for a four-person cabin with kitchenette.

Also three miles east of Cooke City—and right across the road—**Big Bear Lodge** is primarily a fishing lodge but offers nightly accommodations throughout the year. Guests stay in six older but well-kept log cabins, each of which has two double beds. Rates are $55-65 d, and breakfasts are available in the main lodge ($6 per person). The lodge is a popular destination for fly-fishing enthusiasts who come here on three- to six-night package trips that include lodging, meals, and guided horseback rides and fishing. Anglers head into backcountry areas inside Yellowstone, returning each evening to the lodge. In the winter months, Big Bear is a popular overnight rest for skiers and snowmobilers. Get details at www.sandersbigbearlodge.com, or by calling (406) 838-2267.

You'll find spacious, clean, and comfortable rooms and cabins at **High Country Motel,** tel. (406) 838-2272. Rates are $45-57 s or d. Cabins with kitchenettes are $10 extra. Open all year, and recommended.

Antler's Log Cabins, tel. (406) 838-2432, www.yellowstonenationalpark.com, charges $45-70 for a range of cabins, some that include kitchens and lofts. It's open late May-Oct., and Christmas-March.

Alpine Motel, tel. (406) 838-2262, is open all year and has rooms for $55-65 s or d.

Bearclaw Cabins, tel. (406) 838-2336, has cabin rentals (these sleep four) for $58. No kitchenettes, but it is open year-round.

Moderate: Hoosier's Motel, tel. (406) 838-2241, has good rooms for $60 s or d and is open mid-May to mid-October.

Edelweiss Cabins, tel. (406) 838-2304, charges $60 d or $70 for four people for its six cabins, three of which are new. Most of these contain kitchenettes, and one is handicapped-accessible; open year-round.

With 32 guest rooms on two floors, **Soda Butte Lodge,** tel. (406) 838-2251 or (800) 527-6462, is the largest lodging in the area. The hotel contains one of the best restaurants in these parts (Prospector), and guests are welcome to use the small indoor pool and jacuzzi. Rooms with king beds cost $65; those with two queens are $70, and suites that sleep six are $100. Open year-round.

Owned by Beartooth Plateau Outfitters (next door), **Beartooth Plateau Lodge,** tel. (406) 445-2293 or (800) 253-8545, is a comfortable log home with space for six people. It has a full kitchen and bath with clawfoot tub and is open June-September. The house rents for $85 d, plus $10 for each additional person.

Elk Horn Lodge has reasonably priced motel rooms and two cabins. Call (406) 838-2332 for rates. Open all year.

Silver Gate Lodging

Range Riders Lodge, tel. (406) 838-2359, is a classic two-story log building with a bar downstairs and upstairs rooms. Rates are reasonable, $36 d or $46 for four people, but there are no phones or TVs, and the bath is a few steps down the hall. The original 1930s furniture is still here. Range Riders is open Memorial Day to Labor Day. Budget-Inexpensive.

Silver Gate Cabins features eight attractive log cabins from the 1930s that contain kitchenettes and cost $55 s or d. Also here are five motel units for $39-45 s or d. Outside, you'll find barbecue grills, volleyball, and horseshoes, and a playground for kids. It's open May 15-Sept.; call (406) 838-2371 in the summer or (307) 733-3774 in winter. Inexpensive.

Whispering Pines Lodge, tel. (406) 838-2228 or (888) 777-7554, is one of the nicest and quietest places in the area, and it has a clientele that returns year after year. The nine log cabins are off the main road and along a pretty creek. They're rustic outside but modern within; some have kitchenettes. Rates are $45-50 for up to four people. Open Memorial Day through September. Budget-Inexpensive.

Grizzly Lodge is a century-old log building right on the river and close to the Yellowstone border. Guests stay in a variety of rooms (including kitchenette rooms, two-bedroom units, and rooms with lofts) inside the lodge for $45-75. Also here are a sauna and hot tub. Open Memorial Day through October, and Christmas-New Year's. Get details at tel. (406) 838-2219 or www.yellowstonenationalpark.com. Inexpensive-Moderate.

Pine Edge Cabins, tel. (406) 838-2222, has 11 attractive cabins that were originally built in the 1930s. All contain kitchenettes and cost $55 d or $65 for four people. The **Yellowstone Ecosystems Studies Science Center** (www.yellowstone.org) is based here, and the cabins are also used by researchers studying coyotes and water quality in the region. Lectures and educational programs are offered. Because of the researchers, some cabins may not be available to the public. Open year-round. Budget-Inexpensive.

CAMPING AND PUBLIC CABINS

Heading east from Cooke City, you'll find five National Forest campgrounds ($8; open June-Sept.) within 10 miles of town. Closest is **Soda Butte Campground,** just a half mile from town; another mile to the east is **Colter Campground.** Two Forest Service cabins are also in the area. The four-person **Round Lake Cabin** ($20; open July to mid-September and mid-December through April) is four and a half miles north of Cooke City up a jeep/hiking trail. The **Kersey Lake Cabin** ($30; open July to mid-September and mid-December to mid-April) is four miles east of Cooke City. This lakeside cabin has a rowboat and sleeps 10 people, but access requires a one-and-a-half-mile hike. For details on Gallatin National Forest campgrounds and cabins, call (406) 848-7375, or visit www.fs.fed.us/r1/gallatin/recreation.

Park RVs ($15) in Silver Gate at **Whispering Pines Lodge,** tel. (406) 838-2228, or in Cooke City at **Wilson's RV Ranch,** tel. (406) 838-2322. Both are open only in the summer months. Showers are available from Soda Butte Inn for $5.

FOOD

Located inside Cooke City's Soda Butte Lodge, **Prospector Restaurant,** tel. (406) 838-2251, is well-known for prime rib cooked to perfection, but it's also open for breakfast and lunch. Also here is the **Ore House Saloon,** with sports on the TV and video poker and keno machines to take your money. Everything at Soda Butte is open year-round.

The Bistro in Cooke City, tel. (406) 838-2160, is open three meals a day, serving standard American fare the first two of these. Dinner is when this authentic French bistro shines, with quality steaks, veal, lamb, and fish.

Beartooth Cafe in Cooke City, tel. (406) 838-2475, has good sandwiches for lunch, all-American dinners (outstanding free-range Angus beef steaks), and more than 100 kinds of beer. Open summers only. Also in Cooke City, **Pine Tree Cafe,** tel. (406) 838-2213, has reasonable prices, three meals a day, and locally famous milk shakes. This is the best breakfast place in town.

In peaceful Silver Gate, **Log Cabin Cafe,** tel. (406) 838-2367, is a consistent favorite, with well-prepared trout, pasta, barbecued beef, steaks, and homemade soups. Open in the summer and fall only.

Cooke City's **Miner's Saloon,** tel. (406) 838-2214, is a classic Old West bar where the stools are filled with locals and tourists. Pull the handles on the one-armed bandits, or try a game of pool, foosball, or air hockey. The menu includes surprisingly good pizzas and burgers.

Cooke City Bike Shack, tel. (406) 838-2412, cranks out espresso coffees and is a good place to meet locals. For groceries and supplies, head to Cooke City General Store (described under Sights above) or **Summit Provisions** in Silver Gate, tel. (406) 838-2248.

ENTERTAINMENT AND EVENTS

Drinking is the most popular recreational activity in these parts, but **Range Riders Lodge** in Silver Gate, tel. (406) 838-2359, also has live country music on Friday and Saturday nights all summer long. Find a small-town parade and chili cookoff during **Pig Daze** in mid-June. The twin towns have a fun firemen's picnic and 4th of July fireworks, and Silver Gate is home to **Shakespeare in the Parks** in the middle of summer.

RECREATION

Absaroka-Beartooth Wilderness

Yellowstone is less than four miles away and is the obvious site for recreation in the Cooke City-Silver Gate area during the summer months. The Absaroka-Beartooth Wilderness is accessible from Cooke City or various other points to the east along the gorgeous Beartooth Highway. One of the more unusual sights is **Grasshopper Glacier,** eight miles north of Cooke City and 4,000 feet higher. The glacier contains the remains of a swarm of locusts that was apparently caught in a snowstorm while flying over the mountains. (See Beartooth Mountains under Shoshone National Forest below for more on this wilderness.)

Three local outfitters lead summertime horseback rides, pack trips into the Absaroka-Beartooth Wilderness, and guided fly-fishing expeditions: **Beartooth Plateau Outfitters,** tel. (406) 445-2328 or (800) 253-8545; **Castle Creek Outfitters,** tel. (406) 838-2301; and **Skyline Guide Service,** tel. (406) 838-2380. **Greater Yellowstone Flyfishers,** tel. (406) 838-2468, is a full-service fly shop, with lures and other supplies, guided fishing trips, and equipment rentals.

Other Outdoor Fun

Cooke City Bike Shack, tel. (406) 838-2412, is a hub for the outdoor adventure crowd. Owner Bill Blackford is a jack of all trades, running the espresso machine one minute, and fixing a bike or selling outdoor gear the next. In the winter he guides telemarking and cross-country ski trips, costing $125 per person for an all-day trek. Backcountry skiers and snowboarders who want to head out on their own can catch a five-mile snowmobile ride ($15 per person) into the high country at Daisy Pass, gaining 2,100 feet of elevation along the way. This makes for a great day of skiing, not to mention a fun downhill run back to town.

Reminders of the mining era abound in the surrounding country, but not all of it is benign. Reclamation ponds catch toxic runoff from some of these old mines. The visitor center has a brochure showing Jeep/ATV/mountain biking trails through the mining country just north of Cooke City.

Cooke City has become a hub for winter sports. Pick up a map of groomed cross-country ski trails and snowmobile routes at the visitor center. Snowmobile rentals are available from **Cooke City Exxon,** tel. (406) 838-2244, and **Yamaha Shop,** tel. (406) 838-2231 or (800) 527-6462. The local snowmobile club grooms approximately 60 miles of trails in the surrounding mountains; call (406) 838-2272 for information. Be sure to also call the **Avalanche Advisory Hotline** at (406) 838-2341 for the latest on backcountry conditions before heading out, or check its website: www.gomontana.com/avalanche.

INFORMATION AND SERVICES

The **Cooke City-Silver Gate Chamber of Commerce** has a small summertime visitor center in Cooke City that is generally open daily 10 a.m.-5 p.m. from June through mid-September. Call (406) 838-2495 (summers) or (406) 838-2272 (winters). When the visitor center is closed, drop by High Country Motel for local information.

Despite its remoteness, you'll discover three (count-em) **ATMs** in Cooke City. The town also has a laundromat.

Based in Bozeman, **4x4 Stage** offers by-request connections around the park and to surrounding communities, including to Cooke City and Silver Gate. Call 24 hours ahead for reservations, tel. (406) 848-2224 or (800) 517-8243.

SHOSHONE NATIONAL FOREST

Shoshone National Forest encompasses over 2.4 million acres and extends along a 180-mile strip from the Montana border to the Wind River Mountains. Sagebrush dominates at the lowest elevations, but as you climb, lodgepole, Douglas-fir, Engelmann spruce, and subalpine fir cover the slopes. Above 10,000 feet, the land opens into alpine vegetation and barren rocky peaks. The **Shoshone National Forest Supervisor's Office** is in Cody at 808 Meadowlark Ave., tel. (307) 527-6241, www.fs.fed.us/r2/shoshone. Get information and forest maps ($4) at the supervisor's office or from ranger stations in Cody, Dubois, and Lander.

HISTORY

Shoshone is America's oldest national forest. On March 30, 1891, President Benjamin Harrison signed a proclamation creating Yellowstone Park Timberland Reserve adjacent to Yellowstone National Park. At first this title meant very little, but in 1902 President Theodore Roosevelt appointed rancher and artist A.A. Anderson to control grazing and logging and catch poachers. His strong management almost got him lynched. Three years later under Gifford Pinchot, the forest reserves were transferred to the Department of Agriculture and renamed national forests. The land was renamed Shoshone National Forest in 1908.

RECREATION

More than half of Shoshone National Forest lies inside wilderness boundaries; the Absaroka-Beartooth, North Absaroka, and Washakie Wilderness Areas cover much of the country east of Yellowstone National Park, while the Wind River Mountains contain the Fitzpatrick and Popo Agie Wildernesses (see my *Wyoming Handbook* for more on these areas). Part of the credit for the surprising expanse of wilderness areas on the Shoshone National Forest goes to Buffalo Bill Cody. By bringing people into the area to hunt, fish, and explore, he helped create what one author called a "dude's forest." In addition, the Buffalo Bill Dam (which he vociferously supported) prevented logs from being sent down the North Fork of the Shoshone River and thus made logging less prevalent.

Hiking Trails

Over 1,500 miles of trails offer hiking and horseback access to much of this country. Shoshone has more than 50 campgrounds, most costing $9 per night during the summer. Once the water has been shut off for the winter months (generally Oct.-April), you can camp free but have to haul out your own trash. Space is generally available even at the busiest times of year. In addition, free dispersed camping is possible at undeveloped sites throughout the forest, with the exception of heavily traveled US Hwy. 14/16/20, where you must be a half mile off the road.

Though they are uncommon, black bears roam throughout the forest, and grizzlies are found within the northern portions, including the North Absaroka and Washakie Wilderness Areas. Be sure to take the necessary bear precautions anywhere in the backcountry. Bears also sometimes wander into campgrounds along US Hwy. 14/16/20 near Yellowstone National Park. Actually, you are more likely to encounter mosquitoes, deer flies, and horse flies in midsummer, so be sure to bring insect repellent.

BEARTOOTH MOUNTAINS

Spectacular Beartooth Highway (US Hwy. 212) connects Cooke City and Yellowstone National Park with the historic mining town of Red Lodge, Montana. Along the way, it passes through the Beartooth Mountains on a road built by the Civilian Conservation Corps (CCC) in the 1930s. Some have called this the most scenic route in America. If you like alpine country, towering rocky spires, and a landscaped dotted with small lakes and scraggly trees, you're going to love this drive. A small corner (23,750 acres out of a total of 945,334 acres) of

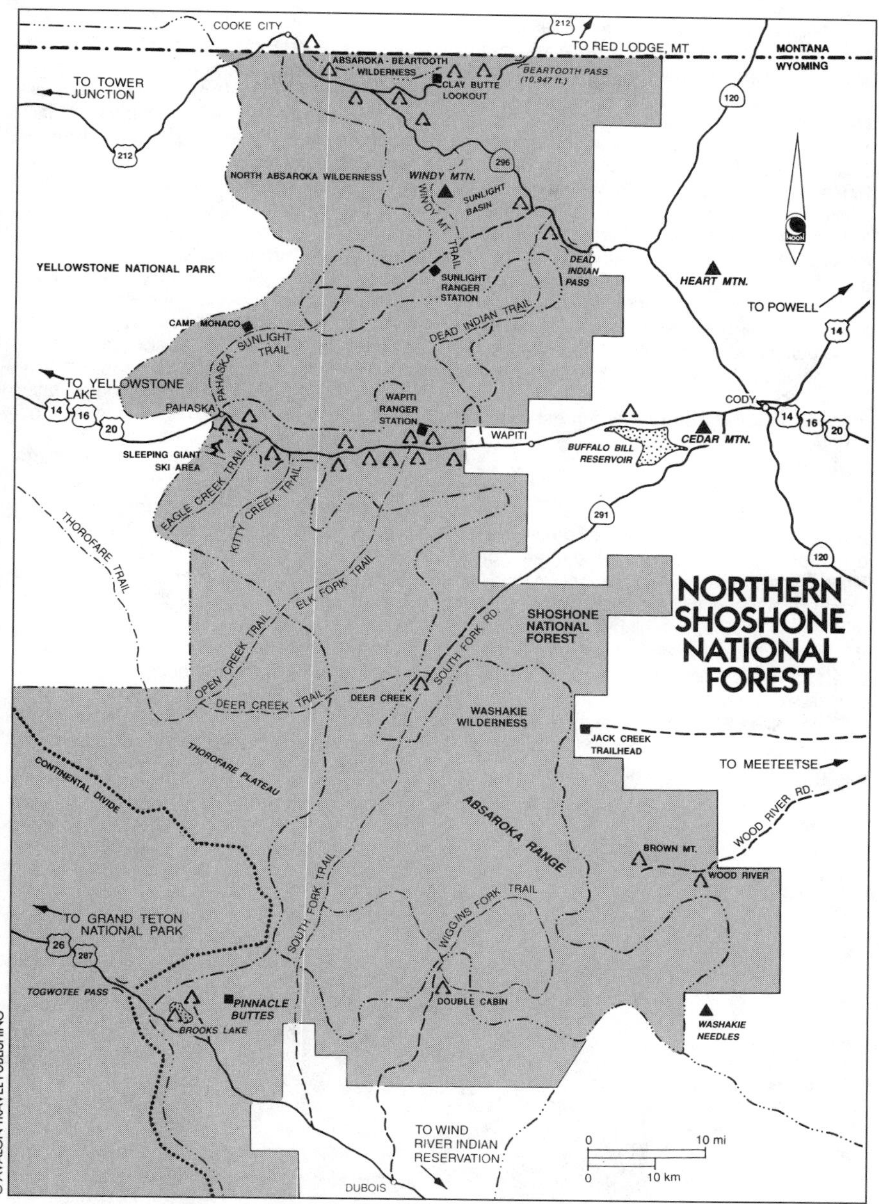
COOKE CITY
TO RED LODGE, MT
MONTANA
WYOMING
ABSAROKA - BEARTOOTH WILDERNESS
BEARTOOTH PASS (10,947 ft.)
CLAY BUTTE LOOKOUT
TO TOWER JUNCTION
212
120
296
NORTH ABSAROKA WILDERNESS
WINDY MTN.
WINDY MT TRAIL
SUNLIGHT BASIN
DEAD INDIAN PASS
YELLOWSTONE NATIONAL PARK
SUNLIGHT RANGER STATION
HEART MTN.
TO POWELL
CAMP MONACO
PAHASKA - SUNLIGHT TRAIL
DEAD INDIAN TRAIL
14
TO YELLOWSTONE LAKE
PAHASKA
WAPITI RANGER STATION
CODY
16
20
WAPITI
CEDAR MTN.
BUFFALO BILL RESERVOIR
SLEEPING GIANT SKI AREA
EAGLE CREEK TRAIL
KITTY CREEK TRAIL
291
THOROFARE TRAIL
ELK FORK TRAIL
SOUTH FORK RD.
NORTHERN SHOSHONE NATIONAL FOREST
SHOSHONE NATIONAL FOREST
OPEN CREEK TRAIL
DEER CREEK TRAIL
DEER CREEK
WASHAKIE WILDERNESS
JACK CREEK TRAILHEAD
TO MEETEETSE
THOROFARE PLATEAU
CONTINENTAL DIVIDE
ABSAROKA RANGE
WOOD RIVER RD.
BROWN MT.
WOOD RIVER
SOUTH FORK TRAIL
WIGGINS FORK TRAIL
TO GRAND TETON NATIONAL PARK
26
287
TOGWOTEE PASS
PINNACLE BUTTES
DOUBLE CABIN
BROOKS LAKE
WASHAKIE NEEDLES
TO WIND RIVER INDIAN RESERVATION
DUBOIS
0
10 mi
0
10 km
MOON

the Absaroka-Beartooth Wilderness lies in Wyoming just north of the highway—the rest is right across the Montana border.

Over the Top

A national scenic byway, Beartooth Highway sails across a high plateau and then over the twin summits of **Beartooth Pass:** the east summit is 10,936 feet, and a short distance farther is the west summit at 10,947 feet. A scenic overlook at west summit provides views of the Absarokas to the south and west, the Beartooths to the north, and Bighorn Basin to the east. Majestic rock faces rise in all directions, the most obvious being Beartooth Mountain (its sharp point resembles the tooth of a bear), Pilot Peak, and Index Peak. This is the highest highway pass in Wyoming and one of the highest in North America.

As the road enters Montana, it passes Beartooth Mountain and begins a rapid elevator ride down folded ribbon curves into the resort town of Red Lodge. On top, keep your eyes open for moose, mule deer, mountain goats, bighorn sheep, marmots, and pikas. Be ready for strange weather at this elevation, including snow at any time of year. The highway is closed with the first heavy snowfall (generally in September) and doesn't open until June. The flowers don't really get going until mid-July.

Twin Lakes Ski Area sits near the Wyoming-Montana border and provides Olympic ski training for high school age kids in June and July. South of the summit is the appropriately named Top-of-the-World Store (see below), and another mile or so south is the turnoff to an old fire lookout tower at **Clay Butte,** where you'll discover horizon-to-horizon views of the surrounding countryside. A narrow gravel road climbs three miles to the tower, at an elevation of 9,811 feet. The small visitor center here is staffed July to mid-September.

Camping and Supplies

There are four developed campgrounds (all $9; open July-Labor Day) along this stretch of US Hwy. 212, and more once you drop into Montana. **Beartooth Lake** and **Island Lake** campgrounds border alpine lakes. In addition, dispersed camping is allowed at no charge once you get off the main roads. Grizzlies inhabit this country, so be sure to store your food safely.

Top of the World Store, tel. (307) 899-2482 or (307) 587-9043, sits along the highway between the two Forest Service campgrounds and is a popular stopping point for cyclists and other travelers over the pass. The general store has a limited selection of food and gifts, plus gas pumps, three motel rooms ($30 d), and a handful of RV spaces ($10). The store and motel generally open in July (when the snow is mostly gone) and close in mid-October.

Hiking

The open country at this elevation is dotted with whitebark pines and Engelmann spruce, and

Sitting atop Wyoming's highest mountain pass, Top of the World Store is a popular stop for supplies.

delivers marvelous cross-country hiking opportunities. Anglers should bring a fishing pole to take a few casts for the brook, cutthroat, and rainbow trout in the alpine lakes. Two major trail systems are found in the High Lakes area.

The **Beartooth High Lakes Trail**—actually a series of trails—connects Island Lake, Beartooth Lake, Beauty Lake, and many smaller alpine ponds and puddles. A good place to start is from the boat ramp at Island Lake; see topographic maps for specific routes. This is a very popular late-summer area for day-hiking or for access to the Beartooth Wilderness. Be sure to bring a compass, topo map, and warm clothes before heading out on a day-hike—the weather can close in very quickly at this elevation, and afternoon thunderstorms are frequent. Always be aware of lightning activity when hiking in this exposed country.

Beartooth Loop National Recreation Trail is just two miles east of Beartooth Pass. This 15-mile loop traverses alpine tundra and passes several lakes and a century-old log stockade of unknown origin.

NORTH ABSAROKA WILDERNESS

The 350,488-acre North Absaroka Wilderness is one of the lesser-known wild places in Wyoming. It abuts Yellowstone National Park to the west and is bordered by the Sunlight Basin and Beartooth Highways to the north and US Hwy. 14/16/20 to the south. North Absaroka Wilderness is primarily used by hunters who arrive on horseback. The few hikers here tend to be quite experienced with backcountry travel and willing to tolerate the lack of trail signs and the steep and frequently washed-out paths. Much of the wilderness is relatively inaccessible, and snow may be present on passes until mid-July. Ask at the ranger stations for current trail conditions, and be sure to get topographic maps before heading out. Large populations of grizzly and black bears, bighorn sheep, moose, and elk are found in the Absaroka Mountains, and golden eagles are a common sight. The tough landscape is of volcanic origin, and the topsoil erodes easily, turning mountain creeks into churning rivers of mud after heavy summer rainstorms.

Hikes

The enormous 1988 Clover-Mist Fire that began in Yellowstone burned through a large portion of the North Absaroka Wilderness, but the land is recovering as young trees and other plants become established. Some areas were also replanted following the fire. Many hikers begin from trailheads near the Crandall Ranger Station along the Chief Joseph Scenic Highway. The **North Crandall Trail** is the most popular, a 16-mile hike up the North Fork of Crandall Creek. It is primarily used by horsepackers and offers great views of Hurricane Mesa along the way. Another popular wilderness path is **Pahaska-Sunlight Trail,** an 18-mile trek that begins at Pahaska Campground on US Hwy. 14/16/20 and heads north through historic Camp Monaco to Sunlight Basin.

SUNLIGHT BASIN

The **Chief Joseph Scenic Highway** (State Hwy. 296) is a 46-mile route through a magnificent Wyoming landscape. Popularly known as Sunlight Basin Road, it is paved and most of it remains open year-round, providing access for backcountry skiers and snowmobilers to the beautiful Beartooth Pass area. (An eight-mile portion between Cooke City, Montana, and Pilot Creek, Wyoming, is not plowed in the winter. It typically opens by early May.) Chief Joseph Highway begins 17 miles north of Cody off State Hwy. 120, with Heart Mountain prominent to the southeast, and climbs sharply up from the dry east side, passing a brilliant red butte en route to **Dead Indian Pass,** named for an incident during an 1878 fight between Bannocks and the U.S. Army. After the battle, Crow scouts found a wounded old Bannock warrior here. They killed and scalped him, burying the body under a pile of rocks. Other tales claim that the name came from the body of an Indian propped up as a ruse to trick the Army during Chief Joseph's attempted escape to Canada in 1877. Chief Joseph *did* lead the Nez Percé through this country, avoiding the cavalry by heading up Clarks Fork Canyon, a route the Army had considered impassable. An overlook on top of Dead Indian Pass provides a panoramic vista of the rugged mountains and valleys below. The river forms

The bridge spanning Sunlight Creek is the highest in Wyoming—300 feet above the water.

a boundary between the volcanic Absarokas to the south and the granitic Beartooth Mountains to the north.

Indians weren't the only ones killed in this era. In 1870, two miners, Marvin Crandall and T. Dougherty headed into the Upper Clarks Fork following reports of gold in the area. When they failed to meet up with other miners, a search party was sent out. The searchers were themselves attacked by Indians who stole their horse. They later found the bodies of Crandall and Dougherty scalped and decapitated, with their heads atop mining picks. In a perverse bit of humor, tin cups sat in front of each skull and the right hand of each man held a spoon. The men had apparently been killed while eating and left as a warning against further white exploration of the area.

West of the overlook, the road switchbacks down hairpin turns into remote and beautiful Sunlight Basin. The name came about in the 1840s. Fur trappers worked this area for beaver and discovered a place flooded with light, but it was so remote that "the only thing that can get into this valley most of the year is sunlight." Today it is considerably more accessible, but still just as beautiful. A gravel side road leads seven miles up the valley to **Sunlight Ranger Station,** built in 1936 by the CCC. It's open summers only. This is some of the finest elk winter range anywhere and the home of a number of scenic old guest ranches (described below).

Back on the main road, a bridge—the highest in Wyoming at 300 feet above Sunlight Creek—spans deep, cliff-walled **Sunlight Gorge.** Sorry, no bungee jumping allowed. The highway then continues northwest past Cathedral Cliffs and through a scenic ranching and timbering valley, offering views into the deep gorge that belongs to the Clarks Fork of the Yellowstone River. In some sections, sheer cliffs tower 1,200 feet above the water. Part of the area burned by the 1988 Clover-Mist Fire is visible near **Crandall Ranger Station.** This area also contains the only large herd of mountain goats in Wyoming. Eventually you reach the junction with US Hwy. 212, the Beartooth Highway (see Beartooth Mountains above for a description of this beautiful route).

Camping and Hiking

The Forest Service's Lake Creek, Hunter Peak, and Dead Indian Campgrounds ($7-9; open mid-May through September) are found along Chief Joseph Scenic Highway. **Dead Indian Trail** (just uphill from Dead Indian Campground) goes two miles to a fine overlook into Clarks Fork Canyon. Also of interest is **Windy Mountain Trail,** which climbs 10,262-foot Windy Mountain. It starts from a trailhead four miles east of the Crandall Ranger Station (interesting old log buildings here), is approximately seven miles one way, and gains 3,700 feet in elevation. Windy Mountain can also be climbed from the other side near the Sunlight Ranger Station. Trailheads into the North Absaroka Wilderness are at the Crandall Ranger Station and beyond the Little Sunlight Campground (free; open year-round) on Forest Road 101.

River Running

Clarks Fork of the Yellowstone River (named for William Clark, of the Lewis and Clark expedition) is Wyoming's only designated Wild and

Scenic River. Experienced kayakers will find a couple of great stretches of class IV-V whitewater in the upper Clarks Fork. However, use considerable caution—there are several big drops. Be sure to pull out before dangerous Box Canyon, which is considered unrunnable. Find more class IV waters farther down the river. Check with the Forest Service for specifics. Below the rapids are quieter stretches. Based in Cody, **Red Canyon River Trips,** 1374 Sheridan Ave., tel. (307) 587-6988 or (800) 293-0148, leads gentle float trips down a scenic 12-mile section of the Clarks Fork. The half-day trip costs $45 per person. These are offered from late May to early August.

Guest Ranches

Located in the heart of beautiful Sunlight Basin, **Seven D Ranch** is a family-oriented guest ranch offering horseback rides, cookouts, fly-fishing, hiking, and pack trips. The setting is spectacular—it's where some of the Marlboro ads were shot—and the cabins are comfortable and cozy. Weekly all-inclusive rates are $2,870 for two people. The ranch has space for a maximum of 32 guests. Open mid-June to mid-September; adults only in September. Get details at (307) 587-9885, or on the web at www.7dranch.com. Luxury.

K Bar Z Guest Ranch is located off the Chief Joseph Scenic Highway in the Crandall Creek area. Nightly log cabin accommodations are available for $75 d, or guests can stay by the week for $1,400 for two people all-inclusive. Horseback rides, Yellowstone sightseeing, backcountry pack trips, cookouts, and guided fishing trips are also offered, along with wintertime snowmobile rentals. In addition to the usual horse adventures, the ranch has a sauna and hot tub and is open year-round. A maximum of 30 guests can stay here. For more information, call (307) 587-4410, or find it on the web at www.agonline.com/KBarZ. Moderate-Luxury.

Hunter Peak Ranch, 4027 Crandall Rd., tel. (307) 587-3711, is located on the banks of the upper Clarks Fork River, offering lodging in rustic log cabins or motel-type rooms. Rates are $80 s or d per night or $400 d per week, with extra charges for meals, horseback rides, and pack trips. The main lodge was built from handhewn logs in 1917. Open year-round. Moderate.

Also in Sunlight Basin, **Elk Creek Ranch** provides a unique opportunity for teenagers to gain a wide range of ranching and wilderness skills. Ranch stays ($2,700 per person all-inclusive for a four-week session) include lots of time on horseback and the opportunity to train horses, build cabins, cut hay, or learn other ranch work. The backpacking adventures ($2,600 per person all-inclusive for a four-week session) give kids plenty of time in the backcountry, where they learn a range of outdoor and mountain climbing skills. Two month-long sessions are offered each summer with a maximum of 30 kids at a time. For more on these adventures, see www.elkcreekranch.com on the web, or call (307) 587-3902 (summers) or (307) 384-5361 (winters).

Other Services

The little settlement called **Painter** is 21 miles southeast of Cooke City on Chief Joseph Hwy., and right along the Clarks Fork River. Here you'll find a general store and gas pumps, along with year-round RV hookups ($20) at **Painter Estates RV Resort,** tel. (307) 527-5248. Not far away is **Cary Inn Restaurant,** tel. (307) 527-5510, serving three meals a day.

WAPITI VALLEY/NORTH FORK

Wapiti Valley provides one of the most popular and scenic routes into or out of Yellowstone National Park, connecting Cody with the park's East Entrance. President Theodore Roosevelt came here often and called it "the most scenic 50 miles in the U.S." Along the way are numerous lodges, dude ranches, and resorts, private summer homes, eating places, Forest Service campgrounds, RV parks, hiking trails, and horseback rides. The fishing is great in the North Fork of the Shoshone River, which US Hwy. 14/16/20 parallels for the entire 50 miles from Yellowstone to Cody. From East Entrance the highway drops through high forests past an array of volcanic pinnacles and cliffs as the country becomes drier and more open. Cottonwoods line the gradually widening river, and Douglas-firs intermix with sage, grass, and rock at lower elevations. Trailheads provide access to two wilderness areas that border the highway, North Absaroka and Washakie. A major reconstruction project that ended in 1999 has left the road in excellent condition the entire distance from Cody to Yellowstone.

Pahaska Tepee

Located less than three miles from Yellowstone's East Entrance (48 miles west of Cody), Pahaska Tepee was built in 1904 to house Buffalo Bill's guests and others on their way to the park. Pahaska—pronounced "pa-HAZ-ka"—was Buffalo Bill's nickname, a Crow Indian word meaning "Long Hair."

The original Pahaska Tepee is a two-story log building that contains a few of his original items, including an old buffalo skull over the stone fireplace and several flags that were given to Buffalo Bill. Although it is no longer used and in need of major repairs, the lodge is open for fascinating free tours on weekdays during the summer. The bar at Pahaska Tepee is small but contains a stunning Thomas Molesworth chandelier that was formerly in the Smithsonian; it's said to be worth $2 million. Look around for other furnishings from Molesworth and a beautiful stained glass window.

On one of Buffalo Bill's many hunting treks with European royalty, he led the Prince of Monaco into the North Fork country. **Camp Monaco,** 15 miles up the Pahaska-Sunlight Trail from Pahaska Tepee, was named in his honor. Unfortunately, the old aspen tree inscribed with the words "Camp Monaco" was killed when the Clover-Mist Fire burned through here in 1988.

Pahaska Tepee Resort has a mix of old and new cabins and small A -frame motel rooms; rates are $96-105 for up to four people. Wintertime guests can use the outdoor jacuzzi. Also here are a restaurant, gift shop, gas pumps, and limited supplies. Pahaska is open May-Oct. and Dec.-March. Expensive. In winter the road is not plowed beyond Pahaska, and the lodge becomes a very popular place to rent snowmobiles and cross-country skis for trips into Yellowstone. Call (307) 527-7701 or (800) 628-7791 for more information on Pahaska, or visit www.pahaska.com.

Skiing and Snowboarding

Located just four miles from Yellowstone's East Gate, **Sleeping Giant Ski Area** is a small family skiing and snowboarding hill with a chairlift and T-bar providing a 500-foot vertical rise. Lifts operate mid-December to early April, and lift tickets cost $20 for adults or $10 for kids. Nordic and alpine skis, along with snowboards, are available for rent. For details, call (307) 587-4044 (Shoshone Lodge), or find Sleeping Giant Ski Area on the web at http://skisleepinggiant.com.

Also based here is **North Fork Nordic Trails,** with 40 km of groomed cross-country ski trails over widely varied terrain. These lead right to the edge of Yellowstone National Park. Call Pahaska Tepee at (307) 527-7701 for specifics.

Down the Road

Below Sleeping Giant Ski Area the road passes a whole series of delightfully weird volcanic rock formations. Signs point out several of the most obvious. Stop at the **Firefighters' Memorial,** honoring 15 firefighters killed nearby in the Blackwater Fire of 1937. The picnic area here has a special pond for anglers with disabilities.

Eight miles farther east is the historic **Wapiti Ranger Station.** Built in 1903, it was the nation's first Forest Service ranger station. Just a few hundred feet away and right along the highway is **Wapiti Wayside Visitor Center,** tel. (307) 587-3925, open Mon.-Fri. 8 a.m.-8 p.m. and Sat.-Sun. 8:30 a.m.-5 p.m. between Memorial Day and Labor Day; closed the rest of the year. Pull in for details on local camping and recreation opportunities, and to watch the informative video on safety in bear country. Check the board for recent bear sightings. A few miles to the west (not marked) is Mummy Cave, where a 10,000-year-old mummified body was discovered in 1957.

Next up is a parking area at **Holy City,** an impressive group of dark red volcanic rocks with the Shoshone River cutting away at their base. Try to pick out Anvil Rock, Goose Rock, and Slipper Rock here. The highway leaves Shoshone National Forest and then passes the scattered settlement called **Wapiti**—an Indian word meaning "elk"—20 miles east of Cody. As you might guess, a large elk herd winters in this valley. An unusual volcanic rock ridge near here is locally called Chinese Wall. The eastern half of the road between Cody and Yellowstone passes through this broad and fertile valley; it's quite a change from the rock-lined route to the west. On the east end, the road borders Buffalo Bill

Reservoir (see "Buffalo Bill State Park" below) before plunging through three tunnels on the descent into Cody.

Camping

Nine different Shoshone National Forest campgrounds provide rustic accommodations along the North Fork of the Shoshone River. Most of these are open mid-May through September (some remain open through October) and cost $9 per site; no reservations. All sites have picnic tables, fire rings, potable water, and outhouses. In areas where bears are a problem, the campgrounds also contain bearproof food storage boxes. All of these Forest Service campgrounds are on the west half of the 50-mile stretch of highway between Cody and Yellowstone. Of these, **Big Game Campground** is closest to Cody at 25 miles to the west, and **Three Mile Campground** is closest to the park, just three miles from Yellowstone's East Gate. Get details on public campgrounds from the Forest Service's Wapiti Wayside Visitor Center (described above). Dispersed camping outside designated campsites is not allowed anywhere between Cody and Yellowstone along US Hwy. 14/16/20.

Two campgrounds are located within Buffalo Bill State Park, described below. Also mentioned below are three Wapiti Valley lodges that have RV park campgrounds: Elk Valley Inn, Wise Choice Motel, and Yellowstone Valley Inn.

Wapiti Valley/North Fork Accommodations

More than 20 lodges, motels, and guest ranches line the road between Yellowstone and Cody. Pahaska Tepee—the closest lodge to Yellowstone—is described above. The places below are arranged by their distance from downtown Cody on US Hwy. 14/16/20, starting with those nearest the East Entrance to Yellowstone. Lodging places west of the midpoint between Cody and Yellowstone are in the more secluded and wooded canyon country of the upper North Fork of the Shoshone River. Places on the eastern half are situated in the broad and beautiful Wapiti Valley and are typically visible from the highway.

Wapiti Valley/North Fork lodges generally do not have TVs or phones in the rooms, but most will provide transportation from Cody upon request. Many also offer family-style meals, BBQ cookouts, horseback rides, pack trips, fishing, hiking, river rafting, and other outdoor recreation. If you aren't staying on an all-inclusive plan, most of these will cost extra. Some amenities—such as horseback rides and meals—are often available to folks who aren't staying at the lodge. Wapiti lodges and guest ranches open in the winter months are favorite bases for snowmobiling and cross-country skiing. See www.yellowstone-lodging.com, or call (307) 587-9595 for more information on Wapiti Valley businesses.

Shoshone Lodge, 46 miles west of Cody (four miles east of Yellowstone), tel. (307) 587-4044, is a classic mountain lodge with rustic log cabins. Home-cooked meals are served in the main lodge. The cabins have been nicely updated with Western furnishings; they range from one to three rooms, some containing kitchens. Nightly rates are $60-90 s or $70-100 d. A variety of horseback rides are offered, including breakfast and dinner rides. Shoshone Lodge is open mid-May through October, and you can find it on the web at www.shoshonelodge.com. Moderate-Expensive. The owners of Shoshone Lodge also run Sleeping Giant Ski Area, located directly across the road; see above for details.

Established in 1898, **Crossed Sabres Ranch,** 42 miles west of Cody (eight miles east of Yellowstone), tel. (307) 587-3750, has a beautiful century-old lodge. There's space for 40 guests in modernized cabins with log furniture and Western decor. After a day of horseback riding, hiking, river rafting, square dancing, or exploring Yellowstone, guests can relax with an evening cookout or soak in the jacuzzi. All-inclusive weekly packages are $2,000 for two people; open June to mid-September. Its website is www.ranchweb.com/csabres. Luxury.

Stay in deluxe log cabins at **Goff Creek Lodge,** 40 miles west of Cody, and just 10 miles east of Yellowstone. Cabins are offered on either a nightly basis ($95-105 d) or by the week; open May-November. A variety of outdoor adventures fill the bill here, including horseback rides, pack trips, fly-fishing, and chuck wagon cookouts. For details, point your mouse to www.goffcreek.com, or call (307) 587-3753 or (800) 859-3985. Expensive.

Elephant Head Lodge, 40 miles west of Cody (10 miles east of Yellowstone), is a no-frills dude ranch with a gracious main lodge built in 1910. Guests stay in a dozen modernized cabins, each with private baths and most with decks. Filling meals are served in the restaurant, and horseback rides are offered each day. Because of its proximity to the park, Elephant Head makes a good base for exploring Yellowstone. Peak season lodging-only rates start at $85 d per day; the largest cabin sleeps eight people for $150 per day and has a kitchenette. All-inclusive packages are $240 for two people per day. The ranch is open June-September. For details, call (307) 587-3980, or visit www.elephantheadlodge.com. Expensive-Luxury.

Just a dozen miles from Yellowstone (38 miles west of Cody), **Absaroka Mountain Lodge** offers old-time hospitality and adventure. Guests stay in comfortable log cabins with private baths and dine in the historic main lodge, built in 1910. Nightly rates are $76-116 d. Horseback rides, breakfast, and lunch are extra. The lodge also has a two-night rate of $250 for two people that includes meals and rides. Open May-September. Get more info by calling (307) 587-3963, or visiting its website: www.absarokamtlodge.com. Moderate-Premium.

Blackwater Creek Ranch, 35 miles west of Cody (15 miles east of Yellowstone), tel. (307) 587-5201, is a fine place to relax amid the natural beauty of the area. Featured attractions include horseback rides, trout fishing, hiking, games, barbecues, and cowboy sing-alongs. The gracious log cabins contain fireplaces, and meals are served in the modern lodge with an Old West atmosphere. Also here are an outdoor pool, a large jacuzzi, and a game room with ping-pong and pool tables. Weekly all-inclusive rates are $2,200 for two people. Open May-September. Find Blackwater Creek Ranch on the web at www.wavecom.net/~bwcranch. Luxury.

A classic Western dude ranch, **UXU Ranch,** tel. (307) 587-2143 or (800) 373-9027, www.uxuranch.com, is 33 miles west of Cody and 17 miles east of Yellowstone. UXU offers horseback riding, hiking, fly-fishing, mountain biking, and day-trips to Yellowstone and Cody. Guests stay in comfortable cabins containing private baths and porches; some also have fireplaces or gas stoves. After a day of trail riding, you can relax in the big jacuzzi or visit with new friends in the main lodge. Special children's programs and Forest Service talks are available, and the food is memorable. All-inclusive weekly stays cost $2,450 for two people; open June-September. Luxury.

Located 25 miles west of Cody (25 miles east of Yellowstone), **Bill Cody Ranch** has graceful log cabins, a comfortable lodge, horseback and wagon rides, creekside cookouts, trout fishing, a jacuzzi, and more. All-inclusive stays are $270 for two people per night; lodging-only rates are $105 d. The guest ranch is open May-September. Get more information by calling (307) 587-6271, or find it on the web at www.billcodyranch.com. Expensive-Luxury.

Rimrock Dude Ranch, 25 miles west of Cody (25 miles east of Yellowstone), tel. (307) 587-3970, is a classic place with creekside log cabins, horse riding, backcountry pack trips, a large swimming pool, river rafting, hearty family-style meals, and grand mountain country. Pack trips into the mountains are a special favorite. In the winter, this is a popular destination for snowmobilers; Rimrock rents them and leads tours into Yellowstone. Summertime weekly rates are $2,400 for two people, all inclusive. Rimrock is open late May-Sept., and Dec.-March. Find it on the web at www.rimrockranch.com. Luxury.

One of the most distinctive Wapiti Valley places is the nonprofit **Breteche Creek Ranch,** tel. (307) 587-3844, a 7,000-acre working cattle ranch. The ranch is 25 miles west of Cody and 25 miles east of Yellowstone. Horseback riding is a staple activity here, but guests also learn about the natural world through workshops in photography, nature writing, and poetry. The ranch lacks electricity. A maximum of 20 people stay in canvas-sided tent cabins set amid the aspen trees and use a central bathhouse. Meals are served family-style in a central lodge. All-inclusive rates are $2,200 for two people per week, or $350 for two people per night. Open June-September. The website is www.guestranches.com/breteche. Luxury.

Lodging places listed below are in the broad and open portion of Wapiti Valley; those listed above (east of the midpoint between Yellowstone and Cody) are in the more secluded and wooded canyon country of the upper river valley.

Located 23 miles west of Cody (27 miles east of Yellowstone), **Trail Inn,** tel. (307) 587-3741, sits off the road and along the North Fork Shoshone River. Rustic cabins with private baths are $60 s or d. Open May-September. Inexpensive.

Wise Choice Motel, 22 miles west of Cody (28 miles east of Yellowstone), tel. (307) 587-5004 or (877) 587-5004, has roadside motel rooms for $55-60 s or d, and RV sites for $15. Open mid-April to mid-November. Inexpensive.

Kinkade Guest Kabin B&B, 21 miles west of Cody (29 miles east of Yellowstone), tel. (307) 587-5905, has a two-bedroom log home with a dining room/living area and private baths. Rates are $65-85 s or d. Also available are bunk beds in the barn for $20 per person, or in a sheepherder wagon for $10 per person. No showers or running water for the wagon, just an outhouse. All of these options include a filling country breakfast served in the cabin. Open year-round. The Kinkade website is www.bbonline.com/wy/guestkabin. Budget-Moderate.

Stay in modern log cabins at **Rand Creek Ranch and Guest Lodge,** 19 miles west of Cody (31 miles east of Yellowstone), tel. (307) 527-7176 or (888) 412-7335. The cabins cost $85 s or d; all-inclusive one-week stays are $2,300 for two people, including horseback rides, fishing, lodging, and three meals per day. Rand Creek's main lodge was built in 1905, the oldest building in the area. Open May-December. Find it on the web at www.randcreekranch.com. Expensive-Luxury.

Elk Valley Inn, 18 miles west of Cody (32 miles east of Yellowstone), tel. (307) 587-4149, has standard motel rooms for $39-59 s or d, and a couple of cabins (one with a kitchenette) for $69 d. Pitch tents ($12) or park RVs ($12-15) at the inn's campground. The private pond has paddleboats for rent, and children will appreciate the fun playground. Open May-September. Inexpensive-Moderate.

Motel rooms cost $75 s or d at **Yellowstone Valley Inn,** 18 miles west of Cody (32 miles east of Yellowstone), tel. (307) 587-3961 or (888) 705-7703. Tent spaces are $10, and RV hookups run $20. The inn sits right on the North Fork Shoshone River and has a coffee shop and lounge, plus summertime horseback rides. Open May-November. Moderate.

Streamside Inn is 15 miles west of Cody (35 miles east of Yellowstone) near the east end of Buffalo Bill Reservoir. Modern motel rooms go for $56 s or $60-64 d, including a continental breakfast and access to the large outdoor pool and stocked fishing pond. Kitchenettes are available for $10 extra. Horseback rides are also offered, and Streamside Inn is open year-round. Get details by calling (307) 587-8242 or (800) 285-1282, or on the web at www.wtp.net/streamside. Moderate.

Just 11 miles west of Cody (39 miles east of Yellowstone), **Red Pole Ranch,** tel. (307) 587-5929 or (800) 326-5928, has motel units for $60-85 s or d, and four-person log cabins with kitchenettes for $100-125; open May-September. Moderate.

BUFFALO BILL STATE PARK

Located six miles west of Cody on US Hwy. 14/16/20, **Buffalo Bill Reservoir** is a very popular place for local boaters and fishermen. Buffalo Bill State Park, tel. (307) 587-9227, encompasses the reservoir and includes two campgrounds ($9 for nonresidents or $4 for Wyoming residents; open May-Sept.) on the north shore. Day-use of the park is $5 for nonresident vehicles, or $2 for those with Wyoming plates.

An impressive **Buffalo Bill Dam visitor center** atop the dam has historical displays and jaw-dropping views into the canyon, which plummets 350 feet below you. The center is open daily 8 a.m.-8 p.m. May-Sept., closed the rest of the year. Even if it's closed, stop for the view over the dam. For more information, call (307) 527-6076, or check its Internet site: www.BBDVC.org.

Fishing is good for rainbow, cutthroat, brown, and Mackinaw trout in Buffalo Bill Reservoir. The lake also offers some of the finest windsurfing conditions anywhere, with nearly constant 30-mph winds; *Outside* magazine once rated it among the country's 10 best spots. The water's cold—you'll need the protection of a wetsuit until mid-June.

History

In 1899, Buffalo Bill Cody acquired the rights to build canals and irrigate some 60,000 acres of land near the new town of Cody. With passage of the Reclamation Act of 1902, the project was taken over by the Reclamation Service and an enormous concrete-arch dam was added to provide water. The 328-foot-high dam was begun in 1904 and required five long years to finish. It cost nearly $1 million and, when finally completed, was the tallest dam in the world. Seven men died along the way—including a chief engineer—and the first two contractors were forced into bankruptcy as a result of bad weather, floods, engineering difficulties, and labor strife. A lack of sand and crushed gravel forced them to manufacture it from granite, and 200-pound boulders were hand-placed into the concrete to save having to crush more gravel.

Originally named Shoshone Dam, the impoundment was renamed in honor of Buffalo Bill in 1946. A hydroelectric plant and a 25-foot addition to the top were completed in 1993, bringing the total dam height to 353 feet and increasing water storage by 50 percent. The dam irrigates more than 93,000 downstream acres through the Shoshone Reclamation Project, making it one of the only Wyoming irrigation schemes that actually benefits the state's farmers to a large extent.

SOUTH FORK AREA

South Fork Road heads southwest from Cody and follows the South Fork of the Shoshone River for 42 miles to the edge of the Washakie Wilderness (described below). It's a beautiful drive through definitive Western country, with tree-covered mountains and the rich valley below.

Lodging

Two dude ranches operate along the South Fork River. **Castle Rock Ranch,** tel. (307) 587-2076 or (800) 356-9965, 17 miles southwest of Cody, has an attractive central lodge with magnificent vistas from the tall windows. Guests stay in log cabins containing handmade furniture and woodstoves or fireplaces; other facilities include an outdoor pool and a sauna. The ranch emphasizes not only horseback riding and fly-fishing but also less-traditional ranch activities such as windsurfing, mountain biking, and even rockclimbing. Special kids' programs are offered. The guest ranch is open June-September.

The **Double Diamond X Ranch** is an excellent family-oriented dude ranch near the South Fork River 34 miles southwest of Cody. The ranch itself only covers 200 acres, but it is surrounded by Shoshone National Forest land. Guests take part in horseback rides, cookouts, square dances, cowboy poetry, and day-trips to Cody. Their kids' program is one of the best around, with entertaining and educational activities every day, and the ranch brings in professional entertainers several times a week. There's space for up to 32 guests. Facilities include remodeled log cabins—some dating to 1914—and lodge accommodations, plus an indoor pool and jacuzzi. Meals are noteworthy. All-inclusive rates are $2,920 for two people for six nights; open May-October. Get more info by calling (307) 527-6276 or (800) 833-7262, or from the website: www.ddxranch.com. Luxury.

WASHAKIE WILDERNESS

Covering 704,529 acres, Washakie Wilderness is one of the largest chunks of wild land in Wyoming. Named for Shoshone Chief Washakie, it lies between US Hwy. 14/16/20 (the road connecting Yellowstone and Cody) and US Hwy. 26/287 (Dubois area). To the west are Yellowstone National Park and Teton Wilderness. The Washakie is a land of deep narrow valleys, mountains of highly erodible volcanic material, and step-like buttes. The mountains—a few top 13,000 feet—are part of the Absaroka Range. About half of the land is forested. One of the unique features of Washakie Wilderness is a petrified forest, a reminder of the region's volcanic past.

Hikes

There are numerous trails through the Washakie Wilderness, but most require that you either return the same way you came or end at a location far from your starting point. Several trails stretch into Yellowstone National Park and are popular for extended horsepacking trips. The most popular Washakie Wilderness hikes are from US Hwy. 14/16/20 in Wapiti Valley. Most folks use them for short day-hikes or horseback rides rather than attempting longer backcountry treks.

Kitty Creek Trail leaves from the Kitty Creek summer home area, nine miles east of Yellowstone. Low-clearance vehicles will need to park along the highway. The trail follows the creek past two large scenic meadows to Flora Lake, 6.5 miles and 2,500 feet higher. This is the shortest hike in the area and one of the most popular.

The 21-mile-long **Elk Fork Trail** starts at Elk Fork Campground and crosses Elk Creek several times en route to remote Rampart Pass at nearly 11,000 feet. It is steep and rocky in the higher elevations. West of the Continental Divide you enter the Teton Wilderness. For the really ambitious, the Open Creek and Thorofare Trails continue on into Yellowstone National Park.

Deer Creek Trail departs from the free Deer Creek Campground, 42 miles southwest of Cody on State Hwy. 291 (South Fork Road). The trail switchbacks very steeply uphill at first and after two miles reaches an attractive waterfall. Continue another eight miles from here to the Continental Divide and the Thorofare portion of the Teton Wilderness. This is probably the quickest route into this remote country and is popular with both horsepackers and hikers.

South Fork Trail takes off from the South Fork Guard Station across the creek from Deer Creek Campground. (Take a signed spur road to get there.) It climbs up along South Fork Creek to Shoshone Pass on the Continental Divide (9,858 feet). From here you can continue on a number of trails to the south, rambling over three more passes to eventually reach Double Cabin Campground, 27 miles north of Dubois. Another long hike into Washakie Wilderness leaves from this campground and follows the **Wiggins Fork Trail** up into a connecting series of paths: Absaroka, Nine Mile, East Fork, and Bug Creek Trails. It ends back at Double Cabin Campground. Total length is 60 miles. Along the way you're likely to see hundreds of elk in the high country as well as bighorn sheep. You won't meet many other hikers.

COURTESY AISLINN RACE

CODY

The city of Cody (pop. 8,800) marks the transition point between the forested mountains of northwest Wyoming and the sage-covered plains of Bighorn Basin. It's a favorite stopping place for Yellowstone tourists heading into or out of the park. The park is just 50 miles from the edge of Cody, and other magnificent country spreads in all directions—the Beartooth Mountains and Sunlight Basin to the north, the Absaroka Range and Wapiti Valley to the west and south. Established as an agricultural and tourism center, Cody retains both roles today, though tourism seems to be gaining in importance with each passing year. The town is one of the few places in Wyoming that continued to grow through the 1990s; only Jackson Hole exceeds Cody as a tourism center. Not surprisingly, both are gateways to the national parks that dominate northwest Wyoming. Cody is also home to a number of mid-size companies, including oil, mining, and logging operations. For details on other towns in the Bighorn Basin, see my *Wyoming Handbook* (Emeryville, CA: Avalon Travel Publishing, www.moon.com).

Cody itself has a number of attractions, including the justly famous Buffalo Bill Historical Center, along with Trail Town and other local

CODY AT A GLANCE

Elevation 5,095 feet

Cody Country Chamber of Commerce, 836 Sheridan Ave., tel. (307) 587-2297 or (800) 393-2639, www.codychamber.org, open daily Memorial Day to Labor Day, and Mon.-Fri. the rest of the year

Shoshone National Forest Supervisor's Office, 808 Meadowlark Ave., tel. (307) 527-6241, www.fs.fed.us/r2/shoshone

Wapiti Valley lodges, tel. (307) 587-9595, www.yellowstone-lodging.com

Buffalo Bill Historical Center, tel. (307) 587-4771 or (800) 227-8483, www.bbhc.org, open daily year-round (except Thanksgiving, Christmas, and New Year's Day)

Cody Area Central Reservations, tel. (307) 587-0200 or (888) 468-6996, www.wtp.net/codyres

Cody Nite Rodeo, tel. (307) 587-5155 or (800) 207-0744, www.westwyoming.com/cody-stampede

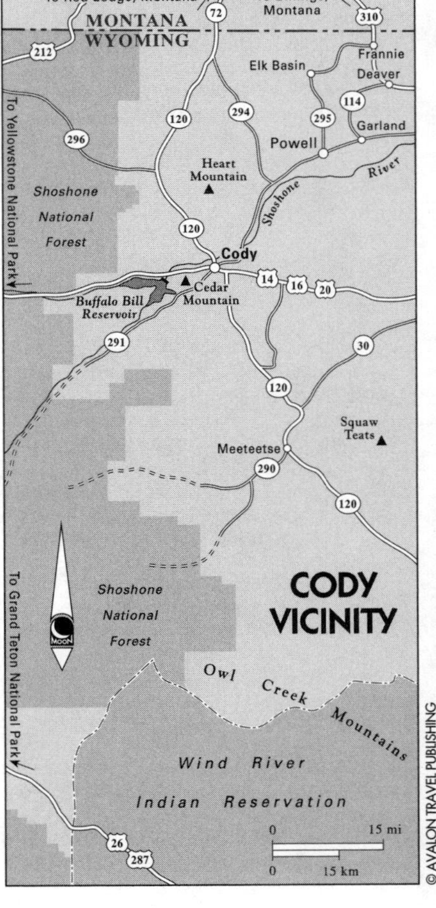

sights. The Shoshone River flows right through town, providing the opportunity for scenic float trips. Lots of events crowd the summer calendar, from nightly rodeos and shootouts to parades and powwows; biggest of all is the annual Cody Stampede in July. The town also takes pride in a long list of artists that includes Charles Cary Rumsey and Harry Jackson. Famed abstract expressionist Jackson Pollock was born here, but he achieved his reputation in New York and never returned to his birthplace.

HISTORY

Immediately west of Cody—past the Wal-Mart, RV parks, fireworks stands, and gas stations—are the Absaroka Mountains, named for the Native Americans who first lived here. They called themselves the Absaroka, or "Children of the Large Beaked Bird." Whites interpreted this as crow, and the natives have been called Crow Indians ever since. Explorer John Colter passed through this region in 1808 while recruiting Indians to supply beaver furs. When Colter returned to the semblance of civilization called Fort Manual Lisa, everyone laughed at his tales of a spectacular geothermal area along the "Stinkingwater River." Soon everyone was calling it "Colter's Hell." But the geysers were real; they still steam along the Shoshone (formerly the Stinkingwater) just west of present-day Cody. Other mountain men came later, followed by miners who found copper and sulfur in Sunlight Basin. The first real settler in the area was a Prussian, Otto Franc, who developed a large cattle spread at the famous Pitchfork Ranch.

Because of desertlike conditions, Bighorn Basin was one of the last parts of Wyoming to be settled, and most of the towns did not spring up until the 1890s. The spark that led to their development was the Carey Act, named for Wyoming Senator Joseph M. Carey. The act allowed the federal government to donate land to the states for reclamation by settlers. Wyoming was the first state to try out the new law, but only 10% of the two million acres in the program were ever patented.

In 1895, William F. "Buffalo Bill" Cody and two partners began plans for the Shoshone Land and Irrigation Company, with headquarters along the Shoshone River just west of the present city of Cody. Cody had spent much time in the Bighorn Basin, guiding parties of wealthy sportsmen, and was convinced that a combination of tourism and irrigated farming could transform this desert land. The name Cody was a natural choice for this new settlement, officially founded in 1896. At the urging of Buffalo Bill, the Chicago, Burlington, & Quincy Railroad arrived in 1901, bringing in tourists who continued west up Shoshone Canyon to Yellowstone by stagecoach. Between 1904 and 1909, construction of massive Buffalo Bill Dam employed hundreds of workers and later provided water to irrigate farmland in the basin. Oil was first discovered near Cody in 1904, and Park County is now the second-largest oil producer in the state.

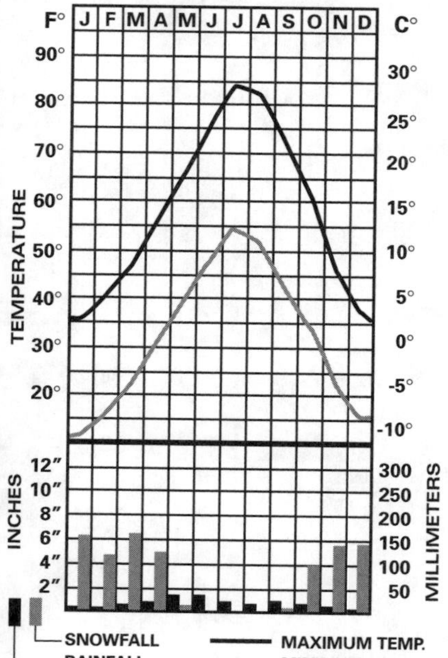

Average Maximum Temp.	**58.8°F**
Average Minimum Temp.	**32.6°F**
Annual Rainfall	**10.03″**
Annual Snowfall	**39″**

Marathon Oil Company has its Rocky Mountain headquarters in Cody and is one of the town's largest employers. Also important are a wallboard manufacturing plant, a lumber mill, and a producer of ranch products.

BUFFALO BILL HISTORICAL CENTER

Each year, more than 300,000 people visit Cody's main attraction, the Buffalo Bill Historical Center. Nowhere else in America is such a major museum in a town with so few people. This is the largest and most impressive museum in Wyoming and the finest Western museum in the world. The late author James Michener once labeled it "the Smithsonian of the West," and his term is even more true today. It's a place where visitors quickly run out of superlatives. The collection focuses—not surprisingly—on the Western frontier and includes thousands of artifacts and works of art spread through more than 237,000 square feet of space. The center actually houses four separate museums, a research library, the boyhood home of Buffalo Bill, and two sculpture gardens.

The original Buffalo Bill Museum opened in 1927 in what is now the chamber of commerce log cabin. Opening in 1959, the Whitney Gallery of Western Art formed a nucleus for the current

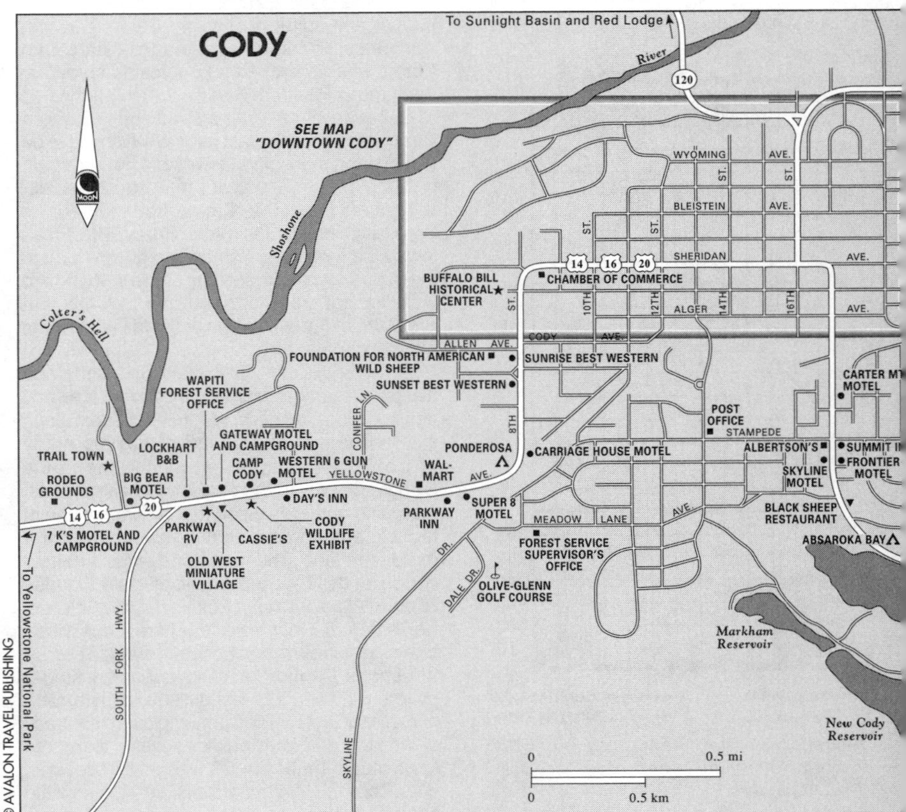

museum location; later additions included the Buffalo Bill Museum, the Plains Indian Museum, and the Cody Firearms Museum. A new natural history museum is under development and should open early in the 21st century. Other facilities at the Buffalo Bill Historical Center include an outstanding gift shop and bookstore, plus a cafe for light meals. Head to the sculpture garden for a lunchtime buffalo burger beneath the aspen trees.

An array of events take place all summer long, ranging from powwows to historical talks to cowboy singing. Of note is the **Larom Summer Institute in Western American Studies,** an in-depth two-week history course offered each June. See Events below for other museum activities.

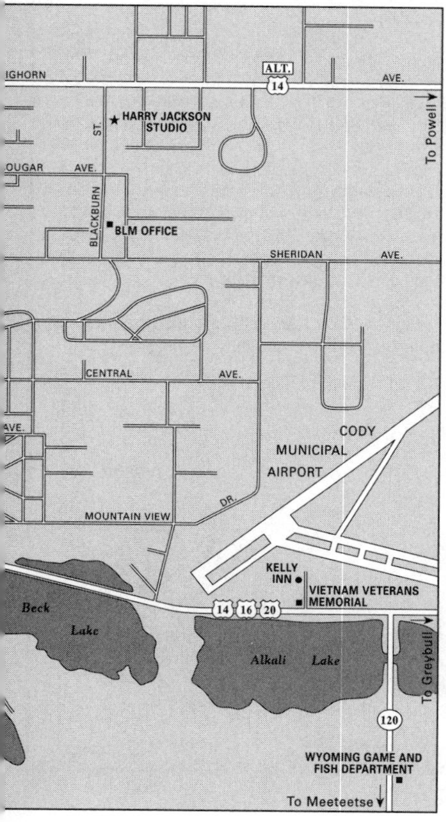

Practicalities

Buffalo Bill Historical Center is open year-round. In the busy summer season from June through mid-September, it's open daily 7 a.m.-8 p.m. At other times, hours are reduced: daily 8 a.m.-5 p.m. mid-September through October and during April; daily 8 a.m.-8 p.m. in May. From November through March the museum is open Tues.-Sun. 10 a.m.-3 p.m. Closed Thanksgiving, Christmas, and New Year's Day.

Admission costs $10 for adults, $6 for students 18 and over, and $4 for ages 6-17. Children under six get in free. The admission is good for two days, and it may well take two days to explore this massive collection! Tours are generally offered only for school groups and VIPs, but the Historical Center often has summertime demonstrations, and the helpful docents can provide additional info. Call (307) 587-4771 or (800) 227-8483 for more on the museum, or visit its website: www.bbhc.org.

Outside

Before heading inside, stop to view Buffalo Bill's **boyhood home,** a tiny yellow building built in 1841 by Isaac Cody. The house stood in LeClarie, Iowa, for almost a century. In 1933 it was sawn in half, loaded on two railcars, and hauled to Cody to be reassembled and refurbished. The house is on your left as you face the museum. Flanking the museum on the opposite side is ***The Scout,*** a dramatic, larger-than-life statue of larger-than-life Buffalo Bill. This huge bronze piece was created by New York sculptress Gertrude Vanderbilt Whitney and was unveiled in 1924. Her family later donated 40 acres of surrounding land to the Buffalo Bill Museum. Directly in front of the historical center are three colorfully painted **tepees,** a treat for kids. Once you enter the museum, ask for directions to the **Visitor's Lounge,** where a 10-minute orientation video provides a good introduction. Just inside the entrance on the left is a magnificent feathered cape made in 1839 by a Mesquakie woman from the Great Lakes area; don't miss it.

Buffalo Bill Museum

The Buffalo Bill Museum is a real joy. In it, the life of Buffalo Bill Cody is briefly sketched with all

BUFFALO BILL CODY

For many people today, the name "Buffalo Bill" brings to mind a man who helped slaughter the vast herds of wild bison that once filled the west. But William F. Cody cannot be so easily pigeonholed, for here was one of the most remarkable men of his or any other era—a man who almost single-handedly established the aura of the "Wild West." More than 800 books—many of them the dime-store novels that thrilled generations of youngsters—have been written about Cody. In many of these, the truth was stretched far beyond any semblance of reality, but the real life of William Cody contains so many adventures and plot twists that it seems hard to believe one person could have done so much.

Young Cody

Born to an Iowa farm family in 1846, William Cody started life as had many others of his era. His parents moved to Kansas when he was six, but his abolitionist father, Isaac Cody, soon became embroiled in arguments with the many slaveholders. While defending his views at a public meeting, Isaac Cody was stabbed in the back and fled for his life. When a mob learned of his father's whereabouts, eight-year-old Will Cody rode on his first venture through enemy lines, galloping 35 miles to warn of the impending attack. Three years later, when Isaac Cody died of complications from the stabbing, 11-year-old Will Cody became the family's breadwinner. There were four other children to feed. Will quickly joined the company of Alexander Majors, running dispatches between his Army supply wagons and giving his $40 monthly wages to his mother. In Cody's autobiography he claimed to have killed his first Indian on this trip, an action that gave him the then-enviable title "youngest Indian slayer of the plains."

On his first long wagon trek west, the Army supply wagons were attacked by Mormon zealots who took all the weapons and horses, forcing Cody to walk much of the thousand miles back to his Kansas home. It was apparently on this walk that Cody met Wild Bill Hickok. At Wyoming's Fort Laramie, young Will sat in awe as famed scouts Jim Bridger and Kit Carson reminisced about their adventures. The experience was a turning point in Cody's life; he resolved to one day become a scout. Cody's next job offered excellent training: he became a rider for the Pony Express. At just 15 years of age he already was one of the finest riders in the West and a crack shot with a rifle. On one of his Pony Express rides Cody covered a total of 320 miles in just 21 hours and 40 minutes—the longest Pony Express ride ever. The Civil War had begun, and at age 18 Cody joined the Seventh Kansas Regiment, serving as a scout and spy for the Union Army.

After the Civil War, Will Cody tried his hand at the hotel business and then briefly joined Gen.

BUFFALO BILL HISTORICAL CENTER

Buffalo Bill with Indian children, 1913—this photo was probably taken during the filming of The Indian Wars.

George Custer as a scout before returning to Kansas to do a little land speculating along the route of the newly built railroad. Cody and a partner bought land and laid out a town that they named Rome. For a short while it boomed. One day a man appeared in Rome, offering to take over the town while leaving Cody with only a small portion of the place he had founded. Thinking it was only intimidation from a shady operator, Cody laughed at the man, not knowing that he was president of the railroad's townsite company. The railroad quickly chose another townsite, and three days later all the inhabitants of Rome moved east to the new site, taking their buildings with them. Cody was left with a worthless patch of land.

Buffalo Hunter and Scout

In 1867, Cody found work hunting buffalo to supply fresh meat for the railroad construction crews, a job that soon made him famous as "Buffalo Bill" and paid a hefty $500 a month. With 75 million bison spread from northern Canada to Mexico, and herds so vast that they took many days to pass one point, it seemed impossible that they could ever be killed off. Cody was one of the best hunters in the West; in just eight months, he slaughtered 4,280 buffalo, often saving transportation by driving the herd toward the camp and dropping them within sight of the workers. Cody's name lives on in the jingle: "Buffalo Bill, Buffalo Bill; never missed and never will; always aims and shoots to kill; and the company pays his buffalo bill . . ."

After this stint, Cody finally got the job he wanted—chief scout for the U.S. Army in the West, a job packed with excitement and danger. Conflicts with Indians had reached a fever pitch as more and more whites moved into the last Indian strongholds. Cody worked as scout for Gen. Philip Sheridan, providing information on the Indians' movements, leading troops in pursuit of the warriors, and joining in the battles, including one in which he supposedly killed Chief Tall Bull. His men considered Buffalo Bill good luck, because he managed to keep them out of ambushes.

During the Indian campaigns, the writer/preacher/scoundrel Ned Buntline began writing of Cody's exploits for various New York papers, giving Buffalo Bill his first taste of national acclaim. Soon Buntline had cranked out several romantic novels loosely based on Cody's adventures. America had a new national hero. European and Eastern gentry began asking Cody to guide them on buffalo hunts. On the trips, Cody referred to them as "dudes" and to his camps as "dude ranches"—perhaps the first time anyone had used the terms for such hunters. One of Wyoming's most unusual businesses had begun. Cody's incredible knowledge of the land and hunting impressed the men, but they were stunned to also discover in him a natural showman. In 1872, the Grand Duke Alexis of Russia came to the U.S., and Cody guided him on a hunt that made national headlines and brought even more fame to the 26-year-old. On a trip to New York in 1872, Cody met Buntline again and watched a wildly distorted theater production called *Buffalo Bill.* Amazingly, Cody adjusted quickly to the new surroundings. Dressed in the finest silk clothes but with his long scout's hair under a Western hat, Cody suddenly entered the world of high society.

In a short while, Cody was on the stage himself, performing with Ned Buntline and fellow scout Texas Jack in a play called *Scouts of the Plains.* Although the play was meant to be serious, the acting of all three proved so atrocious that the play had audiences rolling in the aisles with laughter. A New York reviewer called the play "so wonderfully bad it was almost good. The whole performance was so far aside of human experience, so wonderful in its daring feebleness, that no ordinary intellect is capable of comprehending it." Audiences packed the theaters for weeks on end. But Cody was suddenly called back west, for the Sioux were again on the warpath.

Shortly after Cody had returned to guide Gen. Eugene Carr's forces, they learned of the massacre of Custer's men at the Battle of Little Bighorn. In revenge, Carr's men set out to pursue Indians along the border between Nebraska and Wyoming. Under Cody's guidance, they surprised a group of warriors at War Bonnet Creek. Cody shot the chief, Yellow Hand, and immediately scalped him, raising the scalp above his head with the cry "first scalp for Custer!" (Cody later claimed that he scalped the chief because he was wearing an American flag as a loincloth and had a lock of yellow hair from a white woman's scalp pinned to his clothing.) The Sioux immediately fled. If Cody had been famous before, this event propelled him to even more acclaim. It became the grist for countless dime-store novels and was embellished in so many ways over the years that the true story will never be known.

The Wild West Show

Buffalo Bill's days in the real Wild West were over, and he returned to staging shows, eventually starting his famed Wild West extravaganza. This was un-

(continued on next page)

BUFFALO BILL CODY

(continued)

like anything ever done before—an outdoor circus that seemed to transport all who watched to the frontier. One newspaper remarked that Cody had "out-Barnumed Barnum." There were buffalo stampedes, cowboy bronc riding, Indian camps, a Deadwood stage and outlaws, crack shooting by Annie Oakley, and, of course, Buffalo Bill. At its peak in the late 1890s, the show made Cody more than a million dollars in profit each year.

Amazingly, Sitting Bull and Buffalo Bill became good friends. Cody, who had earlier bragged of his many Indian killings, changed his attitude, eventually saying, "In nine cases out of 10 when there is trouble between white men and Indians, it will be found that the white man is responsible." Cody's other attitudes also continued to evolve. He criticized the buffalo hidehunters of the 1870s and 1880s for their reckless slaughter and later became an ardent supporter of game preserves and limitations on hunting seasons.

The Wild West Show became one of the most popular events anywhere in America and Europe, attracting crowds of up to 40,000 people. Queen Victoria was a special fan (although rumors of an affair are probably false). At the peak of his fame around the turn of the century, Buffalo Bill was arguably the world's best-known man. Cody, however, continued to drink heavily. One day, an obviously drunken Buffalo Bill insisted that his cowboys ride Monarch, a massive and dangerous bison in the entourage. When they refused in front of thousands of spectators, Cody himself climbed on top and was immediately thrown to the ground. He spent the next two weeks in a hospital. For the next decade the show continued to tour but gradually lost its novelty as other forms of entertainment, especially movies, came along. Cody used his money to buy the 40,000-acre TE Ranch in northwestern Wyoming near Yellowstone National Park. For him the Bighorn Basin was paradise. The town that he helped establish here was named Cody in his honor, and he backed the massive Shoshone irrigation project.

A Sad Farewell

Unfortunately, Buffalo Bill seemed to have no comprehension of how to save his wealth. He was a notoriously soft touch and would give money to almost anyone who asked. As his fortune slipped away and his show became more dated, Cody was finally forced to join up with H.H. Tammen, the crooked owner of the *Denver Post*. Tammen used the aging Cody's fame to attract people to his own circus. He forced Cody's Wild West Show into bankruptcy in 1913, sold off all the incredible collection of historical artifacts that had been amassed over the years, and left workers to find their own way home. Buffalo Bill was heartbroken, but, still trusting Tammen (or in desperation), he agreed to join his circus almost as a sideshow act.

Three years later, Cody died while visiting his sister in Denver and was buried on Lookout Mountain near Denver. Cody had wanted to be buried on Cedar Mountain above the town of Cody, but even this wish was denied by Tammen, who apparently paid Cody's widow Louisa $10,000 for the privilege of choosing the burial site (and to use the funeral parade to the burial site as an advertisement for his circus troop). When rumors came that folks from Wyoming intended to dig up Cody's body and take it back to its rightful burial place, Tammen had tons of concrete dumped on top of the grave. Louisa Cody went on to outlive not only her husband, but also all four of her children. She ended up caring for her four grandchildren.

Despite the unhappy ending to Buffalo Bill's life, there are few individuals who lived such a diverse and adventure-filled life and who could count so many people as their friends, from the lowliest beggar to the richest king. Cody's life spanned one of the most remarkable eras in American history, and his impact on American culture is still felt today, not just in the image of the West that he created, which lives on in hundreds of Western movies, but also in the Boy Scouts (an organization inspired partly by his exploits), in the city of Cody, and even in the dude ranches that dot Wyoming.

Late in life, Cody was asked how he wanted to be remembered. He replied: "I don't want to die and have people say 'Oh, there goes another old showman.' When I die I want the people of Wyoming who are living on the land that has been made fertile by my work and expenditure to remember me. I would like people to say, 'This is the man who opened up Wyoming to the best of civilization.'"

sorts of memorabilia from his Wild West Show, including the famous Deadwood Stage, silver-laden saddles, enormous posters, furniture, guns, wagons, and clothing. Be sure to look for "Lucretia Borgia," the Springfield rifle that helped William Cody gain his nickname. Also here are some of the gifts given to Buffalo Bill by European heads of state—including a fur carriage robe from Czar Alexander II—and by Wild Bill Hickok and Sitting Bull. Original film footage from the Wild West Show runs continuously, offering a fascinating and sometimes unintentionally comical glimpse into the past. Amazingly choreographed marching soldiers, fake Indian battles, sign-language conversations, and bucking broncos make it easy to see how the Wild West Show helped inspire Western movies.

Downstairs from the Buffalo Bill Museum is a spacious gallery used for special exhibitions (always worth a look), along with the **Harold McCracken Research Library,** open Mon.-Fri. 8 a.m.-noon and 1-5 p.m. May-October. The library houses thousands of historical photos and books, including more than 300 volumes about Buffalo Bill—mostly dime novels and comic books.

Whitney Gallery of Western Art

The Whitney Gallery contains a stunning collection of masterworks by such Western artists and sculptors as Charles Russell, Frederic Remington, Carl Bodmer, George Catlin, Thomas Moran, Albert Bierstadt, Alfred Jacob Miller, Edgar Paxson, N.C. Wyeth, and others. The studios of Frederic Remington and W.H.D. Koerner have been re-created, and Gertrude Vanderbilt Whitney's *The Scout* is visible from a large window on the north end. The collections of "cowboy artist" Charles Russell and Frederic Remington—best known for his paintings of battles during the Indian wars—are the most complete here; the museum has more than a hundred of each man's paintings. Next to the Whitney Gallery is **Joseph Henry Sharp Garden** where you'll find his "Absarokee Hut" filled with the painter's paraphernalia.

The **Kriendler Gallery of Contemporary Western Art** is upstairs from the entrance to the Whitney Gallery, and it contains a diverse collection of pieces, including several with a delightfully whimsical twist. Well worth the detour.

Cody Firearms Museum

The Cody Firearms Museum houses one of the most comprehensive collections of American firearms in the world, including everything from 16th-century matchlocks to self-loading semiautomatic pistols. This is one museum where the men outnumber the women. Start your visit by viewing "Lock, Stock, & Barrel," a 10-minute video that describes the history of guns and how they work; it's interesting even for those of us who consider the proliferation of guns a national menace. In fact, the entire firearms collection is remarkably informative and well worth taking time to view.

The museum now contains more than 5,000 weapons, but these aren't just rows of guns in glass cases. Some of the more unusual include a 10-shot repeating flintlock rifle made for the New York Militia around 1825 and a 17th-century windlass crossbow. There are all sorts of displays to explore, including a colonial gun shop, a western stage station, a turn-of-the-century firearms factory, and a truly extraordinary collection of embellished arms. One of the most lavish is an intricately carved flintlock sporting carbine presented by Empress Elizabeth I of Russia to King Louis XV of France. The Boone and Crockett Club's collection of trophy animal heads is here, including an elephant-sized moose housed in a re-created hunting lodge. All told, more implements of destruction and mayhem than you're likely to be confronted with at a gathering of Idaho neo-Nazis. Take the elevator to the basement for even more gun displays.

Plains Indian Museum

The largest exhibition space in the historical center encloses the Plains Indian Museum, with items from the Sioux, Cheyenne, Blackfeet, Crow, Arapaho, Shoshone, and Gros Ventre tribes. At first it may seem incongruous that a museum featuring the man once called the "youngest Indian slayer of the plains" should include so much about the culture of Indians, but Cody's later maturity forced him to the realization that Indians had been severely mistreated and that their culture was of great value. His Wild West Shows re-created some semblance of that lost society, if only for show. Some of the more important items here were given to Buffalo Bill by various Indian performers over the years, and the collection of artifacts is now one of the finest in America. Included are an extraordinary painted buffalo robe from 1890 that depicts the Battle of Little Bighorn, elaborately decorated baby carriers, ghost-dance dresses, leather garments, war bonnets, medicine pipes, and even a Pawnee grizzly claw necklace. One of the more unusual items is Lone Dog's Winter Count, with figures representing a 71-year sequence of events affecting the Sioux; it was created in 1877. The moccasin collection fills an entire wall, and one room holds a Sioux camp as it might have appeared in the 1880s. Be sure to check out the exhibit on 10,000-year-old Mummy Cave, discovered in 1957 west of Cody.

OTHER SIGHTS

Trail Town

Point your horses toward the mountains and head 'em two miles west of Cody to a unique collection of historic buildings at Trail Town, tel. (307) 587-5302. The site is open daily 8 a.m.-7 p.m. mid-May to mid-September only; $3 entrance fee (free for kids under 12). This was the original location of "Cody City" in 1895. Trail Town is the creation of Bob and Terry Edgar. (In 1957 Bob Edgar discovered Mummy Cave—one of the most important archaeological finds in the West.) The Edgars bought the old Arland and Corbett trading post that had stood here since the 1880s and began dragging in other historic Wyoming cabins. Some were transported whole, others were disassembled and then put back together at Trail Town. Twenty-two buildings dating from 1879 to 1901, plus 100 wagons, are currently on the site.

For those who love history, Trail Town is an incredible treasure trove without the fancy gift shops and commercial junk that tag along with most such endeavors. This is the real thing, low-key and genuine. Probably the most famous building here is a cabin from the Hole-in-the-Wall country that Butch Cassidy and the Sundance Kid used as a rendezvous spot. Also at Trail Town is the oldest saloon from this part of Wyoming, complete with bullet holes in the door, and a cabin where Jim White—one of the most famous buffalo hunters—was murdered in 1879. The log home of Crow Indian scout Curley stands along Main Street too. (Curley was the only one of General Custer's command who escaped alive from the Battle of Little Bighorn.) Inside the old Burlington Store are a black hearse, arrowheads, a cradleboard, and items from fur traders.

The bodies of buffalo hunter Jim White and several other historic figures have been reinterred in a small graveyard at Trail Town. One of the most interesting of these is Belle Drewry, a prostitute known as "The Woman in Blue." After bouncing around a number of 19th-century mining towns, she ended up in the lawless and now-abandoned town of Arlund, located northwest of Meeteetse. One night in 1897 she shot a cowboy to death during a dance. The following night his outlaw friends took retribution by murdering her. Belle was buried in the blue dress that she always wore. Also buried in the cemetery is **John "Liver Eating" Johnson,** the mountain man portrayed by Robert Redford in the movie *Jeremiah Johnson.* Those who have seen the film will be surprised to learn that Johnson died in 1900 at the Old Soldiers' Home in Los Angeles! Friends sent him there by train from Montana when his health deteriorated, but he only spent a month in California before his death at the age of 76. After the movie came out, schoolchildren in Los Angeles helped promote the moving of Johnson's body closer to his mountain home. Nearly 2,000 people showed up for the reburial in 1974, including Robert Redford. A memorial to explorers John Colter and Jim Bridger also stands near the graveyard. The historic buildings, artifacts, and graves at Trail Town provide a fine counterpoint to the glitzier Buffalo Bill Historical Center.

Irma Hotel

Pick up a copy of the ***Cody Historic Walking Tour*** brochure ($2) at the visitor center for an informative introduction to local buildings and their history. One of the most engaging is the Irma Hotel, named for Buffalo Bill Cody's daughter. It was built in 1902 to house tourists arriving by train and was one of three way stations to Yellowstone built by Cody. The luxurious saloon has a French-made $100,000 cherry wood bar given to Buffalo Bill by Queen Victoria. Many famous people have gathered here over the years.

The **Cody Gunslingers** perform in front of the Irma Mon.-Fri. between Memorial Day and Labor Day. Cody was established long after the era of

The Irma Hotel is named after Buffalo Bill Cody's daughter.

gunfights in the streets, so this isn't particularly authentic, but it does attract a crowd each evening. The gunfight officially starts at 6 p.m., but the first 15 minutes or so are typically wasted on ads for local businesses. You know you're in America when the advertising even delays a gunfight! Call (307) 587-4221 for details on the gunslingers.

Harry Jackson Studio

Cody's best known living artist, Harry Jackson, has a large gallery at 602 Blackburn Avenue. His works cover the palette from abstract expressionist paintings, collages, and cubist studies to his more recent sculptures of traditional Old West figures—cowboys and Indians. Many of his sculptures contain distinctively painted surfaces. The sculptures are his best-known works, including the monumental *Sacajawea* at the Buffalo Bill Historical Center and *Horseman* in Beverly Hills. Jackson's pieces have been exhibited throughout the U.S. and in Italy (where his works are cast). Jackson himself divides his time between Cody and Italy. All bronzes displayed here are for sale (but not his paintings), but they're only for serious art patrons willing to spend thousands of dollars. The gallery is typically open Mon.-Fri. 8 a.m.-5 p.m., but call (307) 587-5508 for the latest.

Art Galleries

The **Buffalo Bill Historical Center** (described above) houses an excellent gift shop with art prints, Indian jewelry, and reproductions of bronze sculptures. Next to the chamber of commerce office at 836 Sheridan Ave. is the **Cody Country Art League,** tel. (307) 587-3597, displaying paintings, sculptures, photos, and crafts for sale. It also offers workshops and juried art shows.

Simpson Gallagher Gallery, 1115 13th St., tel. (307) 587-4022, is one of the finest in Cody, with works that go well beyond the standard Western clichés. **Two Bears at the Irma,** 1192 Sheridan Ave., tel. (307) 587-9400, has a huge selection of silver and turquoise Indian jewelry. Most comes from New Mexico, but a few pieces are from the Wind River Reservation in Wyoming.

Of less interest but possibly worth a peek are two shops with predictable artworks: **Big Horn Gallery,** 1167 Sheridan Ave., tel. (307) 587-6762, and **Kilian Gallery,** 1361 Sheridan Ave., tel. (307) 527-5380.

Old West Miniature Village

Cody has an abundance of offbeat attractions, from talking sheep to sanctified ceilings. The most unusual—and actually worth a visit—is **Old West Miniature Village and Museum** (a.k.a. Tecumseh's Trading Post), 142 W. Yellowstone Ave., tel. (307) 587-5362. Owner Jerry Fick has spent decades creating an enormous diorama that offers a truncated version of Wyoming and Montana history. The term kitsch quickly enters your head when you step inside, but you've got to appreciate the effort that went into creating thousands of hand-carved figures and an array of miniature villages. Of considerably more interest is his collection of artifacts that includes a knife from the Battle of Little Bighorn, old-time cowboy garb, the bow and arrows that belonged to Geronimo, and many Plains Indian artifacts. Entrance is $5 adults or $1 for children; open daily 8 a.m.-8 p.m. May-Sept.; call for winter hours.

Wildlife Exhibits

The **Foundation for North American Wild Sheep** has its national headquarters at 720 Allen Ave. (just south of Buffalo Bill Historical Center), tel. (307) 527-6261. A favorite of wealthy trophy hunters, this nonprofit group funds wild sheep research and conservation. The place is a bit bizarre, however, with oversized bronze rams and a recording that plays out front even when nobody's around. The building is open Mon.-Fri. 8 a.m.-5 p.m.

The **Cody Wildlife Exhibit,** 433 Yellowstone Hwy., tel. (307) 587-2804, has a rather nice display of more than 400 mounted American and African wildlife—all sorts of record-sized critters, from a 17-foot-tall giraffe to a 2,800-pound buffalo. Admission costs $4 (free for kids under age seven); open daily 9 a.m.-8 p.m. June-September.

More Sights

Cedar Mountain, the 7,889-foot-tall summit overlooking Cody from the west, is where Buffalo Bill had wanted to be buried. A winding 4WD trail climbs to the top, but there's no public access at present. Also here is **Spirit Mountain Cave,** one of the first national monuments ever designated (1909). A lack of interest caused the designation to be withdrawn, but the caverns are still on public land. Spelunkers can get permission to enter from the BLM office in Cody.

Southeast of Cody near Beck Lake is the **Wyoming Vietnam Veterans Memorial,** a black granite memorial modeled after the one in Washington. It contains the names of 137 Wyoming men who were killed or declared missing in action.

If you're really desperate for something to do, visit the **Cody Murals** on the domed ceiling of the Latter Day Saints church at 1719 Wyoming Avenue. Tours are available daily during the summer; call (307) 587-3290. No, it isn't the Sistine Chapel. The mural, painted in 1951, offers a rosy-tinted version of Mormon Church history and the Bighorn Basin pioneers.

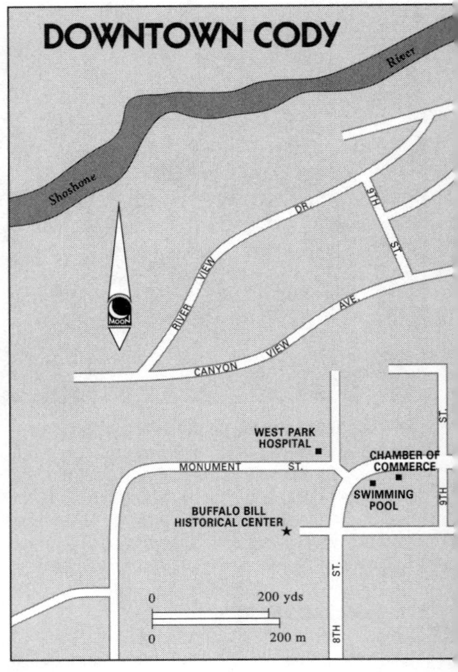

ACCOMMODATIONS

Motels and Hotels

The tourist town of Cody is jam-packed with lodging facilities, but be ready to pay more than anyplace in Wyoming except Jackson Hole. Budget accommodations are nonexistent during the summer, though rates plummet with the first cold nights of fall. The town doesn't have a hostel, but one is definitely needed! Most of the year, lodging in Cody is not a problem as long as you check in before 4 p.m., but during July and August you should reserve a week ahead—and longer for the Cody Stampede in early July.

Cody Area Central Reservations, tel. (307) 587-0200 or (888) 468-6996, makes reservations for many local motels, mountain lodges, and B&Bs at no additional charge, and it is a good one-stop place to plan your trip to the Cody

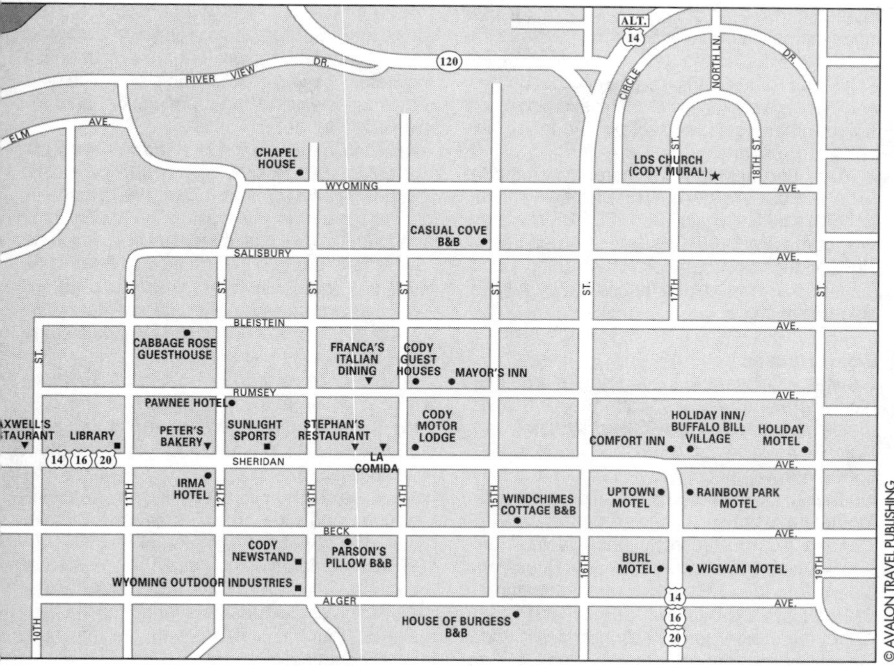

and Yellowstone area. Find it on the web at www.wtp.net/codyres.

A number of local places are described below; see Additional Cody Accommodations in the appendix for rates at other local motels. In addition, you will find many dude ranches and lodges in the mountain country around Cody; these are described above in the Wapiti Valley, Sunlight Basin, and South Fork Area sections.

Cody's least expensive lodging is also its oldest, the **Pawnee Hotel,** 1032 12th St., tel. (307) 587-2239. Built in 1900, the hotel contains 22 refurbished rooms, including four with clawfoot bathtubs. The least expensive accommodations are $22-25 s or $28-32 d and have a shared bath down the hall. Rooms with private baths are $32 s or $38 d, and a four-person suite is $48. Budget-Inexpensive.

Uptown Motel, 1562 Sheridan Ave., tel. (307) 587-4245, is a small motel with well-kept rooms for $50 s or $54-62 d, some of which contain microwaves and fridges. Inexpensive-Moderate.

Stay in very attractive log cabins from the 1920s at **Carriage House Motel,** 1816 8th St., tel. (307) 587-2572 or (800) 531-2572. The cabins are small and don't have phones, but they have been lovingly remodeled. Rates are $50-65 s or d; two-room suites that sleep up to six cost $85-135. Open May-October. Inexpensive.

Buffalo Bill Cody's historic **Irma Hotel,** 1192 Sheridan Ave., tel. (307) 587-4221 or (800) 745-4762, has a great downtown location and all the ambience you could want. It's the real thing, a classic Old West hotel. Its eight suites ($87 s or $94 d) provide updated rooms, or stay in the far less noteworthy motel rooms for $62 s or $69 d. Moderate-Expensive.

Parkway Inn, 720 W. Yellowstone Ave., tel. (307) 587-4208, is a nice place with newly remodeled rooms costing $78-88 s or d. Amenities include a swimming pool and continental breakfast. Open June-September. Moderate-Expensive.

One of the nicest chain motels in town, **Kelly Inn,** tel. (307) 527-5505 or (800) 635-3559, is located a mile east of Cody. Standard but spacious rooms are $89 s or $99 d; six-person family rooms with fridges and microwaves go for $135, and rooms with jacuzzi tubs cost $135 d. Also here is a sauna, jacuzzi, and exercise room. A light breakfast is available in the lobby. Expensive-Premium.

You'll find best-in-town motel accommodations at **Best Western Sunset,** 1601 8th St., tel. (307) 587-4265 or (800) 624-2727, where the rooms are $109-139 s or d. Amenities include indoor and outdoor pools, along with a jacuzzi, playground, and fitness facility. Expensive-Premium.

Guest Houses

Families may want to stay in one of the seven nicely furnished homes, cottages, and apartments managed by **Cody Guest Houses,** 1401 Rumsey Ave., tel. (307) 587-6000 or (800) 587-6560, www.wtp.net/cghouses. Most luxurious is a beautiful three-bedroom Victorian home ($450 for the entire house, sleeps six people, or $120-199 d for individual rooms). Other places include a remodeled 1930s church (Chapel House) that sleeps four for $175, three cottages starting at $110 d up to $150 for four people, and an efficiency apartment for $80 d. In addition, Cody Guest Houses manages Mayor's Inn B&B, described below.

Cabbage Rose Guest House, 1126 Bleistein Ave., tel. (307) 587-4984, is a century-old home with three bedrooms, one bath, and a full kitchen. Eight people can sleep here comfortably. Rates are $120, and children are welcome. Open May-September. Premium.

Cozy Cody Cottages, tel. (307) 587-9253, has two cottages located at 1403 and 1405 Rumsey Avenue. Rates are $80-110 d, and both places contain private baths, full kitchens, and laundry facilities. Moderate-Expensive.

Bed and Breakfasts

Several historic buildings are now part of the Cody B&B scene, offering a taste of the genteel past. **Parson's Pillow B&B,** 1202 14th St., tel. (307) 587-2382 or (800) 377-2348, probably the most interesting, enjoys a good central location. Completed in 1902, the building served for many years as a Methodist-Episcopal Church. Today it's a cozy and well-maintained B&B with antique furnishings, four guest rooms, private baths, and full breakfasts. Kids are accepted (but ask first), and the owners are exceptionally hospitable. Rooms cost $65-85 s or d. The web address is www.cruising-america.com/parsonspillow. Moderate.

Another friendly place is **Windchimes Cottage B&B,** 1501 Beck Ave., tel. (307) 527-5310 or (800) 241-5310, with three guest rooms in the large main house (built in the 1920s as a farmhouse), plus a cottage for families. All rooms have private baths. This is a nice place to stay, with filling country-style breakfasts and attractive rooms containing period decor. Rates are $80 s or d. Groups of five can stay in the cottage for $140. Kids are welcome. Moderate.

Also recommended is **House of Burgess B&B,** 1508 Alger Ave., tel. (307) 527-7208, www.cruising-america.com/burgess. Located on a quiet street just a few blocks from the heart of town, this 1928 brick and frame home features a relaxing and shady backyard, a large living room, and three guest rooms with private baths. Nicest is the treehouse suite ($80 s or $85 d), situated on an upstairs porch; the other rooms are $70 s or $75 d. A light and healthy breakfast is served each morning, and kids are accepted (but call first). A two-night minimum stay is required. Moderate.

For lodging in a classic Cody home, stay at **Mayor's Inn,** built in 1909 by the town's first mayor and restored to its original opulence. The three guest rooms include private baths with jetted tubs, down comforters, terry cloth robes, and heated floors. A full breakfast is served each morning, and children are welcome. Rates are $105-155 d, or $205 d for the suite with a jetted tub. The home is located at 1413 Rumsey Ave.; for details, contact Cody Guest Houses, tel. (307) 587-6000 or (800) 587-6560, www.wtp.net/cghouses. Expensive-Luxury.

Casual Cove B&B, 1431 Salisbury, tel. (307) 587-3622, is a renovated 1908 home with three guest rooms, all with private baths. Room rates are $56-66 s or d, including a full breakfast. No kids under 10. Inexpensive-Luxury.

Lockhart B&B Inn, 109 Yellowstone Ave., tel. (307) 587-6074 or (800) 377-7255, has seven guest rooms with private baths. A full breakfast is served. Rates are $89-98 d including a full breakfast, and kids are welcome. The home once belonged to novelist and newspaper publisher Caroline Lockhart (1871-1962), one of the great characters of the West. It is furnished with antiques, and the baths contain clawfoot tubs and ceiling fans. Family rooms are also available. The B&B went through a series of managers in recent years and the quality suffered greatly. The owner promises improvements, but take a look for yourself before staying here. It's open April to mid-November. Expensive.

Campgrounds and RV Parks

The closest public campground ($9 for nonresidents, or $4 for Wyoming residents) is 11 miles west in Buffalo Bill State Park. Find many more campgrounds (most cost $9) in Shoshone National Forest, but the nearest is 28 miles west of town in Wapiti Valley.

You'll find eight private RV park/campgrounds in Cody, whose rates range widely: $14-27 for RVs, or $10-19 for tents. The two best ones are **Ponderosa Campground,** 1815 8th St., tel. (307) 587-9203, open mid-April to mid-October; and **7 K's RV Park,** 232 W. Yellowstone Ave., tel. (307) 587-5890 or (800) 223-9204, open April-October. Both of these have shade trees. **Cody KOA,** two miles east on US Hwy. 14/16/20, tel. (307) 587-2369 or (800) 562-8507, opened in 1964 as the first franchised KOA. Rates are $21 for tents and $29 for RVs. It's open May-Sept., with an outdoor pool and free pancake breakfasts and "kamping kabins" ($39 d). **Camp Cody,** 415 W. Yellowstone Ave., tel. (307) 587-9730 or (888) 231-2267, has RV hookups but no tent spaces. It's open year-round and includes an outdoor pool.

Other park-it spots include **Gateway Campground,** 203 W. Yellowstone Ave., tel. (307) 587-2561; **Parkway RV Campground** 132 W. Yellowstone Ave., tel. (307) 527-5927 or (800) 484-2365 extension 3881; and **Absaroka Bay RV Park,** US Hwy. 14/16/20 South, tel. (307) 527-7440 or (800) 557-7440. Absaroka's notable for a complete lack of shade; it's located on a windy hill to add to the fun. You can also park RVs at several of the Wapiti Valley lodges (described above), including **Elk Valley Inn, Wise Choice Inn,** and **Yellowstone Valley Inn.** Noncampers can take showers (for a fee) at Gateway Campground, 7 K's RV Park, or Ponderosa Campground.

FOOD

Because Cody is a tourist town, it's no surprise to find many fine places to eat, covering the spectrum from buffalo burgers to Chinese won tons. Of course, Cody also has all the faves—Arby's, Taco John's, Subway, McDonald's, Taco Bell, and more.

Breakfast and Lunch

Hang out with the farmers over breakfast or lunch at **Our Place,** 148 W. Yellowstone, tel. (307) 527-4420. **Cody Coffee Company & Eatery,** 1702 Sheridan Ave., tel. (307) 527-7879, has espresso, pastries, soups, and Italian subs. **Granny's,** 1550 Sheridan Ave., tel. (307) 587-4829, isn't particularly noteworthy but stays open 24 hours a day and serves breakfast anytime.

The ever-popular **Maxwell's Fine Food & Spirits,** 937 Sheridan Ave., tel. (307) 527-7749, dishes up homemade lunches that include sandwiches, pasta, and salads. It's a bright and friendly setting, with a patio for sunny days, and a small bakery/coffeehouse. The dinner menu ($10-18 entrées) features pasta, seafood, chicken, beef, and vegetarian dishes. Closed Sunday.

Peter's Bakery, 1191 Sheridan Ave., tel. (307) 527-5040, bakes breads, cookies, bagels, and turnovers. It's a great place for sub sandwiches and soups. You won't want to go back to Subway after this; the bread is made from scratch, not pulled from the freezer.

Patsy Ann's Pastry & Ladle, 1243 Beck Ave., tel. (307) 527-6297, creates fine sandwiches, homemade soups, and pastries (including great sticky buns).

Sunset House Restaurant, 1651 8th St., tel. (307) 587-2257, is a casual family spot for lunch and also features breakfast and dinner buffets.

Silver Dollar Bar & Grill, 1313 Sheridan Ave., tel. (307) 587-3554, makes the best hamburgers and other cowboy grub in town, served in a Western atmosphere. Guaranteed to fill you up.

Dinner

Proud Cut Saloon, 1227 Sheridan Ave., tel. (307) 587-7343, is a fine old-time Wyoming bar and restaurant offering unusual sandwiches at lunchtime and outstanding steak and prime rib for dinner. It's the real thing, with rustic Old West decor. **Irma Hotel,** 1192 Sheridan Ave., tel. (307) 587-4221, is a long-time favorite of locals for lunch and dinner, but the food is nothing special.

In existence since 1922, **Cassie's Supper Club,** 214 Yellowstone Ave., tel. (307) 527-5500, is famous locally for its steaks, prime rib, and shrimp. The Wednesday lunchtime Mexican specials bring out the crowds.

Stefan's Restaurant, 1367 Sheridan Ave., tel. (307) 587-8511, is an enjoyable place with a diverse menu and three meals a day. Dinner entrées ($10-23) are unconventional takes on such favorites as steaks, filet mignon, baby back ribs, Kung Pao chicken, and shrimp scampi. The atmosphere is a bit upscale, but not stuffy. Be sure to save room for the luscious desserts.

International Eats

You'll find outstanding Northern Italian cuisine at **Franca's Italian Dining,** 1374 Rumsey Ave., tel. (307) 587-5354 or (888) 806-5354. The menu changes throughout the week, with a different fixed-price dinner each evening ($17-26). Completely authentic, right down to the Italian chef. Reservations are essential for this quaint little restaurant; call several days ahead to be assured of a table. Franca's doesn't take credit cards.

Located in the heart of town, **La Comida,** 1385 Sheridan Ave., tel. (307) 587-9556, serves very good Mexican food for reasonable prices. Take in the local scene from the outside patio. On the west side of town, **Zapata's,** 325 W. Yellowstone Ave., tel. (307) 527-7181, offers food with a New Mexican flavor and tasty margaritas. For Chinese food, visit **Hong Kong Restaurant,** 1201 17th St., tel. (307) 587-6420.

Black Sheep Restaurant, on the east end of town at 1901 Mountain View Rd., tel. (307) 527-5895, serves Greek specialties, along with lamb chops, pork loin, steak, seafood, pasta, and hickory smoked ribs. Dinner entrées cost $10-18.

Pizza Hut, 736 Yellowstone Ave., tel. (307) 527-7819, has predictable pizzas and all-you-can-eat lunch buffets.

Grocers and Specialty Foods

Cody's grocers include a **Smith's** at 1526 Rumsey Ave., tel. (307) 587-6289, and a huge **Albertson's,** 1825 17th St., tel. (307) 527-7007. For natural foods and Wyoming-made gifts, head to **Whole Foods Trading Co.,** 1243 Rumsey Ave., tel. (307) 587-3213. **Wyoming Buffalo Company,** 1276 Sheridan Ave. tel. (307) 587-8708 or (800) 453-0636, specializes in buffalo jerky, salami, sausage, and fresh meat, with a variety of gift packages. Stop in for a free sample.

EVENTS AND ENTERTAINMENT

Summer is a busy time in Cody, with special events nearly every weekend. Cody calls itself "Rodeo Capital of the World," and it packs the calendar with nightly summertime rodeos, plus the famous Cody Stampede. The rodeo grounds are a mile west of town on US Hwy. 14/16/20.

Cody Nite Rodeo

After more than 60 years of operation, the Cody Nite Rodeo is still one of the best in a state filled with rodeos. Shows begin nightly at 8:30 p.m. June-August and always attract a big crowd. The best performances take place Friday and Saturday nights, when you'll see events sanctioned by the Professional Rodeo Cowboys Association (PRCA). A crowd favorite is the calf scramble, starring kids from the stands. Tickets cost $10-12 for adults and $4-6 for children. Call (307) 587-5155 or (800) 207-0744 for details, or look on the web at www.westwyoming.com/cody-stampede.

Cody Stampede

Independence Day sets the stage for Cody's main event, the Cody Stampede, held July 1-4. Established in 1922, it attracts thousands of visitors from all over the nation. Parade fans are treated to one each morning (including a kiddie parade), with dozens of marching bands, mountain men, vintage autos, floats, cowboys, and tons of free candy. Special PRCA rodeo performances, a street dance, art shows, running events, fireworks, and a carnival complete the schedule. For more info, call (307) 587-5155 or (800) 207-0744, or visit www.westwyoming.com/cody-stampede.

More Events

At 6 p.m. each evening of the summer, the **Cody Gunslingers** perform downtown at the Irma Hotel. The mock gunfights are entertainment,

Western style. Worth a look if you haven't seen it before, but the players do a more professional job at the Jackson shootout.

Cowboy Songs and Range Ballads is a unique Western musical festival held the second weekend of April at the Buffalo Bill Historical Center. You'll hear true cowboy music (not country-western), along with poetry and stories from cowboys, ranchers, musicians, and folklorists.

Held in the Robbie Powwow Garden in front of the Buffalo Bill Historical Center in late June, the **Plains Indian Powwow** attracts several hundred participants from all over the Rockies and Canada vying for $10,000 in prize money. It includes daylong singing and dancing in tribal regalia and various dance competitions. Visitors can purchase Indian arts and crafts and taste Indian tacos and fry bread.

The **Old West Show & Auction** in mid-June offers the chance for collectors to purchase quality old cowboy gear. It's considered the finest such event in the nation and attracts a wealthy crowd.

Frontier Festival, held in mid-July at the Buffalo Bill Historical Center, is a celebration of the many turn-of-the-century skills that were needed to survive on the frontier. Included are demonstrations of horsepacking, hide tanning, gunsmithing, rawhide braiding, weaving, and other home-grown talents. Various contests, musical performances, and booths make this an enjoyable and popular event.

The **Yellowstone Jazz Festival** in mid-July brings both regional and national jazz groups. The **Buffalo Bill Art Show & Sale** in mid-September is the biggest art event of the year. It features exhibitions, a symposium, receptions, and an auction.

Music and Entertainment

The downtown **City Park bandshell** is the place to be on Friday evenings during the summer; free musical performances start at 6 p.m. **Cassie's,** 214 Yellowstone Ave., tel. (307) 527-5500, has Wednesday night country swing dance lessons, along with country-western and mellow rock tunes nightly throughout the summer. Hang around the bar long enough and you can join in that old Cassie's favorite, barroom brawling. **Angie's,** at the Silver Dollar Bar, 1313 Sheridan Ave., tel. (307) 587-3554, sometimes has rock bands. The big dance floor fills up on weekends. **Gibb's Sports Pub,** 1901 Mountain View Rd. (inside the Black Sheep Restaurant), tel. (307) 527-5895, has a big-screen TV for ESPN fanatics, plus a pool table and darts.

Park Drive In, on the east end of Big Horn Dr., tel. (307) 587-2712, is one of the few drive-in theaters left in Wyoming. Open Thurs.-Sun. only. For the indoor version, head to **Cody Theatre,** 1171 Sheridan Ave., tel. (307) 587-2712, or the four-plex version, **Big Horn Cinemas,** 2525 Big Horn Ave., tel. (307) 587-8009.

the Cody Stampede parade

RECREATION

River Rafting

One of the most popular summertime activities in Cody is floating the class I and II Shoshone River. Beware, however: even with these mild conditions, you should plan on getting soaked in the rapids. Expect to pay around $20 for adults ($18 for kids) for a six-mile run that lasts 90 minutes, or $26 for adults ($24 for kids) for a 13-mile (three-hour) float. For details, contact **Wyoming River Trips,** 233 Yellowstone Hwy., tel. (307) 587-6661 or (800) 586-6661; **River Runners,** 1491 Sheridan Ave., tel. (307) 527-7238 or (800) 535-7238; or **Red Canyon River Trips,** 1374 Sheridan Ave., tel. (307) 587-6988 or (800) 293-0148.

Founded in 1978, Wyoming River Trips are the most experienced folks in Cody. Red Canyon River Trips is newer, but the guides are very experienced and they use smaller rafts for a more personalized trip. Both Wyoming River and Red Canyon offer inflatable kayak trips for those who want to run the rapids on their own power. In addition, Red Canyon leads scenic float trips down the Clarks Fork; see "Sunlight Basin" above for details.

If you want to try rafting or kayaking on your own, you'll find several miles of very technical class IV water with some class V drops below the dam and above DeMaris Springs. Above the dam are stretches of class I and II water with good access from the main highway. Ask locally for flow conditions before heading out since snowmelt and dam releases can dramatically affect water levels. The rafting companies offer half-day whitewater trips down the North Fork above the reservoir for $50 per person including lunch. These trips only run late May through July, when the water level is high.

Most rafters put in three miles west of Cody off Demaris Street. Just upstream from the put-in point is DeMaris Springs, a part of **"Colter's Hell"** that is on private property and not open to the public. The area was once far more active, with hot springs bubbling out of the river and sulfurous smoke rising all around. People actually died from the poisonous gas. Today the geothermal activity has lessened, but the air still smells of sulfur and small hot springs color the cliff faces. Miners worked over nearby hillsides in search of sulfur; the diggings are still apparent. It's also pretty obvious why they first called this the Stinkingwater River.

Horse and Wagon Rides

Horseback rides are available from **Cedar Mountain Trail Rides,** tel. (307) 527-4966, located a mile west of the rodeo grounds; **Gateway Motel and Campground,** 203 Yellowstone, tel. (307) 587-6507; and **Buffalo Bill's Trail Rides,** at the Cody KOA a mile east of the airport, tel. (307) 587-2369. Many of the lodges in Wapiti Valley (see Shoshone National Forest, above) also offer horseback rides as well as longer backcountry pack trips. Get a complete listing of Cody area outfitters and guides from the chamber of commerce, and a list of permitted outfitters from local Forest Service offices.

Located at the Holiday Inn, **Heart 3 Carriage Service,** tel. (307) 899-1484, has downtown carriage rides all summer long; $35 per carriage.

Each August, horse enthusiasts join in a week-long trip called **High Country Trail Ride.** Most folks bring their own horses, but rentals are also available. The route takes participants through Sunlight Basin, with overnight camping, a support staff, veterinarians, catered meals, and entertainment beneath the circus tent. Call (307) 527-7468 for details.

More Recreation

A spacious new recreation center opens on the south side of Cody in 2000, with a large indoor pool and other facilities; call (307) 587-2550 for details. Other swimming options include an **outdoor pool** across from the Buffalo Bill Historical Center at 1240 Beck Ave., tel. (307) 527-7511, and the **Stock Natorium** at 9th St. and Beck Ave., tel. (307) 587-2550.

Cody Rock Gym, 1310 Shoshone, tel. (307) 587-5222, has an indoor climbing wall. **Foote's Mountaineering,** 1280 Sheridan Ave., tel. (307) 527-9937, has a 32-foot-high climbing wall outside in the back and also sells a variety of climbing gear, maps, and other supplies.

Rent mountain bikes from **Olde Faithful Bicycle,** 1231 16th St., tel. (307) 527-5110 or (800) 775-6023. Olde Faithful also offers mountain-bike tours of the area.

The 18-hole **Olive-Glenn Golf and Country Club,** 802 Meadow Lane, tel. (307) 587-5688, is a PGA championship course with a complete golf shop and upscale restaurant. Families enjoy playing **miniature golf** at the downtown city park, tel. (307) 587-3685. It's open summers only.

Outdoor Gear

For quality backcountry equipment—especially if you travel by horse—be sure to drop by **Wyoming Outdoor Industries,** 1231 13th St., tel. (307) 527-6449 or (800) 725-6853. You won't find Gore-Tex jogbras here, just tough equipment for backcountry use (especially horsepacking), including folding woodstoves, pack saddles, bear-resistant panniers, and wall tents. There's also a mail-order catalog.

Sunlight Sports, 1251 Sheridan Ave., tel. (307) 587-9517, is the largest outdoors shop in town, with tents, climbing equipment, clothes, topographic maps, and more. It also rents cross-country and downhill skis, snowboards, and snowshoes during the winter, and this is the place to go for details on ice climbing in the South Fork area. Get topographic maps from **Cody Newsstand,** 1121 13th St., tel. (307) 587-2843.

North Fork Anglers, 1438 Sheridan Ave., tel. (307) 527-7274, has anything you might need for fly-fishing, including a full-service retail shop, professional fishing guides, and fly-tying clinics.

INFORMATION AND SERVICES

Get local info from the **Cody Country Chamber of Commerce** at 836 Sheridan Ave., tel. (307) 587-2297 or (800) 393-2639, or on the web at www.codychamber.org. Hours are Mon.-Sat. 8 a.m.-7 p.m. and Sunday 10 a.m.-3 p.m. Memorial Day to Labor Day; and Mon.-Fri. 8 a.m.-5 p.m. the rest of the year. This log building housed the original Buffalo Bill Museum from 1927 to 1969 and was built as a replica of Cody's TE Ranch in northwestern Wyoming. It's on the National Register of Historic Places. In addition to the chamber's website, you may want to visit www.codynetwork.com for local information.

The BLM's **Cody Resources Office** is at 1002 Blackburn Ave., tel. (307) 587-2216. The Forest Service has two local offices: the **Shoshone National Forest Supervisor's Office** at 808 Meadowlark Ave., tel. (307) 527-6241, and the smaller **Wapiti Ranger District Office** at 203 W. Yellowstone Ave., tel. (307) 527-6921. The Shoshone National Forest website is www.fs.fed.us/r2/shoshone.

Services

Cody's **West Park Hospital,** 707 Sheridan Ave., tel. (307) 527-7501 or (800) 654-9447, is the largest in Bighorn Basin, and one of the best in the state. The hospital's **Urgent Care Clinic** at 702 Yellowstone Ave., tel. (307) 587-7207, is open daily and doesn't require an appointment.

Get fast cash at **ATMs** scattered throughout Cody, including one inside the Buffalo Bill Historical Center and another in the Wal-Mart store.

Wash clothes at **Skippy's Laundromat,** 728 Yellowstone Ave., tel. (307) 527-6001; **Eastgate Laundry,** 1813 17th St., tel. (307) 587-5355; and **Quick Coin-Op Laundromat,** 930 12th St., tel. (307) 587-6519.

Need a dogsitter while you're heading into Yellowstone for a few days? Several local kennels will keep an eye on Spot or Fifi for you: **Chinook Boarding Kennels,** 134 Cooper Lane E., tel. (307) 587-3379; **Cody Veterinary Hospital,** 5524 Greybull Hwy., tel. (307) 587-3151; and **Pet Set,** 2625 Big Horn Powell Hwy., tel. (307) 587-9515.

OTHER PRACTICALITIES

Shopping

As you might expect from a tourist town, Cody has more than its share of shops dealing in clunky jewelry, crass T-shirts, and fake Indian trinkets. Fortunately, it's also home to a number of places with a bit more class.

Corral West Ranchwear, 1202 Sheridan Ave., tel. (307) 587-2122, has a large collection of big game heads and a couple of stuffed nine-foot-tall bears. Oh, yes, it also sells inexpensive Western wear. Get fancy Western duds at **Custom Cowboy Shop,** 1286 Sheridan Ave., tel. (307) 527-7300.

Cody Rodeo Company, 1291 Sheridan Ave., tel. (307) 587-5913, sells cowboy gear and rodeo memorabilia in a fun atmosphere. Decorations include a turn-of-the-century backbar from Hardin, Montana, and a **stuffed bull** that stood in front of the Irma Hotel for many years. Get your picture taken atop the bull for $7. Another fun place is **Crafty Quilter,** 1262 Sheridan Ave., tel. (307) 527-6305, which sells handmade quilts.

Traditions West Antique Mall, 1131 Sheridan Ave., tel. (307) 587-7434, is a good place to look for Western antiques. A block away at 1215 Sheridan Ave., **Old West Antiques,** tel. (307) 587-9014, even serves espresso in the back, where you can sit on old barber chairs.

Books

The **Park County Library** at 1057 Sheridan Ave., tel. (307) 587-6204, has regional titles and computers providing Internet access. New books are available from **Cody Newsstand,** 1121 13th St., tel. (307) 587-2843, and **The Thistle,** 1243 Rumsey Ave., tel. (307) 587-6635. Cody Newsstand also has one of the best magazine selections in Bighorn Basin. **Wyoming Well Book Exchange and Oilfield Supply,** 1902 E. Sheridan Ave., tel. (307) 587-4249, has the oddest combination in town: bodice-buster novels and oil drilling equipment!

Transportation

Yellowstone Regional Airport is just east of town on US Hwy. 14/16/20. **Skywest/Delta,** tel. (307) 587-9740 or (800) 221-1212, has daily flights to Salt Lake City, while **United Express/Great Lakes Aviation,** tel. (307) 527-6443 or (800) 241-6522, connects to Denver. **Spirit Mountain Aviation,** tel. (307) 587-6732, offers scenic flights and charter service. **Phidippides Shuttle Service,** tel. (307) 527-6789, provides shuttle vans to the Billings, Montana, airport.

Rent cars at the airport from **Avis,** (307) 587-5792 or (800) 331-1212; **Budget,** tel. (307) 587-6066 or (800) 527-0700; **Hertz,** tel. (307) 587-2914 or (800) 654-3131; or **Thrifty,** tel. (307) 587-8855 or (888) 794-1025.

Buses from **Powder River/Coach USA,** tel. (800) 442-3682, stop at Daylight Donuts, 1452 Sheridan Ave., providing service to Billings, Montana, along with towns in to northern and eastern Wyoming.

Tours

During the summer, daily lower-loop tours of Yellowstone National Park—$60 for adults, $30 for kids—are available through **Powder River/Coach USA,** tel. (307) 527-3677. You can stay overnight in Yellowstone and return on a later van for no extra charge (on a space-available basis), transfer to Gray Line buses (tel. 307-733-4325 or 800-443-6133) to reach Jackson or West Yellowstone, or catch the vans of 4x4 Stage (tel. 406-388-6404 or 800-517-8243) for Gardiner, West Yellowstone, Cooke City, or Bozeman.

For a more personalized trip, call **Grub Steak Expeditions,** tel. (307) 527-6316 or (800) 527-6316. It leads 12-hour auto tours of the park, along with visits to Sunlight Basin, Wapiti Valley, and the South Fork. Multiday trips are also available. One-day tours cost $300 for two people, plus $75 per person for additional people. These are very popular with families looking for a unique perspective on the park, and some are led by the co-owner, a retired Yellowstone park ranger. Both **Wyoming Touring Adventures,** tel. (307) 587-5136, and **Yellowstone Expedition Services,** tel. 9307) 587-5452 or (888) 808-7990, also offer customized auto tours into Yellowstone with a maximum of six people per group.

DUBOIS

Approaching Dubois (pop. 1,000) from either direction, you drive through the extraordinary red, yellow, and gray badlands that set this country apart. The luxuriant Wind River winds its way down a narrow valley where horses graze in the irrigated pastures and old barns and newer log homes stand against the hills, while the tree-covered Absaroka and Wind River Mountains ring distant views. The town of Dubois consists of a long main street that makes a startlingly abrupt elbow turn and then points due west toward the mountains. The many log buildings and snatches of wooden sidewalk give the place an authentic frontier feel. Locals live in cabins, trailer homes, and simple frame houses. Dubois weather is famously mild; warm Chinook winds often melt any snow that falls. Grand scenery reigns in all directions. Snowmobilers, hunters, and anglers have discovered that Dubois provides a good place to relax in Wyoming's "banana belt" while at the same time remaining close to the more temperamental mountains. The area basks in an average of 300 days of sunshine each year. By the way, Dubois is pronounced "DU-boys"; other pronunciations will reveal your tenderfoot status. Locals sometimes jokingly call it "Dubious."

the badlands near Dubois

HISTORY

Dubois began in the 1880s when pioneer ranchers and more than a few rustlers—including Butch Cassidy—settled in the area, followed by Scandinavian hand-loggers who cut lodgepole for railroad ties. The town that grew up along the juncture of Horse Creek and the Wind River was first known as Never Sweat, but when citizens applied for a post office the Postal Service refused to allow the name and suggested Dubois instead—the name of an Idaho senator who just happened to be on the Senate committee that provided funding for the post office.

Like many edge-of-the-mountain towns, Dubois is in transition. For most of its existence, it served as a logging and ranching center. In 1987, the Louisiana Pacific sawmill shut down, throwing many loggers and millworkers onto the unemployment rolls. Loggers blamed environmentalists and the Forest Service for sharply reducing the timber available; environmentalists countered that the company was simply using the reductions as an excuse to close an aging mill. After everyone ran out of mud to sling, they decided to look at what Dubois had to offer and discovered that, lo and behold, they just happened to be sitting in an almost-undiscovered recreational and retirement gold mine. In the 1990s the town leapt full-force into the tourism business. The transformation of Dubois to a visitor-oriented economy certainly has its downside—elaborate trophy log summer homes are beginning to overrun the lush pastures on both ends of town—but so far this pretty little place has been spared the onslaught of industrial tourism. Stay tuned.

DUBOIS AT A GLANCE

Elevation 6,917 feet

Dubois Chamber of Commerce, 616 W. Ramshorn, tel. (307) 455-2556, www.dteworld.com/duboiscc, open daily Memorial Day to Labor Day, Mon.-Fri. the rest of the year

Shoshone National Forest Wind River Ranger District, one mile west of town, tel. (307) 455-2466, www.fs.fed.us/r2/shoshone

SIGHTS

Museum

The **Dubois Museum** at 909 W. Ramshorn, tel. (307) 455-2284, is open daily 9 a.m.-5 p.m. June-Aug., and daily 10 a.m.-5 p.m. in September; closed the rest of the year. Entrance is $1 for adults, 50 cents for kids under 12, or $3 for the whole family. It houses exhibits on the Sheepeater Indians and various cultural artifacts, petrified wood, and displays on ranch life, natural history, and the tie hacks. Be sure to check out the hilarious photo of 1930s movie star Tim McCoy teaching golf to a rather skeptical group of Shoshone Indians! Out front are five historic log cabins. Upstairs from the museum is the **Headwaters Community Arts and Conference Center,** where a spacious gallery displays the works of local artists.

National Bighorn Sheep Center

Located right next door to the museum, the National Bighorn Sheep Interpretive Center, 907 W. Ramshorn, tel. (307) 455-3429 or (888) 209-2795, www.bighorn.org, houses displays on desert bighorn, Rocky Mountain bighorn, stone sheep, and Dall sheep. The museum details how the population was brought back from the brink of extinction and includes fine hands-on exhibits and interactive displays on how bighorns live. Also here is a diorama of a Sheepeater Indian trap and mounted specimens around a 16-foot-high central "mountain." A theater shows videos on bighorn sheep and other topics, and a gift shop sells books and other items. The center is open daily 9 a.m.-8 p.m. Memorial Day to Labor Day; and Thurs.-Mon. 9 a.m.-4 p.m. the rest of the year. Entrance costs $2 for adults, 75 cents for kids under 13, or $5 for families.

Whiskey Basin

Approximately five miles east of Dubois, a sign points the way to Whiskey Basin. Follow this gravel road two miles to the **Dubois State Fish Hatchery,** where rainbow, cutthroat, golden, brook, and brown trout, as well as grayling, are raised. It's open daily 8 a.m.-5 p.m. The bucolic setting is hard to beat: a tree-lined creek surrounded by sage, mountains, and badlands.

A short distance farther up the road is a wildlife viewing kiosk for the **Whiskey Basin Wildlife Habitat Area.** In winter the valley is home to the largest population of Rocky Mountain bighorn sheep anywhere on earth. Some 900 sheep congregate here because of the mild temperatures and shallow snow. Although you're likely to find sheep all winter, the best time to photograph them is the breeding season, from late November through December. During this period you'll see rams charging head-first into each other over the chance to mate. It's enough to give you a headache, though I doubt the "not tonight—I have a headache" line gets used much by bighorns. Despite any headaches, something must happen, since lambs are born in late May and early June high up on rocky slopes. **Winter wildlife tours** are offered by the National Bighorn Sheep Interpretive Center. These five-hour van trips cost $30 per person and include binoculars and spotting scopes to view the animals. They operate on weekends from mid-November through March; call (307) 455-3429 for reservations (recommended). Bighorn sheep are also sometimes seen in the meadows along the highway or in the hills just above Dubois.

COURTESY AISLINN RACE

Beyond the wildlife viewing kiosk, the road follows Torrey Creek up past a string of three small bodies of water: Torrey, Ring, and Trail Lakes. These were created by retreating glaciers centuries ago, but small dams have enlarged them. State Game and Fish **campsites** (free) are located along Ring and Trail Lakes. **Ring Lake Ranch,** tel. (307) 455-2663, houses an ecumenical religious facility used for a variety of retreats, seminars, and other activities.

A trailhead at the end of the road up Whiskey Basin (12 miles from the turnoff) provides access to the primary route up to Dinwoody Glacier and 13,804-foot Gannett Peak (Wyoming's highest). Keep your eyes open for the osprey nest at mile five. The Audubon Society has a field camp at mile eight.

You'll discover quite a few Indian **pictographs** on large boulders in the Trail Lake vicinity; look for them along the hillside between Trail and Ring Lakes. These figures—some four feet tall—are elaborate otherworldly creations with horns and headdresses, and they are believed to represent shamans performing ceremonies under altered states of consciousness. While their age is unknown, the pictographs are probably at least 2,000 years old and of Athapaskan (a Canadian tribe) rather than Shoshonean origin. This is some of the oldest rock art in Wyoming. Please be very careful to protect these sacred sites.

Other Sights

On the west end of Dubois is a signed turnoff to a **scenic overlook.** The gravel road climbs sharply (no RVs) for approximately a mile to the viewpoint, where signs note the surrounding peaks. Enjoy marvelous views of 11,635-foot Ramshorn Peak from here.

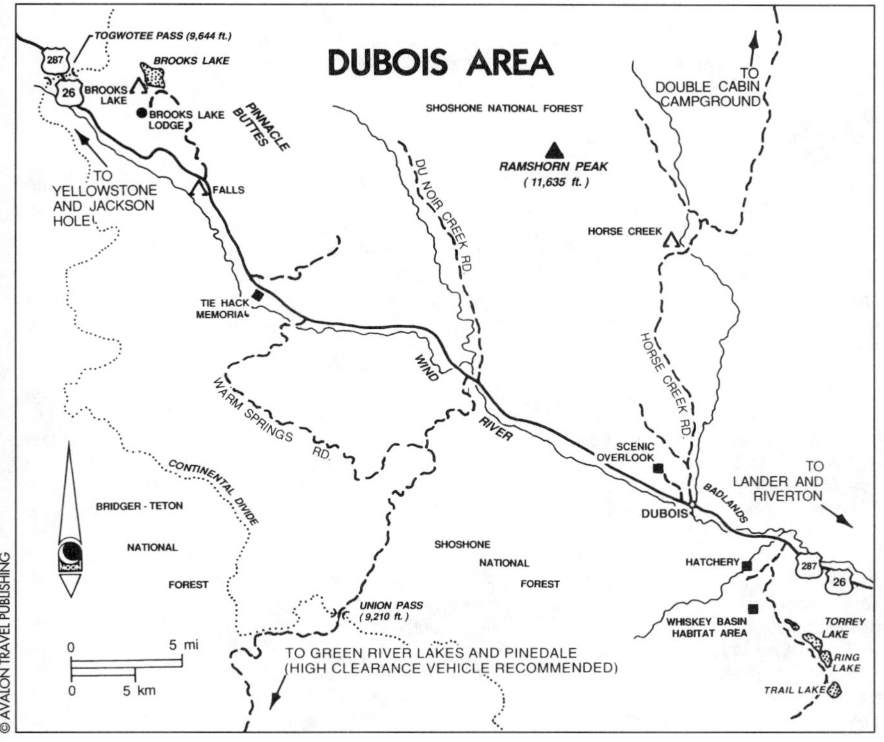

The magnificent badlands on both sides of Dubois—but especially to the east—are well worth exploring. The Bureau of Land Management maintains a fascinating **Badlands Interpretive Trail** up Mason Draw, 2.4 miles northeast of town. Pick up a booklet describing the trail at the visitor center. Depending upon your route, the hike should take an hour or two to complete.

Rock hounds will find all sorts of petrified wood, agates, and other colorful rocks up the Wiggins Fork and Horse Creek drainages; ask at the chamber of commerce for directions.

One thing you certainly would not expect to find in Dubois is a training center for lawyers, but famed Wyoming attorney Gerry Spence has one on his Thunderbird Ranch east of town. His **Trial Lawyers College** puts some 50 lawyers through an intense four-week session each summer, with mock trials and professional actors. Watch your step with all these lawyers around Dubois!

ACCOMMODATIONS

Motels

Dubois makes an excellent stopping point on the way to Yellowstone and Grand Teton National Parks, with lodging prices well below those in Jackson Hole. All places are open year-round unless noted otherwise, and all except Black Bear and Super 8 can be found on the web at www.dteworld.com/wyoming/lodging.htm. Accommodations are listed below from least to most expensive. Add a 7% sales and lodging tax to these rates.

If you're looking for quietude, head three miles east of town to **Riverside Inn & Campground,** tel. (307) 455-2337 or (877) 489-2337, where the motel rooms are $30 s or $40-44 d. The motel has fishing access to a private stretch of the river. Inexpensive.

Located right on the river, **Wind River Motel,** 519 W. Ramshorn, tel. (307) 455-2611 or (877) 455-2621, has a mix of rustic cabins, motel rooms, and suites for $30-75 s or d. Some rooms contain kitchenettes. Open April-November. Budget-Moderate.

Trail's End Motel, 511 Ramshorn, tel. (307) 455-2540 or (888) 455-6660, has recently remodeled rooms for $34-56 s or $42-64 d. Amenities include in-room refrigerators and microwaves, decks facing the Wind River, an exercise facility, and an outdoor jacuzzi. Inexpensive-Moderate.

Located a half mile east of Dubois, **Chinook Winds Mountain Lodge**, tel. (307) 455-2987 or (800) 863-0354, has a variety of rooms. Riverside motel units are $40 s or $50-80 d, and they contain small fridges. Cabins with full kitchens cost $75 d. The Wind River is right out the back door. Inexpensive-Moderate.

Find newly remodeled accommodations at the largest motel in town, **Stagecoach Motor Inn,** 103 Ramshorn, tel. (307) 455-2303 or (800) 455-5090. Rates are $ 45 s or $55-60 d, including an outdoor pool; kitchenette units cost $75 and sleep four. Suites are also available. Inexpensive-Moderate.

For historic rooms stay at **Twin Pines Lodge & Cabins,** 218 Ramshorn, tel. (307) 455-2600 or (800) 550-6332. Built in 1934, and on the National Register of Historic Places, the lodge has modern and rustic cabins for $42 s or $55 d, with fridges in all rooms. Inexpensive.

A fine riverside place is **Black Bear Country Inn,** 505 W. Ramshorn, tel. (307) 455-2344 or (800) 873-2327, where the rooms cost $44-50 s or d, including fridges and microwaves. Kitchenette apartments sleep five people and cost $65. The motel is open mid-May through Thanksgiving. Inexpensive.

Branding Iron Motel, 401 Ramshorn, tel. (307) 455-2893 or (800) 341-8000, www.brandingironinn.com, has cozy and well-maintained duplex log cabins that were built in the 1940s. Rates are $48-53 s or d; kitchenettes cost $6 extra. Inexpensive.

Two miles west of town is **Super 8 Motel,** tel. (307) 455-3694 or (800) 800-8000, where the rooms are $51 s or $54 d, including access to a jacuzzi. Inexpensive.

A mile west of town is **Bald Mountain Inn,** tel. (307) 455-2844 or (800) 682-9323, where spacious motel rooms with kitchenettes are $54 s or d. Two-story townhouse units with fireplaces and kitchens cost $90 a night and can sleep six. Bring your fishing pole; the Wind River is right out back. Inexpensive.

Bed and Breakfasts

Jakey's Fork Homestead has B&B accommodations in a delightful century-old homestead four miles east of town. Located near the bighorn sheep refuge in Whiskey Basin, Jakey's Fork offers extraordinary views of both the Wind River Mountains and nearby badlands. Birdwatchers will find a host of feathered friends in the trees and marsh. Be sure to ask owner Irene Bridges about Butch Cassidy's encounter with Indians nearby. Guests can stay in the modern home or a rustic sod-covered cabin. A sauna and jacuzzi bathtub are available, and the rooms have shared baths. A full breakfast is served. Rates are $85 d in the house, or $110 d ($130 for four people) in the cabin. Weekly rates are also available. Children will enjoy the toy-filled playroom. Get more info at tel. (307) 455-2769, or www.cruising-america.com/jakeysfork. Expensive.

Just two blocks from downtown Dubois is **The Stone House B&B,** 207 South First St., tel. (307) 455-2555. Inside this stately stone home are two guest rooms ($45 s or $50 d) with shared baths, along with a basement suite ($70 d) that has a private bath. A full breakfast is served each morning, and the sitting room faces Whiskey Mountain, a good place to watch for bighorn sheep. Inexpensive-Moderate.

Six miles west of Dubois is **Mountain Top B&B at Triple EEE Ranch,** on 20 acres of land with a modern lodge and duplex cabins. There are fine views of the Wind River Valley. This is primarily a dude ranch (see below for details), but unfilled rooms are offered on a nightly basis for $95 d including a big breakfast. The six guest rooms include private baths and access to a jacuzzi. Horseback rides are available. For more info, call (307) 455-2304 or (800) 353-2555, or check the website: www.dudesville.com. Expensive.

Dude Ranches

Fifteen different dude ranches/mountain lodges are found in the Dubois area. Six are described below, and another nine places are described in the Over Togwotee Pass section below.

Located 10 miles out East Fork Road, **Lazy L&B Ranch** is a century-old ranch offering creekside log cabins, horseback riding, overnight pack trips, cowboy poetry and songs, a swimming pool, hot tub, stocked fishing ponds, kids' programs, volleyball, pool table, fly-fishing, and a rifle range. The ranch excels at horseback rides offered, and guests can choose trips through the badlands or high into the mountains. It is open late May-Sept., with all-inclusive weekly rates of $1,950 for two people. Get more details by calling (307) 455-2839 or (800) 453-9488, or check its website: www.ranchweb.com/lazyl&b. Luxury.

Sixteen miles north of Dubois in gorgeous Dunoir Valley, **Absaroka Ranch,** tel. (307) 455-2275, has all the typical guest ranch offerings: horseback riding, guided fly-fishing, hiking, cookouts, and pack trips. The ranch accommodates just 18 guests and emphasizes the personal touch. It is surrounded by National Forest land and has a comfortable main lodge (built in 1910), attractively restored log cabins, and a redwood sauna. The ranch is open mid-June to mid-September. All-inclusive weekly rates are $2,500 for two people. Luxury.

Bitterroot Ranch, tel. (307) 455-2778 or (800) 545-0019, emphasizes horseback riding for experienced riders; each guest has three horses. The owners breed Arabian horses and offer cross-country jumping courses, pack trips, fly-fishing, and kids' programs. Both French and German are spoken here, attracting an international clientele. The ranch is open June to mid-September and has space for 32 guests in a dozen cabins. The web address is www.ranchweb.com/bitterroot. All-inclusive weekly rates are $2,800 for two people. Luxury.

Located south of Dubois in beautiful Jakeys Fork Canyon, **CM Ranch,** tel. (307) 455-2331 or (800) 455-0721, is one of Wyoming's oldest dude ranches; it's been here since 1927. The ranch offers dramatic badlands topography and a variety of fossils, making it a favorite of geologists (and the amateur version). Trails lead into the adjacent Fitzpatrick Wilderness, a favorite destination for horseback trips. Fishing is another popular activity, and a fishing guide is available. The immaculate lodge buildings have space for 60 guests, and kids love the big outdoor pool. All-inclusive weekly rates at this delightful old-time ranch are $2,000-2,200 for two people. The web address is www.cmranch.com. Luxury.

Operating as a dude ranch since 1920, **T-Cross Ranch** is located 15 miles north of Dubois near Horse Creek and is open June to mid-September. Surrounded by the Shoshone National Forest, this remote ranch offers weekly accommodations for $2,100 for two people, including horseback riding, all meals, activities for kids, trout fishing, and a hot tub. Backcountry pack trips and other activities are also available. Lodging is in comfortable log cabins, and the main lodge has a massive stone fireplace and spacious front porch. Get more information by calling (307) 455-2206, or checking this web address: www.ranchweb.com/tcross. Luxury.

Elk Trails Ranch is a small adult-oriented riding ranch 25 miles northeast of Dubois off East Fork Road. The modern log cabins are surrounded by beautiful mountain country and have space for a maximum of six people. Day rides and fishing are the primary attractions. Rates are $145 per person per day, with a three-night minimum stay required. Get more information at tel. (307) 455-3615 or www.elktrails.com. Luxury.

Camping

The closest public camping spot is **Horse Creek Campground** ($8; open June-Oct.), 12 miles north of Dubois on Horse Creek Road. Three more Forest Service campgrounds are west of Dubois in the Pinnacle Buttes area (see Over Togwotee Pass below), and additional public campsites can be found east of Dubois in Whiskey Creek Basin, described above.

Circle-Up Camper Court, 225 W. Welty, tel. (307) 455-2238, charges $14 for tents (some shade), $19 for RVs, and $25 for basic cabins. Kids love the tepees for $17. Non-campers may use the showers here for $4. Open year-round, this is one of Wyoming's better private campgrounds. You can also park RVs ($20) or pitch tents ($15) at **Riverside Inn & Campground,** three miles east of town, tel. (307) 455-2337 or (877) 489-2337.

FOOD

Cowboy Cafe, 115 E. Ramshorn, tel. (307) 455-2595, has good home-style breakfasts with big helpings of biscuits and gravy. For a real artery-clogger, try the steak and eggs. The Cowboy is extremely popular with both locals and tourists.

The setting is old-fashioned, but **Ramshorn Inn,** 202 E. Ramshorn, tel. (307) 455-2400, serves surprisingly light fare for breakfast and lunch: bagels, sandwiches, and espresso.

Village Cafe/Daylight Donut, 515 W. Ramshorn, tel. (307) 455-2122, is an interesting family place offering doughnuts and coffee in the mornings and steak dinners each evening.

Get malts and sundaes from the old-time soda fountain inside the **Dubois Drugstore,** 126 E. Ramshorn, tel. (307) 455-2300.

Anita's Cafe, 106 E. Ramshorn, tel. (307) 455-3828, sits right along Horse Creek and serves gourmet lunches and dinners. Very nice. Open summer only.

Bernie's Cafe, 1408 Warm Springs Dr., tel. (307) 455-2115, opens at 6 each morning, and doesn't close 'til 10 p.m. You'll find down-home cooking, fast service, and all-American meals for reasonable prices. It's a family favorite.

Rustic Pine Steakhouse, 119 E. Ramshorn, tel. (307) 455-2772, is a carnivore's delight, with prime rib on Friday and Saturday nights; open for dinners only.

Cavallo Creek Grille, 112 E. Ramshorn, tel. (307) 455-3979, offers delicious lunches of salads, soup, and panini sandwiches, along with 10-inch pizzas from its wood-fired oven, served Mon.-Sat. evenings. On Sunday nights, there is an all-you-can-eat pizza feast for $9; a variety of pizzas straight out of the oven are passed around.

You can pick up groceries at **Ramshorn Food Farm,** 610 W. Ramshorn, tel. (307) 455-2402. For fresh-baked pastries, breads, and tasty hardtack made from an old Swedish recipe, stop by **Circle-Up Camper Court,** 225 W. Welty, tel. (307) 455-2238.

FUN AND GAMES

Entertainment

Dubois is a hopping place during the summer, especially on weekends. **Ramshorn Inn,** 202 E. Ramshorn, tel. (307) 455-2400, often has rock bands in the summer, while both **Rustic Pine,** 119 E. Ramshorn, tel. (307) 455-2430, and **Outlaw Saloon,** 204 W. Ramshorn, tel. (307) 455-2387, offer country-western bands. The Rustic Pine is a classic western bar with elk and moose heads, plenty of old wood, and a pool table. Check out the ashtrays, which note "God spends his vacation here." The famous Tuesday night **square dances** bring in dudes from local ranches in July and August. You may want to avoid this night if you don't want to be overwhelmed with fellow visitors.

Events

Dubois is one of 12 stops in early February's **Rocky Mountain Stage Stop Sled Dog Race,** an

all decked out in a black bear coat at the Whiskey Mountain Buckskinners Wind River Rendezvous

event that attracts some of the nation's best mushers with a $100,000 purse. The race begins and ends in Jackson. Call (307) 734-1163 for details, or check its website: www.wyomingstagestop.org.

The Dubois **4th of July** weekend is the biggest local event. The town comes alive with an ice-cream social, parade, western barbecue, fireworks, and rubber-ducky races down the river. The **National Art Show** comes to the arts center on the last week of July, attracting both professionals and amateurs. **Whiskey Mountain Buckskinners Wind River Rendezvous** on the second weekend of August includes some impressive black-powder marksmanship contests. Also don't miss the Dubois firemen's **buffalo barbecue** during rendezvous weekend. Get details on these and other events from the Dubois Chamber of Commerce, tel. (307) 455-2556.

Summer Recreation

Dubois sits at the confluence of the Wind River and Horse Creek, and both streams provide good trout fishing right in town. Hot springs keep the Wind River flowing all year. See the visitor center for descriptions of local fishing holes and brochures from local outfitters who offer pack trips and horseback rides.

The nine-hole **Antelope Hills Golf Course,** tel. (307) 455-2888, is on the western end of Dubois. Rent **mountain bikes** from Double Bar J Guest Ranch, 20 miles west of Dubois, tel. (307) 455-2681.

Winter Recreation

Based in Dubois, **Washakie Outfitting,** tel. (307) 733-3602 or (800) 249-0662, www.dogsled-washakie.com, leads a variety of excellent dogsled tours from Cowboy Village Resort at Togwotee (40 miles west of Dubois), and from Brooks Lake Lodge (23 miles west of Dubois). Iditarod veteran Billy Snodgrass offers half-day ($131), full-day ($175), overnight ($325), and extended trips and also runs teams from Teton Village in Jackson Hole. This is the real thing, with Alaskan huskies racing dogs in some of the most dramatic country imaginable.

Geyser Creek Dog Sled Adventures, tel. (307) 739-0165 or (800) 531-6874, www.dogsledadv.com, also leads dogsled tours of the Brooks Lake area and longer trips, all the way up to a three-day sled trip that includes overnight stops in a tepee and a yurt. All-day rates are $195 for adults, $95 for kids under age 10.

The Absarokas and Wind River Mountains around Dubois are extremely popular with snowmobilers during the winter months, and several places rent "sleds" in town and nearby. Don't expect peace and quiet with all these machines roaring through the backcountry! More than 300 miles of trails head out in all directions. **Cross-country skiers** find trails near Falls Campground and Brooks Lake (both 23 miles west of town) and Cowboy Village Resort at Togwotee (40 miles west), and in backcountry areas off-limits to snowmobiles.

OTHER PRACTICALITIES

Shopping

Sew What, 112 E. Ramshorn, tel. (307) 455-3373, sews authentic old western clothing using its own designs. It also sells Wyoming-made jewelry, baskets, quilts, leather goods, and clothing. Inside the lobby of **Black Bear Country**

Inn, 505 W. Ramshorn, tel. (307) 455-2344 or (800) 873-2327, you'll find more than 500 different teddy bears on display (and for sale). They call it the largest selection of teddy bears in the West. Don't let your two-year-old know about this place!

Trapline Gallery, 120 E. Ramshorn, tel. (307) 455-2800, sells Indian-crafted beadwork, jewelry, and artwork, as well as furs. **Horse Creek Traders,** 104 E. Ramshorn, tel. (307) 455-3345, has an impressive collection of antique trade beads for sale, along with tacky antler carvings and Indian trinkets. A few doors down is a nice bookshop, **Two Ocean Books,** tel. (307) 455-3554. **Water Wheel Gift Shop,** 113 E. Ramshorn, tel. (307) 455-2112, also carries a selection of Wyoming titles.

Purchase topographic maps at historic **Welty's General Store,** 113 W. Ramshorn, tel. (307) 455-2377 (its hours are haphazard—call first), and fishing supplies from **Wind River Fly Shop,** 116 E. Ramshorn, tel. (307) 455-2109, or **Whiskey Mountain Tackle** at 1418 Warm Springs Dr., tel. (307) 455-2587.

Information and Services

The **Dubois Chamber of Commerce,** 616 W. Ramshorn, tel. (307) 455-2556, is open Mon.-Sat. 9 a.m.-7 p.m. and Sunday noon-5 p.m. Memorial Day to Labor Day; and Mon.-Fri. 9 a.m.-5 p.m. the rest of the year. Ask for a self-guided tour map of old logging flumes, tie-hack cabins, and other historic structures. Its web address is www.dteworld.com/duboiscc.

Stop by the Forest Service's **Wind River Ranger District** office at 1403 W. Ramshorn (one mile west of town), tel. (307) 455-2466, for maps of Shoshone and Bridger-Teton National Forests ($4) and info on local trails. The Ranger District also has a listing of local horsepacking outfitters.

Dubois does not have a hospital, but the **Dubois Medical Center,** 706 Meckem, tel. (307) 455-2516, has a nurse practitioner. Wash clothes at the laundromat on W. Ramshorn across from Branding Iron Motel.

Transportation

Wind River Transportation Authority (WRTA), tel. (307) 856-7118 or (800) 439-7118, has on-demand van service to western and southwestern Wyoming. Travelers can call for a ride to Jackson, Salt Lake City, Lander, Riverton, Pinedale, Rock Springs, and other places. **Trail's End Motel,** tel. (307) 455-2540, provides shuttle van service to the airports in Jackson or Riverton.

DUBOIS VICINITY

Anyone who loves the outdoors will discover an abundance of pleasures around Dubois. There's good fishing for rainbow, cutthroat, brown, and brook trout in the Wind River and for rainbow, brook, and Mackinaw trout in the many alpine lakes. You'll also see lots of deer, elk, and bighorn sheep. Hikers and horse-packers will find hundreds of miles of Forest Service trails in the area. Photographers love the brilliantly colored badlands that frame Dubois on both the east and west sides. And each winter, hundreds of 'bilers climb on their "sleds" and cross-country skiers strap on their boards to enter the world of deep powder in the Absarokas.

Horse Creek Area

Horse Creek Road heads north from Dubois and provides scenic views of the Absarokas and nearby badland country. **Horse Creek Campground** ($6; open June-Oct.) is 12 miles north. Forest Road 504 continues another five miles, providing access to the Washakie Wilderness via Horse Creek Trail. Forest Road 508 splits off near Horse Creek Campground and leads another 17 miles to **Double Cabin Campground** ($6; open June-September). Several trails head into the wilderness from here; the most popular are Frontier Creek Trail and the Wiggins Fork Trail. You'll find remnants of a petrified forest six miles up the Frontier Creek Trail, but they have been rather picked over by illegal collectors. (It's unlawful to remove petrified wood from a wilderness area. Please leave pieces where you find them.) For other Washakie Wilderness trails info, ask at the Dubois Ranger Station. Several dude ranches are in the area.

Union Pass

The first road across the Absarokas headed through Union Pass southwest of Dubois. The pass forms a divide between the waters of the Columbia, Colorado, and Mississippi Rivers and marks the boundary of the Absaroka, Wind River, and Gros Ventre mountain ranges. Near the pass are an interpretive sign and a nature trail through a flower-filled meadow. Union Pass Road (gravel) leaves US Hwy. 26/287 approximately nine miles northwest of Dubois and climbs across to connect with State Hwy. 352 north of Pinedale. On the west side of the pass the road becomes rougher and should only be attempted in dry weather. It's not for RVs; high-clearance vehicles are recommended.

The Union Pass area is popular with mountain bikers, cross-country skiers, and far too many wintertime snowmobilers. **Lakes Lodge,** tel. (307) 455-2171 or (888) 655-5253, five miles up Union Pass Road, has condo-style cabins ($45 d), a bar, restaurant, and winter snowmobile rentals. Closed mid-April through May.

A beautiful 20-mile-long side road begins a few miles up Union Pass Road, heads along Warm Springs Creek, and eventually reconnects with US Hwy. 26/287. Find fantastic views of the Absaroka and Wind River Ranges along this route. The remains of an old tie-hack logging flume are visible and a warm spring (85° F) flows into the creek.

OVER TOGWOTEE PASS

The enjoyable drive west from Dubois first cuts through the colorful badlands, playing tag with the Wind River as it begins a long ascent to 9,644-foot Togwotee Pass (pronounced "TOE-go-tee"). The pass is named for a subchief under Chief Washakie. Togwotee was one of the last independent Sheepeater Indians—a branch of the Shoshones—and the man who led a U.S. government exploratory expedition over this pass in 1873. He even guided President Chester Arthur on his month-long visit to Yellowstone in 1883.

Togwotee Pass is one of the most scenic drives imaginable, with Ramshorn Peak peeking down from the north for several miles until the road plunges into dense lodgepole forests (Shoshone National Forest) with lingering glimpses of the Pinnacle Buttes. At the crest it emerges into grass-, willow-, and flower-bedecked meadows with Blackrock Creek winding through. Whitebark pine and Engelmann spruce trees cover the nearby slopes. As the highway drops down the western side into the Bridger-Teton National Forest, another marvelous mountain range—the Tetons—dominates the horizon in dramatic fashion. Snow lies along the roadsides until early July; notice the high posts along the road used by wintertime snowplows. Togwotee Pass is a complete shock after all the miles of sagebrush and grassland that control the heartland of Wyoming. It's like entering another world—a world of cool, forested mountains and lofty peaks instead of the arid land with horizon-wide vistas.

PINNACLE BUTTES AREA

Dominating the view along US Hwy. 26/287 for perhaps 15 miles are the castlelike Pinnacle Buttes. Twenty-three miles west of Dubois, you'll come to the turnoff to Brooks Lake, elevation 9,100 feet. Take it, even if you don't plan on camping or lodging here. A five-mile gravel road leads to the cliff-rimmed lake, and a clear creek flows east and south from here. The Forest Service's excellent **Pinnacles** and **Brooks Lake** campgrounds are along the lakeshore and cost $9 a night; open mid-June to mid-September. Facing the lake is historic Brooks Lake Lodge (see below).

Back on the main highway, you'll want to stop at **Falls Campground** (also $9; open June to mid-September). Here, Brooks Creek tumbles into a deep canyon. Catch very impressive views of **Brooks Creek Falls** along the short trail beginning from the parking lot. In wintertime, cross-country skiers will find an easy but ungroomed ski trail that heads out two miles from here. **Wind River Lake** is another five miles up the hill, just below the pass. It's a gorgeous place for picnics, with deep blue water and the sharp cliffs of Pinnacle Buttes behind.

MOUNTAIN LODGES AND DUDE RANCHES

A number of lodging places and guest ranches are just off the road as you drive west from

Dubois over Togwotee Pass. In addition to those listed below, see Mountain Resorts in the Accommodations section of the Jackson Hole chapter for details on two other notable places, **Brooks Lake Lodge**—on the lake of the same name—and **Cowboy Village Resort at Togwotee**—just west of Togwotee Pass.

Triple EEE Ranch is a recently built facility on a small spread adjacent to Shoshone National Forest. Guests (maximum of 18 people) stay in the lodge or duplex cabins that afford gorgeous views of Wind River Valley. Horseback riding is a favorite activity, but guests also enjoy fishing, hiking, wildlife watching, cookouts, sing-alongs, or simply relaxing in the hot tub. Special children's programs are also offered. Weekly all-inclusive rates are $1,790 for two people. For details, call (307) 455-2304 or (800) 353-2555, or visit www.dudesville.com. Luxury.

Fourteen miles west of Dubois—and right on the Continental Divide Snowmobile Trail—**Timberline Ranch** has wintertime lodging in cabins and condo accommodations. Call (307) 455-2513 for rates. The ranch also rents snowmobiles and has a restaurant and bar. It is open to the public mid-September through March. In the summer, the ranch houses a geology field camp run by Ohio's Miami University.

Sixteen miles west of Dubois is **Mackenzie Highland Ranch,** tel. (307) 455-3415, where accommodations are offered in a variety of cabins and other rustic buildings. Lodging starts at $45 d for the simplest cabin with shared bath, up to a four-bedroom home that sleeps eight with two baths and a full kitchen for $210. There's a three-night minimum stay. Trail rides, meals, and guided fishing trips are offered in the summer, and the ranch is a base for snowmobilers, skiers, dog mushers, and hunters at other times of the year. A portion of Mackenzie Highland Ranch becomes a base for lepidopterology research each summer, with graduate-level classes offered through Sam Houston State University. This unique program is run by professor Karölis Bagdonas, a specialist on moths and butterflies; he discovered the vital importance of moths in the diet of Yellowstone grizzlies.

Crooked Creek Guest Ranch is 16 miles from Dubois along Union Pass Road. In the summer, the ranch has horseback rides, hiking, fly-fishing, barbecues, wagon rides, and other activities. In winter it's the haunt of snowmobilers (the Continental Divide Snowmobile Trail is very close). The ranch rents snowmobiles, sells gas, and has a convenience store. Guests stay in modern log cabins and dine in the main lodge. All-inclusive weekly rates are $1,790 for two people in the summer. Get more information by calling (307) 455-3035 or (888) 238-2647, or pointing your browser to www.ranchweb.com/crookedcreek. Luxury.

Seventeen miles west of Dubois, **Wapiti Ridge Ranch,** tel. (307) 455-2219, has a dozen motel-type units for $40 s or $70 d, including a continental breakfast in summer or full breakfast in winter. The rooms are comfortable and nicely furnished but do not contain televisions or phones. This is a popular spot for hunters in the fall and snowmobilers in winter. No smoking. Moderate.

In the mountains 18 miles west of Dubois, **Triangle C Dude Ranch,** tel. (307) 455-2225 or (800) 661-4928, was established as the first tie-hack camp in the region and now operates as a summertime guest ranch and wintertime snowmobiling and cross-country skiing center. In summer, the main emphasis is horseback riding, but guests will also enjoy fishing, hiking, children's activities, black powder shoots, archery, mountain biking, canoeing, and evening entertainment. Weekly rates are $1,800-2,800 for two people, though shorter three-night visits are possible in the shoulder season. The ranch is open Memorial Day to Labor Day. Find it on the web at www.ranchweb.com/trianglec. Luxury.

Twenty miles west of Dubois is **Pinnacle Buttes Lodge and Campground,** tel. (307) 455-2506 or (800) 934-3569, www.pinnaclebuttes.com, where motel rooms are $70 and cabins with kitchenettes (but no TVs) go for $90. The cabins and motel rooms sleep four people each. You'll also find a restaurant with home-cooked meals, an outdoor pool, jacuzzi, and camping spaces ($10 for tents, $19 for RVs). Open year-round. Moderate-Expensive.

Double Bar J Guest Ranch, 20 miles west of Dubois, tel. (307) 455-2681, has log cabin accommodations, horseback rides, mountain biking, fishing, evening barbecues, and a sauna. Weekly all-inclusive rates in the summer are $1,680 for two people; or stay by the night for $330 d, all inclusive. In the winter the ranch offers cross-country skiing and snowmobiling. Find it on the web at www.doublebarj.com. Luxury.

THE BASICS

ACCOMMODATIONS

Lodging in the Yellowstone and Jackson Hole area is generally at a premium during the summer months and over the Christmas-New Year's holiday. Each chapter of this book details the local situation. During peak summer or winter seasons in Jackson Hole, expect to pay $80-100 for a decent room; even fairly basic rooms with older furnishings fetch $60 a night. Rates are lower in West Yellowstone, Gardiner, Cody, Driggs, Cooke City, and Dubois, but not nearly as cheap as in less-touristy towns in Wyoming, Montana, or Idaho.

Throughout this book I have typically listed only two prices for most lodging places: single, or s (one person), and double, or d (two people). Prices listed are the peak season summertime rates—which are generally the highest of the year. These prices do not include state and local taxes. The prices are, of course, not set in concrete and will certainly head up over time.

Regional Lodging Info

For a complete listing of motels, hotels, bed and breakfasts, dude ranches, and camping places in Wyoming, request a copy of the free ***Wyoming Accommodations Directory*** by calling (307) 777-7777 or (800) 225-5996, or visiting the web at www.wyomingtourism.org. Contact **Jackson Hole Central Reservations,** tel. (307) 733-4005 or (800) 443-6931, www.jacksonholeresort.com, for information and a brochure detailing Jackson Hole's many lodging options.

The ***Montana Travel Planner*** has helpful lodging info for towns in Montana. Get it by calling (406) 444-2978 or (800) 847-4868, or on the web at http://visitmt.com. There is also a separate Yellowstone Country guide that you may want to request.

The ***Idaho Official State Travel Guide*** is available by calling (208) 334-2470 or (800) 847-4842, or browsing over to www.visitid.org.

Motels and Hotels

The motel and hotel scene in the Greater Yellowstone area is geared to travelers with cash to spend, though there are inexpensive hostels in Jackson and West Yellowstone. If you're visiting the region and planning to save money by camping the entire time, do make one or two modifications to your plan by booking at least one night in Yellowstone's Old Faithful Inn or Lake Yellowstone Hotel. Both of these are classics, and Old Faithful Inn occupies a league of its own. Rates are surprisingly reasonable if you're willing to walk down the hall for a shower. Call far ahead for reservations on these! See specific chapters for other great places to spend a night.

Every town in the area has its locally owned small motels or cabins. These motels vary widely in quality and price but tend to offer the best rates and friendliest service. If you're staying in one of the chain motels, always be sure to ask about the sometimes-substantial discounts such as AAA-member rates, senior discounts, corporate or government rates, business travel fares, military rates, or other special deals. Try not to take the first rate quoted at these places, especially if you're calling the chain's 800 number; these "rack rates" are what they charge if they can get away with it. Ask if they have any promotional rates. You may also get better prices by calling the motel directly to bargain with a clerk; they're more likely to be able to dicker over price than the 800 number operators working from their room in a Texas prison.

If in doubt about where to stay, you may want to choose a place that gets the American Automobile Association seal of approval. The annual ***AAA TourBook*** for Idaho, Montana, and Wyoming (free to AAA members) is a helpful guide to the better hotels and motels, offering current prices and accurate ratings. Members often get discounts on lodging rates.

Bed and Breakfasts

Bed and breakfasts are found in most towns described in this book. Favorites of 30- and 40-something professional couples, bed and breakfasts are a fine way to get acquainted with a new area. They're also a good choice if you're traveling alone, since you'll have opportunities to meet fellow travelers in the library, over tea, and at breakfast. Note, however, that the single person rate frequently differs little if at all from the price for couples.

One problem with B&Bs is that they sometimes get a bit too homey and lack the privacy afforded by motels. I've been in some where the owner sits by your table in the morning, feeling it his duty to hold a conversation. This may be fine sometimes, especially if you want to learn more about the local area, but it's not so great if you're looking for a romantic place or just want to read the newspaper in peace. In some places the intense personal attention and strict rules (no hard-soled shoes, no noise after 10 p.m., and so on) get a bit much, making you feel less a guest than an intruder. In others, hosts serve breakfast at precisely 8 a.m. and guests who sleep in miss out. Other B&Bs are more flexible, and some even offer separate cottages or suites for honeymooners seeking privacy.

A number of regional B&Bs don't allow kids and almost none allow pets or smoking inside. Most guest rooms have private baths, and if they don't, one is probably just a few steps away.

Get a detailed listing of Wyoming B&Bs by writing to **Wyoming Homestay & Outdoor Adventures (WHOA),** 1031 Steinle Rd., Douglas, WY 82633. The same info is on its website, www.wyomingbnb-ranchrec.com. For Montana listings, contact the **Montana Bed and Breakfast Association** at tel. (800) 453-8870 or www.mtbba.com. Find connections to Idaho B&Bs on the web at www.visitid.org/accom or www.idaho--lodging.com. Two good websites to find details on B&Bs throughout the region are Cruising America (www.cruising-america.com) and Bed & Breakfast Inns Online (www.bbonline.com).

DUDE RANCHES

An old and respected Western tradition is the dude ranch, which began as a sideline to the

ACCOMMODATIONS RATINGS

In addition to including specific prices, all accommodations in this book are further rated by price category for comparison with other Moon Travel Handbooks. Categories are based on double-occupancy, high-season rates; the categories are:

Budget: under $35
Inexpensive: $35-60
Moderate: $60-85
Expensive: $85-110
Premium: $110-150
Luxury: $150 and up

business of raising cattle. Friends from back east would remember old Jake out there in wild Wyoming, where the buffalo roam and the antelope play, and decide it was time for a visit. So off they would head, living in the rancher's outbuildings and helping with the chores. The "dudes," as they became known, soon told their friends, and Jake found his ranch inundated. After a couple of years of this, the next step was obvious: get those eastern scoundrels to fork over some cash for the privilege of visiting. Pretty soon the dude ranching business was born. At its peak in the 1920s, dude ranching spread through much of the West. Dude ranching saved many cattle ranches from extinction by providing a second source of income and simultaneously brought these magnificent lands to the attention of people who had the money to prevent their development (most notably John D. Rockefeller, Jr., in Grand Teton National Park).

At the older ranches, generations of families have returned year after year for a relaxing and rejuvenating vacation in the Wild West. Many dude ranches now call themselves guest ranches, a term that reflects both the suspicious way people view the word "dude" and the changing nature of the business. Most city folks today lack the desire or skill to actually saddle up their own horses, much less push cattle between pastures. As a result, guest/dude ranches tend to emphasize grand scenery and horseback riding—the centerpiece of nearly every ranch—along with fly-fishing, hiking, hearty meals, campfires, chuck wagon cookouts, sing-alongs, and evenings around the fireplace. Some folks even camp overnight out there in the fearful wilderness, where the coyotes howl and the mice chew into your stash of potato chips. A few ranches still offer the chance to join in on such activities as cattle drives, branding, pregnancy testing, shot-giving, calving, and roundups. For some folks it's a great chance to learn about the real West; others view it as paying good money (sometimes a lot of good money!) to work as a cowhand.

What to Expect

Wyoming has literally dozens of dude ranches and ranch resorts offering accommodations ranging from spartan to so sumptuous that they bear absolutely no resemblance to ranch life. Not all dude ranches are created equal—some are slick and modern with tennis courts and hot tubs while others are funky and old-fashioned with delightful rough edges and trailer-home lodging. The smaller ones offer more personalized service, but in larger ones you're more likely to find someone your own age (particularly important if there are teens in your household). Dudes normally sleep in log cabins. Conditions inside can vary widely, but don't expect TVs or phones in the rooms. The cabins are usually located near a central lodge where meals are served family style. Many also have large libraries, along with outdoor games such as volleyball and horseshoes. Fishing and photography are other big attractions.

Practicalities

Dude ranches generally cost around $2,000 for two people per week, with lower rates for kids and surcharges for those staying by themselves. The price includes all meals, lodging, and horseback rides, but you'll usually pay more for features such as airport shuttles, rafting trips, guided fishing, beer and wine, or backcountry pack trips, not to mention local taxes and tips. The fanciest Jackson Hole resort, Lost Creek Ranch, will set you back over $5,000 for two people per week! Many guest ranches offer discounted rates in early June and late September, and for repeat guests. A few also have special adults-only weeks. Most require that you stay a week, or at least three nights, though a few places offer overnight accommodations. To really get into the comfortably slow pace of ranch life, try to set aside a week or more.

Ask plenty of questions before you visit, such as what activities are available, what to bring in the way of clothing, what sort of meals to expect (vegetarians may have a hard time on some ranches), whether there are additional charges, whether they accept credit cards (many don't), what the living accommodations are like, and how many other guests will likely be there at the same time—some house more than a hundred, others fewer than a dozen. Upon request, the better ranches will provide lists of references from previous clients. Note that it is considered proper to tip the ranch hands, kitchen help, and others who work hard to keep the ranch running; the standard total is 15% of your bill. For many of the workers, this is a way to fund their college educations (or a winter in Belize).

Finding a Dude Ranch

Most dude ranches now have their own websites, and these include photos of their operations to give you an idea of the setting and accommodations. An outstanding source for detailed information about guest ranches is ***Kilgore's Ranch Vacations,*** by Eugene Kilgore (Santa Fe: John Muir Publications). Find it on the web at www.ranchweb.com. Another useful web address is www.guestranches.com/usa, where you'll find links to many dude ranches in the Jackson Hole and Yellowstone area.

Founded in 1926, the **Dude Ranchers' Association** includes only the most established and authentic dude ranches in the nation. Call (970) 223-8440 for a listing of member ranches throughout the West, or visit the association's website, www.duderanch.org, for links to the ranches. Also helpful is **Off the Beaten Path,** tel. (800) 445-2995, www.offthebeatenpath.com, a travel agency that specializes in ranch vacations and other trips for independent travelers.

CAMPING

The Greater Yellowstone Ecosystem is dotted with several dozen Forest Service and Park Service campgrounds. Most of these have drinking water, garbage pick-up, and outhouses, but they generally do not have showers. The fee is typically $9-12 per night, with a 14-day limit on camping at any location. It's generally legal to camp free on undeveloped Forest Service throughout the region, but check with local ranger district offices for any restrictions. Dispersed camping is not allowed in Snake River Canyon south of Jackson, or the North Fork of the Shoshone River west of Cody. The Forest Service and Park Service now contract out the management of certain campgrounds. The effect is not especially noticeable to most visitors, but many of these places charge a higher fee, and a few allow advance reservations. The best source for regional camping information is *Camping Wyoming* by Michael McClure (Atlantic City, WY: WigRaf Publishing).

Every Yellowstone-area town of any size contains at least one private RV park and so-called campground. Most of these are little more than vacant lots with sewer and electrical hookups, showers, and toilet facilities, but a few are quite nice. These private campgrounds generally charge $2-4 for showers if you're not camping there. A better deal in many towns is to use the shower at the local public swimming pool, where you get a free swim thrown in for the entrance charge.

TRANSPORTATION BY CAR

Most summer travelers to the Yellowstone area—and a substantial number of winter visitors—arrive by car. Some fly into Salt Lake City and rent a vehicle, while others head out on a grand road trip from home. The northwest corner of Wyoming is accessible from all sides in the summer months, but most roads inside Yellowstone National Park are closed when the snow flies. Jackson Hole remains accessible year-round, of course, but a massive road reconstruction in the Snake River Canyon (south of Jackson) will continue to create delays for years to come. Other large reconstruction projects will be continuing inside Yellowstone for the next decade or so. Be prepared for delays.

Free state highway maps can be found at visitor centers in Wyoming, Montana, and Idaho, but map aficionados should also purchase one of the excellent statewide topographic map books published by DeLorme Mapping of Freeport, Maine, tel. (800) 511-2459, www.delorme.com. These are indispensable for travelers heading off main routes and are sold in most local bookstores. National forest maps are also very helpful for mountain driving in many parts of Wyoming; buy them in local Forest Service offices.

Car Rentals

You can rent cars at all the larger towns, and those with airports generally have Hertz, Avis, and other national chains. See individual towns in this book for local rental companies. You'll find four-wheel-drive sport utility vehicles available in many locations, including Jackson Hole, but will pay dearly for the privilege.

I've generally found the best car rental rates in the larger cities where there's more competition. You'll pay considerably more in a resort town such as Jackson. If you plan to rent a car for an extended period, it's worth your while to check travel websites such as www.travelocity.com to see which company offers the best rates. Note, however, that these quotes do not include taxes, which can be substantial, especially if you rent from the Salt Lake City airport. Even if you've made a reservation, it pays to call around once more after you arrive at the airport. On a recent visit I saved hundreds of dollars by getting a last-minute quote for a one-month rental. Cool tip: if you're visiting in the summer, try to get a light-colored car; the dark ones can get incredibly hot in the blazing sun!

Winter Road Closures

Most of the roads in Yellowstone National Park are closed to cars when the first heavy snows block the passes, and by the first of November things are generally shut down all over except for the 56 miles between Gardiner and Cooke City. This is the only road within Yellowstone that remains open all year. The roads are groomed for snowmobiles and snowcoaches from mid-December to mid-March. Plowing starts in March, but most park roads don't open for cars again until mid-May and sometimes not until early June. If you're planning a trip early or late in the season, call the park for current road conditions, tel. (307) 344-7381. The same information can be found on the park's webpage: www.nps.gov/yell.

Within Grand Teton National Park, US Hwy. 89/191/287 is plowed from Moran Junction to Flagg Ranch throughout the winter, providing a base for snowcoaches and snowmobiles heading into Yellowstone. Most other roads in Grand Teton are not plowed and are generally closed to cars Nov.-April.

Outside the parks, most regional roads are plowed throughout the winter, including Teton Pass (west of Jackson), Togwotee Pass (northeast of Jackson), and US Hwy. 14/16/20 from Cody to Pahaska Teepee near the East Entrance to Yellowstone. Two roads that are not plowed in winter are US Hwy. 212 over Beartooth Pass (between Cooke City and Red Lodge, Montana) and an eight-mile stretch of Chief Joseph Scenic Highway east of Cooke City and northwest of Cody.

Wintertime Travel

Travelers need to take special precautions in the winter months. Snow tires are a necessity, but you should also have on hand a number of emergency supplies including tire chains, a shovel and bag of sand in case you get stuck, a first-aid kit, booster cables, signal flares, flashlight, lighter and candle, transistor radio, non-perishable foods (granola bars, canned nuts, or dried fruit), a jug of water, an ice scraper, blankets, winter clothes, and a sleeping bag. The most valuable tool may well be a **cell phone** to call for help—assuming you're in an area with reception. If you become stranded in a blizzard, stay in your car. You're more likely to be found, and the vehicle provides shelter from the weather. Run the engine and heater sparingly, occasionally opening a window for ventilation. Don't run the engine if the tailpipe is blocked by snow, or you may risk carbon monoxide poisoning.

For up-to-date road and travel conditions in Wyoming, call (307) 772-0824 or (888) 996-7623, or visit the Department of Transportation on the web at http://wydotweb.state.wy.us. Get Montana road info from tel. (800) 226-7623, http://mdt.mt.gov. For the Idaho road report, call (208) 336-6600 or (888) 432-7623, or head to http://state.id.us/itd.

BY BUS

To Jackson Hole

Southern Teton Area Rapid Transit—better known as **START**—offers local bus service in the Jackson/Teton Village area; call (307) 733-4521. **Jackson Hole Express,** tel. (307) 733-1719 or (800) 652-9510, www.jacksonholebus.com, has daily bus connections to Jackson from Greyhound stations in Salt Lake City and Idaho Falls. **Community and Rural Transportation** (CART), tel. (208) 354-2240 or (800) 657-7439, www.cyberhighway.net/~cartbus, also has daily service between Idaho Falls and Jackson, along with service between Driggs and Rexburg, Idaho. Another option is **Wind River Transportation Authority,** tel. (800) 439-7118, with on-demand service. Travelers can call for a pickup in Jackson, Salt Lake City, Dubois, Pinedale, Rock Springs, and other places.

Two companies provide shuttles in the winter between Jackson Hole and Grand Targhee Ski Resort: **Targhee Express,** tel. (307) 733-3101 or (307) 734-9754, and **Downhill Express,** tel. (307) 734-9525 or (877) 943-3574.

Destinations

Greyhound, tel. (800) 231-2222, www.greyhound.com, has bus service into Salt Lake City, Idaho Falls, West Yellowstone (the closest connection to Yellowstone National Park), Bozeman, and Billings, but not to Jackson, Cody, Gardiner, Driggs, or other towns in the area. They also travel along the I-80 corridor, with stops in both Evanston and Rock Springs, Wyoming.

Powder River/Coach USA, tel. (800) 442-3682, has daily bus service between Billings and Cody and also connects Cody with the eastern and southern parts of Wyoming, continuing all the way to Denver. **Community Bus Service,** tel. (406) 646-7600, provides service between West Yellowstone and Bozeman. **4x4 Stage,** tel. (406) 848-2224 or (800) 517-8243, offers reservation-only van service between Bozeman and Gardiner.

Several options exist for tours of Yellowstone and Grand Teton National Parks from surrounding towns; see the appropriate chapters for details.

BY OTHER MEANS

Air Travel

Commercial airline service is provided to the towns of Cody, Jackson, and West Yellowstone in the region covered by this book. The most direct air access is into the Jackson Hole airport, with American Airlines flights from Chicago or Dallas, Sky West/Delta from Salt Lake City, and United Airlines from Denver or Los Angeles. Cody is served by Sky West/Delta from Salt Lake City and United Express/Great Lakes Aviation from Denver, while West Yellowstone is served by Sky West/Delta out of Salt Lake City.

The airport at Idaho Falls, Idaho, is a 90-mile drive from Jackson and is served by Horizon Air from Boise and Sky West/Delta from Salt Lake City. Farther away are airports in Salt Lake City, Bozeman, and Billings.

Salt Lake City has service from most of the major carriers and is a 275 mile drive from Jackson. Because of its size, this is probably the least expensive regional airport to fly into, and Salt Lake City is a regional hub for Sky West/Delta.

It's an 84-mile drive from Bozeman to Mammoth Hot Springs on the northwest corner of Yellowstone, or 225 miles from Bozeman to Jackson. Direct flights to Bozeman are offered by Sky West/Delta from Salt Lake City, Horizon Air from Seattle, and Northwest Airlines from Minneapolis.

Billings has the largest airport in Montana. It's a 127-mile drive from Billings to the Northeast Entrance to Yellowstone National Park, but this requires going over the 10,947-foot summit of Beartooth Pass (closed in the winter). From Billings to Gardiner, on the northwest corner of Yellowstone, it's 169 miles, and from Billings to Cody the drive is 104 miles (plus another 52 miles to the East Entrance of Yellowstone). Several airlines serve Billings: Sky West/Delta from Salt Lake City, Horizon Air from Seattle, Northwest Airlines from Minneapolis, and United Airlines from Denver.

Train Travel

Amtrak's California Zephyr runs between Chicago and Oakland but does not come close to Jackson Hole or Yellowstone. The closest train station is in Salt Lake City, 275 miles from Jackson. Those traveling by train will need to take a bus, rental car, or plane from Salt Lake into Jackson. Call (800) 872-7245 for details on Amtrak, or visit on the web at www.amtrak.com.

Bike Travel

Bicycles are available for rent in Jackson, Cody, Moose (Grand Teton National Park), and West Yellowstone, but not inside Yellowstone National Park. Excellent paved paths can be found around Jackson and within Teton Valley, and mountain biking trails and dirt roads criss-cross the region, particularly on Forest Service lands. A few of these are described in this book; for others, contact local bike shops or get trail information from Forest Service or Park Service offices. Bikes are prohibited on backcountry trails in both Yellowstone and Grand Teton National Parks, but they are allowed on most main roads and certain other paths.

Many cyclists ride through this part of Wyoming and Montana, but conditions are not the safest, particularly in Yellowstone, where traffic is heavy and the roads are narrow and winding with little or no shoulders. In the summer, the best times to ride are in the morning before traffic thickens or late in the afternoon before the light begins to fade and you become less visible to motorists. September and October are far less crowded than mid-summer. See the Yellowstone chapter for details on riding in the park. **Backroads,** tel. (800) 462-2848, www.backroads.com, leads six-day cycling tours of the Yellowstone area.

The Park Service recommends staying at least 25 yards from bison.

HEALTH AND SAFETY

Medical clinics can be found in most towns in the Yellowstone region, with good hospitals in Jackson and Cody, plus a smaller hospital in Driggs, Idaho. A summertime hospital is located near Lake Yellowstone Hotel within Yellowstone, with clinics at Old Faithful and Mammoth. Inside Grand Teton National Park there's a summertime clinic near Jackson Lake Lodge. See the special topics Bear Country and Lightning Safety for precautions while traveling in the Yellowstone region.

A common annoyance for travelers is insects, especially mosquitoes and blackflies. These are most prevalent in early summer in the mountains; by late August, mosquito populations thin considerably. Use insect repellents containing DEET to help keep them away or wear a head net.

Beaver Fever

Although the lakes and streams of the Greater Yellowstone Ecosystem may appear clean, you are risking a debilitating sickness by drinking the water without treating it first. The protozoan *Giardia lambia* is found throughout the state, spread by both humans and animals (including beaver). The disease is curable with drugs, but it's always best to carry safe drinking water on any trip, or to boil any water taken from creeks or lakes. Bringing water to a full boil is sufficient to kill Giardia and other harmful organisms. Another option—the one I much prefer—is to use one of the water filters sold in camping goods stores. Make sure you buy one that filters out organisms such as *Campylobacter jejuni,* bacteria that are just 0.2 microns in size. Chlorine and iodine are not always reliable, taste foul, and can be unhealthy.

Hypothermia

Anyone who has spent much time in the outdoors will discover the dangers of exposure to cold, wet, and windy conditions. Even at temperatures well above freezing, hypothermia—the reduction of the body's core temperature—can prove fatal.

In the early stages, hypothermia causes uncontrollable shivering, followed by a loss of coordination, slurred speech, and then a rapid descent into unconsciousness and death. Always travel prepared for sudden changes in the weather. Wear clothing that insulates well and that holds its heat when wet. Wool and polypropylene are far better than cotton, and clothes should be worn in layers to provide better trapping of heat and a chance to adjust to conditions more easily. Always carry a wool hat, since your head loses more heat than any other part of the body. Bring a waterproof shell to cut the wind. Put on rain gear *before* it starts raining; head back or set up camp when the weather looks threatening; and eat candy bars, keep active, or snuggle with a friend in a down bag to generate warmth.

If someone in your party begins to show signs of hypothermia, don't take any chances, even if the person denies needing help. Get the victim out of the wind, strip off his clothes, and put him in a dry sleeping bag on an insulating pad. Skin-to-skin contact is the best way to warm a hypothermic person, and that means you'll also need to strip and climb in the sleeping bag. If you weren't friends before, this should heat up the relationship! Do not give the victim alcohol or hot drinks, and do not try to warm the person too quickly since it could lead to heart failure. Once the victim has recovered, get medical help as soon as possible. Of course, you're far better off keeping close tabs on everyone in the group and seeking shelter *before* exhaustion and hypothermia set in.

Frostbite

Frostbite is a less serious but quite painful problem for the cold-weather hiker; it is caused by direct exposure or by heat loss due to wet socks, clothing, and boots. Frostbitten areas will look white or gray and feel hard on the surface, softer underneath. The best way to warm the area is with other skin: put your hand under your arm, your feet on your friend's belly. Don't rub it with snow or warm it near a fire. In cases of severe frostbite, in which the skin is white, quite hard, and numb, immerse the frozen area in water warmed to 99° to 104° until it's thawed. Avoid refreezing the frostbitten area. If you're a long way from medical assistance and the frostbite is extensive, it is better to keep the area frozen and get out of the woods for help; thawing is very painful, and it would be impossible to walk on a thawed foot.

Ticks

Ticks can be a bother in brushy and grassy areas in the spring and early summer. They drop onto unsuspecting humans and other animals to suck blood, and they can spread several potentially devastating diseases, including Rocky Mountain spotted fever, Ehrlichiosis, and Lyme disease. A few cases of these diseases have been reported in the Greater Yellowstone Ecosystem, but they are not common.

Avoid ticks by tucking pant legs into boots and shirts into pants, using insect repellents containing DEET, and carefully inspecting your clothes while outside. Light-colored clothing and socks are less attractive to ticks and make it easier for you to see them, while broad hats keep ticks out of your hair. Check your body while hiking and immediately after the trip. If possible, remove ticks before they become embedded in your skin. If one does become attached, use tweezers to remove the tick, making sure to get the head. Apply a triple antibiotic ointment such as Neosporin to the area, and monitor the bite area for two weeks.

Lyme disease typically shows up as a large red spot with a lighter bulls-eye center and often causes muscle aches, fatigue, headache, and fever. Get medical help immediately if you show these symptoms after a tick bite. Fortunately, the disease can usually be treated with antibiotics. If untreated, it can cause a facial nerve palsy, memory loss, arthritis, heart damage, and other problems. A relatively effective vaccine has been developed for Lyme disease, but it requires a one-year regimen of doses and is quite expensive; check with your doctor for specifics. In northwest Wyoming, where the disease is relatively uncommon, the vaccine is probably not warranted, and it may give a false sense of security since ticks can still spread other—and more dangerous—diseases. There are no vaccinations available against either Rocky Mountain Spotted Fever or Erlichia, both of which sometimes kill people. The best action is to prevent tick bites in the first place. For more on tick-borne diseases, see the Johns Hopkins Institute website at www.intelihealth.com.

SERVICES

Money and Banking

Travelers checks (in U.S. dollars) are accepted without charge in most stores and businesses throughout the Yellowstone region. It's not a good idea to travel with travelers checks in non-U.S. currency; they are only accepted at certain banks in Wyoming and are a time-consuming hassle. If you do arrive with pounds, yen, or Deutsche marks, several banks in Jackson, along with the park hotels inside Yellowstone, will exchange foreign currency for greenbacks.

When traveling, I pay for expenses by credit card whenever possible, but also keep an automated teller machine (ATM) card and a small stash of travelers checks as a backup. Unfortunately, nearly all ATMs now tack on a charge—usually $1.50-2 per transaction—to your own bank's fees, making this an expensive way to get cash. If the bank imposes such a charge it will be posted on the machine. One way to avoid this ripoff is to make a purchase at a grocery store that takes ATM cards and simply ask to get additional cash back. For an up-to-date listing of Cirrus system ATMs, call (800) 424-7787, or visit the website, www.mastercard.com/atm. For the Plus system, call (800) 843-7587, or head to www.visa.com/atms.

The major credit cards—especially Visa and MasterCard—are accepted almost everywhere, even in many grocery stores. This is probably the easiest way to travel—especially if you can get airline mileage credit at the same time. The miles can quickly add up if you make all your purchases in this way, but so can your credit card bill!

Post Offices

Post offices generally open between 7 a.m. and 9 a.m. and close between 5 p.m. and 6 p.m.; only a few are open on Saturday. Their outer doors are usually open, so you can go in to buy stamps from the machines. Some drug or card stores also operate a postal substation where you can purchase stamps or mail packages within the U.S. (you'll have to go to a real post office for mailing to foreign addresses or other special services). Many grocery store checkout counters also sell books of stamps with no markup.

TRAVEL DETAILS

Chambers of commerce information centers are described for each town in this book. A large Wyoming Information Center is located in Jackson, and you'll also find helpful chambers of commerce in all but the tiniest towns in the Yellowstone area.

Wyoming Information

For a helpful overall guide to Wyoming, along with a listing of events, chamber of commerce offices, and lodging and camping places, request a copy of the free ***Wyoming Vacation Directory*** from the Wyoming Division of Tourism and State Marketing, tel. (307) 777-7777 or (800) 225-5996, www.wyomingtourism.org. Both summer and winter versions are available. It also offers free state maps, or pick them up at any local visitor center. For other info, head to the Wyoming state homepage: www.state.wy.us. See my ***Wyoming Handbook*** for the full story on the Cowboy State; it's available from Avalon Travel Publishing (Emeryville, CA, www.moon.com).

Montana Information

Find Montana travel information at tel. (406) 444-2654 or (800) 847-4868, or on the web at http://visitmt.com. Get more specific info for "Yellowstone Country" at tel. (406) 646-4383 or (800) 7336-5276 (West Yellowstone Chamber of Commerce), http://yellowstone.visitmt.com. The state of Montana homepage is www.state.mt.us. The most complete travel guide for the state is ***Montana Handbook,*** by W.C. McRae and Judy Jewell (Emeryville, CA: Avalon Travel Publishing, www.moon.com).

Idaho Information

For more on the state of Idaho, contact the Idaho Division of Tourism Development's website at www.visitid.org or the main state site at www.state.id.us. Reach the Idaho Division of Tourism Development by phone at (208) 334-2470 or (800) 847-4842 to ask for its official state travel guide and a state map. Get complete details on Idaho in ***Idaho Handbook*** by Don Root (Emeryville, CA: Avalon Travel Publishing, www.moon.com).

Land Management Agencies

The following phone numbers and websites provide contact information for major public land management agencies in the Greater Yellowstone Ecosystem.

Grand Teton National Park, Moose, WY, tel. (307) 739-3399, www.nps.gov/grte

Yellowstone National Park, Mammoth Hot Springs, WY, tel. (307) 344-7381, www.nps.gov/yell

National Elk Refuge, Jackson, WY, tel. (307) 733-9212, www.r6.fws.gov/refuges/natlelk

Bridger-Teton National Forest, Jackson, WY, tel. (307) 739-5500, www.fs.fed.us/btnf

Shoshone National Forest, Cody, WY, tel. (307) 527-6241, www.fs.fed.us/r2/shoshone

Targhee National Forest, Driggs, ID, tel. (208) 354-2431, www.fs.fed.us/tnf

Gallatin National Forest, West Yellowstone, MT, tel. (406) 823-6961, or Gardiner, MT, tel. (406) 848-7375, www.fs.fed.us/r1/gallatin

The following national forests have lands on the margins of the Greater Yellowstone Ecosystem and are covered in the Montana and Idaho guidebooks mentioned above.

Beaverhead-Deerlodge National Forest, Dillon, MT, tel. (406) 683-3900, www.fs.fed.us/r1/bdnf

Caribou National Forest, Pocatello, ID, tel. (208) 236-7500, www.fs.fed.us/r4/curlew

Custer National Forest, Red Lodge, MT, tel. (406) 446-2103, www.fs.fed.us/r1/custer

On the Web

The Internet changes rapidly, and by the time you read this a multitude of new sites will exist for businesses and organizations in the Greater Yellowstone region. Most local libraries have computers with Internet access, and if you have a free web-based e-mail service such as Hotmail or Excite, you can check in from almost anywhere. In addition, the towns of Jackson, Cody, Gardiner, and West Yellowstone all have Internet cafes or businesses with computer terminals for rent by the hour.

There are dozens of Internet sites with information on Yellowstone, Grand Teton, and Jackson Hole; just type in the key words and see what your search engine discovers. Excellent places to begin your virtual voyage are the state tourism sites and land management agencies listed above. See specific town descriptions for listings of chambers of commerce websites; these typically have links to local businesses. Also try the following for Wyoming information: www.wyominggold.com, http://home.wyoming.com/wyolinks, www.wyomingvisitor.com, and www.wyomingnetwork. com. For Jackson Hole, head to www.jacksonholechamber.com, www. jackson-hole.com, www.jacksonholenet.com, or www.jacksonnetwork.com. Other useful sites are www.westyellowstonechamber.com and www.westyellowstone.com for the West Yellowstone area, along with www.codychamber.org or www.codynetwork.com for information on the Cody area.

On the Radio

Jackson, Cody, and other towns in the region have local radio stations of varying quality, offering the standard mix of top-40, rock, and country. For a bit more class, turn your dial to one of the local public radio stations that provide in-depth news, insightful call-in shows, and comedic relief. In Jackson, the local Wyoming Public Radio station is KUWJ 90.3 FM, www.uwyo.edu/wpr. In the Yellowstone area and Cody, you're likely to hear "Yellowstone Radio" out of Bozeman, KBMC 102.1 FM. In Idaho's Teton Valley, listen to NPR on KRIC-FM 100.5 from Rexburg, Idaho.

WEIGHTS AND MEASURES

The Metric System

Except for the nutritional information labels on packaged food and beverages, the metric system is just about nonexistent in the United States. For help converting from the modified English measuring system used in the U.S., consult the conversion table at the back of this book.

COURTESY AISLINN RACE

Time Zones

All of Wyoming uses Mountain Standard Time, seven hours behind Greenwich Mean Time. The sprawling continental U.S. contains four time zones. For a specific breakdown of time zone borders in the rest of the country, consult the map in local phone books, which contain combination area code/time zone maps in the front. All states, with the exception of Hawaii, convert to daylight saving time from midnight on the first Sunday in April to midnight on the last Sunday in October. Daylight saving time advances the clock one hour across all U.S. time zones.

Electricity

Electric current in the U.S. is 110-120 volts, 60-cycle; appliances manufactured for use in most Asian and European countries will need an adapter to operate safely outside their typical system of 220-240 volt, 50-cycle current, as well as a plug adapter for the flat two-pin style of the U.S. plug.

APPENDIX

ADDITIONAL JACKSON HOLE ACCOMMODATIONS

See the text for descriptions of many Jackson Hole lodging places, including condos, cabins, bed and breakfasts, hotels, motels, guest ranches, and hostels. This appendix provides brief descriptions of places not included in the text, but that offer good alternatives. Accommodations are listed from least to most expensive, and rates may be considerably lower in the off-season. Add a six percent tax to these rates.

Teton Gables Motel, 1140 W. Broadway, tel. (307) 733-3723; $75-85 s or d; older motel, but will be renovated in late 2000 (prices will probably rise). Moderate.

Four Winds Motel, 150 N. Millward St., tel. (307) 733-2474 or (800) 228-6461; $82-102 s or d; AAA approved. Moderate-Expensive.

Pony Express Motel, 50 S. Millward St., tel. (307) 733-2658 or (800) 526-2658; $85-92 s or d; outdoor jacuzzi and heated pool open all year, AAA approved. Expensive.

Pioneer Motel, 325 N. Cache Dr., tel. (307) 733-3673 or (800) 550-0330, www.pioneermotel.com; $85-115 s or d; microwaves and refrigerators, homemade quilts, AAA approved. Expensive-Premium.

Crystal Springs Inn, in Teton Village, tel. (307) 733-4423 or (800) 735-8342; $86-98 s or d; fridges in rooms. Expensive.

Teton Inn, 165 W. Gill St., tel. (307) 733-3883 or (800) 851-0700; $90 s or d; small and friendly, to be renovated in 2000 (prices will probably rise), AAA approved. Expensive.

Prospector Motel, 155 N. Jackson, tel. (307) 733-4858 or (800) 851-0070, www.jacksonprospector.com; $90-110 s or d; small and friendly motel, outdoor jacuzzi; to be renovated in 2000 (prices will probably rise), AAA approved. Expensive.

Flat Creek Motel, one mile north of town on U.S. Hwy. 89, tel. (307) 733-5276 or (800) 438-9338, www.flatcreekmotel.com; $92-109 s or d for rooms with fridges and microwaves; fully equipped kitchens cost $125 for up to four people; large motel facing Elk Refuge with jacuzzi, sauna, ski waxing room. Expensive.

Village Center Inn, Teton Village, tel. (307) 733-3155 or (800) 735-8342; $92-105 s or d for studio or loft units (sleep five); $134 for two-bedroom units (sleep six); all units with full kitchens. Expensive.

Elk Refuge Inn, one mile north of town on U.S. Hwy. 89, tel. (307) 733-3582 or (800) 544-3582, www.elkrefugeinn.com; $95 s or $98 d; kitchenettes $115 for up to four people; overlooks the National Elk Refuge, horse corrals available, AAA approved. Expensive.

Stagecoach Motel, 291 N. Glenwood, tel. (307) 733-3451 or (800) 421-1447, www.blissnet.com/~stagecoach; $95-110 s or d, kitchen suites for $150 d; older motel but in good condition, fairly small rooms, open June-September. Expensive-Premium.

Ranch Inn, 45 E. Pearl St., tel. (307) 733-6363 or (800) 348-5599, www.ranchinn.com; standard rooms $98 s or $110 d with fridges and microwaves; tower rooms $145 for four; half-suites $165 d; suites with kitchenettes, fireplaces, and balconies $175 d; luxury suites with jacuzzi tubs $180 d; indoor and outdoor jacuzzis, continental breakfast. Expensive-Luxury.

Trapper Inn, 235 N. Cache Dr., tel. (307) 733-2648 or (800) 341-8000, www.trapperinn.com; $98-129 s or d for standard rooms; suites $160-217 for four people (some have jacuzzi tubs and king-size beds); indoor and outdoor jacuzzis, fridges and microwaves in many rooms, AAA approved. Expensive-Premium.

ADDITIONAL JACKSON HOLE ACCOMMODATIONS

(continued)

Virginian Lodge, 750 W. Broadway, tel. (307) 733-2792 or (800) 262-4999, www.virginianlodge.com; $99-109 s or d; kitchenette suites for $135 (sleep four); jacuzzi suites $165 (sleep four); two-bedroom suites $185 (sleep six); big motel with large outdoor pool and jacuzzi, AAA approved. Expensive.

Cache Creek Motel, 390 N. Glenwood, tel. (307) 733-7781 or (800) 843-4788, www.cachecreekmotel.com; $100-110 s or d; suites for $175-200 for up to six; full kitchens in all rooms, outdoor jacuzzi, ski lockers, AAA approved. Expensive.

49'er Inn & Suites (Quality Inn), 330 W. Pearl, tel. (307) 733-7550 or (800) 483-8667, www.townsquareinns.com; $104-172 s, $108-172 d; fireplace and jacuzzi suites with kitchenettes for $172 d; large indoor jacuzzi, sauna, continental breakfast, exercise room, AAA approved. Expensive-Luxury.

Alpenhof Lodge, Teton Village, tel. (307) 733-3242 or (800) 732-3244, www.jacksonhole. com/alpenhof; summer rates: $114-388 d; ski season rates: $138-428 d; wide range of rooms available, along with four-person suites; some rooms with Bavarian furnishings, original artwork, and fireplaces; heated year-round outdoor pool, jacuzzi, sauna, ski lockers, game room. Premium-Luxury.

Golden Eagle Inn, 325 E. Broadway, tel. (307) 733-2042; $115 s or d for standard rooms; two-bedroom house with full kitchen for $235 d ($255 for six); quiet location, outdoor seasonal pool, AAA approved. Premium-Luxury.

Painted Buffalo Inn, 400 W. Broadway, tel. (307) 733-4340 or (800) 288-3866, www.paintedbuffalo.com; $120 s, $125-130 d in standard rooms, $170 d in family units; AAA approved. Premium.

Super 8 Motel, 750 S. US Hwy. 89, tel. (307) 733-6833 or (800) 800-8000, www.super8. com; $130-140 s or d. Premium.

Jackson Hole Lodge, 420 W. Broadway, tel. (307) 733-2992 or (800) 604-9404, www.jacksonholelodge.com; $134 for up to four people in motel rooms; condos, all with kitchens, include studios ($184 for three people), one-bedroom units ($219 for four people), and two-bedroom units ($304 for up to eight people); large indoor pool, wading pool, two jacuzzis, sauna, AAA approved. Premium-Luxury.

Days Inn of Jackson Hole, 1280 W. Broadway, tel. (307) 739-9010 or (800) 329-7466, www.daysinnjacksonhole.com; $159-199 s or d for standard rooms; $219-239 for suites with fireplaces and jacuzzi tubs; expanded continental breakfast, large jacuzzi, sauna, in-room safes, microwaves and fridges in some rooms, AAA approved. Luxury.

The Inn at Jackson Hole (Best Western), Teton Village, tel. (307) 733-2311 or (800) 842-7666, www.innatjh.com; $179-279 s or d; outdoor pool, three outdoor jacuzzis, sauna, ski lockers, some rooms with loft and kitchenette. Luxury.

Wyoming Inn (Red Lion), 930 W. Broadway, tel. (307) 734-0035 or (800) 844-0035, www.wyoming-inn.com; $189-249 s or d; corporate-style motel with ostentatious lobby, large rooms, jacuzzi, light breakfast, some rooms with fireplaces and jacuzzis, free access to health club (across the street), free airport shuttle, AAA approved. Luxury.

Snow King Resort, 400 E. Snow King, tel. (307) 733-5200 or (800) 522-5464, www.snowking.com; $200 s or $210 d for motel rooms; $280 for two-bedroom condos with kitchen, up to $410-430 for four-bedroom condos; heated outdoor pool (open year-round), three outdoor jacuzzis, game room, indoor ice rink, sauna, fitness room, concierge, free airport shuttle, AAA approved. Luxury.

The Lodge at Jackson Hole (Best Western), 80 S. Scott Lane, tel. (307) 739-9703 or (800) 458-3866, www.lodgeatjh.com; $209 s or d for mini-suites; three-story lodge on south end of town, indoor and outdoor heated year-round pools, indoor and outdoor jacuzzis, sauna, continental breakfast, fridges and microwaves, three phones per room, in-room safes, ski lockers, AAA approved. Luxury.

ADDITIONAL CODY MOTELS

The Bighorn Basin chapter contains descriptions of selected Cody lodging places. Listed below from least to most expensive are motels not described elsewhere. Rates may be lower in the off-season. Add an eight percent tax to these rates.

Frontier Motel, U.S. Hwy. 14/16/20 E, tel. (307) 527-7119; $40 s, $44-52 d, kitchenettes for $73 d. Inexpensive-Moderate.

Rainbow Park Motel, 1136 17th St., tel. (307) 587-6251 or (800) 341-8000; $44 s, $47-60 d, kitchenettes $5 extra, AAA approved. Inexpensive-Moderate.

Skyline Motor Inn, 1919 17th St., tel. (307) 587-4201 or (800) 843-8809; $48 s, $56-62 d, $68 for four; outdoor pool, AAA approved. Inexpensive-Moderate.

Wigwam Motel, 1701 Alger Ave., tel. (307) 587-3861; $48-55 s or d; older motel. Inexpensive.

Holiday Motel, 1807 Sheridan Ave., tel. (307) 587-4258 or (800) 341-8000; $51 s, $54-65 d; recently refurbished, AAA approved. Inexpensive-Moderate.

7 K's Motel, 232 W. Yellowstone Ave., tel. (307) 587-5890 or (800) 223-9204; $55-65 s or d; outdoor pool, no phones in rooms, open April-September. Inexpensive-Moderate.

Big Bear Motel, 139 W. Yellowstone Ave., tel. (307) 587-3117 or (800) 325-7163; $55-65 s or d; outdoor pool, no phones in rooms, open April-Oct., AAA approved. Inexpensive-Moderate.

Gateway Motel and RV Park, 203 Yellowstone, tel. (307) 587-2561; motel rooms for $55-70, rustic cabins from 1946 with kitchenettes for $45; no phones in rooms, open April-September. Inexpensive-Moderate.

Carter Mountain Motel, 1701 Central Ave., tel. (307) 587-4295; standard rooms (some with fridges) for $69-79 s or d; suites with full kitchens (largest ones sleep up to nine people) for $89-125; all rooms new or recently remodeled. Moderate.

Western 6 Gun Motel, 433 W. Yellowstone Ave., tel. (307) 587-4835; $69-79 s or d; suites with fridges $92 for four people; open May-September. Moderate.

River's View Motel, 109 W. Yellowstone Ave., tel. (307) 587-6074 or (800) 377-7255; standard rooms $75-95 s or d with microwaves and fridges; cabin $85 d or $120 for six; see rooms first; open April to mid-November. Moderate-Expensive.

Buffalo Bill Village Resort, 1701 Sheridan Ave., tel. (307) 587-5544 or (800) 527-5544; $79-89 s, $89-99 d; refurbished 1920s-era log cabins equipped with modern amenities, small outdoor pool, airport transport, open May-Sept., AAA approved. Expensive.

Comfort Inn at Buffalo Bill Village Resort, 1601 Sheridan Ave., tel. (307) 587-5556 or (800) 329-7466; $79-129 s or d; outdoor pool, continental breakfast, airport transport, AAA approved. Moderate-Premium.

Burl Inn, 1213 17th St., tel. (307) 587-2084 or (800) 388-2084; $80 s or $85 d; honeymoon suite with king bed and jacuzzi tub for $105; handcrafted burled wood beds and lamps, closed January, AAA approved. Expensive.

Super 8 Motel, 730 W. Yellowstone Ave., tel. (307) 527-6214 or (800) 800-8000; $80-115 s or $90-115 d. Expensive-Premium.

Cody Motor Lodge, 1455 Sheridan Ave., tel. (307) 527-6291 or (800) 340-2639; $85-88 s or d; spacious rooms, six-person kitchenettes for $130. Expensive-Premium.

Best Western Sunrise, 1407 8th St., tel. (307) 587-5566 or (800) 528-1234; $85-99 s or d; outdoor pool, continental breakfast, AAA approved. Expensive.

Days Inn, 524 W. Yellowstone Ave., tel. (307) 527-6604 or (800) 325-2525; $85-115 s, $95-125 d; indoor pool, jacuzzi, continental breakfast, AAA approved. Expensive-Premium.

Holiday Inn at Buffalo Bill Village Resort, 1701 Sheridan Ave., tel. (307) 587-5555 or (800) 527-5544; $99-129 s or d; large motel, outdoor pool, airport transport, AAA approved. Expensive-Premium.

BOOKLIST

Note: A number of the books listed below are now out of print. You can find many of them in regional libraries, or check the web for special orders or rare book auctions. Amazon.com, barnesandnoble.com, and other online sites will also search used bookstores for out-of-print titles.

REGIONAL TITLES

Graham, Kenneth Lee. *Fishing Wyoming.* Helena, MT: Falcon Publishing Co., 1998. A 300-page tome that goes far beyond the standard coverage of Yellowstone and Jackson Hole.

Herrero, Stephen. *Bear Attacks: Their Causes and Avoidance* New York, NY: Lyons Press, 1998. An authoritative volume on the lives of bears and staying safe in their country.

Kilgore, Gene. *Gene Kilgore's Ranch Vacations.* Santa Fe: John Muir Publications, 1999. The definitive guide to dude and guest ranches. Includes detailed, up-to-date descriptions of the best places to be a city-slicker cowboy.

McClure, Michael. *Camping Wyoming.* Atlantic City, WY: WigRaf Publishing, 1999. An amazingly detailed guide to virtually every possible Wyoming camping spot.

Petersen, David. *Among the Elk.* Flagstaff, AZ: Northland Publishing, 1988. The story of wapiti, with outstanding photos by Alan D. Carey. Out of print.

Retallic, Ken. *Flyfisher's Guide to Wyoming.* Gallatin Gateway, MT: Wilderness Adventures Press, 1998. An excellent guide; particularly helpful for anglers headed to Yellowstone.

Schneider, Bill. *Bear Aware: Hiking and Camping in Bear Country* Helena, MT: Falcon Publishing Co., 1998. A handy pocket-sized book that is easy to read and up to date.

Onward Travel

The following is a shameless promotion for other Moon Travel Handbooks titles covering the region. All of these are authoritative guides for their respective states. Find Moon Travel Handbooks on the web at www.moon.com.

McRae, W.C., and Judy Jewell. *Montana Handbook.* Emeryville, CA: Avalon Travel Publishing, 1999.

Metzger, Stephen. *Colorado Handbook.* Emeryville, CA: Avalon Travel Publishing, 1999.

Pitcher, Don. *Wyoming Handbook.* Emeryville, CA: Avalon Travel Publishing, 2000.

Root, Don. *Idaho Handbook.* Emeryville, CA: Avalon Travel Publishing, 1997.

Weir, Bill, and W.C. McRae. *Utah Handbook.* Emeryville, CA: Avalon Travel Publishing, 1997.

JACKSON HOLE AND GRAND TETON NATIONAL PARK

Note: A number of natural history and geology books encompass both Yellowstone and Grand Teton National Parks. See "Yellowstone National Park" below for additional titles with overlapping coverage.

History

Betts, Robert B. *Along the Ramparts of the Tetons: the Saga of Jackson Hole, Wyoming.* Boulder, CO: Colorado Associated University Press, 1978. A substantial, detailed, and beautifully written book about the history of Jackson Hole.

Burt, Nathaniel. *Jackson Hole Journal.* Norman, OK: University of Oklahoma Press, 1983. Tales of growing up as a dude in Jackson Hole. Contains some very amusing stories.

Hayden, Elizabeth Wied, and Cynthia Nielsen. *Origins, A Guide to the Place Names of Grand Teton National Park and the Surrounding Area.* Moose, WY: Grand Teton Natural History Association, 1988. A guide to the obscure sources for place names in Grand Teton.

Huidekoper, Virginia. *The Early Days in Jackson Hole.* Boulder, CO: Colorado Associated University Press, 1978. Filled with over 100 photos from old-time Jackson Hole. Out of print.

Righter, Robert W. *Crucible for Conservation: The Creation of Grand Teton National Park.* Boulder, CO: Colorado Associated University Press, 1982. The story of how the Tetons were spared through a half-century battle.

Thompson, Edith M., and William Leigh Thompson. *Beaver Dick: The Honor and the Heartbreak.* Laramie, WY: Jelm Mountain Press, 1982. A touching historical biography of Beaver Dick Leigh, one of the first white men to settle in Jackson Hole. Out of print.

Ringholz, Raye C. *Little Town Blues: Voices from the Changing West.* Salt Lake City, UT: Gibbs-Smith Publisher, 1992. A cautionary note on the consequences of unbridled growth, this important small book visits several small towns in the west—including Jackson—where the rural qualities and beauty that attract visitors are being inundated by tourism and development.

Natural History

Carrighar, Sally. *One Day at Teton Marsh.* Lincoln, NE: University of Nebraska Press, 1979. A classic natural history of life in a Jackson Hole marsh. Made into a movie by Walt Disney. Out of print.

Clark, Tim W. *Ecology of Jackson Hole, Wyoming: A Primer.* Salt Lake City, UT: Paragon Press, 1981. An excellent scientific introduction to ecological interrelationships within Jackson Hole. Out of print.

Murie, Margaret, and Olaus Murie. *Wapiti Wilderness.* Boulder, CO: Colorado Associated University Press, 1986. The lives of two of America's most-loved conservationists in Jackson Hole and their work with elk.

Raynes, Bert. *Birds of Grand Teton National Park and the Surrounding Area.* Moose, WY: Grand Teton Natural History Association, 1984. A guide to local birds. Out of print.

Shaw, Richard J. *Plants of Grand Teton and Yellowstone National Parks.* Salt Lake City, UT: Wheelwright Press, 1981. Photos and descriptions of the most commonly found plants in the parks.

Hiking, Climbing, and Skiing

Carter, Tom. *Day Hiking Grand Teton National Park.* Garland, TX: Dayhiking Press, 1993. A pocket-sized guide to 15 day-treks in the park.

Dufy, Katy and Darwin Wile. *Teton Trails.* Moose, WY: Grand Teton Natural History Association, 1995. A useful guide to more than 200 miles of trails in the park.

Ortenburger, Leigh N., and Reynold G. Jackson. *A Complete Guide to the Teton Range.* Seattle, WA: Mountaineers Books, 1996. The definitive (415 pages!) climbing guide for the Tetons.

Woods, Rebecca. *Jackson Hole Hikes.* Jackson, WY: White Willow Publishing, 1999. An excellent guide that includes trails in Grand Teton National Park and surrounding National Forest areas. Easy to use and informative.

Rossiter, Richard. *Teton Classics: 50 Selected Climbs in Grand Teton National Park.* Evergreen, CO: Chockstone Press, 1997. A small and nicely illustrated guide to 50 climbing routes in the Tetons.

Watters, Ron. *Winter Tales and Trails: Skiing, Snowshoeing and Snowboarding in Idaho, the Grand Tetons and Yellowstone National Park.* Pocatello, ID: Great Rift Press, 1997. A book that combines lucid writing on the area's rich history with guides to winter trails. More than 350 pages of details from an expert in the field.

Geology

Good, John M. and Kenneth L. Pierce. *Interpreting the Landscape: Recent and Ongoing Geology of Grand Teton and Yellowstone National Parks.* Moose, WY: Grand Teton Natural History Association, 1996. This attractive book has the latest geologic research on the parks and presents it in an understandable format with excellent illustrations.

Love, J.D., and John C. Reed, Jr. *Creation of the Teton Landscape: the Geologic Story of Grand Teton National Park.* Moose, WY: Grand Teton Natural History Association, 1995. A small but authoritatively detailed guide to the geology of Jackson Hole and the Tetons.

YELLOWSTONE NATIONAL PARK

Note: A number of natural history and geology books encompass both Yellowstone and Grand Teton National Parks. See "Grand Teton National Park" above for additional titles with overlapping coverage.

Fishing

Charlton, Robert E. *Yellowstone Fishing Guide.* Ketchum, ID: Lost River Press, 1990. A detailed guide to fishing in the park. Leaves no trickle unfished.

Parks, Richard. *Fishing Yellowstone.* Helena, MT: Falcon Publishing, 1998. One of several authoritative guides, this one provides details on fly and lure fishing, along with descriptions of more than 100 sites.

Varley, John D. and Paul D. Schullery. *Yellowstone Fishes: Ecology, History, and Angling in the Park.* Mechanicsburg, PA: Stackpole Books, 1998. The comprehensive guide to the fish of Yellowstone, written by two authorities in the field.

Geology

Bryan, Scott. T. *The Geysers of Yellowstone.* Boulder, CO: University Press of Colorado, 1995. The definitive guide to more than 400 geysers and other geothermal features in Yellowstone.

Fritz, William J. *Roadside Geology of the Yellowstone Country.* Missoula, MT: Mountain Press Publishing Co., 1986. All the park roads are covered in this easy-to-follow Yellowstone geology primer.

Schreier, Carl. *Yellowstone's Geysers, Hot Springs and Fumaroles.* Moose, WY: Homestead Publishing, 1987. An attractive small book filled with color photos and brief descriptions.

Hiking

Bach, Orville E., Jr. *Hiking the Yellowstone Backcountry.* San Francisco, CA: Sierra Club Books, 1998. A pocket-sized guide to hiking, canoeing, biking, and skiing in the park.

Carter, Tom. *Day Hiking Yellowstone.* Garland, TX: Dayhiking Press, 1991. A pocket-sized guide to 20 day-treks, coordinated with the Trails Illustrated topographic maps.

Marschall, Mark C. *Yellowstone Trails: A Hiking Guide.* Yellowstone National Park, WY: The Yellowstone Association, 1999. An excellent, up-to-date, and detailed guidebook to the park's 1,000 miles of hiking trails.

Schneider, Bill. *Hiking Yellowstone National Park.* Helena, MT: Falcon Publishing, 1997. Clear maps and helpful trail profiles make this the most useful book for anyone heading out on Yellowstone hiking routes. Contains descriptions of more than 100 trails.

History

Bartlett, Richard A. *Yellowstone: A Wilderness Besieged.* Tucson, AZ: University of Arizona Press, 1989. The history of Yellowstone and the fight to prevent its destruction by railroad magnates, concessioners, and others.

Haines, Aubrey L., ed. *Journal of a Trapper: Osborne Russell.* Lincoln, NE: University of Nebraska Press, 1965 (reprinted from the 19th-century original volume). The first-person account of a fur trapper's life from 1834 to 1843. A classic and surprisingly well-written book.

Haines, Aubrey L. *The Yellowstone Story: A History of Our First National Park.* Boulder, CO: University Press of Colorado, 1996. A definitive two-volume history of the park. Volume one (history up to the park's establishment) is the most interesting.

Haines, Aubrey L. *Yellowstone Place Names: Mirrors of History.* Boulder, CO: University Press of Colorado, 1996. For the Trivial Pursuit enthusiast, this is 318 pages of detailed descriptions with every possible name from every obscure corner of Yellowstone.

Janetski, Joel C. *Indians of Yellowstone Park.* Salt Lake City, UT: University of Utah Press, 1987. A general overview of the earliest settlers in Yellowstone and their later conflicts with incoming whites.

Milstein, Michael. *Yellowstone Album: 125 Years of America's Best Idea.* Billings, MT: *The Billings Gazette,* 1996. A delightful book filled with historical photographs, along with photos of postcards, souvenirs, and other tourist artifacts.

Schreier, Carl, ed. *Yellowstone: Selected Photographs 1870-1960.* Moose, WY: Homestead Publishing, 1989. An outstanding collection of historic photographs from the park.

Natural History

Craighead, Frank J. *Track of the Grizzly.* San Francisco, CA: Sierra Club Books, 1982. The life of grizzlies in Yellowstone, by one of the most famous bear researchers.

Krakell, Dean, II. *Downriver: A Yellowstone Journey.* San Francisco, CA: Sierra Club Books, 1987. An extraordinarily moving journey down the magnificent Yellowstone River.

McEneaney, Terry. *Birds of Yellowstone.* Boulder, CO: Roberts Rinehart, 1988. A guide to Yellowstone birds and where to find them.

Scott, Douglas M., and Suvi A. Scott. *Wildlife of Yellowstone and Grand Teton National Parks.* Salt Lake City, UT: Wheelwright Press, 1990. A brief descriptive guide to Yellowstone and Grand Teton critters.

Shaw, Richard J. *Wildflowers of Yellowstone and Grand Teton National Parks.* Salt Lake City, UT: Wheelwright Press, 1992. Color photos and short descriptions of more than 100 wildflowers in the Greater Yellowstone Ecosystems.

Schullery, Paul, ed. *Yellowstone Bear Tales.* Boulder, CO: Roberts Rinehart Publishers, 1991. First-person stories of bear encounters from a range of travelers—including President Theodore Roosevelt—between 1880 and 1950.

Wuerthner, George. *Yellowstone: A Visitor's Companion.* Mechanicsburg, PA: Stackpole Books, 1992. A detailed guide to the natural history of Yellowstone.

Other Yellowstone Books

Henry, Jeff. *Yellowstone Winter Guide.* Boulder, CO: Roberts Rinehart Publishers, 1998. A detailed guide to visiting Yellowstone in the winter; especially good for cross-country skiers.

Olsen, Ken, Dena Olsen, and Steve and Hazel Scharosch. *Cross-Country Skiing Yellowstone Country.* Helena, MT: Falcon Publishing, 1994. Detailed descriptions of 200 miles of ski trails in and near the park, including helpful trail profiles.

Reese, Rick and Terry Tempest Williams. *Greater Yellowstone: The National Park and Adjacent Wildlands.* Helena, MT: American Geographic Publishing, 1991. An attractive book with considerable information on ecological conditions in one of the Lower 48's largest intact ecosystems.

Schmidt, Jeremy, and Steven Fuller. *Yellowstone Grand Teton Road Guide: The Essential Guide for Motorists.* Jackson, WY: Free Wheeling Travel Guides, 1998. A nicely done pocket-sized guide to the roads of the two parks, with accurate, up-to-date information.

Schullery, Paul. *Searching for Yellowstone.* New York, NY: Houghton Mifflin Co.: 1997. An eloquently written book by a longtime park ranger whose knowledge of the park goes far beyond the hype. A must-read for anyone who cares about Yellowstone.

CODY AREA

Cook, Jeannie, ed. *Buffalo Bill's Town in the Rockies: A Pictorial History of Cody, Wyoming.* Cody, WY: Park County Historical Society; 1996. A photographic visit to Cody's interesting past.

Rosa, Joseph G. and Robin May. *Buffalo Bill and His Wild West.* Lawrence, KS: University Press of Kansas, 1989. One of the newer books on Buffalo Bill, with a somewhat revisionist take on his life and times. Rich in detail on Cody's Wild West Show.

Russell, Don. *The Lives and Legends of Buffalo Bill.* Norman, OK: University of Oklahoma Press, 1979. The most complete biography on the life of Buffalo Bill Cody.

ACCOMMODATIONS INDEX

RESTAURANT INDEX

INDEX

ART MUSEUMS/GALLERIES

BACKCOUNTRY SPORTS/ RECREATION

BED AND BREAKFASTS

C

CABINS

CAMPGROUNDS/RV PARKS

CROSS-COUNTRY SKIING

D

DOWNHILL SKIING/ SNOWBOARDING

EVENTS

FISH/FISHING

GEYSERS/HOT SPRINGS

GRAND TETON NATIONAL PARK

GUEST RANCHES

HIKING/BACKPACKING

HISTORIC SITES

JACKSON HOLE

KID STUFF

MUSIC VENUES

OUTFITTERS/SPORT SHOPS

QR

TOURS/GUIDES

TRAILS

UV

W

WATERFALLS

XYZ

YELLOWSTONE NATIONAL PARK

ABOUT THE AUTHOR

Born in Atlanta, Georgia, Don Pitcher grew up all over the East Coast—from Florida to Maine. He moved west to attend college and immediately fell in love with its wide open spaces. After receiving a master's degree in fire ecology from the University of California at Berkeley, he worked seasonally for a variety of state and federal agencies. Over the years Don did all sorts of outdoor work: calling spotted owls in northern California, mapping grizzly habitat in Wyoming's Teton Wilderness, and doing a wide range of work in Alaska: building backcountry trails, running salmon weirs, conducting forest fire research, and working with brown bears.

Although trained as an ecologist, Don Pitcher's love of travel led him into the field of writing and photography. In addition to this book, he is author of **Wyoming Handbook,** *Washington Handbook, Alaska-Yukon Handbook,* and *Berkeley Inside/Out.* He has photographed books on Wyoming and Alaska for Compass American Guides, and his photographs have also appeared in numerous books, calendars, magazines, and advertisements. Don bases his travels out of Homer, Alaska, where he lives with his wife, Karen Shemet, and daughter, Aziza Bali. You can contact him at www.donpitcher.com.

For Travelers With Special Interests

Guides

The 100 Best Small Art Towns in America • Asia in New York City
The Big Book of Adventure Travel • Cities to Go
Cross-Country Ski Vacations • Gene Kilgore's Ranch Vacations
Great American Motorcycle Tours • Healing Centers and Retreats
Indian America • Into the Heart of Jerusalem
The People's Guide to Mexico • The Practical Nomad
Saddle Up! • Staying Healthy in Asia, Africa, and Latin America
Steppin' Out • Travel Unlimited • Understanding Europeans
Watch It Made in the U.S.A. • The Way of the Traveler
Work Worldwide • The World Awaits
The Top Retirement Havens • Yoga Vacations

Series

Adventures in Nature
The Dog Lover's Companion
Kidding Around
Live Well

Rick Steves shows you where to travel and how to travel—all while getting the most value for your dollar. His Back Door travel philosophy is about making friends, having fun, and avoiding tourist rip-offs.

Rick's been traveling to Europe for more than 25 years and is the author of 20 guidebooks, which have sold more than a million copies. He also hosts the award-winning public television series *Travels in Europe with Rick Steves*.

Rick Steves' Country & City Guides

Best of Europe
France, Belgium & the Netherlands
Germany, Austria & Switzerland
Great Britain & Ireland
Italy • London • Paris • Rome • Scandinavia • Spain & Portugal

Rick Steves' Phrase Books

French • German • Italian • French, Italian & German
Spanish & Portuguese

More Europe from Rick Steves

Europe 101
Europe Through the Back Door
Mona Winks
Postcards from Europe

WWW.RICKSTEVES.COM

www.travelmatters.com

User-friendly, informative, and fun:

Because travel *matters.*

Visit our newly launched web site and explore the variety of titles and travel information available online, featuring an interactive *Road Trip USA* exhibit.

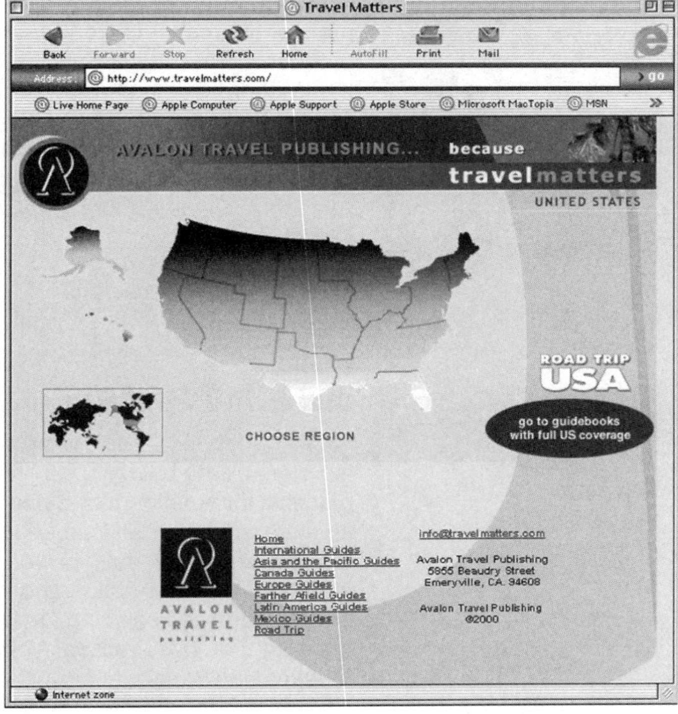

U.S.~METRIC CONVERSION

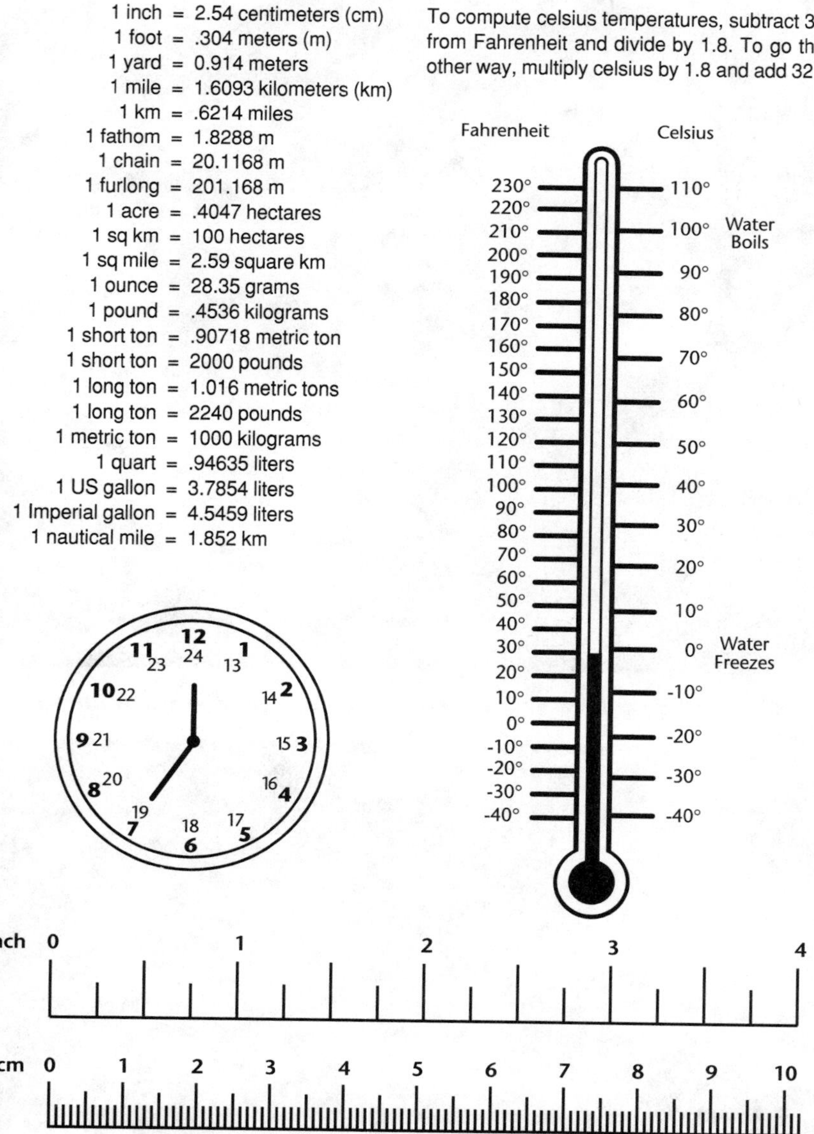